The Technique of Film and Video Editing

Fifth Edition

The Technique of Film and Video Editing

History, Theory, and Practice

Fifth Edition

Ken Dancyger

Focal Press
Taylor & Francis Group

NEW YORK AND LONDON

First published 2011
This edition published 2013
by Focal Press
70 Blanchard Road, Suite 402, Burlington, MA 01803

Simultaneously published in the UK
By Focal Press
2 Park Square, Milton Park, Abingdon, Oxon OX14 4RN

Focal Press is an imprint of the Taylor & Francis Group, an informa business

Notices

Practitioners and researchers must always rely on their own experience and knowledge in evaluating and using any information, methods, compounds, or experiments described herein. In using such information or methods they should be mindful of their own safety and the safety of others, including parties for whom they have a professional responsibility.

To the fullest extent of the law, neither the Publisher nor the authors, contributors, or editors, assume any liability for any injury and/or damage to persons or property as a matter of products liability, negligence or otherwise, or from any use or operation of any methods, products, instructions, or ideas contained in the material herein.

Library of Congress Cataloging-in-Publication Data

Dancyger, Ken.
  The technique of film and video editing : history, theory, and practice / Ken Dancyger — 5th ed.
     p. cm.
  Includes bibliographical references and index.
  ISBN 978-0-240-81397-4 (alk. paper)
  1. Motion pictures—Editing. 2. Video tapes—Editing.
  3. Digital video—Editing. I. Title.
  TR899.D26 2010
  778.5′35—dc22   2010035589

British Library Cataloguing in Publication Data
A catalogue record for this book is available from the British Library

ISBN 13: 978-0-240-81397-4 (pbk)

*For the next generation,
and dedicated to my
contribution to that
generation,
Emily and Erica.*

Contents

ACKNOWLEDGMENTS XV
INTRODUCTION xvii
ABOUT THE WEBSITE XXV

Section 1   History of Film Editing

CHAPTER 1   The Silent Period 3

Edwin S. Porter: Film Continuity Begins 4

D. W. Griffith: Dramatic Construction 5

    International Perspectives 12

Vsevolod I. Pudovkin: Constructive Editing and Heightened Realism 13

Sergei Eisenstein: The Theory of Montage 16

    Metric Montage 17

    Rhythmic Montage 18

    Tonal Montage 18

    Overtonal Montage 20

    Intellectual Montage 20

    Eisenstein: Theoretician and Aesthete 21

Dziga Vertov: The Experiment of Realism 23

Alexander Dovzhenko: Editing by Visual Association 25

Luis Buñuel: Visual Discontinuity 27

Conclusion 32

CHAPTER 2   The Early Sound Film 33

Technological Limitations 33

Technological Improvements 35

Theoretical Issues Concerning Sound 35

Early Experiment in Sound—Alfred Hitchcock's *Blackmail* 36

Sound, Time, and Place: Fritz Lang's *M* 38

The Dynamic of Sound: Rouben Mamoulian's *Applause* 42

Conclusion 44

CHAPTER 3   The Influence of the Documentary 45

Ideas About Society.. 46

    Robert Flaherty and *Man of Aran*.. 46

    Basil Wright and *Night Mail* 49

    Pare Lorentz and *The Plow That Broke the Plains* 51

Ideas About Art and Culture 51

    Leni Riefenstahl and *Olympia*.. 53

    W. S. Van Dyke and *The City*... 54

Ideas About War and Society 56

    Frank Capra and *Why We Fight*... 56

    Humphrey Jennings and *Diary for Timothy* 57

Conclusion... 60

CHAPTER 4   The Influence of the Popular Arts 61

Vaudeville... 61

The Musical... 64

The Theatre... 65

Radio 66

CHAPTER 5   Editors Who Became Directors 71

Robert Wise... 72

    The Set-Up... 74

    I Want to Live! 75

    West Side Story 77

David Lean 79

    Lean's Technique.. 80

    Lean's Art... 83

CHAPTER 6   Experiments in Editing: Alfred Hitchcock 87

A Simple Introduction: Parallel Action.. 88

A Dramatic Punctuation: The Sound Cut 88

Dramatic Discovery: Cutting on Motion.. 89

Suspense: The Extreme Long Shot 89

Levels of Meaning: The Cutaway 90

Intensity: The Close-up.. 90

The Moment as Eternity: The Extreme Close-up.. 91

    Dramatic Time and Pace 92

The Unity of Sound 92

The Orthodoxy of the Visual: The Chase 94

Dreamstates: Subjectivity and Motion.. 95

Conclusion.. 97

CHAPTER 7 New Technologies 99

The Wide Screen 99

Character and Environment 102

Relationships 104

Relationships and the Environment 105

The Background 106

The Wide Screen After 1960 107

Cinéma Vérité 109

CHAPTER 8 International Advances 115

The Dynamics of Relativity 116

The Jump Cut and Discontinuity 118

Objective Anarchy: Jean-Luc Godard 121

Melding Past and Present: Alain Resnais 123

Interior Life as External Landscape 125

CHAPTER 9 The Influence of Television and Theatre 133

Television 133

Theatre 137

CHAPTER 10 New Challenges to Filmic Narrative Conventions 143

Peckinpah: Alienation and Anarchy 143

Altman: The Freedom of Chaos 146

Kubrick: New Worlds and Old 148

Herzog: Other Worlds 150

Scorsese: The Dramatic Document 150

Wenders: Mixing Popular and Fine Art 152

Lee: Pace and Social Action 153

Von Trotta: Feminism and Politics 158

Feminism and Antinarrative Editing 160

Mixing Genres 162

CHAPTER 11 The MTV Influence on Editing I 165

Origins 166

The Short Film 167

Where We Are Now—The State of the MTV Style 167

The Importance of Feeling States 168

The Downgrading of the Plot 168

Disjunctive Editing—The Obliteration of Time and Space 169

The Self-Reflexive Dream State 170

The Media Looks at Itself 171

Oliver Stone's Career 171

Natural Born Killers 172

CHAPTER 12 The MTV Influence on Editing II 177

The Case of *Saving Private Ryan* 178

The Case of Ang Lee's *Crouching Tiger, Hidden Dragon* 182

The Set-Pieces 183

The Case of *In the Mood for Love* 186

The MTV Style of *In the Mood for Love* 187

The Case of *Life Is Beautiful* 188

The Set-Pieces in *Life Is Beautiful* 189

The Case of *Tampopo* 190

The Set-Pieces in *Tampopo* 191

Conclusion 192

CHAPTER 13 Changes in Pace 193

Evolution of Pace in Filmmaking 193

Pace in the Docudrama 194

Pace in the Thriller 195

Pace in the Action-Adventure 198

Pace in the Musical 199

Anti-Pace in Tarantino's *Inglourious Basterds* 200

Conclusion 202

CHAPTER 14 The Appropriation of Style I: Imitation and Innovation 203

Narrative and Style 203

Style for Its Own Sake 205

Breaking Expectations 206

Imitation versus Innovation 207

Imitation and Innovation 208

CHAPTER 15 The Appropriation of Style II: Limitation and Innovation 213

The Elevation of Cinéma Vérité 213

The Return of Mise-en-Scène 217

The Close-Up and the Long Shot 222

Camera Placement and Pace: The Intervention of Subjective States 227

CHAPTER 16 The Appropriation of Style III: Digital Reality 233

Artificial Reality 233

Video Over Film 234

Constructed Artifice 235

The Imagined as the Observational 235

Use of Spectacle 236

Use of Special Effects 237

Realism 237

Section 2   Goals of Editing

CHAPTER 17 Editing for Narrative Clarity 243
The Plot-Driven Film 244
Five Fingers 244
Mountains of the Moon 245
Invictus 246
The Character-Driven Film 248
Hannah and Her Sisters 248
Valmont 249
Hero 249
The Case of *The Hours* 250
The Case of *Atonement* 252

CHAPTER 18 Editing for Dramatic Emphasis 255
United 93 255
The Docudrama Effect 258
The Close-up 258
Dynamic Montage 259
Juxtaposition 260
Pace 260
Frost/Nixon 261
Different Goals, Different Strategies 264
The Close-up 264
Dynamic Montage 265
Juxtaposition 265
Pace 266

CHAPTER 19 Editing for Subtext 267
The Departed 271
Lust, Caution 272
There Will Be Blood 273

CHAPTER 20 Editing for Aesthetics 277
Brighton Rock 278
The Third Man 279
The Passion 282

Section 3   Editing for the Genre

CHAPTER 21 Action 287
The Contemporary Context 289
The General: An Early Action Sequence 292
Raiders of the Lost Ark: A Contemporary Action Sequence 294

The Bourne Ultimatum: The Ultimate Use of Pace in an
Action Sequence 296
Case Study: *A History of Violence*: An Alternative Action Sequence............. 298

CHAPTER 22 Dialog 301
Dialog and Plot.. 302
Dialog and Character... 303
Multipurpose Dialog 304
Trouble in Paradise: An Early Dialog Sequence.............................. 306
Chinatown: A Contemporary Dialog Sequence.............................. 309
Michael Clayton: Dialog as Transformative Device 312

CHAPTER 23 Comedy.. 315
Character Comedy 315
Situation Comedy.. 316
Satire 316
Farce 316
Editing Concerns 316
The Comedy Director... 318
The Past: *The Lady Eve*—The Early Comedy of Role Reversal 320
The Present: *Victor Victoria*—A Contemporary Comedy of
Role Reversal... 321
Forgetting Sarah Marshall: Emotional Role Reversal 324
Conclusion... 325

CHAPTER 24 Documentary 327
Questions of Ethics, Politics, and Aesthetics 328
Analysis of Documentary Sequences—*Memorandum* 329
Simple Continuity and the Influence of the Narrator.................... 329
The Transitional Sequence 330
The Archival Sequence.. 332
A Sequence with Little Narration.. 334
The Reportage Sequence 336

CHAPTER 25 Imaginative Documentary 341
Altering Meaning Away from the Literal.. 341
The Wartime Documentary: Imagination and Propaganda.............. 343
The Case of *Listen to Britain* 344
Conclusion... 347

CHAPTER 26 Innovations in Documentary I.. 349
The Personal Documentary 349
Changes in the Use of Narration 355
The Narrator as Observer... 355
The Narrator as Investigator... 356

The Narrator as Guide..357
The Narrator as Provocateur...359
Conclusion...361

CHAPTER 27 Innovations in Documentary II...363

Section 4 **Principles of Editing**

CHAPTER 28 The Picture Edit and Continuity.....................................371
Constructing a Lucid Continuity 372
Providing Adequate Coverage...372
Matching Action 373
Preserving Screen Direction 375
Setting the Scene 378
Matching Tone 378
Matching Flow Over a Cut..378
Change in Location...379
Change in Scene 380

CHAPTER 29 The Picture Edit and Pace..381
Timing..382
Rhythm 383
Time and Place...387
The Possibilities of Randomness Upon Pace 388

CHAPTER 30 Nonlinear Editing and Digital Technology I 391
The Technological Revolution...391
The Limits of Technology...392
The Aesthetic Opportunities 392
The Nonlinear Narrative..393
Past Reliance on Linearity..393
A Philosophy of Nonlinearity 394
The Artists of Nonlinear Narrative..395

CHAPTER 31 Nonlinear Editing and Digital Technology II 399
The Framework...399
The Case of *The Ice Storm* 400
The Case of *Happiness*..403
The Case of *The Thin Red Line* 405
The Case of *Magnolia*...409

CHAPTER 32 Conclusion 413

APPENDIX: FILMOGRAPHY.. 415

GLOSSARY 435

SELECTED BIBLIOGRAPHY 443

INDEX 445

ONLINE

CHAPTER 1   Ideas and Sound

CHAPTER 2   The Sound Edit and Clarity

CHAPTER 3   The Sound Edit and Creative Sound

CHAPTER 4   Innovations of Sound

Acknowledgments

ACKNOWLEDGMENTS FOR THE FIFTH EDITION

Thanks to Michele Cronin and Elinor Actipis at Focal Press for their work on the fifth edition. Many thanks to the invaluable help from the reviewers who offered many suggestions and critiques, with a special thanks to John Rosenberg and James Joyce.

ACKNOWLEDGMENTS FOR THE FOURTH EDITION

Thanks to Elinor Actipis and Becky Golden-Harrell at Focal Press for their work on the fourth edition. I'd also like to thank my students in the History of Editing class in the Film Department at TISCH School of the Arts, New York University. They have helped me convert that class into a laboratory where ideas about editing can by explored.

ACKNOWLEDGMENTS

Many people have been helpful in the preparation of this manuscript.

At Focal Press I thank Karen Speerstra for suggesting the project to me, and Sharon Falter for her ongoing help. I'm grateful to the following archives for their help in securing the stills for this book: the British Film Institute, the French Cinematheque, the Moving Image and Sound Archives of Canada, and the Museum of Modern Art, New York. For their generous financial support I thank the Faculty of Fine Arts, York University, and the Canada Council. This book could not have been written on the scale attempted without the financial support of the Canada Council. This project was complex and challenging in the level of support services it required. From typing and shipping to corresponding with archives and studios on rights clearances, I have been superbly supported by my assistant, Steven Sills, in New York, and my friend and colleague, George Robinson, in Toronto. I thank them both. Finally, I thank my wife, Ida, for being so good-natured about the demands of this project.

Introduction to the Fifth Edition

In this fifth edition of the *Technique of Film and Video Editing*, I have added a new section called "The Goals of Editing."

As this book expanded through editions one to four, it became a history of editing as well as a theory-practice book on different genres—documentary for example—as well as different types of sequences—action, dialogue, comedy. Along the way, my students at New York University and in my workshops abroad reminded me that what was being overlooked were the fundamentals, the purposes editing served. An article I wrote for Cineaste on *Editing for Subtext* pulled into focus what I had been including in my lectures but not highlighting in this book. And so, in this fifth edition I have chosen to fix on those goals of editing to highlight their centrality in the editing process.

The new chapters are about editing for narrative clarity, editing for dramatic emphasis, editing for subtext, and editing for aesthetic purpose. All chapters take a case study approach to illustrate the goal.

These goals lie behind the evolution of the history of editing and make more precise the exercise of pace, juxtaposition and the use of particular editing choices from the close-up to jump cutting. Although there are distinct trends or styles in how a film is edited, the underlying goal remains the same—to move the audience into and out of a narrative or documentary or experimental narrative in the manner that best conveys the editorial intention of the creators. This is why this new section is so important to the evolution of this text. The new edition refocuses the book's audience on what editing can and should achieve.

I have also added examples of recent films to update pace, purpose, and the means used to edit action, dialogue, and comedy sequences.

I am excited about these changes in the fifth edition. I hope you will be too.

INTRODUCTION

It has been half a century since Karel Reisz, working with a British Film Academy committee, wrote *The Technique of Film Editing*. Much has happened in those 50 years. Television is pervasive in its presence and its influence, and cinema, no longer in decline because of television, is more influential than ever. The videocassette recorder (VCR) made movies, old and new, accessible, available, and ripe for rediscovery by another generation. The director is king, and film is more international than ever.

In 1953, Reisz could not foresee these changes, but he did demonstrate that the process of film editing is a seminal factor in the craft of filmmaking and in the evolution of film as an art form. If anything, the technological changes and creative high points of the past 50 years have only deepened that notion.

Reisz's strategic decision to sidestep the theoretical debate on the role of editing in the art of film allowed him to explore creative achievements in different film genres. By doing so, he provided the professional and the student with a vital guide to the creative options that editing offers. One of the key reasons for the success of Reisz's book is that it was written from the filmmaker's point of view. In this sense, the book was conceptual rather than technical. Just as it validated a career choice for Reisz (within 10 years, he became an important director), the book affirmed the key creative role of the director, a view that would soon be articulated in France and 10 years later in North America. It is a widely held view today. The book, which was updated in 1968 by Gavin Millar (now also a director), remains as widely read today as it was when first published.

It was my goal to write a book that is, in spirit, related to the Reisz–Millar classic but that is also up to date with regard to films and film ideas. I also refer to the technical achievements in film, video, and sound that have expanded the character of modern films and film ideas. This update illustrates how the creative repertoire for filmmakers has broadened in the past 50 years.

POINT OF VIEW

A book on film and video editing can be written from a number of points of view. The most literal point of view is, of course, that of the film editor, but even this option isn't as straightforward as it appears. *When the Shooting Stops . . .* , by Ralph Rosenblum and Robert Karen, is perhaps the most comprehensive approach to the topic by a film editor. The book is part autobiography, part editing history, and part aesthetic statement. Other editing books by film editors are strictly technical; they discuss cutting room procedure, the language of the cutting room, or the mechanics of offline editing. With the growth of high-technology editing options, the variety of technical editing books will certainly grow as well.

This book is intended to be practical, in the sense that editing an action sequence requires an appreciation of which filmic elements are necessary to make that sequence effective. Also needed is a knowledge of the evolution of editing, so that the editor can make the most effective choices under the circumstances. This is the goal of the book: to be practical, to be concerned about aesthetic choices, but not to be overly absorbed with the mechanics of film editing. In this sense, the book is written from the same perspective as Reisz's book—that of the film director. It is my hope, however, that the book will be useful to more than just directors. I have enormous admiration for editors; indeed, I agree with Ralph Rosenblum, who suggests that if editors had a different temperament and more confidence, they would be directors. I also agree with his implication that editing is one of the best possible types of training for future directors.

One final point: By adopting the director's point of view, I imply, as Reisz did, that editing is central in the creative evolution of film. This perspective allows me to examine the history of the theory and the practice of film editing.

TERMS

In books about editing, many terms take on a variety of meanings. *Technique*, *art*, and *craft* are the most obvious. I use these terms in the following sense.

Technique, or the technical aspect of editing, is the physical joining of two disparate pieces of film. When joined, those two pieces of film become a sequence that has a particular meaning.

The *craft* of film editing is the joining of two pieces of film together to yield a meaning that is not apparent from one or the other shot. The meaning that arises from the two shots might be a continuity of a walk (exit right for shot one and enter left for shot two), or the meaning might be an explanation or an exclamation. The viewer's interpretation is clarified by the editor practicing her craft.

What about the art? I am indebted to Karel Reisz for his simple but elegant explanation. The *art* of editing occurs when the combination of two or more shots takes meaning to the next level—excitement, insight, shock, or the epiphany of discovery.

Technique, *craft*, and *art* are equally useful and appropriate terms whether they are applied to visual material on film or videotape, or are used to describe a visual or a sound edit or sequence. These terms are used by different writers to characterize editing. I have tried to be precise and to concentrate on the artistic evolution of editing. In the chapters on types of sequences—action, dialog, comedy, documentary—I am as concerned with the craft as with the art. Further, although the book concentrates on visual editing, the art of sound editing is highlighted as much as possible.

Because film was for its first 30 years primarily a silent medium, the editing innovations of D. W. Griffith, Sergei Eisenstein, and V. I. Pudovkin were visual. When sound was added, it was a technical novelty rather than a creative addition. Not until the work of Basil Wright, Alberto Cavalcanti, Rouben Mamoulian, and Orson Welles did sound editing suggest its creative possibilities. However, the medium continued to be identified with its visual character—films were, after all, called "motion pictures." In reality, though, each dimension and each technology added its own artistic contribution to the medium. That attitude and its implications are a basic assumption of this book.

THE ROLE OF EXPERIMENTAL AND DOCUMENTARY FILMS

Although the early innovations in film occurred in mainstream commercial movies, many innovations also took place in experimental and documentary films. The early work of Luis Buñuel, the middle period of Humphrey Jennings, the cinéma vérité work of Unit B of the National Film Board of Canada, and the free associations of Clement Perron and Arthur Lipsett (also at the National Film Board), contributed immeasurably to the art of editing.

These innovations in editing visuals and sound took place more freely in experimental and documentary filmmaking than in the commercial cinema. Experimental film, for example, was not produced under the scrutiny of commercial consideration. Documentary film, as long as it loosely fulfilled a didactic agenda, continued to be funded by governments and corporations.

Because profit played a less central role for the experimental and documentary films, creative innovation was the result. Those innovations were quickly recognized and absorbed by mainstream filmmaking. The experimental film and the documentary have played an important role in the story of the evolution of editing as an art; consequently, they have an important place in this book.

THE ROLE OF TECHNOLOGY

Film has always been the most technology-intensive of the popular arts. Recording an image and playing it back requires cameras, lights, projectors, and chemicals to develop the film. Sound recording has always relied on technology. So, too, has editing. Editors needed tape, a splicer, and eventually a motorized process to view what they had spliced together. Moviolas, Steenbecks, and sophisticated sound consoles have replaced the more basic equipment, and editroids, when they become more cost effective, may replace Steenbecks. The list of technological changes is long and, with the high technology of television and video, it is growing rapidly. Today, motion pictures are often recorded on film but edited on video. This gives the editor more sophisticated choices.

Whether technological choice makes for a better film or television show is easily answered. The career of Stanley Kubrick, from *Paths of Glory* (1957) to *Full Metal Jacket* (1987), is telling. Kubrick always took advantage of the existing technology, but beginning with *2001: A Space Odyssey* (1968), he began to challenge convention and to make technology a central subject of each of his films. He proved that technology and creativity were not mutually exclusive. Technology in and of itself need not be used creatively, but, in the right hands, it can be. Technology plays a critical role in shaping film, but it is only a tool in the human hands of the artists who ply their ideas in this medium.

THE ROLE OF THE EDITOR

It is an overstatement for any one person involved in filmmaking to claim that his or her role is the exclusive source of creativity in the filmmaking process. Filmmaking requires collaboration; it requires the skills of an army of people. When filmmaking works best, each contribution adds to the totality of our experience of the film. The corollary, of course, is that any deficit in performance can be ruinous to the film. To put the roles into perspective, it's easiest to think of each role as creative and of particular roles as more decisive—for example, the producer, the writer, the director, the cinematographer, the actors, and the editor. Sound people, gaffers, art designers, costumers, and special effects people all contribute, but the front-line roles are so pervasive in their influence that they are the key roles.

The editor comes into the process once production has begun, making a rough assembly of shots while the film is in production. In this way, adjustments or additional shots can be undertaken during the production phase. If a needed shot must be pursued once the crew has been dispersed and the set has been dismantled, the cost will be much greater.

The editor's primary role, however, takes place in the postproduction phase. Once production has been completed, sound and music are added during this phase, as are special effects. Aside from shortening the film, the editor must find a rhythm for the film; working closely with the director and sometimes the producer, the editor presents options, points out areas of confusion, and identifies redundant scenes. The winnowing process is an intuitive search for clarity and dynamism. The film must speak to as wide an audience as possible. Sound, sound effects, and music are all added at this stage.

The degree of freedom that the editor has depends on the relationship with the director and the producer. Particular directors are very interested in editing; others are more concerned with performance and leave more to the editor. The power relationship between editor and director or editor and producer is never the same; it always depends on the interests and strengths of each. In general terms, however, editors defer to directors and producers. The goals of the editor are particular: to find a narrative continuity for the visuals and the sound of the film, and to distill those visuals and sound shots that will create the dramatic emphasis so that the film will be effective. By choosing particular juxtapositions, editors also layer that narrative with metaphor and subtext. They can even alter the original meaning by changing the juxtapositions of the shots.

An editor is successful when the audience enjoys the story and forgets about the juxtaposition of the shots. If the audience is aware of the editing, the editor has failed. This characterization should also describe the director's criteria for success, but ironically, it does not. Particular styles or genres are associated with particular directors. The audience knows an Alfred Hitchcock film or a Steven Spielberg film or an Ernst Lubitsch film. The result is that the audience expects a sense of the director's public persona in the film. When these directors make a film in which the audience is not aware of the directing, they fail that audience. Individual directors can have a public persona not available to editors.

Having presented the limits of the editor's role in a production, I would be remiss if I didn't acknowledge the power of editors in a production and as a profession. The editor shares much with the director in this respect.

Film and television are the most powerful and influential media of the century. Both have been used for good and for less-than-good intentions. As a result, the editor is a very powerful person because of his or her potential influence. Editing choices range from the straightforward presentation of material to the alteration of the meaning of that material. Editors also have the opportunity to present the material in as emotional a manner as possible. Emotion itself shapes meaning even more.

The danger, then, is to abuse that power. A set of ethical standards or personal morality is the rudder for all who work in film and television. The rudder isn't always operable. Editors do not have public personae that force them to exercise a personal code of ethics in their work. Consequently, a personal code of ethics becomes even more important. Because ethics played a role in the evolution of the art of editing and in the theoretical debate about what is art in film, the issue is raised in this book.

ORGANIZATION OF THIS BOOK

This book is organized along similar lines to the Reisz–Millar book. However, the first section, the history section, is more detailed not only because the post-1968 period had to be added, but also because the earlier period can now be dealt with in a more comprehensive way. Research on the early cinema and on the Russian cinema and translations of related documents allowed a more detailed treatment than was available to Karel Reisz in 1952. Many scholars have also entered the theoretical debate on editing as the source of film art. Their debate has enlivened the arguments, pro and con, and they too contribute to the new context for the historical section of this book.

The third part of the book, on the principles of editing, uses a comparative approach. It examines how particular types of scenes are cut today relative to how they were cut 60 years ago. Finally, the section on the practice of editing details specific types of editing options in picture and sound.

A WORD ABOUT VIDEO

Much that has evolved in editing is applicable to both film and video. A cut from long shot to close-up has a similar impact in both media. What differs is the technology employed to make the physical cut. Steenbecks and tape splicers are different from the offline video players and monitors deployed in an electronic edit. Because the aesthetic choices and impacts are similar, I assume that those choices transcend differing technologies. What can be said in this context about film can also be said about video. With the proviso that the technologies differ, I assume that what can be said about the craft and art of film editing can also be said about video editing.

A WORD ABOUT FILM EXAMPLES

When Reisz's book was published, it was difficult to view the films he used as examples. Consequently, a considerable number of shot sequences from the films he discussed were included in the book.

The most significant technological change affecting this book is the advent of the VCR and the growing availability of films on videotape, videodisc, DVD, and Blu-ray. Because the number of films available on video is great, I have tried to select examples from these films. The reader may want to refer to the stills reproduced in this book but can also view the sequence being described. Indeed, the opportunity for detailed study of sequences on video makes the learning opportunities greater than ever. The availability of video material has influenced both my film choices and the degree of detail used in various chapters.

Readers should not ignore the growing use of Blu-ray and DVDs. This technology is now accessible for most homes, and more and more educational institutions are realizing the benefit of this technology. Most videodisc and DVD players come with a remote that can allow you to slow-forward a film so that you can view sequences in a more detailed manner. The classics of international cinema and a growing number of more recent films on videodisc can give the viewer a clearer picture and better sound than ever before technologically possible.

This book was written for individuals who want to understand film and television and who want to make film and television programs. It will provide you with a context for your work. Whether you are a student or a professional, this book will help you move forward in a more informed way toward your goal. If this book is meaningful to even a percentage of the readers of the Reisz–Millar book, it will have achieved its goal.

About the Website

The website features four exclusive chapters covering the principles of sound in editing:

Ideas in Sound
The Sound Edit and Clarity
The Sound Edit and Creative Sound
Innovations in Sound

Please be sure to visit!

http://www.focalpress.com/9780240813974

History of Film Editing

1. The Silent Period 3
2. The Early Sound Film 33
3. The Influence of the Documentary 45
4. The Influence of the Popular Arts 61
5. Editors Who Became Directors 71
6. Experiments in Editing: Alfred Hitchcock 87
7. New Technologies 99
8. International Advances 115
9. The Influence of Television and Theatre 133
10. New Challenges to Filmic Narrative Conventions 143
11. The MTV Influence on Editing I 165
12. The MTV Influence on Editing II 177
13. Changes in Pace 193
14. The Appropriation of Style I: Imitation and Innovation 203
15. The Appropriation of Style II: Limitation and Innovation 213
16. The Appropriation of Style III: Digital Reality 233

CHAPTER 1

The Silent Period

Film dates from 1895. When the first motion pictures were created, editing did not exist. The novelty of seeing a moving image was such that not even a screen story was necessary. The earliest films were less than a minute in length. They could be as simple as *La Sortie de l'Usine Lumière* (*Workers Leaving the Lumière Factory*) (1895) or *Arrivée d'un Train en Gare* (*Arrival of a Train at the Station*) (1895). One of the more popular films in New York was *The Kiss* (1896). Its success encouraged more films in a similar vein: *A Boxing Bout* (1896) and *Skirt Dance* (1896). Although George Méliès began producing more exotic "created" stories in France, such as *Cinderella* (1899) and *A Trip to the Moon* (1902), all of the early films shared certain characteristics.

Editing was nonexistent or, at best, minimal, in the case of Méliès. What is remarkable about this period is that in 30 short years, the principles of classic editing were developed. In the early years, however, continuity, screen direction, and dramatic emphasis through editing were not even goals. Cameras were placed without thought to compositional or emotional considerations. Lighting was notional (no dramatic intention meant), even for interior scenes. William Dickson used a Black Maria.[1] Light, camera placement, and camera movement were not variables in the filmic equation.

In the earliest Auguste and Louis Lumière and Thomas Edison films, the camera recorded an event, an act, or an incident. Many of these early films were a single shot.

Although Méliès's films grew to a length of 14 minutes, they remained a series of single shots: tableaus that recorded a performed scene. All of the shots were strung together. The camera was stationary and distant from the action. The physical lengths of the shots were not varied for impact. Performance, not pace, was the prevailing intention. The films were edited to the extent that they consisted of more than one shot, but *A Trip to the Moon* is no more than a series of amusing shots, each a scene unto itself. The shots tell a story, but not in the manner to which we are accustomed. It was not until the work of Edwin S. Porter that editing became more purposeful.

3

The Technique of Film and Video Editing: History, Theory, and Practice. DOI: 10.1016/B978-0-240-81397-4.00001-7

EDWIN S. PORTER: FILM CONTINUITY BEGINS

The pivotal year in Porter's work was 1903. In that year, he began to use a visual continuity that made his films more dynamic. Méliès had used theatrical devices and a playful sense of the fantastic to make his films seem more dynamic. Porter, impressed by the length and quality of Méliès's work, discovered that the organization of shots in his films could make his screen stories seem more dynamic. He also discovered that the shot was the basic building block of the film. As Karel Reisz suggests, "Porter had demonstrated that the single shot, recording an incomplete piece of action, is the unit of which films must be constructed and thereby established the basic principle of editing."[2]

Porter's *The Life of an American Fireman* (1903) is made up of 20 shots. The story is simple. Firemen rescue a mother and child from a burning building. Using newsreel footage of a real fire, together with performed interiors, Porter presents the six-minute story from the view of the victims and their rescuers.

In six minutes, he shows how the mother and child are saved. Although there is some contention about the original film, a version that circulated for 40 years presents the rescue in the following way. The mother and daughter are trapped inside the burning building. Outside, the firemen race to the rescue. In the version that circulated from 1944 to 1985, the interior scenes were intercut with the newsreel exteriors. This shot-by-shot alternating of interior and exterior made the story of the rescue seem dynamic.

The heightened tension from the intercutting was complemented by the inclusion of a close-up of a hand pulling the lever of a fire alarm box. The inclusion of the newsreel footage lent a sense of authenticity to the film. It also suggested that two shots filmed in different locations, with vastly different original objectives, could, when joined together, mean something greater than the sum of the two parts. The juxtaposition could create a new reality greater than that of each individual shot.

Porter did not pay attention to the physical length of the shots, and all of the shots, excluding that of the hand, are long shots. The camera was placed to record the shot rather than to editorialize on the narrative of the shot. Porter presented an even more sophisticated narrative in late 1903 with *The Great Train Robbery*. The film, 12 minutes in length, tells the story of a train robbery and the consequent fate of the robbers. In 14 shots, the film includes interiors of the robbery and exteriors of the attempted getaway and chase. The film ends very dramatically with an outlaw in subjective midshot firing his gun directly toward the audience. There is no match-cutting between shots, but there are location changes and time changes. How were those time and location changes managed, given that the film relies on straight cuts rather than dissolves and fades, which were developed later?

Every shot presents a scene: the robbery, the getaway, the pursuit, the capture. No single shot in itself records an action from beginning to end. The audience enters or exits a shot midway. Here lies the explanation for the time and location changes. For narrative purposes, it is not necessary to see the shot in its entirety to understand the purpose of the shot. Entering a shot in midstream suggests that time has passed. Exiting the shot before the action is complete and viewing an entirely new shot suggest a change in location.

Time and place shifts thus occur, and the narrative remains clear. The overall meaning of the story comes from the collectivity of the shots, with the shifts in time or place implied by the juxtaposition of two shots. Although *The Great Train Robbery* is not paced for dramatic impact, a dynamic narrative is clearly presented. Porter's contribution to editing was the arrangement of shots to present a narrative continuity.

D. W. GRIFFITH: DRAMATIC CONSTRUCTION

D. W. Griffith is the acknowledged father of film editing in its modern sense. His influence on the Hollywood mainstream film and on the Russian revolutionary film was immediate. His contributions cover the full range of dramatic construction: the variation of shots for impact, including the extreme long shot, the close-up, the cutaway, and the tracking shot; parallel editing; and variations in pace. All of these are ascribed to Griffith. Porter might have clarified film narrative in his work, but Griffith learned how to make the juxtaposition of shots have a far greater dramatic impact than his predecessor.

Beginning in 1908, Griffith directed hundreds of one- and two-reelers (10- to 20-minute films). For a man who was an unemployed playwright and performer, Griffith was slow to admit more than a temporary association with the new medium. Once he saw its potential, however, he shed his embarrassment, began to use his own name (initially, he directed as "Lawrence Griffith"), and zealously engaged in film production with a sense of experimentation that was more a reflection of his self-confidence than of the potential he saw in the medium. In the melodramatic plot (the rescue of children or women from evil perpetrators), Griffith found a narrative with strong visual potential on which to experiment. Although at best naïve in his choice of subject matter,[5] Griffith was a man of his time, a nineteenth-century southern gentleman with romanticized attitudes about societies and their peoples. To appreciate Griffith's contribution to film, one must set aside content considerations and look to those visual innovations that have made his contribution a lasting one.

Beginning with his attempt to move the camera closer to the action in 1908, Griffith continually experimented with the fragmentation of scenes. In *The Greaser's Gauntlet* (1908), he cut from a long shot of a hanging tree (a woman has just saved a man from being lynched) to a full body shot of the man thanking the woman. Through the match-cutting of the two shots, the audience enters the scene at an instant of heightened emotion. Not only do we feel what he must feel, but the whole tenor of the scene is more dynamic because of the cut, and the audience is closer to the action taking place on the screen.

Griffith continued his experiments to enhance his audience's emotional involvement with his films. In *Enoch Arden* (1908), Griffith moved the camera even closer to the action. A wife awaits the return of her husband. The film cuts to a close-up of her face as she broods about his return. The apocryphal stories about Biograph executives panicking that audiences would interpret the close-up as decapitation have displaced the historical importance of this shot. Griffith demonstrated that a scene could be fragmented into long shots, medium shots, and close shots to allow the audience to move gradually into the emotional heart of the scene. This dramatic orchestration has become the standard editing procedure for scenes. In 1908, the effect was shocking and effective. As with all of Griffith's innovations, the close-up was immediately adopted for use by other filmmakers, thus indicating its acceptance by other creators and by audiences.

In the same film, Griffith cut away from a shot of the wife to a shot of her husband far away. Her thoughts then become visually manifest, and Griffith proceeds to a series of intercut shots of wife and husband. The cutaway introduces a new dramatic element into the scene: the husband. This early example of parallel action also suggests Griffith's experimentation with the ordering of shots for dramatic purposes.

In 1909, Griffith carried this idea of parallel action further in *The Lonely Villa*, a rescue story. Griffith intercuts between a helpless family and the burglars who have invaded their home and the husband who is hurrying home to rescue his family. In this film, Griffith constructed the scenes using shorter and shorter shots to heighten the dramatic impact. The resulting suspense is powerful, and the rescue is cathartic in a dramatically effective way. Intercutting in this way also solved the problem of time. Complete actions needn't be shown to achieve realism. Because of the intercutting, scenes could be fragmented, and only those parts of scenes that were most effective needed to be shown. Dramatic time thus began to replace real time as a criteria for editing decisions.

Other innovations followed. In *Ramona* (1911), Griffith used an extreme long shot to highlight the epic quality of the land and to show how it provided a heightened dimension to the struggle of the movie's inhabitants. In *The Lonedale Operator* (1911), he mounted the camera on a moving train. The consequent excitement of these images intercut with images of the captive awaiting rescue by the railroad men again raised the dramatic intensity of the sequence. Finally, Griffith began to experiment with film length. Although famous for his one-reelers, he was increasingly looking for more elaborate narratives. Beginning in late 1911, he began to experiment with two-reelers (20 to 32 minutes), remaking *Enoch Arden* in that format. After producing three two-reelers in 1912—and spurred on by foreign epics such as the 53-minute *La Reine Elizabeth* (*Queen Elizabeth*) (1912) from France and *Quo Vadis* (1913) from Italy—Griffith set out to produce his long film *Judith of Bethulia* (1913). With its complex biblical story and its mix of epic baffles and personal drama, Griffith achieved a level of editing sophistication never before seen on screen.

Griffith's greatest contributions followed. *The Birth of a Nation* (1915) and *Intolerance* (1916) are both epic productions: each screen story lasts more than two hours. Not only was Griffith moving rapidly beyond his two-reelers, but he was also now making films more than twice the length of *Judith of Bethulia*. The achievements of these two films are well documented, but it is worth reiterating some of the qualities that make the films memorable in the history of editing.

Not only was *The Birth of a Nation* an epic story of the Civil War, but it also attempted in two and a half hours to tell in melodramatic form the stories of two families: one from the South, and the other from the North. Their fate is the fate of the nation. Historical events such as the assassination of Lincoln are intertwined with the personal stories, culminating in the infamous ride of the Klan to rescue the young southern woman from the freed slaves. Originally conceived of as a 12-reel film with 1544 separate shots, *The Birth of a Nation* was a monumental undertaking. In terms of both narrative and emotional quality, the film is astonishing in its complexity and range. Only its racism dates the film. *The Birth of a Nation* displays all of the editing devices Griffith had developed in his short films. Much has been written about his set sequences, particularly about the assassination of Lincoln[6] and the ride of the Klan. Also notable are the battle scenes and the personal scenes. The Cameron and Stoneman family scenes early in the film are warm and personal in contrast to the formal epic quality of the battle scenes. These disparate elements relate to one another in a narrative sense as a result of Griffith's editing. In the personal scenes, for example, the film cuts away to two cats fighting—one is dark and the other is light gray. Their fight foreshadows the larger battles that loom between the Yankees (the Blues) and the Confederates (the Grays). The shot is simple, but it is this type of detail that relates one sequence to another.

In *Intolerance*, Griffith posed for himself an even greater narrative challenge. In the film, four stories of intolerance are interwoven to present a historical perspective. Belshazzar's Babylon, Christ's Jerusalem, Huguenot France, and modern America are the settings for the four tales. Transition between the time periods is provided by a woman, Lillian Gish, who rocks a cradle. The transition implies the passage of time and its constancy. The cradle implies birth and the growth of a person. Cutting back to the cradle reminds us that all four stories are part of the generational history of our species. Time and character transactions abound. Each story has its own dramatic structure leading to the moment of crisis when human behavior will be tested, challenged, and questioned. All of Griffith's tools—the close-ups, the extreme long shots, the moving camera—are used together with pacing.

The film is remarkably ambitious and, for the most part, effective. More complex, more conceptual, and more speculative than his former work, *Intolerance* was not as successful with audiences. However, it provides a mature insight into the strengths and limitations of editing. The effectiveness of all four stories is undermined in the juxtaposition. The Babylonian story and the modern American story are more fully developed than the others and seem to overwhelm them, particularly the St. Bartholomew's Day Massacre in Huguenot France. At times the audience is confused by so many stories and so many characters serving a metaphorical theme. The film, nevertheless, remains Griffith's greatest achievement in the eyes of many film historians. Because *The Birth of a Nation* and *Intolerance* are so often subjects of analysis in film literature, rather than refer to the excellent work of others, the balance of this section focuses on another of Griffith's works, *Broken Blossoms* (1919).

Broken Blossoms is a simple love story set in London. A gentle Chinese man falls in love with a young Caucasian woman. The woman, portrayed by Lillian Gish, is victimized by her brutal father (Donald Crisp), who is aptly named Battler. When he learns that his daughter is seeing an Oriental (Richard Barthelness), his anger explodes, and he kills her. The suitor shoots Battler and then commits suicide. This tragedy of idealized love and familial brutality captures Griffith's bittersweet view of modern life. There is no place for gentleness and purity of spirit, mind, and body in an aggressive, cruel world.

The two cultures—China and Great Britain—meet on the London waterfront and in the opium dens (Figures 1.1 and 1.2). On the waterfront, the suitor has set up his shop, and here he brings the young woman (Figures 1.3 and 1.4). Meanwhile, Battler fights in the ring (Figure 1.5). Griffith intercuts the idyllic scene of the suitor attending to the young woman (Figure 1.6) with

FIGURE 1.1
Broken Blossoms, 1919. Still provided by British Film Institute.

FIGURE 1.2
Broken Blossoms, 1919. Still provided by Moving Image and Sound Archives.

FIGURE 1.3
Broken Blossoms, 1919. Still provided by British Film Institute.

FIGURE 1.4
Broken Blossoms, 1919. Still provided by British Film Institute.

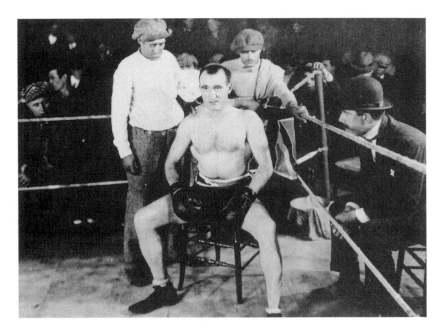

FIGURE 1.5
Broken Blossoms, 1919. Still provided by British Film Institute.

FIGURE 1.6
Broken Blossoms, 1919. Still provided by Moving Image and Sound Archives.

Battler beating his opponent. The parallel action juxtaposes Griffith's view of two cultures: gentleness and brutality. When Battler finishes off his opponent, he rushes to the suitor's shop. He is led there by a spy who has informed him about the whereabouts of the young woman. Battler destroys the bedroom, dragging the daughter away. The suitor is not present.

At home, Battler menaces his daughter, who hides in a closet. Battler takes an ax to the door. Here, Griffith intercuts between three locations: the closet (where the fearful, trapped young woman is hiding), the living room (where the belligerent Battler is attacking his daughter), and the suitor's bedroom (where he has found the room destroyed). The suitor grabs a gun and leaves to try to rescue the young woman. Finally, Battler breaks through the door. The woman's fear is unbearable. Griffith cuts to two subjective close-ups: one of the young woman, and one of Battler (Figures 1.7 and 1.8). Battler pulls his daughter through the shattered door (Figure 1.9). The scene is terrifying in its intensity and in its inevitability. Battler beats his daughter to death. When the suitor arrives, he finds the young woman dead and confronts Battler (Figure 1.10), killing him. The story now rapidly reaches its denouement: the suicide of the suitor. He drapes the body of the young woman in silk and then peacefully accepts death.

Horror and beauty in *Broken Blossoms* are transmitted carefully to articulate every emotion. All of Griffith's editing skills came into play. He used close-ups, cutaways, and subjective camera placement to articulate specific emotions and to move us through a personal story with a depth of feeling rare in film. This was Griffith's gift, and through his work, editing and dramatic film construction became one.

FIGURE 1.7
Broken Blossoms, 1919. Still provided by British Film Institute.

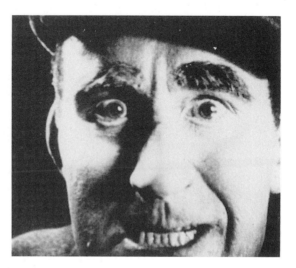

FIGURE 1.8
Broken Blossoms, 1919. Still provided by British Film Institute.

FIGURE 1.9
Broken Blossoms, 1919. Still provided by British Film Institute.

International Perspectives

There is little question that D. W. Griffith was the first great international filmmaker and that the drop in European production during World War I helped American production assume a far greater international position than it might have otherwise. It should not be surprising, then, that in 1918 Griffith and his editing innovations were the prime influence on filmmakers around the world. In the Soviet Union, Griffith's *Intolerance* was the subject of intense study for its technical achievements as well as for its ideas about society. In the 10 years that followed its release, Sergei Eisenstein wrote about Griffith,[7] V. I. Pudovkin studied Griffith and tried to perfect the theory and practice of communicating ideas through film narrative, and Dziga Vertov reacted against the type of cinema Griffith exemplified.

FIGURE 1.10
Broken Blossoms, 1919. Still provided by British Film Institute.

FIGURE 1.11

Dos Cabinet des Dr. Caligari, 1919. Still provided by Moving Image and Sound Archives.

In France and Germany, filmmakers seemed to be as influenced by the other arts as they were by the work of other filmmakers. The influence of Max Reinhardt's theatrical experiments in staging and expressionist painting are evidenced in Robert Wiene's *The Cabinet of Dr. Caligari* (1919) (Figure 1.11). Sigmund Freud's ideas about psychoanalysis join together with Griffith's ideas about the power of camera movement in F. W. Murnau's *The Last Laugh* (1924). Griffith's ideas about camera placement, moving the camera closer to the action, are supplemented by ideas of distortion and subjectivity in E. A. Dupont's *Variety* (1925). In France, Carl Dreyer worked almost exclusively with Griffith's ideas about close-ups in *The Passion of Joan of Arc* (1928), and produced one of the most intense films ever made. Griffith accomplished a great deal. However, it was others in this silent period who refined and built upon his ideas about film editing.

VSEVOLOD I. PUDOVKIN: CONSTRUCTIVE EDITING AND HEIGHTENED REALISM

Although all of the Soviet filmmakers were deeply influenced by Griffith, they were also concerned about the role of their films in the revolutionary struggle. Lenin himself had endorsed the importance of film in supporting the revolution. The young Soviet filmmakers were zealots for that revolution. Idealistic, energetic, and committed, they struggled for filmic solutions to political problems.

Perhaps none of the Soviet filmmakers was as critical of Griffith as V. I. Pudovkin.[8] As Reisz suggests, "Where Griffith was content to tell his stories by means of the kind of editing construction we have already seen in the excerpt from *The Birth of a Nation*, the young Russian directors felt that they could take the film director's control over his material a stage further. They planned, by means of new editing methods, not only to tell stories but to interpret and draw intellectual conclusions from them."[9]

Pudovkin attempted to develop a theory of editing that would allow filmmakers to proceed beyond the intuitive classic editing of Griffith to a more formalized process that could yield greater success in translating ideas into narratives. That theory was based on Griffith's perception that the fragmentation of a scene into shots could create a power far beyond the character of a scene filmed without this type of construction. Pudovkin took this idea one step further. As he states in his book,

> The film director [as compared to the theater director], on the other hand, has as his material, the finished, recorded celluloid. This material from which his final work is composed consists not of living men or real landscapes, not of real, actual stage-sets, but only of their images, recorded on separate strips that can be shortened, altered, and assembled according to his will. The elements of reality are fixed on these pieces; by combining them in his selected sequence, shortening and lengthening them according to his desire, the director builds up his own "filmic" time and "filmic" space. He does not adapt reality, but uses it for the creation of a new reality, and the most characteristic and important aspect of this process is that, in it, laws of space and time invariable and inescapable in work with actuality become tractable and obedient. The film assembles from them a new reality proper only to itself.[10]

Pudovkin thereby takes the position that the shot is the building block of film and that is the raw material of which the ordering can generate any desired result. Just as the poet uses words to create a new perception of reality, the film director uses shots as his raw material.

Pudovkin experimented considerably with this premise. His early work with Lev Kuleshov suggested that the same shot juxtaposed with different following shots could yield widely different results with an audience. In their famous experiment with the actor Ivan Mosjukhin, they used the same shot of the actor juxtaposed with three different follow-up shots: a plate of soup standing on a table, a shot of a coffin containing a dead woman, and a little girl playing with a toy. Audience responses to the three sequences suggested a hungry person, a sad husband, and a joyful adult, yet the first shot was always the same.

Encouraged by this type of experiment, Pudovkin went further. In his film version of *Mother* (1926), he wanted to suggest the joy of a prisoner about to be set free. These are Pudovkin's comments about the construction of the scene:

> I tried to affect the spectators, not by the psychological performances of an actor, but by the plastic synthesis through editing. The son sits in prison. Suddenly, passed in to him surreptitiously, he receives a note that the next day he is to be set free. The problem was the expression, filmically, of his joy. The photographing of a face lighting up with joy would have been flat and void of effect. I show, therefore, the nervous play of his hands and a big close-up of the lower half of his face, the corners of the smile. These shots I cut in with other and varied material—shots of a brook, swollen with the rapid flow of spring, of the play of sunlight broken on the water, birds splashing in the village pond, and finally a laughing child. By the junction of these components our expression of "prisoner's joy" takes shape.[12]

In this story of a mother who is politicized by the persecution of her son for his political beliefs, a personal approach is intermingled with a political story. In this sense, Pudovkin was similar in his narrative strategy to Griffith, but in purpose he was more political than

Griffith. He also experimented freely with scene construction to convey his political ideas. When workers strike, their fate is clear (Figure 1.12); when fathers and sons take differing sides in a political battle, the family (in this case, the mother) will suffer (Figure 1.13); and family tragedy is the sacrifice necessary if political change is to occur (Figure 1.14).

FIGURE 1.12
Mother, 1926. Still provided by Museum of Modern Art/Film Stills Archives.

FIGURE 1.13
Mother, 1926. Still provided by Museum of Modern Art/Film Stills Archives.

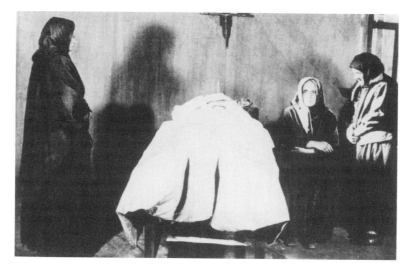

FIGURE 1.14
Mother, 1926. Still provided by Museum of Modern Art/Film Stills Archives.

Pudovkin first involves us in the personal story and the narrative, and then he communicates the political message. Although criticized for adopting bourgeois narrative techniques, Pudovkin carried those techniques further than Griffith, but not as far as his contemporary Sergei Eisenstein.

SERGEI EISENSTEIN: THE THEORY OF MONTAGE

Eisenstein was the second of the key Russian filmmakers. As a director, he was perhaps the greatest. He also wrote extensively about film ideas and eventually taught a generation of Russian directors. In the early 1920s, however, he was a young, committed filmmaker.

With a background in theatre and design, Eisenstein attempted to translate the lessons of Griffith and the lessons of Karl Marx into a singular audience experience. Beginning with *Strike* (1924), Eisenstein attempted to theorize about film editing as a clash of images and ideas. The principle of the dialectic was particularly suitable for subjects related to prerevolutionary and revolutionary issues and events. Strikes, the 1905 revolution, and the 1917 revolution were Eisenstein's earliest subjects.

Eisenstein achieved so much in the field of editing that it would be most useful to present his theory first and then look at how he put theory into practice. His theory of editing has five components: metric montage, rhythmic montage, tonal montage, overtonal montage, and intellectual montage. The clearest exposition of his theory has been presented by Andrew Tudor in his book *Theories on Film*.[13]

Metric Montage

Metric montage refers to the length of the shots relative to one another. Regardless of their content, shortening the shots abbreviates the time the audience has to absorb the information in each shot. This increases the tension resulting from the scene. The use of close-ups with shorter shots creates a more intense sequence (Figures 1.15 and 1.16).

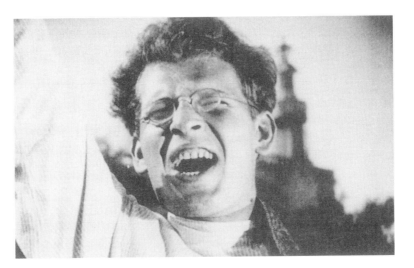

FIGURE 1.15
Potemkin, 1925. Courtesy Janus Films Company. Still provided by British Film Institute.

FIGURE 1.16
Potemkin, 1925. Courtesy Janus Films Company. Still provided by British Film Institute.

Rhythmic Montage

Rhythmic montage refers to continuity arising from the visual pattern within the shots. Continuity based on matching action and screen direction are examples of rhythmic montage. This type of montage has considerable potential for portraying conflict because opposing forces can be presented in terms of opposing screen directions as well as parts of the frame. For example, in the Odessa Steps sequence of *Potemkin* (1925), soldiers march down the steps from one quadrant of the frame, followed by people attempting to escape from the opposite side of the frame (Figures 1.17 to 1.21).

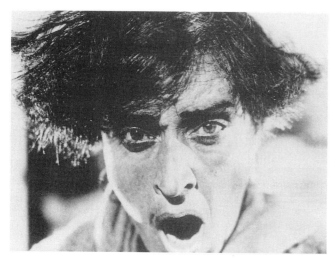

FIGURE 1.17
Potemkin, 1925. Courtesy Janus Films Company. Still provided by British Film Institute.

Tonal Montage

Tonal montage refers to editing decisions made to establish the emotional character of a scene,

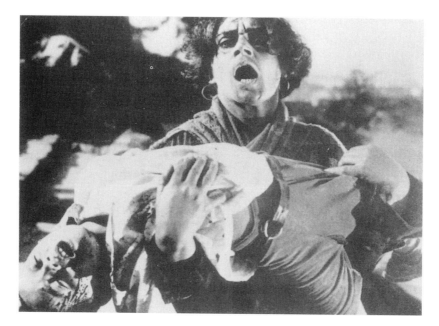

FIGURE 1.18
Potemkin, 1925. Courtesy Janus Films Company. Still provided by British Film Institute.

FIGURE 1.19

Potemkin, 1925. Courtesy Janus Films Company. Still provided by British Film Institute.

FIGURE 1.20

Potemkin, 1925. Courtesy Janus Films Company. Still provided by British Film Institute.

FIGURE 1.21
Potemkin, 1925. Courtesy Janus Films Company. Still provided by British Film Institute.

which may change in the course of the scene. Tone or mood is used as a guideline for interpreting tonal montage, and although the theory begins to sound intellectual, it is no different from Ingmar Bergman's suggestion that editing is akin to music, the playing of the emotions of the different scenes.[14] Emotions change, and so too can the tone of the scene. In the Odessa Steps sequence, the death of the young mother on the steps and the following baby carriage sequence highlight the depth of the tragedy of the massacre (Figures 1.22 to 1.27).

Overtonal Montage

Overtonal montage is the interplay of metric, rhythmic, and tonal montages. That interplay mixes pace, ideas, and emotions to induce the desired effect from the audience. In the Odessa Steps sequence, the outcome of the massacre should be the outrage of the audience. Shots that emphasize the abuse of the army's overwhelming power and the exploitation of the citizens' powerlessness punctuate the message (Figure 1.28).

Intellectual Montage

Intellectual montage refers to the introduction of ideas into a highly charged and emotionalized sequence. An example of intellectual montage is a sequence in *October* (1928). George Kerensky, the Menshevik leader of the first Russian Revolution, climbs the steps just as quickly as he ascended to power after the czar's fall. Intercut with his ascent are shots of a

FIGURE 1.22
Potemkin, 1925. Courtesy Janus Films Company. Still provided by Moving Image and Sound Archives.

FIGURE 1.23
Potemkin, 1925. Courtesy Janus Films Company. Still provided by Moving Image and Sound Archives.

FIGURE 1.24
Potemkin, 1925. Courtesy Janus Films Company. Still provided by Moving Image and Sound Archives.

mechanical peacock preening itself. Eisenstein is making a point about Kerensky as politician. This is one of many examples in *October* (1928).

Eisenstein: Theoretician and Aesthete

Eisenstein was a cerebral filmmaker, an intellectual with a great respect for ideas. Many of his later critics in the Soviet Union believed that he was too academic and his respect for ideas

FIGURE 1.25
Potemkin, 1925. Courtesy Janus Films Company. Still provided by Moving Image and Sound Archives.

FIGURE 1.26
Potemkin, 1925. Courtesy Janus Films Company. Still provided by Moving Image and Sound Archives.

FIGURE 1.27
Potemkin, 1925. Courtesy Janus Films Company. Still provided by British Film Institute.

would supersede his respect for Soviet realism, that his politics were too aesthetic, and that his aesthetics were too individualistic.

It is difficult for modern viewers to see Eisenstein as anything but a committed Marxist. His films are almost as naïve as those of Griffith in their simple devotion to their own view of

FIGURE 1.28
Potemkin, 1925. Courtesy Janus Films Company. Still provided by Moving Image and Sound Archives.

life. In the 1920s, regardless of whether he was aware of it, Eisenstein discovered the visceral power of editing and of visual composition, and he was a master of both. He was dangerous in the same sense that every artist is dangerous: He was his own person, a unique individual. Today, Eisenstein is greatly appreciated as a theoretician, but, like Griffith, he was also a great director. That is the extent of his crime.

DZIGA VERTOV: THE EXPERIMENT OF REALISM

If Eisenstein illustrated an editing theory devoted to reshaping reality to incite the population to support the revolution, Dziga Vertov was as vehement that only the documented truth could be honest enough to bring about true revolution.

Vertov described his goals in the film *The Man with a Movie Camera* (1929) as follows: "*The Man with a Movie Camera* constitutes an experiment in the cinematic transmission of visual phenomena without the aid of intertitles (a film with no intertitles), script (a film with no script), theater (a film with neither actors nor sets). Kino-Eye's new experimental work aims to create a truly international film—language, absolute writing in film, and the complete separation of cinema from theater and literature."[15]

Pudovkin remained interested in bourgeois cinema, and Eisenstein was too much the intellectual. Neither was sufficiently radical for Vertov, whose devotion to the truth is exemplified by his documentary *The Man with a Movie Camera*. Because the film was the story of one day in the life of a film cameraman, Vertov repeatedly reminds the viewer of the artificiality and nonrealism of cinema. Consequently, nonrealism, manipulation, and all of the technical elements of film become part of this self-reflexive (looking on the director's own intentions and using film to explore those intentions and make them overt) film. Special effects and fantasy were part of those technical elements (Figures 1.29 to 1.32).

Although on paper Vertov seems doctrinaire and dry, on film he is quite the opposite. He edits in a playful spirit that suggests filmmaking is pleasurable as well as manipulative. This sense of fun is freer than the work of Pudovkin or Eisenstein. In attitude, Vertov's work is more experimental and freeform than the work of his contemporaries. This sense of freedom and free

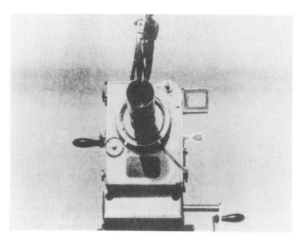

FIGURE 1.29
The Man with a Movie Camera, 1929. Still provided by British Film Institute.

FIGURE 1.30
The Man with a Movie Camera, 1929. Still provided by Moving Image and Sound Archives.

FIGURE 1.31

The Man with a Movie Camera, 1929. Still provided by Moving Image and Sound Archives.

association becomes particularly important in the work of Alexander Dovzhenko in the Ukraine and Luis Buñuel in France.

In terms of editing, Vertov is more closely aligned with the history of the experimental film than with the history of the documentary. In terms of his ideas, however, he is a forerunner of the cinéma vérité movement in documentary film, a movement that awaited the technical achievements of World War II to facilitate its development.

FIGURE 1.32

The Man with a Movie Camera, 1929. Still provided by Moving Image and Sound Archives.

ALEXANDER DOVZHENKO: EDITING BY VISUAL ASSOCIATION

In his concept of intellectual montage, Eisenstein was free to associate any two images to communicate an idea about a person, a class, or a historical event. This freedom was similar to Vertov's freedom to be playful about the clash of reality and illusion, as illustrated by the duality of the filmmaking process in *The Man with a Movie Camera*. Alexander Dovzhenko, a Ukranian filmmaker, viewed as his goal neither straight narrative nor documentary. His film *Earth* (1930) is best characterized as a visual poem. Although it has as its background the class struggle between the well-to-do peasants (in the era of private farms) and the poorer farmers, *Earth* is really about the continuity of life and death. The story is unclear because of its visual indirectness, and it leads us away from the literal meaning of the images to a quite different interpretation.

The opening is revealing. It begins with a series of still images—tranquil, beautiful compositions of rural life: a young woman and a wild flower, a farmer and his ox, an old man in an apple orchard, a young woman cutting wheat, a young man filled with the joy of life. All of these images are presented independently, and there is no apparent continuity (Figures 1.33 to 1.37). Gradually, however, this visual association forms a pattern of pastoral strength and tranquility. The narrative finally begins to suggest a family in which the grandfather is preparing to die, but dying surrounded by apples is not quite naturalistic.

FIGURE 1.33
Earth, 1930. Still provided by Museum of Modern Art/Film
Stills Archives.

FIGURE 1.34
Earth, 1930. Still provided by Museum of Modern Art/Film
Stills Archives.

FIGURE 1.35
Earth, 1930. Still provided by Museum of Modern Art/Film
Stills Archives.

FIGURE 1.36
Earth, 1930. Still provided by Museum of Modern Art/Film
Stills Archives.

FIGURE 1.37
Earth, 1930. Still provided by Museum of Modern Art/Film Stills Archives.

The cutting is not direct about the narrative intention, which is to illustrate the death of the grandfather while suggesting this event is the natural order of things—that is, life goes on. The presence of the apples surrounding him in the images takes away from the sense of loss and introduces a poetic notion about death. The poetic sense is life goes on in spite of death. The old man returns to the earth willingly, knowing that he is part of the earth and it is part of him.

The editing is dictated by visual association rather than by classic continuity. Just as the words of a poem don't form logical sentences, the visual pattern in *Earth* doesn't conform to a direct narrative logic. Initially, the absence of continuity is confusing, but the pattern gradually emerges, and a different editing pattern replaces the classic approach. It is effective in its own way, but Dovzhenko's work is quite different from the innovations of Griffith. It does, however, offer a vastly different option to filmmakers, an option taken up by Luis Buñuel.

LUIS BUÑUEL: VISUAL DISCONTINUITY

Surrealism, expressionism, and psychoanalysis were intellectual currents that affected all of the arts in the 1920s. In Germany, expressionism was the most influential, but among the artistic community in Paris, surrealism had an even greater influence. Salvador Dali and Luis Buñuel, Spanish artists, were particularly attracted to the possibility of making surrealist film. Like Vertov in the Soviet Union, Buñuel and Dali reacted first against classic film narrative, the type of storytelling and editing represented by Griffith. Like Eisenstein, Buñuel particularly viewed the use of dialectic editing and counterpoint, setting one image off in reaction to another, as a strong operating principle.

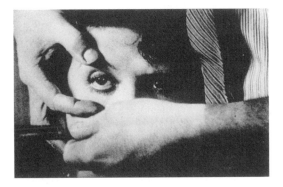

FIGURE 1.38
Un Chien d'Andalou, 1929. Still provided by Moving Image and Sound Archives.

The filmic outcome was *Un Chien d'Andalou* (*An Andalusian Dog*) (1929). Buñuel particularly was interested in making a film that destroyed meaning, interspersed with the occasional shock. Suddenly, a woman's eye is being slashed, two donkeys are draped across two pianos, a hand exudes ants or caresses a shoulder (Figures 1.38 to 1.41).

FIGURE 1.39
Un Chien d'Andalou, 1929. Still provided by British Film Institute.

FIGURE 1.40
Un Chien d'Andalou, 1929. Still provided by British Film Institute.

The fact that the film has become as famous as it has is a result of what the film represents: a satirical set of shocks intended to speak to the audience's unconscious. Whether the images are dreamlike and surreal or satiric remains open to debate. The importance of the film is that it represents the height of asynchronism: It is based on visual disassociation rather than on the classical rules of continuity. Consequently, the film broadens the filmmaker's options: to make sense, to move, to disturb, to rob of meaning, to undermine the security of knowing.

To frame Buñuel's contribution to film editing in another way, consider classic narrative storytelling as a linear progression. The plot begins with the character's achievement or final failure of achieving that goal. The plot follows the progress of the character in a linear fashion.

Buñuel, in undermining narrative expectations, creates in essence a nonlinear plot. A character may be replaced by a new character or by a new goal for the old character. This nonlinearity can be frustrating for the viewer. But it also can open up the story to a new series of story options and consequent experiences for the audience.

In this sense, Buñuel creates at least philosophically a nonlinear experience for his audience. And he uses editing to do so. Buñuel and Dali followed up *Un Chien d'Andalou* with a film that is a surreal narrative, *L'Age d'Or* (*The Golden Age*) (1930). In this film, a couple is overwhelmed by their passion for one another, but society, family, and church stand against them and prevent them from being together. This is a film about great passion and great resistance to that passion. Again, the satiric, exaggerated imagery of surrealism interposes a nonrealistic commentary on the behavior of all. Passion, anger, and resistance can lead only to death. The film's images portray each state (Figures 1.42 to 1.46).

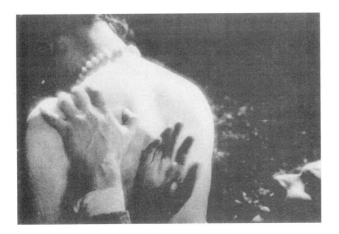

FIGURE 1.41
Un Chien d'Andalou, 1929. Still provided by Moving Image and Sound Archives.

FIGURE 1.42
L'Age d'Or, 1930. Still provided by Moving Image and Sound Archives.

FIGURE 1.43
L'Age d'Or, 1930. Still provided by Moving Image and Sound Archives.

FIGURE 1.44
L'Age d'Or, 1930. Still provided by Moving Image and Sound Archives.

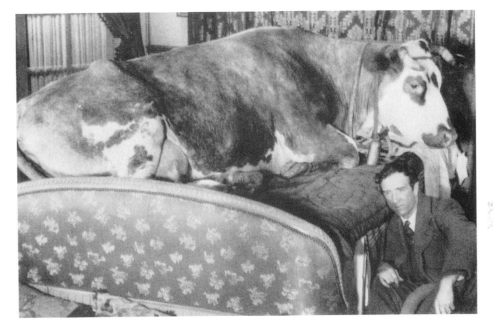

FIGURE 1.45
L'Age d'Or, 1930. Still provided by Moving Image and Sound Archives.

FIGURE 1.46
L'Age d'Or, 1930. Still provided by Moving Image and Sound Archives.

CONCLUSION

The silent period, 1885–1930, was an age of great creation and experimentation. It was the period when editing, unfettered by sound, came to maturity and provided a full range of options for the filmmaker. They included considerations of visual continuity, the deconstruction of scenes into shots, the development of parallel editing, the replacement of real time by a dramatic sense of time, poetic editing styles, the assertive editing theories of Eisenstein, and the asynchronous editing styles of Vertov and Buñuel. All of these became part of the editing repertoire.

One of the best examples of a filmmaker who combined the style of Griffith with the innovations of the Soviets was King Vidor. In his silent work, *The Big Parade* (1925) and *The Crowd* (1928), and then in his early sound work, *Billy the Kid* (1930) and *Our Daily Bread* (1934), he presented sequences that were narrative-driven, like Griffith's work, and idea- or concept-driven, like Eisenstein's. Both Griffith and Eisenstein were influential on the mainstream cinema, and their influence extended far beyond the silent period.

NOTES/REFERENCES

1. The Black Maria was an irregularly shaped building with a movable roof that could be raised to allow natural light to enter. Inside, the building was draped in black to prevent light reflection. The only light source was the roof, which could be moved to accommodate the location of the sun.

2. K. Reisz, G. Millar, The Technique of Film Editing, Focal Press, Boston, 1968, p. 19.

3. The history of the debate over which version is Porter's original is fully described by D. A. Cook in A History of Narrative Film, W. W. Norton, New York, 1990.

4. Porter's contribution to crosscutting for pace remains open to debate.

5. The controversy about racism in his work stems from *The Birth of a Nation* (1915), but as a subject, it is notable from his first film, *The Adventures of Dolly* (1908). Griffith, a southern gentleman, tended to be paternalistic and racist about slaves and slavery.

6. A full analysis of the 55-shot assassination sequence can be found in Cook, Narrative Film, pp. 84–88.

7. See S. Eisenstein, Dickens, Griffith and the Film Today, in: Film Form, Harcourt Brace Jovanovich, New York, 1977, pp. 195–255.

8. Pudovkin's ideas about editing are fully presented in his book Film Technique and Film Acting, Vision Press, London, 1968.

9. K. Reisz, G. Millar, The Technique of Film Editing, Focal Press, Boston, 1968, p. 27.

10. V. Pudovkin, Film Technique and Film Acting, Vision Press, London, 1968, pp. 89–90.

11. Ibid., 24–25.

12. V. Pudovkin, Film Technique and Film Acting, Vision Press, London, 1968, p. 27.

13. A. Tudor, Theory of Film, Viking, 1974.

14. I. Bergman, Introduction. Four Screenplays of Ingmar Bergman, Simon & Shuster, New York, 1960, pp. xv–xviii, xxi–xxii. Reprinted in: R. D. MacCann (Ed.), Film, a Montage of Theories, E. P. Dutton & Co., New York, 1966, pp. 142–146.

15. A. Michaelson (Ed.), Kino Eye, The Writings of Dziga Vertov, University of California Press, Berkeley, 1984, p. 283.

CHAPTER 2

The Early Sound Film

A great many innovations in picture editing were compromised with the coming of sound. The early sound films have often been called *filmed plays* or *radio plays with pictures* as a result of the technological characteristics of early sound. In this period, however, there was an attempt to come to grips with the theoretical meaning of sound as well as an attempt to find creative solutions to overcome its technological limitations and to return to a more dynamic style of editing. It is to these early experiments in sound and picture editing that we now turn our attention.

TECHNOLOGICAL LIMITATIONS

Although experiments in sound technology had been conducted since 1895, it was primarily in radio and telephone transmission technology that advances were made. By 1927, when Warner Brothers produced the first sound (voice) feature film, *The Jazz Singer* with Al Jolson, at least two studios were committed to producing sound films. The Warner Brothers system, Vitaphone, was a sound-on-disk system. The Fox Corporation invested in a sound-on-film system, Movietone. Photophone, an optical system produced by RCA, eventually became the industry standard. In 1927, though, Photophone had not yet been tested in an actual production, whereas Warner Brothers had used Vitaphone in *The Jazz Singer* and Fox had produced the popular Movietone news.

To use sound on film, several technological barriers had to be overcome. The problems revolved around the recording system, the microphone quality and characteristics, the synchronization of camera and sound disk playback, and the issue of sound amplification.

In the production process, the microphones used to record sound had to be sufficiently directional so that the desired voices and music were not drowned out by ambient noise.

A synchronization process was also needed. The camera recording the image and the disk recording the voice or music had to be in continuous synchronization so that, on playback, picture and sound would have a direct and constant relationship to one another. This system had to be carried through so that during projection the sound disk and the picture were synchronized. In sound-on-film systems, the sound reader had to be located on the projector so

33

The Technique of Film and Video Editing: History, Theory, and Practice. DOI: 10.1016/B978-0-240-81397-4.00002-9

that it was read precisely at the instant when the corresponding image was passing under the light of the projector.

Finally, because film was projected in an auditorium or theatre, the amplification system had to be such that the sound playback was clear and, to the extent possible, undistorted.

The recording of sound was so daunting a task that picture editing took second place. Dialog scenes on disk could not be edited without losing synchronization. A similar problem existed with the Movietone sound-on-film movies. A cut meant the loss of sound and image. Until rerecording and multiple camera use became common, editing was restricted to silent sequences. Consequently, the coming of sound meant a serious inhibition for editing and the loss of many of the creative gains made in the silent period.

This did not mean that film and film production did not undergo drastic changes in the early sound period. Suddenly, musicals and their stars became very important in film production. Stage performers and playwrights were suddenly needed. Journalists, novelists, critics, and columnists were in demand to write for the new dimension of speech on film. Those who had never spoken, the actors and their writers, fell from favor. The careers of the greatest silent stars—John Gilbert, Pola Negri, Emil Jannings, Norma Talmadge—all ended with the coming of sound. Many of the great silent comedians—Buster Keaton, Fatty Arbuckle, Harry Langdon—were replaced by verbal comedians and teams. W. C. Fields and the Marx Brothers were among the more successful. It was as if 30 years of visual progress were dismissed to celebrate speech, its power, and its influence.

Returning to the editing gains of the silent period, it is useful to understand why sound and picture editing today provides so many choices. The key is technological development. Today, sound is recorded with sophisticated unidirectional microphones that transmit sound to quarter-inch magnetic tape. Recording machines can mix sounds from different sources or record sound from a single source. The tape is transferred to magnetic film, which has the same dimensions as camera film and can be edge-numbered to coincide with the camera film's edge numbers. Original sound on tape is recorded in sync with the camera film so that camera film and magnetic film can be easily synchronized. Editing machines can run picture and sound in sync so that if synchronization is lost during editing it can be retrieved. Finally, numerous sound tracks are available for voice, sound effects, and music, and each is synchronized to the picture. Consequently, when those sound tracks are mixed, they remain in sync with the edited picture. When the picture negative is conformed to the working copy so the prints can be struck, an optical print of the sound is married to those prints from the negative. The married print, which is in sync, is used for projection.

The modern situation allows sound and picture to be disassembled so that editing choices in both sound and picture can proceed freely. Synchronization in picture and sound recording is fundamental to later synchronization. In the interim phases, the development of separate tracks can proceed because a synchronized relationship is maintained via the picture edit. Projection devices in which the sound head is located ahead of the picture allow the optical reading of sound to proceed in harmony with the image projection.

TECHNOLOGICAL IMPROVEMENTS

This freedom did not exist in 1930. It awaited a wide variety of technological improvements in addition to the decision to run sound and film at 24 frames per second (constant sound speed) rather than the silent speed of 16 frames per second (silent speed of film).

By 1929, camera blimps were developed to rescue the camera from being housed in the "ice box," a sound-proofed room that isolated camera noise from the action being recorded. As camera blimps became lighter, the camera itself became more mobile, and the option of shooting sound sequences with a moving camera became realistic.

Set construction materials were altered to avoid materials that were prone to loud, crackling noises from contact. Sound stages for production were built to exclude exterior noise and to minimize interior noise.

Carbon arc lights, with their constant hum, were initially changed to incandescent lights. More sophisticated circuitry eventually allowed a return to quieter arc light systems.

By 1930, a sound and picture editing machine, the Moviola, was introduced. In 1932, "edge numbering" allowed sound and picture to be edited in synchronization. By 1933, advances in microphones and mixing allowed sound tracks to use music and dialog simultaneously without loss of quality.

By 1936, the use of optical sound tracks was enhanced by new developments in optical light printers, which now provided distortionless sound. Quality was further enhanced by the development of unidirectional microphones in 1939.

Between 1945 and 1950, the use of magnetic recording over optical improved quality and permitted greater editing flexibility. Magnetic film began to replace optical film for sound editing.

Larger film formats, such as CinemaScope and TODD-AO, provided space on film for more than one optical track. Stored sound offered greater sound directionality and the sense of being surrounded by sound.

THEORETICAL ISSUES CONCERNING SOUND

The theoretical debate about the use of sound was a deliberate effort to counter the observation that the sound film was nothing more than a filmed play complete with dialog. It was an attempt to view the new technology of sound as a gain for the evolution of film as an art. Consequently, it was not surprising that the first expression of this impulse came from Eisenstein, Pudovkin, and Grigori Alexandrov. Their statement was published in a Leningrad magazine in 1928.[1]

Eisenstein, Pudovkin, and Alexandrov were concerned that the combination of sound and image would give the single shot a credibility it previously did not have. They worried that the addition of sound would counter the use of the shot as a building block that gains meaning when edited with other shots. They therefore argued that sound should not be used to enhance naturalism, but rather that it be used in a unsynchronized or asynchronous fashion. This contrapuntal use of sound would allow montage to continue to be used creatively.

The next year, Pudovkin argued in his book *Film Technique and Film Acting* for an asynchronous use of sound. He believed that sound has far greater potential and that new layers of meaning can be achieved through the use of asynchronous sound. Just as he saw visual editing as a way of building up meaning, he viewed sound as an additional element to enrich meaning. In the early work of Alfred Hitchcock, Pudovkin's ideas are put into practice. We will return to Hitchcock later in this chapter.

Later, directors Basil Wright and Alberto Cavalcanti experimented with the use of sound in film. In the early 1930s, each argued that sound could be used not only to counteract the realistic character of dialog, but also to orchestrate a wide variety of sound sources—effects, narration, and music—to create a new reality. They viewed sound as an element that could liberate new meanings and interpretations of reality. Because both worked in documentary film, they were particularly sensitive to the "realism" affected by the visuals.

For the most part, these directors were attempting to find a way around the perceived tyranny of technology that resulted in the distortion of the sound film into filmed theatre. In their theoretical speculations, they pointed out the direction that enabled filmmakers to use sound creatively and to resume their attempts to find editing solutions for new narratives.

EARLY EXPERIMENT IN SOUND—ALFRED HITCHCOCK'S *BLACKMAIL*

Alfred Hitchcock's *Blackmail* (1929) has many of the characteristics of the earliest sound films. It was shot in part as a silent film and in part as a sound film. The silent sequences have music and occasional sound effects. These sequences are dynamic—the opening sequence, which shows the apprehension and booking of a criminal by the police, is a good example. Camera movement is fluid, images are textured, and the editing is fast-paced. The sound sequences, on the other hand, are dominated by dialog. The camera is static, as are the performers. The mix of silent and sound sequences of this sort typifies the earliest sound films. Hitchcock didn't let sound hamper him more than necessary, however. This story of a young woman, Alice (Anny Ondra), who kills an overzealous admirer (Cyril Ritchard) and is protected from capture by her Scotland Yard beau is simple on the surface, but Hitchcock treated it as a tale of desire and guilt. Consequently, these very subjective states are what he attempted to create through a mix of visuals and sound.

After the murder (Figures 2.1 to 2.3), Alice wanders the streets of London. A neon sign advertises Gordon's Gin cocktail mix, but instead of a cocktail shaker, Alice sees the stabbing motion of a knife. Later, this subjective suggestion is carried even further. She arrives home and pretends that she has spent the night there.

Her mother wakes her for breakfast, mentioning the murder. She changes and goes to the confectioner's store, where a customer begins to gossip about the murder. The customer

FIGURE 2.1

Blackmail, 1929. Still provided by British Film Institute.

follows her into the breakfast room behind the store, continuing to talk about the murder instrument. The dialog begins to focus on the word *knife*. The image we see is of Alice trying to contain herself. The dialog over the visual of Alice is as follows: "Never use a knife . . . now mind you a knife is a difficult thing to handle . . . I mean any knife . . . knife . . . knife . . . knife. . . ." The word *knife* is now all that we (and Alice) hear, until she takes the knife to slice the bread. As she picks up the knife, the pitch and tone of the word changes from conversational to a scream of the word *knife*, and suddenly, she drops the knife.

This very subjective use of dialog, allowing the audience to hear only what the character hears, intensifies the sense of subjectivity. As we identify more strongly with Alice, we begin to feel what she feels. The shock of the scream seems to wake us to the fact that there is an objective reality here also. Alice's parents are here for breakfast, and the customer is here for some gossip. Only Alice is deeply immersed in the memory of the murder the night before, and her guilt seems to envelop her.

Hitchcock used sound as Pudovkin had envisioned, to build up an idea just as one would with a series of images. In *Blackmail*, sound is used as another bit of information to develop a narrative point: Alice's guilt over the murder. This early creative use of sound was achieved despite the

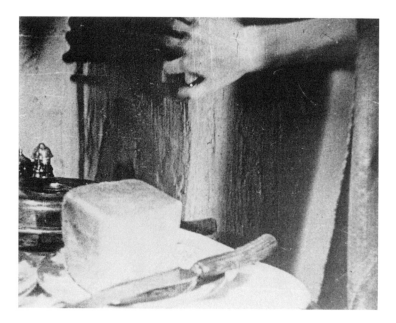

FIGURE 2.2
Blackmail, 1929. Still provided by British Film Institute.

technological limitations of dialog scenes and despite silent sequences presented with music and simple sound effects. It was a hindrance because the static results of sound recording—no camera movement, no interference with the literal recording of that sound—means literal rather than creative use of sound. In *Blackmail*, Hitchcock transcends those limitations.

FIGURE 2.3
Blackmail, 1929. Still provided by British Film Institute.

SOUND, TIME, AND PLACE: FRITZ LANG'S *M*

Fritz Lang's *M* (1931), although made only two years after Hitchcock's *Blackmail*, seems much more advanced in its use of sound, even though Lang faced many of the same technological limitations that Hitchcock did. Like *Blackmail*, Lang's film contains

FIGURE 2.4
M, 1931. Still provided by British Film Institute.

both dialog sequences and silent sequences with music or sound effects. How did Lang proceed? In brief, he edited the sound as if he were editing the visuals.

M is the story of a child murderer, of how he paralyzes a German city, and of how the underworld finally decides that if the police can't capture him, they will. The criminals and the police are presented as parallel organizations that are interested primarily in self-perpetuation. Only the capture of the child murderer will allow both organizations to proceed with business as usual. We are introduced to the murderer in shadow (Figure 2.4) when he speaks to a young girl, Elsie Beckmann. We hear the conversation he makes with her, but we see only his shadow, which is ironically shown on a reward poster for his capture.

Lang then sets up a parallel action sequence by intercutting shots of the murderer (Peter Lorre) with the young girl and shots of the young girl's mother. The culmination of this scene relies wholly on sound for its continuity. The mother calls out for her child. Each time she calls for Elsie, we see a different visual: out the window of the home, down the stairs, out into the yard where the laundry dries, to the empty dinner table where Elsie would sit, and finally far away to a child's ball rolling out of a treed area and to a balloon stuck in a telephone line. With each shot, the cries become more distant. For the last two shots, the mother's cries are no more than a faint echo.

Later in the film, Lang elaborates on this use of sound to provide the unifying idea for a sequence. In one scene, the minister complains to the chief of police that they must find the killer of Elsie Beckmann. The conversation reveals the scope of the investigation. As they speak, we see visual details of the search for the killer. The visuals show a variety of activities, including the discovery of a candy wrapper at the scene of the crime and the subsequent investigation of candy shops. Geographically, the police investigation moves all around the town and takes place over an extended period of time. These time and place shifts are all coordinated through the conversation between the minister and the chief of police.

In terms of screen time, the conversation is five minutes long, but it communicates an investigation that takes place over many days and in many places. We sense the police department's commitment but also its frustration at the lack of results.

What follows is the famous scene of parallel action where Lang intercuts two meetings. The police and the criminal underworld meet separately, and the leaders of both organizations discuss their frustrations about the child murderer and devise strategies for capturing him.

Rather than simply relying on visual parallel action, Lang cuts on dialog at one point, starting a sentence in the police camp and ending it in the criminal meeting. The crosscutting is all driven by dialog. There are common visual elements: the meeting setting, the smoky room, the seating, the prominence of one leader in each group. Despite these visual cues, it is the dialog that is used to set up the parallel action and to give the audience a sense of progress. Unlike Griffith's chase, there is no visual dynamic to carry us toward a resolution, nor is there a metric montage. The pace and character of the dialog establish and carry us through this scene.

Lang used sound as if it were another visual element, editing it freely. Notable is how Lang used the design of sound to overcome space and time issues. Through his use of dialog over the visuals, time collapses and the audience moves all about the city with greater ease than if he had straight-cut the visuals (Figures 2.5 to 2.7).

FIGURE 2.5

M, 1931. Still provided by British Film Institute.

FIGURE 2.6
M, 1931. Still provided by British Film Institute.

FIGURE 2.7
M, 1931. Still provided by British Film Institute.

THE DYNAMIC OF SOUND: ROUBEN MAMOULIAN'S *APPLAUSE*

As Lucy Fischer suggests, "Mamoulian seems to 'build a world'—one that his characters and audience seem to inhabit. And that world is 'habitable' because Mamoulian vests it with a strong sense of space. Unlike other directors of the period, he recognizes the inherent spatial capacities of sound and, furthermore, understands the means by which they can lend an aspect of depth to the image."[2]

Applause (1929) is a tale of backstage life, and it creates a world surrounded by sound (Figures 2.8 and 2.9). Even in intimate moments, the larger world expunges the characters. To capture this omnipresent sense of sound, Rouben Mamoulian added wheels to the sound-proof booth that housed the camera. As his characters moved, so did the camera and the sound. He also recorded two voices from two sources simultaneously. This challenge to technological limitations characterizes Mamoulian's attitude toward sound. Mamoulian realized that the proximity of the microphones to the characters would affect the audience's sense of closeness to the characters. Consequently, he used proximity and distance to good effect. Proximity meant that the characters (and the viewers) were surrounded and invaded by sound. Distance meant the opposite: total silence. Mamoulian used silence in Kitty's (Helen Morgan) suicide scene.

FIGURE 2.8
Applause, 1929. Still provided by British Film Institute.

FIGURE 2.9
Applause, 1929. Still provided by British Film Institute.

In this sense, Mamoulian used sound as a long shot (silence) and close-up (wide open sound). It wasn't necessary to use sound and picture in synchrony. By using sound in counterpoint to the images, Mamoulian was able to heighten the dramatic character of the scenes.

This operating principle was elaborated and made more complex three years later in Mamoulian's *Dr. Jekyll and Mr. Hyde* (1932). The Robert Louis Stevenson novel was adapted with a Freudian interpretation. Repressed sexuality leads Dr. Jekyll (Frederic March) to free himself to become the uninhibited Mr. Hyde. The object of his desire (and later his wrath) is Ivey (Miriam Hopkins).

To create an interior sense of Dr. Jekyll and to enhance the audience's identification with him, Mamoulian photographed the first five minutes with a totally subjective camera. We see what Dr. Jekyll sees. Consequently, we hear him but don't see him until he steps in front of the mirror. Poole, Jekyll's butler, announces that he will be late for a lecture at the medical school. We hear Jekyll as if we were directly beside him. The microphone's proximity gives us, in effect, "close-up" sound. Poole, on the other hand, is distant from the audience. At one point, the drop in sound is quite pronounced, a "long shot" sound.

This sense of spatial separation and character separation is continued when Jekyll enters the carriage that will take him to the medical school, but now the reverse begins to occur. The "close-up" sound is of the driver, and it is Jekyll who sounds distant. This continues when he is greeted by the medical school attendant.

Jekyll is now in the classroom, and all is silent. Then whispers by students and faculty can be heard. Only when Jekyll begins to lecture do the sound levels become more natural. When the film cuts to a closer visual of Jekyll, the sound also becomes a "close-up." Consequently, what Jekyll is saying about the soul of man is verbally presented with as much emphasis as if it were a visual close-up.

Later, when Jekyll rescues Ivey from an abusive suitor, Mamoulian returns to this use of "visual" sound. He advises bed rest for her injuries. When she slips off her garter and her stockings, there is sudden silence, as though Jekyll were silenced by her sensuality. He tucks her into bed, and she embraces and kisses him just as his colleague, Lagnon, enters the room. Misunderstanding and embarrassment lead Jekyll and Lagnon to leave as Ivey, with one leg over the bed, whispers "Come back soon."

As Jekyll and Lagnon walk into the London night, Ivey and her provocative thigh linger as a superimposed image and the soundtrack repeats the whisper, "Come back soon." The memory of Ivey and the desire for Ivey are recreated through the sound. Throughout the film, subjectivity, separation, desire, and dreams are articulated through the use of sound edits.

CONCLUSION

In their creative work, Mamoulian, Lang, and Hitchcock attempted to overcome the technological limitations of sound in this early period. Together with the theoretical statements of Eisenstein, Pudovkin, and the documentary filmmakers, they prepared the industry to view sound not as an end in itself, but rather as another element that, along with the editing of the visuals, could help create a narrative experience that was unique to film.

NOTES/REFERENCES

1. Reprinted in: E. Weis, J. Belton (Eds.), Film Sound: Theory and Practice, Columbia University Press, New York, 1985, pp. 83–85. An entire section of the book is devoted to sound theory; see pp. 73–176.
2. L. Fischer, *Applause*: The Visual and Acoustic Landscape, in: E. Weis, J. Belton (Eds.), Film Sound, pp. 232–246.

CHAPTER 3

The Influence of the Documentary

D. W. Griffith and his contemporaries were part of a growing commercial industry of which the prime goal was to entertain. This meant that the ideas presented in their films were subordinate to their entertainment value. Griffith attempted to present conceptual material about society in *Intolerance* and failed. Although other filmmakers—such as King Vidor (*The Crowd*, 1928), Charlie Chaplin (*The Gold Rush*, 1925), and F. W. Murnau (*Sunrise*, 1927)—blended ideas and entertainment values more successfully, the commercial film has more often been associated primarily with entertainment.

The documentary film, on the other hand, has always been associated with the communication of ideas first and with entertainment values a distant second. Griffith was very successful in using editing techniques to involve and entertain. He was less successful in developing editing techniques that would help communicate ideas. Which editing theories and techniques facilitate the communication of ideas? How do ideas work with the emotional power implicit in editing techniques?

Because the documentary film was less influenced by market forces than commercial film was and because the filmmakers attracted to the documentary had different goals from commercial filmmakers, often goals with social or political agendas, the techniques they used often displayed a power not seen in the commercial film. Subsidized by government, these filmmakers blended artistic experimentation with political commitment, and their innovations in the documentary broadened the repertoire of editing choices for all filmmakers.

The documentary, or "film of actuality," had been important from the time of the Lumière brothers in France, but it was not until the 1920s that the work of the Russian filmmakers—Eisenstein, Pudovkin, and the National Film School under Kuleshov—and the release of Robert Flaherty's *Nanook of the North* (1922) prompted John Grierson in England to consider films of actuality and "purposive filmmaking."[1] As Paul Swann suggests, "Grierson was prompt to note Lenin's belief in 'the power of film for ideological propaganda.' Grierson's great innovation was to adapt this revolutionary dictum to the purpose of social democracy."[2]

The Technique of Film and Video Editing: History, Theory, and Practice. DOI: 10.1016/B978-0-240-81397-4.00003-0

Grierson was very affected by the power of the editing in *Potemkin* and the method Eisenstein used to form, present, and argue about ideas visually (intellectual montage). There is little question that a dialectic between form and content became a working principle as Grierson produced his own film, *The Drifters* (1929), and moved on to produce the work of many others at the British Marketing Board.

Grierson took the principle of social or political purpose and joined it with a visual aesthetic. Greatly aided by the coming of sound after 1930, the documentary as propaganda developed into an instrument of social policy in England, in Germany, and temporarily in the United States. In their work, the filmmakers applied editing solutions to complex ideas. Through their work, the options for editing broadened almost exponentially.

IDEAS ABOUT SOCIETY

The coming of sound was closely followed by shattering world events. In October 1929, the U.S. stock market crash signaled the onset of the Great Depression. Political instability led to the rise of fascist governments in Italy and Germany. The aftereffects of World War I undermined British and French society. The United States maintained an isolationist position. The period, then, was unpredictable and unstable. The documentary films of this time searched for a stability and strength not present in the real world. The efforts of these filmmakers to find positive interpretations of society were the earliest efforts to communicate particular ideas about their respective societies. Grierson was interested in using film to bring society together. Working during the Great Depression, a fracturing event, he and others wanted to use film to heal society. In this sense, he was an early propagandist.

Robert Flaherty and *Man of Aran*

Robert Flaherty's *Man of Aran* (1934) closely resembles a commercial film. In this fictionalized story of the Aran Islands off the coast of Ireland, Flaherty used actual islanders in the film, but he created the plot according to his goals rather than basing it on the lives of the islanders.

Man of Aran tells the story of a family that lives in a setting where they are dwarfed by nature and challenged by the land and sea. Flaherty used two shark hunts to suggest the bravery of the islanders, and the storm at the end of the film illustrates that their struggle against nature makes them stronger, worthy adversaries in the hierarchy of natural beings. People, not being supreme in the natural hierarchy, are shown to be worthy adversaries for nature when the challenge is considerable. In essence, a poetic interpretation of people's struggle with nature makes them look good.

This idea of the nobility of humanity and of its will to live despite the elements was Flaherty's creation. The Aran Islanders didn't live as he presented them. For example, the sharks they hunted are basking sharks, a species that is harmless to humans (the film implies that they are maneaters). Of course, Flaherty's production of such a film in 1934 in the midst of the Great Depression suggests how far he roamed from the issues of the day. Like Griffith, he had a particular mythic vision of life, and he recreated that vision in all of his films.

In terms of its editing, *Man of Aran* is similar to the early sound films of Mamoulian and Hitchcock. Music and simple sound effects are used as sound coverage for essentially silent sequences. There is no narrative, and where dialog is used, it is equivalent to another sound effect. The actual dialog is not necessary to the progress of the story. The film has a very powerful visual character, which is presented in a very formal manner. Although the film offers opportunity for dialectical editing, particularly in the shark hunts, the actual editing is deliberate and avoids developing a strong identification with the characters. In this sense, the intimacy so vital to the success of a film like *Broken Blossoms* is of no interest to Flaherty (Figures 3.1 to 3.4). Instead, Flaherty tries to create an archetypal struggle of humanity against nature, and dialectics seem inappropriate to Flaherty's vision. Consequently, the editing is secondary to the cumulative, steady development of Flaherty's personal ideas about the struggle. The fact that the film was made in the midst of the Great Depression adds a level of irony. It makes *Man of Aran* timeless; this quality was a source of criticism toward the film at the time.

For our purposes, however, *Man of Aran* presents the documentary film in a form similar to the commercial film. Performance, pictorial style, and editing serve a narrative: in this case, Flaherty's version of the life of the Aran Islanders. It is not purposive filmmaking, as Grierson proposed, but nor is it the Hollywood film he so vehemently criticized.

FIGURE 3.1
Man of Aran, 1934. Still provided by Moving Image and Sound Archives.

FIGURE 3.2

Man of Aran, 1934. Still provided by Moving Image and Sound Archives.

FIGURE 3.3

Man of Aran, 1934. Still provided by British Film Institute.

FIGURE 3.4
Man of Aran, 1934. Still provided by British Film Institute.

Basil Wright and *Night Mail*

Night Mail (1936), produced by John Grierson and the General Post Office film unit and directed by Basil Wright, was certainly purposive, and it used sound particularly to create the message of the film. The film itself is a simple story of the delivery of the mail by train from London to Glasgow, but it is also about the commitment and harmony of the postal workers. If the film has a simple message, it's the importance of the job of delivering the mail. The sense of harmony among the workers is secondary.

Turning again to the events of the day, 1936 was a dreadful time in terms of employment. Political and economic will were not enough to overcome the international protectionism and the strains of the British Empire. Consequently, *Night Mail* is not an accurate reflection of feeling among postal workers. It is the Grierson vision of what life among the postal workers should be.

For us, the film's importance is the blend of image and sound and how the sound edit is used to create the sense of importance and harmony. As in all of these films, there is a visual aesthetic that is in itself powerful (Figures 3.5 and 3.6), but it is the sound work of composer Benjamin Britten, poet W. H. Auden (who wrote the narration), and above all Alberto Cavalcanti (who designed the sound) that affects the purposeful message Grierson intended.

FIGURE 3.5
Night Mail, 1936. Still provided by Moving Image and Sound Archives.

FIGURE 3.6
Night Mail, 1936. Still provided by British Film Institute.

The sound of the train simulating a cry or the rhythm of the narration trying to simulate the urgent, energetic wheels of the train rushing to reach Glasgow create a power beyond the images themselves. The reading, although artificial in its nonrealism, acts as Dovzhenko's visuals did—to create a poetic idea that is transcendent. The idea is reinforced by the music and by the shuffling cadence of the narration. Together, all of the sound, music, words, and effects elevate the images to achieve the unifying idea that this train is carrying messages from one part of the nation to another, that commerce and personal well-being depend on the delivery of those messages, and that those who carry those messages, the workers, are critical to the well-being of the nation. This idea, then, is the essence of the film, and it is the editing of the sound that creates the dimensions of the idea.

Pare Lorentz and *The Plow That Broke the Plains*

A more critical view of society was taken by Pare Lorentz in *The Plow That Broke the Plains* (1936), a film sponsored by the Resettlement Administration of the U.S. government. Lorentz looked at the impact of the Depression on the agricultural sector. The land and the people both suffered from natural as well as human-made disasters. The purposive message of the film is that government must become actively involved in recovery programs to manage these natural resources. Only through government intervention can this sort of suffering be alleviated.

To give his message impact, Lorentz relied on the photojournalist imagery made famous by Walker Evans and others during the Great Depression. In terms of the visual editing, the film is imitative of Eisenstein, but the sequences aren't staged as thoroughly as Eisenstein's were. Consequently, the sequences as a whole don't have the power of Eisenstein's films. They resemble more closely the work of Dovzhenko, in which the individual shots have a power of their own (Figures 3.7 and 3.8).

It is the narration and the music by Virgil Thomson that pull the ideas together. Lorentz has to rely on direct statement to present the solution to the government. In this sense, his work is not as mature propaganda as the later work of Frank Capra or the earlier work of Leni Riefenstahi. Lorentz was more successful in his second film, *The River* (1937). As Richard Meran Barsam states about Lorentz, "While (his films) conform to the documentary problem—solution structure, these films rely on varying combinations of repetition, rhythm, and parallel structure, so that problems presented in the first part of the films are solved in the second part, but solved through such an artistic juxtaposition of image, sound, and motif that their unity and coherence of development set them distinctly apart."[3]

IDEAS ABOUT ART AND CULTURE

Flaherty, Grierson, and Lorentz had specific views about society that helped shape their editing choices. Other filmmakers, although they also held particular political views, attempted to deal with more general and more elusive ideas. How they achieved that aesthetic goal is of interest to us.

FIGURE 3.7
The Plow That Broke the Plains, 1936. Still provided by Moving Image and Sound Archives.

FIGURE 3.8
The Plow That Broke the Plains, 1936. Still provided by British Film Institute.

Leni Riefenstahl and *Olympia*

It would be simple to dismiss Leni Riefenstahl's work as Nazi propaganda (Figure 3.9). Although Riefenstahl's *Olympia Parts I and II* (1938) are films of the 1936 Olympics held in Berlin and hosted by Adolph Hitler's Nazi government, Riefenstahl's film attempts to create a sensibility about the human form that transcends national boundaries. Using 50 camera operators and the latest lenses, Riefenstahl had at her disposal slow-motion images, micro-images, and images of staggering scale. She presented footage of many of the competitions in the expected form—the competitors, the competition, the winners—but she also included numerous sequences about the training and the camaraderie of the athletes. *Part II* opens with an idyllic early morning run and the sauna that follows the training. Riefenstahl used no narration, only music, and she didn't focus on any individual. She focused only on the beauty of nature, including the athletes and their joy.

This principle is raised to its height in the famous diving sequence near the end of *Part II*. This five-minute sequence begins with shots of the audience responding to a dive and shots of competitors from specific countries. Then Riefenstahl cuts to the mechanics of the dive. Gradually, the audience is no longer shown. Now we see one diver after another. She concentrates on the grace of the dive, then she begins to use slow motion and shows only the form and completion of the dive. The shots become increasingly abstract.

We no longer know who is diving. She begins to follow in rapid succession dives from differing perspectives. The images are disorienting. She begins to fragment the dives. We see only the beginning of dives in rapid succession.

Then the dives are in silhouette, and they seem like abstract forms rather than humans. Two forms replace one. She cuts from one direction to another, one abstract form to another. Are they diving into water or jumping into the air? The images become increasingly abstract, and eventually, we see only sky.

FIGURE 3.9

Olympia, 1938. Still provided by British Film Institute.

In five minutes, Riefenstahl has taken us from a realistic document of an Olympic dive (complete with an audience) to an abstract form leaping through space—graceful beauty in motion. Through the sequence, we hear only music and the splash of water as the diver hits the surface. Riefenstahl's ideas about beauty and art are brilliantly communicated in this sequence. No narration was necessary to explain the idea. Editing and music were the tools on which Riefenstahl relied.

W. S. Van Dyke and *The City*

In the late 1930s, the American Institute of Planners commissioned a film about the future city to be shown at the 1939 World's Fair in New York City. W. S. Van Dyke and Ralph Steiner, working from a script by Henwar Rodakiewicz and Lewis Mumford (and an outline by Pare Lorentz), fashioned a story about the future that arises out of the past and present. The urgency of the new city is born out of contemporary problems of urban life. The images of those problems are in sharp contrast to the orderly prosperous character of the future city (Figures 3.10 to 3.12).

In *The City* (1939), ideas about politics are mixed with ideas about the culture of the city: urban life as a source of power as well as oppression. Unfortunately, the images of oppression are so memorable and so human that they overwhelm the suburban utopia presented later. In the third section of the film, featuring New York City, Van Dyke and Steiner portray the travails of the lunch hour in the big city. Everyone is on the run with the inevitable congestion and indigestion. All this is portrayed in the editing; the pace and the music capture the charm and the harm of lunch on the run. This metaphor is carried through to the conclusion through images of the icons of the large city—the signs that, instead of

FIGURE 3.10
The City, 1939. Still provided by Museum of Modern Art/Film Stills Archives.

FIGURE 3.11
The City, 1939. Still provided by Museum of Modern Art/Film Stills Archives.

FIGURE 3.12
The City, 1939. Still provided by Museum of Modern Art/Film Stills Archives.

giving the city balance, imply a rather conclusive improbability about one's future in the city of the present. This sequence prepares us for the city of the future.

As in *The Plow That Broke the Plains*, the American documentary structure follows a point−counterpoint flow that is akin to making a case for the position put forward in the concluding sequence, in this case, the city of the future. The film unfolds as a case for the prosecution would in a trial. It's a dramatic device differing from the slow unfolding of many documentaries. As in the Lorentz film, music is very important. Another similarity is the strength of the individual shots. Van Dyke and Steiner, as still photographers, bring a power to the individual images that undermines the strength of the sequences. However, the film does succeed in creating a sense that the city is important as more than an economic center. The urban center becomes, in this film, a place to live, to work, and to affiliate, and a cultural force that can shape or undermine the lives of all who live there. Van Dyke's city becomes more than a place to live. It becomes the architectural plan for our quality of life.

IDEAS ABOUT WAR AND SOCIETY

The shaping of ideas became even more urgent when the purpose of the film was to help win a war fought for the continued existence of the country. Grierson provided the philosophy for the propaganda film, and Eisenstein and Pudovkin provided the practical tools to shape and sharpen an idea through editing. In the 1930s, such filmmakers as Riefenstahl put the philosophy and techniques to the practical test. Her film *Triumph of the Will* (1935) became the standard against which British and American war documentaries were measured. The work of Frank Capra, William Wyler, and John Huston in the United States and of Alberto Cavalcanti, Harry Watt, and Humphrey Jennings in Great Britain displayed a mix of personal creativity and national purpose. Their films drew on national traditions, and in their own way, each advanced the role of editing in shaping ideas effectively.

Consequently, the power of the medium seemed to be without limit, and thus dangerous. This perception shaped both the fascination with and the suspicion of the media, particularly film and television, in the postwar period.

Frank Capra and *Why We Fight*

Frank Capra, one of Hollywood's most successful directors, was commissioned by then−Chief of Staff George C. Marshall to produce a series of films to prepare soldiers inducted into the army for going to war. The *Why We Fight* series (1943−1945), seven films produced to be shown to the troops, are among the most successful propaganda films ever made. As Richard Dyer MacCann suggests about the films, "They attempted (1) to destroy faith in isolation, (2) to build up a sense of the strength and at the same time the stupidity of the enemy, and (3) to emphasize the bravery and achievements of America's allies. Their style was a combination of a sermon, a between-halves pep talk, and a barroom bull session."[4]

Capra used compilation footage, excerpts from Riefenstahl's *Triumph of the Will*, recreated footage, and excerpts from Hollywood films to create a sense of actuality and credibility. To make dramatic points, Capra resorted to animation. Maps and visual analogies—such as the juxtaposition of two globes, and a white earth (the Allies) and a black earth (the Axis), in *Prelude to War* (1943)—illustrate the struggle for primacy. Capra used the animation to make a dramatic point with simple pictures.

The narration is colloquial, highly personalized, and passionate about characterizing each side in terms of good and evil. The narration features slang, rather than objective language. Read by Walter Huston, it illustrates and deepens the impact of the images.

Picture and sound complement one another, and where possible, repetition follows a point made in a rapid visual montage. The pace of the film is urgent. Whether the scene has to do with the subversion necessary from within in the takeover of Norway or the more complex portrayal of French capitulation and Nazi perfidy and consequent glee (the repetitive shot of Hermann Göring rubbing his hands together), Capra highlighted victim and victimizer in the most dramatic terms (Figures 3.13 to 3.15).

Capra also used visual and sound editing in a highly dramatized way. A great deal of information is synthesized into an "us against them" structure. Eisenstein's dialectic ideas have rarely been used more effectively.

Humphrey Jennings and *Diary for Timothy*

By the time he produced *Diary for Timothy* (1945), Humphrey Jennings had already directed two of the greatest war documentaries, *Listen to Britain* (1942) and *Fires Were Started* (1943). Whereas Capra in his films concentrated on the combatants and the war, Jennings, in his work, concentrated on the home front.

FIGURE 3.13
Divide and Conquer, 1945. Still provided by Museum of Modern Art/Film Stills Archives.

FIGURE 3.14
Divide and Conquer, 1945. Still provided by Museum of Modern Art/Film Stills Archives.

FIGURE 3.15
Divide and Conquer, 1945. Still provided by Museum of Modern Art/Film Stills Archives.

Diary for Timothy is a film about a baby, Timothy, born in 1944. The film speculates about what kind of world Timothy will grow up in. The film's tone is anxious about the future. As with all of Jennings's work, this film tends to roam visually, not focusing on a single event,

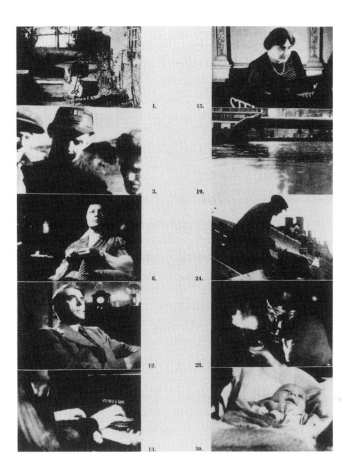

FIGURE 3.16

Diary for Timothy, 1945. Stills provided by British Film Institute.

place, or person. To create a sense of the society as a whole, Jennings includes many people at work or at home with their families. This general approach poses the problem of how to unify the footage (Figure 3.16).

In this film, the baby, at different ages, acts as a visual reference point, and the narration addressed to Timothy (read by Michael Redgrave, written by E. M. Forster) personalizes and attempts to shape a series of ideas rather than a plot. The film contains six sections. Although there is a temporal relationship, there is no clear developmental character. Instead of a story, as Alan Lovell and Jim Hillier suggest, "*A Diary for Timothy* depends for its effect on highly formal organization and associative montage."[5] Within the montage sections, the sum is greater than the parts. Again quoting from Lovell and Hillier:

> With the wet reflection of a pit-head and "rain, too much rain," the film launches into a
> further sequence of images and events: Tim's mother writing Christmas cards, rain on

Bill's engine, rain in the fields, Tim's baptism, Peter learning to walk again, Goronwy brought up from the pit on a stretcher. It is of course possible to attempt an intellectual analysis of the sequence of images but such analysis rarely takes us far enough. Jennings seems to have reached such a pitch of personal freedom in his association of ideas and shifts of mood that we lose the precise significance of the movement of the film and respond almost completely emotionally.[6]

This emotion is charged with speculation in the last sequence. Instead of a hopeful, powerful conclusion, as in *Listen to Britain*, or a somber, heroic conclusion, as in *Fires Were Started*, Jennings opted for an open-ended challenge.

He put the challenge forward in the narration:

Well, dear Tim, that's what's been happening around you during your first six months. And, you see, it's only chance that you're safe and sound. Up to now, we've done the talking; but, before long you'll sit up and take notice.... What are you going to say about it and what are you going to do? You heard what Germany was thinking, unemployment after the war and then another war and then more unemployment. Will it be like that again? Are you going to have greed for money or power ousting decency from the world as they have in the past? Or are you going to make the world a different place—you and all the other babies?[7]

CONCLUSION

Perhaps more than any other genre, the documentary has been successful in communicating ideas. The interplay of image and sound by filmmakers such as Riefenstahl, Capra, and Jennings has been remarkably effective and has greatly enhanced the filmmaker's repertoire of editing choices. These devices have found their way back into the fictional film, as evidenced in the work of neorealist filmmakers and the early American television directors whose feature film work has been marked by a pronounced documentary influence.

NOTES/REFERENCES

1. P. Swann, The British Documentary Film Movement, 1926–1946, Cambridge University Press, Cambridge, 1989, p. 9.

2. Ibid., 7.

3. R. M. Barsam (Ed.), Nonfiction Film: A Critical History, E. P. Dutton, New York, 1973, pp. 99–100.

4. R. D. MacCann, World War II: Armed Forces Documentary, in: R. M. Barsam (Ed.), Nonfiction Film: Theory and Criticism, E. P. Dutton, New York, 1976, p. 139.

5. A. Lovell, J. Hillier, Studies in Documentary, Martin Secker and Warburg, London, 1972, 105.

6. Ibid., 108.

7. Quoted from the shot-by-shot analysis of *Diary for Timothy* in: E. Cameron. An analysis of 'A Diary for Timothy.' *Cinema studies*, Spring, 1967.

CHAPTER 4

The Influence of the Popular Arts

Film as a narrative form had numerous influences, particularly the popular novel of the nineteenth century[1] and the theatrical genres of spectacle, pantomime, and melodrama.[2]

The character and narrative conventions of those forms were adapted for film through editing. The types of shots required and how they were put together are the subject of Chapter 1. This chapter is concerned with the ongoing development in the popular arts and how they affected editing choices. In some cases (radio, musicals), they expanded those choices, and in others (vaudeville, theatre), they constrained those choices.

The interaction of these popular forms with film broadened the repertoire for film and eventually influenced other arts. However, film's influence on theatre, for example, took much longer. That influence was not apparent in theatrical production until the 1960s. In the 1920s and 1930s, it was the influence of theatre and radio that shaped film and film editing.

VAUDEVILLE

In the work of Griffith and Vidor, narrative goals affected editing choices. In the subsequent work of Eisenstein and Pudovkin, political goals influenced editing choices. Vaudeville, as in the case of the documentary, presented yet another set of priorities, which in turn suggested different goals for editing. Vaudeville, whether associated with burlesque or, later, with the more respectable theatre, offered a different audience experience than the melodramas and epics of Griffith or the polemics of the Russian revolutionary filmmakers. Vaudeville embraced farce as well as character-based humor, and physical humor as well as verbal humor. As Robert C. Allen suggests, diversity was a popular characteristic of vaudeville programs: "A typical vaudeville bill in 1895 might include a trained animal act, a slapstick comedy routine, a recitation of 'inspirational' poetry, an Irish tenor, magic lantern slides of the wilds of Africa, a team of European acrobats, and a twenty-minute dramatic 'playlet' performed by a Broadway star and his/her company."[3]

Vaudeville skits didn't have to be realistic; fantasy could be as important as an everyday situation. Character was often at the heart of the vaudeville act. Pace, character, humor, and

61

The Technique of Film and Video Editing: History, Theory, and Practice. DOI: 10.1016/B978-0-240-81397-4.00004-2

entertainment were all goals of the act. In the early period, the audience for vaudeville, just like the early audience for film, was composed of the working class and often immigrants.[4] Pantomime and visual action were thus critical to the success of the production because routines had to transcend the language barrier.

We see the influence of vaudeville directly in the star system. Both Charlie Chaplin and Buster Keaton began in vaudeville. In their film work, we see many of the characteristics of vaudeville: the victim, the routine, the performance, and a wide range of small set-pieces (brief dramatized comic scenes) that are either standalone routines or parts of a larger story. What unifies the Chaplin and Keaton films is their characters and the people they represent: in both cases, ordinary men caught up in extraordinary situations. In terms of editing, the implications are specific. First, the routine is important and must be clearly articulated so that it works. Second, the persona of the star—Chaplin or Keaton—must remain central; there can be no distractions from that character.

The easiest way to illustrate these principles is to look at Charlie Chaplin's films. Structurally, each film is a series of routines, each carefully staged through Chaplin's pantomime performance. Chaplin called *City Lights* (1931) "a comedy romance in pantomime." The opening sequence, the unveiling of a city statue on which Chaplin's character, "the little tramp," is sleeping, is both absurd and yet logical. Why is a man sleeping in the arms of a statue? Yet this very absurdity emphasizes the homelessness of the character. He is in every sense a public ward. This type of absurdity is notable in many of Chaplin's sequences, for example, the eating of shoelaces as spaghetti in *The Gold Rush* (1925) and the attempted suicide in *City Lights*. Absurdity is often at the heart of a sequence when Chaplin is making a point about the human condition. Perhaps the most absurd is the scene in *The Great Dictator* (1940) in which the dictator plays with a globe as if it were a beach ball. Absurdity and logic are the key elements to these vaudeville-like routines in Chaplin's films.

Perhaps no film by Chaplin is as elaborate in those routines as *Modern Times* (1936). The structure is a series of routines about factory life and personal life during the Great Depression. The first routine focuses on the assembly line. Here, the little tramp is victimized first by the pace and regimentation of the line and then by a lunch machine. He suffers an emotional breakdown, is hospitalized and released, and when he picks up a red flag that has fallen off a passing truck, he is arrested as a Communist. In jail, he foils a jail break, becomes a hero, and is released back into society. He meets a young woman, fantasizes about domestic life with her, and sets about getting a job to achieve that life. His attempt as a night watchman fails. When the factories reopen, he takes a job as a mechanic's assistant. A strike ends the job, but after another spell in jail, he gets a job as a singing waiter. He succeeds, but the young woman must flee for breaking the law. In the end, the tramp is on the road again, but with the young woman. Their life is indefinite, but he tries to smile.

Every scene in the film is constructed as a vaudeville routine. It has an internal logic and integrity. Each is visual and often absurd, and at its core is Chaplin portraying the little tramp. The scene in which Chaplin works as a mechanic's assistant presents an excellent example. Chaplin tries to be helpful to the mechanic (portrayed by Chester Conklin), but at each step, he hinders his boss. First, the oil can is crushed in the press, and eventually all of the mechanic's tools are crushed. Even the mechanic is swallowed up by the machinery (Figure 4.1). Now the absurdity twists away from the mechanic's fate; the lunch whistle blows, so the tramp attempts to feed the mechanic, who at this stage is upside down. To help him drink the coffee, he uses an oil spigot. He discards it for a whole chicken of which the shape works as a funnel. As absurd as the situation seems, by using a chicken, the mechanic can be fed coffee. Finally, lunch is over and the mechanic can be freed from the machine. Once freed, however, the job ends due to a strike.

In terms of editing, the key is enough screen time to allow the performance to convince us of the credibility of the situation. The emphasis throughout the scene is on the character's reaction to the situation, allowing us to follow through the logic of the scene. In every case, editing is subordinate to setting and performance. Pace is not used for dramatic purposes. Here, too, performance is the key to the pacing.

If one looks at the work of Keaton, Langdon, or Harold Lloyd in the silent period or the Marx Brothers, Abbott and Costello, or other performer—comedians in the sound period, the same editing pattern is apparent. Editing is determined by the persona of the character, and affirmation of that persona is more important than the usual dramatic considerations for editing. In a sense, vaudeville continued in character in the films that starred former vaudeville performers. Beyond the most basic considerations of continuity, the editing in these

FIGURE 4.1
Modern Times, 1936. Still provided by British Film Institute.

films could take any pattern as long as it supported the persona of the actor. Within that range, realism and surrealism might mix, and absurdity was as commonplace as realism. This style of film transcends national boundaries, as we see in the films of Jacques Tati and Pierre Etaix of France and the Monty Python films of England.

THE MUSICAL

The musical's importance is underlined by the success of *The Jazz Singer* (1927), the first sound picture. As mentioned earlier, however, the early sound films that favored dialog-intensive plots tended to be little more than filmed plays.

By the early 1930s, however, many directors experimented with camera movement to allow for a more dynamic approach, and postsynchronization (adding sound after production is completed) freed the musical from the constraints of the stage. As early as 1929, King Vidor postsynchronized an entire musical, *Hallelujah* (1929). However, it was the creative choreography of Busby Berkeley in *Gold Diggers of 1933* (1933) that pointed the direction toward the dynamic editing of the musical. Berkeley later became one of the great directors of the musical film.

The musical posed certain challenges for the editor. The first was the integration of a dramatic story with performance numbers. This was most easily solved by using dramatic stories about would-be performers, thus making the on-stage performance appear to be more natural. The second challenge was the vaudeville factor: the need for a variety of routines in the film, comedy routines as well as musical routines. This was the greater challenge because vaudeville routines could not be integrated as easily into the dramatic story as could a few musical numbers. Another dimension from vaudeville was the persona of the character. Such actors as Fred Astaire and Edward Everett Horton had to play particular characters. The role of the editor was to match the assembly of images to the star's persona rather than to the drama itself. Despite these limitations, the musical of the 1930s and beyond became one of the most dynamic and visual of the genres.

A brief examination of *Swing Time* (1936) illustrates the dynamism of the musical. The director, George Stevens, tells the dramatic story of a performer–gambler Lucky Garnett (Fred Astaire) and his relationship to performer Penny Carroll (Ginger Rogers). The dramatic story reflects the various stages and challenges of the relationship. This dimension of the film is realistic and affecting and the editing is reminiscent of *Broken Blossoms* or *The Big Parade*.

The editing of the musical numbers, on the other hand, follows the rhythm of Jerome Kern's music and highlights the personae of Astaire and Rogers. The scale of these numbers is closer to the Zeigfield Follies than to vaudville and consequently the editing of these numbers could have differed markedly from the editing of the balance of the film. However, because Stevens tended to be a more "realistic" director than Berkeley, these numbers are edited in a manner similar to that of the dramatic portion of the film. There is thus little dissonance between the performance and dramatic sections of the film.

All of the musical numbers—the dancing lesson, the winter interlude, the nightclub sequence, "Bojangles"—have a gentle quality very much in key with Kern's music. Other directors—notably Vincente Minnelli, George Sydney, Stanley Donen, and Gene Kelly—were more physical and assertive in their editing, but this style complemented the persona of frequent star Gene Kelly. Later, directors Robert Wise in *West Side Story* (1961) and Bob Fosse in *Cabaret* (1972) were even freer in their editing, but their editing decisions never challenged the rhythm of the music in their films. The scores were simply more varied, and where the music was intense, the director could choose a more intensified editing style, thus using editing to help underscore the emotions in the music.

The musical was a much freer form to edit than films such as *Modern Times*. The narrative, the persona of the performer—star, and the character of the music influenced the editing style. Together with the strengths of the film director, the editing could be "stage-bound" or free.

THE THEATRE

Like the musical, the theatre became an important influence on film with the coming of sound. Many plays, such as Oscar Wilde's *The Marriage Circle* (1924), had been produced as silent films, but the prominence of dialog in the sound movies and the status associated with the stage provided the impetus for the studios to invite playwrights to become screenwriters. Samuel Raphaelson, who wrote *The Jazz Singer*, and Ben Hecht and Charles MacArthur, who wrote *The Front Page* (1931), are among those who accepted. Eugene O'Neill, Maxwell Anderson, and Billy Wilder were also invited to write for the screen.

There was, in the 1930s, a group of playwrights whose work exhibited a new political and social realism. Their form of populist art was well suited to the most populist of mediums: film. The works of Robert Sherwood, Sidney Kingsley, Clifford Odets, and Lillian Hellman were rapidly adapted to film, and in each case, the playwrights were invited to write the screenplays.

How did these adaptations influence the way the films were edited? Two examples suggest the influence of the theatre and how the transition to film could be made. Kingsley's *Dead End* (1937) and Hellman's *The Little Foxes* (1941) were both directed by William Wyler.

Dead End is the story of adolescents who live in a poor neighborhood in New York. They can go the route of trouble and end up in jail, or they can try to overcome their environment. This naturalistic movie features an ensemble of characters: a gang of youths (as the Dead End Kids, the group went on to make a series of films), an adult who is going "bad," and an adult who is trying to do the right thing. No single character dominates the action. Characters talk about their circumstances and their options. There is some action, but it is very little by the standards of the melodrama or gangster genres. Consequently, the dialog is very important in characterization and plot advancement.

The editing of this film is secondary to the staging. Cutting to highlight particular relationships and to emphasize significant actions is the extent of the editing for dramatic purposes. Editing is minimalist rather than dynamic. *Dead End* is a filmed play.[5] In *The Little Foxes*, Wyler moved away from the filmed play. He was greatly aided by a play that is character-driven rather than polemical. The portrayal of the antagonist, Regina (Bette Davis), establishes the relationships within a family as the heart of the play. Behavior can be translated into action as a counterweight to the primacy of dialog, as in *Dead End*. Because relationships are central to the story, Wyler continually juxtaposed characters in foreground/background, side frame/center frame variations. The editing thus highlights the characters' power relationships or foreshadows changes in those relationships. The editing is not dynamic as in a Pudovkin or an Eisenstein film, but there is a tension that arises from these juxtapositions that is at times as powerful as the tension created by dynamic editing. Wyler allowed the protagonist—antagonist struggle to develop without relying solely on dialog, and he used staging of the images to create tension. This method foreshadowed the editing and framing relationships in such Cinemascope films as *East of Eden* (1955).

Although its style of editing is not dynamic as in such films as *M* or restricted as in such films as *Dead End*, *The Little Foxes* illustrates a play that has been successfully recreated as a film. Because of the staging and importance of language over action, character over event, in relative terms the film remains more strongly influenced by the conventions of the theatre and less by the evolving conventions of film than were other narrative sources with more dynamic visual treatment. Westerns and traditional gangster films are very visual rather than verbal.

RADIO

Whether film or radio was a more popular medium in the 1930s is related to the question of whether film or television is a more popular medium today. There is little question today that the influence of television is broader and, because of its journalistic role, more powerful than film. The situation was similar with radio in the 1930s.

Radio was the instrument of communication for American presidents (for example, Franklin D. Roosevelt's "fireside chats") and for entertainers such as Jack Benny and Orson Welles. In a sense, radio shared with the theatre a reliance on language. Both heightened (or literary) language and naturalistic language were readily found in radio drama. Beyond language, though, radio relied on sound effects and music to create a context for the characters who spoke that dialog.

Because of its power and pervasiveness, radio was bound to influence film and its newly acquired use of sound. Perhaps no one better personifies that influence than Orson Welles, who came to film from a career in theatre and in radio. Welles is famous for two creative achievements: one in film (*Citizen Kane*, 1941), the other in radio (his 1937 broadcast of H. G. Wells's *The War of the Worlds*).

As Robert Carringer suggests,

> Welles' background in radio was one of the major influences on *Citizen Kane*. Some of the influence is of a very obvious nature—the repertory approach, for instance, in which roles are created for specific performers with their wonderfully expressive voices in mind. It can also be seen in the exaggerated sound effects. The radio shows alternated between prestigious literary classics and popular melodrama.
>
> Other examples of the radio influence are more subtle. Overlapping dialog was a regular feature of the Mercury radio shows, as were other narrative devices used in the film—the use of sounds as aural punctuation, for instance, as when the closing of a door cues the end of a scene, or scene transitions in mid-sentence (a device known in radio

as a cross fade), as when Leland, talking to a crowd in the street, begins a thought, and Kane, addressing a rally in Madison Square Garden, completes it.[6]

Indeed, from the perspective of narrative structure, *Citizen Kane* is infused by the influence of radio. The story is told via a narrator, a dramatic shaping device central to radio drama. Welles used five narrators in *Citizen Kane*.[7] Although the story proceeds as a flashback from Kane's death, it is the various narrators who take us through key events in Kane's life. To put the views of those narrators into context, however, Welles used a newsreel device to take us quickly through Kane's life. With this short newsreel (less than 15 minutes), the film implies that Kane was a real and important man whose personal tragedies superseded his public achievements. The newsreel leaves us with an implicit question, which the first narrator, the newsreel reporter, poses: What was Kane's life all about? The film then shifts from newsreel biography to dramatic mystery. This is achieved through a series of radio drama devices.

In Movietone fashion, a narrator dramatizes a visual montage of Kane's life; language rather than image shapes the ideas about his life. The tone of the narration alternates between hyperbole and fact. "Xanadu, where Kublai Khan decreed his pleasure dome" suggests the quality of Kane's estate, and the reference to "the biggest private zoo since Noah" suggests its physical scale. The language is constantly shifting between two views of Kane: the private man and the public man. In the course of the newsreel, he is called "the emperor of newsprint," a Communist and a Fascist, an imperialist and a pacifist, a failed husband and a failed politician. Throughout, the character of language drives the narrative.

The music throughout the newsreel shifts the focus and fills in what is not being said. Here, too, Welles and composer Bernard Herrmann used music as it was used in radio. The other narrators in the film—Thatcher, Leland, Bernstein, and Susan (Kane's second wife)—are less forthcoming than the newsreel narrator. Their reluctance helps to stimulate our curiosity by creating the feeling that they know more than they are telling. The tone and language of the other narrators are cautious, circumspect, and suspicious—far from the hyperbole of the newsreel. The implication is dramatically very useful because we expect to learn quite a lot if only they will tell us.

Beyond the dramatic effect of the narration device, the use of five narrators allowed Welles and screenwriter Herman I. Mankiewicz to tell in two hours the story of a man whose life spanned 75 years. This is the principle benefit of using the narrators: the collapse of real time into a comprehensive and believable screen time.

This challenge of collapsing time was taken up by Welles in a variety of fascinating ways. Here, too, radio devices are the key. In the famous Kane–Thatcher scene, the completion of one sentence by the same character bridges 17 years. In one shot, Kane is a boy and Thatcher wishes him a curt "Merry Christmas," and in the next shot, 17 years later, Thatcher is dictating a letter and the dialog is "and a Happy New Year." Although the device is audacious, the audience accepts the simulation of continuity because the complete statement is a well-known one and both parts fit together. Because Thatcher looks older in the second shot and refers to Kane's twenty-fifth birthday, we accept that 17 years have elapsed.

The same principle applies to the series of breakfast table shots that characterize Kane's first marriage. The setting—the breakfast table—and the time—morning—provide a visual continuity while the behavior of Kane and his wife moves from love in the first shot to hostility and silence in the last. In five minutes of screen time, Kane and editor Robert Wise collapse eight years of marriage. These brief scenes are a genuine montage of the marriage, providing insights over time—verbal punctuations that, as they change in tone and language, signal the rise and fall of the marriage. Here, too, the imaginative use of sound over image illustrates the influence of radio. See Figure 4.2.

Welles used the sound cut to amuse as well as to inform. As David Bordwell describes it, "When Kane, Leland and Bernstein peer in the *Chronicle* window, the camera moves up the picture of the *Chronicle* staff until it fills the screen; Kane's voice says 'Six years ago I looked at a picture of the world's greatest newspaper staff . . .' and he strides out in front of the same men, posed for an identical picture, a flashbulb explodes, and we are at the *Inquirer* party."[8] Six years pass as Kane celebrates his human acquisitions (he has hired all the best reporters away from his competition) with sufficient wit to distract us from the artificiality of the device. Finally, like Fritz Lang in *M*, Welles used sound images and sound cuts to move us to a different location. Already mentioned is the shift from Leland in the street to Kane at

FIGURE 4.2
Citizen Kane, 1941. ©1941 RKO Pictures, Inc. All Rights Reserved. Still provided by British Film Institute.

Madison Square Garden, in which Kane finishes the sentence that Leland had started. The sound level shifts from intimate (Leland) to remote (Kane), as the impassioned Kane tries harder to reach out and move his audience. The quality of the sound highlights the differences between the two locations, just as the literal continuity of the words spoken provides the sense of continuity.

Another example of location shift together with time shift is the opera scene. Initially Kane's second wife, Susan Alexander, is seen being instructed in singing opera. She is not very good. Her teacher all but throws up his hands. Kane orders him to continue. Susan tries to reach higher notes, even higher in pitch than she has managed so far. In the next shot the orchestration of the music is more elaborate. Susan is reaching for an even higher note. And visually she is on stage surrounded by her fellow actors and singers. The opera is approaching its climax—the death scene.

Again, Welles has used sound to provide both continuity—Susan singing in training to Susan singing in the performance of the opera—and drama—the stakes are far higher in performance than in training. As we anticipate, both Susan and Kane are humiliated by the performance. Just as Kane did not accept the advice of the teacher, he vows not to accept the views of the audience and his main critic, Jed Leland. Only Susan is left trapped in humiliation.

In the opera scene, time and place change quickly, in a single cut, but the dramatic continuity of growing humiliation and loss demark another step in the emotional descent of *Citizen Kane*.

These radio devices introduced by Welles in a rather dramatic fashion in *Citizen Kane* became part of the editor's repertoire, but they awaited the work of Robert Altman and Martin Scorsese, more than 30 years later, to highlight for a new generation of filmmakers the scope of sound editing possibilities and the range that these radio devices provide.

NOTES/REFERENCES

1. S. Eisenstein, Film Form: Essays in Film Theory, Harcourt, Brace and Company, New York, 1949, pp. 195−255.

2. A. N. Vardac, Stage to Screen, Harvard University Press, Cambridge, MA, 1949, pp. 1−88.

3. R. C. Allen, The Movies in Vaudeville, in: T. Balio (Ed.), The American Film Industry, 1905−1914, University of Wisconsin Press, Madison, 1976, pp. 57−82.

4. R. Merritt, Nickolodeon Theaters, Building an Audience for the Movies. In T. Balio (Ed.), The American Film Industry, 1905−1914, pp. 83−102.

5. The logical conclusion of the approach is the play filmed entirely in a single shot; Hitchcock attempted this in *Rope* (1948). He moved the camera to avoid editing.

6. R. L. Carringer, The Making of Citizen Kane, University of California Press, Berkeley, 1985, pp. 100−101.

7. See the full discussion of the film's narrative structure in: D. Bordwell, K. Thompson, Film Art: An Introduction, Third ed., McGraw-Hill, New York, 1990, pp. 72−84.

8. D. Bordwell, *Citizen Kane*, in: B. Nichols (Ed.), Movies and Methods: An Anthology, University of California Press, Berkeley, 1976, p. 284.

CHAPTER 5

Editors Who Became Directors

One of the more interesting career developments in film has been the transition from editors to directors. Two of the most successful, Robert Wise and David Lean, are the subjects of this chapter.

Is it necessary and natural for editors to become directors? The answer is no. Is editing the best route to directing? Not necessarily, but editing can be invaluable, as demonstrated by the subjects of this chapter. What strengths do editors bring to directing? Narrative clarity, for one: Editors are responsible for clarifying the story from all of the footage that the director has shot. This point takes on greater meaning in the following sampling of directors who have entered the field from other areas. From screenwriting, the most famous contemporary writer who has tried his hand at directing is Robert Towne (*Personal Best*, 1982; *Tequila Sunrise*, 1988). Before Towne, notable writer–directors included Nunnally Johnson (*The Man in the Gray Flannel Suit*, 1956) and Ben Hecht (*Specter of the Rose*, 1946). All of these writers are great with dialog, and their screenplays spark with energy. As directors, however, their work seems to lack pace. Their dialog may be energetic, but the performances of their actors are too mannered. In short, these exceptional writers are unexceptional directors. This, of course, does not mean that all writers become poor directors; consider Preston Sturges, Billy Wilder, and Joseph Mankiewicz, for example. What it does imply, though, is that the narrative skill of writing doesn't lead directly to a successful directing career.

A similar conclusion can be drawn from cinematography. The visual beauty of the camerawork of Haskell Wexler has not translated into directorial success (*Medium Cool*, 1969); nor have William Fraker (*Monte Walsh*, 1970) or Jack Cardiff (*Sons and Lovers*, 1958) found success. Even Nicolas Roeg (*Don't Look Now*, 1973; *Walkabout*, 1971; *Track 29*, 1989) has a problem with narrative clarity and pace in his directed films, although he has won a following. There are, however, a few exceptions worth noting. Jan de Bout had great success with *Speed* (1994), and Barry Sonnenfield has been developing a distinctive style (*The Addams Family*, 1991; *Get Shorty*, 1995).

Producers from David Selznick (*A Farewell to Arms*, 1957) to Irwin Winkler (*Guilty by Suspicion*, 1991) have tried to direct with less success than expected. Again, the problems of narrative clarity and pace have defeated their efforts.

The Technique of Film and Video Editing: History, Theory, and Practice. DOI: 10.1016/B978-0-240-81397-4.00005-4

Only actors have been as successful as editors in their transition to directors. From Chaplin and Keaton to Charles Laughton (*The Night of the Hunter*, 1955), Robert Redford (*Ordinary People*, 1980), and Kevin Costner (*Dances with Wolves*, 1990), actors have been able to energize their direction, and for them, the problems of pace and clarity have been less glaring. Nor are actors singular in their talents. Warren Beatty has been very successful directing comedy (*Heaven Can Wait*, 1977). Diane Keaton has excelled in psychological drama (*Unstrung Heroes*, 1995). Mel Gibson has excelled in directing action (*Braveheart*, 1995). And Clint Eastwood has crossed genres, directing exceptional Westerns (*Unforgiven*, 1992) and melodrama (*The Bridges of Madison County*, 1995). Most notable in this area has been the work of Elia Kazan, director of (*On the Waterfront*, 1954) and (*East of Eden*, 1955), who was originally an actor, and John Cassavetes (*Gloria*, 1980; *Husbands*, 1970; *Faces*, 1968).

The key is pace and narrative clarity. These concerns, which are central to the success of an editor, are but one element in the success of a director. Equally important and visible are the director's success with performers and crew, ability to remain on budget (shooting along a time line rather than on the basis of artistic considerations alone), and ability to inspire confidence in the producer. Any of these qualities (and, of course, success with the audience) can make a successful director, but only success with the building blocks of film—the shots and how they are put together—will ensure an editor's success. Again, we come back to narrative clarity and pace, and again these can be important elements for the success of a director.

Thus, editing is an excellent preparation for becoming a director. To test this idea, we now turn to the careers of two directors who began their careers as editors: Robert Wise and David Lean.

ROBERT WISE

Wise is probably best known as the editor of Orson Welles's *Citizen Kane* (1941) and *The Magnificent Ambersons* (1942). Within two years, he codirected his first film at RKO. As with many American directors, Wise spent the next 30 years directing in all of the great American genres: the Western (*Blood on the Moon*, 1948), the gangster film (*Odds Against Tomorrow*, 1959), the musical (*West Side Story*, 1961), and the sports film (*The Set-Up*, 1949). He also ventured into those genres made famous in Germany: the horror film (*The Body Snatcher*, 1945), the science-fiction film (*The Day the Earth Stood Still*, 1951), and the melodrama (*I Want to Live!*, 1958).

These directorial efforts certainly illustrate versatility, but our purpose is to illustrate how his experience as an editor was invaluable to his success as a director. To do so, we will look in detail at three of his films: *The Set-Up*, *I Want to Live!*, and *West Side Story*. We will also refer to *Somebody Up There Likes Me* (1956), *The Day the Earth Stood Still*, and *The Body Snatcher*.

When one looks at *Citizen Kane* and *The Magnificent Ambersons*, the work of the editor is very apparent. Aside from audacious cutting that draws attention to technique ("Merry

Christmas . . . and a Happy New Year"), the breakfast scene, and the opening introduction to the characters and the town stand out as tours de force: set-pieces that impress us. They contribute to the narrative but also stand apart from it, as did the Odessa Steps sequence in *Potemkin*. Although this type of scene is notable in many of Wise's directorial efforts, the deeper contribution of the editor to the film is not to be intrusive, but rather to edit the film so that the viewer is clearly aware of the story and its evolution, not the editing.

The tension between the invisible editor and the editor of consciously audacious sequences is a tension that runs throughout Wise's career as a director. The equivalents of the breakfast scene in *Citizen Kane* emerge often in his work: the fight in *The Set-Up*, the dance numbers in *West Side Story*, and the opening of *I Want to Live!*. As his career as a director developed, he was able to integrate the sequences into the narrative and make them revealing. A good example of this is the sampan blockade of the American ship in *The Sand Pebbles* (1966).

Another use Wise found for the set-piece is to elaborate a particular idea through editing. For example, in *The Day the Earth Stood Still*, Wise communicated the idea that every nation on Earth can be unified in the face of a great enough threat. To elaborate this idea, he cut sound and picture to different newsrooms around the world. The announcers speak different languages, but they are all talking about the same thing: an alien has landed, threatening everyone on the planet. Finally, the different nationalities are unified, but it has taken an alien threat to accomplish that unity. The idea is communicated through an editing solution, not quite a set-piece, but an editing idea that draws some attention to itself.

Wise used the same editing approach in *Somebody Up There Likes Me* to communicate the wide support for Rocky Graziano in his final fight. His family, his Hell's Kitchen friends, and his new fans are all engaged in "praying" at their radios that his fate in the final fight will mean something for their fate. By intercutting between all three groups, Wise lets us know how many people's dreams hang on the dream of one man. Here, too, the editing solution communicates the idea. Not as self-conscious as the breakfast scene in *Citizen Kane*, this sequence is nevertheless a set-piece that has great impact.

The principle of finding an editing solution to an idea surfaces early in Wise's career as a director. In *The Body Snatcher*, Wise had to communicate that Grey (the title character) has resorted to murder to secure a body for dissection at the local medical school. We don't see the murder, just the street singer walking through the foggy night-bound Edinburgh street. Her voice carries on. Grey, driving his buggy, follows. Both disappear. We see the street and hear the voice of the street singer. The shot holds (continues visually), as does the voice, and then nothing. The voice disappears. The visual remains. We know that the girl is dead and a new body will be provided for "science." The scene has the elements of a set-piece, an element of self-consciousness, and yet is extremely effective in heightening the tension and drama of the murder that has taken place beyond our sight.

We turn now to a more detailed examination of three of Wise's films, beginning with *The Set-Up*.

The Set-Up

The Set-Up (1949) is the story of Stoker Thompson's last fight. Stoker is 35 and nearing the end of his career; he is low on the fight card but has the will to carry on. He fights now in a string of small towns and earns little money.

This screen story takes place entirely on the evening of the fight. Stoker's manager has agreed to have his fighter lose to an up-and-coming boxer, Tiger Nelson. But the manager, greedy and without confidence in Stoker, keeps the payoff and neglects to tell Stoker he is to lose.

Struggling against the crowd, against his wife who refuses to watch him beaten again, and against his manager, Stoker fights, and he wins. Then he faces the consequences. He has been true to himself, but he has betrayed the local gangster, Little Boy, and he must pay the price. As the film ends, Stoker's hand is broken by Little Boy, and the fighter acknowledges that he'll never fight again.

The Set-Up may be Wise's most effective film. The clarity of story is unusual, and a powerful point of view is established. Wise managed to establish individuals among the spectators so that the crowd is less impersonal and seems composed of individuals with lives before and after the fight. As a result, they take on characteristics that make our responses to Stoker more varied and complex.

Like *Citizen Kane*, the narrative structure poses an editing problem. With *Citizen Kane*, two hours of screen time must tell the story of one man's 75-year life. In *The Set-Up*, the story takes place in one evening. Wise chose to use screen time to simulate real time. The 72 minutes of the film simulate those 70 or so minutes of the fight, the time leading up to it, and its aftermath.

As much as possible, Wise matched the relationship between real time and screen time. That is not to say that *The Set-Up* is a documentary. It is not. It is a carefully crafted dramatization of a critical point in Stoker's life: his last fight.

To help engage us with Stoker's feelings and his point of view, Wise used subjective camera placement and movement. We see what Stoker sees, and we begin to feel what he must feel. Wise was very pointed about point of view in this film.

This film is not exclusively about Stoker's point of view, however. Wise was as subjective about Stoker's wife and about seven other secondary characters who are highlighted: a newspaper seller (probably a former boxer), a blind man, a meek man, an obese man, and a belligerent housewife. With the exceptions of the newspaper seller and the obese man, all have companions whose behavior stands out in contrast to their own.

The film introduces each of these spectators before the fight and cuts away to them continually throughout the fight. The camera is close and looks down or up at them (it is never neutral). Wise used an extreme close-up only when the housewife yells to Stoker's opponent, "Kill him!" All of the spectators seem to favor Nelson with much verbal and physical expression. If they could be in the ring themselves, they would enjoy the ultimate identification.

Only when the fight begins to go against Nelson do they shift allegiances and yell their support for Stoker. The spectators do not appear superficially to be bloodthirsty, but their behavior in each case speaks otherwise.

Wise carried the principle of subjectivity as far as he could without drawing too much attention to it. He used silence as Hitchcock did in *Blackmail*. Before the fight, individual disparaging comments about his age and his chances are heard by Stoker. As he spars with his opponent, the two become sufficiently involved with one another that they can actually exchange words in spite of the din. Between rounds, Stoker is so involved in regrouping his physical and mental resources that for a few brief seconds, he hears nothing. Almost total silence takes over until the bell rings Stoker, and us, back into the awareness that the next round has begun. Sound continues to be used invasively. It surrounds, dominates, and then recedes to simulate how Stoker struggles for some mastery within his environment.

In *The Set-Up*, Wise suggested that Stoker's inner life with its tenacious will to see himself as a winner contrasts with his outer life, his life in society, which views him as a fighter in decline, one step removed from being a discard of society. So great is the derision toward him from the spectators that the audience begins to feel that they too struggle with this inner life—outer life conflict and they don't want to identify with a loser. These are the primary ideas that Wise communicates in this film, and by moving away from simple stereotypes with most of the people in the story, he humanizes all of them. These ideas are worked out with editing solutions. Both picture and sound, cutaways and close-ups, are used to orchestrate these ideas.

I Want to Live!

In *I Want to Live!* (1958), Wise again dealt with a story in which the inner life of the character comes into conflict with society's view of that person (Figure 5.1). In this case, however, the consequences of the difference are dire. In the end, the main character is executed by society for that difference. Barbara Graham enjoys a good time and can't seem to stay out of trouble. She perjures herself casually and thus begins her relationship with the law.

She lives outside the law but remains a petty criminal until circumstance leads her to be involved with two men in a murder charge. Now a mother, her defiant attitude leads to a trial where poor judgment in a man again deepens her trouble. This time she is in too far. She is sentenced to be executed for murder. Although a psychologist and reporter try to save her, they are too late. The film ends shortly after she has been executed for a murder she did not commit.

I Want to Live! is a narrative that takes place over a number of years. Wise's first challenge was to establish an approach or attitude that would set the tone but also allow for an elaborate narrative. Wise created the equivalent of a jazz riff. Set to Gerry Mulligan's combo performance, he presented a series of images set in a jazz club. The combo performs. The customers pair off, drink, and smoke. This is an atmosphere that tolerates a wide band of

FIGURE 5.1

I Want to Live!, 1958. ©1958 United Artists Corporation. All rights reserved. Still provided by Museum of Modern Art/Film Stills Archives.

behavior, young women with older men, young men at the margin of the law. A policeman enters looking for someone, but he doesn't find her. Only his determination singles him out from the rest.

This whole sequence runs just over two minutes and contains fewer than 20 shots. All of the images get their continuity from two sources: the combo performance and the off-center, deep-focus cinematography. All of the images are shot at angles of up to 30 degrees. The result is a disjointed, unstable feeling. There is unpredictability here; it's a visual presentation of an off-center world, a world where anything can happen. There is rhythm but no logic here, as in a jazz riff. The pace of the shots does not help. Pace can direct us to a particular mood, but here the pace is random, not cueing us about how to feel. Randomness contributes to the overall mood. This is Barbara Graham's world. This opening sequence sets the tone for what is to follow in the next two hours.

After this prologue, Wise still faced the problem of a screen story that must cover the next 8 to 10 years. He chose to straight-cut between scenes that illustrate Graham's steady decline. He focused on those periods or decisions she made that took her down the road to execution. All of the scenes center around her misjudgments about men. They include granting ill-considered favors, committing petty crime, marrying a drug addict, returning to criminal companions, and a murder charge for being found with those companions. Once charged, she mistrusts her lawyer but does trust a policeman who entraps her into a false confession about her whereabouts on the night of the murder. Only when it is too late does her judgment about a male psychologist and a male reporter suggest a change in her perception, but by relentlessly thumbing her nose at the law and society, she dooms herself to death (this was, after all, the 1950s).

By straight-cutting from scene to scene along a clear narrative that highlights the growing seriousness of Graham's misjudgments, Wise blurred the time issue, and we accept the length of time that has passed. There are, however, a few notable departures from this pattern—departures in which Wise introduced an editorial view. In each case, he found an editing solution.

An important idea in *I Want to Live!* is the role of the media, particularly print and television journalism, and the role they played in condemning Graham. Wise intercut the murder trial with televised footage about it. He also intercut direct contact between Graham and the print press, particularly Ed Montgomery. By doing this, Wise found an editing solution to the problem of showing all of the details of the actual trial on screen and also found a way to illustrate the key role the media played in finding Graham guilty. This is the same type of intercutting seen in *The Day the Earth Stood Still* and *Somebody Up There Likes Me*.

Another departure is the amount of screen time Wise spent on the actual execution. The film meticulously shows in close-up all of the details of the execution: the setting, its artifacts, the sulfuric acid, how it works, the cyanide, how it works, how the doctor checks whether Barbara is dead. All of these details show an almost clinical sense of what is about to happen to Barbara and, in terms of the execution, of what does happen to her. This level of detail draws out the prelude to and the actual execution. The objectivity of this detail, compared to the randomness of the jazz riff, is excruciating and inevitable—scientific in its predictability. This sequence is virtually in counterpoint to the rest of the film. As a result, it is a remarkably powerful sequence that questions how we feel about capital punishment. The scientific presentation leaves no room for a sense of satisfaction about the outcome. Quite the contrary, it is disturbing, particularly because we know that Graham is innocent.

The detail, the pace, and the length of the sequence all work to carry the viewer to a sense of dread about what is to come, but also to editorialize about capital punishment. It is a remarkable sequence, totally different from the opening, but, in its way, just as effective. Again, Wise found an editing solution to a particular narrative idea.

West Side Story

Leonard Bernstein's *West Side Story* (1961) is a contemporary musical adaptation of Shakespeare's *Romeo and Juliet*. Instead of the Montagues and the Capulets, however, the conflict is between two New York street gangs: the Sharks and the Jets (Figure 5.2). The Sharks are Puerto Rican. Their leader is Bernardo (George Chakiris). The Jets are American, although there are allusions to their ethnic origins as well. Their leader is Riff (Russ Tamblyn). The Romeo and Juliet of the story are Tony (Richard Beymer), a former Jet, and Maria (Natalie Wood), Bernardo's sister. They fall in love, but their love is condemned because of the animosity between the two gangs. When Bernardo kills Riff in a rumble, Tony kills Bernardo in anger. It's only a matter of time before that act of street violence results in his own death.

West Side Story was choreographed by Jerome Robbins, who codirected the film with Robert Wise. Although the film is organized around a Romeo and Juliet narrative and Bernstein's brilliant musical score, the editing is audacious, stylized, and stimulating.

FIGURE 5.2
West Side Story, 1961. ©1961 United Artists Pictures, Inc. All rights reserved. Still provided by British Film Institute.

The opening sequence, the introduction to New York and the street conflict of the Sharks and the Jets, runs 10 minutes with no dialog. In these 10 minutes, the setting and the conflict are introduced in a spirited way. Wise began with a series of helicopter shots of New York. There are no street sounds here, just the serenity of clear sightlines down to Manhattan. For 80 seconds, Wise presented 18 shots of the city from the helicopter. The camera looks directly down on the city. The movement, all of it right to left, is gentle and slow, almost elegant. Little sound accompanies these camera movements. Many familiar sights are visible, including the Empire State Building and the United Nations. We move from commercial sights to residential areas. Only then do we begin to descend in a zoom and then a dissolve.

The music comes up, not too loud. We are in a basketball court between two tenements. A pair of fingers snap and we are introduced to Riff, the leader of the Jets, and then to another Jet and then to a group of Jets. The earlier cutting had no sound cues; now the cuts occur on the beat created by the snap of fingers. The Jets begin to move right to left, as the helicopter did. This direction is only violated once—to introduce the Jets's encounter with Bernardo, a Shark. The change in direction alludes to the conflicts to come.

The film switches to the Sharks, and as Bernardo is joined by his fellow gang members, they are introduced in close-ups, now moving left to right. When the film cuts to longer shots, we notice that the Sharks are photographed with less context and more visual entrapment.

For example, as they move up alleys, the walls on both sides of the alley trap them in mid-frame. This presentation of the Sharks also differentiates them from the Jets, who appear principally in midshot with context and with no similar visual entrapment.

The balance of the sequence outlines the escalating conflict between the two gangs. They taunt and interfere with each other's activities. Throughout, the Jets are filmed from eye level or higher, and the Sharks are usually filmed from below eye level. The Jets are presented as bullies exploiting their position of power, and the Sharks are shown in a more heroic light. The sequence culminates in an attack by the Sharks on John Boy, who has been adding graffiti to Shark iconography. For the first time in the sequence, the Sharks are photographed from above eye level as they beat and maim John Boy. This incident leads to the arrival of the police and to the end of this 10-minute introduction. The conflict is established.

Because of the length of this sequence, the editing itself had to be choreographed to explain fully the conflict and its motivation and to differentiate the two sides. Wise was even able to influence us to side with the outsiders, the Sharks, because of the visual choices he made: the close-ups, the sense of visual entrapment, and the heroic camera angle. All suggest that we identify with the Sharks rather than with the Jets.

The other interesting sequence in *West Side Story* is the musical number "Tonight." As with the opera sequence in *Citizen Kane* and the fight sequence in *Somebody Up There Likes Me*, Wise found a unifying element, the music or the sounds of the fight, and relied on the sound carry-over throughout the sequence to provide unity.

"Tonight" includes all of the components of the story. Bernardo, Riff, the Sharks, and the Jets get ready for a rumble; Tony and Maria anticipate the excitement of being with one another, Anita prepares to be with Bernardo after the fight, and the lieutenant anticipates trouble. Wise constructed this sequence slowly, gradually building toward the culmination of everyone's expectations: the rumble. Here he used camera movement, camera direction, and increasingly closer shots (without context) to build the sequence. He also used a faster pace of editing to help build excitement.

Whereas in the opening sequence, pace did not play a very important role, in the "Tonight" sequence, pace is everything. Cross-cutting between the gangs at the end of the song takes us to the moment of great anticipation—the rumble—with a powerful sense of preparation; the song has built up anticipation and excitement for what will happen next. The music unifies this sequence, but it is the editing that translates it emotionally for us.

DAVID LEAN

Through his experience in the film industry, including his time as an assistant editor and as an editor, David Lean developed considerable technical skill. By the time he became codirector of *In Which We Serve* (1942) with Noel Coward, he was ready. As a director, he developed a visual strength and a literary sensibility that makes his work more complex than the work of Robert Wise. Lean's work is both more subtle and more ambitious. His experience as an

editor is demonstrable in his directing work. Although Lean made only 15 films in a career of more than 40 years, many of those films have become important in the popular history of cinema. His pictorial epics, *Lawrence of Arabia* (1962) and *Doctor Zhivago* (1965), remain the standard for this type of filmmaking. His romantic films, *Brief Encounter* (1945) and *Summertime* (1955), are the standard for that type of filmmaking. His literary adaptations, *Great Expectations* (1946) and *Hobson's Choice* (1954), are classics, and *The Bridge on the River Kwai* (1957) remains an example of an intelligent, entertaining war film with a message. Lean may have made few films, but his influence has far exceeded those numbers. The role of editing in his films may help explain that influence.

To establish context for his influence, it is critical to acknowledge Lean's penchant for collaborators: Noel Coward worked on his first three films, Anthony Havelock Allan and Ronald Neame collaborated on the films that followed, and Robert Bolt and Freddie Young worked on *Lawrence of Arabia* and the films that followed (except *Passage to India*, 1984). Also notable are Lean's visual strengths. Few directors have created more extraordinary visualizations in their films. The result is that individual shots are powerful and memorable. The shots don't contradict Pudovkin's ideas about the interdependency of shots for meaning, but they do soften the reliance on pace to shape the editorial meaning of the shots. Lean seems to have been able to create considerable impact without relying on metric montage. That is not to say that there is no rhythm to his scenes. When he wished to use pace, he did so carefully (as he did in the British captain's war memories in *Ryan's Daughter*, 1970). However, Lean seems to have been sufficiently self-assured as a director that his films rely less on pace than is the case with many other directors.

To consider his work in some detail, we will examine *Brief Encounter*, *Great Expectations*, *The Bridge on the River Kwai*, *Lawrence of Arabia*, and *Doctor Zhivago*.

Lean's Technique

Directors who are powerful visualists are memorable only when their visuals serve to deepen the story. The same is true about sound. Good directors involve us with the story rather than with their grasp of the technology. Editing is the means used to illuminate the story's primary meaning as well as its levels of meaning. By looking at Lean's style, we can see how he managed to use the various tools of editing.

Sound

In his use of sound, Lean was very sophisticated. He used the march, whistled and orchestrated, in *The Bridge on the River Kwai*, and in each case, its meaning was different. His use of Maurice Jarre's music in *Lawrence of Arabia*, *Doctor Zhivago*, and *Ryan's Daughter* is probably unprecedented in its popular impact. However, it is in the more subtle uses of sound that Lean illustrated his skill. Through an interior monologue, Laura acts first as narrator and then confessor in *Brief Encounter*. Her confession creates a rapid identification with her.

A less emphatic use of sound occurs in *Great Expectations*. As Pip's sister is insulting the young Pip, Lean blurred the insults with the sound of an instrument. The resulting distortion makes

the insults sound as if they were coming from an animal rather than a human. She is both menacing and belittled by the technical pun.

A similar surprise occurs in an action sequence in *The Bridge on the River Kwai*. British commandos are deep in the Burmese forest. Their Burmese guides, all women, are bathing. A Japanese patrol happens upon them. The commandos hurl grenades and fire their machine guns. As the noise of murder grows louder, the birds of the area fly off frightened, and as Lean cut visuals of the birds in flight, the sound of the birds drown out the machine guns. At that instant, nature quite overwhelms the concerns of the humans present, and for that moment, the outcome of human conflict seems less important.

Narrative Clarity

One of the problems that editing attempts to address is to clarify the storyline. Screen stories tend to be told from the point of view of the main character. There is no confusion about this issue in Lean's stories. Not only was he utterly clear about the point of view, he introduced us to that point of view immediately. In *Great Expectations*, Pip visits the graveyard of his parents and runs into a frightening escaped convict (who later in the story becomes his surrogate father). The story begins in a vivid way; the point of view subjectively presented is that of the young boy. Through the position of the camera, Lean confirmed Pip's point of view. We see from his perspective, and we interpret events as he does: The convict is terrifying, almost as terrifying as his sister.

Lean proceeds in a similar fashion in *Lawrence of Arabia*. The film opens with a three-minute sequence of Lawrence mounting his motorbike and riding through the British countryside. He rides to his death. Was it an accident, or, given his speed on this narrow country road, was it willful? Who was this man? Because the camera is mounted in front of him and sees what he sees, this opening is entirely subjective and quite powerful. By its end, we are involved, and the character has not said a word.

In *Brief Encounter*, the opening scene is the last time that the two lovers, Laura (Celia Johnson) and Alex (Trevor Howard), will be together. Because of a chatty acquaintance of Laura's, they can't even embrace one another. He leaves, and she takes the train home, wondering whether she should confess all to her husband. This ending to the relationship becomes the prologue to her remembrance of the whole relationship, which is the subject of the film. We don't know everything after this prologue, but we know the point of view— Laura's—and the tone of loss and urgency engages us in the story. The point of view never veers from Laura. Lean used a similar reminiscence prologue in another romantic epic, *Doctor Zhivago*.

Subjective Point of View

The use of subjective camera placement has already been mentioned, but subjective camera placement alone doesn't account for the power Lean's sequences can have. The burial scene in *Doctor Zhivago* illustrates this point. In 32 shots running just over three minutes, Lean recreated the five-year-old Yuri Zhivago's range of feelings at the burial of his mother. The sequence begins in extreme long shot. The burial party proceeds. Two-thirds of the frame are filled by sky and mountains. The procession is a speck on a landscape. The film cuts to a moving track shot in front of a five-year-old child. In midshot, at the boy's line of vision, we see him march behind a casket carrying his mother. He can barely see her shape. Soon, he stands by the graveside. A priest presides over the ceremony. Adults are in attendance, but the boy sees only his mother and the trees. When she is covered and then lowered into the ground, he imagines her under the ground, he sees her, he is beside her (given the camera's point of view), and he is aware of the rustle of trees. There is much feeling in this scene, yet Yuri does not cry. He doesn't speak, but we understand his depth of feeling and its lack of comprehension. We are with him. Camera, editing, and music have created these insights into the young Yuri at this critical point in his life.

The subjective point of view is critical if the narrative is to be clear and compelling.

Narrative Complexity

A clear narrative doesn't mean a simple narrative. Indeed, one characteristic of Lean's work that continues to be apparent as his career unfolds is that he is interested in stories of great complexity: India, Arabia, Ireland during troubled times. Even his literary adaptations are ambitious, and he always faces the need to keep the stories personally engaging.

The consequence has been a style that takes advantage of action sequences that occur in the story when they add to the story. The revolt of the army against its officers in *Doctor Zhivago* adds meaning to the goal of the revolution—the destruction of the class hierarchy—and this is central to the fate of Yuri and Lara. Can love transcend revolution?

The two sequences involving the capture of the convict–patron in *Great Expectations* also share complex narrative goals. In the first sequence, Pip is the witness to the soldier's tracking down the man to whom he had brought food. The sequence is filled with sky and the foreboding of the marsh fog. Later in the story, Pip himself is trying to save the convict from capture. He has come to view this man as a father, and he feels obligated to help. Now, at sea again, the escape is foiled by soldiers. The dynamism of this sequence is different from the first sequence, but it is horrifying in another way. It confirms the impossibility of rising above one's circumstances, a goal Pip has been attempting for 20 years of his short life. The action, the escape attempt, is dynamic, but its outcome is more than failure; it becomes a comment on social opportunity.

Pace

Lean did not rely on pace as much as other directors working in similar genres. That is not to say that the particular sequences he created don't rely on the tension that more rapid pace implies. It's just that it is rare in his films. One such sequence of which the success does rely on pace is all the more powerful because it's a complex sequence, and as the climax of the film, it is crucial to its success: the climax of *The Bridge on the River Kwai*.

The group of three commandos has arrived in time to destroy the bridge as the Japanese troop train crosses it. They had laid explosive charges under the bridge that night. Now they await day and the troop train. The injured commando (Jack Hawkins) is atop the hill above the bridge. He will use mortars to cover the escape. A second commando (Geoffrey Horne) is by the river, ready to detonate the charge that will destroy the bridge. The third (William Holden) is on the other side of the river to help cover his colleagues' escape.

It is day, and there are two problems. First, the river's water level has gone down, and some of the detonation wires are now exposed. Second, the proud Colonel Nicholson (Alec Guinness) sees the wires and is concerned about the fate of the bridge. He is proud of the achievement. His men have acted as men, not prisoners of war. Nicholson has lost sight of the fact that his actions, helping the enemy, might be treason. He calls to Saito (Sessue Hayakawa), the Japanese commander, and together they investigate the source of the demolition wires. He leads Saito to the commando on demolition. The intercutting between the discovery and the reaction of the other commandos—"Use your knife, boy" (Hawkins) and "Kill him" (Holden)—leads in rapid succession to Saito's death and to the commando's explanation that he is here to destroy the bridge and that he's British, too. The explanation is to no avail. Nicholson calls on the Japanese to help. The commando is killed. Holden swims over to kill Nicholson, but he too is killed. Hawkins launches a mortar that seriously injures Nicholson, who, at the moment of death, ponders on what he has done. The troop train is now crossing the bridge. Nicholson falls on the detonator and dies. The bridge explodes, and the train falls into the Kwai River. The mission is over. All of the commandos but one are dead, as are Nicholson and Saito. The British doctor (a prisoner of war of the Japanese) comments on the madness of it all. Hawkins reproaches himself by throwing the mortar into the river. The film ends.

The tension in this long scene is complex, beginning with whether the mission will be accomplished and how. Who will survive? Who will die? The outcomes are all surprising, and as the plot turns, the pacing increases and builds to the suspenseful end.

Lean added to the tension by alternately using subjective camera placement and extreme long shots and midshots. The contrast adds to the building tension of the scene.

Lean's Art

Like all directors, David Lean had particular ideas or themes that recurred in his work. How he presented those themes or integrated them into his films is the artful dimension of his work.

Lean made several period films and used exotic locations as the backdrop for his stories. For him, the majesty of the human adventure lent a certain perspective that events and behavior are inscrutable and noble, the very opposite to the modern-day penchant for scientific rationalism. Whether this means that he was a romantic or a mystic is for others to determine; it does mean that nature, the supernatural, and fate all play roles, sometimes cruel roles, in his films. He didn't portray cruelty in a cynical manner but rather as a way of life. His work is the opposite of films by people—such as Stanley Kubrick—for whom technology played a role in meeting and molding nature.

How does this philosophy translate into his films? First, the time frame of his film is large: 20 years in *Great Expectations* and *Lawrence of Arabia*, 40 years in *Doctor Zhivago*. Second, the location of his films is also expansive. *Oliver Twist* (1948) ranges from countryside to city. *Lawrence of Arabia* ranges from continent to continent. The time and the place always have a deep impact on the main character. The setting is never decorative but rather integral to the story.

A powerful example of Lean's use of time, place, and character can be found in *Lawrence of Arabia*. In one shot, Lawrence demonstrates his ability to withstand pain. He lights a match and, with a flourish, douses it with his fingers. As the flame is extinguished, the film cuts to an extreme long shot of the rising sun in the desert. The bright red glow dominates the screen. In the lower part of the screen, there are a few specks, which are identified in a follow-up shot as Lawrence and a guide. The cut from a midshot of the match to an extreme long shot of the sun filling the screen is shocking but also exhilarating. In one shot, we move 500 miles into the desert. We are also struck in these two shots by the awesome, magnificent quality of nature and of the insignificance of humanity. Whether this wonderment speaks to a supernatural order or to Lawrence's fate in the desert, we don't know, but all of these ideas are generated by the juxtaposition of two images. The cut illustrates the power of editing to generate a series of ideas from two shots. This is Lean's art: to lead us to those ideas through this juxtaposition.

An equally powerful but more elaborate set of ideas is generated by the attack on the Turkish train in *Lawrence of Arabia*. Using 85 shots in 6 minutes and 40 seconds, Lean created a sense of the war in the desert. The visuals mix beauty (the derailment of the train) and horror (the execution of the wounded Turkish soldier). The sequence is dynamic and takes us through a narrative sequence: the attack, its details, the aftermath, its implications for the next campaign, Lawrence's relationship to his soldiers. When he is wounded, we gain an insight into his masochistic psychology. Immediately thereafter, he leaps from train car to train car, posing shamelessly for the American journalist (Arthur Kennedy). In the sequence, we are presented with the point of view of the journalist, Lawrence, Auda (Anthony Quinn), Sharif Ali (Omar Sharif), and the British captain (Anthony Quayle).

This sequence becomes more than a battle sequence; Lean infused it with his particular views about heroes and the role they play in war (Figure 5.3). The battle itself was shot using many point-of-view images, principally Lawrence's point of view. Lean also used angles that give the battle a sense of depth or context. This means compositions that have foreground and background. He also juxtaposed close and medium shots with extreme long shots. Finally, Lean used compositions that include a good deal of the sky—low angles—to relate the action on the ground to what happens above it. Looking up at the action suggests a heroic position. This is particularly important when he cut from a low angle of Lawrence atop the train to a high-angle tracking shot of Lawrence's shadow as he leaps from train car to train car. By focusing on the shadow, he introduced the myth as well as the man. The shot is a vivid metaphor for the creation of the myth. This battle sequence of less than seven minutes, with all of its implied views about the nature of war and the combatants, also contains a subtextual idea

FIGURE 5.3
Lawrence of Arabia, 1962. © 1962, Revised 1990, Columbia Pictures Industries, Inc. All rights reserved. Still provided by British Film Institute.

about mythmaking—in this case, the making of the myth of Lawrence of Arabia. This, too, is the art of Lean as editoer–director.

David Lean and Robert Wise provide us with two examples of editors who became directors. To take us more deeply into the relationship of the editor and the director, we turn now to the work of Alfred Hitchcock.

CHAPTER 6

Experiments in Editing: Alfred Hitchcock

Few directors have contributed as much to the mythology of the power of editing as has Alfred Hitchcock. Eisenstein and Pudovkin used their films to work out and illustrate their ideas about editing, but Hitchcock used his films to synthesize the theoretical ideas of others and to deepen the repertoire by showcasing the possibilities of editing. His work embraces the full gamut of editing conceits, from pace to subjective states to ideas about dramatic and real time. This chapter highlights a number of set-pieces that he devoted to these conceits. Before beginning, however, we must acknowledge that Hitchcock may have experimented extensively with editing devices, but he was equally experimental in virtually every filmic device available to him.

Influenced by the visual experiment of F. W. Murnau and G. W. Pabst in the expressionist Universum Film Aktiengesellschaft (UFA) period, Hitchcock immediately incorporated the expressionist look into his early films. Because of the thematic similarities, elements of his visual style recur from *Blackmail* (1929) to *Frenzy* (1972). Particularly notable in the areas of set design and special effects are *Spellbound* (1945) and *The Birds* (1963). In *Spellbound*, Hitchcock turned to Salvador Dali to create the sets that represented the dreams of the main character, an amnesiac accused of murder. The sets represented a primary key to his repressed observations and feelings. Although not totally faithful to the tenets of psychoanalysis, Hitchcock's visualization of the unconscious remains a fascinating experiment.

Equally notable for its visual experiments is the animation in *The Birds*. This tale of nature's revenge on humanity relies on the visualization of birds attacking people. The attack was created with animation. Again, the impulse to find the visual equivalent of an idea led Hitchcock to blend two areas of filmmaking—imaginative animation with live action—to achieve a synthesized filmic reality.

Hitchcock experimented with color in *Under Capricorn* (1949) and *Marnie* (1964). In *Rear Window* (1954), he made an entire film shot from the point of view of a man confined to a wheelchair in his apartment. Robert Montgomery experimented with subjective camera placement in *Lady in the Lake* (1946), but rarely had subjectivity been used as effectively as in *Rear Window*. Hitchcock was less successful in his experiment to avoid editing in *Rope* (1948), but

87

The Technique of Film and Video Editing: History, Theory, and Practice. DOI: 10.1016/B978-0-240-81397-4.00006-6

the result is quite interesting. In this film, camera movement replaces editing; Hitchcock continually moved his camera to follow the action of the story.

Turning to Hitchcock's experiments in editing, what is notable is the breadth and audacity of the experimentation. Ranging from the subjective use of sound in *Blackmail*, which was discussed in Chapter 2, to the experiment in terror in the shower scene in *Psycho* (1960), Hitchcock established very particular challenges for himself, and the result has a sophistication in editing rarely achieved in the short history of film. To understand that level of sophistication, it is necessary to examine first the orthodox nature of Hitchcock's approach to the storytelling problem and then to look at how editing solutions provided him with exciting aesthetic challenges.

A SIMPLE INTRODUCTION: PARALLEL ACTION

Strangers on a Train (1951) is the story of two strangers who meet on a train; one is a famous tennis player (Farley Granger), the other is a psychopath (Robert Walker). Bruno, the psychopath, suggests to Guy, the tennis player, that if they murdered the person who most hampers the progress of the other's life, no one would know. There would be no motive.

So begins this story of murder, but before the offer is made, Hitchcock introduced us to the two strangers in a rather novel way. Using parallel editing, Hitchcock presented two sets of feet (we see no facial shots). One is going right to left, the other left to right, in a train station. The only distinguishing feature is that one of them wears the shoes of a dandy, the other rather ordinary looking shoes. Through parallel cutting between the movements right to left and left to right, we get the feeling that the two pairs of shoes are approaching one another. A shot of one of the men walking away from the camera toward the train dissolves to a moving shot of the track.

The train is now moving. The film then returns to the intercutting of the two sets of feet, now moving toward each other on one car of the train. The two men seat themselves, still unidentified. The dandy accidentally kicks the other and finally the film cuts to the two men seated. The conversation proceeds.

In this sequence of 12 shots, Hitchcock used parallel action to introduce two strangers on a train who are moving toward one another. As is the case in parallel action, the implication is that they will come together, and they do.

A DRAMATIC PUNCTUATION: THE SOUND CUT

Hitchcock found a novel way to link the concepts of trains and murders in *The 39 Steps* (1935). Richard Hannay (Robert Donat) has taken into his home a woman who tells him she is a spy and is being followed; she and the country are in danger. He is woken up by the woman, who now has a knife in her back and a map in her hand. To escape a similar fate, he pretends to be a milkman, sidesteps the murderers who are waiting for him, and takes a train to Scotland, where he will follow the map she has given him.

Hitchcock wanted to make two points: that Hannay is on his way to Scotland and that the murder of his guest is discovered. He also wanted to link the two points together as Hannay will now be a suspect in the murder investigation. The housekeeper opens the door to Hannay's apartment. In the background, we see the woman's body on the bed. The housekeeper screams, but what we hear is the whistle of the train. In the next shot, the rushing train emerges from a tunnel, and we know that the next scene will take place on the train.

The key elements communicated here are the shock of the discovery of the body and the transition to the location of the next action, the train. The sound carry-over from one shot to the next and its pitch punctuate how we should feel about the murder and the tension of what will happen on the train and beyond. Hitchcock managed in this brief sequence to use editing to raise the dramatic tension in both shots considerably, and their combination adds even more to the sense of expectation about what will follow.

DRAMATIC DISCOVERY: CUTTING ON MOTION

This sense of punctuation via editing is even more compelling in a brief sequence in *Spellbound*. John Ballantine (Gregory Peck) has forgotten his past because of a trauma. He is accused of posing as a psychiatrist and of killing the man he is pretending to be. A real psychiatrist (Ingrid Bergman) loves him and works to cure him. She has discovered that he is afraid of black lines across a background of white. Working with his dream, she is convinced that he was with the real psychiatrist who died in a skiing accident. She takes her patient back to the ski slopes, where he can relive the traumatic event, and he does. As they ski down the slopes, the camera follows behind them as they approach a precipice. The camera cuts closer to Ballantine and then to a close-up as the moment of revelation is acknowledged.

The film cuts to a young boy sliding down an exterior stoop. At the base of the stoop sits his younger brother. When the boy collides with his brother, the young child is propelled onto the lattice of a surrounding fence and is killed. In a simple cut, from motion to motion, Hitchcock cut from present to past, and the continuity of visual motion and dramatic revelation provides a startling moment of discovery.

SUSPENSE: THE EXTREME LONG SHOT

In *Foreign Correspondent* (1940), Johnnie Jones (Joel McCrea) has discovered that the Germans have kidnapped a European diplomat days before the beginning of World War II. The rest of the world believes that the diplomat was assassinated in Holland, but it was actually a double who was killed. Only Jones knows the truth. Back in London, he attempts to expose the story and unwittingly confides in a British politician (Herbert Marshall) who secretly works for the Nazis. Now Jones's own life is threatened. The politician assigns him a guardian, Roley, whose actual assignment is to kill him. Roley leads him to the top of a church (a favorite Hitchcock location), where he plans to push Jones to his death.

Roley holds a schoolboy up to see the sights below more clearly. The film cuts to a vertical shot that emphasizes how far it is to street level. The boy's hat blows off, and Hitchcock cuts to the hat blowing toward the ground. The distance down is the most notable element of the shot. The schoolboys leave, and Jones and Roley are alone until a tourist couple interferes with Roley's plans. Shortly, however, they are alone again. Jones looks at the sights. The next shot shows Roley's outstretched hands rushing to the camera until we see his hands in close-up. Hitchcock then cuts to an extreme long shot of a man falling to the ground. We don't know if it's Jones, but as the film cuts to pedestrians rushing about on the ground, a sense of anticipation builds about Jones's fate. Shortly, we discover that Jones has survived because of a sixth sense that made him turn around and sidestep Roley. For the moment that precedes this information, there is a shocking sense of what has happened and a concern that some-one has died. Hitchcock built the suspense here by cutting from a close-up to an extreme long shot.

LEVELS OF MEANING: THE CUTAWAY

In *The 39 Steps*, Hannay is on the run from the law. He has sought refuge for the night at the home of a Scottish farmer. The old farmer has a young wife that Hannay mistakes for his daughter. When the three of them sit down for dinner, the farmer prays. Hannay, who has been reading the paper, notices an article about his escape and his portrayal as a dangerous murderer. As he puts down the paper at the table, the farmer begins the prayer. The farmer, suspecting a sexual attraction developing between his young wife and Hannay, opens his eyes as he repeats the prayer. Hannay tries to take his mind away from his fear. He eyes the wife to see if she suspects.

Here, the film cuts to the headlined newspaper to illustrate Hannay's concern. The next shot of the wife registers Hannay's distraction, and as her eyes drift down to the paper, she realizes that he is the escaped killer. Hitchcock then cuts to a three-shot showing the farmer eyeing Hannay and the wife now acknowledging visually the shared secret. These looks, however, confirm for the husband that the sexual bond between Hannay and the wife will soon strengthen. He will turn out this rival, not knowing that the man is wanted for a different crime.

In this sequence, the cutaway to the newspaper solidifies the sense of concern and communi-cation between Hannay and the wife and serves to mislead the husband about their real fears and feelings.

INTENSITY: THE CLOSE-UP

In *Notorious* (1946), Alicia (Ingrid Bergman) marries Alex (Claude Rains) in order to spy on him. She works with Devlin (Cary Grant). Alex is suspected of being involved in nefarious activities. He is financed by former Nazis in the pursuit of uranium production. He is the leading suspect pursued by Devlin and the U.S. agency he represents. Alicia's assignment is to discover what that activity is. When she becomes suspicious of a locked wine cellar in the home, she alerts Devlin. He suggests that she organize a party where, if she secures the key, he will find out about the wine cellar.

In a 10-minute sequence, Hitchcock created much suspense about whether Devlin will find out about the contents of the cellar, whether Alicia will be unmasked as a spy, and whether it will be Alex's jealousy or a shortage of wine at the party that will unmask them. Alicia must get the key to Devlin, and she must show him to the cellar. Once there, he must find out what is being hidden there.

In this sequence, Hitchcock used subjective camera placement and movement to remind us about Alex's jealousy and his constant observation of Alicia and Devlin's activities. Hitchcock used the close-up to emphasize the heightened importance of the key itself and of the contents of a shattered bottle. He also used close-up cutaways of the diminishing bottles of party champagne to alert us to the imminence of Alex's need to go to the wine cellar. These cutaways raise the suspense level about a potential uncovering of Alicia and Devlin.

Hitchcock used the close-up to alert us to the importance to the plot of the key and of the bogus wine bottles and their contents. The close-up also increases the tension building around the issue of discovery.

THE MOMENT AS ETERNITY: THE EXTREME CLOSE-UP

There is perhaps no sequence in film as famous as the shower scene in *Psycho*.[1] The next section details this sequence more precisely, but here the use of the extreme close-up will be the focus of concern.

The shower sequence, including prologue and epilogue, runs two minutes and includes 50 cuts. The sequence itself focuses on the killing of Marion Crane (Janet Leigh), a guest at an off-the-road motel run by Norman Bates (Anthony Perkins). She is on the run, having stolen $40,000 from her employer. She has decided to return home, give the money back, and face the consequences, but she dies at the hands of Norman's "mother."

The details of this scene, which takes place in the shower of a cheap motel bathroom, are as follows: the victim, her hands, her face, her feet, her torso, her blood, the shower, the shower head, the spray of water, the bathtub, the shower curtain, the murder weapon, the murderer.

Aside from the medium shots of Crane taking a shower and the murderer entering the inner bathroom, the majority of the other shots are close-ups of particular details of the killing. When Hitchcock wanted to register Crane's shock, her fear, and her resistance, he resorted to an extreme close shot of her mouth or of her hand. The shots are very brief, less than a second, and focus on a detail of the preceding, fuller shot of Crane. When Hitchcock wanted to increase the sense of shock, he cut to a subjective shot of the murder weapon coming down at the camera. This enhances the audience's shock and identification with the victim. The use of the extreme close-ups and the subjective shots makes the murder scene seem excruciatingly long. This sequence seems to take an eternity to end.

Dramatic Time and Pace

In real time, the killing of Marion Crane would be over in seconds. By disassembling the details of the killing and trying to shock the audience with the killing, Hitchcock lengthened real time. As in the Odessa Steps sequence in *Potemkin*, the subject matter and its intensity allow the filmmaker to alter real time.

The shower scene begins with a relaxed pace for the prologue: the shots of Crane beginning her shower. This relaxed pacing returns after the murder itself, when Marion, now dying, slides down into the bathtub. With her last breath, she grabs the shower curtain and falls, pulling the curtain down over her. These two sequences—in effect, the prologue and epilogue to the murder—are paced in a regular manner. The sequence of the murder itself and its details rapidly accelerate in pace. The shot that precedes the murder runs for 16 seconds, and the shot that follows the murder runs for 18 seconds. In between, there are 27 shots of the details of the murder.

These shots together run a total of 25 seconds, and they vary from half a second— 12 frames—to up to one second—24 frames. Each shot is long enough to be identifiable. The longer shots feature the knife and its contact with Crane. The other shots of Crane's reaction, her shock, and the blood are shorter. This alternating of shorter shots of the victim and longer shots of the crime is exaggerated by the use of point-of-view shots: subjective shots that emphasize Crane's victimization. Pace and camera angles thus combine to increase the shock and the identification with the victim.

Although this sequence is a clear example of the manipulative power of the medium, Hitchcock has been praised for his editing skill and his ability to enhance identification. As Robin Wood suggests about the shower sequence, "The shower bath murder [is] probably the most horrific incident in any fiction film."[2] Wood also claims that "*Psycho* is Hitchcock's ultimate achievement to date in the technique of audience participation."[3]

THE UNITY OF SOUND

The remake of *The Man Who Knew Too Much* (1956) is commendable for its use of style to triumph over substance. If *Psycho* is the ultimate audience picture, filled with killing and nerve-wrenching unpredictability, *The Man Who Knew Too Much* is almost academic in its absence of emotional engagement despite the story of a family under threat. Having witnessed the killing of a spy, Dr. McKenna (James Stewart) and his wife Jo (Doris Day) are prevented from telling all they know when their son is kidnapped. The story begins in Marrakesh and ends in London, the scene of the crime.

Although we are not gripped by the story, the mechanics of the style are underpinned by the extensive use of sound, which is almost unmatched in any other Hitchcock film. This is best illustrated by looking at three sequences in the film.

In one sequence, Dr. McKenna is following up on information that the kidnappers have tried to suppress. McKenna was told by the dying spy to go to Ambrose Chapel to find the would-be killers of the prime minister. He mistakenly goes to Ambrose Chappell, a taxidermist, and doesn't realize that it is a false lead. He expects to find his son.

In this sequence, Hitchcock relies on a very low level of sound. Indeed, compared to the rest of the film, this sequence is almost silent. The audience is very aware of this foreboding silence. The result is the most tense sequence in the film. Hitchcock used moving camera shots of McKenna going warily toward the address. The streets are deserted except for one other man. The two eye each other suspiciously (we find out later that he is Ambrose Chappell, Jr.). The isolation of McKenna, who is out of his own habitat in search of a son he fears he'll never see again, is underscored by the muted, unorchestrated sound in the sequence.

Another notable sequence is one of the last in the film. The assassination of the prime minister has been foiled, and the McKennas believe that their last chance is to go to the foreign embassy where they suspect their son is being held. At an embassy reception, Jo, a former star of the stage, is asked to sing. She selects "Que Sera, Sera," a melody that she sang to the boy very early in the film. She sings this lullaby before the diplomatic audience in the hope of finding her son.

The camera moves out of the room, and Hitchcock begins a series of shots of the stairs leading to the second floor. As the shots vary, so does the tone and loudness of the song. The level of sound provides continuity and also indicates the distance from the singer. Finally, on the second floor, Hitchcock cuts to a door, and then to a shot of the other side of the door. Now we see the boy trying to sleep. His mother's voice is barely audible.

The sequence begins a parallel action, first of the mother trying to sing louder and then the boy with his captor, Mrs. Drayton, beginning to hear and to recognize his mother. Once that recognition is secure, the boy fluctuates between excitement and frustration. His captor encourages him to whistle, and the sound is heard by mother and father. Dr. McKenna leaves to find his son; Jo continues to sing. We know that the reunion is not far off. The unity of this sequence and the parallel action is achieved through the song.

The final sequence for this discussion is the assassination attempt, which takes place at an orchestra concert at Albert Hall. This rather droll, symphonic shooting is the most academic of the sequences; the unity comes from the music, which was composed and conducted by Bernard Herrmann. In just under 12½ minutes, Hitchcock visually scored the assassination attempt.

The characters of Hitchcock's symphony are Jo McKenna, her husband, the killer, his assistant, the victim, the prime minister and his party, conductor Herrmann, his soloist, his orchestra (with special emphasis on the cymbalist), and, of course, the concert-goers. Hitchcock cuts between all of these characters, trying to keep us moving through the symphony, which emphasizes the assassination with a clash of the cymbals. Through Jo, Hitchcock tried to keep the audience alert to the progress of the assassination attempt: the positioning of the killer, the raising of the gun. To keep the tension moving, Dr. McKenna arrives a few moments before the assassination, and it is his attempt to stop the killer that adds a little more suspense to the proceedings.

Hitchcock accelerated the pace of the editing up to the instant of the killing and the clash of the cymbals, which the killers hope will cover the noise of the gun being fired. Just before the clash, Jo screams, and the gunman fires prematurely. Her scream prompts the prime minister to move, and in doing so, he is wounded rather than killed by the shot. Although the death of the assassin follows after the struggle with Dr. McKenna, the tension is all but over once the cymbals clash. As in the other two sequences, the unity comes from the sound: in this case, the symphony performed in Albert Hall.

THE ORTHODOXY OF THE VISUAL: THE CHASE

The famous cornfield sequence in *North by Northwest* (1959) is unembellished by sound (Figure 6.1). Without using music until the end of the sequence, Hitchcock devoted a 9½-minute sequence to man and machine: Roger Thorndike (Cary Grant) chased by a biplane. As usual in Hitchcock's films, the death of one or the other is the goal.

FIGURE 6.1
North by Northwest, 1959. ©1959 Turner Entertainment Company. All Rights Reserved. Still provided by Moving Image and Sound Archives.

In this sequence of 130 shots, Hitchcock relied less on pace than one might expect in this type of sequence. In a sense, the sequence is more reminiscent of the fun of the Albert Hall sequence in *The Man Who Knew Too Much* than of the emotional power of the shower sequence in *Psycho*. It may be that Hitchcock enjoyed the visual challenge of these sequences and his film invites us to enjoy the abstracted mathematics of the struggle. The odds are against the hero, and yet he triumphs in the cornfield and in Albert Hall. It's the opposite of the shower sequence: triumph rather than torture.

In the cornfield sequence, Hitchcock used much humor. After Thorndike is dropped off on an empty Iowa road, he waits for a rendezvous with George Caplan. We know that Caplan will not come. Indeed, his persecutors think Thorndike is Caplan. Cars pass him by. A man is dropped off. Thorndike approaches him, asking whether he is Caplan. He denies it, saying he is waiting for a bus. Just as the bus arrives, he tells Thorndike that the biplane in the distance is dusting crops, but there are no crops there. This humor precedes the attack on Thorndike, which follows almost immediately.

Throughout the attack, Thorndike is both surprised by the attack and pleased by how he thwarts it. It is not until he approaches a fuel truck that the attack ends, but not before he is almost killed by the truck. As the biplane crashes into the truck, the music begins. With the danger over, the music grows louder, and Thorndike makes his escape by stealing a truck from someone who has stopped to watch the fire caused by the collision.

In this sequence of man versus machine, the orthodoxy of the visual design proceeds almost mathematically. The audience feels a certain detached joy. Without the organization of the sound, the battle seems abstract, emotionally unorchestrated. The struggle nevertheless is intriguing, like watching a game of chess; it is an intellectual battle rather than an emotional one.

The sequence remains strangely joyful, and although we don't relate to it on the emotional level of the shower scene, the cornfield sequence remains a notable accomplishment in pure editing.

DREAMSTATES: SUBJECTIVITY AND MOTION

Perhaps no film of Hitchcock's is as complex or as ambitious as *Vertigo* (1958), which is the story of a detective, Scottie (James Stewart), whose fear of heights leads to his retirement (Figure 6.2). The detective is hired by an old classmate to follow his wife, Madeleine (Kim Novak), whom he fears is suicidal, possessed by the ghost of an ancestor who had committed suicide.

She does commit suicide by jumping from a church tower, but not before Scottie has fallen in love with her. Despondent, he wanders the streets of San Francisco until he finds a woman who resembles Madeleine and, in fact, is the same woman. She, too, has fallen in love, and she allows him to reshape her into the image of his lost love, Madeleine. They become the same, but in the end, he realizes that, together with Madeleine's husband, she duped him.

FIGURE 6.2

Vertigo, 1958. Copyright © by Universal City Studios, Inc. Courtesy of MCA Publishing Rights, a Division of MCA Inc. Still provided by Museum of Modern Art/Film Stills Archives.

They knew he couldn't follow her up the church stairs because of his fear of heights. He was the perfect witness to a "suicide." Having uncovered the murder, he takes her back to the church tower, where she confesses and he overcomes his fear of heights. In the tower, however, she accidentally falls to her death, and Scottie is left alone to reflect on his obsession and his loss.

This very dark story depends on the audience's identification with Scottie. We must accept his fear of heights and his obsession with Madeleine. His states of delusion, love, and discovery must all be communicated to us through the editing.

At the very beginning of the film, Hitchcock used extreme close-ups and extreme long shots to establish the source of Scottie's illness: his fear of heights. Hitchcock cut from his hand grabbing for security to long shots of Scottie's distance from the ground. As Scottie's situation becomes precarious late in the chase, the camera moves away from the ground to illustrate his loss of perspective. Extreme close-ups, extreme long shots, and subjective camera movement create a sense of panic and loss in his discovery of his illness. The scene is shocking not only for the death of a policeman but also for the main character's loss of control over his fate. This loss of control, rooted in the fear of heights, repeats itself in the way he falls in love with Madeleine. Assigned to follow her, he falls in love with her by watching her.

Scottie's obsession with Madeleine is created in the following way. Scottie follows Madeleine to various places—a museum, a house, a gravesite—and he observes her from his subjective viewpoint. This visual obsession implies a developing emotional obsession. What he is doing is far beyond a job. By devoting so much film to show Scottie observing Madeleine, Hitchcock cleverly forced the audience to relate to Scottie's growing obsession. A midshot, full face shot of Scottie in the car, is repeated as the base in these sequences. The follow-up shots of Madeleine's car moving down the streets of San Francisco are hypnotic because we see only a car, not a close-up or a midshot of Madeleine. All we have that is human is the midshot of Scottie. With these sequences, Hitchcock established Scottie's obsession as irrational—given his distance from Madeleine—as his fear of heights.

Another notable sequence takes place in the church tower, where Madeleine commits suicide as Scottie watches, unable to force himself up the stairs. Scottie's fear of heights naturally plays a key role. The scene is shot from his point of view. He sees Madeleine quickly ascend the stairs.

She is a shadow, moving rapidly. He looks up at her feet and body as they move farther away. Scottie's point of view is reinforced with crosscut shots of Scottie looking down. The distance is emphasized. When he is high enough, the fear sets in, and as in the first sequence, the sense of perspective changes as a traveling shot emphasizes the apparent shifting of the floor. These shots are intercut with his slowing to a stop on the stairs. The fear grows.

The ascending Madeleine is then intercut with the slowing Scottie and the ascending floor. Soon Scottie is paralyzed, and rapidly a scream and a point-of-view shot of a falling body follow. Madeleine is dead. Point of view, pace, and sound combine in this sequence to create the sense of Scottie's panic and then resigned despair because he has failed. The editing has created that sense of panic and despair. All that now remains is for *Vertigo* to create the feeling of rebirth in Scottie's increasingly interior dream world.

This occurs after Scottie has insisted that Judy allow herself to be dressed and made up to look like Madeleine. Once her hair color is dyed and styled to resemble Madeleine's, the following occurs.

From Scottie's point of view, Judy emerges from the bedroom into a green light. Indeed, the room is bathed in different colors from green to red. She emerges from the light and comes into focus as Madeleine reborn. Scottie embraces her and seems to be at peace. He kisses her passionately, and the camera tracks around them. In the course of this 360-degree track, with the two characters in medium shot, the background of the room goes to black behind them. Later in the track, the stable where Scottie and Madeleine originally embraced comes into view. As the track continues, there is darkness and the hotel room returns as the background. In the course of this brief sequence, love and hope are reborn and Scottie seems regenerated.

Because this is a Hitchcock film, that happiness will not last. The scene in the church tower quickly proceeds, and this time Judy dies. In the sequence featuring Judy's makeover as Madeleine, Hitchcock used subjectivity, camera motion, and the midshot in deep focus to provide context. The editing of the scene is not elaborate. The juxtapositions between shots and within shots are all that is necessary.

CONCLUSION

Hitchcock was a master of the art of editing. He experimented and refined many of the classic techniques developed by Griffith and Eisenstein. Not only did he experiment with sound and image, but he enjoyed that experimentation.

His enjoyment broadened the editor's repertoire while giving immeasurable pleasure to film audiences. His was a unique talent.

NOTES/REFERENCES

1. This statement could be challenged using the Odessa Steps sequence in *Potemkin* or the final shoot-out in *The Wild Bunch* (1969). All are sequences about killing, and their relationship to Eisenstein's ideas and films must be acknowledged. Which is the greatest seems to be beside the point; all are remarkable.

2. R. Wood, Hitchcock's Films Revisited, Columbia University Press, New York, 1989, p. 146.

3. Ibid., 147.

CHAPTER 7

New Technologies

The 1950s brought many changes to film. On the economic front, the consent decrees of 1947 (antitrust legislation that led to the studios divesting themselves of the theatres they owned) and the developing threat of television suggested that innovation, or at least novelty, might help recapture the market for film. As was the case with the coming of sound in the late 1920s, new innovations had considerable impact on how films were edited, and the results tended to be conservative initially and innovative later.

This chapter concentrates on two innovations, each of which had a different impact on film. The first was the attraction to the wide screen, including the 35 mm innovations of Cinerama, CinemaScope, Vistavision, and Panavision and the 70 mm innovations of TODD-AO, Technirama, Supertechnirama, MGM 65, and later IMAX. Around the world, countries adopted similar anamorphic approaches, including Folioscope. If the goal of CinemaScope and the larger versions was to increase the spectacle of the film experience, the second innovation, cinéma vérité, with its special lighting and unobtrusive style, had the opposite intention: to make the film experience seem more real and more intimate, with all of the implications that this approach suggested.

Both innovations were technology-based, both had a specific goal in mind for the audience, and both had implications for editing.

THE WIDE SCREEN

To give some perspective to the wide screen, it is important to realize that before 1950 films were presented in Academy aspect ratio; that is, the width-to-height ratio of the viewing screen was 1:1.33 (Figure 7.1).

This ratio was replicated in the aperture plate for cameras as well as projectors. There were exceptions. As early as 1927, Abel Gance used a triptych approach, filming particular sequences in his *Napoleon* (1927) with three cameras and later projecting the images simultaneously. The result was quite spectacular (Figure 7.2).

99

The Technique of Film and Video Editing: History, Theory, and Practice. DOI: 10.1016/B978-0-240-81397-4.00007-8

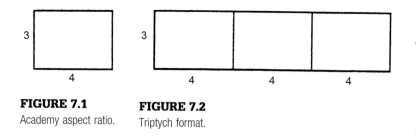

FIGURE 7.1
Academy aspect ratio.

FIGURE 7.2
Triptych format.

In these sequences, the aspect ratio became 1:3. The impact of editing in these sequences was startling. How did one use a close-up? What happened when the camera moved? Was a cut from movement to movement so jarring or awkward that the strength of these editing conventions became muted? The difficulties of Gance's experiment didn't pose a challenge for filmmakers because his triptych technique did not come into wide use.

Other filmmakers continued to experiment with screen shape. Eisenstein advocated a square screen, and Claude Autant-Lara's *Pour Construire un Feu* (1928) introduced a wider screen in 1928 (the forerunner of CinemaScope). The invention of CinemaScope itself took place in 1929. Dr. Henri Chretien developed the anamorphic lens, which was later purchased by Twentieth Century Fox.

It was not until the need for innovation became economically necessary that a procession of gimmicks, including 3D, captured the public's attention. The first widescreen innovation of the period was Cinerama. This technique was essentially a repeat of Gance's idea: three cameras record simultaneously, and a similar projection system (featuring stereophonic sound) gave the audience the impression of being surrounded by the sound and the image.[1] Cinerama was used primarily for travelogue-type films with simple narratives. These travelogues were popular with the public, and at least a few narrative films were produced in the format. The most notable was *How the West Was Won* (1962). The system was cumbersome, however, and the technology was expensive. In the end, it was not economically viable.

Twentieth Century Fox's CinemaScope, however, was popular and cost-effective, and did prove to be successful. Beginning with *The Robe* (1953), CinemaScope appeared to be viable and the technology was rapidly copied by other studios. Using an anamorphic lens, the scenes were photographed on the regular 35 mm stock, but the image was squeezed. When projected normally, the squeezed image looked distorted, but when projected with an anamorphic lens, the image appeared normal but was presented wider than before (Figure 7.3).

The other notable widescreen process of the period was VistaVision, Paramount Pictures's response to CinemaScope. In this process, 35 mm film was run horizontally rather than vertically. The result was a sharper image and greater sound flexibility. The recorded image was twice as wide as the conventional 35 mm frame and somewhat taller. For VistaVision, Paramount selected a modified widescreen aspect ratio of 1:1.85, the aspect ratio later adopted as the industry standard.

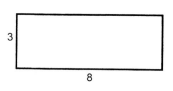

FIGURE 7.3
CinemaScope. Aspect ratio 1:2.55 (later reduced to 1:2.35).

The larger 70 mm, 65 mm, TODD-AO, and Panavision 70 formats had an aspect ratio of 1:2.2, with room on the film for four magnetic sound tracks. Not only did the larger frame make possible a bigger sound, but it also allowed sharper images despite the size of the screen. IMAX is similar to VistaVision in that it records 70 mm film run horizontally. Unlike VistaVision, which had a normal vertical projection system, IMAX is projected horizontally and consequently requires its own special projection system. Its image is twice as large as the normal 70 mm production, and the resultant clarity is striking.

Of all of the formats, those that were economically viable were the systems that perfected CinemaScope technology, particularly Panavision. The early CinemaScope films exhibited problems with close-ups and with moving shots. By the early 1960s, when Panavision supplanted CinemaScope and VistaVision, those imperfections had been overcome, and the widescreen had become the industry standard.[2]

Today, standard film has an aspect ratio of 1:1.85; however, films that have special releases—the big-budget productions that are often shot in anamorphic 35 mm and blown up to 70 mm—are generally projected 1:2.2 so that they are wider-screen presentations. Films such as *Hook* (1991) or *Terminator 2* (1991) are projected in a manner similar to the early CinemaScope films, and the problems for the editor are analogous.[3]

In the regular 1:1.33 format, the issues of editing—the use of close-ups, the shift from foreground to background, and the moving shot—have been developed, and both directors and audiences are accustomed to a particular pattern of editing. With the advent of a frame that was twice as wide, all of the relationships of foreground and background were changed.

In Figure 7.4, two characters, one in the foreground and the other in the background, are shown in two frames, one a regular frame and the other a CinemaScope frame. In the CinemaScope frame, the characters seem farther apart, and there is an empty spot in the frame, creating an inner rectangle. This image affects the relationship implied between the two characters. The foreground and background no longer relate to one another in the same way because of the CinemaScope frame. Now the director also has the problem of the middle ground. The implications for continuity and dramatic meaning are clear. The wider frame changes meaning. The director and editor must recognize the impact of the wider frame in their work.

The width issue plays equal havoc for other continuity issues: match cuts, moving shots, and cuts from extreme long shot to extreme close-up. In its initial phase, the use of the anamorphic lens was problematic for close-ups because it distorted objects and people positioned too close to the camera. Maintaining focus in traveling shots, given the narrow depth of field of the lens, posed another sort of problem. The result, as one sees in the first CinemaScope film, *The Robe*, was cautious editing and a slow-paced style.

Some filmmakers attempted to use the wide screen creatively. They demonstrated that new technological developments needn't be ends unto themselves, but rather opportunities for innovation.

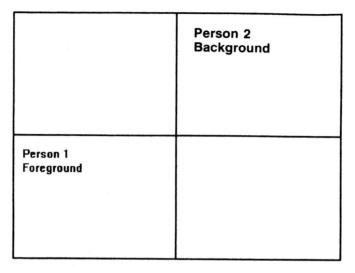

(A)

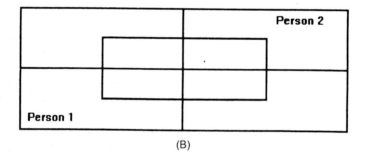

(B)

FIGURE 7.4
Foreground—background relationship in (A) Academy and (B) widescreen formats.

Character and Environment

A number of filmmakers used the new widescreen process to try to move beyond the action-adventure genres that were the natural strength of the wide screen. Both Otto Preminger and Anthony Mann made Westerns using CinemaScope, and although Mann later became one of the strongest innovators in its use, Preminger, in his film *River of No Return* (1954), illustrated how the new foreground—background relationship within the frame could suggest a narrative subtext critical to the story.

River of No Return exhibits none of the fast pacing that characterizes the dramatic moments in the Western *Shane* (1953), for example. Nor does it have the intense close-ups of *High Noon* (1952), a Western produced two years before *River of No Return*. These are shortcomings of the widescreen process. What *River of No Return* does illustrate, however, is a knack for using shots to suggest the characters' relationship to their environment and to their constant struggle with it. To escape from the Indians, a farmer (Robert Mitchum), his son, and an acquaintance (Marilyn Monroe) must make their way down the river to the nearest town. The rapids of the river and the threat of the Indians are constant reminders of the hostility of their environment. The river, the mountains, and the valleys are beautiful, but they are neither romantic nor beckoning. They are constant and indifferent to these characters. Because the environment fills the background of most of the images, we are constantly reminded about the characters' context.

Preminger presented the characters in the foreground. The characters interact, usually in medium shot, in the foreground. We relate to them as the story unfolds; however, the background, the environment, is always present. Notable also is the camera placement. Not only is the camera placed close to the characters, but the eye level is democratic. The camera neither looks down or up at the characters. The result doesn't lead us; instead, it allows us to relate to the characters more naturally.

The pace of the editing is slow. Preminger's innovation was to emphasize the relationship of the characters to their environment by using the film format's greater expanse of foreground and background.

Preminger developed this relationship further in *Exodus* (1960). Again, the editing style is gradual even in the set-piece: the preparation for and the attack on the Acre prison. Two examples illustrate how the use of foreground and background sets up a particular relationship while avoiding the need to edit (Figure 7.5).

FIGURE 7.5

Exodus, 1960. ©1960 United Artists Pictures, Inc. All Rights Reserved. Still provided by Moving Image and Sound Archives.

Early in the film, Ari Ben Canaan (Paul Newman) tries to take 600 Jews illegally out of Cyprus to Palestine. His effort is thwarted by the British Navy. When the British major (Peter Lawford) or his commanding officer (Ralph Richardson) communicate with the *Exodus*, they are presented in the foreground, and the blockaded *Exodus* is presented in the same frame but in the background.

Later in the film, Ari Ben Canaan is showing Kitty, an American nurse (Eva Marie Saint), the location of his home. The scene takes place high atop a mountain overlooking the Jezreel Valley, the valley in which his home is located as well as the village of his Arab neighbors. In this shot, Ari explains to the nurse about the history of the valley, and the two of them acknowledge their attraction to one another. Close to the camera, Ari and Kitty speak and then embrace. The valley they speak about is visible in the background. Other filmmakers might have used an entire sequence of shots, including close-ups of the characters and extreme long shots of the valley. Preminger's widescreen shot thus replaces an entire sequence.

Relationships

In *East of Eden* (1955), Elia Kazan explored the relationship of people to one another rather than their relationship to the environment. The film considers the barriers between characters as well as the avenues to progress in their relationships.

East of Eden is the story of the "bad son" Cal (James Dean). His father (Raymond Massey) is a religious moralist who is quick to condemn his actions. The story begins with Cal's discovery that the mother he thought dead is alive and prospering as a prostitute in Monterey, 20 miles from his home.

Kazan used extreme angles to portray how Cal looks up to or down on adults. Only in the shots of Cal with his brother, Aaron, and his fiancée, Abra (Julie Harris), is the camera nonjudgmental, presenting the scenes at eye level. Whenever Cal is observing one of his parents, he is present in the foreground or background, and there is a barrier—blocks of ice or a long hallway, for example—in the middle. Kazan tilted the camera to suggest the instability of the family unit. This is particularly clear in the family dinner scene. This scene, particularly the attempt of father and son to be honest about the mother's fate, is the first sequence where cutting between father and son as they speak about the mother presents the distance between them.

The foreground–background relationship is broken, and the two men so needy of one another are separate. They live in two worlds, and the editing of this sequence portrays that separateness as well as the instability of the relationship.

One other element of Kazan's approach is noteworthy. Kazan angled the camera placement so that the action either approaches the camera at an angle or moves away from the camera. In both cases, the placement creates a sense of even greater depth. Whereas Preminger usually had the action take place in front of the camera and the context directly behind the action of the characters, there appears a studied relationship of the two. Kazan's approach is more emotional, and the extra sense of depth makes the widescreen image seem even wider. On one level, Kazan may have been exploring the possibilities, but in terms of its impact, this placement seems to increase the space, physical and emotional, between the characters.

Relationships and the Environment

No director was more successful in the early use of the widescreen format than John Sturges, whose 1955 film *Bad Day at Black Rock* is an exemplary demonstration that the wide screen could be an asset for the editor. Interestingly, Sturges began his career as an editor.

John McCready (Spencer Tracy) is a one-armed veteran of World War II. It is 1945, and he has traveled to Black Rock, a small desert town, to give a medal to the father of the man who died saving his life. The problem is that father and son were Japanese-Americans, and this town has a secret. Its richest citizen, Reno Smith (Robert Ryan), and his cronies killed the father, Kimoko, in a drunken rage after the attack on Pearl Harbor. The towns people try to cover up this secret, but McCready quickly discovers the truth. In 48 hours, McCready's principal mission, to give the Medal of Honor to a parent, turns into a struggle for his own survival.

The characters and the plot of Sturges's film are tight, tense, and terse. In terms of style, Sturges used almost no close-ups, and yet the tension and emotion of the story remain powerful. Sturges achieved this tension through his intelligent use of the wide screen and his application of dynamic editing in strategic scenes.

Two scenes notable for their dynamic editing are the train sequence that appears under the credits and the car chase scene in the desert. The primary quality of the train sequence is the barrenness of the land that the train travels through. There are no people, no animals, no signs of settlement. The manner in which Sturges filmed the train adds to the sense of the environment's vastness. Shooting from a helicopter, a truck, and a tracking shot directly in front of the train, Sturges created a sense of movement. By alternating between angled shots that demonstrate the power of the train breaking through the landscape and flat shots in which train and landscape seem flattened into one, Sturges alternated between clash and coexistence. His use of high angles and later low angles for his shots adds to the sense of conflict.

Throughout this sequence, then, the movement and variation in camera placement and the cutting on movement creates a dynamic scene in which danger, conflict, and anticipation are all created through the editing. Where is the train going? Why would it stop in so isolated a spot? This sequence prepares the audience for the events and the conflicts of the story. After introducing us to John McCready, Sturges immediately used the wide screen to present his protagonist in conflict with almost all of the townspeople of Black Rock. Sturges did not use close-ups; he favored the three-quarter shot, or American shot. This shot is not very emotional, but Sturges organized his characters so that the constant conflict within the shots stands in for the intensity of the close-up. For example, as McCready is greeted by the telegraph operator at the train station, he flanks the left side of the screen, and the telegraph operator flanks the right. The camera does not crowd McCready. Although he occupies the foreground, the telegraph operator occupies the background. In the middle of the frame, the desert and the mountains are visible. The space between the two men suggests a dramatic distance between them. As in other films, Sturges could have fragmented the shot and created a sequence, but here he used the width of the frame to provide dramatic information within a single shot without editing.

Sturges followed the same principle in the interiors. As McCready checks into the hotel, he is again on the left of the frame, the hotel clerk is on the right, and the middle ground is unoccupied. Later in the same setting, the sympathetic doctor occupies the background, local thugs occupy the middle of the frame, and the antagonist, Smith, is in the left foreground. Sturges rarely left a part of the frame without function. When he used angled shots, he suggested power relationships opposed to one another, left to right, foreground to background. When he used flatter shots, those conflicting forces faced off against one another in a less interesting way, but nevertheless in opposition. Rather than relying on the clash of images to suggest conflict and emotional tension, Sturges used the widescreen spaces and their organization to suggest conflict. He avoided editing by doing so, but the power and relentlessness of the conflict is not diminished because the power within the story is constantly shifting, as reflected in the visual compositions. By using the wide screen in this way, Sturges avoided editing until he really needed it. When he did resort to dynamic editing, as in the car chase, the sequence is all the more powerful as the pace of the film dramatically changes.

By using the wide screen fully as a dramatic element in the film, Sturges created a story of characters in conflict in a setting that can be used by those characters to evoke their cruelty and their power. The wide screen and the editing of the film both contribute to that evocation.

The Background

Max Ophuls used CinemaScope in *Lola Montes* (1955). Structurally interesting, the film is a retrospective examination of the life of Lola Montes, a nineteenth-century beauty who became a mistress to great musicians and finally to the King of Bavaria. The story is told in the present. A dying Lola Montes is the main attraction at the circus. As she reflects on her life, performers act out her reminiscences. Flashbacks of the younger Lola and key phases are intercut with the circus rendition of that phase. Finally, her life retold, Lola dies.

Ophuls, a master of the moving camera, was very interested in the past (background) and the present (foreground), and he constantly moved between them. For example, as the film opens, only the circus master (Peter Ustinov) is presented in the foreground. Lola (Martine Carol) and the circus performers are in the distant background. As the story begins, Lola herself is presented in the foreground, but as we move into the past story (her relationship with Franz Liszt, her passage to England, and her first marriage), Lola seems uncertain whether she is important or unimportant. What she wants (a handsome husband or to be grown up) is presented in the middle ground, and she fluctuates toward the foreground (with Liszt and later on the ship) or in the deep background (with Lieutenant James, who becomes her first husband). Interestingly, Lola is always shifting but never holding on to the central position, the middle of the frame. In this sense, the film is about the losses of Lola Montes because she never achieves the centrality of the men in her life, including the circus master.

The widescreen shot is always full in this film, but predominantly concerns the barriers to the main character's happiness. The editing throughout supports this notion. If the character is in search of happiness, an elusive state, the editing is equally searching, cutting on movement of the character or the circus ensemble and its exploration/exploitation of Lola. The editing in this sense follows meaning rather than creates it.

By using the wide screen as he did, Ophuls gave primacy to the background of the shot over the foreground, to Lola's search over her success, to her victimization over her victory. The film stands out as an exploration of the wide screen. Ophuls's work was not often imitated until Stanley Kubrick used the wide screen and movement in a similar fashion in *Barry Lyndon* (1975).

The Wide Screen After 1960

The technical problems of early CinemaScope—the distortion of close-ups and in tracking shots—were overcome by the development of the Panavision camera. It supplanted CinemaScope and VistaVision with a simpler system of which the anamorphic projections offered a modified widescreen image with an aspect ratio of 1:1.85, and in its larger anamorphic use in 35 mm or 70 mm, it provided an image aspect ratio of 1:2.2. With the technical shortcomings of CinemaScope overcome, filmmakers began to edit sequences as they had in the past. Pace picked up, and close-ups and moving shots took on their past pattern of usage.

A number of filmmakers, however, made exceptional use of the wide screen and illustrated its strengths and weaknesses for editing. For example, Anthony Mann in *El Cid* (1961) used extreme close-ups and extreme long shots as well as framed single shots that embrace a close shot in the foreground and an extreme long shot in the background. Mann presented relationships, usually of conflict, within a single frame as well as within an edited sequence. The use of extreme close-ups and extreme long shots also elevated the nature of the conflict and the will of the protagonist. Because the film mythologizes the personal and national struggles of Rodrigo Díaz de Bivar, the Cid (Charlton Heston), those juxtapositions within and between shots are critical.

Mann also used the width of the frame to give an epic quality to each combat in which Rodrigo partakes: the personal fight with his future father-in-law, the combat of knights for the ownership of Calahorra, and the large-scale final battle on the beach against the Muslim invaders from North Africa. In each case, the different parts of the frame were used to present the opposing force. The clash, when it comes, takes place in the middle of the frame in single shots and in the middle of an edited sequence when single shots are used to present the opposing forces. Mann was unusually powerful in his use of the widescreen frame to present forces in opposition and to include the land over which they struggle. Few directors have the visual power that Mann displayed in *El Cid*.

In his prologue in *2001: A Space Odyssey* (1968), Stanley Kubrick presents a series of still images that, together, are intended to create a sense of vast, empty, unpopulated space. This is the Earth at the dawn of humanity. Given the absence of continuity—the editing does not follow narrative action or a person in motion—the stills have a random, discontinuous quality, a pattern of shots such as Alexander Dovzhenko used in *Earth* (1930). Out of this pattern, an idea eventually emerges: the vast emptiness of the land. This sequence leads to the introduction of the apes and other animals. From our vantage point, however, the interest is in the editing of the sequence. Without cues or foreground–background relationships, these shots have a genuine randomness that, in the end, is the point of the sequence. There is no scientific gestalt here because there is no human here. The wide screen emphasizes the expanse and the lack of context.

A number of other filmmakers are notable for their use of the wide screen to portray conflict. Sam Peckinpah used close-ups in the foreground and background by using lenses that have a shallow depth of field. The result is a narrowing of the gap between one character on the left and another character, whether it be friend or foe, on the right. The result is intense and almost claustrophobic rather than expansive. Sergio Leone used the same approach in *The Good, the Bad, and the Ugly* (1967). In the final gunfight, for example, he used close-ups of all of the combatants and their weapons. He presented the subject fully in two-thirds of the frame, allowing emptiness, some background, or another combatant to be displayed in the balance of the frame. Leone seemed to relish the overpowering close-ups, as if he were studying or dissecting an important event.

John Boorman, on the other hand, was more orthodox in his presentation of combatants in *Hell in the Pacific* (1968). The story, set in World War II, has only two characters: a Japanese soldier who occupies an isolated island and an American flyer who finds himself on the island after being downed at sea. These two characters struggle as combatants and eventually as human beings to deal with their situation. They are adversaries in more than two-thirds of the film, so Boorman presented them in opposition to one another within single frames (to the left and right) as well as in edited sequences. What is interesting in this film is how Boorman used both the wide screen and conventional options, including close-ups, cut-aways, and faster cutting, to maintain and build tension in individual sequences. When he used the wide screen, the compositions are full to midshots of the characters. Because he didn't want to present one character as a protagonist and the other as the antagonist, he did not exploit subjective placement or close-ups. Instead, whenever possible, he showed both men in the same frame, suggesting the primacy of their relationship to one another. One may have power over the other temporarily, but Boorman tried to transcend the nationalistic, historical struggle and to reach the interdependent, human subtext. These two characters are linked by circumstance, and Boorman reinforced their interdependence by using the wide-screen image to try to overcome the narrative conventions that help the filmmaker demonstrate the victorious struggle of the protagonist over the lesser intentions of the antagonist.

Other notable filmmakers who used the wide screen in powerful ways include David Lean, who illustrated again and again the primacy of nature over character (*Ryan's Daughter*, 1970). Michelangelo Antonioni succeeded in using the wide screen to illustrate the human barriers to personal fulfillment (*L'Avventura*, 1960). Luchino Visconti used the wide screen to present the class structure in Sicily during the Risorgimento (*Il Ovottepordo*, 1962). Federico Fellini used the wide screen to create a powerful sense of the supernatural evil that undermined Rome (*Fellini Satyricon*, 1970). Steven Spielberg used subjective camera placement to juxtapose potential victim and victimizer, human and animal, in *Jaws* (1975), and Akira Kurosawa used color and foreground—background massing to tell his version of King Lear's struggle in *Ran* (1985). Today, the wide screen is no longer a barrier to editing but rather an additional option for filmmakers to use to power their narratives visually.

CINÉMA VÉRITÉ

The wide screen forced filmmakers to give more attention to composition for continuity and promoted the avoidance of editing through the use of the foreground—background relationship. Cinéma vérité promoted a different set of visual characteristics for continuity.

Cinéma vérité is the term used for a particular style of documentary filmmaking. The postwar developments in magnetic sound recording and in lighter, portable cameras, particularly for 16 mm, allowed a less intrusive filmmaking style. Faster film stocks and more portable lights made film lighting less intrusive and in many filmmaking situations unnecessary. The cliché of cinéma vérité filmmaking is poor sound, poor light, and poor image. In actuality, however, these films had a sense of intimacy rarely found in the film experience, an intimacy that was the opposite of the widescreen experience. Cinéma vérité was rooted in the desire to make real stories about real people. The Italian neorealist filmmakers—such as Roberto Rossellini (*Open City*, 1946), Vittorio DeSica (*The Bicycle Thief*, 1948), and Luchino Visconti (*La Terra Trema*, 1947)—were the leading influences of the movement.

Cinéma vérité, then, was a product of advances in camera and sound recording technology that made filmmaking equipment more portable than had previously been possible. That new portability allowed the earliest practitioners to go where established filmmakers had not been interested in going. Lindsay Anderson traveled to the farmers' market in Covent Garden for *Every Day Except Christmas* (1957), Karel Reisz and Tony Richardson traveled to a jazz club for *Momma Don't Allow* (1955), Terry Filgate followed a Salvation Army parish in Montreal in *Blood and Fire* (1959), and D. A. Pennebaker followed Bob Dylan in *Don't Look Back* (1965). In each case, these films attempted to capture a sense of the reality of the lives of the characters, whether public figures or private individuals. There was none of the formalism or artifice of the traditional feature film.

How did cinéma vérité work? What was its editing style? Most cinéma vérité films proceeded without a script. The crew filmed and recorded sound, and a shape was found in the editing process.[4] In editing, the problems of narrative clarity, continuity, and dramatic emphasis became paramount. Because cinéma vérité proceeded without staged sequences and with no artificial sound, including music, the raw material became the basis for continuity as well as emphasis.

Cinéma vérité filmmakers quickly understood that they needed many close-ups to build a sequence because the conventions of the master shot might not be available to them. They also realized that general continuity would come from the sound track rather than from the visuals. Carrying over the sound from one shot to the next provided aural continuity, and this was sometimes the only basis for continuity in a scene. Consequently, the sound track became even more important than it had been in the dramatic film. Between the close-ups and the sound, continuity could be maintained. Sound could also be used to provide continuity among different sequences. As the movement gathered steam, cinéma vérité filmmakers also used intentional camera and sound mistakes, acknowledgments of the filmmaking experience, to cover for losses of continuity. The audience, after all, was watching a film, and acknowledgment of that fact proved useful in the editing. It joined audience and filmmaker in a moment of confession that bound the two together. The rough elements of the filmmaking process, anathema in the dramatic film, became part of the cinéma vérité experience; they supported the credibility of the experience.[5] The symbols of cinéma vérité were those signposts of the handheld camera: camera jiggle and poor framing.

Before exploring the editing style of cinéma vérité in more detail, it might be useful to illustrate how far-reaching its style of intimacy with the subject was to become. Beginning with the New Wave films of François Truffaut and Jean-Luc Godard, cinéma vérité had a wide impact. Whatever their subject, young filmmakers across the world were attracted to this approach. In Hungary, Istvan Szabo (*Father*, 1966); in Czechoslovakia, Milos Forman (*Fireman's Ball*, 1968); and in Poland, Jerzy Skolimowski (*Hands Up*, 1965) all adopted a style of reportage in their narrative films. Because the handheld style of cinéma vérité had found its way into television documentary and news the style adopted by these filmmakers suggested the kind of veracity, of weightiness, of importance, found in the television documentary. They were not making television documentaries, though. Nor were John Frankenheimer in *Seconds* (1966) or Michael Ritchie in *The Candidate* (1972), and yet the handheld camera shots and the allusions to television gave each film a kind of veracity unusual in dramatic films.[6] The same style was taken up in a more self-exploratory way by Haskell Wexler in *Medium Cool* (1969). In these three films, the intimacy of cinéma vérité was borrowed and applied to a dramatized story to create the illusion of reality. In fact, the sense of realism resulting because of cinéma vérité made each film resemble in part the evening news on television. The result was remarkably effective.

Perhaps no dramatic film plays more on this illusion of realism deriving from cinéma vérité than *Privilege* (1967). Peter Watkins recreated the life of a rock star in a future time. Using techniques (even lines of dialog) borrowed from the cinéma vérité film about Paul Anka (*Lonely Boy*, 1962), Watkins managed to reference rock idolatry in a manner familiar to the audience.

Watkins's attraction to cinéma vérité had been cultivated by two documentary-style films: *The Battle of Culloden* (1965) and *The War Game* (1967). Complete with on-air interviews and off-screen narrators, both films simulated documentaries with cinéma vérité techniques. However, both were dramatic recreations using a style that simulated a post-1950 type of reality. The fact that *The War Game* was banned from the BBC suggests how effective the use of those techniques were.

To understand how the cinéma vérité film was shaped given the looseness of its production, it is useful to look at one particular film to illustrate its editing style.

Lonely Boy was a production of Unit B at the National Film Board (NFB) of Canada. That unit, which was central in the development of cinéma vérité with its Candid Eye series, had already produced such important cinéma vérité works as *Blood and Fire* (1958) and *Back-Breaking Leaf* (1959). The French unit at the NFB had also taken up cinéma vérité techniques in such films as *Wrestling* (1960). *Lonely Boy*, a film about the popular young performer Paul Anka, brought together many of the talents associated with Unit B. Tom Daley was the executive producer, Kathleen Shannon was the sound editor, John Spotton and Guy L. Cote were the editors, and Roman Kroitor and Wolf Koenig were the directors. Each of these people demonstrated many talents in their work at and outside the NFB. Kathleen Shannon became executive producer of Unit D, the women's unit of the NFB. John Spotton was a gifted cinematographer (*Memorandum*, 1966). Wolf Koenig played an important role in the future of animation at the NFB. Tom Daley, listed as the executive producer on the film, has a reputation as one of the finest editors the NFB ever produced.

Lonely Boy is essentially a concert film, the predecessor of such rock performance films as *Gimme Shelter* (1970), *Woodstock* (1970), and *Stop Making Sense* (1984). The 26-minute film opens and closes on the road with Paul Anka between concerts. The sound features the song "Lonely Boy." Within this framework, we are presented with, as the narrator puts it, a "candid look" at a performer moving up in his career. To explore the "phenomenon," Kroiter and Koenig follow Paul Anka from an outdoor performance in Atlantic City to his first performance in a nightclub, the Copacabana, and then back to the outdoor concert. In the course of this journey, Anka, Irving Feld (his manager), Jules Podell (the owner of the Copacabana), and many fans are interviewed. The presentation of these interviews makes it unclear whether the filmmakers are seeking candor or laughing at Anka and his fans. Their attitude seems to change. Anka's awareness of the camera and retakes are included here to remind us that we are not looking in on a spontaneous or candid moment but rather at something that has been staged (Figures 7.6 to 7.8).

FIGURE 7.6
Lonely Boy, 1962. Courtesy National Film Board of Canada.

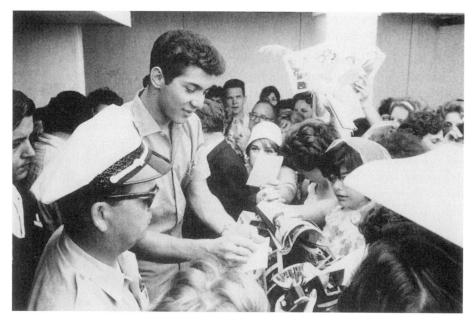

FIGURE 7.7
Lonely Boy, 1962. Courtesy National Film Board of Canada.

FIGURE 7.8
Lonely Boy, 1962. Courtesy National Film Board of Canada.

The audience is exposed to Anka, his manager, and his fans, but it is not until the penultimate sequence that we see Anka in concert in a fuller sense. The screen time is lengthy compared to the fragments of concert performance earlier in the film. Through his performance and the reaction of the fans, we begin to understand the phenomenon. In this sequence, the filmmakers seem to drop their earlier skepticism, and in this sense, the sequence is climactic.

Throughout the film, the sound track unifies individual sequences. For example, the opening sequence begins on the road with the song "Lonely Boy" on the sound track. We see images of Atlantic City, people enjoying the beach, a sign announcing Paul Anka's performance, shots of teenagers, the amusement park, and the city at night. Only as the song ends does the film cut to Paul Anka finishing the song. Then we see the response of his audience.

The shots in this sequence are random. Because many are close-ups intercut with long shots, unity comes from the song on the sound track. Between tracking shots, Kroiter and Koenig either go from movement within a shot, such as the sign announcing Anka's performance, to a tracking shot of teenagers walking—movement of the shot to movement within the shot. Again, overall unity comes from the sound track.

In the next sequence, Anka signs autographs, and the general subject (how Anka's fans feel about him) is the unifying element. This sequence features interviews with fans about their zeal for the star.

In all sequences, visual unity is maintained through an abundance of close-ups. A sound cue or a cutaway allows the film to move efficiently into the next sequence.

In the final sequence, the concert performance, the continuity comes from the performance itself. The cutaways to the fans are more intense than the performance shots, however, because the cutaways are primarily close-ups. These audience shots become more poignant when Kroiter and Koenig cut away to a young girl screaming and later fainting. In both shots, the sound of the scream is omitted. We hear only the song. The absence of the sound visually implied makes the visual even more effective. The handheld quality of the shots adds a nervousness to the visual effect of an already excited audience. In this film, the handheld close-up is an asset rather than a liability. It suggests the kind of credibility and candor of which cinéma vérité is capable.

Lonely Boy exhibits all of the characteristics of cinéma vérité: for example, too much background noise in the autograph sequence and a jittery handheld camera in the backstage sequence where Anka is quickly changing before a performance. In the latter, Anka acknowledges the presence of the camera when he tells a news photographer to ignore the filmmakers. All of this—the noise level, the wobbly camera, the acknowledgment that a film is being made—can be viewed as technical shortcomings or amateurish lapses, or they can work for the film to create a sense of candor, insight, honesty, and lack of manipulation: the agenda for cinéma vérité. The filmmakers try to have it all in this film. What they achieve is only the aura of candor. The film is fascinating, nevertheless.

Others who used the cinéma vérité approach—Allan King in *Warrendale* (1966), Fred Wiseman in *Hospital* (1969), Alfred and David Maysles in *Salesman* (1969)—exploited cinéma vérité fully. They achieved an intimacy with the audience that verges on embarrassing but, at its best, is the type of connection with the audience that was never possible with conventional cinematic techniques.

Cinéma vérité must be viewed as one of the few technological developments that has had a profound impact on film. Because it is so much less structured and formal than conventional filmmaking, it requires even greater skill from its directors and, in particular, its editors.

NOTES/REFERENCES

1. A six-sprocket system also made the Cinerama image taller. The result was an image six times larger than the standard of the day.

2. Directors often shot their films with the television ratio in mind (the old Academy standard of 1:1.33). The result was shots with the action centered in the frame. When projected on television, the parts of the frame outside the television aspect ratio were cut off. Filmmakers have abandoned shots framed with characters off to the side of the frame or have skewed the foreground–background relationship to the sides rather than to the center.

3. For the television broadcast of large-scale epics shot with a ratio of 1:2.2, the films were optically rephotographed for television. Optical zooms and pans were used to follow actions and movements of characters within shots. The results were aesthetically bizarre and questionable, but they allowed the television audience to follow the action.

4. An excellent description of the process is found in: D. Bordwell, K. Thompson. Film Art: An Introduction, Third ed., McGraw-Hill, New York, 1990, pp. 336–342. The authors analyze the form and style of Fred Wiseman's *High School* (1968), a classic cinéma vérité film. With the Maysles brothers (*Salesman*, 1969; *Gimme Shelter*, 1970), Fred Wiseman epitomized the cinéma vérité credo and style.

5. For a full treatment of the attractiveness of the veracity and objectivity implicit in cinéma vérité, see K. Reisz, G. Millar, The Technique of Film Editing, Second ed., Focal Press, Boston, 1968, pp. 297–321.

6. The orgy scene in *Seconds* was filmed as if it were occurring.

CHAPTER 8

International Advances

The year 1950 is a useful point to demarcate a number of changes in film history, among them the pervasive movement for change in film. Nowhere is this more apparent than in the growth in achievement and importance on an international level. Just as Hollywood experimented with the wide screen in this period, a group of British filmmakers challenged the orthodoxy of the documentary, a group of French writers who became filmmakers suggested that film authorship allowed personal styles to be expressed over industrial conventions, and young Italian filmmakers simplified narratives and film styles to politicize a popular art form. All sought alternatives to the classic style.

The classic style is best represented by such popular Hollywood filmmakers as William Wyler, who made *The Best Years of Our Lives* (1946). The film has a powerful narrative, and Wyler's grasp of style, including editing, was masterful but conventional. There were more exotic stylists, such as Orson Welles in *The Lady from Shanghai* (1948), but the mainstream was powerful and pervasive and preoccupied with more conventional stories. By 1950, the Allies had won the war, and just as victory had brought affirmation of values and a way of life to the United States, the war and its end brought a deep desire for change in war-torn Europe. Nowhere was this impulse more quickly expressed than in European films. The neorealist movement in Italy and the New Wave in France were movements dedicated to bringing change to film.

That is not to say that foreign films had not been influential before World War II. The contributions of Eisenstein, Pudovkin, and Vertov from the Soviet Union, F. W. Murnau and Fritz Lang of Germany, and Abel Gance and Jean Renoir of France were important to the evolution of the art of film. However, the primacy of Hollywood and of the various national cinemas was such that only fresh subject matter treated in a new and interesting style would challenge the status quo. These challenges, when they came, were of such a provocative and innovative character that they have profoundly broadened the editing of films. The challenges were broadly based: new ideas about what constitutes narrative continuity, new ideas about dramatic time, and a new definition of real time and its relationship to film time. All this came principally from those international advances that can be dated from 1950.

115

The Technique of Film and Video Editing: History, Theory, and Practice. DOI: 10.1016/B978-0-240-81397-4.00008-X

FIGURE 8.1
Rashomon, 1951. Courtesy Janus Films Company. Still provided by British Film Institute.

THE DYNAMICS OF RELATIVITY

When Akira Kurosawa directed *Rashomon* (1951), he presented a narrative story without a single point of view. Indeed, the film presents four different points of view. *Rashomon* was a direct challenge to the conventions that the narrative clarity that the editor and director aim to achieve must come from telling the story from the point of view of the main character and that the selection, organization, and pacing of shots must dramatically articulate that point of view (Figure 8.1).

Rashomon is a simple period story about rape and murder. A bandit attacks a samurai traveling through the woods with his wife. He ties up the samurai, rapes his wife, and later kills the samurai. The story is told in flashback by a small group of travelers waiting for the rain to pass. The film presents four points of view: those of the bandit, the wife, the spirit of the dead samurai, and a woodcutter who witnessed the events. Each story is different from the others, pointing to a different interpretation of the behavior of each of the participants. In each story, a different person is responsible for the death of the samurai. Each interpretation of the events is presented in a different editing style.

After opening with a dynamic presentation of the woodcutter moving through the woods until he comes to the assault, the film moves into the story of the bandit Tajomaru (Toshiro Mifune). The bandit is boastful and without remorse. His version of the story makes him out to be a powerful, heroic figure. Consequently, when he fights the samurai, he is doing so out of respect to the wife who feels she has been shamed and that only a fight to the death between her husband and the bandit can take away the stain of being dishonored.

The presentation of the fight between the samurai and Tajomaru is dynamic. The camera moves, the perspective shifts from one combatant to the other to the wife, and the editing is lively. Cutting on movement within the frame, we move with the combat as it proceeds. The editing style supports Tajomaru's version of the story. The combat is a battle of giants, of heroes, fighting to the death. The editing emphasizes conflict and movement. The foreground–background relationships keep shifting, thereby suggesting a struggle of equals rather than a one-sided fight. This is quite different from all of the other versions presented.

The second story, told from the point of view of the wife, is much less dynamic; indeed, it is careful and deliberate. In this version, the bandit runs off, and the wife, using her dagger, frees the samurai. The husband is filled with scorn because his wife allowed herself to be raped. The question here is whether the wife will kill herself to save her honor. The psychological struggle is too much, and the wife faints. When she awakes, her husband is dead, and her dagger is in his chest.

The wife sees herself as a victim who wanted to save herself with as much honor as she could salvage, but tradition requires that she accept responsibility for her misfortune. Whether she killed her husband for pushing her to that responsibility or whether he is dead by his own hand is unclear. With its deliberateness and its emphasis on the wife's point of view, the editing supports the wife's characterization of herself as a victim. The death of her husband remains a mystery.

The third version is told from the point of view of the dead husband. His spirit is represented by a soothsayer who tells his story: The shame of the rape was so great that, seeing how his wife lusts after the bandit, the samurai decided to take his own life using his wife's dagger.

The editing of this version is dynamic in the interaction between the present—the soothsayer—and the past—her interpretation of the events. The crosscutting between the soothsayer and the samurai's actions is tense. Unlike the previous version, there is a tension here that helps articulate the samurai's painful decision to kill himself. The editing helps articulate his struggle in making that decision and executing it.

Finally, there is the version of the witness, the woodcutter. His version is the opposite of the heroic interpretation of the bandit. He suggests that the wife was bedazzled by the bandit and that a combat between Tajomaru and the samurai did take place but was essentially a contest of cowards. Each man seems inept and afraid of the other. As a result, the clash is not dynamic but rather amateurish. The bandit kills the samurai, but the outcome could as easily have been the opposite.

The editing of this version is very slow. Shots are held for a much longer time than in any of the earlier interpretations. The camera was close to the action in the bandit's interpretation, but here it is far from the action. The result is a slow, sluggish presentation of a struggle to the death. There are no heroes here.

By presenting a narrative from four perspectives, Kurosawa suggested not only the relativity of the truth, but also that a film's aesthetic choices—from camera placement to editing style—must support the film's thesis. Kurosawa's success in doing so opens up options in terms of the flexibility of editing styles even within a single film. Although Kurosawa did not pursue this multiple perspective approach in his later work, *Rashomon* did show audiences the importance of editing style in suggesting the point of view of the main character. An editing style that could suggest a great deal about the emotions, fears, and fantasies of the main character became the immediate challenge for other foreign filmmakers.

THE JUMP CUT AND DISCONTINUITY

The New Wave began in 1959 with the consecutive releases of François Truffaut's *The 400 Blows* and Jean-Luc Godard's *Breathless*, but in fact its seeds had developed 10 years earlier in the writing of Alexandre Astruc and André Bazin and the film programming of Henri Langlois at the Cinémathèque in Paris. The writing about film was cultural as well as theoretical, but the viewing of film was global, embracing film as part of popular culture as well as an artistic achievement. What developed in Paris in the postwar period was a film culture in which film critics and lovers of film moved toward becoming filmmakers themselves. Godard, Eric Rohmer, Claude Chabrol, Alain Resnais, and Jacques Rivette were all key figures, and it was Truffaut who wrote the important article "Les Politiques des Auteurs," which heralded the director as the key creative person in the making of a film.

These critics and future filmmakers wrote about Hitchcock, Howard Hawks, Samuel Fuller, Anthony Mann, and Nicholas Ray—all Hollywood filmmakers. Although he admired Renoir enormously, Truffaut and his young colleagues were critical of the French film establishment.[1] They criticized Claude Autant-Lara and Rene Clement for being too literary in their screen stories and not descriptive enough in their style. What they proposed in their own work was a personal style and personal stories—characteristics that became the hallmarks of the New Wave.

In his first film, *The 400 Blows*, Truffaut set out to respect Bazin's idea that moving the camera rather than fragmenting a scene was the essence of discovery and the source of art in film.[2] The opening and the closing of the film are both made up of a series of moving shots, featuring the beginning of Paris, the Eiffel Tower,[3] and later the lead character running away from a juvenile detention center. The synchronous sound recorded on location gives the film an intimacy and immediateness only available in cinéma vérité.

It was the nature of the story, though, that gave Truffaut the opportunity to make a personal statement. *The 400 Blows* is the story of Antoine Doinel, a young boy in search of a childhood he never had. The rebellious child is unable to stay out of trouble at home or in school. The adult world is very unappealing to Antoine, and his clashes at home and at school lead him to reject authority and his parents. The story may sound like a tragedy that inevitably will lead to a bad end, but it is not. Antoine does end up in a juvenile detention center, but when he runs away, it is as rebellious as all of his other actions. Truffaut illustrated a life of spirit and suggested that challenging authority is not only moral, but it is also necessary for avoiding tragedy. The film is a tribute to the spirit and hope of being young, an entirely appropriate theme for the first film of the New Wave.

How did the stylistic equivalents of the personal story translate into editing choices? As already mentioned, the moving camera was used to avoid editing. In addition, the jump cut was used to challenge continuity editing and all that it implied.

The jump cut itself is nothing more than the joining of two noncontiguous shots. Whether the two shots recognize a change in direction, focus on an unexpected action, or simply don't show the action in one shot that prepares the viewer for the content of the next shot, the result of the jump cut is to focus on discontinuity. Not only does the jump cut remind viewers that they are watching a film, but it is also jarring. This result can be used to suggest instability or lack of importance. In both cases, the jump cut requires the viewer to broaden the band of acceptance to enter the screen time being presented or the sense of dramatic time portrayed. The jump cut asks viewers to tolerate the admission that we are watching a film or to temporarily suspend belief in the film. This disruption can help the film experience or harm it. In the past, it was thought that the jump cut would destroy the experience. Since the New Wave, the jump cut has simply become another editing device accepted by the viewing audience. They have accepted the notion that discontinuity can be used to portray a less stable view of society or personality or that it can be accepted as a warning. It warns viewers that they are watching a film and to beware of being manipulated. The jump cut was brought into the mainstream by the films of the New Wave.

Two scenes in *The 400 Blows* stand out for their use of the jump cut, although jump cutting is used throughout the film. In the famous interview with the psychologist at the detention center, we see only Antoine Doinel. He answers a series of questions, but we neither hear the questions nor see the questioner.[4] By presenting the interview in this way, Truffaut was suggesting Antoine's basic honesty and how far removed the adult world is from him. Because we see what Antoine sees, not viewing the psychologist is important in the creation of Antoine's internal world.

At the end of the film, Antoine escapes from the detention center. He reaches the seashore and has no more room to run. There is a jump cut as Antoine stands at the edge of the water. The film jumps from long shot to a slightly closer shot and then again to midshot. It freeze-frames the midshot and jump cuts to a freeze-frame close-up of Antoine. In this series of four jump cuts, Truffaut trapped the character, and as he moved in closer, he froze him and trapped him more. Where can Antoine go? By ending the film in this way, Truffaut trapped the character and trapped us with the character. The ending is both a challenge and an invitation in the most direct style. The jump cut draws attention to itself, but it also helps Truffaut capture our attention at this critical instant.

Truffaut used the jump cut even more dynamically in *Jules et Jim* (1961), a period story about two friends in love with the same woman. Whenever possible, Truffaut showed all three friends together in the same frame, but to communicate how struck the men are upon first meeting Catherine (Jeanne Moreau), Truffaut used a series of jump cuts that show Catherine in close-up and in profile and that show her features. This brief sequence illustrates the thunderbolt effect Catherine has on Jules and Jim (Figures 8.2 and 8.3).

FIGURE 8.2
Jules et Jim, 1961. Courtesy Janus Films Company. Still provided by British Film Institute.

FIGURE 8.3
Jules et Jim, 1961. Courtesy Janus Films Company. Still provided by Moving Image and Sound Archives.

Whether the jump cut is used to present a view of society or a view of a person, it is a powerful tool that immediately draws the viewer's attention. Although self-conscious in intent when improperly used, the jump cut was an important tool of the filmmakers of the New Wave. It was a symbol of the freedom of film in style and subject, of its potential, and of its capacity to be used in a highly personalized way. It inspired a whole generation of filmmakers, and may have been the most lasting contribution of the New Wave.[5]

OBJECTIVE ANARCHY: JEAN-LUC GODARD

Perhaps no figure among the New Wave filmmakers raised more controversy or was more innovative than Jean-Luc Godard.[6] Although attracted to genre films, he introduced his own personal priorities to them. As time passed, these priorities were increasingly political. In terms of style, Godard was always uncomfortable with the manipulative character of narrative storytelling and the camera and editing devices that best carried out those storytelling goals. Over his career, Godard increasingly adopted counterstyles. If continuity editing supported what he considered to be bourgeois storytelling, then the jump cut could purposefully undermine that type of storytelling. If sound could be used to rouse emotion in accordance with the visual action in the film, Godard would show a person speaking about a seduction, but present the image in midshot to long shot with the woman's face totally in shadow. In shadow, we cannot relate as well to what is being said, and we can consider whether we want to be manipulated by sound and image. This was a constant self-reflexivity mixed with an increasingly Marxist view of society and its inhabitants. Rarely has so much effort been put into alienating the audience! In doing so, Godard posed a series of questions about filmmaking and about society.

Perhaps Godard's impulse toward objectification and anarchy can best be looked at in the light of *Weekend* (1967), his last film of this period that pretended to have a narrative. *Weekend* is the story of a Parisian couple who seem desperately unhappy. To save their marriage, they travel south to her mother to borrow money and take a vacation. This journey is like an odyssey. The road south is littered with a long multicar crash, and that is only the beginning of a journey from an undesirable civilization to an inevitable collapse leading, literally, to cannibalism. The marriage does not last the journey, and the husband ends up as dinner (Figures 8.4 and 8.5).

How does one develop a style that prepares us for this turn of events? In all cases, subversion of style is the key. A fight in the apartment parking lot descends into absurdity. The car crash, instead of involving us in its horror, is rendered neutral by a slow, objective camera track. In fact, once the camera has observed the whole lengthy crash, it begins to move back over the crash, front to back. When a town is subjected to political propaganda, the propagandists are interviewed head-on. Later, in a more rural setting, the couple comes across an intellectual (Jean-Pierre Leaud) who may be either mad or just bored with contemporary life. He reads aloud in the fields from Denis Diderot. Eventually, when revolution is the only alternative, the wife kills and eats the husband with her atavistic colleagues deep in the woods. At each stage, film style is used to subvert content. The result is a constant contradiction between objective film style and absurdist content or anarchistic film style and objective content.

FIGURE 8.4
Weekend, 1967. Still provided by British Film Institute.

FIGURE 8.5
Weekend, 1967. Still provided by British Film Institute.

In both cases, the film robs the viewer of the catharsis of the conventional narrative and of the predictability of its style and meaning. There are no rules of editing that Godard does not subvert, and perhaps that is his greatest legacy. The total experience is everything; to achieve that total experience, all conventions are open to challenge.

MELDING PAST AND PRESENT: ALAIN RESNAIS

For Alain Resnais, film stories may exist on a continuum of developing action (the present), but that continuum must include everything that is part of the main character's consciousness. For Resnais, a character is a collection of memories and past experiences. To enter the story of a particular character is to draw on those collective memories because those memories are the context for the character's current behavior. Resnais's creative challenge was to find ways to recognize the past in the present. He found the solution in editing. An example illustrates his achievement.

Hiroshima Mon Amour (1960) tells the story of an actress making a film in Hiroshima. She takes a Japanese lover who reminds her of her first love, a German soldier who was killed in Nevers during the war. She was humiliated as a collaborator when she was 20 years old. Now, 14 years later, her encounter with her Japanese lover in the city destroyed to end the war takes her back to that time. The film does not resolve her emotional trauma; rather, it offers her the opportunity to relive it. Intermingled with the story are artifacts that remind her of the nuclear destruction of Hiroshima.

The problem of time and its relationship to the present is solved in an unusual way. The woman watches her Japanese lover as he sleeps. His arm is twisted. When she sees his hand, Resnais cut back and forth between a close-up of the hand and a midshot of the woman. After moving in closer, he cuts from the midshot, of the woman to a close-up of another hand (a hand from the past), then back to the midshot, and then to a full shot of the dead German lover, his hand in exactly the same position as that of the Japanese lover. The full shot shows him bloodied and dead and the film then cuts back to the present (Figures 8.6 to 8.8).

The identical presentations of the two hands provides a visual cue for moving between the past and the present. The midshot of the woman watching binds the past and present.

Later, as the woman confesses to her contemporary lover, the film moves between Nevers and Hiroshima. Her past is interwoven into her current relationship, and by the end of the film, the Japanese lover is viewed as a person through whom she can relive the past and perhaps put it behind her. Throughout the film, it is the presence of the past in her present that provides the crucial context for the woman's affair and for her view of love and relationships. The past also comes to bear, in a less direct way, on the issues of war and politics and how a person can become immersed in them. The fluidity and formal quality of Resnais's editing fuses past and present for the character.

The issue of time and its relationship to behavior is a continuing trend in most of Resnais's work. From the blending of the past and present of Auschwitz in *Night and Fog* (1955), to

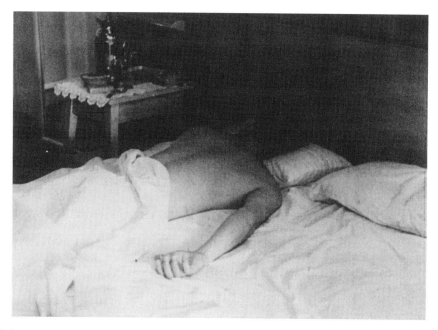

FIGURE 8.6
Hiroshima Mon Amour, 1960. Courtesy Janus Films Company. Still provided by British Film Institute.

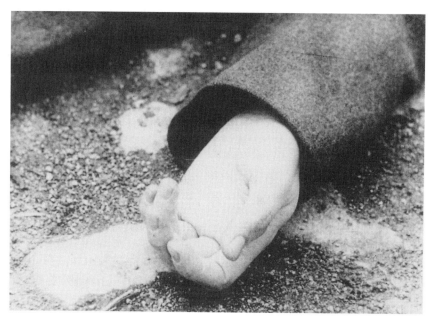

FIGURE 8.7
Hiroshima Mon Amour, 1960. Courtesy Janus Films Company. Still provided by British Film Institute.

FIGURE 8.8
Hiroshima Mon Amour, 1960. Courtesy Janus Films Company. Still provided by British Film Institute.

the role of the past in the present identity of a woman in *Muriel* (1963), to the elevation of the past to the self-image of the main character in *La Guerre est Finie* (1966), the exploration of editing solutions to narrative problems has been the key to Resnais's work. Resnais carried on his exploration of memory and the present in *Providence* (1977), which embraces fantasy as well as memory. Later, he used the intellect, fantasy, and the present in *Mon Oncle d'Amerique* (1980).

The greater the layers of reality, the more interesting the challenge for Resnais. Always, the solution lies in the editing.

INTERIOR LIFE AS EXTERNAL LANDSCAPE

The premise of many of Resnais's narratives—that the past lives on in the character—was very much the issue for both Federico Fellini and Michelangelo Antonioni. They each found different solutions to the problem of externalizing the interior lives of their characters.

When Fellini made *8½* in 1963, he was interested in finding editing solutions in the narrative. In doing so, he not only produced a film that marked the height of personal cinema, he also explored what had been, until that time, the domain of the experimental film: a thought rather than a plot, an impulse to introspection unprecedented in mainstream filmmaking (Figure 8.9).

8½ is the story of Guido (Marcello Mastroianni), a famous director. He has a crisis of confidence and is not sure what his next film will be. Nevertheless, he proceeds to cast it and build sets, and he pretends to everyone that he knows what he is doing. He is in the midst of a personal crisis as well as a creative one. His marriage is troubled, his mistress is demanding, and he dreams of his childhood. *8½* is the interior journey into the world of the past, of Guido's dreams, fears, and hopes. For two and a half hours, Fellini explores this interior landscape.

To move from fantasy to reality and from past to present, Fellini must first establish the role of fantasy. He does so in the very first scene. Guido is alone in a car, stuck in a traffic jam. The traffic cannot be heard, just the sounds Guido makes as he breathes anxiously. The images begin to seem absurd. Suddenly we see other characters, older people in one car, a young woman being seduced in another. Are they dreams or are they reality? What follows blurs the distinction. The camera angle seems to indicate that she is looking straight at Guido (we later learn that she is his mistress). Suddenly, the car begins to fill with smoke. Guido struggles to get out, but people in other cars seem indifferent to his plight. His breathing is very labored now. Then he is out of the car and floating out of the traffic jam. We see a horseman, and Guido floats high in the air. An older man (we find out later that he is Guido's producer) suggests that he should come down. He pulls on Guido's leg, and he falls thousands of feet to the water below (Figure 8.10).

FIGURE 8.9
8½, 1963. Courtesy Janus Films Company. Still provided by British Film Institute.

FIGURE 8.10
8½, 1963. Courtesy Janus Films Company. Still provided by British Film Institute.

The film then cuts to neutral sound, and we discover that Guido has been having a night-mare. The film returns to the present, where Guido is being attended to in a spa. His creative team is also present. In this sequence, the fantasy is supported by the absurdist juxtaposition of images and by the absence of any natural sound other than Guido's breathing. The sound and the editing of the images provide cues that we are seeing a fantasy. This is a strategy Fellini again and again uses to indicate whether a sequence is fantasy or reality. For example, a short while later, Guido is outside at the spa, lining up for mineral water. The spa is popu-lated by all types of people, principally older people, and they are presented in a highly regi-mented fashion. In a close-up, Guido looks at something, dropping his glasses to a lower point on his nose. The film cuts to a beautiful young woman (Claudia Cardinale), dressed in white, gliding toward him. The sound is suspended. Guido sees only the young woman. She smiles at him and is now very close. The film cuts back to the same shot of Guido in close-up. This time he raises his glasses back onto the bridge of his nose. At that instant, the sound returns, and the film cuts to a midshot of a spa employee offering him mineral water. Again, the sound cue alerts us to the shift into and out of the fantasy (Figure 8.11).

Throughout the film, Fellini also relies on the art direction (all white in the fantasy sequences) and on the absurdist character of the fantasies, particularly the harem-in-revolt sequence, to differentiate the fantasy sequences from the rest of the film. In the movement from present to past, a sound phrase—such as Asa-Nisi-Masa—is used to transport the con-temporary Guido back to his childhood. Fellini also uses sound effects and music as cues. In 8½, Guido's interior life is as much the subject of the story as is his contemporary life.

FIGURE 8.11

8½, 1963. Courtesy Janus Films Company. Still provided by British Film Institute.

Although the film has little plot by narrative standards, the concept of moving around in the mind of a character poses enough of a challenge to Fellini that the audience's experience is as much a voyage of discovery as his seems to be. After that journey, film editing has never been defined in as audacious a fashion (Figure 8.12).

Michelangelo Antonioni chose not to move between the past and the present even though his characters are caught in as great an existential dilemma as Guido in 8½. Instead, Antonioni included visual detail that alludes to that dilemma. His characters live in the present, but they find despair in contemporary life. Whether theirs is an urban malaise born of upper-middle-class boredom or whether it's an unconscious response to the modern world, the women in his films are as lost as Guido. As Seymour Chatman suggests, "The central and distinguishing characteristic of Antonioni's mature films (so goes the argument of this book) is narration by a kind of visual minimalism, by an intense concentration on the sheer appearance of things—the surface of the world as he sees it—and a minimalization of exploratory dialogue."[7]

We stay with Antonioni's characters through experiences of a variety of sorts. Something dramatic may happen in such an experience—an airplane ride, for example—but the presentation of the scene is not quite what conventional narrative implies it will be. In conventional narrative, an airplane ride illustrates that the character is going from point A to point B, or it illustrates a point in a relationship (the airplane ride being the attempt of one character to

FIGURE 8.12
8½, 1963. Courtesy Janus Films Company. Still provided by British Film Institute.

move along the relationship with another). There is always a narrative point, and once that point is made, the scene changes.

This is the point in *L'Eclisse* (*The Eclipse*) (1962), for example. The airplane ride is an opportunity for the character to have an overview of her urban context: the city. It is an opportunity to experience brief joy, and it is an opportunity to admire the technology of the airplane and the airport. Finally, it is an opportunity to point out that even with all of the activity of a flight, the character's sense of aloneness is deep and abiding.

The shots that are included and the length of the sequence are far different than if there had been a narrative goal. Also notable are the number of long shots in which the character is far from the camera as if she is being studied by the camera (Figures 8.13 and 8.14).

L'Eclisse is the story of Vittoria (Monica Vitti), a young woman who is ending her engagement to Roberto as the film begins. She seems depressed. Her mother is very involved in the stock market and visits her daily to check on her health. Although Vittoria has friends in her apartment building, she seems unhappy. The only change in her mood occurs when she and her friends pretend they are primitive Africans. She can escape when she pretends.

One day, she visits her mother at the stock exchange. The market crashes and her mother is very bitter. Vittoria speaks to her mother's stockbroker, Piero (Alain Delon). He seems quite interested in her, and a relationship develops. The relationship seems to progress; the film ends inconclusively when she leaves his apartment, promising to meet in the evening. Her leave-taking is followed by a seven-minute epilogue of shots of life in the city. The epilogue

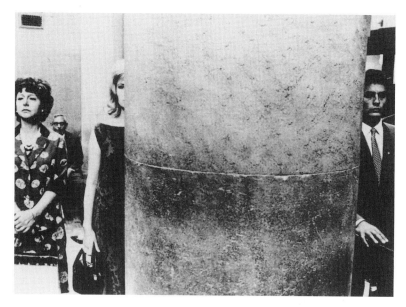

FIGURE 8.13
L'Eclisse, 1962. Courtesy Janus Films Company. Still provided by British Film Institute.

has no visual reference to either Vittoria or Piero. Whether one feels that the film is a condemnation of Piero's determinism and amorality or a meditation on Vittoria's existential state or her search for an alternative to a world dominated by masculine values, the experience of the film is unsettling and open. What is the meaning of the stock market? Vittoria says, "I still don't know if it's an office, a marketplace, a boxing ring, and maybe it isn't even necessary." Piero's vitality seems much more positive than her skepticism and malaise. What is the meaning of the role of family? We see only her mother and her home. The mother is interested only in acquiring money. The family is represented by their home. They are personified by the sum of their acquisitiveness. What is meant by all of the shots of the city and its activity without the presence of either character? One can only proceed to find meaning based on what Antonioni has given us. We have many scenes of Vittoria contextualized by her environment, her apartment, Roberto's apartment, Piero's two apartments, her mother's apartment, and the stock exchange. In these scenes, there is a foreground–background relationship between Vittoria, her habitat, and her relationship to others: her friends, Roberto, Piero, her mother. Antonioni alternated between objective and subjective camera placement to put the viewer in a position to identify with Vittoria and then to distance the viewer from Vittoria in order to consider that identification and to consider her state.

Space is used to distance us, and when Vittoria exits into the city, these spaces expand. Filmed in extreme long shot with a deep-focus lens, the context alternates between Vittoria in midshot in the foreground and Vittoria in the deep background dwarfed by her surroundings, by the human-made monuments, the buildings, and the natural monuments (the trees, the river, the forest).

FIGURE 8.14
L'Eclisse, 1962. Courtesy Janus Films Company. Still provided by British Film Institute.

Antonioni used this visual articulation, which for us means many slowly paced shots so that there is considerable screen time of Vittoria passing through her environment, rather than acting upon it as Piero does. What is fascinating about Antonioni is his ability in all of these shots to communicate Vittoria's sense of aloneness, and yet her sensuality (life force) is exhibited in the scene with her friends and in the later scenes with Piero. In these sequences, Antonioni used two-shots that included elements of the apartment: a window, the drapes. Because of the pacing of the shots, the film does not editorialize about what is most important or least important. All of the information, artifacts, and organization seem to affect Vittoria, and it is for us to choose what is more important than anything else.

If Antonioni's goal was to externalize the internal world of his characters, he succeeded remarkably and in different ways than did Fellini. Two sequences illustrate how the present is the basis for suggesting interior states in *L'Eclisse*.

When the relationship between Vittoria and Piero begins, Antonioni abandons all of the other characters. The balance of the film, until the very last sequence, focuses on the two lovers. In a series of scenes that take place in front of her apartment, at the site of his car's recovery from the river, in his parents' apartment, in a park, and in his pied-à-terre, Vittoria gradually commits to a relationship with Piero. Although there is some uncertainty in the last scene as to whether the relationship will last, the film stays with the relationship in scene after scene. There is progress, but there isn't much dialog to indicate a direct sense of progress in the relationship. The scenes are edited as if they were meditations on the relationship rather than as a plotted progression. The editing pattern is slow and reflective. The final sequence with the characters ends on a note of invasion from outside and of anxiety. As Vittoria leaves, Piero puts all of the phones back on the hook. As she descends the stairs, she hears as they begin to ring. The film cuts to Piero sitting at his desk wondering whether to answer them. In a very subtle way, this ending captures the anxiety in their relationship: Will it continue, or will the outside world invade and undermine it?

The epilogue of the film is also notable. In the last shot of the preceding sequence, Vittoria has left Piero's apartment. She is on the street. In the foreground is the back of her hand as she views the trees across the road. She turns, looks up, and then looks down, and she exits the frame, leaving only the trees.

The epilogue follows: 7 minutes without a particular character; 44 images of the city through the day. Antonioni alternates between inanimate shots of buildings and pans or tracks of a moving person or a stream. If there is a shape to the epilogue, it is a progression through the day. This sequence ends on a close-up of a brilliant street lamp. Throughout the sequence, sound becomes increasingly important. The epilogue relies on realistic sound effects and, in the final few shots, on music.

The overall feeling of the sequence is that the life of the city proceeds regardless of the state of mind of the characters. Vittoria may be in love or feeling vulnerable, but the existence of the tangible, physical world objectifies her feelings. To the extent that we experience the story through her, the sequence clearly suggests a world beyond her. It is a world Antonioni alluded to throughout the film. Early on, physical structures loom over Vittoria and Roberto. Later, when we see Vittoria and Piero for the first time, a column stands between them. The physical world has dwarfed these characters from the beginning. The existential problem of mortal humanity in a physically overpowering world is reaffirmed in this final sequence. Vittoria can never be more than she is, nor can her love change this relationship to the world in more than a temporal way. The power of this sequence is that it democratizes humanity and nature. Vittoria is in awe of nature, and she is powerless to affect it. She can only coexist with it. This impulse to democratization—identification with the character and then a distancing from her—is the creative editing contribution of Michelangelo Antonioni.

NOTES/REFERENCES

1. Just as Anderson, Reisz, and Richardson railed against the British film establishment during this period, Truffaut, Godard, and Chabrol were critical of Claude Autant-Lara, Rene Clement, and the other established directors of the French film industry.

2. *Mise-en-scène*, or the long take, meant moving the camera to record the action rather than ordering the action by fragmenting and editing the sequence.

3. The personalized reference in this prologue is typical of the New Wave. One of the moving shots travels by the Cinémathèque, and the Eiffel Tower is in the background.

4. The jarring effect of the jump cut is softened in this sequence with dissolves.

5. The worldwide influence of the New Wave can be seen in the film movements of the last 30 years. It can be seen in the Czech New Wave, the work of Milos Forman and Jiri Menzel. It can be seen in Yugoslav film, particularly in the work of Dusan Makavejev. It can be seen in the work of Glauber Rocha in Brazil and in the work of Fernando Solanas in Argentina. The New Wave also influenced the work of Pier Paolo Pasolini and the Taviani brothers in Italy. In the United States, Arthur Penn and Mike Nichols were strongly encouraged to experiment by the success of the New Wave.

6. There is an excellent account of Godard's editing style in K. Reisz, G. Millar, The Technique of Film Editing, Focal Press, Boston, 1968, pp. 345–358.

7. S. Chatman, Antonioni, or the Surface of the World, University of California Press, Berkeley, 1985, p. 2.

CHAPTER 9

The Influence of Television and Theatre

TELEVISION

No postwar change in the entertainment industry was as profound as the change that occurred when television was introduced. Not only did television provide a home entertainment option for the audience, thereby eroding the traditional audience for film, but it also broadcast motion pictures by the 1960s. By presenting live drama, weekly series, variety shows, news, and sports, television revolutionized viewing patterns, subject matter, the talent pool,[1] and eventually how films were edited.

Perhaps television's greatest asset was its sense of immediacy, a quality not present in film. Film was consciously constructed, whereas television seemed to happen directly in front of the viewer. This sense was supported by the presentation of news events as they unfolded as well as the broadcasting of live drama and variety shows. It was also supported by television's function as an advertising medium. Not only were performers used in advertising, but the advertising itself—whether a commercial of one minute or less—came to embody entertainment values. News programs, commercials, and how they were presented (particularly their sense of immediacy and their pace) were the influences that most powerfully affected film editing.

One manifestation of television's influence on film can be seen in the treatment of real-life characters or events. Film had always been attracted to biography; Woodrow Wilson, Lou Gehrig, Paul Ehrlich, and Louis Pasteur, among others, received what has come to be called the "Hollywood treatment." In other words, their lives were freely and dramatically adapted for film. There was no serious attempt at veracity; entertainment was the goal. After television came on the scene, this changed. The influence of television news was too great to ignore. Veracity had to in some way be respected. This approach was supported by the postwar appeal of neorealism and by the cinéma vérité techniques. If a film looked like the nightly news, it was important, it was real, it was immediate.

Peter Watkins recognized this in his television docudramas of the 1960s (*The Battle of Culloden*, 1965; *The War Game*, 1967). He continued with this approach in his later work on Edward Munch. In the feature film, this style began to have an influence as early as John Frankenheimer's *The Manchurian Candidate* (1962) and was continued in his later films, *Seven Days in May* (1964) and *Black Sunday* (1977). Alan J. Pakula took a docudrama

133

The Technique of Film and Video Editing: History, Theory, and Practice. DOI: 10.1016/B978-0-240-81397-4.00009-1

approach to Watergate in *All the President's Men* (1976), and Oliver Stone continues to work in this style, from *Salvador* (1986) to *JFK* (1991). The docudrama approach, which combines a cinéma vérité style with jump-cut editing, gives films a patina of truth and reality that is hard to differentiate from the nightly news. Only the pace differs, heightening the tension in a way rarely seen on television news programs. Given that the subject, character, or event already has a public profile, the filmmaker need only dip back into that broadcast-created impression by using techniques that allude to veracity to make the film seem real. This is due directly to the techniques of television news: cinéma vérité, jump cutting, and on- or off-air narrators. The filmmaker has a fully developed repertoire of editing techniques to simulate the reality of the nightly news.

The other manifestation of the influence of television seems by comparison fanciful, but its impact, particularly on pace, has been so profound that no film, television program, or television commercial is untouched by it. This influence can be most readily seen in the 1965–1970 career of one man, Richard Lester, an expatriate American who directed the two Beatles films, *A Hard Day's Night* (1964) and *Help!* (1965) in Great Britain. Using techniques widely deployed in television, Lester found a style commensurate with the zany mix of energy and anarchy that characterized the Beatles. One might call his approach to these films the first of the music videos.

Films that starred musical or comedy performers who were not actors had been made before. The Marx Brothers, Abbott and Costello, and Mario Lanza are a few of these performers. The secret for a successful production was to combine a narrative with opportunities for the performers to do what they did best: tell anecdotes or jokes or sing. Like the Marx Brothers's films, *A Hard Day's Night* and *Help!* do have narratives. *A Hard Day's Night* tells the story of a day in the life of the Beatles, leading up to a big television performance. *Help!* is more elaborate; an Indian sect is after Ringo for the sacred ring he has on his finger. They want it for its spiritual significance. Two British scientists are equally anxious to acquire the ring for its technological value. The pursuit of the ring takes the cast around the world.

The stories are diversions from the real purpose of the films: to let the Beatles do what they do best. Lester's contribution to the two films is the methods he used to present the music. Notably, no two songs are presented in the same way.

The techniques Lester used are driven by a combination of cinéma vérité techniques with an absurdist attitude toward narrative meaning. Lester deployed the same techniques in his famous short film, *Running, Jumping and Standing Still* (1961).

Lester filmed the Beatles's performances with multiple cameras. He intercut close-ups with extreme angularity—for example, a juxtaposition of George Harrison and Paul McCartney or a close-up of John Lennon—with the reactions of the young concert-goers.

The final song performed in *A Hard Day's Night* is intercut with the frenzy of the audience. Shots ranging from close-ups to long shots of the performers and swish pans to the television control booth and back to the audience were cut with an increasing pace that adds to the building excitement. The pace becomes so rapid, in fact, that the individual images matter less than the feeling of energy that exists between the Beatles and the audience. Lester used editing to underscore this energy.

Lester used a variety of techniques to create this energy, ranging from wide-focus images that distort the subject to extreme close-ups. He included handheld shots, absurd cutaways, sped-up motion, and obvious jump cuts.

When the Beatles are performing in a television studio, Lester began the sequence with a television camera's image of the performance and pulled back to see the performance itself. He intercut television monitors with the actual performance quite often, thus referencing the fact that this is a captured performance. He did not share the cinéma vérité goal of making the audience believe that what they are watching is the real thing. He set songs in the middle of a field surrounded by tanks or on a ski slope or a Bahamian beach. The location and its character always worked with his sense of who the Beatles were.

A Hard Day's Night opens with a large group of fans chasing the Beatles into a train station. The handheld camera makes the scene seem real, but when the film cuts to an image of a bearded Paul McCartney sitting with his grandfather and reading a paper, the mix of absurdity and reality is established. Pace and movement are always the key. Energy is more important in this film than realism, so Lester opted to jump cut often on movement. The energy that results is the primary element that provides emotional continuity throughout the film (Figure 9.1).

Lester was able to move so freely with his visuals because of the unity provided by the individual songs. Where possible, he developed a medley around parallel action. For example, he intercut shots of the Beatles at a disco with Paul's grandfather at a gambling casino. By finding a way to intercut sequences, Lester moved between songs and styles. He didn't even need to have the Beatles perform the songs. They could simply act during a song, as they do in "All My Loving." This permitted some variety within sequences and between sequences. All the while, this variety suggests that anything is possible, visually or in the narrative. The result is a freedom of choice in editing virtually unprecedented in a narrative film. Not even Bob Fosse in *All That Jazz* (1979) had as much freedom as Lester embraced in *A Hard Day's Night*.

Lester's success in using a variety of camera angles, images, cutaways, and pace has meant that audiences are willing to accept a series of diverse images unified only by a sound track. The accelerated pace suggests that audiences are able to follow great diversity and find meaning faster. The success of Lester's films suggests, in fact, that faster pace is desirable. The increase in narrative pace since 1966 can be traced to the impact of the Beatles films.

Narrative stories have accelerated,[2] and so too has the pace of the editing. As can be seen in Sam Peckinpah's *The Wild Bunch* (1969) and Martin Scorsese's *Raging Bull* (1980), individual

FIGURE 9.1
A Hard Day's Night, 1964. Still provided by British Film Institute.

shots have become progressively shorter. This is nowhere better illustrated than in contemporary television commercials and music videos.

Richard Lester exhibited in the "Can't Buy Me Love" sequence in *A Hard Day's Night*, the motion, the close-ups, the distorted wide-angle shots of individual Beatles and of the group, the jump cutting, the helicopter shots, the slow motion, and the fast motion that characterize his work. Audience's acceptance and celebration of his work suggest the scope of Lester's achievement—freedom to edit for energy and emotion, uninhibited by traditional rules of continuity. By using television techniques, Lester liberated himself and the film audience from the realism of television, but with no loss of immediacy. Audiences have hungered for that immediacy, and many filmmakers, such as Scorsese, have been able to give them the energy that immediacy suggests.

Lester went on to use these techniques in an uneven fashion. Perhaps his most successful later film was *Petulia* (1968), which was set in San Francisco. In this story about the breakup of a conventional marriage, Lester was particularly adept at moving from past to present and back to fracture the sense of stability that marriage usually implies. The edgy moving camera also helped create a sense of instability (Figure 9.2). Lester's principal contribution to film editing was the freedom and pace he was able to achieve in the two Beatles films.

FIGURE 9.2
Petulia, 1968. ©1968 Warner Bros. Seven Arts and Petersham Films (Petulia) Ltd. All Rights Reserved. Still provided by Moving Image and Sound Archives.

THEATRE

If the influence of television in this period was related to the search for immediacy, the influence of theatre was related to the search for relevance. The result of these influences was a new freedom with narrative and how narrative was presented through the editing of film.

During the 1950s, perhaps no other filmmaker was as influential as Ingmar Bergman. The themes he chose in his films—relationships (*Lesson in Love*, 1954), aging (*Wild Strawberries*, 1957), and superstition (*The Magician*, 1959)—suggested a seriousness of purpose unusual in a popular medium such as film. However, it was in his willingness to deal with the supernatural that Bergman illustrated that the theatre and its conventions could be accepted in filmic form. Bergman used film as many had used the stage: to explore as well as to entertain. Because the stage was less tied to realism, the audience was willing to accept less reality-bound conventions, thus allowing the filmmaker to explore different treatments of subject matter. When Bergman developed a film following, he also developed the audience's tolerance for theatrical approaches in film.

This is not to say that plays were not influential on film until Bergman came on the scene. As mentioned in Chapter 4, they had been. The difference was that the 1950s were notable for the interest in neorealist or cinéma vérité film. Even Elia Kazan, a man of the theatre, experimented with cinéma vérité in *Panic in the Streets* (1950). In the same period, however, he made *A Streetcar Named Desire* (1951). His respect for the play was such that he filmed it as a play, making no pretense that it was anything else.

Bergman, on the other hand, attempted to make a film with the thematic and stylistic characteristics of a play. For example, Death is a character in *The Seventh Seal* (1956). He speaks like other characters, but his costume differentiates him from them. Bergman's willingness to use such theatrical devices made them as important for editing as the integration of the past was in the films of Alain Resnais and as important as fantasy was in the work of Federico Fellini.

Bergman remained interested in metaphor and nonrealism in his later work. *From the Life of the Marionettes* (1980) uses the theatrical device of stylized repetition to explore responsibility in a murder investigation. Bergman used metaphor to suggest embryonic Nazism in 1923 Germany in *The Serpent's Egg* (1978). Both films have a sense of formal design more closely associated with the theatrical set than with the film location. In each case, the metaphorical approach makes the plot seem fresh and relevant. At the same time that Bergman was influencing international film, young critics-turned-filmmakers in England were also concerned about making their films more relevant than those made in the popular national cinema tradition. Encouraged by new directors in the theatre, particularly the realist work of John Osborne, Arnold Wesker, and Shelagh Delaney, directors Tony Richardson, Lindsay Anderson, and Karel Reisz—filmmakers who began their work in documentary film—very rapidly shifted toward less naturalistic films to make their dramatic films more relevant. They were joined by avant-garde directors, such as Peter Brook, who worked in both theatre and film and attempted to create a hybrid embracing the best elements of both media. This desire for relevance and the crossover between theatre and film has continued to be a central source of strength in the English cinema. The result is that some key screenwriters have been playwrights, including Harold Pinter, David Mercer, David Hare, and Hanif Kureishi. In the case of David Hare, the crossover from theatre to film has led to a career in film direction. Had Joe Orton lived, it seems likely that he, too, would have become an important screenwriter.

All of these playwrights share a serious interest in the nature of the society in which they live, in its class barriers, and in the fabric of human relationships that the society fosters. Beginning with Tony Richardson and his film adaptation of Osborne's *Look Back in Anger* (1958), the filmmakers of the British New Wave directed realist social dramas. Karel Reisz followed with *Saturday Night and Sunday Morning* (1960), and Lindsay Anderson followed with *This Sporting Life* (1963). With the exception of the latter film, the early work is marked by a strong cinéma vérité influence, as evidenced by the use of reallocations and live sound full of local accents and a reluctance to intrude with excessive lighting and the deployment of color. This "candid eye" tradition was later carried on by Ken Loach (*Family Life*, 1972) until recently. The high point for the New Wave British directors, however, came much earlier with Richardson's *The Loneliness of the Long Distance Runner* (1962). Later, each director yielded to the influence of the theatre and nonrealism. Indeed, the desertion of realism suggests that it was the seriousness of the subject matter of the early realist films rather than the philosophical link to the cinéma vérité style that appealed to Richardson, Anderson, and Reisz. In their search for an appropriate style for their later films, these filmmakers displayed a flexibility of approach that was unusual in film. The result again was to broaden the organization of images in a film.

The first notable departure from realism was Tony Richardson's *Tom Jones* (1963). Scripted by playwright John Osborne, the film took a highly stylized approach to Henry Fielding's novel. References to the silent film technique—including the use of subtitles and a narrator—framed the film as a cartoon portrait of social and sexual morality in eighteenth-century England.

To explore those mores, Richardson used fast motion, slow motion, stop motion, jump cutting, and cinéma vérité handheld camera shots. He used technique to editorialize upon the times that the film is set in, with Tom Jones (Albert Finney) portrayed as a rather modern nonconformist. In keeping with this sense of modernity, two characters—Tom's mother and Tom—address the audience directly, thus acknowledging that they are characters in a film. With overmodulated performances more suited for the stage than for film, Richardson achieved a modern cartoon-like commentary on societal issues, principally class. Tom's individuality rises above issues of class, and so, in a narrative sense, his success condemns the rigidity of class in much the same way as Osborne and Richardson had earlier in *Look Back in Anger*. The key element in *Tom Jones* is its sense of freedom to use narrative and technical strategies that include realism but are not limited by a need to seem realistic. The result is a film that is far more influenced by the theatre than Richardson's earlier work. Richardson continued this exploration of form in his later films, *The Loved One* (1965) and *Laughter in the Dark* (1969).

Karel Reisz also abandoned realism, although thematically there are links between *Saturday Night and Sunday Morning* and his later *Morgan: A Suitable Case for Treatment* (1966) and *Isadora* (1969). *Morgan: A Suitable Case for Treatment* tells the story of the mental disintegration of the main character in the face of the disintegration of his marriage. Morgan (David Warner), a life-long Marxist with working-class roots, has married into the upper class. This social and political layer to his mental collapse is largely a factor in the failure of Morgan's marriage, but it is his reaction to the failure that gives Reisz the opportunity to visualize that disintegration. Morgan sees the world in terms of animals. He sees himself as a gorilla. A beautiful woman on a subway escalator is a peacock; a ticket seller is a hippopotamus. When he makes love with his ex-wife, they are two zebras rolling around on the veldt. Conflict, particularly with his ex-wife's lover, is a matter for lions. Whenever Morgan finds himself in conflict, he retreats into the animal world.

Reisz may have viewed Morgan's escape as charming or as a political response to his circumstances. In either case, the integration of animal footage throughout the film creates an allegory rather than a portrait of mental collapse. The realist approach to the same subject was taken by Ken Loach in *Family Life* (sometimes called *Wednesday's Child*). Reisz's approach, essentially metaphorical, yields a stylized film. In spite of the realist street sense of much of the footage, David Mercer's clever dialog and the visual allusions create a hybrid film.

The same is true of *Isadora*, a biography of the great dancer Isadora Duncan (Vanessa Redgrave). Duncan had a great influence on modern dance, and she was a feminist and an aesthete. To recreate her ideas about life and dance, Reisz structured the film on an idea grid. The film jumps back and forth in time from San Francisco in 1932 to France in 1927. In between these jumps, the film moves ahead, but always in the context of looking at Duncan in retrospect to the scenes of 1927 in the south of France.

Reisz was not content simply to tell Duncan's biography. He also tried to recreate the inspiration for her dances. When she first makes love to designer Edward Gordon Craig (James Fox), the scene is crosscut with a very sensual dance. The dance serves as an expression of Duncan's feelings at that moment and as an expression of her inspiration. Creation and feeling are linked. The film flows back and forth in time and along a chronology of her artistic development. Although much has been made of the editing of the film and its confusion, it is clearly an expression of its ambition. Reisz attempted to find editing solutions for difficult abstract ideas, and in many cases, the results are fascinating. The film has little connection to Reisz's free cinema roots, but rather is connected to dance and the theatre.

Lindsay Anderson was the least linked to realism of the three filmmakers. *O'Dreamland* (1953) moves far away from naturalism in its goals, and in his first feature, *This Sporting Life*, Anderson showed how far from realism his interests were. This story about a professional rugby player (Richard Harris) is also about the limits of the physical world. He is an angry man incapable of understanding his anger or of accepting his psychic pain. Only at the end does he understand his shortcomings. Of the three filmmakers, Anderson seems most interested in existential, rather than social or political, elements. At least, this is the case in *This Sporting Life*.

When he made *If . . . .* (1969), Anderson completely rejected realism. For this story about rebellion in a public boy's school, Anderson used music, the alternating of black and white with color, and stylized, nonrealistic images to suggest the importance of freedom over authority and of the individual over the will of the society. By the end of the film, the question of reality or fantasy has become less relevant. The film embraces both fantasy and reality, and it becomes a metaphor for life in England in 1969. The freedom to edit more flexibly allowed Anderson to create his dissenting vision.

Anderson carried this theatrical approach even further in his next film, *O Lucky Man!* (1973). This film is about the actor who played Mick in *If . . . .* It tells the story of his life up to the time that he was cast in *If . . . .* The film is not so much a biography as it is an odyssey. Mick Travis is portrayed by Malcolm McDowell, but in *O Lucky Man!* he is presented as a Candide-like innocent. His voyage begins with his experiences as a coffee salesman in northern England, but the realism of the job is not of interest. His adventures take him into technological medical experimentation, nuclear accidents, and international corporate smuggling. Throughout, the ethics of the situation are questionable, the goals are exploitation at any cost: human or political. At the end of the film, the character is in jail, lucky to be alive.

Throughout *O Lucky Man!*, Anderson moved readily through fact and fantasy. A man who is both pig and man is one of the most repellent images. To provide a respite between sequences, Anderson cuts to Alan Price and his band as they perform the musical sound track of the film. Price later appears as a character in the film.

The overall impact of the film is to question many aspects of modern life, including medicine, education, industry, and government. The use of the theatrical devices of nonrealism, Brechtian alienation, and the naïve main character allowed Anderson freedom to wander away from the narrative at will. The effect is powerful. When he was not making films, Anderson directed theatre. *O Lucky Man!*, with its focus on ideas about society, is more clearly a link to that theatrical experience than to Anderson's previous film, *Every Day Except Christmas* (1957).

Not to be overlooked in this discussion of British directors is John Schlesinger. He also began in documentary. He produced an award-winning documentary, *Terminus* (1960); went on to direct a realist film, *A Kind of Loving* (1962); and, like his colleagues, began to explore the nonrealist possibilities.

Billy Liar (1963) is one of the most successful hybrid films. Originally a novel and then a play by Keith Waterhouse and Willis Hall, the story of Billy Fisher is the quintessential film about refusing to come of age. Billy Fisher (Tom Courtenay) lies about everything: his family, his friends, his talents. Inevitably, those lies get him into trouble, and his charm cannot extricate him. He retreats into his fantasy world, Ambrosia, where he is general, king, and key potentate.

The editing is used to work Billy's fantasies into the film. Schlesinger straight-cut the fantasies as if they were happening as part of the developing action. If Billy's father or employer says something objectionable to Billy, the film straight-cuts to Billy in uniform, machine-gunning the culprit to death. If Billy walks, fantasizing about his fame, the film straight-cuts to the crowds for a soccer match. Schlesinger intercuts with the potentate Billy in uniform speaking to the masses. Before the speech, they are reflective; after it, they are overjoyed. Then the film cuts back to Billy walking in the town or in the glen above the town.

Billy is inventive, charming, and involving as a main character, but it is the integration of his fantasy life into the film that makes the character and the film engage us on a deeper level. The editing not only gives us insight into the private Billy, it also allows us to indulge in our own fantasies. To the extent that we identify with Billy, we are given license to a wider range of feeling than in many films. By using nonrealism, Schlesinger strengthened the audience's openness to theatrical devices in narrative films. He used them extensively in his successful American debut, *Midnight Cowboy* (1969).

No discussion of the influence of theatre on film would be complete without mention of Peter Brook. In a way, his work in film has been as challenging as his work in theatre. From *Marat/Sade* (1966) to his more recent treatment with Jean-Claude Carriere of *Maharabata* (1990), Brook has explored the mediation between theatre and film. His most successful hybrid film is certainly *Marat/Sade*.

The story is best described by the full title of the play: *Marat/Sade (The Persecution and Assassination of Jean-Paul Marat as Performed by the Inmates of the Asylum of Charenton under the Direction of the Marquis de Sade)*. The playwright Peter Weiss was interested in the interfaces between play and audience, between madness and reality, and between historical fact and fiction. He used the set as well as the dramaturgy to provoke consideration of his ideas, and he mixed burlesque with realism. He used particular characters to "debate" positions, particularly the spirit of revolution and its bloody representative, Marat, and the spirit of the senses and its cynical representative, the Marquis de Sade.

The play, written and produced 20 years after World War II, ponders issues arising out of that war as well as issues central to the 1960s: war, idealism, politics, and a revolution of personal expectations. The work blurs the questions of who is mad, who is sane, and whether there is a difference.

The major problem that Brook faced was how to make the play relevant to a film audience. (The film was produced by United Artists.) Brook chose to direct this highly stylized theatrical piece as a documentary.[3] He used handheld cameras, intense close-ups, a reliance on the illusion of natural light from windows, and a live sound that makes the production by the inmates convincing. Occasionally, the film cuts to an extreme long shot showing the barred room in which the play is being presented. It also cuts frequently to the audience for the performance: the director of the asylum and two guests. Cutaways to nuns and guards in the performance area also remind us that we are watching a performance.

In essence, *Marat/Sade* is a play within a play within a film. Each layer is carefully created and supported visually. When the film cuts to the singing chorus, we view *Marat/Sade* as a play. When it cuts to the audience and intercuts their reactions with the play, *Marat/Sade* is a play within a play. When Charlotte Corday (Glenda Jackson in her film debut) appears in a close-up, a patient attempts to act as Corday would, or the Marquis de Sade (Peter Magee) directs his performers, and *Marat/Sade* becomes a film.

Because *Marat/Sade* is a film about ideas, Brook chose a hybrid approach to make those ideas about politics and sanity meaningful to his audience. The film remains a powerful commentary on the issues and a creative example of how theatre and film can interface.

NOTES/REFERENCES

1. In the drama genre, young writers such as Rod Serling, Reginald Rose, and Paddy Cheyefsky, and young directors such as John Frankenheimer, Sidney Lumet, and Arthur Penn developed their creative skills in television. Writers such as Carl Reiner and Woody Allen came out of television variety shows, and many performers got their start in television comedy. This continues to this day: Bill Murray, Chevy Chase, John Belushi, Gilda Radner, and Dan Ackroyd all entered the movie industry based on their success on *Saturday Night Live*.

2. In Changes in Narrative Structure, 1960–80: A Study in Screenwriting, a paper presented at the Popular Culture Conference, March, 1984, Toronto, I noted that master scenes in *The Apartment* (1960) were five minutes long. By 1980, the length of the average master scene was two minutes.

3. Bob Fosse decided to direct *Cabaret* (1972) as film noir. He combined opposites—musical and film noir, theatre and documentary. This seems a contradiction, but in both cases, it works to clarify one medium by using another.

CHAPTER 10

New Challenges to Filmic Narrative Conventions

The international advances of the 1950s and the technological experiments in widescreen and documentary techniques provided the context for the influence of television and theatre in the 1960s and 1970s. The sum effect was twofold: to make the flow of talent and creative influence more international than ever and, more important, to signal that innovation, whether its source was new or old, was critical. Indeed, the creative explosion of the 1950s and 1960s was nothing less than a gauntlet: a challenge to the next generation to make artful what was ordinary and to make art from the extraordinary. The result was an explosion of individualistic invention that has had a profound effect on how the partnership of sound and image has been manipulated. The innovations have truly been international, with a German director making an American film (*Paris, Texas*, 1984) and an American director making a European film (*Barry Lyndon*, 1975).

This chapter reviews many of the highlights of the period 1968–1988, focusing primarily on those films and filmmakers who challenged the conventions of film storytelling. In each case, the editing of sound and image is the vehicle for that challenge.

PECKINPAH: ALIENATION AND ANARCHY

Sam Peckinpah's career before *The Wild Bunch* (1969) suggested his preference for working within the Western genre, but nothing in the style of his earlier Westerns, *Ride the High Country* (1962) and *Major Dundee* (1965), suggested his overwhelming reliance on editing in *The Wild Bunch*. Thematically, the passing of the West and of its values provides the continuity between these films and those that followed, primarily *The Ballad of Cable Hogue* (1970) and *Junior Bonner* (1972). Peckinpah's later films, whether in the Western genre (*Bring Me the Head of Alfredo Garcia*, 1974) or the gangster genre (*The Getaway*, 1972) or the war genre (*Cross of Iron*, 1977), refer back to the editing style of *The Wild Bunch*; theme and editing style fuse to create a very important example of the power of editing.

The Wild Bunch was not the first film to explore violence by creating an editing pattern that conveyed the horror and fascination of the moment of death. The greatest filmmaker to explore the moment of death, albeit in a highly politicized context, was Sergei Eisenstein. The death of the young girl and the horse on the bridge in *October* (1928) and, of course, the

143

Odessa Steps sequence in *Potemkin* (1925) are among the most famous editing sequences in history. Both sequences explore the moment of death of victims caught in political upheavals. Kathryn Bigelow's *Hurt Locker* (2008) represents a contemporary film that uses a similar mix of pace and juxtaposition editing for shock about warriors and war in Iraq.

Earlier films, such as Fred Zinnemann's *High Noon* (1952), focus on the anticipation and anxiety of that moment when death is imminent. Robert Enrico's *An Occurrence at Owl Creek* (1962) is devoted in its entirety to the desire-to-live fantasy of a man in the moment before he is hanged. The influential *Bonnie and Clyde* (1967), Arthur Penn's exploration of love and violence, no doubt had a great impact on Peckinpah's choice of editing style.

Peckinpah's film *The Wild Bunch* recounts the last days of Bishop Pike (William Holden) and his "Wild Bunch," outlaws who are violent without compunction—not traditional Western heroes. Pursued by railroad men and bounty hunters, they flee into Mexico, where they work for a renegade general who seems more evil than the outlaws or the bounty hunters. Each group is portrayed as lawless and evil. In this setting of amorality, the Wild Bunch become heroic. No description can do justice to Peckinpah's creation of violence. It is present everywhere, and when it strikes, its destructive force is conveyed by all of the elements of editing that move audiences: close-ups, moving camera shots, composition, proximity of the camera to the action, and, above all, pace. An examination of the first sequence in the film and of the final gunfight illustrates Peckinpah's technique.

In the opening sequence, the Wild Bunch, dressed as American soldiers, ride into a Texas town and rob the bank. The robbery was anticipated, and the railroad men and bounty hunters, coordinated by Deke Thornton (Robert Ryan), a former member of the Wild Bunch, have set a trap for Bishop Pike and his men. Unfortunately, a temperance meeting begins to march toward the bank. The trap results in the deaths of more than half of the Wild Bunch, but many townspeople are also killed. Pike and four of his men escape. This sequence can be broken down into three distinct phases: the 5½-minute ride into town, the 4½-minute robbery, and the 5-minute fight to escape from the town. The pace accelerates as we move through the phases, but Peckinpah relies on narrative techniques to amplify his view of the robbery, the law, and the role of violence in the lives of both the townspeople and the criminals. Peckinpah crosscuts between four groups throughout the sequence: the Wild Bunch, the railroad men and the bounty hunters, the religious town meeting, and a group of children gathered on the outskirts of town. The motif of the children is particularly important because it is used to open and close the sequence.

The children are watching a scorpion being devoured by red ants. In the final phase, the children destroy the scorpion and the red ants. If Peckinpah's message was that in this world you devour or are devoured, he certainly found a graphic metaphor to illustrate his message. The ants, the scorpion, and the children are shown principally in close-ups. In fact, close-ups are extensively used throughout the sequence.

In terms of pace, there is a gradual escalation of shots between the first two phases. The ride of the Wild Bunch into town has 65 shots in 5½ minutes. The robbery itself has 95 shots in

4½ minutes. In the final phase, the fight to escape from the town, a 5-minute section, the pace rapidly accelerates. This section has 200 shots with an average length of 1½ seconds.

The final sequence is interesting not only for the use of intense close-ups and quick cutting, but also for the number of shots that focus on the moment of death. Slow motion was used often to draw out the instant of death. One member of the Wild Bunch is shot on horseback and crashes through a storefront window. The image is almost lovingly recorded in slow motion.

What message is imparted? The impact is often a fascination with and a glorification of that violent instant of death. The same lingering treatment of the destruction of the scorpion and the ants underscores the cruelty and suffering implicit in the action.

The opening sequence establishes the relentless violence that characterizes the balance of the film. The impact of the opening sequence is almost superseded by the violence of the final gunfight. In this sequence, Pike and his men have succeeded in stealing guns for the renegade General Mapache. They have been paid, but Mapache has abducted the sole Mexican member of the Wild Bunch, Angel (Jaime Sanchez). Earlier, Angel had killed Mapache's mistress, a young woman Angel had claimed as his own. Angel had also given guns to the local guerrillas who were fighting against Mapache. Mapache has tortured Angel, and Pike and his men feel that they must stand together; they want Angel back. In this last fight, they insist on Angel's return. Mapache agrees, but slits Angel's throat in front of them. Pike kills Mapache. A massacre ensues in which Pike and the three remaining members of the Wild Bunch fight against hundreds of Mapache's soldiers. Many die, including all of the members of the Wild Bunch.

The entire sequence can be broken down into three phases: the preparation and march to confront Mapache, the confrontation with Mapache up to the deaths of Angel and Mapache, and the massacre itself (Figure 10.1). The entire sequence is 10 minutes long. The march to Mapache runs 3 minutes and 40 seconds. There are 40 shots in the march sequence; the average shot is almost 6 seconds long. In this sequence, zoom shots and camera motion are used to postpone editing. The camera follows the Wild Bunch as they approach Mapache.

The next phase, the confrontation with Mapache, runs 1 minute and 40 seconds and contains 70 shots. The unpredictability of Mapache's behavior and the shock of the manner in which he kills Angel leads to greater fragmentation and an acceleration of the pace of the sequence. Many close-ups of Pike, the Wild Bunch, and Mapache and his soldiers add to the tension of this brief sequence.

Finally, the massacre phase runs 4½ minutes and contains approximately 270 shots, making the average length of a shot 1 second. Some shots run 2 to 3 seconds, particularly when Peckinpah tried to set up a key narrative event, such as the characters who finally kill Pike and Dutch (Ernest Borgnine). Those characters are a young woman and a small boy dressed as a soldier and armed with a rifle.

Few sequences in film history portray the anarchy of violence as vividly as the massacre sequence at the end of *The Wild Bunch*. Many close-ups are used, the camera moves, the camera is placed very close to the subject, and, where possible, juxtapositions of foreground and background are

FIGURE 10.1
The Wild Bunch, 1969. ©1969 Warner Bros. Seven Arts. All Rights Reserved. Still provided by British Film Institute.

included. Unlike the opening sequence, where the violence of death seemed to be memorialized in slow motion, the violence of this sequence proceeds less carefully. Chaos and violence are equated with an intensity that wears out the viewer. The resulting emotional exhaustion led Peckinpah to use an epilogue that shifts the point of view from the dead Bishop Pike to the living Deke Thornton. For five more minutes, Peckinpah elaborated on the fate of Thornton and the bounty hunters. He also used a reprise to bring back all of the members of the Wild Bunch. Interestingly, all are images of laughter, quite distant from the violence of the massacre.

Rarely in cinema has the potential impact of pace been so powerfully explored as in *The Wild Bunch*. Peckinpah was interested in the alienation of character from context. His outlaws are men out of their time; 1913 was no longer a time for Western heroes, not even on the American–Mexican border. Peckinpah used pace to create a fascination and later a visual experience of the anarchy of violence. Without these two narrative perspectives—the alienation that comes with modern life and the ensuing violence as two worlds clash—the pace could not have been as deeply affecting as it is in *The Wild Bunch*.

ALTMAN: THE FREEDOM OF CHAOS

Robert Altman is a particularly interesting director whose primary interest is to capture creatively and ironically a sense of modern life. He does not dwell on urban anxiety as Woody

Allen does or search for the new altruism à la Sidney Lumet in *Serpico* (1973) and *Prince of the City* (1981). Altman uses his films to deconstruct myth (*McCabe and Mrs. Miller*, 1971) and to capture the ambience of place and time (*The Long Goodbye*, 1973). He uses a freer editing style to imply that our chaotic times can liberate as well as oppress. To be more specific, Altman uses sound and image editing as well as a looser narrative structure to create an ambience that is both chaotic and liberating. His 1975 film, *Nashville*, is instructive.

Nashville tells the story of more than 20 characters in a five-day period in the city of Nashville, a center for country music. A political campaign adds a political dimension to the sociological construct that Altman explores. He jumps freely from the story of a country star in emotional crisis (Ronee Blakley) to a wife in a marriage crisis (Lily Tomlin), and from those who aspire to be stars (Barbara Harris) to those who live off stars (Geraldine Chaplin and Ned Beatty) to those who would exploit stars for political ends (Michael Murphy). Genuine performers (Henry Gibson and Keith Carradine) mix career and everyday life uneasily by reaching an accord between their professional and personal lives.

In the shortened time frame of five days in a single city, Nashville, Altman jumped from character to character to focus on their goals, their dreams, and the reality of their lives. The gap between dream and actuality is the fabric of the film. How to maintain continuity given the number of characters is the editing challenge.

The primary editing strategy Altman used in this film was to establish the principle of randomness. Early in the film, whether to introduce a character arriving by airplane or one at work in a recording studio, Altman used a slow editing pace in which he focused on slow movement to catch the characters in action in an ensemble style. Characters speak simultaneously, one in the foreground, another in the background, while responding to an action: a miscue in a recording session, a car accident on the freeway, a fainting spell at the airport. Something visual occurs, and then the ensemble approach allows a cacophony of sound, dialog, and effects to establish a sense of chaos as we struggle to decide to which character we should try to listen to. As we are doing so, the film cuts to another character at the same location.

After we have experienced brief scenes of four characters in a linked location, we begin to follow the randomness of the film. Randomness, rather than pace, shapes how we feel. Instead of the powerful intensity of Peckinpah's *The Wild Bunch*, we sense the instability that random action and response suggests in Altman's film. The uneasiness grows as we get to know the characters better, and by the time the film ends in chaos and assassination, we have a feeling for the gap between dreams and actuality and where it can lead.

Altman's *Nashville* is as troubling as Peckinpah's *The Wild Bunch*, but in *Nashville*, a random editing style that uses sound as a catalyst leads us to a result similar to that of pace in *The Wild Bunch*.

Sound itself is insufficient to create the power of *Nashville*. The ensemble of actors who create individuals is as helpful as the editing pattern. Given its importance to the city, music is another leitmotif that helps create continuity. Finally, the principle of crosscutting, with its implication of meaning arising from the interplay of two scenes, is carried to an extreme, becoming a device that is repeatedly relied upon to create meaning. Together with the randomness of the editing pattern and the overcrowded sound track, crosscutting is used to create meaning in *Nashville*.

KUBRICK: NEW WORLDS AND OLD

Stanley Kubrick has made films about a wide spectrum of subjects set in very different time periods. Coming as they did in an era of considerable editing panache, Kubrick's editing choices, particularly in *2001: A Space Odyssey* (1968) and *Barry Lyndon* (1975), established a style that helped create the sense of the period.

2001: A Space Odyssey begins with the vast expanse of prehistoric time. The prologue proceeds slowly to create a sense of endless time. The images are random and still. Only when the apes appear is there editing continuity, but that continuity is slow and deliberate and not paced for emotional effect. It seems to progress along a line of narrative clarification rather than emotional intensity. When an ape throws a bone into the air, the transition to the age of interplanetary travel is established by a cut on movement from the bone to a space station moving through space.

As we proceed through the story, which speculates on the existence of a deity in outer space, and through the conflict of humanity and machine, the editing is paced to underline the stability of the idea that humanity has conquered nature; at least, they think they have. The careful and elegant cuts on camera movement support this sense of world order. Kubrick's choice of music and its importance in the film also support this sense of order. Indeed, the shape of the entire film more closely resembles the movements of a symphony rather than the acts of a screen narrative.

Only two interventions challenge this sense of mastery. The first is the struggle of the computer HAL to kill the humans on the spaceship. In this struggle, one human survives. The second is the journey beyond Jupiter into infinity. Here, following the monolith, conventional time collapses, and a different type of continuity has to be created.

FIGURE 10.2

2001: A Space Odyssey, 1968. © Turner Entertainment Company. All Rights Reserved. Still provided by British Film Institute.

In the first instance, the struggle with HAL, all the conventions of the struggle between protagonist and antagonist come into play; crosscutting, a paced struggle between HAL and the astronauts leads to the outcome of the struggle, the deaths of four of the astronauts. This struggle relies on many close-ups of Bowman (Keir Dullea) and HAL as well as the articulation of the deaths of HAL's four victims. A more traditional editing style prevails in this sequence (Figure 10.2).

In the later sequence, in which the spaceship passes through infinity and Bowman arrives in the future, the traditional editing style is replaced by a series of jump cuts. In rapid succession, Bowman sees himself as a middle-aged man, an old man, and then a dying man. The setting, French Provincial, seems out of place in the space age, but it helps to link the future with the past. As Bowman lies dying in front of the monolith, we are transported into space, and to the strains of "Thus Speak Zarathustra," Bowman is reborn. We see him as a formed embryo, and as the film ends, the life cycle has come full circle. In Kubrick's view of the future, real time and film time become totally altered. It is this collapse of real time that is Kubrick's greatest achievement in the editing of *2001: A Space Odyssey*.

Barry Lyndon is based on William Thackeray's novel about a young Irishman who believes that the acquisition of wealth and status will position him for happiness. Sadly, the means he chooses to succeed condemn him to fail. This eighteenth-century morality tale moves from Ireland to the Seven Years War on the continent to Germany and finally to England.

To achieve the feeling of the eighteenth century, it was not enough for Kubrick to film on location. He edited the film to create a sense of time just as he did in *2001: A Space Odyssey*. In *Barry Lyndon*, however, he tried to create a sense of time that was much slower than our present. Indeed, Kubrick set out to pace the film against our expectations (Figure 10.3).[1]

In the first portion of the film, Redmond Barry (Ryan O'Neal) loves his cousin, Nora, but she chooses to marry an English captain. Barry challenges and defeats the captain in a duel. This event forces him to leave his home; he enlists in the army and fights in Europe.

FIGURE 10.3
Barry Lyndon, 1975. © 1975 Warner Bros. Inc. All Rights Reserved. Still provided by British Film Institute.

The first shot of Barry and Nora lasts 32 seconds, the second shot lasts 36 seconds, and the third lasts 46 seconds. When Barry and Nora walk in the woods to discuss her marriage to the captain, the shot is 90 seconds long. By moving the camera and using a zoom lens, Kubrick was able to follow the action rather than rely on the editing. The length of these initial shots slows down our expectations of the pacing of the film and helps the film create its own sense of time: a sense of time that Kubrick deemed appropriate to transport us into a different period from our own.

Kubrick used this editing style to recreate that past world. The editing is psychologically as critical as the costumes or the language. In a more subtle way, the editing of *Barry Lyndon* achieves that other-world quality that was so powerfully captured in *2001: A Space Odyssey*.

HERZOG: OTHER WORLDS

Stanley Kubrick was not alone in using an editing style to create a psychological context for a place or a character. Werner Herzog created a megalomania that requires conquests in *Aguirre: The Wrath of God* (1972). The Spanish conquistador Aguirre is the subject of the film. Even more challenging was Herzog's *The Enigma of Kaspar Hauser* (1974), a nineteenth-century story about a foundling who, having been kept isolated, has no human communication skills at the onset of the story. He is taken in by townspeople and learns to speak. He becomes a source of admiration and study, but also of ridicule. He is unpredictable, rational, and animistic.

Herzog set out to create an editing style that simulated Kaspar's sense of time and of his struggle with the conventions of his society. Initially, the shots are very long and static. Later, when Kaspar becomes socialized, the shots are shorter, simulating real time. Later, when he has relapses, there are gaps in the logic of the sequencing of the shots that simulate how he feels. Finally, when he dies, the community's sense of time returns. In this film, Herzog succeeded in using editing to reflect the psychology of the lead character just as he did in his earlier film.

In both films, the editing pattern simulates a different world view than our own, giving these films a strange but fascinating quality. They transport us to places we've never before experienced. In so doing, they move us in ways unusual in film.

SCORSESE: THE DRAMATIC DOCUMENT

Martin Scorsese's *Raging Bull* (1980) is both a film document about Jake LaMotta, a middle-heavyweight boxing champion, and a dramatization of LaMotta's personal and professional lives. The dissonance between realism and psychological insight has rarely been more pronounced, primarily because the character of LaMotta (played by Robert De Niro) is a man who cannot control his rages. He is a jealous husband, an irrational brother, and a prize fighter who taunts his opponents; he knows no pain, and his scorn for everyone is so profound that it seems miraculous that the man has not killed anyone by the film's end (Figure 10.4).

FIGURE 10.4

Raging Bull, 1980. Courtesy MGM/UA. Still provided by British Film Institute.

That is not to say that the film is not slavish in its sense of actuality and realism. De Niro, who portrays LaMotta over almost a 20-year period, appears at noticeably different weights. It's difficult to believe that the later LaMotta is portrayed by the same actor as was the early LaMotta.

In the nonfight scenes, Scorsese moved the camera as little as possible. In combination with the excellent set designs, the result is a realistic sense of time and place rather than a stylized sense of time and place.

In the fight sequences, Scorsese raised the dramatic intensity to a level commensurate with LaMotta's will to win at any cost. LaMotta is portrayed as a man whose ego has been set aside; he is all will, and his will is relentless and cruel. This trait is not usually identified with complex, believable characters.

The fight genre has provided many metaphors, including the immigrant's dream in *Golden Boy* (1939), the existential struggle in *The Set-Up* (1949), the class struggle in *Champion* (1949), the American dream in *Somebody Up There Likes Me* (1956), and the American nightmare in *Body and Soul* (1947). All of these stories have dramatic texture, but none has attempted to take us into the subjective world of a character who must be a champion, because if he weren't, he'd be in prison for murder. This is Scorsese's goal in *Raging Bull*.

To create this world, Scorsese relies very heavily on sound. This is not to say that his visuals are not dynamic. He does use a great deal of camera motion (particularly the smooth hand-held motion of a Steadicam), subjective camera placement, and close-ups of the fight in slow motion. However, the sound envelops us in the brutality of the boxing ring. In the ring, the wonderful operatic score gives way to sensory explosions. As we watch a boxer demolished in slow motion, the punches resound as explosions rather than as leather-to-flesh contact.

In the Cerdan fight, in which LaMotta finally wins the championship, image and sound slow and distort to illustrate Cerdan's collapse. In the Robinson fight, in which LaMotta loses his title, sound grinds to a halt as Robinson contemplates his next stroke. LaMotta is all but taunting him, arms down, body against the ropes. As Robinson looks at his prey, the sound drops off and the image becomes almost a freeze-frame. Then, as the raised arm comes down on LaMotta, the sound returns, and the graphic explosions of blood and sweat that emanate from the blow give way to the crowd, which cries out in shock. LaMotta is defiant as he loses his title. By elevating and elaborating the sound effects and by distorting and sharpening the sounds of the fight, Scorsese developed a dramatized envelopment of feeling about the fight, about LaMotta, about violence, and about will as a factor in life.

In a sense, Scorsese followed an editing goal similar to those of Francis Ford Coppola in *Apocalypse Now* (1979) and David Lynch in *Blue Velvet* (1986). Each used sound to take us into the interior world of their main characters without censoring that world of its psychic and physical violence. The interior world of LaMotta took Scorsese far from the superficial realism of a real-life main character. Scorsese seems to have acknowledged the surface life of LaMotta while creating and highlighting the primacy of the interior life with a pattern of sound and image that works off the counterpoint of the surface relative to the interior. Because we hear sound before we see the most immediate element to be interpreted, it is the sound editing in *Raging Bull* that signals the primacy of the interior life of Jake LaMotta over its surface visual triumphs and defeats. The documentary element of the film consequently is secondary in importance to the psychic pain of will, which creates a more lasting view of LaMotta than his transient championship.

WENDERS: MIXING POPULAR AND FINE ART

Wim Wenders's *Paris, Texas*, written by Sam Shepard, demonstrates Wenders's role as a director who chooses a visual style that is related to the visual arts and a narrative style that is related to the popular form sometimes referred to as "the journey." From *The Odyssey* to the road pictures of Bob Hope and Bing Crosby, the journey has been a metaphor to which audiences have related.

Wenders used the visual dimension of the story as a nonverbal roadmap to understanding the characters, their relationships, and the confusion of the main character. This nonverbal dimension is not always clear in the narrative. Because Wenders used a layered approach to the unfolding understanding of his story, pace does not play a major role in the editing of this film. Instead, the visual context is critical to understanding the film's layers of meaning. The foreground–background juxtaposition is the critical factor.

Paris, Texas relates the story of Travis (Harry Dean Stanton), a man we first meet as he wanders through the Texas desert. We soon learn that he deserted his family four years earlier. The first part of the film is the journey from Texas to California, where his brother has been taking care of Travis's son, Hunter. The second part concerns the father–son relationship. Although Hunter was four when his parents left him, his knowledge seems to transcend his age. In the last part of the film, Travis and Hunter return to Texas to find Jane (Nastassia Kinski), the wife and mother. In Texas, Travis discovers why he does not have the qualities necessary for family life, and he leaves Hunter in the care of his mother.

A narrative summary can outline the story, but it cannot articulate Travis's ability to understand his world and his place in it. The first image Wenders presents is the juxtaposition of Travis in the desert. The foreground of a midshot of Travis contrasts with visual depth and clarity of the desert. The environment dwarfs Travis, and he seems to have little meaning in this context. Nor is he more at home in Los Angeles. Throughout the film, Travis searches for Paris, Texas, where he thinks he was conceived. Later in the film, when he visits the town, it doesn't shed light on his feelings.

Wenders sets up a series of juxtapositions throughout the film: Travis and his environment, the car and the endless road, and, later, Travis and Jane. In one of the most poignant juxtapositions, Travis visits Jane in a Texas brothel. He speaks to her on a phone, with a one-way mirror separating them. He can look at her, but she cannot see him. In this scene, fantasy and reality are juxtaposed. Jane can be whatever Travis wants her to be. This poignant but ironic image contrasts to their real-life relationship in which she couldn't be what he wanted her to be.

These juxtapositions are further textured by differing light and color in the foreground–background mix. Wenders, working with German cameraman Robbie Muller, fashioned a netherworld effect. By strengthening the visual over the narrative meaning of individual images, he created a line somewhere between foreground and background. That line may elucidate the interior crisis of Travis or it may be a boundary beyond which rational meaning is not available. In either case, by using this foreground–background mix, Wenders created a dreamscape out of an externalized, recognizable journey popular in fiction and film. The result is an editing style that deemphasizes direct meaning but implies a feeling of disconnectedness that illustrates well Travis's interior world.

LEE: PACE AND SOCIAL ACTION

As a filmmaker, Spike Lee has constantly experimented with narrative convention. In *She's Gotta Have It* (1986), Lee had the main character address his audience directly. The narrative structure of that film was open-ended and rather more a meditation on relationships than a prescription for relationships. The narrative structure of *Mo' Better Blues* (1990) is also meditative but does not parallel the earlier film. Rather, its structure approximates the rhythm of a spontaneous blues riff. A film between the two is even more different. The narrative structure of *Do the Right Thing* (1989) is analogous to an avalanche rushing down a steep mountain. Racial bigotry is the first rock, and the streets of Brooklyn the valley inundated with the inevitable destructive force of the results of that first rock falling.

There is no question that Spike Lee has as his goal to reach first an African-American audience, then an American audience and an international audience.

His themes are rooted in the African-American experience, from the interpersonal (*Crooklyn*, 1994) to the interracial (*Jungle Fever*, 1991), the political (*Malcolm X*, 1992), and the politics of color (*School Daze*, 1988). He is concerned about man–woman relationships (*She's Gotta Have It*) and about family relationships (*Jungle Fever*, *Crooklyn*). Always he is interested in ideology and education, first and foremost in the African-American community (Figures 10.5 and 10.6).

FIGURE 10.5

Crooklyn, 1994. Courtesy Forty Acres and a Mule Filmworks/Spike Lee.

FIGURE 10.6

Crooklyn, 1994. Courtesy Forty Acres and a Mule Filmworks/ Spike Lee.

But Lee is also a filmmaker interested in the aesthetic possibilities of visual expression. Although we will focus on his experiments with pace to promote social action, he has also explored the excitement of camera motion (following the character he plays in *Malcolm X* across the streets of Harlem), the possibilities of slow circular motion in the interview scene in *Jungle Fever*, and the possibilities of distortion of color using reversal film as the originating material in *Clockers* (1995). He is always exploring the possibilities of the medium.

The greatest tool, however, that Spike Lee has turned to is pace. Given his agenda for social change, one might anticipate that he would be attracted to pace as he is in *Do the Right Thing* to raise public ire and anger about racism. Although he uses pace very effectively in that film to promote a sense of outrage, it is actually his other less predictable experiments with pace that make his work so interesting.

FIGURE 10.7

Jungle Fever, 1991. Copyright ©1991 Universal Studios, Inc. All rights reserved. Courtesy Forty Acres and a Mule Filmworks/Spike Lee.

Jungle Fever, his exploration of an interracial relationship between an African-American male and an Italian-American female, is notable in how Lee backs away from using pace to create an us-against-them, hero–villain sense in the film (Figure 10.7). In fact, he only resorts to the expected sense of pace around the excitement of the initial sexual encounter of the couple. After that, with family hostility to the relationship growing, we might expect a growing sense of tension with the arc of the interracial relationship. But it doesn't happen. Instead, the tension and consequent use of pace shifts to those around the two lovers. In the Italian community, Angela, the young Italian-American woman (Annabella Sciorra), is beaten by her father upon discovery of the relationship. Pace, as expected, is an important expression of the emotion in the scene. Later, when Angela's spurned boyfriend, Pauly, speaks for tolerance toward the African-American community, the tension in his soda and newspaper shop is palpable. His customers are intolerant about the new black mayor of New York and Pauly asks politely if they voted. And when he is kind to a young African-American female customer, these same customers are filled with rage and sexual aggression. Pace again plays an important role in the scene.

With regards to the African-American lover (Wesley Snipes), his community also expresses its tension about his new relationship. Whether it is his wife's female friends' discussions about black men and white women, or his visit to the Taj Mahal crack house to retrieve his parents' color television from his brother, Gator, in both scenes pace plays an important role to create tension about the potential outcomes of interracial as well as interfamilial relationships.

In relative terms, the exercise of a slower pace in the scenes between the two lovers creates a sense of reason and tolerance that doesn't exist in either the Italian-American community or the African-American community. Although the relationship in the end fails, by using pace in a way that we don't expect, Lee has created a meditation on interracial relationships rather than a prescriptive statement on those relationships.

In *Crooklyn*, the focus is less on two people than on a family in Brooklyn. And Lee has a different goal in the film—to suggest the strengths of the family and of the community.

Pace can be used to create tension, to deepen the sense of conflict between individuals, families, or communities. Pace can also be used to suggest excitement, energy, power. It is this latter use of pace to which Lee turns in *Crooklyn*. He wants to suggest the energy and positive force of family and community. The opening 15 minutes of *Crooklyn* are instructive here. Children play in the streets adjacent to their home. The day is bright and the feeling is positive. He cuts on movement to make the energy seem more dynamic and positive.

In the home proper, the Carmichael family includes mother (Alfre Woodard), the father (Delroy Lindo), their five children, and a dog. The family scenes, whether they are meals together or watching television or sharing news about the future, are energetic and dynamic. The feeling of the scenes is directed by the way Lee uses pace. At times, even the chaos seems appealing because of the way pace is used.

These domestic scenes intercut with the less stable elements of the community, strengthen the feeling of the importance of family, of having a mother and a father, even one where the parents have divergent views about discipline.

Throughout the opening scenes, pace is used to affirm a positive, energetic sense of the Carmichael family in the Brooklyn community they are part of. Here, pace is used to underline the values of family so often the sources of tension in *Jungle Fever*.

Family and its values are also at the heart of the narrative in *Clockers* (Figures 10.8 and 10.9). Because *Clockers* is in its form a crime story, in this case the murder of a fast-food manager, we expect the investigation and prosecution of the perpetrator to dictate a particular pace to the film. The expected pace is cut faster as we move to the climax, the exciting apprehension of the perpetrator of the crime. The baptism scene at the end of *The Godfather* is a classic example of the use of pace to create a sense of climax and release in such a scene.

Lee sidesteps the entire set of expectations we bring to the crime story. Instead, he fleshes out the narrative of an African-American family, the eldest son having been accused of the crime; but it is the youngest son in the family, the son deeply involved in the traffic of drugs, who we expect is the real killer, and it is this son who is the focus of the police investigation. In order to discourage his audience from the celebration of violence inherent in the crime film, in order to educate his audience about the real crimes—drugs, mutual exploitation, the increasingly young perpetrators of violent crime in our ghettoes—Lee turns away from pace as a narrative tool.

FIGURE 10.8
Clockers, 1995. Courtesy Forty Acres and a Mule Filmworks/Spike Lee.

Just as he replaces scenes of characterization for scenes of action, he more slowly cuts those scenes of action when they occur. He also focuses far more on the victims of emotional and physical violence and undermines the potential heroic posture for the perpetrators, the drug king (Delroy Lindo) and the police investigator (Harvey Keitel).

By doing so, Lee risks disappointing his audience, who are accustomed to the fast pace of the crime story. But by doing so, he is pushing into the forefront his educational goals over his entertainment goals. Social action, a new rather than expected action, is Spike Lee's goal in *Clockers*. And pace, albeit not as expected, plays an important role in *Clockers*.

FIGURE 10.9
Clockers, 1995. Courtesy Forty Acres and a Mule Filmworks/Spike Lee.

VON TROTTA: FEMINISM AND POLITICS

In the 1970s, Margarethe von Trotta distinguished herself as a screenwriter on a series of films directed by her husband, Volker Schlondorff. They codirected the film adaptation of the Henrich Böll novel *The Lost Honor of Katharina Blum* (1975). In 1977, von Trotta began her career as a writer–director with *The Second Awakening of Crista Klages*.

All of her work as a director is centered on female characters attempting to understand and act upon their environment. Von Trotta is interesting in her attempt to find a narrative style suitable to her work as an artist, a feminist, and a woman. As a result, her work is highly political in subject matter, and when compared to the dominant male approach to narrative and to editing choices, von Trotta appears to be searching for alternatives, particularly narrative alternatives. Before examining *Marianne and Julianne* (1982), it is useful to examine von Trotta's efforts in the light of earlier female directors.

In the generation that preceded von Trotta, few female directors worked. Two Italians who captured international attention were Lina Wertmüller and Liliana Cavani. Wertmüller (*Swept Away . . .* , 1975; *Seven Beauties*, 1976) embraced a satiric style that did not stand out as the work of a woman. Her work centered on male central characters, and in terms of subject—male–female relationships, class conflicts, regional conflicts—her point of view usually reflected that of the Italian male. In this sense, her films do not differ in tone or narrative style from the earlier style of Pietro Germi (*Divorce—Italian Style*, 1962).

Liliana Cavani (*The Night Porter*, 1974) did make films with female central characters, but her operatic style owed more to Luchino Viscontithan to a feminist sensibility. If Wertmüller was concerned with male sexuality and identity, Cavani was concerned with female sexuality and identity.

Before Wertmüller and Cavani, there were few female directors. However, Leni Riefenstahl's experimentation in *Olympia* (1938) does suggest an effort to move away from a linear pattern of storytelling.

Although generalization has its dangers, a number of observations about contemporary narrative style set von Trotta's work in context in another way. There is little question that filmmaking is a male-dominated art form and industry, and there is little question that film narratives unfold in a pattern that implies cause and effect. The result is an editing pattern that tries to clarify narrative causation and create emotion from characters' efforts to resolve their problems.

What of the filmmaker who is not interested in the cause and effect of a linear narrative? What of the filmmaker who adopts a more tentative position and wishes to understand a political event or a personal relationship? What of the filmmaker who doesn't believe in closure in the classic narrative sense?

This is how we have to consider the work of Margarethe von Trotta. It's not so much that she reacted against the classic narrative conventions. Instead, she tried to reach her audience using an approach suitable to her goals, and these goals seem to be very different from those of male-dominated narrative conventions.

It may be useful to try to construct a feminist narrative model that does not conform to classic conventions, but rather has different goals and adopts different means. That model could be developed using recent feminist writing. Particularly useful is the book *Women's Way of Knowing: The Development of Self, Voice and Mind.*[2] Mary Field Belenky and her coauthors suggest that women "that are less inclined to see themselves as separate from the 'theys' than are men, may also be accounted for by women's rootedness in a sense of connection and men's emphasis on separation and autonomy."[3] In comparing the development of an inner voice in women to that of men, the authors suggest the following: "These women reveal that their epistemology has shifted away from an earlier assumption of 'truth from above' to a belief in multiple personal truths. The form that multiplicity (subjectivism) takes in these women, however, is not at all the masculine assertion that 'I have the right to my opinion'; rather, it is the modest inoffensive statement, 'it's just my opinion.' Their intent is to communicate to others the limits, not the power, of their own opinions, perhaps because they want to preserve their attachments to others, not dislodge them."[4] The search for connectedness and the articulation of the limits of individual efforts and opinions can be worked into an interpretation of *Marianne and Julianne.*

Marianne and Julianne are sisters. The older sister, Julianne, is a feminist writer who has devoted her life to living by her principles. Even her decision not to have a child is a political decision. Marianne has taken political action to another kind of logical conclusion: she has become a terrorist. In the film, von Trotta was primarily concerned by the nature of their relationship. She used a narrative approach that collapses real time. The film moves back and forth between their current lives and particular points in their childhoods. Ironically, Julianne was the rebellious teenager, and Marianne, the future terrorist, was compliant and coquettish.

The contemporary scenes revolve around a series of encounters between the sisters; Marianne's son and Julianne's lover take secondary positions to this central relationship. Indeed, the nature of the relationship seems to be the subject of the film. Not even Marianne's suicide in jail slows down Julianne's effort to confirm the central importance of their relationship in her life.

Generally, the narrative unfolds in terms of the progression of the relationship from one point in time to another. Although von Trotta's story begins in the present, we are not certain how much time has elapsed by the end. Nor does the story end in a climactic sense with the death of Marianne.

Instead, von Trotta constructed the film as a series of concentric circles with the relationship at the center. Each scene, as it unfolds, confirms the importance of the relationship but does not necessarily yield insight into it. Instead, a complex web of emotion, past traumas, and victories is constructed, blending with moments of current exchange of feelings between the sisters. Intense anger and love blend to leave us with the sense of the emotional complexity of the relationship and to allude to the sisters' choice to cut themselves off emotionally from their parents and, implicitly, from all significant others.

As the circles unfold, the emotion grows, as does the connection between the sisters. However, limits are always present in the lives of the sisters: the limits of social and political responsibility, the limits of emotional capacity to save each other or anyone else from their fate. When the film ends with the image of Julianne trying to care for Marianne's son, there is no resolution, only the will to carry on.

The film does not yield the sense of satisfaction that is generally present in classic narrative. Instead, we are left with anxiety for Julianne's fate and sorrow for the many losses she has endured. We are also left with a powerful feeling for her relationship with Marianne.

Whether von Trotta's work is genuinely a feminist narrative form is an issue that scholars might take up. Certainly, the work of other female directors in the 1980s suggests that many in the past 10 years have gravitated toward an alternative narrative style that requires a different attitude to the traditions of classic editing.

FEMINISM AND ANTINARRATIVE EDITING

Although some female directors have chosen subject matter and an editing style similar to those of male directors,[5] there are a number who, like von Trotta, have consciously differentiated themselves from the male conventions in the genres in which they choose to work.

For example, Amy Heckerling has directed a teenage comedy from a girl's perspective. *Fast Times at Ridgemont High* (1982) breaks many of the stereotypes of the genre, particularly the attitudes about sex roles and sexuality. Another film that challenges the conventional view of sex roles and sexuality is Susan Seidelman's *Desperately Seeking Susan* (1985). The narrative editing style of this film emulates the confusion of the main character (Rosanna Arquette). Seidelman was more successful in using a nonlinear editing pattern than was Heckerling, and the result is an originality unusual in mainstream American filmmaking.

Outside of the mainstream, Lizzie Borden created an antinarrative in *Working Girls* (1973), her film about a day in the life of a prostitute. Although the subject matter lends itself to emotional exploitation, as illustrated by Ken Russell's version of the same story in *Whore* (1991), Borden decided to work against conventional expectations.

She focused on the banality of working in a bordello, the mundane conversation, the contrast of the owner's concerns and the employees' goals, and the artifice of selling the commodity of sex. Borden edited the film slowly, contrary to our expectations. She avoided close-ups, preferring to present the film in midshots to long shots, and she avoided camera motion whenever possible. As a result, the film works against our expectation, focusing on the ironic title and downplaying the means of their livelihood. Borden concentrated on the similarities of her characters' lives to those of other working women.

Another antinarrative approach adopted by women directors is to undermine the notion of a single voice, that of the main character in the narrative. Traditionally, the main character is the dramatic vehicle for the point of view, the point of empathy and the point of identification. By sidestepping a single point of view, the traditional arc of the narrative is undermined. Two specific examples will illustrate this.

Agnieszka Holland was already established as a director who explored new narrative approaches (she uses a mixed-genre approach in her film *Europa, Europa*, 1991; see next section on mixing genres) when she made *Olivier, Olivier* (1992).

Olivier, Olivier is a story about a family tragedy. In rural France, a middle-class family has two children, an older daughter and a young son. The boy is clearly the focal point of the family for the mother. The older sibling is ignored. She is also the family member who doesn't quite fit in, a role that often evolves into the scapegoat in family dynamics. One day, the young boy is sent off to deliver lunch to his father's mother. He never returns. In spite of extensive investigation, there is no trace of the boy. The family disintegrates. The local detective is transferred to Paris, determined not to give up on the case. Six years later, he finds a street kid, aged 15, who looks like the disappeared Olivier. He is certain he has found the boy. So is the mother. Only the sister is suspicious. The father, who had left the family to work in Africa, returns. Just as Olivier returns, the family seems to heal, to be whole again. The mother, who had all but fallen apart and blamed the father for Olivier's disappearance, for the first time in years is happy.

The new Olivier seems happy, eccentric, but not poorly adjusted, given his trauma. He wants to be part of this family. But one day he discovers the neighbor molesting a young boy and when the police are called, Olivier confesses that he is not the original Olivier and the neighbor admits to killing the original Olivier. What is to happen to this family who have already endured so much tragedy? Will they relive the original tragedy with all its profound loss? Or will the mother deny again the loss and try for a new life with the new Olivier?

What is interesting about Holland's narrative approach is that she does not privilege any one character over any other. The story presents the point of view of the mother, the father, the sister, Olivier, and the new Olivier.

If Holland had chosen a single point of view, a sense of resolution might have resulted in the discovery of the fate of Olivier. Without a single point of view, we have far less certainty. Indeed, we are left totally stranded in this family tragedy. And the consequence is a profound shock at the end of *Olivier, Olivier*. This is the direct result of the multiple perspectives Holland has chosen.

Julie Dash follows a singular narrative path in her film *Daughters of the Dust* (1991). However, her purpose is quite different from Agnieszka Holland. Whereas Holland is looking to destabilize our identification with the multiple points of view in *Olivier, Olivier*, Julie Dash wants to stabilize and generalize the point of view: The multiple perspectives together represent the African-American diaspora experience in the most positive light.

Daughters in the Dust takes place in a single summer day in 1902, in the Sea Islands of the South, which are off the coast of South Carolina and Georgia. On the islands, life has become a hybrid, not African and not American. The elderly matriarch of the family will stay behind, but she has encouraged her children to go north to the mainland to make a life. She has also told them not to forget who they are. She will remain to die in her home at Ibo Landing.

Julie Dash deals with the feelings that surround this leave-taking with the points of view of the matriarch, her daughters, a niece from the mainland (called Yellow Mary), and an unborn granddaughter who narrates the beginning and end of the story. No single voice is privileged over any other. The conflicts around behavior—a granddaughter has been impregnated via a rape, Yellow Mary may have made her way on the mainland through prostitution, a granddaughter has an Indian-American lover with whom she may want to remain on the island—all dim next to the conflict-ridden future these migrants may face when they move north.

In order to create a sense of tolerance and power in the women, Dash presents the men as the weaker, more emotional sex. She also empowers a matriarch as the focal center of the life of the entire family. By doing so, she diminishes the sense of tension and conflict among the women and emphasizes their collective power and stability. Together they are the family and the purveyors of continuity for the family. And by giving one of the voices—the unborn child—the privileged position of early and closing narrator, Dash frames a voice for the future. But even that voice depends on the continuity of family for life.

Consequently, in *Daughters in the Dust*, Julie Dash uses multiple points of view to sidestep linearity and to instead emphasize the circularity of the life cycle. It is strong, stable, and ongoing.

Although these directors did not proceed to a pattern of circular narrative as von Trotta did, there is no question that each is working against the conventions of the narrative tradition.

MIXING GENRES

Since the 1980s, writers and directors have been experimenting with mixing genres. Each genre represents particular conventions for editing. For example, the horror genre relies on a high degree of stylization, using subjective camera placement and motion. Because of the nature of the subject matter, pace is important. Although film noir also highlights the world of the nightmare, it tends to rely less on movement and pace. Indeed, film noir tends to be even more stylized and more abstract than the horror genre. Each genre relies on visual composition and pace in different ways. As a result, audiences have particular emotional expectations when viewing a film from a particular genre.

When two genres are mixed in one film, each genre brings along its conventions. This can sometimes make an old story seem fresh. However, the results for editing of these two sets of conventions can be surprising. At times, the films are more effective, but at other times, they simply confuse the audience. Because the mixed-genre film has become an important new narrative convention, its implications for editing must be considered.

There were numerous important mixed-genre films in the 1980s, including Jean-Jacques Beineix's *Diva* (1982) and Ethan Coen and Joel Coen's *Raising Arizona* (1987), but the focus here is on three: Jonathan Demme's *Something Wild* (1986), David Lynch's *Blue Velvet*, and Errol Morris's *The Thin Blue Line* (1988).

Something Wild is a mix of screwball comedy and film noir. The film, about a stockbroker who is picked up by an attractive woman, is the shifting story of the urban dream (love) and the urban nightmare (death). Screwball comedies tend to be rapidly paced, kinetic expressions of confusion. Film noir, on the other hand, is slower, more deliberate, and more stylized. Both genres focus sometimes on love relationships.

The pace of the first part of *Something Wild* raises our expectations for the experience of the film. The energy of the screwball comedy, however, gives way to a slower-paced dance of death in the second half of the film. Despite the subject matter, the second half seems anticlimactic. The mixed genres work against one another, and the result is less than the sum of the parts.

David Lynch mixed film noir with the horror film in *Blue Velvet*. He relied on camera placement for the identification that is central to the horror film, and he relied on sound to articulate the emotional continuity of the movie. In fact, he used sound effects the way most filmmakers use music, to help the audience understand the emotional state of the character and, consequently, their own emotional states.

Lynch allowed the sound and the subjectivity that is crucial in the horror genre to dominate the stylization and pacing of the film. As a result, *Blue Velvet* is less stylized and less cerebral than the typical film noir work. Lynch's experiment in mixed genre is very effective. The story seems new and different, but its impact is similar to such conventional horror films as William Friedkin's *The Exorcist* (1973) or David Cronenberg's *Dead Ringers* (1988).

Errol Morris mixed the documentary and the police story (the gangster film or thriller) in *The Thin Blue Line*, which tells the story of a man wrongly accused of murder in Texas. The documentary was edited for narrative clarity in building a credible case. With clarity and credibility as the goals of the editing, the details of the case had to be presented in careful sequence so that the audience would be convinced of the character's innocence. It is not necessary to like or identify with him. The credible evidence persuades us of the merits of his cause. The result can be dynamic, exciting, and always emotional.

Morris dramatized the murder of the policeman, the crime that has landed the accused in jail. The killing is presented in a dynamic, detailed way. It is both a shock and an exciting event. In contrast to the documentary film style, many close-ups are used. This sequence, which was repeated in the film, was cut to Phillip Glass's musical score, making the scene evocative and powerful. It is so different from the rest of the film that it seems out of place. Nevertheless, Morris used it to remind us forcefully that this is a documentary about murder and about the manipulation of the accused man.

The Thin Blue Line works as a mixed-genre film because of Glass's musical score and because Morris made clear the goal of the film: to prove that the accused is innocent.

Mixing genres is a relatively new phenomenon, but it does offer filmmakers alternatives to narrative conventions. However, it is critical to understand which editing styles, when put together, are greater than the sum of their parts and which, when put together, are not.

NOTES/REFERENCES

1. Our expectation for an adventure film of this period was probably established by Tony Richardson's *Tom Jones* (1963) and Richard Lester's *The Three Musketeers* (1974). In both films, the sense of adventure dictated a rapid and lively pace, the opposite of Kubrick's Barry Lyndon.

2. M. F. Belenky, B. M. Cliachy, N. R. Goidherger, J. M. Torule, Women's Way of Knowing: The Development of Self, Voice and Mind, Basic Books, New York, 1986.

3. Ibid., pp. 44–45.

4. Ibid., p. 66.

5. Kathryn Bigelow, for example, directed *Blue Steel* (1989) and *Point Break* (1991), both of which were edited in the action style we expect from the well-known male directors who specialize in this genre.

CHAPTER 11

The MTV Influence on Editing I

What I have called the MTV influence on editing is principally associated with that phenomenon of the past 30 years, the music video. Initially viewed as a vehicle to sell records, those 3- to 30-minute videos have captured a young audience looking for quick, evocative visual stimuli presented as a background for the aural presentation of a single song or series of songs.

Although this style of film was further popularized by films such as *Flashdance* (1983) and repopularized by Baz Luhrman's *Moulin Rouge* (2005), the form has its roots in more experimental filmmaking and certainly in the success of the short form, the television commercial. The MTV style is today principally associated with television, although its influence has superseded television. By sidestepping the traditional set of narrative goals, which include a linear narrative and a focus on plot and character, the MTV style has instead replaced it with a multilayered approach. There may be a story. There may be a single character. But the likelihood is that place, feeling, or mood will be the primary layer of the music video. It is also likely that the traditional sense of time and place with the conventions that are used to reference film time to real time will be replaced by a far less direct correlation. In fact, many music videos attempt to establish their own reference points between reality and film time. This may mean great leaps in time and place and it is the vividness of the resulting imagery that provides the new correlation. In the world of the music video, real place is far less important. In fact, they are not as important as references to other media and other forms, to the landscapes of science fiction, and to the horror film. And with regard to time: Time in the music video is any time. With time and place obliterated, the film and video makers are free to roam in the world of their imagined media meditation. And their audience, young and rebellious, is free to feel the simulation of their freedom and to celebrate their rejection of tradition—from our perspective, the rejection of the tradition of narrative.

Because the MTV style sidesteps traditional narrative, it is of interest to us. How does the form coalesce to capture its audience? By focusing on the most aggressive stylist of our day, Oliver Stone, we will try to understand how the MTV style can be used and why it has such a powerful grip on the public imagination.

165

The Technique of Film and Video Editing: History, Theory, and Practice. DOI: 10.1016/B978-0-240-81397-4.00011-X

ORIGINS

Although Luis Buñuel's early antinarrative experiments in *Un Chien d'Andalou* (1929) and *L'Age d'Or* (1930) bear certain similarities to the contemporary music video, the more critical shaping device is music that has a narrative as well as emotional character. This means that we have to look to the two early Beatles films, *A Hard Day's Night* (1964) and *Help!* (1965), for a starting point in the mid-1960s. Very quickly, the Lester films were joined by John Boorman's film with the Dave Clark Five, *Having a Wild Weekend* (1965). Later, Lester's *A Funny Thing Happened on the Way to the Forum* (1966) and the nonmusical series of Monty Python films that followed in the 1970s (*And Now for Something Completely Different*, 1972; *Monty Python and the Holy Grail*, 1975; and *Life of Brian*, 1979) added stylistic elements to the new genre.

How these films differed from traditional narratives and musicals needs to be articulated. Traditional musicals generally presented a narrative together with interspersed musical or dance numbers. Films such as *The Pirate* (1948), *An American in Paris* (1951), and *Invitation to the Dance* (1957) were exceptions. The best of the musicals, such as *Singin' in the Rain* (1952), *Funny Face* (1957), and *West Side Story* (1961), found a visual style to match the energy and emotion of the narratives.

Turning to the Lester films, *A Hard Day's Night* and *Help!*, on one level, they are musicals, for the main characters are performers. The music is integral to our understanding of the film narratives. But whereas there is a narrative that is elaborate and character-driven in the traditional musical, we must accept the fact that the narratives in *A Hard Day's Night* and *Help!* have far more modest goals. In fact, we are hard-pressed to find common sense as well as feeling arising out of the narratives of these films. In essence, the narratives were an excuse for the musical numbers, which themselves were used to highlight what the Beatles represented—inventiveness, anarchy, energy. These feeling states were far more important to director Richard Lester than a narrative about a concert or about the disappearance of a ritual ring from India and the efforts by a cult to retrieve it.

Here there are the first stylistic elements of the music video. The shaping device is the music. Narrative is less important; a feeling state is more important. From an editing standpoint, this translates as making the jump cut more important than the match cut. It also implies a centrality for pace. Given the low involvement quotient of the narrative, it is to pace that the role of interpretation falls. Consequently, pace becomes the source of energy and new juxtapositions that suggest anarchy and inventiveness.

When we move to the Monty Python films, we add a literary base for reference and a self-reflexing acknowledgment that the characters can step in and out of character and speak to the audience directly. This process results in the acknowledgment of media, of manipulation, and the more subtle notion that in spite of self-reflexivity, the form can be even more manipulative as you let your audience in on it—it's a joke, it's funny, and you, the audience, have been let in on the construction of the joke—which in turn privileges the viewer and involves the viewer in a more conscious manner. These elements, the literary metaphor and the self-reflexive, fill out the repertoire of the music video. But over time the referent points move beyond literature and film to other media: television, journalism, the world of comic books, and now the world of computer games.

The Short Film

The short film and its relationship to the short story, as well as to the world of the visual arts, has yielded many explorations of form, the creations of particular styles. The work of Luis Buñuel, Maya Daren, and the more recent work of Stan Brakhage and Andy Warhol are marked by a number of characteristics we now find in the MTV style. So too video art. The antinarrative position of Buñuel and the stream of consciousness visual style of Maya Daren have far more in common with the MTV style than they do with mainstream filmmaking. Filmmakers such as Stan Brakhage are interested in layering images—not to create a special effect but rather in a self-reflexive way to suggest this media experience, this film, is both a manipulation and reflection upon the tolls of that manipulation. And few filmmakers take a stylistic position as minimalist as Andy Warhol. Indeed, the position is so clearly about style as opposed to content, that the experience of his films becomes a comment on the medium more than any other interpretation (i.e., society, the art world).

All of these filmmakers also create a distinctive style, and once their audience is in tune with their intentions, they create as powerful an identification of the audience with their work as did Richard Lester in his Beatles films. The only difference between these filmmakers and the MTV style is the role of sound, particularly music, as a shaping device. From a visual point, however, the MTV style has a great deal in common with the short film, particularly the experimental film.

WHERE WE ARE NOW—THE STATE OF THE MTV STYLE

Because of the volume of music videos produced to promote records and because TV stations and international networks welcome programming that appeals to the 15- to 25-year-old audience, MTV is not only here to stay, but it is actually a powerful force in broadcasting. Its interrelationship with advertising underpins its influence.

Consequently, we must view the MTV style as a new form of visual storytelling. Part narrative, part atmosphere, sound-intensive, and image-rich, the form has a remarkable appeal to the new generation of filmmakers and videomakers whose media viewing experience is preponderantly television.

Although the MTV style has not made a broad entry into the feature film, it has characterized much of the style of those directors who began in commercials—Adrian Lyne (*Flashdance*, 1983), Tony Scott (*Top Gun*, 1986), and Ridley Scott (*Thelma & Louise*, 1991). It has also accounted for the success of at least one new director, Ben Stiller, in his debut film, *Reality Bites* (1994). Newer directors, such as Richard Linklater (*Dazed and Confused*, 1993), and older directors, such as Luc Besson (*La Femme Nikita*, 1990), are attracted to the ideology and style of MTV. But few filmmakers have leaped as headlong into the MTV style as Oliver Stone did in his film *Natural Born Killers* (1994). We will look at *Natural Born Killers* in some detail later in the chapter, but before we do, it's necessary to highlight the key characteristics of the MTV style.

The Importance of Feeling States

One of the central features of the MTV style is the importance of creating a definite feeling state. This is not an issue of the need to challenge the primacy of plot. Rather, it begins with the close relationship of the MTV style with music.

Music—particularly without lyrics—synthesizes human emotion. The brain processes sound. It was Bergman who stated the goal of the film experience—it should be like music. This equation of music with heightened emotional experience was applied by Bergman to the overall experience of film. The sound of music in this sense is even more concentrated than the film experience itself. And the music of a single short song can be viewed as an even greater concentration of emotion.

When we add the lyrics of a song, which tend to the poetic, we are given a direction for the emotion of the music. If there is a sense of narrative, it yields from those poetic lyrics. But to repeat: The purpose of music and lyrics is to give a defined emotional state to the feeling state that is created.

A feeling state can be sharp and deep or can be developmental and dreamlike. In either case, the state creates a disjunctive, disconnected sense to a narrative. Because of the depth of feeling of a single sequence associated with a single piece of music, it is difficult to create a continuum of narrative. Rather, we have in the longer MTV-style film a series of disjunctive sequences, memorable in and of themselves, but hardly organized on an effectively rising arc of action characteristic of the narrative film. This is why there are moments one remembers in films like *Flashdance* or *Top Gun*, but one is left without a powerful sense of the characters or the story. This does not diminish the overall film, but it does make it a different kind of experience than the conventional film.

Feeling states can also appeal as dream fragments—pleasurable, but not entirely real, in the way the experience of a traditional narrative tends to be. Clearly, a film that concentrates on feeling states will appeal only to an audience accustomed to it—that young audience that views and enjoys a series of visualized music videos one after the other, that have no narrative connection but each of which provides a distinct sensation or feeling. This audience does not mind the fragmentation or the pace or the brevity of the experience. For this audience, the feeling state is a desirable audiovisual experience.

The Downgrading of the Plot

It's not that this new audience is disinterested in plot. The success of films such as Amy Heckerling's *Clueless* (1995) and Ang Lee's *Sense and Sensibility* (1995) with a young audience is proof that the narrative drive and energy in both of these love stories appeals to that audience. Ironically, both are based upon the novels of Jane Austen. But these films, although popular, are not "icons" to this young audience. Those filmic icons are *Reality Bites*, *Natural Born Killers*, and *Slacker* (1991). These icons are notable for their put-down of plot, of the elevation of adolescent rage and anarchy over the continuum of the happy ending in *Clueless* and *Sense and Sensibility*.

When plot is less important, incident, or scene, takes on a different meaning, and character becomes everything. When the logic of plot progression is less pressing, set-pieces can stand more readily. Mood, alternating shifts of mood, fantasy, play, nightmare, all can be juxtaposed more readily because their contribution to the plot progression is unnecessary.

Add to that a character who stands against the prevailing values of the society, and for the destruction of those values, and you have the hero/main character of the MTV-style film: Ethan Hawke in *Reality Bites*, Woody Harrelson in *Natural Born Killers*, Anne Parillaud in *La Femme Nikita*. It's as if the Brando character in *The Wild One* (1954) has returned and again answered the 1950's question, "What are you rebelling against?" The answer: "What have you got?"

In a standard plotted narrative, such a main character would seem reactive and immature, rootless and without a goal. In the fragmented narrative of the MTV-style film, the character is a hero in a fragmented world, a hero who can recite poetry and kill in the same breath, a hero who can't be held accountable. It's his world that has made him so.

Having a degraded (or downgraded) plot simulates the world of these heroes. Their audience recognizes that world with ease. It's the world they live in, the TV world, the videogame world. They see it as a game to cope with the incomprehensibility of that world. For them, the MTV style is a tool, a stimuli, and a philosophy. Less plot facilitates the audience entry into the MTV world view.

Disjunctive Editing—The Obliteration of Time and Space

In order to create feeling states and to downgrade plot and its importance, the filmmaker must also undermine the gestalt impulse—to make sense of what we see. To put in another way, the viewer will organize a pattern of sounds and images into a progression of thought—an applied linearity—even if one is not available on the surface.

To counteract the impulse to organize those images and sounds into the narrative that may not be present, the filmmaker must challenge the impulse more deeply. She must undermine the sense of time and space in the MTV-style film or video.

To understand how this is done, we must back up to some issues raised in Chapters 8, 9, and 10. In the work of Kurosawa, we saw him visually play with the idea that the truth was relative, that it was influenced by whoever was telling the story (*Rashomon*, 1951). In Resnais's work memory, the past and its intervention posed the question about time and its continuum. If a character is gripped by events of the past, what does this mean for their current conduct and perception (*Hiroshima, Mon Amour*, 1960)? Fellini went even further to suggest not simply the past, but the character's fantasy/fantasies about the past overshadowed the present (*8½*, 1963). In the case of Antonioni, place and the environment overwhelms character and perception. Place obliterates the time gestalt of thinking and replaces it with the objective power of place. *Will*, an expression of character's goals, is replaced by *will not*, *cannot*; place replacing time in importance (*L'Eclisse*, 1962).

Peter Brook poses questions about reality through his exploration of performance, and his understanding of history (*Marat/Sade*, 1966). Again, time and place are reconfigured. They become relative and less important. Herzog and Wenders both challenge the notions of personal history and objective reality (*The Enigma of Kaspar Hauser*, 1974; *Paris, Texas*, 1984).

Together these filmmakers and numerous others have challenged conventional notions of time and place in their work. Their artistic advances in turn opened up options for those working with the MTV style. Central to that style is the obliteration of a conventional sense of time and place. Even though Tony Scott's *Top Gun* has a location for the story (the Southwest) and a time (the 1980s, the last phase of the Cold War), its actual dream state—the marine pilot as invincible hero and lover—actually bears little resemblance to training, to the history of the 1980s; rather, it resembles a cartoon, or a piece of advertising. To succeed, Scott has to pay lip service to time and place but little more.

By focusing on the feeling state, by mixing dream and fear, by obliterating history, and replacing it with a new mythology, Scott uses style to move us into a less narrative experience, a more sensation experience. And he succeeds because of the work of Fellini, Antonioni, Kurosawa, and Brook in their challenges to our sense of time and place.

What we haven't focused on until now is the mechanical editing choices that help the filmmaker obliterate time and place. The first choice is to use many more close-ups than long shots. This choice withdraws the context that, when present, lends credibility to the sequence. The second choice is to emphasize foreground over background in the frame. Whether this is done by using telephoto shots rather than side-angle shots or through the crowding of the character into the front of the frame, which can, with a wide-angle shot, distort the character, both choices yield the same result—withdrawal of visual context. Add the art direction—lighting choices that move away from realism—the sepia of *Top Gun*, the gauzed images of *Flashdance*, the hot reds alternating with the cool blues in Tony Scott's *Crimson Tide* (1995)—when combined with the oversize of the close-up and of the foreground image, all undermine context. Add the use (where possible) of the jump cut and the overuse of pace and we have the mechanical editing repertoire of the obliteration of time and place.

The Self-Reflexive Dream State

To create a dream state is to imply that the viewer temporarily loses oneself in that state. The self-reflexive dream state suggests that on another level, viewers watch or reflect upon themselves dreaming, or to put it another way, to be simultaneously very involved and not involved at all.

Turning back to the Monty Python films, as well as the Beatles films, there is in both the acknowledgment by the characters that they are performing as well as participating. Almost ironic in tone, these performances veer wildly from viewing the characters as innocents and then as having enough mastery over the situation, that they step out of the role and address us, the audience, directly.

Whether the technique is Brechtian or closer to Beckett, the device allows for a range of genres—adventure to satire—that helps the MTV-style film transcend what could easily become marginalized to pictures for the music. It reinforces an attitude in its audience—the will to reconfigure their world via their dreams, all the while acknowledging, "Just playing, folks!"

But the self-reflexivity plays another, more serious, role in the MTV style. Because self-reflexivity acknowledges that it is a film being watched (as opposed to reality), this creates a tolerance for ranging more widely. It pulls the film closer to theatre, where the suspension of belief is far higher than in film (which looks real). This freedom allows for shifts in feeling, narrative, fantasy, and so on without needing to make those shifts plausible. It is, after all, only a film that you are watching. "Go with it," is the message to its audience, and knowing that it is a media event (unlike a real dream), the audience is tolerant of those shifts in tone, time, place, and so on that are undertaken.

The Media Looks at Itself

Just as the character stands apart and comments on himself within the film, so too does the media. The MTV style embraces a self-reflexivity of the particular form, film or video, upon itself, its power, and its manipulative techniques. The MTV style also embraces a referential base to comment upon as well as to include other media.

Top Gun deploys and celebrates the techniques of the TV commercial; the recent music videos of Madonna reference the paintings of Frida Kahlo; and Michael Jackson's music video *Thriller* is a mix of *West Side Story* meets *The Wiz* (1978), which in turn is based on *The Wizard of Oz* (1939). *Flashdance* is itself a long series of music videos.

One can imagine music videos referencing key journalistic events (an election, a revolution), famous TV situation comedies, and various other media renderings of historical events: the deaths of Abraham Lincoln, John F. Kennedy, and Mahatma Gandhi, for example, as well as media interpretations of serious social issues (AIDS, racism, spousal abuse). The MTV style will mimic and comment upon the other media's presentation of such key events or issues.

By doing so, a reductive view can be confirmed and transcended. It says to its audience, "Everything can be criticized and by using this style, even the critics can be criticized." Rather than providing the audience with the restorative power of the classic narrative, the MTV style plays to paranoia and to narcissism. By criticizing the media itself, the MTV style criticizes the power of the media and confirms in its audience the suspicion that there is no trust out there and the last element of the society that is trustworthy is the media itself.

Having looked at the elements of the MTV style, we're ready to turn our attention to a detailed look at Oliver Stone, who represents the most artistic use of the style to date.

OLIVER STONE'S CAREER

After leaving the film program at New York University, Oliver Stone made his way as a screenwriter. His credits include *Midnight Express* (1978), *Scarface* (1983), and *Year of the Dragon* (1985). As a writer–director, Stone is responsible for *Salvador* (1986), *Platoon* (1986), *Wall Street* (1987), *Born on the Fourth of July* (1989), *JFK* (1991), *Natural Born Killers* (1994), and *Nixon* (1995).

He has made at least three films about the Vietnam War (including *Heaven and Earth*, 1993), two films about American presidents, and at least two other films about the media and violence (*Salvador* and *Natural Born Killers*). Aside from the seriousness of the subject matter and a good deal of narrative bravado, Stone has a very distinctive style—lots of camera motion and pace. He has often been criticized for manipulating—whether it is in *JFK* or *Nixon*, he is quite willing to use editing, juxtaposition, and pace to make whatever point he wishes. Although powerfully fascinated by the forceful nature of the medium, Stone is not beyond criticizing those forceful tools he himself uses. This is the source of the great controversy in *JFK*. He uses simulated footage of real-life events, rephotographs them, and then proceeds to declare that he is using those same tools to reveal "the truth." In this sense, he is the ideal self-reflexive filmmaker.

But to be fair to Stone, he is also part of a tradition from Eisenstein to Peckinpah of directors who see editing as the real art of directing. In *Natural Born Killers*, Stone uses this self-reflexivity to create a multilayered film experience. Using the MTV style, Stone creates an explosive, creative commentary on family, violence, and the media in America.

Natural Born Killers

Natural Born Killers, from a story by Quentin Tarantino, tells the story of two mass murderers, Mickey and Mallory Knox (Woody Harrelson and Juliette Lewis). The film begins with a killing spree, then moves back to their meeting and their three-week sweep through the Southwest. In those three weeks, they kill 52 people. They are captured, after being snakebitten, while looking for snakebite serum in a drugstore. Their captor, Detective Jack Scagnetti, seems as pathological as the two young killers. The story flashes forward a year to the maximum-security prison where they are held.

It seems that a television journalist, Wayne Gale (Robert Downey, Jr.) has a television show, *American Maniacs*, where he profiles serial killers. The public is quite fascinated by Mickey and Mallory, and Wayne has fed the fascination. He proposes to Mickey and to the warden (Tommy Lee Jones) that he, Wayne, interview Mickey live on Super Bowl Sunday. Both parties are agreeable, but the warden wants Mickey and Mallory put away for good. They have incited trouble in the prison; the other prisoners idealize them. He invites Jack Scagnetti to take both out of prison and dispose of them right after the interview.

This doesn't happen, because the interview is so inflammatory. Mickey celebrates that he does what he does so well because he was born to it—he's a natural-born killer. Upon hearing this, the prison erupts, the convicts go on a rampage. In the confusion, Mickey disarms a guard and begins to kill again. He takes hostages, including Wayne Gale, and they free Mallory and kill Jack Scagnetti, while the majority of hostages are killed by police fire. Using a guard and Wayne Gale as human shields, while Gales's TV camera records it all, Mickey and Mallory make good their escape. In the woods, on live TV, they kill Wayne Gale, who they claim is worse than a killer, a parasite, and they go on, it seems, to live happily ever after. Mallory speaks of it being time to have a family.

This narrative description can't give more than an outline of *Natural Born Killers*. The film is actually organized in a series of set-pieces—in the precredit introduction to Mickey and Mallory in a roadside diner, they kill all but one of the customers. A television situation comedy show follows. It introduces Mickey and Mallory, her abusive father, the impotent mother, and the young brother. This show is complete with laugh track. The show is called *I Love Mallory*. The next sequence introduces Australian-American reporter Wayne Gale and his television show, *American Maniacs*. On the show, they do a dramatic reenactment of two Mickey and Mallory killings. London, Tokyo—the media spreads the fame of these killers around the world.

A set-piece of Mickey and Mallory in a motel room follows. They have a spat and he amuses himself with a female hostage; she amuses herself with a gas station attendant. When he recognizes her, she kills him. A sequence with an Indian who handles rattlesnakes follows. The Indian seems to be the first person Mickey respects. Accidentally, Mickey kills the Indian.

As the lovers run away, both are bitten by snakes. A set-piece in a drug mart follows. Both are ill. In this sequence, the lovers are captured by the police. A year later in jail, Wayne Gale requests an interview with Mickey. Mickey agrees. In this sequence, the hero worship of Mickey and Mallory by young people is highlighted. The interview is the next set-piece. Jack Scagnetti's parallel encounter with Mallory is the next. The strong sexual current of this sequence is juxtaposed with the romantic dimension of the first part of the live interview with Mickey—the theme is that love can tame the demon.

The prison riot is the next set-piece, followed by Mickey's escape. Shortly thereafter is a final sequence in Mallory's cell. The next sequence captures their escape from prison. In the woods, the last taping of Wayne Gale's show ends with his murder on camera. The title sequence that follows is a merging of past and future images. They imply that Mickey and Mallory survive and have a family.

Looking at the sequences in a general way, one notices how much each resembles a music video. Music is the overall shaping device. The first sequence begins with Leonard Cohen's "Waiting for a Miracle." The last sequence is shaped by Cohen's "The Future." Thirty songs are used in between. Each sequence has within itself remarkable latitude to use images of the characters, images of animals, and theatrical images of monsters, dragons, and headless bodies, presented in a highly stylized manner: black and white, natural color, filtered color (usually blood red), TV images of the Menendez brothers and O. J. Simpson trials, TV images from the 1950s, filmic images from *The Wild Bunch* (for example), and animated cartoon-like drawings. Add to this distortions from morphing, highlight shifting to low light, and you have a range of images that runs the gamut from natural to unnatural. Often these images are thrown together in the same sequence.

The capacity to reflect on the media itself is ever-present. Beyond the references to other films, much is made in the film of the role of television in American life. The introduction of Mickey and Mallory's meeting is presented in the form of a situation comedy. Three of their clashes with the law are presented in the form of a Saturday morning cartoon. And the actuality television style of Wayne Gale's television show, *American Maniacs*, to sketch their career and to demonstrate its power on the young as well as the convicts in prison, is a frightening condemnation of the role of television in the promotion of violence.

Finally, each sequence uses black-and-white and color images intertwined to pose the question: Which is imagined and which is real? The crossover doesn't make the answer any clearer. Sometimes the black-and-white images seem to be remembrances of Mickey's childhood. At other times, they reference in a journalistic way the faces and feelings of the other convicts in maximum-security prison. In terms of color, it starts with the unreal use of green as a motif in the diner sequence that opens the film. The green is the key lime pie Mickey eats, and it is the cartoon color of the diner. That green can alternate with black and white or with blood red. In each case, the sharp shifts in color create a sense of stylization that affirms this is a media event and manipulation you are watching. Enjoy! The black-and-white newsreel interspliced goes with the confusion between reality and dream this film plays with.

These are the general elements of the MTV style in *Natural Born Killers*. More specifically, we can look at any sequence and see how Oliver Stone pushes the feeling state over the narrative linearity of plot. In the opening sequence, for example, one is aware of the extreme close-ups intercut with long shots. It is the dead eye of a deer in close-up cutting to a distorted wide-angle shot of the truck in front of the diner, complete with dead deer on its roof. Mickey is eating his pie in color and remembering his past in black and white. The camera studies him in close. The back of his head crowds the front of the camera. Mallory, on the other hand, is presented in a long shot dancing alone initially to the music of the jukebox. The camera undulates side to side, as unstable as she is. When she is joined by one of the men from the truck, she is seductive and suggestive and soon lethal. Here, Stone jump cuts her attack on the male, details it, and makes it more violent through the use of the jump cuts.

The pace increases as the killing begins, only to be slowed down when Mickey throws a knife at the man outside. The camera tracks the trajectory of the knife, emphasizing the unreality of the killing. Only the man's death brings back the sense of realism via sound. The next death, the stylized death of the waitress, is presented in almost farcical terms. The camera sways with the choosing of the last victim between the waitress and the last male.

When the choice is made, Mickey shoots her, but his bullet hits the pan she is holding. The impact of the pan kills her. It seems a comic moment in its presentation. She is the fourth victim of Mickey and Mallory in the diner. The movement of the camera, the extreme close-ups, and the foreground crowding of character in the frame alternating with extreme wide-angle shots of action and character in the background give the sequence a tension that Stone uses to make the sequence function on a stylized as well as narrative level. The color shifts increase the stylization. And the occasional images of nature—tarantulas, rabbits—contextualize the events with the natural world. Whether Stone is implying the similarities or differences becomes clearer later in the Indian sequence when he uses both perspectives in nature and man's behavior. Mickey also refers to the natural order of things in his live interview with Wayne Gale.

This pattern of viewing each sequence as a music video unto itself, when put together on a two-hour narrative frame, yields the sense that Stone has put together a narrative that is a music video and that comments on the ethics of the music video. His style, as well as the unappealing actions and goals of the main characters, gives us little choice but to consider *Natural Born Killers* as Oliver Stone's meditation on violence and the media in American society.

Stone has always been a vigorous filmmaker interested in ideas, society, and history, but nothing before has prepared us for the artfulness of the challenge he meets and transcends in *Natural Born Killers*. As much as we don't like to acknowledge it, Stone has created in *Natural Born Killers* a meditation on what he does—manipulates—and he both celebrates and condemns the power of the media. The MTV style, along with its qualities and its goals, have never been used in so creative a way.

CHAPTER 12

The MTV Influence on Editing II

In the previous chapter, we explored the characteristics of the MTV style in editing. Whereas linear narratives proceed by focusing a viewer's identification with a main character, the MTV approach proceeds using a less specific focus. Consequently, pace, subjectivity, and the close-up are not used to build an identification with the main character. In the MTV style, they are used to generate a less specific intensity. Pace and subjectivity in general are not used to move us up a dramatic arc; instead, they are used to intensify in effect a set-piece that may or may not contribute to a dramatic arc.

The MTV style is more clearly understood if the developmental narrative structure of the linear narrative is set aside, and if instead the narrative is seen as a series of set-pieces that each embodies a dramatic arc of their own. You might even consider the set-pieces to be the equivalent of short films strung together by a loose-shaping device. The most important point is that the editing implications of the MTV style shifts the focus from character and the structure of the narrative as a whole to the set-piece itself. In a sense, the MTV style subverts the linear experience and elevates the scene over a sequence, an act, or indeed the whole film.

Within the scene itself, the MTV style focuses on feeling over the progress of the narrative. In the previous chapter we looked at a single example, Oliver Stone's *Natural Born Killers* (1994). In this chapter, we expand this exploration to look at different narrative conventions that have emerged from the influence of MTV style. In the case of Wong Kar-wai's *In the Mood for Love* (2000), the filmmaker has taken a classic melodrama, a doomed love story, and by adopting an MTV-style approach, he alters the specificity of the narrative to become an existential meditation on yearning and loneliness. Similarly, Ang Lee's MTV-style editing of the fight sequences in *Crouching Tiger, Hidden Dragon* (2000) transforms a kung fu action film into a feminist melodrama about the clash of the "traditional" with the "modern." Very often, the MTV style self-reflexively uses the media itself as a character in the narrative.

Juzo Itami in his film *Tampopo* (1987) uses this characteristic to both frame his narrative and interrupt the main story line. By doing so, he uses the MTV style to interject his own voice into the story line, thereby giving a layered, more complex experience to what is otherwise a simple story. In the case of *Life Is Beautiful* (1998), Roberto Benigni uses his own character in the narrative as the focus for the set-pieces that together propose a philosophy at odds with

177

The Technique of Film and Video Editing: History, Theory, and Practice. DOI: 10.1016/B978-0-240-81397-4.00012-1

the plot. Here the MTV style transgresses plot to yield a powerful but very different interpretation of the narrative.

In Chapter 31, *Nonlinear Editing and Digital Technology II*, we will look at the use of the set-piece in the nonlinear film. In both Terence Malick's *The Thin Red Line* (1998) and P. T. Anderson's *Magnolia* (1998), the filmmakers create powerful and intense set-pieces. Although there are similarities between these two films and those discussed in this chapter on the MTV editing approach to the set-piece, they also differ from the films discussed here in two areas. First, each of these two films uses a single character as opposed to multiple characters as a vehicle for the narrative. Second, these MTV-influenced films move to resolution, whereas the nonlinear film more often has an open ending.

To begin our deliberation of the influence of MTV style, we turn first to the D-Day set-piece that occurs early in Steven Spielberg's *Saving Private Ryan* (1997).

THE CASE OF *SAVING PRIVATE RYAN*

Steven Spielberg's *Saving Private Ryan* is a traditional war film framed by a modern prologue. The former Private Ryan, with his wife, children, and grandchildren, visit the American cemetery where so many who died on D-Day and in its immediate aftermath are buried. He is there to visit the grave of Captain John Miller, who died on the rescue mission that saved Ryan's life. The body of the narrative focuses on D-Day and the mission to save Ryan, after the War Department receives word that his three brothers have all been killed in action. Army Chief of Staff George Marshall issues the command: Save the one remaining Ryan so that his mother will not have lost all four sons fighting for their country. Captain Miller and his men are given the tough assignment, and six of the eight will die in carrying out the mission, including Miller himself. While he is dying, Captain Miller exhorts Ryan to live a worthy life or, put another way, to "make my sacrifice worthwhile." In the epilogue, Ryan in deepest sorrow tells us he has lived up to Miller's invocation.

This brief description can't capture the powerful emotions created by the experience of the film. *Saving Private Ryan* is a classic war film, and the goal for Miller, the main character, is to try to survive. His conscious self-sacrifice to save Ryan elevates the premise of the narrative to a meditation on the question of what is worth dying for, and the film implies that there are issues and events in life that are worth dying for. Whether this notion is romantic or realistic is not the point we're concerned with here. Our concern is how Spielberg elevates the narrative beyond a conventional war story. An important if not vital contributor to this shift is the MTV style that Spielberg employs in the D-Day landing sequence. This 24-minute sequence is the subject to which we now turn. The place is Omaha Beach, Dog Green Sector.

The sequence proceeds under the following subheadings. Lengths (rounded off) are noted:

1. In the Landing Craft: 2 minutes
2. In the Water: 2 minutes
3. At the Edge of the Beach—What Do We Do: 2 minutes
4. Movement Off the Beach: 3 minutes

5. Up to the Perimeter (Barbed Wire): 3 minutes
6. Gather Weapons: 3 minutes
7. Advance on the Pillbox—Take Machine Gun Emplacement: 3 minutes
8. Take the Pillbox and the Surrounding Environment: 3 minutes
9. The Beach Is Taken—Stop Shooting: 3 minutes

Before we turn to the individual sequences, here are a number of general observations that drive the overall sequence. The first observation is that although mastery of a sort is achieved by the characters by the end of the sequence, the emphasis is on the casualties, their extensive number, the pervasiveness of death on the beach, the chaos of trying to survive on the beach, and the horror of how mutilating death can be when it occurs in war. Second, Spielberg has adopted a cinéma vérité style involving handheld shots, a lot of telephoto images where context is flattened to emphasize crowding, and the creation of the effect that there is nowhere to hide from the steady machine gun and mortar fire. Spielberg also uses close-ups to a far higher proportion than he usually does when presenting an action sequence. Finally, as expected, pace plays a very important part in the experience of the sequence as a whole.

FIGURE 12.1
Saving Private Ryan (1998). Dreamworks/Photofest. ©Dreamworks.

Now we turn to the individual sequences.

1. In the Landing Craft
   The emphasis in this sequence is on intensity. We begin in a close-up of Captain Miller's shaking hands as he takes some water from his canteen. Whether it is fear of dying or just

fear, the camera pulls back to other expressions of fear. A man vomits; another kisses his crucifix. Miller and his sergeant bark short, clear orders. They are in command and they have the experience few men on the landing craft have. Point-of-view shots and close-ups build the intensity. As the landing craft opens its front to allow the men to move onto the beach, those upfront are greeted with instant death. They are cut down by enemy machine-gun fire. A cutaway to the German pillbox atop the beach positions the killers' point of view. To save his men, Miller orders them over the side, into the water. It's the only way to survive the enemy fire. Pace, movement, and the telephoto cutaway together create the claustrophobia of imminent death in this sequence. The feeling is one of intensity and fear.

2. In the Water

Men are pushed or jump over the side. As they enter the water and sink under the surface, the sounds of combat are lost and everything slows down. Men grapple to shed the equipment that weighs them down. A rifle falls to the sea floor. Bullet tracers reach their mark and kill two soldiers as they struggle with their gear. There is a macabre beauty to their deaths. Another soldier simply drowns. Survivors emerge from the water and head for the beach. The sounds of combat return only to be muted again as underwater shots of the footsteps of soldiers are intercut with the struggle above water. Miller makes his way out of the water. He helps a soldier but to no avail. The soldier catches a bullet in his chest and his struggle not to drown is over. The feeling in this sequence is surprise—surprise that death can't be evaded. There are fewer close-ups and less pace used in this sequence.

3. At the Edge of the Beach

Here the pace and camera position change. The pace quickens and close-ups return. The cutaway to the German pillbox position presents the source of the killing in a dominant (foreground) position. The throughline for this sequence is the chaos on the beach. Miller loses his hearing from a shrapnel hit close by. He looks about on the beach. A soldier with a flamethrower blows up. Another soldier loses his arm. The soldier searches out his arm and carries it looking for someone to help him. A landing craft is on fire. The soldiers on it exit ablaze. Miller empties his helmet of blood. His face is splattered with blood. The overall feeling of this sequence is beauty, stillness; there shouldn't be so much blood and death, but there is. But it's a stylized death, almost abstract. The feeling in this sequence is surprise that death can't be evaded and, as a consequence, a feeling of helplessness, of victimization. Close-ups and less pace are used in this sequence.

4. Movement Off the Beach

Now the sequences increase in length. Until now there have been modest narrative goals in each of the sequences; in essence, they have been more about creating a feeling than about narrative complexity. This sequence begins as a soldier in close-up tries to speak to Miller. Miller's hearing returns and his message is simple—get off this beach or die. Here the camera sits low and the telephoto lens compresses and cramps the men. The cutaway to the German machine gun creates a sense of proximity—they can't miss the Americans on the beach. The wounded scream. The shot of a gut-shot soldier is lengthy, almost endlessly painful. Miller attempts to drag a wounded man up to medical attention on the beach. By the time he reaches his goal, the wounded man is hit by shrapnel and all that is left is a body part. The feeling state is one of overwhelming chaos, violent death, and growing helplessness. So far the landing is an unmitigated disaster.

5. Up to the Perimeter

If the earlier sequences were characterized by victimization, chaos, and death, this next sequence begins specifically to move the audience away from the sense of victimization and helplessness that has prevailed until now. The focus is on Captain Miller and on movement. Handheld movement from Miller's point of view, complete with his breathlessness, creates the feeling level of this sequence. Miller reaches the barbed wire at the hill embankment where he attempts to assess the situation. He establishes radio contact with Command and lets them know that Dog One of Dog Green Sector is not open. His men—those who have survived—are pinned down. He takes a count of those alive and at the embankment. Sergeant Horvath confirms the situation. There is enormous frustration—the radio man is killed. Medics attending to the wounded on the beach are frustrated and angry as the wounded are killed where they lie as the medics try to stabilize them. This sequence is a transitional sequence; it is the first where there is a feeling of power rather than powerlessness, which is emphasized by the handheld movement up to the embankment. On the other hand, the slaughter of Americans continues.

6. Gather Weapons

The call to action in this scene is marked by quick cuts. The call creates a dynamic sense. Bangalore explosives are rushed to the scene. They are maneuvered into position; again, the handheld shot yields a powerful sense of assertion. The explosives are effectively detonated, creating a path to move up toward the pillbox. Meanwhile, men continue to die. A young soldier takes a bullet in his helmet. Shocked and grateful to be alive, he removes the helmet to admire where the bullet hit. He is shot in the head and dies. Nevertheless there is a dynamic sense in this sequence, a feeling that there have been survivors in Miller's company and that they are beginning to take action against the German enemy. The prevailing feeling of the sequence is dynamic and forceful. The feeling of victimization lessens.

7. Advance on the Pillbox

The throughline in this sequence is attack. In a strategic assessment of the situation, Miller organizes his men and coordinates the attack. In this sequence, his men successfully take the machine gun emplacement to the right of the pillbox. The individual members of Miller's company (later patrol members) are also characterized in this sequence. Jackson the sharpshooter is a religious man; he kisses his crucifix prior to moving up. Fish the Jew provides the captain with gum so that he can create a makeshift periscope using a piece of glass gummed to his bayonet. The action in this sequence is highly fragmented. Spielberg uses many close-ups to identify the individual soldiers and to create the elements that will underscore the attack, particularly the view of the pillbox through the makeshift periscope. Quick images of the pillbox itself suggest its daunting quality from the point of view of these soldiers. Miller is also characterized as experienced and professional in this work. The feeling state in this sequence is mastery. Miller, his sergeant, and those he's working with closely, at least, are professional soldiers. There is a feeling of hope for the first time within the larger 24-minute sequence.

8. Take the Pillbox and the Surrounding Environment
   The sense of action escalates. The members of Miller's company advance their attack on the pillbox. Sharpshooter Jackson eliminates a number of the machine-gunners. He also fires a grenade at the bunker. Closer to the pillbox, grenades are thrown into it. As soldiers exit, they are shot. A torch-thrower advances and burns out the bunker. Burning German soldiers fall from the front of the bunker that had been the platform for firing down on the Americans. As we move through this sequence, the number of telephoto shots that compress context begin to give way to more long shots with visual context. We no longer have the sense that the camera is crowding us. That greater sense of freedom begins to imply that the chaos and killing that have marked the sequences so far is coming to an end.

9. The Beach Is Taken
   Although sporadic shooting continues, this sequence focuses on the men who have survived. Again in close-up, Captain Miller's hands shake as he opens his canteen and drinks from it. Sergeant Horvath packs earth into a tin container marked *France*. He puts it into his knapsack where we see similar cans marked *Italy* and *Africa*. Private Fish simply cries, finally allowing his fear to emerge. The beach, littered with the dead, now becomes the focus of the sequence. There are so many. A long crane shot moves slowly in on one body whose knapsack reads his name, S. Ryan. This sequence is marked by lingering close-ups. The pace is very deliberate, even slow, to bring us to the end of Spielberg's 24-minute minifilm about the D-Day landing.

To sum up, the 24-minute sequence uses the MTV style to create a feeling: what it was like to be on Omaha Beach as an American combatant. The experience is quite unlike any created by a previous war film. This is due to the power of the MTV style.

THE CASE OF ANG LEE'S *CROUCHING TIGER, HIDDEN DRAGON*

The set-piece as a challenge for filmmakers is as old as Griffith's *Intolerance* (1916). The set-piece has ranged from sensational to more purposeful intentions. The attack on the train in Lean's *Lawrence of Arabia* (1962) is spectacle attuned to mythmaking. The cornfield sequence in Hitchcock's *North by Northwest* (1959), on the other hand, is almost academic in its confident approach to the chase. Ranging in between we have the final shootout in Peckinpah's *The Wild Bunch* (1969) and the car chase in Friedkin's *The French Connection* (1971). Filmmakers have even begun to parody those set-pieces. Witness the Spaghetti Westerns of Sergio Leone and the homages of Brian de Palma. The kung fu films of Hong Kong have used such set-pieces to make superheroes of their main characters.

Ang Lee has overtly made a kung fu film in *Crouching Tiger, Hidden Dragon* (2000), but his primary intent is not to create superheroes. He is far more ambitious in his intentions for the set-piece. To explore those intentions, we now turn to *Crouching Tiger, Hidden Dragon*.

Ostensibly the plot revolves around the theft of a famous sword called Green Destiny. Its owner, the great warrior Li Mu Bai, has grown weary of battle; as if in a mood of existential doubt, he decides to give the sword to Sir Te, a trustworthy custodian. He asks Shu Lein, a woman he has long admired, to take the sword to Sir Te. Although Li Mu Bai was trained at Wudan Mountain, a center known for creating the greatest fighters, Shu Lein is also a very capable warrior. From their conversation, we understand that only one who is worthy of carrying it can possess the Green Destiny sword. Two more narrative notations are made in this sequence—that Shu Lein and Li Mu Bai yearn to be together, but something holds them back. The second point is that Li Mu Bai has one adversary, Jade Fox, a woman who killed his master.

The sword is delivered to Peking, and its custodian shows it to Governor Yu, but in short order the sword is stolen. Shu Lein suspects the thief is the Governor's daughter Jen. Jen, who is much younger and very willful, indeed is the thief, but much to our surprise her housekeeper is Jade Fox. Jen is unhappily scheduled to marry, in a politically opportune marriage. She is disinterested, as we discover, because she loves the bandit Lo, known as Dark Cloud. In a flashback into the past, Dark Cloud stole Jen's comb, and she pursued him into his home territory. There on the desert steppes of China they fought and fell in love.

The story line then follows the Green Destiny sword. First it is recovered by Li Mu Bai, who attempts to encourage Jen to become his student. (He admires her skills.) Jen in turn steals the sword again after Dark Cloud breaks up her wedding party. She runs off but soon encounters Shu Lein and then Li Mu Bai. She is captured by Jade Fox, drugged, and has to be rescued by Li Mu Bai. There Jade Fox is finally killed, but not before she has poisoned Li Mu Bai with a poison dart. Jen attempts to make the antidote for the poison but returns too late. Shu Lein sends her to her love, Dark Cloud, who waits for her on Wudan Mountain. The young lovers are reunited, and Jen, asking Lo to make a wish, leaps into the air, to descend to the desert where they can once again be alone and together. The older would-be lovers, Li Mu Bai and Shu Lein, have earlier sworn loyalty and love to one another and express the wish to be reunited together in heaven.

Crouching Tiger, Hidden Dragon, ostensibly an action-adventure film, is actually also a melodrama about two capable women, Shu Lein and Jen. They struggle with traditional values and modern values, the society and the individual. Jen represents modern values, and she alone achieves a union with her lover Lo (Dark Cloud). Shu Lein, on the other hand, represents the forces of tradition; because, years before, her fiancé died before they married, she could not accept Li Mu Bai's attentions, nor could he offer them as he wished. Both were bound by tradition, and consequently their love was always platonic rather than physically manifest. Together, these two women represent the deep struggle for so many women in the world today: Should I make my own way above all, or should the family and tradition take precedence? This is the context for the set-pieces in *Crouching Tiger, Hidden Dragon*.

The Set-Pieces

The set-pieces are approached with the MTV style. They are, in effect, self-contained, stand-alone experiences. They may or may not add to the progress of the narrative. They may or may not help the narrative build. It's my contention that the set-pieces in *Crouching Tiger,*

Hidden Dragon bend the narration away from the traditional exciting impact of a superhero saving society from a supervillain. To understand where Ang Lee takes us instead, we need to begin by examining the set-pieces in a more general manner. First, of the six set-pieces in *Crouching Tiger*, a woman participates in each of them. In two of the six, the combatants are both women. A second observation is that a clear death occurs in only one of the set-pieces. This is important because kung fu set-pieces are conventionally marked by multiple deaths in every set-piece. A third observation is that three of the set-pieces take place at night, and of the three that take place in daylight, the environment is unusual and open: one of these takes place in the desert, the other up in the trees.

A final observation is that at least three of the participants—Li Mu Bai, Shu Lein, and Jen—are trained in Wudan; they can move up buildings, fly, and stop, by hand, a poison dart so small it's barely visible to the human eye. Their skills, in other words, go far beyond weaponry and introduce a kinesis not generally associated with skilled warriors. Whether this is supernatural or mind over body, it allows a woman to be strong beyond the weight and muscle of her male opponent, and it also narrows the field of worthy opposition. Only the best, only the most worthy, can fight as these three can.

If the set-pieces are not about primacy through killing, then, what are they about? If I had to articulate the purpose of the set-pieces in *Crouching Tiger, Hidden Dragon*, I would say they have much to do with the four characters who dominate the narrative: the two main characters, Shu Lein and Jen, and their two love choices, Li Mu Bai and Lo. All four are skilled in matters of war, whether from the point of view of self-defense or of attack. But Li Mu Bai in particular is looking for much more. In his restless search, he has chosen to understand and experience the meaning of life first through the sword and later to move beyond the sword. If Li Mu Bai looks for meaning in the sword, Lo sees the sword or combat as a means to an end—to get what you want, whether it is material gain or social status, and be associated with freedom, ferocity, and banditry. Jen seems to want to prove that she is as good as any man. And Shu Lein seems to accept the responsibility and limits of combat—she seems to be the most mature in her articulation of what combat can and does mean.

Each of these characters exhibits skill beyond the ordinary. Their identity issues, confusions, and aspirations imbue the set-pieces with an emotion that the fighting in and of itself cannot yield. The dignity each deports in the fight implies grace, and it is this sense of grace that resonates from the majority of set-pieces. Only the fight at the inn between Jen and a multitude of men does not display such grace; it's the only set-piece that is almost comical in a slight woman's primacy over many large, heavily armed men.

Thus, grace is Ang Lee's goal in the remaining set-pieces. In a practical sense, that sense of grace is achieved through a series of visual strategies. The range of shots moves between medium shots and extreme long shots. Movement is a distinct feature of the shots—movement of the camera as well as movement within the frame. Cutting on movement makes the movement seem more dynamic. Rather than focusing on the immediate danger, Lee is anxious to see the mechanics of the fight-thrust and counterthrust. More distance allows that skill to be in the foreground, as opposed to an anxiety as to who will survive. Overall there is a formal quality to the set-pieces—a quality that makes them ethereal, as if we were watching the combat of two gods rather than a thief and a protector of private property. To get a more detailed sense of this, I turn to the first set-piece in the film—the robbery of the Green Destiny sword.

The First Set-Piece

This set-piece, detailing the robbery of the Green Destiny sword and the consequent escape of its thief, is six minutes long. The theft itself is quick, and the thief quickly overcomes the guard. Once the thief escapes, Shu Lein is alerted and she becomes the primary pursuer. The guard at Sir Te's house also continues the pursuit and is puzzled by the fact that he is led to the house of Governor Yu. The thief will eventually get away when Jade Fox fires a poison dart at Shu Lein. Although she catches the dart, the shift of focus allows the thief to evade capture or harm. Additionally, although we have not been shown the identity of the thief, we note that the thief is slight, and that Jen was shown the Green Destiny sword, as was her father. We also note that Jen's governess is dismissive of people like Shu Lein, although this is not the case for Jen. Consequently, we believe the thief to be Jen. The only surprise is the level of her skill, which is considerable.

The major portion of the set-piece is Shu Lein's pursuit of the thief. They seem equally skilled and inventive in the combat. They also alone have the capacity to climb buildings and to leap or fly in pursuit. The height of the buildings, or their number, don't seem to be a barrier. Both master space in a fashion unavailable to any of the other pursuers. In this sense, until Jade Fox tries to kill Shu Lein, they are in effect alone. Hands, feet, movement, and artifacts all become weapons in the combat. Jen even uses her whole body against Shu Lein.

The feeling that the set-piece creates is that these two women are special warriors; they have a knowledge and skill available to few. Shu Lein also does not kill. She only wants the return of the stolen sword. This implies her values. She doesn't exploit her powers to show her power. She uses her power in service of something worthwhile: the retrieval of the sword. Jen, on the other hand, is less mature. She wants to get away with the theft. Because the subtext of the story is teaching Jen higher values that are in accord with her talent, this exchange with Shu Lein will be her first lesson.

Whereas the narrative has proceeded in a kind of stillness and serenity until now, the tone shifts in the set-piece. First, the theft is exciting. Camera movement and cutting on movement makes the scene dynamic. The flight, particularly of Shu Lein pursuing Jen across rooftops and up the sides of buildings, is utterly graceful. The values of power or violence are nowhere to be seen in the set-piece. The camera moves a good deal; it is often close to the action or, when an extreme long shot is used, the action moves away from the camera position. Again, there is a formal beauty to what we are watching. Once the fighting gets in close, Lee resorts to medium close-ups rather than extreme close-ups. This is not a fight to the death, as in the combat between El Cid and his would-be father-in-law, the King's Champion, in Anthony

Mann's *El Cid* (1961), a scene in which extreme close-ups were integral. Movement, pattern, move, and countermove are more important in Lee's combat than the exercise of power. What more powerful notion can he apply to these two women? Who will be his two main characters? The fight scene is not about primacy; it's about character. This is the subtext to this set-piece as well as to the final one—between Jen and Shu Lein and then Jen and Li Mu Bai.

The six minutes of this set-piece create the feeling that will become the real theme of *Crouching Tiger, Hidden Dragon*. In a world of violence, deceit, and power, grace and inner beauty are offsetting critical values that must prevail, as they certainly do in this narrative.

THE CASE OF *IN THE MOOD FOR LOVE*

Wong Kar-wai's *In the Mood for Love* is ostensibly a very simple love story set in 1962 Hong Kong. Overcrowding leads two young couples to rent rooms with other families. The man, Chow Mo Wan, works in a newspaper office. The woman, Su Li Zhen, works as a secretary for the head of a business. We never see his wife or her husband, but eventually we understand that his wife and her husband have been carrying on an affair. The marriages dissolve, and Chow Mo Wan and Su Li Zhen begin their own affair. The body of the film follows the course of their relationship. The relationship ends when he goes to Singapore. A few years later, he returns and revisits the apartment where she used to live. He discovers that she had a son, and it is implied that the son is his. The film ends with his trip to Cambodia, where he deposits a note in a prayer box.

What is important to say about this film is that Wong Kar-wai is an unusual filmmaker who prefers to work in the experimental narrative form. Like Tom Tykwer in *Run Lola Run* (1999) and Peter Greenaway in *The Draughtsman's Contract* (1982), style is more important than the actual content. The struggle between style and content creates a powerful forum for the voice of the director. The experimental narrative is thus very much about voice. So what is it that Wong Kar-wai wants to say in this simple romantic melodrama? Before we examine how the MTV style helps create his voice, a number of observations need to be put forward.

The first observation is that a story of a romantic relationship between a man and a woman conventionally has a particular progression. They meet, he or she pursues the other, they reach a hurdle, somehow that hurdle is overcome, another crisis develops, and finally the relationship is or is not a success. The story is structured with a beginning, middle, and end, and it is approached through character. Status, background, shared goals, and other elements all factor in to the success or failure of the romance, with all versions of *Romeo and Juliet* at the tragic end of the spectrum, and Nora Ephron's *Sleepless in Seattle* (1993) at the successful end of the spectrum. Wong Kar-wai's narrative follows the expected progression, but he constructs his key scenes out of minute details without actually showing the expected scenes. Consequently, the relationship is alluded to in its progression rather than treated conventionally.

A second observation is that the place, Hong Kong in 1962, is implied rather than actually seen. No cinéma vérité here. Hong Kong is represented by a dark street, a crowded hallway, a restaurant table, and two workstations. There is no sense of crowding beyond the fact that the two couples are renting rooms in the apartments of others. The time, 1962, is implied through the cut of clothing, the hairstyles, and the look of a clock or a restaurant. Time and place are implied rather than pronounced, as was the case with the narrative progression.

A third is that the visual focus is on Chow Mo Wan and Su Li Zhen. His wife and her husband are never seen, and aside from his landlady, his colleague at work, and her boss, there are few other characters on view. This is a Hong Kong that is implied without its mass of people. Perhaps Wong Kar-wai means for it to be a dreamt Hong Kong.

This idea brings us to the director's intention. The narrative is austere, the dialog is austere, and the pace and camera movement are an austere equivalent. But the color, the lingering close-ups of the two characters, and the stylized movements are not austere; they are rich and create the mood appropriate for passion. So too is the music. Wong Kar-wai, through the dissonance between style and content, is trying to create the mood of a doomed love story. Whether he is trying to say that loneliness is the human condition or whether his Hong Kong is a unique barrier to "being together" is for you to decide. What can be said is that Wong Kar-wai employs MTV style to show how passion can only be sustained for a short time in a relationship.

The MTV Style of *In the Mood for Love*

Wong Kar-wai uses two pieces of music a number of times in *In the Mood for Love*. One is a Spanish number sung by Nat King Cole, the other a romantic lament without lyrics. These pieces of music provide the shape for the set-pieces. Within the set-piece, the music creates an aura of tremendous anticipation and romanticism. Visually, Wong Kar-wai presents movement.

Chow Mo Wan smokes a cigarette under a street light. The smoke focuses our attention on his sense of anticipation. Su Li Zhen walks by. The visuals focus on the rhythm of her movement. It's as if she glides. She is swinging a pot of soup, and it too has a rhythm that Wong Kar-wai notes. His stillness, the movement of the smoke, her movement, the soup pot—all project an erotic possibility of their meeting. The movement is slowed down, the smoke is slowed down, and both together with the music build a sense of anticipation. What the sequence leaves us with is a mood, a feeling of desire, of his desire for her.

Wong Kar-wai puts forward similar sequences as Chow Mo Wan and Su Li Zhen joust early in their relationship, then bicker later in the relationship, as one feels disappointed in the other. All the while, Wong Kar-wai shows us duplicity in other male–female relationships. Nevertheless, the prevailing focus is the moods that mark the phases of the main characters' relationship. The short movements, the extreme close-ups, and the clarity of composition, together with the romantic lighting, all support the overall romantic feeling—the longing—that pervades the set-pieces. This longing in turn becomes the overall feeling accentuated by the dominance of style over content in *In the Mood for Love*.

THE CASE OF *LIFE IS BEAUTIFUL*

Roberto Benigni's *Life Is Beautiful* (1997) is unusual in that its set-pieces are concept-driven and their pace has almost no role in their effectiveness. They are, nevertheless, an example of the MTV style. Rather than looking to the historical examples mentioned earlier in this chapter, it's more meaningful to look at Charlie Chaplin's *Modern Times* (1936) and Woody Allen's *Sleeper* (1975).

Like those comedies, which were built up around the persona of the actor–director, *Life Is Beautiful* is a fable of which the moral is that love can sustain us through terrible life experiences. Guido Orefice is a young man who comes to the city of Arezzo to follow his dream: to set up a bookstore. But the time is 1939 and Guido, as we discover 40 minutes into the story, is a Jew. The narrative is organized in two distinct sections. The first half is 1939 Arezzo, and the focus is Guido's pursuit of his dreams, particularly to catch his princess, Dora. He achieves his goal, snatching Dora from the arms of a local bureaucrat on the very evening of her engagement party. This part of the narrative focuses on the barriers to Guido's dreams: He needs a permit to open a bookstore—a permit that has to be signed by the very same bureaucrat who is to marry Dora; he is a Jew, an already persecuted minority; he takes work of low status when he becomes a waiter. Nevertheless, his persistence and his inventiveness win over his princess, who is not Jewish.

The second half of the film takes place in 1944. He is now married to Dora, and they have a young son, Joshua. He also has a bookstore, albeit not commercially successful. But he does have a wonderful, playful relationship with his son. In short order, he and his son are picked up and shipped off to a concentration camp in northern Italy. Dora chooses to go as well. At the camp the issue is survival, as the old and the young are quickly gassed and their bodies burned. Guido makes up a game to help his son: If you earn 1000 points, you will win a real tank. But to do so Joshua must listen, pretend he doesn't want snacks with jam, and generally follow his father's enthusiastic lead. Guido also finds various ways to communicate with the women's barracks that he and Joshua are alive. In this sense, he keeps both his wife and his son alive. The game continues to the last night in the concentration camp, when the Germans kill all the prisoners they can before they abandon the camp due to the arrival of the Americans. Guido dies, but not before he has saved his son. Even at this last stage, he has made a game of survival.

Before we look at the three set-pieces composing the body of the narrative, let me make a few points. First, the tone, as one would expect in a fable, is not realistic. It is formal and rather fantastic, as one finds in hyperdramas[1] such as Volker Schlöndorff's *The Tin Drum* (1979) and Robert Zemeckis's *Forrest Gump* (1994).

Second, the concept that shapes the set-pieces arises out of the fable's moral. The narrative as a whole, as well as the set-pieces, follows the same progression: a character is hopeful, even enthusiastic; a misfortune befalls him and then, arising out of the misfortune, he finds good fortune. In other words, goodness and love prevail in spite of personal loss of economic status, freedom, and even life itself. It's as if the Holocaust itself cannot dim the will of a father that his child be a child, that games, playfulness, and creativity can actually crowd out deprivation, pain, loss, and tragedy. To understand how Benigni conveys the moral, we turn to three set-pieces in different phases of the narrative.

The Set-Pieces in *Life Is Beautiful*

The first set-piece we examine occurs in the early part of the film. Guido has come to the city office, where he will apply for a permit to establish a bookstore. He has only recently arrived in the city. The first phase of the set-piece is Guido's enthusiasm to get on with his dream. He is told that it's lunchtime and the person who needs to sign will now go for lunch. When he complains, he is told that the next person who can sign will arrive in one hour. Guido quickly gets into an argument with the bureaucrat, who now leaves. Upset, Guido looks out the window, accidentally pushing a flowerpot off the window ledge. The pot shatters on the head of the bureaucrat.

Guido rushes out to apologize. He places his hat, which has raw eggs in it, on an adjacent car. The bureaucrat tells Guido he will never get the needed signature, mistakenly picks up the hat with the eggs, and puts it on his head. The eggs crack and the bureaucrat, humiliated again, is infuriated. He begins to pursue Guido, who borrows a bicycle. As he flees he crashes into the woman of his dreams, Dora, whom he refers to as princess. This is their second accidental meeting. The misfortune of losing the chance to apply for the bookstore and of being pursued by an angry bureaucrat turns into the good fortune of finding Dora again. Throughout the set-piece, Guido has maintained a high level of energy, first as enthusiasm, then as indignation, and finally as passion. The feeling created by the set-piece is that his career will persevere in spite of setbacks.

The next set-piece I will refer to as the Engagement Party. The set-piece occurs in the restaurant where Guido works as a waiter. Tonight the bureaucrat will announce his engagement to the reluctant Dora. She is clearly being prompted by her mother to be enthusiastic about this relationship.

The set-piece begins with the reluctant Dora hiding in her dress under her bedcovers, and ends with her riding off on a horse with Guido. The scene is filled with signs of misfortune for Guido: his uncle's white horse has been painted green to designate it as a Jewish horse; a stuffed ostrich sits atop the celebratory "Ethiopian" engagement cake (a reference to Italy's territorial ambitions); and a live poodle ends up decorating Guido's serving tray. The scene has a serious intention, but absurdity abounds. Finally, to get away from the absurdity, Dora sees Guido hiding under her table and decides to join him in order to declare her love. He is clearly her type of man. He takes her home and, within the same shot, five years have passed. We understand that time has passed because a child emerges from the door that Guido and

Dora just entered. The feeling created in this set-piece is that society is becoming absurd and that Guido's imaginative nonconformity seems sane in comparison.

The third set-piece takes place late in the film. I will call it A Good Lunch in the Concentration Camp. Guido now works as a waiter in the mess hall. A German doctor he knew in Arezzo is now the camp doctor. That day, a group of officer's children are brought to the camp. They play on the grounds and Guido encourages Joshua to play as well. When the children are called to lunch, a matron mistakes Joshua for a German child. Guido tells him to be silent, for any speech would give away that he is Italian. And so Joshua goes to lunch where his father will be one of the waiters, but he is playing the "be quiet game," according to his father. As he is offered food and being polite, he says "grazie" to the German waiter. The waiter rushes for the matron—an Italian boy is among the Aryan youngsters. Guido hastily organizes a game among the German children. By the time the matron and waiter appear, all the children are saying "grazie." Playing a children's game has saved Joshua. Satiated with food, the boy goes to sleep at the table. Guido then puts Offenbach on the gramophone and points it out of the windows.

His wife hears and goes to the window. Guido is saving her as well, in this case by keeping her spirits up—he and their son are alive, and seemingly well. Once again Guido's attitude and his active imagination have saved his family. The feeling in this set-piece is that play, in essence, children's games, are curative.

None of these set-pieces are fast-paced; in fact, each is very deliberate, even slow. But each has a concept at its core, and each confirms the moral of the fable—that love can help you overcome any adversity.

THE CASE OF *TAMPOPO*

The MTV style was used to create a chaotic context for the main character in *Saving Private Ryan*. The result is to pose the question—*how* will he survive?—rather than the traditional question about the main character in a war film—*will* he survive? In *Crouching Tiger, Hidden Dragon*, the MTV style realigns our expectations of the kung fu adventure film. And in *Life Is Beautiful*, the MTV style reiterates the central theme of the narrative. In each case, the MTV style has had a relation to the narrative, either deepening or altering that narrative. The MTV style is deployed for an altogether different purpose in Juzo Itami's *Tampopo* (1987). In *Tampopo*, the MTV style is altogether distinct from the narrative. What it does add is the powerful statement of mood: a mood that acts against the narrative content. The ironic tone created is the vehicle for Itami's voice.

The main narrative follows how a stranger helps a young widow transform her ordinary noodle shop into the "best noodle shop in Tokyo." This seems like a modest enough tale, but Itami approaches the story by borrowing heavily from Kurosawa and his epic "Western" *Seven Samurai* (1954), which was later remade by John Sturges as *The Magnificent Seven* (1960).

This epic treatment means that the mentor character, here called Goro, has to assemble a group that can help Tampopo "save" her shop. They include an impudent young man, a "fallen" older doctor, a rich man's valet, and a rough and tumble builder. Tampopo's young son is also a member of these unlikely helpers. Goro, by the way, always appears in the film wearing a cowboy hat. The opposition to Tampopo is composed of other noodle shop owners, and, appropriately, each acts as if he were a cattle baron whose wealth is under threat from the suspicious Goro and the modest Tampopo. Soup preparation, noodle composition, pork fat—each is treated like the weaponry in a Western.

The tone Itami uses is ironic and filled with allusion to the Western genre. Occasionally Itami will also reference the gangster film. Itami effectively establishes the tone by framing the narrative, first as a film and then as a pulp novel. In the opening, a gangster, dressed like a dandy, enters a cinema with his retinue. He sets up in the first row, complete with champagne. He acknowledges that a film will be seen, then he issues a warning to a viewer: No loud eating during the film; it's rude and will lead to the viewer's violent end at the gangster's hand. Then he allows the film to proceed. In the next scene, a young man is instructed on how to eat good noodle soup. This extended introduction to soup is then acknowledged as the visualization of a book being read by a truck driver. The truck drivers are hungry and decide to stop at a noodle shop. One of them is Goro, and what follows is his introduction to Tampopo. Later in the narrative, whenever Itami feels the need (there is no logic to these set-pieces), he wanders away from the narrative into an MTV set-piece. Each set-piece has something to do with eating. A number of set-pieces have to do with the gangster from the opening. Others simply stand alone.

Before we proceed to look at two of these set-pieces, here is a summary of their context:

1. A narrative that is essentially a melodrama is treated as a Western.
2. The Itami voice is highlighted by a sense of irony about Japanese social conventions as well as filmic narrative conventions.
3. Food—its importance and its elevation to a status beyond simple eating—unites the narrative as well as the set-pieces.
4. The tone is extreme, running from playful to absurd; to put it another way, the tone is widely variable.

The Set-Pieces in *Tampopo*

The first set-piece, which occurs in the first third of the film, focuses on dining. A group of Japanese businessmen eats in the exclusive dining room of a high-class hotel. The cuisine is French. The group is principally elderly with the exception of one young man. As the waiter requests everyone's order one of the elderly gentlemen places his—a simple fish dish, beer and soup, and no salad. As the waiter moves around the table, others replicate the order of the "leader" of the group. As the waiter comes to the young man clearly the pressure is on—conform. But he doesn't. He recognizes the menu as a replication of the number one restaurant in Paris. He then proceeds to order snails and a special champagne, much to the consternation of his colleagues. Clearly, he is an individual among corporate conformists.

The scene shifts to another dining room in the hotel. A "group leader" is teaching young Japanese women the etiquette of eating spaghetti. The procedure is formal, slow, and silent.

The young women are very attentive. Close by, an American is served spaghetti. He proceeds to eat it vigorously and messily. The young women are taken with his zeal, and they proceed to noisily eat their spaghetti. Finally the group leader succumbs. She too begins to eat her spaghetti noisily.

This set-piece is all about conformity among the upper class. What Itami is saying is "enjoy yourself—conventions be damned." What is important is to be yourself and to enjoy yourself. The set-piece is ironic and humorous. It's difficult to remember, but as he reminds us: it's only lunch.

The second set-piece takes place early in the second half of the film. All efforts to learn the secret of making exceptional broth for the noodle soup have failed, and so Goro takes Tampopo to see "the doctor." He is an old man and a homeless person, living among other vagrants—in effect a community of the homeless. The "doctor" left his practice and family for this new life. Goro enlists the doctor in Tampopo's cause. As Tampopo's son is hungry, one of the doctor's colleagues, a "chef," takes the boy to the local hotel. There he breaks into the kitchen and proceeds to make him a rice omelet. The cooking is precise, and the effort yields perfection. They steal away as the hotel security guard inspects the kitchen where a light suggests mischief. They get away and the boy has a great meal.

The notion that a cooking genius resides in a group of homeless people offers the opposite end of the social spectrum from the first set-piece. Indeed, the sense of togetherness, respect, and aesthetic cooking sensibility all suggest the opposite of the earlier scene, in which conformity and class were the order in approaching the what and how of eating.

Again, irony abounds in this set-piece, but what is also critical at its core is the sense of an aesthetic about food, its creation, and its consumption. As in the first set-piece, there is considerable surprise here—surprise at individual behavior and surprise about individual values. Finally, as in the first set-piece, there is enormous humor. The creation of an omelet is treated with a reverence deserving of the creation of something far greater. Or perhaps Itami is saying that it all stops here, at the eye, the mouth, and the stomach. In the end, we are what we eat and how we eat it. The feeling state Itami is working with is to elevate originality in all its aspects.

CONCLUSION

Whether the purpose of the set-piece is to highlight the voice of the author, as in the case of Itami, or to subvert the genre expectation, as in Ang Lee's *Crouching Tiger, Hidden Dragon*, the MTV set-piece is a powerful tool in the filmmaker's tool box. Its use often alters conventional narrative. Used strategically, that alteration can add meaning to the narrative, as in Spielberg's *Saving Private Ryan*, or it can tilt our experience toward feeling and mood rather than narrative, as in Wong Kar-wai's *In the Mood for Love*. In either case, the MTV style has a powerful impact.

NOTE/REFERENCE

1. See discussion of hyperdrama in K. Dancyger. The Centrality of Metagenre in Global Scriptwriting, Focal Press, Boston, 2001, pp. 197–208. Hyperdrama is a genre structured as a moral fable for adults. It is plot-driven, varying in tone, and usually far from realism. It is characterized by the distinctive voice of its author.

CHAPTER 13

Changes in Pace

Pace has been a critical editing tool since D. W. Griffith perfected the chase sequence. Although an existing dramatic climax was Griffith's goal, the purpose of pace has proved far more diverse over time. The context of this diversity begins with Sergei Eisenstein. German expressionists such as F. W. Murnau moved the camera to avoid editing; Eisenstein built upon Griffith's ideas about pace and brought more rapid editing into filmmaking with a political rather than an entertainment agenda. In films memorializing the revolutionary spirit (*Stachka* [*Strike*], *Bronenosets Potyomkin* [*Potemkin*]) and collectivization (*Staroye inovoye* [*The General Line*]), Eisenstein worked out his theory of montage: pace, or metric montage, was one of its central traits. The core issue for Eisenstein was conflictual—the ordinary sailor against his officers, the oppressed workers against their rulers, the people against the czar. Pace was used to juxtapose oppression and political action in the most powerful fashion. Eisenstein was not afraid to exploit the emotionalism inherent in the audience's relationship with the film medium. Pace promoted that emotionalism and its exploitation.

EVOLUTION OF PACE IN FILMMAKING

Eisenstein opened the door on the issue of pace, and a wide variety of filmmakers walked through that door. King Vidor effectively used pace to build an aesthetic tension in the march through the woods sequence in *The Big Parade* (1925). Walter Ruttmann used pace to capture the energy of the city in *Berlin: Symphony of a Great City* (1927). And Frank Capra used pace to energize his dialog-heavy narrative in *You Can't Take It with You* (1938). The great leaps forward, however, would await the 1950s. In that decade, with Akira Kurosawa's dynamic use of pace in *Rashomon*—together with Alfred Hitchcock's set-pieces in *The Man Who Knew Too Much* and, in 1960, *Psycho*—new pathways emerged, suggesting that pace could be used for more diverse purposes.

In *Rashomon*, Kurosawa presents four versions of the same story, each from a different person's point of view. The interpretations vary widely. Kurosawa's main editing device to underscore the differences in view is variation in the pace of each of the four stories. In the Hitchcock instance, the shower scene in *Psycho* has become the second most famous set piece

193

in the history of film, and at its editing core the changes in pace are what move the sequence from anticipation, to the violence of the killing, to the stillness of death.

The next significant development in the use of pace was seen in the work of Richard Lester in the Beatles films *A Hard Day's Night* and *Help!*. Their dynamic mixture of movement, jump-cutting, and variations in point of view (performers, audience, and the media) created a filmic persona of youthful energy and joyful anarchy. There is little question that the effective use of pace in these films accelerated—dare I say—the *pace* of pace in film. After *A Hard Day's Night*, commercials and feature films were cut faster.

The next step in the use of pace seemed on one level a reversion to the ideas of Eisenstein. Sam Peckinpah's *The Wild Bunch*—particularly in its opening and climactic set-pieces, a robbery and a massacre—relies on modulation of pace to create a sense of the chaos of violence. Building out from the death scene in Arthur Penn's *Bonnie and Clyde*, the massacre that ends in the death of the final four members of *The Wild Bunch* seems the ultimate use of pace to mesmerize and simultaneously horrify its audience. At this point, pace seems to affiliate with particular genres—the police story in *The French Connection* (1971), the gangster film in *Scarface* (1983), the thriller in *Jaws* (1975), and the war film in *Apocalypse Now* (1979). In each genre and film, a different purpose might be served, but, in general, the mix of excitement and insight into the fragmented psychology of the main character captures the intent.

Perhaps no filmmaker best encapsulated both of these agendas—excitement and insight—as did Oliver Stone in his 25 years of work as a director, from *Salvador* (1986) through *Natural Born Killers*. Stone, in his use of pace, seems to be the direct descendant of Sergei Eisenstein by way of Sam Peckinpah.

For each of these filmmakers, pace was the primary editing strategy for their storytelling agenda. Each wanted to move their audience by marrying an aggressive editing style to highly political, or at least politicized, content.

Although pace has been more recently affiliated with action directors such as McG (*Charlie's Angels*) and Tony Scott (*Man on Fire*), the most aggressive use of pace has been demonstrated by John Woo in his action-adventure renditions of police and gangster films (*The Replacement Killers*). The most consistent exploration of pace and its possibilities can be found in the work of Steven Spielberg, from *Saving Private Ryan* (1998) to *War of the Worlds* (2005). In order to clarify the changes in the use of pace, we now turn to its use in four different genres, starting with the docudrama.

Pace in the Docudrama

Jean-Pierre and Luc Dardenne made *Rosetta* in 1999. Since then, they have continued to refine their approach in *Le Fils* (*The Son*) (2003) and *L'Enfant* (*The Child*) (2005). The style is essentially a cinéma vérité approach—handheld camera and the absence of lights and music.

Rosetta is the story of a 17-year-old girl. The film begins with her being forced from a factory job, and essentially the film follows her efforts to secure a full-time job in order to stabilize a life marked by a trailer-park existence caring for an alcoholic mother. A young man (Riquet) who works at a local waffle stand is interested in Rosetta. He confides in her and shelters her. In the end, she betrays him to his boss to secure his job. Riquet has been making waffles at home and selling them at the stand—in effect, stealing from his boss. Rosetta reports him and gets his job, but life is too challenging. She gives up the job and the film ends with Rosetta unsure about the future—not knowing whether she should take up with the young man or continue her hand-to-mouth existence.

The locations for *Rosetta* are the workplace, the waffle stand, the young man's apartment, and the trailer park. The trailer park particularly seems rural and cut off from the city. A muddy-bottomed river that passes through the trailer park represents a constant threat to it; there is no pastoral sense in this film.

The Dardenne brothers rely on a handheld camera positioned close to the characters, particularly Rosetta. They stay close, yielding few long or locating shots. Their preferences are close-ups, but they occasionally include midshots to allow for two characters in the frame. Pace is accelerated by a reliance on jump cutting, both in simple locations and between locations. In *Rosetta*, the Dardenne brothers are using pace principally to capture Rosetta's fierceness, her means to have what she calls "a job in order to have a normal life." This fierceness is illustrated in the opening. Rosetta is fired from her factory job. Her resistance is powerful as she tries to stay, in the end requiring security to escort her out when the efforts of the boss prove insufficient. The moving camera, the jump cutting, and the pace of this sequence palpably demonstrate Rosetta's fierceness. This quality seems to be the primary purpose of pace in the film.

A secondary purpose of the pace is to capture the instability of Rosetta's life. Her mother's condition leads the mother to be promiscuous with the caretaker of the trailer park. The caretaker plies the mother with liquor, while Rosetta attempts to moderate her drinking. Rosetta is, at different points in the narrative, facing a dire financial situation. At one point, she sells her clothes to raise cash. Her attempt to do so takes her to various secondhand outlets. Then there is a point in the film when Rosetta secures a job assisting the baker who owns the waffle outlet. The job ends after a few days, when the baker chooses to employ his ne'er-do-well son instead.

Rosetta's desperation and her refusal to accept the situation are desperate moments for her character—she wants nothing more than a normal life. At each of these points in the film, the Dardenne brothers use pace to capture the instability of Rosetta's situation. Her reactions, together with the pace, serve to demonstrate the depth of her desire and desperation. Pace has rarely so powerfully evoked the inner life of a character.

Pace in the Thriller

The docudrama as a genre tends to emphasize the voice of the filmmakers. How we feel about the conflict between Rosetta's fierce desire for a normal life and the very instability of her life is the space the Dardennes want their audience to occupy. How do we feel about the space they have trapped us in? The thriller as a genre has quite a different goal. Above all, it's a more entertainment-oriented goal and, consequently, pace takes on differing purposes in the thriller.

For the most part, the thriller is the story of an ordinary person caught in extraordinary circumstances. If he doesn't figure out by who and why he is being pursued, he will, in short order, be dead. If he prevails, he will be a hero. In Paul Greengrass's *The Bourne Supremacy* (2004), the main character, Bourne, isn't ordinary. He's a CIA-trained killer. But his adversaries are not the usual run-of-the-mill killers, either. Here, Bourne is being pursued by the CIA and a Russian supercriminal. Before this thriller begins to sound like the ultimate action-adventure film, a number of character and story details will serve to humanize the main character.

Jason Bourne has amnesia, and Marie, the woman he lives with, tries to help piece together his past. He knows he has killed others. He also knows he has instincts that help protect life, but he can't save Marie. In the first 10 minutes of the film, he is blamed for killing two CIA operatives in Berlin. The real killer has planted Bourne's fingerprint at the scene. And he tracks Bourne down in Goa, India. There, in his attempt to kill Bourne, he kills Marie instead. In the balance of the film, Bourne will attempt to stop the CIA, who he believes is trying to kill him. He will also recover the memory of his last time in Berlin. There, his first assignment was to kill a Russian dissident politician. Finding the politician's wife in the room, Bourne killed her as well. Realizing his past deeds, he goes to Moscow to seek out the daughter of his two victims. He tells her how her parents died, in the hope that the truth (she was led to believe at the time of her parents' deaths that the two were a murder–suicide) will help the teenager. In Moscow, Bourne is pursued, in a high-speed chase, by Marie's killer. During that chase, the killer is killed.

What is also useful to the sense of the story is that the women in the film (Marie; Pamela Landy and Nicky, both with the CIA; and the Russian victims' daughter), each in their way, are helpful to Bourne. All of the men (Russian, American, and German) are against him. Paul Greengrass, the director, also made the docudramas *Bloody Sunday* (2002) and *United 93*, and his approach to *The Bourne Supremacy* is to treat events and people as realistically as possible. Pace plays a very important role in the creation of that sense of realism.

Let's look at the way Greengrass characterizes Bourne's struggle against his loss of memory. The film opens with a series of quick images—city lights, a hotel room, a body. The images pass by quickly. They are presented as recaptured fragments of Bourne's memory. They are fleeting and they are frustrating. Together, they yield a logical explanation. As we move farther into the narrative and to Bourne's return to the city where the crime took place, and to the room where he killed the diplomat and his wife, the pace slows down and we're given fuller information. But the movement—from the fragmentary opening to the gains in memory Bourne makes—illustrates how Greengrass opts to use pace. He's using it to give us insight into the personal problem, which is the memory loss, and into the means by which the character recovers his memory. Pace is the key to the pictorialization of the problem and to its solution.

Another purpose for the use of pace is to illustrate Bourne's instinctual survivalist skills. On one level, his are lethal skills. But on the level of characterization, they illustrate a level of training that has made him anticipate and react instantly to that threat. There is a point in the film at which Bourne has been apprehended by customs officials in Naples. He is traveling under his own name rather than under the assumed identity he so often uses. A CIA operative has entered the room to interrogate Bourne. Bourne is nonresponsive. A call comes in telling the agent that Bourne is dangerous. As soon as the agent begins to reach for his gun, a rapid-fire Bourne disarms and disables him as well as the two Italian Customs police.

The characteristic instinct is even more rapid when Bourne visits another CIA "killer" in Munich. They are the only two of their kind still alive. Yet each is wary of the other. Bourne has the man secure his own hands. Nevertheless, a fight to the death ensues. This proceeds so speedily and with such a clear goal—each striving to ensure the death of the other—that the pace is breathtaking, all in the service of conveying just how dangerous and capable these men are. This editing approach is used at least a half-dozen times; each time it's exhilarating and convinces us that Jason Bourne is not a man to go quietly into the night.

A third and perhaps the most dramatic use of pace in this thriller is in the narrative, particularly in the plot. The scene in which Marie is killed is a pursuit, a car chase through Goa's streets, back alleys, and bridges. Greengrass must keep the narrative clear, yet capture Bourne's determination to escape as well as the killer's goal, the killing of Bourne. Greengrass focuses on the details such as Bourne switching out of the driver's seat in order to be able to return fire. The killer fires at the driver and kills Marie. The pace of this scene focuses on chaos and credibility, while including those critical shots needed to clarify the narrative progression of the scene. The pace is appropriate and effective to the narrative goals of the characters.

This editing idea is even more dynamically present in the climactic confrontation between Bourne and the killer on the streets of Moscow. The information that the killer is from the Secret Service, that he has telephone communication about Bourne's whereabouts, and that he all but owns the streets of Moscow, contrasted with a wounded Bourne (shot by the killer) commandeering a cab and fleeing for his life through the streets of the city. Add to this a high-speed chase that ends in an underground tunnel in a shootout between Bourne and the killer. When Bourne shoots out the killer's tires, the killer's car smashes into a concrete pillar.

The pace of this chase differs from the car chase in *The French Connection*, in which the goal was to emphasize the crazy determination of a policeman in pursuit of a French gangster who tried to kill him. It also differs from the chase in *Bullitt* (1968), which is all about the excitement and the thrills of a pursuit through the hilly streets of San Francisco. In *The Bourne Supremacy*, the pace is deployed to make the chase realistic, and to keep the chaotic narrative utterly clear. Greengrass succeeds in these goals. As in the other uses of pace in the film, Greengrass never forgets that editing is in service of a larger directorial idea, in this case making that narrative seem utterly realistic.

Pace in the Action-Adventure

Another genre that has used pace as an important feature is the action-adventure film. Pace has long been an exciting feature of the action-adventure films, some of the best examples being found in the opening and the horse-truck chase in *Raiders of the Lost Ark*. Here the thrill of the chase is vitalized by the use of pace. Pace has been used to heighten the tension and amplify the stakes in Michael Bay's *Armageddon* (1997) and Roland Emmerich's *Independence Day* (1996). And pace has been used to amplify the status of the main character, in essence, to verify that he and his colleagues are superheroes, as in Antoine Fuqua's *King Arthur* (2004). But Zhang Yimou uses pace in a more subtle and surprising way in his film *Ying xiong* (*Hero*) (2002).

Hero uses stillness and pace juxtaposed to create a more formal quality to the narrative. *Hero* is the story of a nameless assassin (played by Jet Li). His ostensible role is to be rewarded by the Emperor for destroying the Emperor's most powerful enemies, Sky, Flying Snow, and Broken Sword. By giving the broken silver spear of Sky to the Emperor, the assassin gains access and proximity to the Emperor. Although he has been thoroughly searched, the assassin's proximity will allow him to quickly capture the Emperor's own sword and kill him with it. The film unfolds in the recounting of the assassin's heroic actions in defeating the above-mentioned powerful adversaries of the Emperor. Each story moves the assassin from the initial 100 paces away from the Emperor, finally to within 10 paces from the Emperor. When he has finally reached his goal of 10 paces, the assassin finds he cannot kill a man who has proved to have intelligence and vision as a leader. In the end, the assassin leaves the palace and is killed by the Emperor's archers. It is as heroic a death as his three accomplices had achieved. The film ends alluding to the greatness of the Emperor, who during his reign united all of China. Zhang Yimou stages his film as a meditation on what a hero truly is.

Although his focus is upon four assassins and an Emperor, and a plot by the four to kill the Emperor, he is more interested in the inner life of each person, rather than the outcome. In short, this action-adventure film is all about character. Inner life is about passion, whether it is love of another or love of one's country. Each of these characters, including the Emperor, has passion to burn. Consequently, outer life—who wins material goods or honors or competitions—is less valued than is the fire that burns within.

Zhang Yimou uses a strategy about pace in order to pictorialize the inner life and the outer life. Because the outer life is less subtle, we turn to pace and life in the world first. The aspects of outer life—essentially, the battle of the Emperor's army of invasion, the palace guard protecting the Emperor, and the battle of the assassin with Sky and later with Flying Snow—are dynamic and staged with a static camera and much cutting between extreme long shots and close-ups. The juxtaposition is dynamic but the stillness of the camera position modifies the pace. It is dynamic, but formal—far from the chaos that pace creates in *The Wild Bunch*. Here the pace almost stylizes the battles. Clearly, personal power and military power are at stake, but the formal pace does not exploit the clash of powerful people or armies. Rather, the pace juxtaposes those sources of power, creating wonderment rather than conflict, beauty rather than strength.

Zhang Yimou's use of pace to create the inner sense of the character is far more subtle. Here he jump cuts in on the character's faces, almost seeking revelation or true emotion or intention. The fight between Sky and the assassin is revealing: Zhang Yimou jump cuts into the eyes or face at oblique angles, so that we don't see the whole face. Something is revealed, but, visually, part of the face is also withheld. Or the focus is on the clash of the weapons—sword and spear. The weapons become part of each combatant's body, providing an insight into how each man views his weapon. It is not a killing instrument, it is part of him. Again, pace reveals the inner life of Sky. Zhang Yimou uses the same approach to Broken Sword's calligraphy. The intent is to move away from the man as assassin and to reveal what is most meaningful to him. The use of pace in the attack on the calligraphy school, and Broken Sword's response to being under attack from a barrage of arrows from the Emperor's army, tell us much about Broken Sword. Pace is used to reveal not his tension, but rather his inner tranquility.

Pace in the Musical

We turn now to the musical, a genre that is essentially a wish-fulfillment narrative focusing on "putting on the show" and a main character that is a performer who is unseasoned or overseasoned. The show will launch or relaunch the main character's career and secure a relationship with the leading lady. On both the plot and the character relationship levels, the character gets what he wants.

Most classic musicals, including George Stevens's *Swing Time* (1936) and Stanley Donen's *Singin' in the Rain* (1952), follow the Busby Berkeley lead and take a mise-en-scène approach to the edit, essentially avoiding editing to capture the choreography of performance, rather than fragmenting the performance using the edit. In this sense, editing is seen as an intervention into the performance.

Moving the camera was the preferred choice. Everything changed when Bob Fosse made *Cabaret* (1972), and later *All That Jazz* (1979; not quite a musical). In these films, pace became a dynamic option that Fosse integrated into the choreography of a performed song. Alan Parker followed with *Fame* (1980), Adrian Lyne followed with *Flashdance* (1983), and a kind of MTV approach became an important framework for actively using pace in the musical.

When Baz Luhrmann made *Moulin Rouge!* (2001), the use of pace in the musical changed again. Luhrmann's agenda was to use pace to not only play with his love of the musical, but also to articulate the joy of love, the pain of love, and the depth of desire. Of course, he also wanted to articulate the love of performance as well as love for people.

Moulin Rouge! tells the story of Christian, a writer who comes to Paris to write about love. But he doesn't know anything about love. In Montmartre, he falls in with a group of Bohemian housemates—performers, writers, musicians. When the group's writer is overtaken by his condition, narcolepsy, they turn to Christian to write their musical "Spectacular, Spectacular." And they want the famous courtesan-actress, Satine, to play the lead.

That night at the theatre, the leader of the Bohemian team, Toulouse-Lautrec, introduces Christian to Satine. At the same time, Harold Zidler, impresario-master of ceremonies, wants Satine to meet the Duke, a rich financier, who has the means to save Zidler's theatrical ambitions. Satine mistakenly believes Christian is the Duke. She finds out soon enough that the Duke is the real Duke, but not before Christian has fallen in love. In short order, Satine falls in love with Christian. The Duke, an insanely jealous rich man, falls in love with Satine. He finances the play to buy Satine, but, as they say, you can't buy love. The lovers defy the Duke, the show goes on, and Satine, incurably ill, dies, and Christian has learned enough about love to feel that he is now a writer.

FIGURE 13.1
Moulin Rouge (2001). 20th Century Fox/Photofest. ©20th Century Fox.

Before we plunge into pace and love and jealousy, it is important to acknowledge that whether love and jealousy are about a performance or about a person, each translates into energy. Desire, competition, and hatred also translate into energy, and here is where pace becomes important. Pace, by its nature, creates energy or tension when it accelerates and creates calm when it goes from fast to slower. Luhrmann first establishes energy when Christian arrives by train in Paris. Christian is excited. And whether he keeps hearing his father criticize his decision to come to Paris or seeks out an apartment in Montmartre, Luhrmann's use of pace articulates Christian's feeling of excitement.

When Christian meets the eccentric Bohemians who will become colleagues and friends, again pace is used. Here it's not so much Christian's excitement, but rather his disbelief that such people exist. Disbelief turns to fascination and again pace, together with art direction, including hair and makeup, both individuates and makes these characters passionate artists, ready to march forward into their culture war, a musical production.

Finally, Christian is taken to the theatre to meet Satine. A performance is underway. Here the pace quickens to the point of frenzy. Movement, dance, singing, performance, passion—all mix as we get a pastiche of the joyful aspects of being a performer. Pace makes this sequence one of the most dynamic in the film. We in the audience, who may never have dreamed of dancing and singing professionally for the length of this introduction, entertain all possibilities. The scene is nothing less than a seduction of the senses. Christian is hooked and so are we.

The pace is no less powerfully deployed later in the film in the Roxanne number. Here the purpose is to illustrate the pain of passion. Jealousy is rife as both the narcoleptic Bohemian and Christian experience a deep bout of jealousy. By crosscutting between Christian and the narcoleptic, between the lovers of each man, and by images of their rivals or imagined rivals, Luhrmann uses an accelerating pace to capture the cascading feeling of being overwhelmed with desire and jealousy. The pain in the scene is palpable and Luhrmann uses pace to measure the characters' descent into the depths of their pain. Again Luhrmann is using pace operatically to calibrate feeling—in this case, pain; in the earlier case, pleasure and desire. In all cases, pace is playing the key editing role in modulating the characters' feelings.

ANTI-PACE IN TARANTINO'S *INGLOURIOUS BASTERDS*

For the most part, changes in pace have meant increases in the pace of films. One filmmaker has decided to slow pace down. What is interesting about Quentin Tarantino's *Inglourious Basterds* (2009) is that although the actual pace is diminished, the tension he is able to create in a scene is not diminished at all. On the contrary, using camera placement and performance, Tarantino achieves a powerful impact. The opening scene of *Inglourious Basterds* makes the point.

The scene at 19½ minutes is almost as lengthy as the D-Day invasion set piece in Spielberg's *Saving Private Ryan* (see Chapter 12). That 24-minute set piece tells a complex narrative using hundreds of shots. The Tarantino sequence is essentially a two-character scene employing 134 cuts in 19½ minutes. There a few cuts that are a second or less, but the majority of shots average 30 seconds or more. This is not slow pace; it is almost no deployment of pace.

In terms of content, the scene establishes that a farmer, Pierre La Padite, is visited in 1941 France by a German S.S. colonel, Hans Landa. Landa is accompanied by three soldiers who remain outside. The farmer's three daughters wait outside while the two men talk.

Pleasantries are exchanged. The German drinks milk, both men smoke a pipe. Eventually the colonel gets to the point. He is hunting for Jews. One Jewish family is not accounted for: the Dreyfus family. Does the farmer know where they are? After some exchange about the family, the colonel gets to the point. If the farmer will cooperate in finding the Dreyfus family, the colonel will be grateful and not act against the farmer's family. Reluctantly, painfully, the farmer acknowledges that he is hiding the family in his basement. The three German guards are invited in, and they fire their automatic weapons into the floor. The eldest Dreyfus girl, Shoshanna escapes. The colonel considers shooting her, but refrains.

Another dimension to the content is the tone. The colonel and the farmer speak French initially, switch to English, and end in French again. The politeness of the colonel, his familiarity, and his ironic menace and pleasure in his work contribute to the tension in the scene. The delay in getting to the point of the scene, the hunt for Jews, until halfway through the scene, adds a sense of treading water that is amusing and menacing at the same time. Essentially, given that this is a war film—a realistic genre—the tone makes us uneasy, posing the question: Is this a war film, or a soft satire on the war film?

The most useful way to consider Tarantino's narrative strategy and consequently his editing strategy is analogous to saying that there is a bomb planted in a building at the outset and then to allow ordinary activity that we know will end in destruction and death to proceed— indeed, to crowd out anything else but the knowledge that something terrible will inevitably occur.

In the Tarantino scene, the planting of the bomb is the arrival of a German S.S. officer and his men at the farm of a Frenchman and his family. The social exchange and the pleasantries about milk and smoking only delay the inevitable—the true reason for the colonel's visit. And once the colonel shares his nickname—Jew hunter, and asks about the Dreyfus family, the bomb is closer to detonation. Finally, when the colonel threatens the farmer's family, we know the blast is imminent.

Tarantino's editing strategy follows this logic. With the arrival of the German colonel, the action moves into the farmhouse. Long shots in deep focus are replaced by midshots. The background is lost; the lighting becomes more dramatic. Eventually we move closer, and the scene becomes more emotional. Tarantino alters the visuals occasionally with a slow track or a tilt shot downward, but for the most part, he relies on long takes. Close-ups and reaction shots essentially punctuate the farmer's reactions to the colonel's questions about the Jews. When he gives them up, we are close enough to see the tear fall from the farmer's eye. And death, when it comes, does so in close-up. The scene ends outside the house, once again in deep focus, so that Tarantino can hold the shot of Shoshanna fleeing longer.

Because the lengthy scene is essentially a two-character piece, Tarantino places the camera close to the characters. They are most often presented singly (adversarial) in the frame, although there are shots in which both the farmer and the Colonel appear together. This scene is an excellent example of how tremendous tension can be achieved even when pace is set aside as a key tool. The tradeoff, however, is that performance, dialog, and camera placement become even more central. Tarantino provides us with a reminder that effectiveness in film can be achieved by varied means.

CONCLUSION

In this chapter, I have communicated an array of uses of pace. When linked to a genre, pace deepens the audience's sense experience of the docudrama, the thriller, the action-adventure film, and the musical. The repertory for pace has broadened; its use now is sophisticated, rather than coarse. Although much has happened since those initial forays into pace by D. W. Griffith, we must not forget the key contributions of those early pioneers, Griffith and Eisenstein.

CHAPTER 14

The Appropriation of Style I: Imitation and Innovation

In this chapter, we explore a new phenomenon: the movie of which the style is created from the context of movie life rather than real life. The consequence is twofold—the presumption of deep knowledge on the part of the audience of those forms such as the gangster films or Westerns, horror films or adventure films. And that the parody or alteration of that film creates a new form, a different experience for the audience. This imitative and innovative style is a style associated with the brief but influential directing career of Quentin Tarantino (*Reservoir Dogs*, 1992; *Pulp Fiction*, 1994). In order to suggest the limits of imitation and a more startling kind of innovation, we look at Milcho Manchevski's film, *Before the Rain* (1994). Like *Pulp Fiction*, it is three stories in a single film.

In order to contextualize the theme of style, imitation, and innovation, we turn to earlier examples of filmmakers whose style was pronounced.

NARRATIVE AND STYLE

Style in and of itself can contribute to the narrative or can undermine the narrative if it is not clearly dramatically purposeful. The elements of style most obvious to the viewer are compositional elements—camera placement, movement, juxtaposition of foreground and background people or things, light, sound, and, of course, editing. Whether the filmmaker relies on the editing, the pace, to explain the narrative, or she avoids editing, moving the camera, using the planes within the frame to explain the narrative. More often style is associated with composition—naturalistic or stylized; however, editing, as I hope is illustrated in this book, has its own style, ranging from directly expository to elliptical and metaphorical.

Two filmmakers who use a distinct style that serves the narrative well are Max Ophuls and George Stevens. In *Caught* (1949), Ophuls uses camera composition to create a style that beautifully fleshes out the narrative. A young woman, Leonora (Barbara Bel Geddes), wants to marry rich—and she does. She marries Smith Ohlrig (Robert Ryan). He proves to be sadistic and cruel. She runs off and works for a Dr. Quinada (James Mason), in a poor, urban district of New York. They fall in love and the triangle is set. Will she find

203

The Technique of Film and Video Editing: History, Theory, and Practice. DOI: 10.1016/B978-0-240-81397-4.00014-5

happiness or be destroyed for her original goal, material wealth? Ophuls uses the composition of Leonora and Smith at the outset to show his power over her. Whenever they are together, the compositions suggest control rather than love. Early in the film, Ophuls uses a similar composition while Smith is seeing his psychoanalyst. But here the power position in the composition belongs to the analyst. In the scene, Smith is so upset by an allegation that he wouldn't marry the girl that he in fact calls and arranges the marriage.

He will leave analysis and enter marriage to show the analyst that he himself is in control, not the analyst. The composition affirms the contrary. Later in the film, when Leonora leaves her husband, she works for Dr. Quinada. One evening, he takes her out for dinner. They dance and he proposes marriage. She tells him she loves him but that she has to clarify issues in her life (Ohlrig and the pregnancy she has just discovered). The commitment to and a visual rendering of the quality of the relationship is recorded in a single shot. Ophuls moves the camera as the lovers, in close-up, dance on the crowded dance floor. This gentle, elegant shot communicates everything about the future of this relationship.

The following shot uses three planes. In the foreground, Leonora's desk, as we pan to the left from the desk we see one partner, the obstetrician in the office, panning to the other side, Dr. Quinada. The two men talk about Leonora's disappearance and about Quinada's proposal. The obstetrician, knowing she is pregnant, suggests Quinada forget about her. The camera pans one direction or the other at least twice, but all the while Leonora's desk is in the close-up or middle-ground of the frame. Consequently, whatever the dialog, we never forget what is being spoken about—Leonora. These two shots use movement, placement, and composition to create a sense of an entire relationship. This is style in brilliant service of the narrative purpose.

In George Stevens's *A Place in the Sun* (1951), the agenda is more complex. George Eastman (Montgomery Clift) comes east to take a job with his rich uncle. His own parents were religious and poor. He comes from a different class in spite of sharing the name Eastman. Early in the film, George is invited to the Eastman home. Having just arrived in town, he buys a suit. He then goes to see his mentor-to-be and his family. The wife and the two grown children are totally snobbish toward their poor cousin. In order to create the sense of status or lack thereof, Stevens has George Eastman enter what seems to be a cavernous room. In the foreground, the wealthy Eastmans are seated. The patriarch is the only one to offer him a hand. In a series of carefully staged images, Stevens portrays the separateness of George Eastman from his relations. Stevens uses camera placement and a deep-focus image. George Eastman is at the back of the frame. They also occupy the center, while George is often placed to the side. When another guest, Angela Vickers (Elizabeth Taylor), arrives, she sweeps into the room—not even seeing George Eastman. By the staging, and using the planes of the composition, Stevens suggests that George Eastman is the forgotten man. He simply does not have the status to be a "real" Eastman. Again, the compositional style underscores the theme of the narrative.

STYLE FOR ITS OWN SAKE

It is not always the case that style supports the narrative. Often style is presented as a substitute for a weak narrative or is, in the view of the director, a necessary overmodulation simulating the thematic extremes of the narrative. To be specific about style, we need only look to films such as *Fellini Satyricon* (1970) or Cornel Wilde's *Beach Red* (1967) to see style overwhelming the content. On the other hand, in each case, the style spoke to the director's view of ancient Rome or about war. In both cases, "excess" was too mild a term to describe the director's view. There are times when this can work, as in *Fellini Satyricon*, but there are other instances, such as Richard Lester's *Petulia* (1968), when the style totally overwhelms the content of the film.

A good example of a film with a feeble narrative, but a remarkable style, is Orson Welles's *Touch of Evil* (1958), one of Welles's great works. The story of a murder and its investigation in a Texas border town is simply too trite for description. But the shot that begins the film with a three-minute tracking shot of a bomb being planted in a car on the Mexican side of the border and ending with its explosion on the American side is simply a tour de force.

In the course of the shot, Welles also introduces the main character, the Mexican investigator, Vargas (Charlton Heston). The murder of a Mexican drug lord (Akim Tamiroff) by the sheriff (Welles), the assault on Vargas's wife, the final recording of the guilty sheriff and his death—each of these sequences is a remarkable exercise in style. Using to excess the wide-angle lens, low camera placements, and a crowding of the foreground of the frame, Welles created a style more appropriate to film noir than to a police story. It is a style that is garish, even corrupt. In its power, it conveys something the narrative lacks—conviction.

An example of eclectic but extreme style is Stanley Kubrick's *A Clockwork Orange* (1971). The story of a futuristic England beset by violent youth and a mind-controlling government, Kubrick's version of the Anthony Burgess novel is to use style as a counterpoint to the action. The camera pans gradually over an ongoing rape. Extreme close-ups of the assault on the man character's eyes forces sympathy as the victimizer becomes the victim. Kubrick tracks and zooms with an equanimity totally absent in the narrative. Eventually we are worn out by the violence and by the ironic style, left to consider our own world and its future.

A third example of style overwhelming the subject is the apocalyptic tale, *Twelve Monkeys* (1995). Terry Gilliam, better known for *Brazil* (1985), another highly stylized tale of the future, portrays the future and the present with a fish-eye lens view. Distortion is everywhere and a key to Gilliam's treatment of Chris Marker's *La Jetee* (1962). Can one prevent the future from happening? Are we all destined to be the future's victims? These are the central issues of *Twelve Monkeys*. Biological research, wealth, and psychiatry all form the nexus of human-made madness that preordains the fate of the world—destruction. Few, if any, filmmakers, with the exception of John Frankenheimer in *Seconds* (1966), have relied so heavily on a distorting lens to filter their narrative. The result of using a lens that makes the world less natural, more distorted, is to distance us form the narrative and to position us for a strongly visual, highly unnaturalistic experience. The result is that we become less involved and possibly lose the apocalyptic message of *Twelve Monkeys*. This is the upshot of a surplus of style.

BREAKING EXPECTATIONS

Perhaps no filmmakers represent as great a break from expectations as a trio of filmmakers with the independent filmmaking spirit—Martin Scorsese, Spike Lee, and Oliver Stone.

In his work in *Raging Bull* (1980), Martin Scorsese uses a metaphor to create a style. This tale is of a man whose aggression was so great that prizefighting was simply an extension of his life. The metaphor Scorsese borrows is from opera. Many nineteenth-century operas included a ballet within the opera. Using the music from Verdi's *La Forza del Destino*, Scorsese opens the film with LaMotta (Robert De Niro) prepping for a fight. There, in slow motion, the beauty of the physical movements of arms, legs, and body becomes ballet-like. The emphasis in this section of the "ballet" is on beauty. Later, as LaMotta actually fights, the shift is to physical clash and brutality, but the way in which the action in the ring is filmed makes it another phase of the ballet—the combat phase.

Scorsese's metaphor set to Verdi's music creates a layer of meaning to LaMotta's life that pushes the story beyond the biography of Jake LaMotta, champion middleweight, to the battle of the titans, the gods, the kings so often invoked as the central subject of opera. Here, Scorsese's stylistic choices break the expectations that *Raging Bull* will be a boxing film about a famous boxer, albeit flawed as a human being. By breaking our expectations, Scorsese creates a modern opera—the equivalent of Verdi's *La Forza del Destino*.

Spike Lee also challenges expectations in much of his work. In *Jungle Fever* (1991), a film with a distinct style, Lee portrays the world of two families—an African-American family and an Italian-American family. The catalytic event is an interracial love affair between an African-American man and an Italian-American woman. The style of the film is far from documentary. When two men speak to one another, Lee photographs them from a heroic camera placement, midshot. Only the background moves.

This stylized shot forces us to think about what they are saying rather than engaging us by what we see. Later, the main character's visit to a crack house in search of his brother is akin to a series of Hieronymus Bosch paintings. Again unreality, but the power comes from the sense of how far from reality the house's occupants want to be. What we expect from Spike Lee in *Jungle Fever* is a sexual exploration of stereotypes of black men and white women; what we get instead is a meditation on racism, on family, on love, and on responsibility. By using a highly stylized approach, Lee undermines our expectations and provides us with a much greater experience.

Oliver Stone has always relied on a powerful style. Using pace, a roving camera, and an excess of close-ups, he has clearly used style to press his editorial view—war, politics, and controversial issues in American history. He is not a director who layers the case, as does

Fred Wiseman in his documentaries. Instead, Stone uses style to promote his view of the case. His style is so effective that the only question the viewer can ask is why every advertiser in the country doesn't line up to hire Stone to direct their commercials!

We expect Oliver Stone to carry on this tradition of staking out an editorial position of force. In *Natural Born Killers* (1994), however, he so broadens the definition of stylistic choices that we no longer know what to expect from Oliver Stone. How can a filmmaker known for excessive style find a style even more excessive? Given the subject matter—young killers on a killing spree, followed and exploited by the media and, in turn, exploiting the media—Stone anticipates the tough question of identification by using an MTV-style, cartoonish sitcom format, as well as mixing a black-and-white newsreel look with overly decorous color. *Natural Born Killers* is awash in style. Yet we are both offended and moved by this postmodern visitation to media land's today in the United States. Using the story thread of the rise and fall of two young lover-killers, Stone deploys style to create a satire of the American relationship with guns and violence. Few films have more effectively used a surplus of style to create a new interpretation on the American dream and the American nightmare. By moving beyond our expectations of excessive style, Stone outdoes himself. He finds a style suited to his view of the subject.

IMITATION VERSUS INNOVATION

There is a definite demarcation point between imitation and innovation. Imitation is simply referential; we have seen it before, and the implication is we've seen it too often. It's become somewhat of a cliché. The gunfight in George Stevens's *Shane* (1953) is a good example. The gunfight between Shane (Alan Ladd) and his antagonist (Jack Palance) is staged in a careful manner. It is referential to many other gunfights we have seen. The result is predictable, and imitative. That is not to say that *Shane*, as a film, is an uncreative film. On the contrary: Stevens has respected the Western myth and affirmed in this tale that primitivism will have no place next to civilization. But the gunfight itself is imitative of other gunfights in other Western films.

More novel is the gunfight at the O.K. Corral in John Ford's *My Darling Clementine* (1946) or the gunfight at the end of Howard Hawks's *Rio Bravo* (1959). Some Westerns prefer to reference earlier films—the killing of a miner in town in Clint Eastwood's *Pale Rider* (1985) references the murder of a homesteader in Stevens's *Shane*. Others choose to parody earlier films.

The train sequence at the beginning of Sergio Leone's *Once Upon a Time in America* (1984) references the opening of Fred Zinnemann's *High Noon* (1952). The point here is that in order to create a new insight to a point of view, straight imitation does not do the trick; it's necessary to alter the narrative or visual style of the scene to make it seem new. The very length of the train sequence in the Leone film creates a tension about the anticipated arrival as powerful as the arrival of the train in *High Noon*. The length and the exaggerated interplay of extreme close-ups and extreme long shots in Leone's film make the train sequence and the shoot-out that follows it fitting prologue to the epic that will follow. Leone makes something new by imitating a famous sequence from the earlier Western film.

My point here is that there is a relationship between imitation and innovation. But the film-maker has to recognize that our engagement with the imitation will depend on his making it seem novel and innovative.

IMITATION AND INNOVATION

The heart of this chapter lies in the great and novel success of a film like Quentin Tarantino's *Pulp Fiction*. In terms of classical story forms, *Pulp Fiction* is a classic gangster film in its generic origin, but this is where the comparison ends. Tarantino also feels free to relate *Pulp Fiction* to the ebb and flow of movies and television on that popular culture. A character refers to himself as "I'm *The Guns of Navarone*." Another character portraying a Vietnam veteran recently released from a prisoner-of-war camp, who is portrayed by Christopher Walken, tells a powerful story about preserving a gold watch while a prisoner-of-war. The reference here is to the film that made Walken's career, Michael Cimino's *The Deer Hunter* (1978), where he portrayed an American fighting in Vietnam, imprisoned by the Vietnamese.

Elsewhere in the film, a restaurant is hosted by an Ed Sullivan imitator. A waiter is Buddy Holly; a waitress is Marilyn Monroe; a performer is Ricky Nelson. Just as the gangster film is one point of reference for *Pulp Fiction*, popular culture since 1950 is another key referent point.

If these were its only narrative virtues, there would be little to write about. *Pulp Fiction* is also organized around three stories, a prologue, and an epilogue. The prologue is continued in terms of time in the epilogue. The time frame for *Pulp Fiction* thus resembles the circle rather than the straight line. Tarantino uses this frame to break our expectations of a linear treatment of the gangster genre. If the film were linear, the story would follow a rise and fall story line. Given the circularity of the story line, Tarantino can meditate on the pursuit of work and pleasure in the world of the gangster. Both are fraught with a fatalism that underscores the fragility of life and, in the case of one of the characters, Jules (Samuel Jackson), causes him to give up the life for a pursuit that will be more spiritual.

The actual story line is, in reality, three story lines—Vincent Vega and Marsellus Wallace's wife, the Gold Watch, and the Bonnie Situation. Characters from each story line appear in the other stories. The first story is the story of Vincent Vega (John Travolta), who, with his partner, Jules, proceeds to kill some young dealers who have betrayed their employer, Marsellus.

The second part of this story is the "date" Vincent has with Mia (Uma Thurman), Marsellus's wife. This drug-induced date sees Mia overdose and Vincent rescue her with the help of his drug dealer (Eric Stoltz). The overall tone of this first story is a druglike trance. The killers, Vincent and Jules, approach their work like ministers meditating on life values and loyalty. The second phase is a cocaine-hazed seduction without sex. But playing with fire, whether it's sex or drugs, has consequences. Vincent is always aware of doing the right thing: of not crossing the line. Self-preservation is his philosophy in a profession in which the long view is the short run.

The second story is the story of Butch (Bruce Willis). His gold watch has been passed down for generations of heroic but dead soldiers in his family. For him the watch represents the father and grandfather he never knew. Butch is a boxer who has agreed to throw a fight for Marsellus, the local Los Angeles crime boss. Instead, he wins the fight and the money he bet on it. But now Marsellus wants to kill him. His escape is well planned, except that his girlfriend left his gold watch in his apartment. Fate pulls him back in the direction of Marsellus. Back at the apartment to retrieve the watch, he finds Vincent in the washroom, his gun in the kitchen. Butch kills Vincent, but as he escapes, he literally runs into Marsellus on the street. They try to kill one another. Absurdly, they are taken into captivity by a pawn shop owner who proceeds, with the help of a friend, to rape Marsellus. Rescued by Butch, Marsellus forgives him, but Butch must leave town.

The third story returns to the killing of the first story. It seems there was a hidden gunman in the backroom. He is killed by Vincent and Jules, but not before he has fired five shots, all of which miss their target. Jules is certain that divine intervention has saved his life. He will give up the life of crime. With a young black man taken from the apartment, they leave. En route, Vincent accidentally kills the young man, splaying blood and matter all over the car and themselves. Now endangered, they proceed to the home of a friend (Quentin Tarantino). The friend tells them they must leave quickly before his wife returns. They call on Marsellus for help. He dispatches Mr. Wolf (Harvey Keitel) to help fix the situation. He does so, cleaning them and the car for reentry into the world.

Hungry, they go out for breakfast, to a diner where the robbery that has begun in the prologue is now played out as an epilogue. Jules has said that he will no longer kill and advises the robbers how to leave with their booty and their lives. The film ends at this point, although, in terms of chronology, the gold watch story is to take place at a future point.

To understand the imitative dimensions of *Pulp Fiction*, we look at the references to popular culture, particularly television. It is not only the references to particular characters; it is also the attitudes expressed. Butch is a product of a *Leave It to Beaver* family; he becomes a boxer, the result of "Beaver" being orphaned. He is the analogue to the persona who grows up without a father—Jimmie (Quentin Tarantino) is a house-husband, a "Mr. Brady" without the Bunch; Marsellus is Othello to Mia's Desdemona; and Vincent is Iago's younger brother. All three are contemporary visions of a 1950's *Playhouse 90* revisited in the 1990s. Wolf is a George C. Scott character out of *The Hustler* (1961) and Jules is a character who has walked right out of a Sinclair Lewis novel made for television. The imitative dimensions of *Pulp Fiction*, although presented with great wit, would not be enough to suggest innovation.

The innovative storytelling dimension of *Pulp Fiction* has more to do with genre violation. Not only does Tarantino use black humor as the tone for *Pulp Fiction*, but he actually satirizes the form's violence and its fastidious devotion to testosterone. Both Vincent and Jules, although killers, are sensitive to one another and, in Vincent's case, remarkably sensitive to Mia, Marsellus's wife. Their devotion to language, its nuances and its elegance, makes them the most unusual of hit men. In a story form known for action and a devotion to quick solutions, this obsession with language can be interpreted only as a satire on the male propensity for action. By substituting language for action, Tarantino is also substituting one for the other, thereby undermining a key motif of the genre. Consequently, the shape of the dramatic action becomes less cause and effect and more meditation, even a search for goals.

The result, given the circularity of the narrative and the substitution of dialog for action, is to shift the narrative heart of *Pulp Fiction* from material goals to spiritual goals for each of the main characters. First, Vincent simply wants to eschew sexuality for survival; Butch wants a piece of his family, perhaps all of his family, as represented by his father's gold watch, instead of money; and finally, Jules wants to leave the life he leads for a better one; the Lord has shown him the way to save himself—divine intervention, he calls it. Whether any of these characters will indeed find happiness, we will never know (although we do witness Vincent's fate: he is right to be cautious). The key result of the innovations Tarantino introduces is to shift us from a focus on cause and effect, or linear narrative, to a different kind of narrative: a circular narrative. The focus, consequently, shifts to character over action, and to spiritual values over material values.

All of this is presented in a tone that allows Tarantino to find humor in a form not known for humor and to step outside the dramatic limitations of the form into a new kind of experience, where a self-reflexive meditation on the medium occurs as well as the narrative.

The layered experience of *Pulp Fiction* consequently allows us to be inside the film, and outside the film. The result is that Tarantino has moved far beyond imitation to a work that is remarkable for its innovation.

To give some sense of perspective on how creative *Pulp Fiction* is, we turn to another tripartite story, Milcho Manchevski's *Before the Rain*. Set in Macedonia in 1993, *Before the Rain* is essentially three love stories: two set in rural Macedonia and one in London. Each focuses on a love that is forbidden by the surrounding society and each ends tragically, as religious bigotry leads to murder. The combatants in each case are Macedonian and Albanian, Christian and Muslin.

The first story, Words, focuses on a priest, Father Kiril, who has taken a vow of silence. He finds a young Albanian woman in his room. Her hair has been shorn. She looks young, not more than eighteen. She is being pursued by Macedonians who accuse her of murder. The priest hides her, against the wishes of his superiors. The Macedonians search the grounds but do not find her. When she's found out, the priest is thrown out with her. They cannot communicate because each speaks a different language. But a bond has formed. They are discovered by the girl's grandfather and his men. The priest is sent away while the girl is beaten and accused of being a slut. She professes love and runs after him. The girl is killed by her own brother.

The second story, Faces, takes place in London. A British woman, Anne, an executive in a photography agency, has a lover, a Pulitzer Prize–winning photographer. Alexander, the photographer, is Macedonian. He wants her to return to Macedonia with him, but she refuses. She is pregnant by the husband she has left for the photographer. He leaves, and she meets her husband at a restaurant. She tells him she's pregnant by him, but stills wants a divorce. In the background, an argument grows in intensity. It is between an ethnic waiter and an ethnic customer. The argument mushrooms. The implication is a replay of the Macedonian–Albanian enmity in London. Both are thrown out. The angry customer returns and shoots indiscriminately, killing the waiter as well as Anne's husband.

Pictures, the third story, is Alexander's story. He returns after 16 years to his home in Macedonia. He is greeted by his relatives. Only when they recognize him do they drop their enmity. Everyone seems to carry guns. Alexander visits Hana, a school friend, a woman he clearly loves. She is Albanian. He is greeted with great hostility, but clearly she was the love of his life, and he has returned to see if his love is returned by her. Her father is respectful, but her son threatens to kill him. He leaves. Alexander's cousin is killed and Hana's daughter is accused. She asks if he can find her daughter. He finds and releases her, but in doing so, he is killed by his own cousin. The young woman runs off to a monastery, the very monastery of the first story.

The three stories of *Before the Rain* form a circle of time, another circle of religious hatred, and a circle of love. Each story has the same theme, and in each, the hatred destroys the love. Only time continues, but in Manchevski's world, it comes full circle, in order to repeat itself with another circle of opportunity, love, and religious hatred.

In each story, the characters of the other appear. And in each story, the meditation of the main character fails to puncture the circles.

Like Tarantino in *Pulp Fiction*, Manchevski has chosen a nonlinear frame in order to layer his story. Where Tarantino used the structure to comment on the form—the gangster film—Manchevski uses the nonlinear frame to create a fable about issues larger than Macedonia or the former Yugoslavia.

His goal is to say something about the struggle between the life instinct and the death instinct and to warn us that, in Macedonia, this archetypal struggle is moving toward a victory for death. Manchevski doesn't portray religion or social structures as the enemy. He shows both sides victimized and caught in a circle of self-destruction. In this film, the nonlinear structure and style help Manchevski distance himself from the particular and to suggest the general. He uses the structure to create a modern parable.

Manchevski's film is innovative in every way. There is little imitation of story form. He strikes a fresh chord. Although this struggle has been told before—specifically, in Elia Kazan's *America, America* (1963)—it has never been told in such a novel fashion. Manchevski's style in *Before the Rain* presents an ideal example of how a style can be so innovative as to seem uniquely original.

Both these films—*Pulp Fiction* and *Before the Rain*—rely on a nonlinear structure to move them beyond imitation and to suggest a new innovative style for film narrative. It is not the case that every story is well served by this approach. However, as these two films illustrate, the options for film narrative have been expanded by Tarantino and Manchevski.

CHAPTER 15

The Appropriation of Style II: Limitation and Innovation

This chapter continues the exploration begun in the previous chapter, which looked at the tension between style and content and how that tension generates first a distinct voice for the narrative. This voice is first articulated in the compositional choices and consequently in the organization and orchestration of those images. Style may refer to genre or it may reconsider the organization of shots into a different narrative frame, such as the nonlinear frame Quentin Tarantino uses in *Pulp Fiction* (1994). In this chapter, we examine four stylistic interventions that on one level appear to be a return to former forms—in a sense, a creative reaction to the radical experience of the nonlinear story. On another level, however, these interventions represent a deepening of long-evolving tendencies in film narrative. In this sense, they work with the limitations of those tendencies, not so much imitating them as trying to stretch the boundaries those tendencies may have. We begin with the most conservative of these tendencies, the elevation of cinéma vérité.

THE ELEVATION OF CINÉMA VÉRITÉ

Cinéma vérité, beginning with its ideological underpinnings in the work of Dziga Vertov (see Chapter 1), has been principally viewed as affiliated with the documentary. Indeed, together with the personal documentary and the educational–political documentary, cinéma vérité is one of the three principal ideologies of the documentary. Its affiliation with the dramatic film dates from the 1960s: the British kitchen-sink dramas, the New Wave films of Jean-Luc Godard, and the docudramas of Peter Watkins and Ken Loach.[1] More recently, there has been a resurgence of interest and activity in the use of the cinéma vérité style. The results of that interest have led to the most profitable film of all time (in terms of percentage of revenue to cost), *The Blair Witch Project* (1999), and to the most talked-about school of filmmaking of the 1990s, Dogme 95. Cinéma vérité has also had a pronounced impact on the lively Belgian school, the films of Luc and Jean-Pierre Dardenne (*Rosetta*, 1999) and Frederick Fonteyne (*An Affair of Love*, 2000), and the move to hyperrealism in the work of Erick Zonca (*The Dreamlife of Angels*, 1998) in France. The earlier work of Remy Belvaux (*Man Bites Dog*, 1992) is formative in the Belgian embrace of cinéma vérité. Turning to the Dogme films, a background note will contextualize the movement.

213

The Dogme filmmakers are led by the Danish filmmaker Lars Von Trier. Their "dogma" echoes the ethos of the New Wave declaration that their films would be a creative reaction to the dominant studio films of the day and that the style of their films would be free of those conventions. In the case of Dogme 95, that means a return to cinéma vérité. Von Trier, Thomas Vinterberg, Søren Kragh-Jacobsen, and Kristian Levring have committed themselves to making films without artifice. That means no tripods, artificial light, or music. As much as possible, naturalism must prevail. There is a script and there are actors, but all else looks and feels like cinéma vérité.

The style is critical to the experience. Making it feel real, albeit a stylistic posture, is the central tenet of Dogme 95. The subject matter of the films, the fact that they are scripted, and the fact that actors are portraying the characters makes the content classic melodrama. The style, however, is the style of cinéma vérité. Since the declaration and the release of a number of Dogme films, at least one major filmmaker has embraced the Dogme style. Mike Figgis has produced *Time Code* (2000), and there are certainly independent filmmakers such as Kevin Smith (*Clerks*, 1994) who echo the principles of Dogme.

To understand the conflict of style and content, we turn to Thomas Vinterberg's film *The Celebration* (released in Europe as *Festen*, 1998). The film covers a crucial 24-hour period in the life of one Danish family. The patriarch, a successful businessman named Helge, is turning 60, and the celebration of the title brings together all the extended intergenerational members of his family. Such an event is a mark of success, but the title is essentially used ironically. For Helge's three surviving children (there was a recent suicide by the only adult child still living at home), Christian, Helene, and Michael, the issue is whether to celebrate silently and continue living depressed and disparate lives, or whether tonight is the time to expose the family's ugly secret. The suicide was Christian's twin sister, and Christian decides to challenge the status quo. At the party, as he toasts his father, he congratulates him for being the man who continually raped him and his sister when they were children. This statement initiates a chain reaction that results in all the children turning against their father. At the very end the mother joins them, banishing Helge from the celebratory breakfast. It has been the night that changed the power structure in this family. The children at last can assume a different position—hopefully, a more successful position in their emotional lives.

The Celebration is about secrets, it is about anxiety, and it is about guilt within a family. How does the cinéma vérité style contribute to the veracity of the emotional states? How do the camera placements, the shot selections, and the organization of the shots create the feeling states that underline the narrative?

The cinéma vérité approach creates a general sense of veracity. It seems to capture the edgy personalities of characters unmasked—the insecurity and rage of Michael, the depression and special position in the family of Christian, the power and confidence of Helge, the provocative rebelliousness of Helene, the superficiality and extroversion of the mother. But the style goes further; it also seems to catch the sense of minor characters, such as the manager of the hotel who knows his place and is the voice of the owner and no more. The chef is outspoken and ironic; he doesn't accept his place.

The waitress, with her openness and charming sexuality, contrasts with the closed Christian, whom she has always adored. The cinéma vérité style captures character and makes each of them seem more credible than they might if the style didn't promote a sense of actuality.

Perhaps even more striking is that the camera becomes an active participant in creating the sense of the emotional core of the characters. When Helge is photographed, it's in midshot. He's always in the center of the frame, and there is a stillness to the shot. Vinterberg also holds the shot longer than he does with other characters. The result is that we feel Helge's power, his control over others. In the case of Michael, the images are quite the opposite. Michael is more than insecure; he is filled with rage, and his anger, although inappropriate to the moment, is explosive. Here, Vinterberg uses a camera in close to Michael, looking down and at him—almost glaring at him. The camera also moves in jerking movements toward the object of his rage, usually his wife and often other women. The camera motion is kinetic, just as are his emotions. Vinterberg also uses quick cuts, whether they are jump cuts or cutaways, to simulate Michael's emotional state.

Although Christian and the children are ultimately victorious, Vinterberg never exploits the emotional power shift via image or editing. There are no quick emotional fixes here. Toward the end, the camera placement and cutting vis-à-vis Michael slows down and becomes more calm, just as Michael calms down and actually assumes a leadership role in his new position in relation to his father. The result is that we experience the new Michael as more solid, more stable, and more a man with a sense of dignity than the man who was controlled by fear and anger earlier in the narrative.

This transition is particularly critical because Michael seemed the most damaged of the three surviving children. Different camera placement and a pace that lacks the staccato cutting surrounding Michael in Act I, indicate how far the grown children have come in these 24 hours.

One more observation about the editing style of *The Celebration* is important. *The Celebration* is not an action film or a plot-driven film. Consequently, it would be expected that the editing style would be relatively slow. It's not. Because *The Celebration* is about the emotional turmoil that surrounds a key family event, and because it focuses on a 24-hour period, Vinterberg cuts the film as if it's a thriller. In Act I, all that happens prior to Christian's inflammatory toast to his father, is that we are introduced to the situation and to the characters. To make these 30 minutes dynamic, Vinterberg rapidly cuts between the arrival of the three children, then the guests, and the preparations of each of the adult children for the party. By rapidly cutting between them, Vinterberg adds pace to the narrative purpose.

He individuates the three children, giving each their own pace that is driven by their character. Christian is depressed, so the pace is slow, the camera distant, and the deep focus of the shots makes him seem very far away. Michael, as mentioned, is nervous, almost undone by having to prepare for the party. He berates his wife for leaving his black shoes behind, but minutes later needs to have sex with her (to lie down for five minutes) to calm down. He trips in the shower, and he trips while running to meet his father. He is a man on the verge of a nervous breakdown. Helene, on the other hand, is in a room, the room where her sister recently committed suicide. The manager of the hotel is with her. She begins to search for her sister and eventually finds the suicide note left by her. This sequence is one of distance and observation in Helene's search for her sister. The shots are longer and the movement subjectively echoes Helene's point of view.

The pace is faster than the Christian sequence but not as hectic as the shots relating to Michael. Overall, the pace here creates a sense of dynamism but also emotional tension. The restlessness of the camera echoes the emotional out-of-breath quality of Helge's children. We don't yet know why, but by the end of Act I, we are emotionally exhausted and the party is just about to really begin. This is the power of the editing style Vinterberg employs. He uses cinéma vérité to add a layer of veracity to the narrative.

This impulse is magnified fivefold in Erick Zonca's *The Dreamlife of Angels* (1998). Isa and Marie are twentysomething young women. The narrative takes place in Lille, France, today. Isa is from the South. Both are marginal in the sense that they are uneducated, unskilled young women. Although Isa is more the drifter, she has a more optimistic personality. Marie is negative and angry. In *The Dreamlife of Angels*, Zonca frames the narrative with the friendship of these two women, and like any relationship, this one has the arc of meeting, growing closer, growing apart, and ending the relationship. Within this metastructure, Zonca explores two relationships: Isa's relationship with a young girl in a coma, and Marie's with a rich young man. The apartment in which the women live is owned by the young girl's mother, who died as a consequence of the car accident that left the young girl in a coma. The relationship between Isa and the girl in a coma would appear to be an impossible one but it isn't. In the case of Marie, Zonca follows her relationship with a rich young man who is clearly a womanizer. He is a poor choice for Marie, and when he abandons her, leaving Isa to give Marie the news, Marie at first blames Isa, pushes Isa away, and then finally commits suicide.

The style Zonca chooses reflects in a general way cinéma vérité—a handheld camera, tight two-shots (in cramped spaces), lots of close-ups of functional activity such as writing in a journal. The footage has a captured quality, as opposed to one that is staged, and this too is symptomatic of cinéma vérité. But Zonca has more in mind than to observe two marginalized young women. He wants the level of observation to promote a love for his characters rather than an assessment of them. To promote this level of involvement with his two main characters, Zonca needs to adopt what I call *hyper-realism*, a much more intense experience than the veracity yielded from cinéma vérité. As a consequence, Zonca first truncates scenes.

He doesn't move from an establishing shot into midshots of interactions between characters, to a cutaway for a new idea, to a close-up for dramatic emphasis, to midshot to long shot as he concludes the scene. Rather he is very selective. Scenes are constructed of fewer shots, and the shots that are employed are used to emotionally heat up the experience of the scene. This means that scenes are mostly presented in midshots and close-ups. It also means that the camera placement crowds the action. There is very little space between us and the characters.

In one scene, for example, Isa is offering breakfast coffee to Marie. They are recent acquaintances. Marie, at Isa's request, has allowed Isa to sleep in the apartment. Call this a breakthrough-in-the-relationship scene—the two will be friends. There is no detail of the bedroom's geography in the scene, only the two young women. It's as if Zonca wants to push us toward them, the last two human beings on Earth. In this scene, Zonca creates a sense of togetherness as well as isolation from geography, the apartment, and other people. Most of his scenes proceed with this level of intimacy vis-à-vis the young women and this level of isolation from society at large. When we do see the young women with others— Marie with an early corpulent lover or Isa with the young girl in a coma—Zonca approaches the scenes with the same sense of inclusion and exclusion. The result is intense, emotional, and involving—the hyper-realism that goes beyond cinéma vérité.

THE RETURN OF MISE-EN-SCÈNE

As a style, mise-en-scène is associated with Orson Welles in *Citizen Kane* (1941) and *Touch of Evil* (1958), and with Max Ophuls in *Letter from an Unknown Woman* (1948) and *Lola Montès* (1955). These filmmakers, building upon the work of F. W. Murnau in the 1920s (*The Last Laugh*, 1924), essentially moved the camera to avoid editing. The elegance of their camera movement recorded performance and added a more subtle editorial direction.

In Welles's case, a sense of aesthetic virtuosity was created; in the case of Ophuls, it was a sense of romantic longing and energy. The former impulse, that of technical virtuosity and the filmic aesthetic, infuse the early camera movement in the career of Stanley Kubrick (*Paths of Glory*, 1957). Only later would Kubrick use the camera movement to slow down the pace of the film in order to recreate the seventeenth-century sense of time and place in *Barry Lyndon* (1975) or the accelerated sense of the future in *2001: A Space Odyssey* (1968). The latter impulse, the moody romanticism of Ophuls, resonates in the mise-en-scène work of Roberto Rossellini and Luchino Visconti. But none of these filmmakers was as effective at using the moving camera to conjure the inner emotional state of the main character as was F. W. Murnau. Hitchcock tried to capture the feeling but was more effective when he resorted to a cutaway or subjective sound.

What about mise-en-scène today, in the era of rapid pace and authorial intervention? Today the work of Luc Besson, Oliver Stone, and John Frankenheimer reflects the influence of Eisenstein rather than Murnau. But in spite of the preference for the fast cut, there is a renewed interest in mise-en-scène, particularly in the work of Stanley Kubrick and Martin Scorsese, and it is to this work that we now turn.

Stanley Kubrick's last film *Eyes Wide Shut* (1999) differs substantially from his previous work. Kubrick principally gravitated to genre work, which gave him an opportunity to explore aesthetic challenge and moral failure.

This dialectic operates in his war films, *Paths of Glory* and *Full Metal Jacket* (1987); his satires, *Lolita* (1962) and *Dr. Strangelove* (1963); his horror film, *The Shining* (1979); his science-fiction film, *2001: A Space Odyssey*; his gangster film, *The Killing* (1969); and his epics, *Spartacus* (1960) and *Barry Lyndon*. As mentioned earlier, Kubrick enjoyed the challenge of mise-en-scène and employed it with a panache rare among filmmakers. For the most part, however, the movement of the camera seemed to be a creative challenge Kubrick warmed to. How else does one understand the lengthy tracking shot that follows the Master Sergeant about the barracks, introducing his ethos to the young recruits, in *Full Metal Jacket*? Movement does energize the scene, but it is the aesthetic virtuosity of the lengthy shot that stays with the viewer. Here the style of the scene seems to be far more important than its content. This approach to mise-en-scène is echoed in the long tracking shots in *The Shining* and in the trenches and in the chateaux in *Paths of Glory*. As I mentioned earlier, there is a deeper purposefulness to the deployment of mise-en-scène in *2001: A Space Odyssey* and in *Barry Lyndon*.

Turning to *Eyes Wide Shut*, we first note that it is neither a classic genre film nor a classic satire. Instead, Kubrick has turned to a moral fable for adults. The Harfords are a materially successful New York professional couple. Bill Harford is a caring physician; Alice is a caring mother. But each is more in love with their own self-image than they are with one another.

Consequently, to feed the personal excitement of her narcissism, Alice plants a seed of doubt in her husband's mind: there was and may be another man in her life. The notion excites her but fills him with doubt and jealousy, and he begins a search, a desperate search, for excitement and illicit thrills. But his journey becomes a nightmare. Outrageous behavior, even murder, are the results of the narcissism he encounters in others, and in the end he is rather undone while his wife is reconciled to a relationship without ecstasy, the desired goal of self-love.

The New York the Harfords inhabit is as much a spiritual wasteland as are the chateaux of France in *Paths of Glory*. Material abundance implies that spirituality is flesh-bound, but this is not what Kubrick implies in *Eyes Wide Shut*. On the contrary, what the Harfords encounter is emptiness, and here lies the moral of Kubrick's tale. The culture of narcissism leads away from spiritual fulfillment, not toward it. The question for us is how Kubrick uses a particular style that may or may not conflict with the content, to create the sense of narcissism, ennui, and the illusion that sexual adventure can satisfy the longings of self-love. These are complex and interior feelings. How does this plot-oriented director create these interior states of mind?

The options here are performance, art direction, and/or camera movement. Kubrick, of course, uses all of the above. Our interest, however, is on his use of camera movement. Here he doesn't disappoint. Kubrick's camera moves in a restless, probing, searching movement.

Two examples will illustrate how Kubrick has gone further with mise-en-scène than did the work of F. W. Murnau. To contextualize these two examples from *Eyes Wide Shut*, it's useful to look at Murnau's use of mise-en-scène in *The Last Laugh*. In 1924 Murnau made this film about an older gentleman who gained great status from his position as the doorman at a major urban hotel. But in the first act, we see his pride, the sense of power he derives from his position. A turn of events sees him removed from his position; he lies to his neighbors and to his daughter—he is still a doorman.

To be convincing he needs a uniform, and so he steals it and begins his pretense—the precursor to his tragic downfall. When he enters the hotel, the camera is with him, but as he proceeds to steal the coat, the camera moves ahead of him, stopping at the coat, the object of his desire. Murnau has used mise-en-scène to pictorialize both the psychology of the old man, desperation, and his desire to do anything to regain his status. The camera movement, which is subjective and labored, then filled with a desire that outsteps the old man, provides a full sense of his inner life.

This is what Kubrick achieves in the following early sequence in *Eyes Wide Shut*. The scene is a party given by a wealthy client-friend of Bill. The first camera movement is the arrival of the Harfords. The movement, directly in front of the Harfords, is a glide fairly close to them. Both sides of the frame capture the mirrors that line the entry, and beautiful people are seen close to the periphery. The track captures the Harfords in midshot. They are looking at the guests and the mirrors to the sides. They are looking at themselves in the mirrors and beautiful people are looking at them. Are they comparing themselves to the other guests? It doesn't appear so. What they note is that others are looking at them, rather than each of them taking an interest in others. The effect of the tracking shot is excessive but very much directed at the subjects midframe: the Harfords. What we are left with is a powerful sense of their self-absorption, their unbridled, unfiltered narcissism that feeds on the image of themselves watching themselves and being watched. It's as if the main characters are becoming, in this single shot, their own objects of desire.

Our second example is also found in the same party scene. Bill has been called upstairs. The host's mistress has overdosed upstairs; his wife ministers to the guests downstairs. He calls upon Bill, his medical friend, to save the situation by saving the girl's life. Bill obliges and does so. Alice, meanwhile, is gently accosted by an older man with a distinctly elegant, illicit aura. He is not only trying to meet her, but is also trying to talk her into having an affair with him. Here the mise-en-scène is a tracking shot that follows Alice dancing with the Lothario. What is critical is that this movement also proceeds in midshot and the camera is placed even closer to Alice and her would-be lover. This crowding accomplishes two things.

First, it gives the shot a sense of intimacy, the movement of seduction. Second, the camera, by staying close, excludes all the others. She is the only woman in this world, and he is the only man. The consequence in this case is to withdraw context. It's no longer a party in a very wealthy man's home; it's an erotic encounter. The exclusion of context heightens the intensity and narcissism of both characters. In the first tracking shot, discussed previously, the narcissism was a barrier; here it is shared. In the first track there was no erotic quality, only self-absorption; in the second track, it's all erotic, directed at stimulating Alice in a way she wasn't with her "familiar" husband. In essence, Kubrick has created a sexualized dream state by using camera movement with the same intense purposefulness used by F. W. Murnau. But the focus in *Eyes Wide Shut* is the self as the subject and object of desire.

Martin Scorsese sets himself quite a different task in *Kundun* (1997). In essence, Scorsese uses mise-en-scène to create a spiritual dream state appropriate to a biography of the Dalai Lama. Scorsese used camera movement to energize the bar scene in *Mean Streets* (1973) and to establish a sense of power (albeit posturing) for the main character's entry and movement about a restaurant in *Goodfellas* (1990). But in *Kundun* the goal of the movement is far more interior and complex.

Kundun follows the life of the current Dalai Lama from his discovery as the next Dalai Lama at age three to his leaving Tibet, now invaded and occupied by China, 30 years later. The historical conflicts among his advisors, the Chinese invasion, his meeting with Mao, the decision to accept exile in India—all this is covered in the narrative. But that is plot and not of central interest to Scorsese. These events are events of the secular world, the political world. Scorsese is more interested in the spiritual world, the inner life of the Dalai Lama. The challenge is to concretize this spiritual sensibility. Robert Bresson and Carl Dreyer both took up this challenge in their work, and both used a mise-en-scène approach to create the conflict between the outer-world conflict and the inner strength and belief of their characters. Bresson's *Diary of a Country Priest* (1945) and Dreyer's *The Passion of Joan of Arc* (1929) exemplify their methodology.

The first notable quality of the camera movement is that it simulates the eye line and point of view of the Dalai Lama. When we first encounter the boy, he is lying down, and we see the adult world upside down. As he rises, the camera rights itself and begins to move at the pace of the young boy's movement. Because he is always running, the camera moves at a fast pace. The young boy is curious, and the camera movement is not only subjective but also takes in objects and people. In every sense, the camera movement identifies the point of view with the attitudes and interests of the three-year-old boy. It is important that Scorsese moves the camera along this subjective arc.

When he uses cutaways, they are clearly from the boy's point of view. By doing so excessively in the first scenes, Scorsese is establishing ownership by the character of Dalai Lama, but also subjectivity in the most inclusive sense. The shot selection in these scenes represents the sense memory of the little boy, which creates the context for what will follow. The progression of shots doesn't follow logic but rather the feelings and interior "monologue" of a young boy with himself. What sense does he make of adults, parents, the tests the priests put to him to prove or disprove he is the chosen one, or Kundun? This is the aesthetic and psychological rationale for the shots chosen. It is also the driving notion for how and when camera movement is used to avoid editing.

To complement this subjective camera movement, Scorsese uses a variety of images of the natural world. Usually he incorporates them into a sequence of travel, as when the young boy is transported to Lhasa or when his father dies and his body is disassembled for burial, which consists of feeding him to the scavengers of nature, the vultures. In these cutaways, in effect, Scorsese is always concerned with the scale of man in nature. And so the image may be the boy's caravan as a speck in the frame, with the rest of the image filled with the sun and the desert. Or the image will be of snowcapped mountains that reach to the sky. Or birds in flight from valley to mountain. Or a river that is endless until it reaches the sky at the horizon.

The images are always contextual: Human beings are not the masters of nature, only one of many who inhabit nature. These natural cutaways are the practical context for the actions and deliberations of men. Kundun or the Chosen One is one of many ongoing elements of natural life. The contrast of these images clashing with the subjective camera movements of a young boy provide a dialectic of the inner and the outer worlds that carries us into the notion that both exist in an ongoing and harmonious balance.

Beyond the subjective camera movement juxtaposed with the cutaways of nature, Scorsese must create a sense of a dream state: in this case, a spiritual one. Here it is pattern that is important. Acknowledging the repetition of various aural patterns in the score by Philip Glass, Scorsese harmonizes the camera movements with the score. They too tend to follow a pattern, a rhythmic repetition. The crowning of the young Dalai Lama provides a good example. A young boy arrives in Lhasa. Crowds are present, in awe of their new spiritual leader. The boy's parents are present. His advisors are present.

The movement first enters the frame, then cuts away to side-to-side movements of his family, for example, and then cuts to the camera moving again into frame with the seated boy stationary. These rhythmic movements set up and follow a pattern, and they instill a formal discovery: that this young boy is making the transition from being a citizen to being Kundun, from the human to the spiritual. It is this pattern, this rhythm of the movements, that creates a special sense, a spiritual sense of the occasion of the crowning of the country's spiritual leader. What is critical here is that real time and naturalism are subverted and replaced with a feeling that is not practical or easy to articulate. It is spiritual.

Before we leave this section on mise-en-scène, it is worth mentioning other notable work that tries to use the moving camera in a manner not associated with a Hitchcock, a Polanski, or a Spielberg—the thriller or action directors, in other words—or for identification or the tension inherent in the use of the moving camera in an action sequence. (See Chapter 17.) Two of the most interesting directors are Andrei Tarkovsky (*Andrei Rublev*, 1969; *The Sacrifice*, 1986) and Miklós Jancsó (*The Round-Up*, 1965; *The Red and the White*, 1967). In both cases, the filmmaker moves the camera to avoid editing. The lengthy takes in *The Red and the White* and *The Sacrifice* become as much an aesthetic challenge as a source of insight into the narrative. The voice of the filmmaker is as important here as the narrative elements. An example will illustrate the point, *The Red and the White*, a story of the civil war that followed the 1918 Bolshevik revolution in Russia as it spills over into mid-Europe. Jancso's camera moves from one side of the battlefield to the other and back. Geography doesn't mean a lot; neither does rank. Nothing protects the combatants from the inevitability of mutual extinction. This is the voice of Jansco: neither side is better than the other. This idea is achieved through his use of the moving camera.

Working at about the same time, Mike Nichols explores ideas about human-made machines, airplanes, killing machines, and the environment. Are they natural or unnatural? They look like birds in the sky, yet they kill not for food but for more human reasons. These are the ironic notions Mike Nichols is working with as he uses zooms and camera movement to follow these manmade "birds" in *Catch 22* (1970). Nichols takes a similar ironic approach to relationships in *Carnal Knowledge* (1971). Again, the camera movement both follows the action and distances us from the characters so that we consider the nature of those male–female and male–male relationships.

More recently, Quentin Tarantino has taken up camera movement in *Pulp Fiction* (1994). In keeping with the genre subversion he is seeking, the moving camera maintains an even flow of energy as opposed to the upward arc of action and violence so central to the gangster film. Tarantino's first subversion is to replace action with dialog. His second is to move the camera rather than to build up a sequence through pace and close-ups. In this sense, his use of camera movement is supportive of his voice (as in the case of Jansco) rather than in support of the dramatic arc of the narrative.

THE CLOSE-UP AND THE LONG SHOT

D. W. Griffith created a pattern of fragmentation of shots that differentiated long shots, or shots that established location and context, and close shots, or shots that were emphatic, emotional, and intense. Eisenstein built on Griffith's innovations by using the juxtaposition of images to create conflict. In effect, this meant a polarization of the kind of shots used, with Eisenstein using more close-ups than had been the practice. Those directors who sidestepped mise-en-scène and chose to be more directive about audience emotions gravitated to a disproportionate use of close-ups. Sam Peckinpah, Oliver Stone, and feature directors coming from the world of TV commercials, such as Michael Bay (*Armageddon*, 1997), favored the close-up. In fact, all of the above-mentioned directors also embraced extreme close-up shots in which there is no context—shots that make sense only in juxtaposition to the other shots in the scene. Needless to say, these directors also embraced pace with vigor, which brings us to the issue of this section: What are filmmakers today doing with the juxtaposition of the long shot and the closeup? As I will focus on the work of Shekhar Kapur, particularly *Elizabeth* (1998) and *Bandit Queen* (1994), we need first to look at other epic filmmakers to understand how they dealt with the issue of juxtaposition.

All filmmakers have a logic for their shot selection. Otto Preminger in *Exodus* (1960), for example, uses wide-angle shots with his main character in the foreground and the ship, the *Exodus*, or the attack on Acre Prison ongoing in the background. He doesn't use close-ups as much as the deep-focus CinemaScope frame as a whole to advance his narrative. He is not all that interested in the juxtaposition of the long shot and the close-up. In this sense, his is a mise-en-scène approach to the issue.

Anthony Mann, on the other hand, is interested in juxtaposition. Whether it's *El Cid* (1961) or *The Heroes of Telmark* (1965), he will very often move from an intense close-up to an extreme long shot. Indeed, the angles he chooses for the long shot give them scale, a heroic proportion. In a sense, the shots aren't so much dramatic (although they are) as they are scaled to create an epic or heroic sense about character or action or both.

Turning to David Lean, whether it is the burial scene in *Doctor Zhivago* (1965) or the attack on the train in *Lawrence of Arabia* (1962), or, for that matter, *The Bridge on the River Kwai* (1957), one notices how sparingly Lean uses close-ups. But when he does, we are emotionally overwhelmed by them.

Think of the trees swaying at the funeral in *Doctor Zhivago*, or the hands pushing the detonator in *Lawrence of Arabia*, or the cross driven into the ground in *Bridge on the River Kwai*. The shots are dramatically very important to the evolution of the scene that is to follow. If there is an observation to be made about Lean's close-ups, it's that he uses them to plunge us into a scene, as opposed to the punctuation for the middle of a scene. In terms of his long shots, very few filmmakers have used the long shot as effectively, whether it is the winter wonderland of *Doctor Zhivago* or the scale of man crossing the magnificent fierce desert in *Lawrence of Arabia*. Unlike Anthony Mann, whose images grip us, impress us, and give us a sense of the hero, Lean uses the long shot as he does the close shot—for dramatic impact.

Another way to look at this issue is to contrast this work to that of Carl Dreyer, whose *The Passion of Joan of Arc* (1929) proceeds almost entirely in close shots. What we experience is first the disorientation of a loss of context, then the intensity of the close shots. Placed next to Carl Dreyer, John Ford's *The Searchers* (1956) is principally composed of long shots and midshots. We are left with the epic sense of the search for young family members who survived an Indian massacre. The long shots give the film a poetic, formal quality, quite different from the Dreyer experience. Perhaps the best balance of long shot and close shot is George Stevens's *A Place in the Sun* (1951). This intensely romantic tragedy modulates feeling through the use of the long shot and the close shot. Here the close shots provide point of view and dramatic emphasis. In the close shots we see Angela, the object of George Eastman's desire; in the long shots we have the perspective of class and social position and see where George fits in. Initially he is at the bottom of the social ladder. Stevens uses the shots, both close and long, to articulate the layers of the narrative. He subsumes his voice deeply in the narrative (the antithesis of Anthony Mann).

The recent filmmaker who uses long shots and close shots in a manner closest to Stevens is Steven Spielberg. Throughout *Saving Private Ryan* (1998), we are led to narrative clarity and emotional pitch through shot selection and balance. The recent filmmaker who uses long shots and close shots akin to the Anthony Mann style is Ridley Scott. Ironically, Scott's *Gladiator* (2000) is a retelling of Anthony Mann's *The Fall of the Roman Empire* (1964), with a shift in emphasis from plot to character. These, then, are the models facing Shekhar Kapur: To stick with the narrative, as do Stevens and Spielberg, or, at the other extreme, to create a heroic epic with a distinct authorial voice that pushes the narrative to an aesthetic that may look intriguing, but that may be out of scale with the content of the narrative or at the very least push a less apparent interpretation of the narrative.

Kapur lies somewhere in between, but at times he expresses one or the other of the extremes. Just as Mann will occasionally use an extremely stylized long shot, so too does Kapur. *Elizabeth* is rife with extreme long shots from a point of view high above the characters. Does this represent Kapur's artistic perspective or an authorial comment? Whichever it is, the extreme long shots draw considerable attention to themselves. To coax out the meaning of this and other options, we must first turn to his film *The Bandit Queen* (1994).

The film, which is based on a real character, begins with Phoolan, at the age of 11, being promised by her father to an adult in a marriage of low caste. The family needs the money that it will gain from the marriage. Phoolan, a spirited young girl, accompanies her husband. Even at this age, she smarts at the injustice of boys and men who verbally and otherwise abuse her because of her low social status. When the husband insists on sexual relations (she has not yet entered puberty), she rebels and runs backs to her parents. There shame follows her through adolescence. As a young woman, now living with her parents, the head villager's son tries to rape her in a field. She fights him off, but he accuses her of seducing him. The consequence, in a hearing of the village elders, is that Phoolan is banished from the village. Again, men have been unjust and only she has paid the consequences.

Phoolan joins a band of low-caste bandits and becomes the lover of its leader. In this relationship, she experiences for the first time a relationship of equals. It doesn't last because he is killed and she is raped by one of his criminal patrons. The experience is so humiliating that she is consumed with a need for revenge. Her criminal career grows, as does her notoriety when she returns to the village where she was raped and kills 10 of its men. The perpetrator, however, eludes her revenge. Eventually she is hunted down and imprisoned, but her fame is such that she is pardoned by the government and freed at last. Phoolan's story is the biography of a low-caste woman.

In fact, Kapur makes the film much more. It's an incitement to change women and the caste system. All must change. There is too much injustice. This is the theme of Kapur's film.

How does the deployment of long shots and close-ups, their use in a pattern of juxtaposition, help articulate the narrative? And how does Kapur present a layered view of Phoolan rather than a simplistic hero—villain approach?

The first challenge for Kapur is to lead the viewer to identify with Phoolan. Initially, he uses close-ups to show us her emotive quality. All the other characters are relatively impassive or guarded, but Phoolan is open and expressive, particularly in her reaction to personal injustice. Here the close-up is deployed to differentiate Phoolan from the other characters. Kapur does not make of her a romanticized heroine or a pathetic victim; he focuses on her spirit, and he treats her character in a realistic manner.

Nor does Kapur make a case that Phoolan shares a bond with other women, that her story is their story. He is far more specific. This is Phoolan's story. She is rebellious and she is unusual. The other women seem more resigned to their status in the family and in their communities. Her mother-in-law, for example, is assertive, cold, and cruel to this 11-year-old bride. She is the privileged one in Phoolan's new home; even her son, the husband, conforms to her view of Phoolan as lazy and uncooperative. In this sense, Kapur's portrait is very specific. Phoolan is the exception rather than a symbol. He creates a believable, understandable, admirable character. She doesn't want to be anyone's victim.

To give the narrative an epic feeling, Kapur resorts to extreme long shots—Phoolan crossing a bridge with her new husband, or Phoolan in the hilly badlands that house the bandits. These images add a formal sense of the context for Phoolan's life; that context is the southern Indian subcontinent, a vast space where people can lose themselves. This aspect of Kapur's approach is very different from the cinéma vérité approach, in which the characters' environment is less the focus than the characters' relationships. By alternating between the emotional close shots of Phoolan with the formal impassivity of the long shots, one gets the sense that there will be no help for Phoolan. There is no romantic Fordian vision of the land to be had here. The next dimension of the use of close shots and long shots is the variety of viewpoints of Phoolan that Kapur seeks. I suggest that Kapur wants to give us as diverse a portrait of Phoolan as he can. By doing so, he begins to make the more general case that, on one level, Phoolan's story is every woman's story. This means that he needs to establish the powerful Phoolan as well as the powerless Phoolan. He needs to show her as woman, daughter, lover, and leader. He needs to show every aspect of Phoolan in order that the general case of women be made. He thus has to be both specific for Phoolan's identification and layered for Phoolan to become every woman.

I have already illustrated Phoolan as the defiant daughter and the naïve young girl who believes that if you tell the truth, justice should prevail. In spite of being truthful about the assault by the village elder's son, she is still banished from her home. When Kapur shows us Phoolan the lover, with her lover the bandit leader, the shots he chooses emphasize the equivalence of man and woman. They are first related to each other in the same frame (foreground and background), and as they grow intimate they are presented on the same plane. Kapur uses close shots to punctuate the passion in the relationship. Phoolan the lover is presented emotionally in the use of the close shot. The camera placement is also intimate.

Later, when Phoolan is raped by the local crime boss, the camera placement is more distant. And when she is humiliated, walking naked through the village, the placement is high and the camera is far from her. The long shot records her humiliation. Here Phoolan is the victim of unbridled, cruel male power.

When Phoolan does exact revenge on the men of her village and has 10 of them executed by her own men, the camera is in close to Phoolan. It's as if we have to feel her power as a woman seeking revenge on the men who contributed to her past humiliation.

By moving to different visual perspectives on Phoolan using close shots and extreme long shots, and by varying the placement of the camera from looking down on her after the rape (victim) to looking close at her as an executioner, Kapur gives us multiple perspectives on Phoolan. By doing so he individuates her as a strong personality. He also creates a portrait of the various roles of women in a man's world: victim, lover, daughter, mother, powerless castaway, powerful leader.

Kapur takes up another story of a woman in *Elizabeth*, but in this case she is the sixteenth-century queen of England rather than a woman from the lowest caste in India. But there are similarities between the two films, both dramatically and in terms of shot selection. First, a summary of the narrative.

Elizabeth begins with Elizabeth's half-sister, Mary, on the throne. Mary is a Catholic and Elizabeth is a Protestant. Religious differences and alliances pit sister against sister, and in the first act of the film, Elizabeth's life is under threat. At the end of Act I, Mary dies and the Protestant Elizabeth assumes the throne. But as a woman and as a Protestant, she is surrounded by enemies. The highest nobleman, Norfolk, is Catholic, and he wants to be king. Elizabeth's advisors suggest an alliance—marry the King of Spain or a Prince of France, both Catholic monarchies. Even Elizabeth's lover counsels an alliance. In the end, she trusts one Protestant advisor, Walsingham, who—as a Protestant cleric and nobleman—is interested in her survival as a Protestant queen. The thread through the narrative is that all men (but Walsingham) treat her as a woman rather than as a monarch. In the end, she realizes she must choose to be a woman or a monarch. She can't be both. She renounces her feminine (read: weak) side and assumes the role of an asexual but successful monarch.

The prologue sets the directorial pattern as it applies to the conflict of Catholic versus Protestant. In an intense close-up, a woman's head is being shaved. In a close-up of her accuser, a Catholic bishop condemns her as a heretic to be burned at the stake. Quickly the scene moves to three heretics tied to a stake and observed by a crowd. Wood is heaped and a fire is set. The heretics complain that they burn too slowly. More wood is thrown on the fire and they perish. The scene is presented principally in intense close-up, with close-shot cutaways to the crowd and to the Catholic officials. Interspersed are a few establishing shots. Kapur cuts away to a point of view shot from above—is this his point of view, or God's point of view? Whatever it represents, it interjects a "watching" perspective. The conflict between Catholic and Protestant is being observed. The scene is very intense and unforgettably establishes the stakes in this conflict. It also sets the directorial pattern: a preponderance of close-shots with a few long shots for context, and the introduction of a third-person perspective from above the action.

When we meet Elizabeth in the next scene, it is in a close-up. She is dancing with her ladies-in-waiting—in a field, awaiting the return of her lover, Sir Robert. The image of Elizabeth is soft and feminine, in sharp contrast to the presentation of Elizabeth at the end of the film, where the shots are three-quarter shots to long shots, and the distant camera placement is hard-edged and powerful but not sexual, as is the presentation when we first see her. In these opening shots, Kapur uses a telephoto lens to blur the context, giving Elizabeth not only a softness, but also an openness of expression that seems so opposed to the cruelty of the preceding scene.

In this scene, Elizabeth is arrested and taken to the Tower of London. For the most part, we see Elizabeth in close, either via camera placement or as she approaches the camera, or the shot is a close-up. The images of the court, particularly in the queen's chambers, are distant and more long shots prevail. When Norfolk moves through the queen's castle toward her chamber, the point of view is again from high above. He and his retinue look very small indeed. The extreme long shots from a third person or from a distant on-high perspective creates an epic perspective: The struggle is not just men struggling for power, but there is something bigger at stake. The implication is that an epic struggle is being observed by the gods. This alternation of very intense close-ups for emotion (the death of the Protestant heretics) or identification (Elizabeth) is alternated with extreme long shots to give the sense of a struggle that is epic.

In the scene that follows, Elizabeth is called to the queen's chamber from her jail cell. There in the chamber, Mary weighs Elizabeth's fate. They are half-sisters, but of different religions.

Mary acknowledges that Elizabeth will be the queen when she dies (she is now ill), but only if Mary doesn't sign Elizabeth's death warrant. Here both power and emotion are played out.

There are long shots of the chamber that remind us that Mary as queen has absolute power. And there are close-ups of Elizabeth and Mary where Elizabeth appeals to her as a sister not to condemn her to death. The shift from long shot to close-up, from power to emotion, captures the layers of this narrative extremely well. It is both the emotional story of a woman concerned about love, about relationships, about dignity, and it is a story about power, its scale and its absolutism. Relationships, love, and dignity have no place beside power, and in the narrative Elizabeth will eventually have to choose.

Kapur uses close-ups for the emotion, for the femininity, for the sexuality of Elizabeth (and others), and he uses the long shot to articulate power issues, whether they are about Protestant versus Catholic, or monarchy versus church, or England versus France or Spain. He also uses the extremé long shot from a third person or on-high point of view to lend an epic scale to all the struggles listed.

CAMERA PLACEMENT AND PACE: THE INTERVENTION OF SUBJECTIVE STATES

Numerous filmmakers have used a subjective camera placement and/or shifts in pace to alert us that the narrative has shifted into a subjective or dream or unreal state as opposed to the in-the-world, real state that has preceded it. Beginning with Georges Méliès, best known for his film *A Trip to the Moon* (1902), subjective states have been a narrative concern and creative challenge. Luis Buñuel simply ignored the distinction between the objective and subjective from his first film, *Un Chien Anadalou* (1929), in which he simply cut directly into an altered state. Other filmmakers were more aesthetically elegant. Rouben Mamoulian used the subjective camera to establish point of view in *Dr. Jekyll and Mr. Hyde* (1932). Alfred Hitchcock used sound and the close-up in *Blackmail* (1929). Federico Fellini used sound, or its absence, and the subjective point of view, together with shifts in art direction and, of course, a narrative absurdity to assure that we would understand the difference between the objective and the subjective.

Filmmakers such as Alain Resnais, on the other hand, blurred the line between them in their work. Others used black and white and color to differentiate one from the other. To examine this issue we begin with Elem Klimov's *Come and See* (1985) and then look at Darren Aronofsky's *Requiem for a Dream* (2000).

Elem Klimov's *Come and See* is a war film set in German-occupied Byelorussia. The time is 1943. The main character, Florya, is a young adolescent who volunteers to fight for the partisans. The narrative is experienced and envisioned through his eyes. The story begins with Florya finding a gun, the prerequisite for joining the partisans (to provide your own weapon). He leaves home and joins them. The story ends, perhaps days or weeks later, after his initial experiences of war; he is shooting his gun for the first time and moving off into the woods with the partisans. In between, he experiences the horrors of war and wartime occupation. He is left on guard duty in the woods with a young woman only a few years older than himself. The partisans move off to fight the Germans; then, he and the young woman experience a German aerial bombardment resulting in his temporary deafness.

The two flee to his home, but his mother and sisters have disappeared. He doesn't know it, but they have been killed by the Germans in an exercise in ethnic cleansing. He and the young woman go to an island where he is certain he will find his mother and sisters; there are many survivors but none of his family. He then goes off with a soldier to find food for the people on the island. They steal a cow, but both the soldier and the cow are killed by artillery fire. A peasant farmer hides him, but soon the Germans take him.

They round up everyone in the village, including Florya, and herd them into a barn. He is allowed to leave the barn before the Germans burn the barn with its hundreds of occupants. He is threatened with death, but it is only for the photograph a German is taking—as a souvenir. The Germans leave, and he has survived. Soon the same Germans who burnt the barn are captured. We learn that half of them are in fact fellow Russians. Sentiment among the partisans is to burn them, but they are all shot instead. Florya now fires his rifle at a portrait of Hitler. This is intercut with historical footage of the rise of Hitler. As we move through this sequence, and as the shooting proceeds, we realize that chronologically the historical footage is moving backwards in time and backwards in presentation, as if it is being eliminated. The narrative ends with a statement that more than 600 villages were burned by the Nazis as they moved through Byelorussia.

This narrative summary is a chronology of the events of the film. What is more important, however, is how Klimov creates the subjective state of Florya, the young main character. How does he feel about war, about this war, about himself, about what is happening to him and his family? Klimov is more interested in giving us the feelings of the boy. Camera placement, shot selection, and sound combine to create the internal state of Florya. The consequence is a film experience that is constantly on the verge of the unbearable, and of the unbelievable. The question for us is how does Klimov create the subjective state of the main character? Whether it is real or imagined, an expression of his fear or of his hopes, is beside the point. Klimov's task is to transport us into the inner life of an adolescent as it is shaped by external events—the losses, the possibility of imminent death, the manner of observed violence. How does he process all of these events, and how does Klimov take us into the feeling state that the boy experiences?

First Klimov begins from afar, observing Florya. He is guided by another boy in his search for a gun. This search seems almost absurd, a war game played by boys. It becomes real only when Florya digs up a gun. All we see is that the gun is attached to a hand and rigor mortis has made pulling the gun from its dead possessor a very difficult task. This absurd narrative piece sets up the paradox—a real task, getting a gun, is born out of absurd, surreal circumstance. The fun is buried, together with its previous owner, on a beach that seems an ideal setting for two kids to be playing out a war game. It's play, it's real, and it's surreal.

Shortly, a glider floats by. This cutaway, also surreal, will be repeated throughout the film as a prologue to the intrusion of the real war, a German attack, which will follow. At this point, the glider seems a tranquil, childlike part of the war game. We will learn its true meaning after a few more repetitions of the shot.

The narrative proceeds with the induction of the boy into the partisans. His mother pleads with him that he doesn't need to and shouldn't go. A partisan officer says that they need men with guns; he has fulfilled the recruitment requirement, and he must go. Cutaways of food being prepared and the boy's twin sister flesh out a realistic sequence. He is excited. Like all young people, the act of going to war makes him feel older, and proud of it. He leaves. In the forest, Klimov's subjective strategy begins. The bombardment catches Florya and the young girl in a playful mood, but the mood changes quickly. Klimov uses the sound of the descending bombs to set the tone. The pitch is high and loud, and the images are in themselves descriptive of a bombing. But as the bombing proceeds, he cuts to very long takes of the main character. As his eardrums are damaged, the close-up of his face focuses on his pain. The sound of the bombs then becomes louder and more distorted.

The focus on Florya, on his pain, on the intensity and distortion of the sound, and on the growing distortion of constant noise, suddenly gives us the subjective aural experience of the character. Later the girl will explain that he has become crazy because he can't hear. In a sense this is what we begin to experience—his inner sense of pain and isolation from the world.

Klimov now alternates scenes of the real and the subjective. The next scene shows Florya taking the young woman to his home for protection, but no one is home. There is still warm soup on the table. Florya eats and tells the girl that his mother makes good soup. This very naturalistic scene ends with Florya's notion that his mother and sisters have escaped to the island not far away. They run off, but as they do the young woman looks over her shoulder and sees naked bodies piled up behind a barn. This glimpse reveals to us that the mother and sisters have been killed. This scene proceeds naturalistically, but it is followed by the almost surreal journey to the island. The water surrounding the island is thick with oil tar that retards the progress of the characters' flight. They wade through water. The tar coats their bodies and faces. The pace slows way down, and it seems the oil tar will sink them. When they finally emerge, they look inhuman.

They soon find other villagers who tell Florya that his mother is dead. They are covered with oil and tar, and a close-up registers his attempt to scream. Does he scream? Is it inner or outer reality? Florya seems demented, and the girl says he is crazy from the damage to his ears. This scene seems entirely subjective and unnaturalistic. This pattern will be repeated with each scene: the search for food, his capture by the Germans, the barn burning, the execution of the Germans. By moving back and forth, Klimov creates a tension between the outer reality and the inner feeling state of the boy.

The concluding sequence continues to heighten the tension between outer and inner reality. When the boy fires his gun at the portrait of Hitler, he is trying to exorcise his anger and the source of his pain—Adolph Hitler. By cutting between the boy firing and the history of the Third Reich, Klimov is giving him a target. By running the footage of the Third Reich in reverse, he is implying that the boy's firing is turning back and erasing history. Regardless of whether this is a catharsis or a wish, the sequence is very much a subjective adolescent notion—that the boy can, by firing his gun, turn back the destruction done to his family and to his country. This subjective idea and state is then offset by the return to reality. The boy moves off to join the partisans and we are told with a title how many villages in Byelorussia were destroyed by fire by the advancing German army.

Sound, camera placement, and shot selection—particularly close-up shots where the camera is very close to the subject—create the subjective state of this young person in war. Pace plays a secondary role in particular sequences, such as crossing to the island and the artillery attack that kills the soldier and the cow intended to feed the people on the island.

Darren Aronofsky's *Requiem for a Dream* (2000) is also concerned with subjective states—states that are induced by drugs. The narrative focuses on four characters: Harry, his mother Sara Goldfarb, his girlfriend Marion, and his friend and business partner, Tyrone. Harry and Tyrone are, as Harry calls it, in the distribution business—the distribution of drugs. Marion becomes addicted to heroin and Harry's mother, Sara Goldfarb, becomes addicted to diet pills. Initially, every character has some degree of control over their lives, but by the end, each loses control and each does what they have to do to survive. Aronofsky gives each character a well-defined character arc. For Harry, it's being a guilty caretaker, torn between self-interest and responsibility to others.

For Sara Goldfarb, it's loneliness or a search for acknowledgment by others (her friends, her son, the community at large, as represented by her quest for public recognition through a television appearance). For Marion, it's rebellion, first against her parents and later by blaming whomever she depends upon for money to buy drugs. For Tyrone, it's being a man torn by the need for praise, yet impulsive to a degree that undermines any achievement. In the course of their drug dependency, the characters will lose everything physically and mentally, and will be left with very little dignity.

The creative issue for Aronofsky is how to portray the shift from living in a community to living in your head. To manage the transition, Aronofsky uses a full range of devices—sound, pace, camera placement, the distortion of a fisheye, wide-angle images, pixilation, and lots of camera movement.

The issue for us is first to see an outer/inner visual dialectic, and then to differentiate how Aronofsky illustrates the transition for each of the characters so that he creates a subjective state that is distinct for each. First we'll look at the outer/inner dynamic that contextualizes and prepares us for the shift to a subjective state. Aronofsky uses two devices: the alternation between extreme close-up and extreme distance from the action, and the narrative device of intercutting reality with a fantasy.

When we first meet Harry and his mother, he is taking her television with the help of Tyrone. He pawns it to buy drugs—as he calls it "a stake"—to get his business going again. When we see Harry and Sara Goldfarb, both are in intense close-up. Aronofsky uses a split screen so they are together within the big frame but separated by the split. When Harry and

Tyrone are moving the TV through the streets, the camera moves with them but is located at a distance. The use of a fisheye lens makes them seem even farther away.

Aronofsky often cuts between these two extremes so that we feel very close and then very distant from the characters. He repeats this pattern when Harry and Tyrone take drugs. The drugs are shot in three quick close-up shots: of heroin dissolving under a flame, of the pump of heroin moving through an injection device, and then of a breakdown of the drug—whether it's in a vein in the body or externally we are uncertain. Aronofsky then cuts to Harry and Tyrone in a wide-angle shot that is initially in slow motion, then in accelerating motion. The use of an extremely wide-angle lens gives some distortion to the shot. Aronofsky repeats this sequence of shots when Harry, Tyrone, and Marion get high. Here the additional use of pixelation makes the sense of drug-induced motion powerful and unnaturally fast.

Aronofsky also uses the narrative device of a fantasy insert to create a sense of the dissonance between the outer and inner world. Sara Goldfarb will often see herself as a character in the TV game show she watches religiously. Harry dreams of stealing a policeman's gun. Tyrone dreams of his childhood, of its perfection and his idealized relationship with his mother. When Marion is having dinner with her therapist (he is clearly interested in her sexually), she dreams of driving a fork through his hand as it reaches out to her. These inserts clarify the thoughts of the characters, but principally they articulate the desire to be or to do what they cannot be or do in real life.

To create distinctive subjective states for each of these characters, Aronofsky initially uses pace to illustrate their individual goals. They all energetically want something: Sara Goldfarb wants to be thin; Harry wants to be helpful; Tyrone wants to be successful; and Marion, principally, wants thrills, including the thrill of being high. Having established their goals, Aronofsky will explore what thwarts their goals. This involves close-ups.

For Sara, it's a close-up of chocolates. Following the shot of the chocolates, Sara gets a phone call informing her that she has been chosen to be on television. It is clearly a sales come-on for something, but to her it's the beginning of a new opportunity. Immediately she gets her hair colored so she will look younger and tries to get into her red dress, but she can't. This introduces the issue of diet. When she visits a doctor he puts her on medication—amphetamines to lose weight, and sleeping pills to sleep—and her journey into a distorted world begins. Now Aronofsky uses a visual shorthand: the mailbox close-up registers her anticipation of the TV invitation or the application to appear.

The fridge far away represents the objects of desire—food. The pills in close-up represent the means to the end—her appearance in the red dress. But her hallucinations become more frequent; she sees and hears fragments. When she visits the doctor late in her experience, her pills are working less well. She sees him far away, his movements are pixelated, and his voice is distant and distorted. We now have a representation of an extremely dissociative state. The establishment of this state precedes her final act of desperation: her appearance at the TV station, disheveled and demanding to appear on TV. This act develops along the path of disconnectedness, and Sara is taken off to Bellevue for involuntary confinement and shock treatment. She has lost touch with reality; she is totally within her own subjective state.

Aronofsky parallel cuts between the descent of Harry, Tyrone, and Marion together with Sara. Their arcs proceed downward into loss and humiliation. By using the alternation of very close and extremely long shots (with a fisheye lens to make us seem even further), and by using sound and image and changes in pace, Aronofsky brings us into the inner world and the descent into the self that characterizes the effect of drugs on these four characters. The style is critical in creating our feeling for each of these characters from the most internal subjective perspective.

A final comment: There is a great deal of energy in this film. Pace and movement energize these characters even though they are caught in an inertia brought on by drugs. Each of them acts, but the inappropriateness of their actions harms rather than helps them. These are characters who can't save themselves or each other in spite of their desire to help the others.

NOTE/REFERENCE

1. The American experience with cinéma vérité techniques in dramatic films is strongly identified with the work of John Cassavetes in films such as *Shadows* (1959) and *Faces* (1968). Haskell Wexler in his film *Medium Cool* (1969) and later Michael Ritchie in his films *Downhill Racer* (1969) and *The Candidate* (1972) also experimented with the form.

CHAPTER 16

The Appropriation of Style III: Digital Reality

From the earliest days, film has struggled with two opposite impulses—to make its narratives as realistic as possible and to create the fantastic, the reimagined reality. These two impulses were represented in the late 1890s and early 1900s by Louis Lumière and his brother, and by George Méliès. Now, over 100 years later, digitization of the image, including special effects and postproduction, has fused the two opposite worlds. Now images can look real, yet originate out of an imagined reality rather than out of a captured (filmed) reality. In this chapter, our goal is to examine how artifice has become real and how realism of the old-fashioned sort has taken on a new meaning in the film experience.

What needs to be said at the outset is that editing has always actively supported both impulses. The extreme long shot and the long shot were the primary means editors and directors first used to articulate imagined reality and the fantastic. The long shot, the close-up, and the cutaway were used to convey both physical and emotional reality. In terms of editing styles, the jump cut and pace have been used to create imagined reality, while seamless continuity cutting—parallel action, match cutting—follow the principles of screen direction and have supported a sense of physical and emotional realism.

Immediately, the contributions of digital reality challenged both sides. The consequence has been an increased effort to create and exploit imagined reality and physical reality. As editors and directors appropriate new stylistic choices to gain advantage in one direction or the other, audiences are left in a state of suspended belief. For them, the issues become: "What is real?" or "I can't believe anything!" or "I surrender to the film, knowing it's not real." This begins to sound cynical, but it is not meant to be. Editors and directors are taking more extreme stylistic positions and the result is a kind of transparency about pushing artifice or pushing realism. Peter Jackson (*King Kong*, 2005) is having lots of fun on that island, as a giant gorilla, numerous dinosaurs, and innumerable giant insects all pursue the humans. And so are we having fun. But we know it is digitized reality.

ARTIFICIAL REALITY

To understand this "imagined reality" more deeply, it's best to consider the operational choices different filmmakers have used to achieve an imagined reality by pushing artifice.

233

The Technique of Film and Video Editing: History, Theory, and Practice. DOI: 10.1016/B978-0-240-81397-4.00016-9

Consider five options as pathways to what I will call *artificial reality*. These pathways are the use of video rather than film, the use of constructed artifice, the use of the imagined over the observational, the use of spectacle, and the use of special effects. Each of these options is clearly artificial. At times, the director's goal is playful, as it was in the case of Peter Jackson in *King Kong*. More often, the director has a greater purpose in mind, ranging from a Brechtian intervention in Lars von Trier's *Manderlay* (2005) and *Dogville* (2003) to rescale the story, to making it larger, as Ridley Scott does in *Gladiator*. I turn now to these options.

Video Over Film

The first pathway is the choice of *video over film*. Film, in its finer grain, has a depth and sharpness that projects realism. Video, on the other hand, has a flatness and a tendency to desaturate color, resulting in a pastel quality that projects artifice. Filmmakers sometimes opt for video as a cheaper option to film. In the case of Michael Mann in *Collateral* (2004) and of Coline Serreau in *Chaos* (2001), the choice was aesthetic—the choice was to use artifice in their conceptualization of the narrative.

Coline Serreau's *Chaos*, a fable of contemporary life in France, focuses on two women, the Caucasian Hélène and the Algerian Malika. Both are in trouble because they are women. The film opens when Hélène and her husband witness the severe beating of the young prostitute, Malika. The husband insists they do nothing and Hélène complies. But she feels so guilty and outraged that she seeks out the critically ill Malika and stays by her side until she is almost recovered. Hélène has to contend with an indifferent, selfish husband and son. Malika has to contend with the criminal ring that has exploited her and the father who wanted to sell her into marriage with an older man. The two women, with the help of Hélène's mother-in-law, claim justice and revenge against all of the men who have so callously controlled and depreciated their lives.

Serreau's concept is to present the women differently. Hélène has the typical hurried life of the upper middle class. All of the men in her life view her as "serving" them. Husband, son, boss—all see Hélène as in service to them, to be tolerated, rather than as a partner and an equal. Serreau plays on this characterization of Hélène until late in the film, when, as a lawyer, she is helpful to Malika. Until that point, she is presented as the men see her—subservient. Serreau's approach is light and comic, as if Hélène's life is a soap opera, a *comedic* soap opera. Using video and fast cutting emphasizes the plastic, unreal quality of her life and her life as a wife, mother, and employee. She is clearly capable and living an upper-middle-class life. The use of video here trivializes that life, focusing on its hurried and harried qualities. The use of video contributes to the notion of trivialization and also makes light, rather than tragic, her role in the family.

In the case of Malika, her life is anything but light; indeed, it verges on the tragic. When we learn about her life, it begins with the suicide of her mother in Algeria. In France, she is shunned by her father's new wife and in short order is sold into marriage with an elderly Algerian. When she escapes, she is without a passport or resources. She is forced into prostitution by a man who buys her food. As she moves up the prostitution ladder, her intelligence and her ability to exploit her skills bring her into conflict with her "owners." An elderly client wills her his fortune and the mob claims ownership. Malika's refusal to accept this leads to the beating and to their relentless pursuit of her. Hélène saves Malika from the mob's clutches, and Malika and Hélène plan revenge. They also plan to save Malika's younger sister from the fate of loveless marriage and from the same exploitation planned for her as it had been for Malika.

The use of video does not lighten the Malika story. But it does help the audience experience her story as a fable. Serreau uses the story form to present her ideas about contemporary women as a cautionary tale. Malika, as in the case of Hélène, is a modern French woman, albeit from a more traditional culture. Serreau is saying that women from whichever culture they come from must act to save each other. They cannot rely on men. Mothers, wives, and sisters: All women must stand together in a modern war against tradition and a male power structure that will only use them.

By using video, Serreau enhances the artifice of the story and emotionally distances us from Hélène and Malika. They become symbols in the battle of women and men. Video helps Serreau move the fable into a representation about modern life, rather than being only a slice of modern life. Artifice and certain story forms, such as the fable, enhance one another. In this sense, video, by making Malika's story as unreal as Hélène's is, moves the film into a stylistic choice that strengthens its message.

Constructed Artifice

A second pathway to imagined reality is what I will call *constructed artifice*. Lars von Trier's *Dogville* and *Manderlay* provide useful examples of constructed artifice. *Dogville* is set in an imaginary Appalachian town in the 1930s. Thematically, a city woman, an outsider, comes to town. She is running away from her life and her family. The town is very suspicious of strangers: Even a man attracted to the outsider will, in the end, side with his fellow citizens against her. Small-town thinking and its purveyors, the citizens, punish her. Only when her father, a mob boss, arrives to reclaim her, will she act as he would and punish her persecutors. "Like father, like daughter" proves to be the revealing cliché that ends *Dogville*.

The constructed artifice is created as follows: The film is made on a large set. Houses are demarked by masking tape. Lighting is antidramatic. Long takes give the film the appearance of a play being workshopped prior to sets being built for the production. Everything about the film oozes artifice, as opposed to any sort of realism. The result tests our capacity for imagined reality, but eventually we get past the nonhouses and enter the lives of the characters. One can see *Dogville* as another mischievous film from Lars von Trier, or one can see it as an upshot of digital reality, a reaction to it, a film that openly and stylistically states, "It's not real." Constructed artifice is the second pathway to an imagined reality. What I will call *the imagined as the observational* is the third pathway.

The Imagined as the Observational

Steven Spielberg's *War of the Worlds* (2005) provides an excellent example of the imagined as the observational. The story is a straightforward tale of survival. A father who has been a so-so parent (Tom Cruise) has his two children for the weekend. The children's tolerance of their father verges on contempt. In short order, Earth is invaded by hostile and otherworldly beings. The focus is Bayonne, New Jersey, but reports allude to a widespread invasion. The fate of father and children is challenged and in the course of their flight, the father will be heroic and restored as a good father.

The artifice of *War of the Worlds* is to make the invasion and the first attack essentially an observable, credible reality, although in fact it's imagined. No constructed artifice here. Rather, Spielberg attempts to make this invasion as credible as the Normandy landing in *Saving Private Ryan*. Moving from a lightning storm in the sky, to wind coming in from the Atlantic, the invasion proceeds with rumbling sounds coming from beneath the surface, the appearance of a sink hole, the slow emergence of what appears to be a giant spaceship, and the laser-like attack and the consequent vaporization of humans and the destruction of property. Eventually, the scale of the attack intensifies, and cars, buildings, and even the Bayonne Skyway give way under the attack. Each stage threatens the main character and he and his children provide the human guide focus for the action. Each of these actions is presented in a developmental credible fashion, although each is imagined.

The slow, incremental development of the threat and the attack makes it more observational. Later in the film, when the creatures from outer space are introduced as giant, wormlike beings, we are in imagined artifice, and the credible observational sense of the first attack is lost. In the first attack, however, we have an excellent example of the imagined and the observational merging to form a very credible sense of the threat to the world.

Use of Spectacle

A fourth pathway to pushing artifice is to sidestep the observational and to embrace the imagined reality for purposes of creating *spectacle*. Useful examples here include Ridley Scott's *Kingdom of Heaven* (2005) and *Gladiator* (2000). Both are epic struggles, the first the Christian–Muslim war for control of Jerusalem, the second the struggle between the Roman General Maximus and the Roman Emperor Commodus. In *Gladiator*, a dying Emperor Marcus Aurelius names Maximus to succeed him; Marcus Aurelius's disappointed son, Commodus, kills his father, and orders Maximus killed.

Maximus, enslaved, becomes a gladiator, eventually to great fame. When he is invited to fight at the Colosseum in Rome, he confronts the Emperor Commodus. Only one man will triumph. In the end, Maximus, although seriously injured, kills Commodus. He has achieved his goal, vengeance, but dies from his wounds.

In *Gladiator*, Ridley Scott uses imagined reality to increase the epic scale of the personal struggle. It's not important to Scott that the settings be believable. The battle against the German barbarians, the arena in the desert, and the Roman Colosseum are each presented in a highly designed artificial visualization. Each is intended to give scale to the personal struggle of Commodus and Maximus and, in an imagined way, each does precisely that. Scott isn't seeking believability. Rather, his goal is larger than life—epic.

By relying on a highly stylized set of extreme long shots of the battle, of the Colosseum, and of the arena in the desert, Scott is allowing imagined reality to contextualize the personal story, making the imagined reality of the battle for Jerusalem more schematic than, and not as effective as is the use of imagined reality and personal conflict in *Gladiator*. This illustrates the importance of the linkage of pushing artifice to effective narrative goals. Without the linkage, the artifice proves to be empty rather than effective.

Use of Special Effects

The last pathway we discuss to push artifice is the use of *special effects* to animate the narrative. Here *The Lord of the Rings* provides a useful example. Peter Jackson uses a large palette to pictorialize Tolkien's classic tale. The three films of the Tolkien trilogy tell the story of good versus evil in a mythical land, Middle Earth. At the wizard level, Gandalf represents good and Sauron represents the forces of darkness. Kings and kingdoms and noblemen focus on the kingdoms of Gondor and Rohan. The commoners are represented by the little people—specifically, the hobbits. The humans, kings, and hobbits struggle against the nonhuman orcs and their giant vultures and elephants. Serpents abound between human lands. The plot follows the effort to transport a ring that has power that corrupts the men who possess it. The hobbit Frodo, the epitome of good will, is sent on this mission. His friend Sam goes along with Frodo to aid him. En route, they meet Sméagol (now known as Gollum), who has been corrupted by the possession of the ring. Gollum is a creature torn between corrupt action and moral action. A group of knights accompany the warrior Aragorn to protect the passage of Frodo. Frodo and Aragorn are separated and reunite only at the end of the journey. Aragorn returns to the kingship of Gondor, and Frodo succeeds in the destruction of the ring. Each man is changed by the journey, but in the end human and humane values overcome the forces of evil and destruction, and Middle Earth survives.

In order to pictorialize such an epic tale of an imagined world, Peter Jackson used special effects in order to create the imagined reality of Middle Earth. The city Minas Tirith, capital of Gondor, and Mordor, the dead city, are pictorialized as the centers for good and for evil. The armies of Mordor and the armies that fight to save Minas Tirith are presented via special effects and their presentations animate metaphorical visions of good and evil. The giant vultures, the elephants, and the orcs ooze repellent qualities, while the king of Rohan and the to-be king of Gondor, Aragorn, ooze nobility, the best of human qualities. As for Frodo and the hobbits, they begin as innocents, but increasingly gain a more complex view of the world; short people and ugly monsters are all pictorialized using special effects technology. Much of the film is thus artifice.

As in the case of *Gladiator*, the artifice works because it is linked to personalized dramatic tensions—for example, the relationships of Frodo, Sam, and Sméagol are conflictual and complex. Without the emotions arising out of these relationships, the scale of the special effects would have far less meaning. When linked to effect-emotionalized narrative, however, the special effects amplify the characters' struggles. In this case, artifice contributes powerfully to the audience experience.

REALISM

The other stylistic choice filmmakers have taken up is pushing realism. In their way, they have pursued realism as aggressively as Ridley Scott and Peter Jackson have pursued an imagined realism that openly embraced artifice. The most useful start point for this impulse is to reiterate that cinéma vérité staked a position in narrative film starting in the 1940s, in location shoots such as those of Elia Kazan's *Boomerang!* (1947) and *Panic in the Streets* (1950), through the late 1950s, as captured in the reality filmmaking of Karel Reisz in *Saturday Night and Sunday Morning* (1960) and John Cassavetes's *Shadows* (1959). In the 1960s, Arthur Penn (*Mickey One*, 1965), John Frankenheimer (*Seconds*, 1966), and Sydney Lumet (*The Pawnbroker*, 1965) favored a cinéma vérité approach to their subjects, and in the 1970s, Michael Ritchie took up the style (*Downhill Racer*, 1969). By the 1990s, appearance of the Danish Dogme films (Dogma films and Docudrama in the U.K.; Ken Loach's *Land and Freedom*, 1995) and the work of Mike Leigh had made cinéma vérité an accepted stylistic tool for dramatic material.

Thomas Vinterberg's *Festen* (*The Celebration*) launched the Dogme films, exemplified by no artificial lights, no artificial sound, and no tripod, as mentioned earlier. Lone Scherfig's *Italiensk for begyndere* (*Italian for Beginners*) (2000) and Kristian Levring's *The King Is Alive* (2000) consolidated the reputation of cinéma vérité at the turn of the century. At the same time, Belgian filmmakers began to use the docudrama style for a wide variety of story forms, from gangster (*Man Bites Dog: It Happened in Your Neighborhood*, 1992) to melodrama (*Rosetta*). Cinéma vérité as a style became mainstream when Woody Allen used it in *Husbands and Wives* (1992) and Steven Spielberg used it in *Schindler's List* (1993) and *Saving Private Ryan*.

If spectacle—the epic—underscores imagined realism, it is the human scale, both in inner life and outer life, that is the goal of those styles undertaken to push realism. In Vinterberg's *Festen* (*The Celebration*), jump cutting is used to create the chaotic lives of two of three living siblings. The stillness of the camera and the longer takes illustrate the cold-bloodedness of a patriarch who continually raped his twins when they were children. If the Dogme films have once again popularized realism, particular filmmakers have worked with variants of style to seek out levels of realism. The most orthodox in their goals are the Dardenne brothers, who in a series of films—*La Promesse* (1996), *Rosetta*, *Le Fils* (*The Son*) (2002), and *L'Enfant* (*The Child*) (2005)—have made an art of the observational. Their focus is the smallest of behaviors, actions, and goals.

In each of the Dardenne films, the world is made up of children and adults. In *Rosetta*, a mother is nothing but an alcoholic barrier to the teenage daughter, Rosetta. In *Le Fils* (*The Son*), an adult who works with troubled teenage boys is the main character. Goals and relationships are grounded in small actions—working, preparing a meal, moving from work to home or from home to work. Nothing extreme occurs and yet there is an intensity to these films quite unlike a film grounded in one catastrophe after another—*The Poseidon Adventure*, for example. The handheld camera movement, the proximity to the character, the movement, and the jump cutting together produce a heightened sense of each action, each behavior, and each interaction. The cumulative effect of a Dardenne brothers' film is an excruciating level of pain and pathos. We feel we have lived through a human war and are drained by the experience. Here the active observance of character makes the experience participatory for us.

The next level of the observational principle is to strip away the empathic style of the Dardenne brothers and to replace it with an alternative action style that is active without empathy. This approach is best captured by Philippe Grandrieux in his film *Sombre* (1998). *Sombre* tells the story of a serial killer in rural France. He kills throughout the film, and neither remorse nor psychological explanation is offered. Instead, Grandrieux presents the killings using a handheld camera. Jump cuts alternately voyeuristically show the action and avoid showing the action, creating the feeling that what is in fact shown is accidental. The result is disturbing.

In between the killings, Grandrieux has long tracking shots from the point of view of the killer. Traveling through the mountains, the rural population selling, working in their recreation, is captured but not understood. No empathy for the population, or for the killer, is evoked: only the sadness of not being connected. The pace, when it changes, implies that the killer needs the excitement of contact, and then of empowerment, and then of domination and destruction. The shot selection and the edit pattern create the feeling of desire and alienation and disturbance of the murderer. Nothing is explained. Psychology is sidestepped. Only the actions are presented, and those actions, habitual desire and destruction, are disturbingly captured by the moving camera by the proximity of its placement, its point of view, and the jump cuts. Here style suggests or implies psychology: I can't help myself. I love it. And I hate it. This is the upshot of the observational aggressive realism of that style. *Sombre* is well titled. Pushing realism here is powerful, troubling. The human scale, although not understood, is experienced by the audience. *Sombre* and action direction represent the second pathway to pushing realism as a style.

The third pathway is to explore the option of heightened realism. By heightened realism, I have in mind a sense of inner realism. What if Philippe Grandrieux took us into the mind of the serial killer in *Sombre*? The recent explosion of biographical films centering on personalities—Howard Hughes (*The Aviator*, 2004), Ray Charles (*Ray*, 2004), Johnny Cash (*Walk the Line*, 2005), and Truman Capote (*Capote*, 2005)—provides the insight here. In each case, the plot is about a career or a critical phase of a career—the writing of *In Cold Blood* in *Capote*, for example. But the sense of heightened realism comes from the inner life of the character: What motivates their behavior, their achievement? For Howard Hughes, it's a pathological fear of the hygienic danger of the other. For Ray Charles, it's the question of whether blindness is a barrier in life or a motivation. For Johnny Cash, it's the guilt and anger he feels about the death of his father's favored son. And for Truman Capote, it's a malignant ambition that drives the author to creative heights and to personal depths.

In order for the sense of heightened realism to be credible, the complexity of two relationships needs to be explored. In *Capote*, those relationships are between Truman and one of the killers, Perry, and between Truman and Harper Lee, his old friend. In the case of Harper Lee, she accepts Truman, his strengths and his weaknesses. She represents, in her acceptance, the option of Capote's creative potential. Perry, the killer who Capote befriends in order to exploit for career purposes, represents the personal depth Capote reaches in order to further his ambition. Both relationships help create an inner complexity to an outwardly clever, vain writer. It is the inner complexity that gives *Capote* a heightened realism. The other biographies are equally adept at providing the relationships to explore the inner life of their creative, driven subjects. Without this sense of an inner life, these films wouldn't resonate as emotionally with their audiences. Heightened realism is the critical pathway to creating output of each of these accomplished characters.

Another pathway to pushing realism is to opt for the docudrama as the story form. Here, Steven Spielberg's *Munich* (2005) provides a good example. The template for the film is the terrorist massacre of Israeli athletes at the 1972 Olympics. The attack on the athletic residence and the consequent murders are presented in a fragmented sequential series of scenes, with the massacre itself in the final sequence of the film. The more contemporary plot is the commissioning of a team of Israeli assassins to hunt down and kill the perpetrators. The leader of the team is Avner (Eric Bana), and his Mossad handler is Ephraim (Geoffrey Rush). From the commissioning of the killings by Prime Minister Golda Meir, together with the Army and Intelligence chiefs, through the creation of the team, the film unfolds through a series of killings until Avner, having lost half his team, loses his will to kill and begins to question the eye-for-an-eye philosophy that initiated the revenge killings. In the last scene of the film, a paranoid Avner has joined his family in Brooklyn. Against a New York skyline that includes the Twin Towers (which we, the audience, know will be destroyed in the future, on September 11, 2001), Ephraim tries to convince Avner to return to Israel. Avner refuses and the film ends inconclusively: among those Palestinians responsible for the Munich attacks, a number have survived; among the Israelis, a number of the assassins have died.

In *Munich*, Spielberg is exploring the case for "an eye for an eye" and is suggesting that "an eye for an eye" is not the answer. Implicitly, he is making the case for political rather than quasimilitary action as the only path to peace. In the film, Spielberg pushes a sense of realism that is credible and complex. Avner may be a killer, but he's also a family man who cares deeply about his wife and baby daughter. He also cares about the daughter of a Palestinian he plans to kill. Avner is also presented in a number of scenes with his mother. Those scenes imply the difficulty of growing up as the son of a military hero. His complexity as a character is attuned to the complexity of his victims as well as of his accomplices, inside and outside Mossad. Being a son, being a father, being a husband, and being a man, each layer of Avner contributes to the complexity of our response to the film.

In *War of the Worlds*, Spielberg made imagined reality and artifice observational, credible. In *Munich*, he tried to make real events and real people credible. I've already mentioned the complexity of character. Killing is also complex. Spielberg made every effort to portray the killing of the athletes in Munich realistically. Because it was a real turning point in global terrorism, he spreads the murders out through the entire film. By doing so, he makes the event inevitable and iconic—more important than it would have seemed if the killings had simply opened the film. In the same sense, by presenting the conclusion of the film against the backdrop of the Twin Towers, again Spielberg is making the conversation more important and iconic. It's a reminder to current audiences that the Munich killings and the attack on the Twin Towers are a continuum. We all are linked—Israelis, Americans, and citizens of the world—by these attacks. Whether they occur in Munich or in New York, they form phases in a struggle that has been ongoing for more than 40 years. Spielberg wants us to consider that continuum and to reflect upon the eye-for-an-eye response: It hasn't worked all these years—time for a different response. This is the upshot of the use of the docudrama in *Munich*. Its pushes realism and it strengthens the voice of the writers and of its director.

Goals of Editing

17. Editing for Narrative Clarity... 243
18. Editing for Dramatic Emphasis 255
19. Editing for Subtext.. 267
20. Editing for Aesthetics.. 277

CHAPTER 17

Editing for Narrative Clarity

Complete narratives have been an editing challenge since D. W. Griffith's *Intolerance* (1916). But narrative clarity is a more complicated challenge than leading the audience through complex narratives. Stories can have complicated characters or multiple characters. Who is important to the narrative outcome: one or all of the characters, or multiple characters? Who is important to the narrative outcome: one or all of the characters? Is the antagonist as important as the main character? Is it important to understand which secondary character is transformative for the main character as the narrative begins and he or she changes from the character in crisis to the changed character we leave as the narrative resolves? And what about the tone of the narrative, that accumulation of detail that helps us to interpret the narrative? Must the tone be consistent or varied? The answers to all of these questions must be addressed and answered in the edit. Only by doing so in a consistent and specific manner can the goal of narrative clarity be effectively met and achieved.

The challenge for the editor begins with an articulation of the premise. Whether the narrative is complex or simple, the first task for the editor is to reveal the premise and to make sure that it resonates emotionally in every scene and that its prime carrier is the main character. A simple narrative will serve to exemplify how this works. The film I use to highlight the issues involved is John Hillcoat's *The Proposition* (2006).

The Proposition is a Western set in 1880's Australia. It opens with the capture of a notorious outlaw, Charlie Burns, and his younger brother Mikey. Captain Stanley, the law in the area, makes Charlie a proposition: If he tracks down and kills his older brother, Arthur, in the next week, Mikey will live. If he does not, Mikey will hang. Either Charlie will save his brother Mikey or he will not. To save him is to preserve family, but to do so he must destroy another part of his family. The premise is to save or to destroy, love or violence.

This theme of love or violence will be echoed in Charlie's relation to Mikey, Arthur's relation to Charlie, and in Captain Stanley's relation to his wife Martha. In each case, the character will make a choice. And throughout, the paradox of violence and cruelty toward those outside the family is ongoing, as if it's the prevailing behavior overriding civil and familial feeling. Violence, when it comes, is sudden, shocking. To convey the feeling, Hillcoat moves from extreme long shots to extreme close-ups. Half-butchered, half-human images crowd

243

The Technique of Film and Video Editing: History, Theory, and Practice. DOI: 10.1016/B978-0-240-81397-4.00017-0

foregrounds, partial visuals allow the imagination to proceed to the worst possibility, and great beauty cuts to great horror. Juxtapositions of those sorts assure the audience's fear of the violence when it comes. Long takes, on the other hand, create the stability of family, the enduring quality of love. Both polarities articulate the premise for Charlie, for Arthur, for Captain Stanley. The consequence is a tense experience that positions love and violence as the two gatekeepers of feeling for the main character and his two adversaries. In a very elemental visual and editing style, Hillcoat has positioned his audience in the narrative from the outset, and he has made us understand on a feeling level what is at stake for each of the characters. The power of the film is the notion that love and family feeling could exist in so violent an environment.

The Proposition illustrates narrative clarity in simple narrative. Joachim Trier's *Reprise* (2006) illustrates narrative clarity when the primary goal is a mood or feeling other than a progressive, plot-driven narrative. *Reprise* is about one dimension of being 23. Two young men, attractive and intelligent, want to be writers. Rather than focus on the artistic goal, Trier instead chooses to create the anxiety each feels about being age 23. Their work and their relationships provide the narrative material, but there are no resolutions here—only the feeling state of being 23 and uncertain and anxious. Trier creates the mood by using a narrator and fast-paced montages that detail how each young man has over time come to feel as he does. The visuals and the narration are energetic; they are 23, and unreliably ironic. In each case, the combination creates uncertainty and ambivalence around the behavior of each young man. The consequence is an appealing energy and a fearful inertia coexistent in the same characters. Neither writer is mocked by the editing device; the audience is not put off by their self-absorption. We simply see them as what they are: 23 and uncertain about work and love. Trier's editing choices help create the mood and elevate the mood to an importance beyond the narrative events of *Reprise*. In this film, a clarity to this pervasive mood is the narrative.

Turning to more complex narratives, the challenge is commensurately more difficult for the editor. Those challenges differ in plot-driven narratives as compared to character-driven narratives.

THE PLOT-DRIVEN FILM

The first challenge in the plot-driven film is to keep the plot moving along with a building momentum and appropriate surprises, twists, and turns. The more subtle issue in the plot-driven film is to clarify the premise for the main character and to assure that the plot sustains appropriate pressure in conflict with the main character's goal. To illustrate both the challenges and the strategies for clarity, I look at three films with elaborate plots that mask a premise that complicates the narrative.

Five Fingers

Joseph Mankiewicz's *Five Fingers* (1952) tells a story of the espionage set in Ankara, Turkey, three months before the Allied invasion of Europe. The Germans desperately want to know where the invasion will take place. The valet of the British Ambassador to Turkey wants to sell them that information, as well as many additional top secrets as he can. He does sell them the information about the invasion. As he puts it, whether they will put the information to good use is wholly another matter. This is the plot of *Five Fingers*.

The personal story and the premise of *Five Fingers* is the story of the spy Diello, a valet who wants to move up in class. Politics are meaningless to him; money is his ideology. But he is surrounded by people brimming with belief—the Nazis, the British, and a Polish countess who's down on her luck. (Diello had been in the past her husband's valet.) The question of money versus ideology is the premise throughout the narrative. Class affiliates at different times with money or ideology. It is the elusive goal of Diello.

Each element of the premise can be seen as power. Money gives power to its owner, as does ideology. Consequently, the visual compositions, the ordering of the shots, and their juxtapositions imply power relationships. Mankiewicz doesn't opt for pace to create opposition or conflict, but instead relies on composition. Diello and his Nazi contact Moyzisch; Moyzisch and the Nazi ambassador; Von Papen, Diello, and Anna, the Polish countess; Diello and the British ambassador are all present in foreground–background relationships. Power gravitates to the foreground, with the background representing the opposition to that power. It is rare in the film to be presented with equals. Even when Anna becomes Diello's lover, the presentation is in terms of unequal powers.

Surprises, when they come—Anna's letter to the British ambassador telling him Diello is a Nazi spy, a cleaning woman's thoroughness tripping the alarm to the ambassador's safe, thereby identifying Diello as the Nazi spy, the news that the Nazi payments to Diello and Anna have been in counterfeit British pounds—are each revelations that are presented in a cutaway rather than in pace. Mankiewicz uses reaction shots of Diello in each case to register their meaning for Diello.

By using a visual compositional style that highlights shifting power relationships and cutaways and reaction shots to register the surprises in the narrative, Mankiewicz keeps the plot and the articulation of the premise for the main character clear and emotionally resonant throughout the film. *Five Fingers* is narrative clarity in sophisticated top form.

Mountains of the Moon

Bob Rafelson's *Mountains of the Moon* (1990) focuses on the British exploration in the 1850s to find the source of the Nile. There are two main characters: the upper-class lieutenant John Hanning Speke and the Irish travel writer and anthropologist Captain Richard Burton. Although they have different interests, backgrounds, and goals, they also have different skills. Speke is very much the hunter and Burton the intellectual explorer. The search is above all dangerous—hostile tribes, animals, disease, and the unforgiving land pose almost insurmountable challenges.

The premise of *Mountains of the Moon* pits friendship against fame as options for the two. Class, conformity, and conquest are all at play in the narrative, but they are always filtered through the meaning of friendship and the ambition for fame. Friendship knows no bounds—loyalty, love, and even homoerotic love are subsumed in friendship. Fame, on the other hand, is competitive, rivalrous, and exclusive, and there doesn't seem to be room for both, at least for John Hanning Speke and the characters who influence him. Burton, on the other hand, opts always for friendship even at the cost of fame.

To clarify the two polarities of the premise, the journey in search of the Nile is presented in terms of a series of crises where one man saves the other. Early on, when their camp is attacked by horrible natives, it is Speke's skill with weapons that saves both men. Later, when Speke is afflicted with an insect in his ear burrowing toward his brain, it is Burton who nurses him back to health. When Burton is afflicted with a blood disorder, it is Speke who nurses him to health.

As the threatening events occur, the men grow closer, and it is clear that theirs is virtually a commitment equivalent to love. In the progression of these scenes, Rafelson moves in closer from longer shots to close-ups. The shot selection itself presents the growing commitment and intensity of the relationship. Rafelson uses these scenes to progressively illustrate the growing bond between the two men.

Rafelson uses relationships to press both characters toward the fame option and both are carried forward by "lovers." In the case of Speke, it is the young publisher Oliphant, and in the case of Burton, his wife Isabel. In both cases the framing of Speke—Oliphant and Burton—Isabel is looser and more adversarial in positioning when compared to the shots that depict friendship. The latter are framed not only with characters on the same plane but with closer proximity to the camera. The result is an intimacy in the shots depicting friendship, and a coolness, a more distant and even adversarial sense to those shots depicting the quest for fame. Rather than use pace with either fame or friendship, Rafelson opts for close-ups for friendship and three-quarter shots for fame. Throughout the film, both Speke and Burton are foregrounded relative to other characters so that their points of view are more critical around the premise, rather than the views of others. Together with the focus on the issues of friendship and fame, the characters as well as the plot provide the opportunity to explore friendship and fame clearly and powerfully.

Invictus

Clint Eastwood's *Invictus* (2009) tells the true story of the early presidency of Nelson Mandela. Having emerged from almost 20 years of imprisonment, Nelson Mandela is in short order elevated to the presidency of the new South Africa. White apartheid has failed, but white—black fears and anger remain. The national rugby team, the Springboks, symbolizes the former regime—Black South Africans celebrate their losses, and White South Africans see the team as theirs, a continuum from the White South Africa of the past.

President Mandela faces this racial divide as he takes office. Next year, 1995, the World Championship Rugby games will be held in South Africa. He believes that if he can rally the country around the Springboks and if they win the World Cup he will be able to move the country past the divided country it is and to the united country that he hopes it will become. But he has to overcome the team's losing ways, and the powerful divide between blacks and whites. The film ends with the Springboks winning the World Cup in 1995.

Although the Mandela character drives the narrative, it is Francois Pienaar who is the main character dealing with the premise of a divided, antagonistic (past-directed) view of South Africa, or a unified, forgiving (future-directed) view of South Africa. The former views South Africa through the primacy of color, white or black power and its attendant hatred of the other, while the latter—the view held by Nelson Mandela—is that a country can't be built upon payback for past grievances, that forgiveness is necessary to become "the master of one's destiny." Mandela's is the transformative character for Pienaar, just as he is for the nation.

Of the three films we examine here, *Invictus* is the only one to opt for an editing solution to execute the premise of the film. Essentially, it means using specific narrative characters to illustrate the divide in the country in the early phase and to later use some of the same characters to illustrate how change takes place. That change is linked to the fate of the Springboks in the World Rugby competition, with Francois Pienaar being the focal point for change, but by no means is he used to imply the extent of that change.

More specifically, the divide between black and white focuses on Pineaar's family, whose maid is black, and on the security forces, whose new leadership is black, but the security experience resides with the whites. The introduction by Mandela of previous Presidential Security men who happen to be white is strongly objected to by the new black leaders of the Presidential Security team. Additional objections to Mandela's plan come from his daughter, the Black Sports Association that nominates the team that will represent South Africa in the Games, a well-known white sportscaster, and more general black and white sports fans in stadiums, pubs, or workplaces.

The transformation of Francois Pienaar takes place through a series of meetings and visitations that bring Pienaar together with Nelson Mandela. In those meetings, Mandela confides in Pienaar about his hopes, and in essence enlists him to the president's view about the importance of forgiveness and the extent of the challenge. The enlistment is complete when Pienaar and his wife visit Robbin Island and Pienaar stands in the cell that confined Mandela for 17 years. Skepticism about Pineaar's changing attitude comes from his family and his teammates.

The change for the nation takes place against the backdrop of the final game against New Zealand. Eastwood uses parallel editing to focus first on the divide between two security men watching the president watch the game, one white and the other black. Outside the stadium, a poor black boy is chased away by two white security men who sit in their car listening to the game. Inside, the black maid sits with Pineaar's white family. The sequence also focuses on Mandela's daughter, workers in black settings, and white workers all listening to or watching the game.

As the game begins, the focus is on the separateness, but as the game proceeds, the enthusiasm and hopes bring the adversaries closer. The poor black boy now listens to the game on the police car radio. He is not chased away.

As the game concludes with the Springbok win, the black boy is now sharing tea and sitting on the hood of the police car. Blacks and whites embrace each other. The two presidential security guards, former adversaries, now embrace, as do each of the adversaries that have been highlighted in the parallel action. Their reaction shots tell it all, the country is united behind their black president and it is left to Pienaar to punctuate that all South Africans, black and white, share in the team's victory. Here it is an editing solution that clarifies the intentions of the narrative.

THE CHARACTER-DRIVEN FILM

By its nature, the character-driven film often relies on screenwriting and performance to convey the complexity and dramatic intention of the characters. One would assume that this leaves the editor with a lower order of responsibility. That's not the case. Not only does the editor have to edit for a clear, coherent performance, but she also has to pay attention to tonal consistency. A narrative with serious intentions is too easily undermined by tonal variation, specifically a tone at variance with the narrative intention.

Here again, we look at three examples to highlight consistency as well as inconsistency of tone.

Hannah and Her Sisters

In Woody Allen's *Hannah and Her Sisters* (1986), Hannah is the most successful of three sisters. She is successful in her career and in her marriage. Her middle sister, Holly, an actress, is struggling in her career and in her love life. Her younger sister, Lee, is in a relationship with an older man, but has no career. The narrative follows each sister, including Hannah as well as her current husband Elliot, and her former husband, Mickey, in their search for satisfaction in love and in their work. Two Thanksgiving dinners, a few years apart, flank the narrative. They serve as a portrait of these five characters at that point in time.

The major story line follows the relationship of Elliot and Lee, with both being unfaithful to their partners and the attendant fallout of the affair. All other relationships, whether work or love, emanate out the dissatisfaction of the five characters, essentially the shared premise of the individual narratives. Each character is dissatisfied with his or her life, and each will make a change that may or may not be helpful.

What makes the narratives real and affecting is that Woody Allen reveals in each case the private source of disaffection with their lives. Holly needs to be acknowledged for who she is, but acknowledgment eludes her inside and outside the family. Lee needs to be sexually desired, the only state in which she feels accepted. Hannah, the most successful sister and the eldest, is a caretaker, a state that masks her need to be loved for herself rather than for what she provides for others. Elliot needs to be in the state of love (as opposed to married) to feel vital. Without it, he cannot be in a relationship. As for Mickey, he is existentially unsettled; he needs meaning to calm his anxieties. Neither his job as a TV writer nor his relationships have helped him. Consequently, he is a man searching for answers about his place in the world.

Because each of these people is dissatisfied and searching, they remain within the shared premise. Because Woody Allen deals with their despair and their search to overcome it realistically, we remain in the narrative and the narrative remains in focus and clear. Woody Allen's use of parallel narratives for the five characters is not problematic because each follows the same pattern: dissatisfaction, reaction, potential solution, result. This pattern in the case of Holly, Lee, and Mickey is repeated more than once, while Hannah and Elliot have the single crisis of Elliot's affair, and its threat to the marriage. *Hannah and Her Sisters* is a good example of a complex character-driven narrative that proceeds clearly because of the sharpness of the shared premise, the insight into the characters' dissatisfaction, its source internal to each of their characters (as opposed to being caused by another party), and the consistent tone, the mood of emotional realism.

Valmont

Milos Forman's *Valmont* (1989) is essentially the same narrative as Stephen Frears's *Les Liaisons Dangereuses* (1988). The films, however, differ in premise and tone. *Les Liaisons Dangereuses* is a realistic treatment of sexual politics in eighteenth-century France, and *Valmont*, which takes on the premise of love or sex as the important dimension of relationships, is treated in a lighter tone. The problem in *Valmont* is that the lighter approach to the narrative undermines the tragic fate of its main character.

The narrative is complex. The Marquise is a woman who views her sexuality and that of others as weapons of power and punishment. She asks a sometime lover, Valmont, to deflower the young fiancée, Cecile, as revenge against her current lover, who she discovers has become engaged to Cecile. Cecile is in fact in love with her young music teacher. Valmont is actually in love with a married woman, Madame de Tourvel, whom he meets at the estate of his aunt. His goal is to conquer her and to win her love.

If this sounds like musical beds, it is. For Valmont, the discovery he makes is that there's more to life than sex; there's love. The discovery can be treated seriously or lightly, but the outcome, Valmont's death as a result of a duel, can be seen as penance for him, and as tragedy for the Marquise, who discovers love late as well (for her, in the person of Valmont). In order for us to understand the tragedy of loss of life and loss of love, the tone has to lead us to the feeling of loss and of caring about the loss. Unfortunately, the tone moves from romantic realism to farce. Casting, performance, and narrative event each contribute to this shifting tone. When Valmont is initially romancing Madame de Tourvel, the approach is farcical; so too the final duel that costs him his life. The variance from farce to the realistic pain of discovering love for the first time (in Valmont's case) undermines the poignancy of Valmont's discovery. This example is but one instant of many where tonal shifts serve to undermine the clarity of this complex narrative. *Valmont* exemplifies failed narrative clarity.

Hero

Stephen Frears's *Hero* (1992) is an even more complex narrative than *Valmont.* The central event that pulls the character stories together is a plane crash due to bad weather. The passengers are rescued by a "hero" who, after saving the most trapped passenger (a well-known TV reporter, Gale Gayley), leaves one of his shoes behind. Gale launches an all-out search for this modern Cinderella, a hero. She does find someone, a tramp, who has the other shoe, and she begins to transform him into "the ideal hero." The one problem is that he knows he's not the hero, and when the real rescuer steps forward, the lowly, unheroic petty criminal Bernie LaPlante, the question of truth has to be set aside so that the public can keep the hero it wants.

Each of the three characters exhibits questionable behavior. Bernie is a compulsive liar; the tramp, although a war veteran, is essentially decent but down on his luck, and indulges in the big lie about being the rescuer; and the reporter Gale Gayley is always after the big TV story, even when it's not necessarily the truth. All these heroes exhibit unheroic behavior in how they deal with the truth. The option of telling the truth might mean failure: in Bernie's case, keeping the admiration of his son; in the tramp's case, in changing the material elements of his life; in the reporter's case, in continuing to be as successful as she has been. In each case, the truth can hurt each of these characters.

Where this leaves us is that each character is less moral, more human, and less heroic in the case of public views of heroes—war veterans and media personalities. The true hero in this film is immoral, very human, and not at all admirable. In terms of the narrative, this leaves the audience with no clear answer as to who is a hero. Indeed, it leaves the audience wondering whether heroism is accidental rather than characterological. Perhaps this is the place writer David Webb Peoples and director Stephen Frears wanted to take us. If so, *Hero* in all its complexity offers the example of how difficult narrative clarity can become, when the narrative goal becomes more ambitious than the more traditional linear narrative.

The point we have reached, then, is the point of suggesting how narrative clarity is achieved and how difficult it can remain, in spite of the editing strategies undertaken. We turn now to a test of these ideas on two films that are quite complex. One represents a successful example of narrative clarity; the other, a failure. By presenting each, my goal is to highlight the strategies that can help the editor succeed and the choices that can be made that undermine success.

The Case of *The Hours*

Stephen Daldry's *The Hours* (2002) is a very complex narrative based on Michael Cunningham's novel. The narrative is really three different stories set in 1923, 1951, and 2001. Each story takes place in the course of a single day. The 1923 narrative, Virginia Woolf's story, takes place in Richmond, England. The 1951 narrative, Laura Brown's story, takes place in Los Angeles. The 2001 narrative, Clarissa Vaughan's story, takes place in New York. All the stories echo Virginia Woolf's novel *Mrs. Dalloway*, in that they take place on one day, that Mrs. Dalloway is to have a party, that she is undergoing a spiritual crisis, that she contemplates suicide, that the novel muses about the meaning of living and dying, that all things are part of the natural world, that the natural world has an order (beginning, living, and dying) to it, and that the musings throughout are in fact a search for meaning. The 1941 suicide of Virginia Woolf opens and closes the film along with the writing and reading of her departing note to her husband, Leonard Woolf.

Virginia Woolf's story in 1923 starts with her beginning to write *Mrs. Dalloway*. She is taken up with the writing throughout the day. Her husband, very much her caretaker, concerns himself primarily with her safety. They have moved here to control her unpredictable moods and to prevent another madness and its attendant suicide attempt. During the day, there is not so much a party as a visit from her sister Vanessa and her three children. Her loneliness is illustrated throughout the visit, and her yearning for contact is so great that she kisses her sister Vanessa on the lips. Vanessa flees back to London altogether overwhelmed by the degree of her sister's neediness. The crisis that ensues is a confrontation with Leonard; she wants to return to London. Richmond is worse than death for her. He agrees sorrowfully, feeling that his efforts to save his dear wife will fail.

Laura Brown's story in 1951 takes place on the day of her husband's birthday. She is pregnant. Her young son seems very attached to his mother. A neighbor comes over to ask that she look in on her dog. She has to have a procedure; she has a growth in her uterus. Laura seems deeply pained. She kisses her neighbor on the mouth and the neighbor quickly leaves. Laura's attempt at baking a birthday cake is a failure. She trashes it. She takes her son to a sitter; he is resistant. She checks into a hotel to attempt suicide. She reads the novel *Mrs. Dalloway*. She decides against suicide, picks up her son, and has the birthday party for her husband. Her despair does not seem to have diminished.

Clarissa Vaughan (Clarissa is also Mrs. Dalloway's first name) lives with a female lover, has a birth daughter, and has a passionate commitment to Richard, a former lover, now deathly ill with AIDS. Today she will host a party for Richard. He is to be awarded a prize recognizing his life contribution in poetry. He has also written a novel in which Clarissa has a prominent part. Richard has nicknamed her "Mrs. Dalloway." In her morning visit, she is upset by his state, and by his despair. He teases her that he is dying and maybe he will miss her party. She is undone by his threats but proceeds with the arrangements. Richard's former lover, Lewis, visits. He shares with her his sense of freedom when he left Richard. She returns in the afternoon, early, to help Richard prepare. Instead he says goodbye—he lived so long only for her. He commits suicide by falling from his window. Clarissa is uncertain whether to be liberated or to be bereft. She is reflective. Richard's mother arrives at her home. She is Laura Brown. She tells Clarissa that abandoning her children was the only way for her to survive, to live. The narrative ends with Clarissa's acknowledgment that she herself is pleased that she has a love relationship with Sally. She kisses Sally on the lips.

Daldry does a great deal to link these three stories one to the other. The frame of the narrative being the suicide of Virginia Woolf, author of *Mrs. Dalloway*, at the front and back ends provides a general linking to Virginia Woolf. The fact that Virginia Woolf is writing *Mrs. Dalloway*, that Laura Brown is reading *Mrs. Dalloway*, and that Clarissa is referred to by Richard as "Mrs. Dalloway," all serve to link the stories in a general way. There are shared details of a party being planned; the spiritual crisis of the main character; the confusion of need and desire the main character exhibits; and the blame ascribed to being confined, jailed, frozen by another—Leonard in Virginia's story, the son Richard in Laura's story, and Richard, the adult, in Clarissa's story. Together with a mood of deep anxiety, even spiritual crisis, on this day emanates powerfully from each of the three main characters.

But to make the linkages more unmistakable, Daldry uses classic editing devices; seeing the three characters in the same position or action links them visually early in the film. Flowers brought into a room, put into a vase in one story shifts into a similar image in the next. Morning rituals for the women, from awaking to the sound of an alarm, to wrapping one's hair, to washing one's face, are other visual linkages from one story to the next. In a sense, the match-cutting from one to another connects the stories further. When she's writing the book, the first sentence is repeated from the Virginia Woolf story, repeated in the reading in the Laura Brown story, and then loosely adopted in the Clarissa Vaughan story. "I think I'll buy the flowers myself" also serves to link one story to the next.

But it is the ephemeral depth of feeling about the fragility of life, the loneliness, the sense of abandonment, the emotional chaos that marks the inner life of each of these characters, and the capacity of each of these characters to reflect on that chaos, all create a mood that essen-

FIGURE 17.1

The Hours (2002). Miramax Films/Paramount Pictures/Photofest. © Miramax Films/Paramount Pictures.

tially makes each of these stories about those moments the characters live suspended between life and death. More than anything else, this sad embrace of those hours in between makes the three stories and their three characters feel like one another. *The Hours* (Figure 17.1) is an excellent example of a very complex narrative that is clear and powerful in its emotional clarity.

The Case of *Atonement*

Joe Wright's *Atonement* (2007) is as complex as Daldry's *The Hours*. It also takes place in three distinct time frames: 1935, 1940, and 1999. Rather than following different characters in each time frame, the characters in each remain common to each period. They are Briony Tallis, her older sister Cecilia, and Robbie Turner, son of the housekeeper on the Tallis estate. Robbie and Cecilia are lovers torn apart by Briony's accusation in 1935 of rape, for which he is jailed. Both Robbie and Cecilia die during the war. In 1999, Briony writes a novel called *Atonement* in which the two lovers are reunited; they live in her novel and achieve what her accusation prevented in life.

Wright's film, based on the Ian McEwan novel, attempts to present the film from two points of view—Briony's, and that of the romantic couple; the novel awards each of the three main characters their own points of view. To understand the flow in the clarity of the film version, it's best to lay out the narrative initially from the points of view articulated in the film. Because the central catalyst of the film is Briony, we turn first to her narrative.

In 1935, Briony is a 13-year-old girl. As in the case of each of the Tallis children, nonconformity seems both a goal and a virtue. Briony is a young person with a very active imagination. As the film opens, she is to perform a play she has written, using her cousins and later her family as her audience. The main action takes place in one day. Briony seems very interested in her sister Cecilia and in Robbie. She witnesses a scene where Cecilia disrobes to jump into the fish pool that fronts the house. She emerges wet, seminaked, with

Robbie standing there. Before a dinner party she intercepts a note from Robbie to Cecilia. The note is sexually raw. Later she enters the library to see Robbie mounting Cecilia. In her view, he is raping her. During the dinner party with Robbie present, her twin cousins have run off. A search is mounted. While Briony is out in the dark, she sees her 15-year-old cousin Lola being raped. The twins are found and returned to the house by Robbie, but not before Briony has accused Robbie of being the rapist. She shows his letter to Cecilia, further proof of who he really is.

In 1940, the 18-year-old Briony is a nurse in training. She tries to contact her sister, also a nurse, but is rebuffed. She sees a wedding announcement—her cousin Lola has married Paul Marshall. She now remembers that Paul was a guest of her brother Leon, at the 1935 dinner party, and that it was Paul, not Robbie, who raped Lola. She also remembers the time when she was 13 and jumped into a deep pond on her estate. Her actions were a test to see if her love, Robbie, would rescue her. He does, but he chastises her for being a silly little girl to put herself into such danger.

In 1999, Brittany is 77. In a TV interview, she talks of her book *Atonement* where she has altered the fate of Robbie and Cecilia. In the fictional version, they live and are together. In life, each died in 1940—Robbie at Dunkirk, Cecilia in a bombed subway tunnel in London. Now dying, Briony is seeking closure for her 1935 actions that ruined their life together.

The other point of view is the romance of Cecilia Tallis and Robbie Turner. Cecilia, Cambridge-educated upper-class beauty, and Robbie Turner, the housekeeper's smart, ambitious (he wants to study medicine in college) son, make an unlikely couple. Class poses an all but unbridgeable barrier between them. Nevertheless, they are in love. But the relationship is fraught with tensions. Nervous Robbie accidentally breaks a family heirloom, a vase, and drops it in the fish pool that stands before the house. Outraged Cecilia strips and jumps into the pool to retrieve the vase, as if she is upholding the family values.

Later, when her brother Leon has brought home a friend, Paul, as a potential and suitable suitor for Cecilia, she is cool to the approach. Leon has invited Robbie to join them for dinner. Cecilia does not feel it was a good idea. Robbie again seems awkward in his approach to Cecilia. He wants to write her a note, but fluctuates between polite formality and prurient provocation. By mistake, he sends her the provocative note. Briony is his messenger.

When he arrives at the house, he is led by Cecilia into the library. There they pounce on each other. They are interrupted by Briony. Later at dinner, they caress hands under the table while the dinner proceeds. Still later, it is Robbie who finds the disappeared twin cousins—only to find himself arrested for rape.

The scene shifts to 1940. Robbie is now in the army, the alternative to remaining in prison. He meets Cecilia before he ships out. They profess renewed love for one another in spite of her family's objection. She will wait for him to return.

In Europe, Robbie, now wounded, leads the remnants of his troops to Dunkirk. Speaking French, he clearly takes command but formally as a former prisoner he cannot be commissioned as an officer. At Dunkirk they wait for transport, but Robbie dies of blood poisoning. He and Cecilia are never reunited, except in an imagined scene where Briony attempts to apologize to Robbie and Cecilia.

The central question about clarity in *Atonement* is whether the narrative is a romantic elegy to a past cross-class love, or whether it is a narrative about sexual desire, that is Briony's toward Robbie Turner. Because of her love thwarted by her sister, and her age, she takes revenge when given the opportunity one night in 1935. Five years later, she realizes she has made a false accusation, ruined Robbie's life (he had planned to study medicine), and separated him from Cecilia. Rebuffed in 1940 by her sister, she spends her life wishing to atone. Her last novel, which brings the lovers back to life, is her attempt to atone.

I believe Joe Wright, the director, wants it both ways. He builds up the romance by giving romantic musculature to Robbie and his advances toward Cecilia, as well as his journey in war. Wright treats the Dunkirk beachhead as a peak romantic experience. He uses a six-minute tracking shot that mixes Robbie's point of view with Felliniesque spectacle—men, animals, and artifacts are organized to give scale and meaning to war as an absurdity, albeit brimming with beauty. Even Cecilia's death from drowning in a subway tunnel echoes beauty over tragedy, composition over horror.

If Wright wanted to point the blame at Briony for destroying life petulantly out of pique born of her own thwarted desire for Robbie, why does he reveal this central motivation an hour into the film, rather than at the very beginning? The consequence is a murky narrative. Although Wright tries to show us that there are two points of view here—he repeats the vase scene first from Briony's point of view, somewhat later from the point of view of Robbie and Cecilia. He does the same in the case of the sexual tryst in the library.

Further confusing the issue is the role of class in Cecilia's behavior, of nonconformity as a motivation for behavior throughout the Tallis family, and the absence of a more rounded portrayal of Robbie in 1935. The consequence is that he simply seems awkward and predatory in 1935, yet the Robbie presented in 1940 is sympathetic, helpful, caring, and effective.

Finally, what is most needed for narrative clarity in *Atonement* is a single point of view—Briony's or Robbie's, preferably—so that we understand the film thematically. Is it in the end about the primacy of class over love? Is it about the tragedy of war and how it destroys worthy lives? Or is it about how something small is all that is necessary to destroy lives, particularly when the people such as Robbie are dependent upon their rich patrons, and women such as Cecilia are pushed to act according to class lineage rather than personal preference? The fact that so many questions arise out of the experience of *Atonement* suggests the lack of narrative clarity in the film.

CHAPTER 18

Editing for Dramatic Emphasis

Editors and their directors use dramatic emphasis to point out to their audience that what they are now experiencing—image and sound—is more important to them than what has preceded it and, possibly, what is to follow. Whether the event is a clue, a revelation, or simply the feeling state of a character, the dramatic emphasis strategy deployed orchestrates how you and I should feel at that moment. The editor also needs to orchestrate these moments in the rising action that allows the audience to move along to that peak moment: the resolution of the film. In this sense, moments of dramatic emphasis tend to be more intense as we move closer to the resolution of the film.

Important markers in the evolution of dramatic emphasis range from the subjective, menacing close-ups of the father and the Chinaman in Griffiths's *Broken Blossoms* to the shower scene in Hitchcock's *Psycho*. Significant contributors to the repertoire of sounds and images for dramatic emphasis include Carl Dryer's *The Passion of Joan of Arc*. His extensive use of close-ups to the exclusion of establishing shots created the pathway for the importance of the close-up for dramatic emphasis. Frank Capra's use of a dynamic montage that creates excitement and chaos in the opening of *Lost Horizons* (1937) illustrates another option for the creation of dramatic emphasis. Music and juxtaposition of shots create a unique dramatic tension in Sergei Eisenstein's *Alexander Nevsky*. And the modulation of pace creates an unbearable dramatic climax in Sam Peckinpah's *The Wild Bunch*.

In this chapter, we will look at the deployment of all these strategies—the close-up, the dynamic montage, the juxtaposition of sound and image, and the use of pace for dramatic emphasis in two films, Paul Greengrass's *United 93* (2006) and Ron Howard's *Frost/Nixon* (2008), to illustrate how dramatic emphasis is used to deepen our experience of these films.

UNITED 93

The narrative of *United 93* sidesteps conventional narrative strategies such as the use of a main character for a docudrama approach to the story. The consequence is a detailed reconstruction of the tragic flight and of the tragic events of September 11, 2001.

255

The Technique of Film and Video Editing: History, Theory, and Practice. DOI: 10.1016/B978-0-240-81397-4.00018-2

The film opens as the terrorists prepare. It is the morning of September 11, 2001, but there is no reference to the date. Because there is no main character, the designation of the leader of the terrorists, together with three accomplices, becomes the narrative goal. The activities of preparation, from prayer to luggage to passports and tickets, become the details of the sequence. The leader of the group calls his wife to say goodbye. He seems tense, and his compatriots share the feeling.

The narrative proceeds to the terrorists at the airport. They and their luggage pass through security. The first danger point has been passed. Simultaneously, we are introduced to other passengers who will be on United 93, which will leave Newark to proceed to a California destination. We are also introduced to the air traffic control center for Newark, as well as for the country at large. There, a man who is the manager for the whole system is introduced. He is friendly and grandfather-like, a benevolent presence. As United 93 is prepared for passengers, we are introduced to its pilots and flight crew. Conversation is casual and friendly all around.

The narrative shifts to preparations for takeoff. There is heavy traffic in Newark, and the taxiing of United 93 is slowed down. The pilot is told that he is fourteenth in line for takeoff. While this is going on, a suspicious transmission is picked up from American Flight 11 out of Boston. A controller at Central Air Traffic Control believes he heard foreign voices. He alerts his superiors of a possible hijacking in progress. The Military Air Command is introduced as it is alerted about the possible hijacking. United 93 edges closer to takeoff; finally, the plane is allowed to depart.

From this point on, the fate of American Flight 11 from Boston, the first plane to crash into one of the World Trade Center towers, becomes a greater focus. Initially, the aircraft turns south away from its flight path to Los Angeles. Is the plane returning to its base, or tracking south toward New York? The clarity of a hijacking is brought into focus as another plane, American Flight 79, no longer responds to the air controller. That plane also changes course.

Air Traffic Control continues to try to communicate with the hijacked airliners. An in-air collision is narrowly avoided. Flight 11 is flying lower, eventually disappearing from the radar screen. The Military Command Center continues to scramble planes and seek guidance from the political leadership, but none is forthcoming. The military seems more undone by the events than Air Traffic Control. Smoke rises from one of the World Trade towers. A news report suggests a small private plane has struck one of the towers. A third hijacking is reported, and tensions escalate.

The focus shifts to the whereabouts of the second hijacked plane. It has suddenly disappeared from the radar screen. Activity on United 93 is banal. Stewards gossip, the two copilots, more serious, converse about their families in more elevated tones, the conversation nevertheless being relaxed—in essence, filler for the long flight. Suddenly there is clarification from city officials—a commercial airliner has apparently hit one of the Twin Towers, rather than the rumored crash of a private smaller airplane.

Suddenly, we are mesmerized by the second hijacked plane, as it approaches and hits the second Twin Tower. Here is the tragedy brought home via CNN—is it a staged entertainment or live television? At that instant news (television) and real life coincide and transcend entertainment and politics, replaced by death and destruction.

Shock ensues at Military Command Center and Air Traffic Control Center. What can they do? Suddenly, there is word that as many as five airliners may have been hijacked. The top man at Air Traffic Control Center decides to ground all planes. Planes from outside the United States must be turned back, and the thousands of planes in the air are ordered to land. The military is paralyzed, as it has not been given authority to fire on planes that may now become flying bombs. Smoke emanates from the Pentagon; it is clear that it too has been hit by an airplane.

At this stage of the film, the pressure from some of the hijackers prompts an escalation of the hijacking on United 93. Taking his carry-on bag, one of the hijackers goes to the washroom and there puts together a bomb-vest with a handheld trigger device. He hides the apparatus under the coat he wears. Another hijacker urges the leader of the group to take action. The leader puts him off; it is not yet the moment. It is unclear whether the leader fears the moment or welcomes it. The sense of urgency grows among the hijackers, and finally, one acts. This prompts the other to rush to the front of the plane. There they kill the pilots, and the stewardess. The leader of the group takes over as the pilot.

As the passengers see what is unfolding, fear grips the main cabin. Conciliation, panic, outrage—what to feel and how to deal? Each passenger tries to absorb the dangerous events unfolding. A stewardess has used an airplane phone to call home. Others are using cell phones to call 911 or to loved ones. News comes back about the two World Trade Center towers having been hit by commercial airliners. One of the passengers says this plane too will be used as a bomb against a prominent target. Yet others acknowledge that the fate of United 93 is not to return to Newark as claimed by one of the hijackers. The plane turns and is no longer moving west. Cleveland Air Traffic Control Center reports to Central. It appears to the passengers that their plane has changed direction. At the Military Command Center, there is anger and some panic. Their planes have launched in the wrong direction, away from United 93, and they do not yet have permission to fire on the commercial airliner. At Central Air Traffic Control, the head of the operation is frustrated with the military liaison officer. Where is the military at this crucial and dangerous moment in the history of commercial flight? In the cockpit of United 93, the hijackers are growing nervous. When the bodies of the pilots and the stewardess were moved, those activities were noticed by the other passengers. This is not on the hijackers' side.

Passengers begin to gather at the rear of the plane—specifically, the younger, more formidable males. The stewardesses pass out knives, fire extinguishers, anything that could be used as a weapon. Other passengers, seeing what is about to unfold, make calls to their loved ones to say goodbye. One of the passengers has piloted smaller planes. He is designated to pilot the plane once a takeover has been achieved. One of the passengers seems to emerge as the leader. Speed is of the essence. They must kill the hijackers quickly if they are to have any hope. The lead hijacker takes the plane lower to avert a takeover. The stakes are now higher. The likelihood of mutual failure, for the passengers and the hijackers, grows. Feelings grow to a fever pitch.

The passengers, now armed, move down toward the hijacker wielding a bomb. They take him and rip away the bomb vest. It was a phony bomb. For an instant, there is hope. They use a serving cart to batter away at the door to the cockpit. In the cockpit, fear and resignation mix. As the serving cart manages to get through the door, the passengers grab at the hijackers, while the pilot-hijacker begins to pray and reiterate his farewell to his family. As he is grabbed by the passengers, he moves the flying gear into a vertical descent. The passengers reach him and suddenly the plane is in freefall. The film ends as the plane reaches the ground. The screen goes black, announcing that the plane crashes into a Pennsylvania field. Fifteen minutes later, the White House gives permission to shoot down any civilian airliner that threatens Washington, DC. But we know that with the downing of United 93, the commercial airline threat to the United States is over.

The Docudrama Effect

Paul Greengrass uses a docudrama approach to give *United 93* both veracity and the "captured" look. Performance, sets, and camera work all support both the look and the feeling of immediacy. The story is filmed as if it's just happening before our eyes.

This means shorter takes, handheld shots, and the use of sound to provide continuity within scenes, just as would be the editing style of a cinéma vérité documentary. To counter the "performance" dimension, particularly of the hijackers, Greengrass also uses jump cuts as if extending behaviors as captured in close-ups. Whether it's fear, anxiety, or impulsiveness, Greengrass cuts in closer from a midshot or a close-up of a hijacker; at times the jump cut punctuates a feeling, at other times it seems to question the impression of the preceding shot. In both cases, the jump cut elongates the feeling of the initial hijacker reaction shot.

Greengrass avoided the inclusion of narrators to offer an opinion on the events of September 11, 2001. He could have used footage of the political leadership, from President George W. Bush to Mayor Rudy Giuliani, to the leader of Al Qaeda, Osama bin Laden. But he does not. Nor is there a journalist, excepting a CNN broadcaster. The consequence is a total absence of speeches of any sort; no editorial or political opinion shapes our interpretation of that day's events. Instead, we have the portrait of ordinary people—passengers, pilots, air traffic controllers, military personnel, and, of course, the hijackers themselves. But each person is presented small and personal rather than as heroic, dramatic, or tragic. Greengrass's approach is to make the dialog as everyday as his presentation of the people. Not even the music track is used to overdramatize.

The consequence is an immediacy that is startling and a narrative that, contrary to possibility, conveys an aura of authenticity rather than manipulation. The docudrama approach contributes mightily to this feeling.

The Close-up

The close-up, when used sparingly, clearly is a more emphatic shot. When the close-up is used extensively, however, we need to look more closely as to how it is used to discern dramatic emphasis. To simulate the documentary, short close-ups, as a component of a sequence or scene, are important reference devices. Further, the absence of a main character—antagonist narrative device undermines the use of the close-up to underscore the key points of that struggle. What this leaves us with is a narrower band of purposes for the use of the close-up. It also means that the close-up will be used in a subtler, but no less effective, fashion.

In *United 93*, Paul Greengrass uses the close-up in a special way to distinguish the leadership in the four key groups in the film—among the air traffic controllers, the military, the passengers and crew on United 93, and the hijackers.

For the leaders, Greengrass uses a greater number of close-ups than he does for the other members of the group. He also tends to position them at the front of the frame; in the case of the leadership in Air Traffic Control and the military, he places subordinates in each setting deeper into the background of the shot. In order to provide us with a sense of the relative effectiveness within these two groups, Greengrass combines the close-up with a moving shot (more dynamic) in the case of the leadership at the Air Traffic Control Center; the leadership at the Military Command Center is presented in a more static close-up. The consequence is to visually imply effectiveness or lack thereof. Greengrass uses the same combination of movement and camera proximity to imply which passengers are defiant and leaders, and which are fatalistic and victims.

Greengrass uses a similar strategy when he presents the attack on the cockpit, a critical dramatic moment. The pilots are not shown full-face, whereas the terrorists are. He focuses the shots of the pilots on their backs and then their wounds. In that scene, the primary close-ups are also given over to the terrorist leader, taking over as pilot of the airliner. Within this scene, the details of the killings and the takeover of the plane are more important than any other visual detail, and consequently these narrative elements dominate in the close-ups used in this scene.

The other area of choice where close-ups are important and revealing is their use to establish critical specific events that detail the tragic trajectory of the flight and the day. The shot of the luggage of the hijackers passing through airport security, the disappearance of Flight 11 from the radar screen at the Air Traffic Control Center, the creation of the bomb that the hijacker will use to intimidate the passengers of United 93, the signage the leader of the hijackers put up in the cockpit detailing their destination—Washington, DC. By using close-ups to be specific about the turning points in the narrative, Greengrass is conveying critical visual information to the audience.

Dynamic Montage

A second strategy Paul Greengrass uses for dramatic emphasis is to rely on a dynamic montage to highlight pivotal moments in the narrative: the challenge of airport security, the traffic jam at Newark Airport, the bustling activity of an airport traffic control center, the chaotic takeover of United 93 by the hijackers, and the even more chaotic recapture of the United 93 by the passengers of the airplane from its hijackers. Each of these sequences is pivotal to the story, but in different cases the narrative purpose differs. In the security and traffic jam sequences, the intention is to add to the tension of the film. Will the hijackers get through security? Will traffic gridlock at Newark Airport prevent United 93 from taking off on its fateful journey?

In the case of the airplane takeover and the recapture of the airliner, the narrative goals of the scene and the use of a dynamic montage approach is more complex. In these scenes, the focus is to prompt the audience to grasp at enough details to assure they know what's going on. But more important is to give the audience the sense of chaos that ensues in these violent pivotal moments. The feeling of chaos prevails to horrify us, the audience, and to instill the notion that not only is violence chaotic, but also that in the chaos, the outcome can go either way. The chaos blurs the certainty of the outcome and invites the audience to hope for the best, knowing full well that the worst will ensue. The dynamic montage creates a cloud of energy and dramatic intensity within which both hope and dread can coexist, a state that makes the dynamic montage doubly purposeful.

Juxtaposition

Juxtaposition can involve two visuals to illustrate intense conflict, as in Eisenstein's Odessa Steps sequence, or involve a sound and an image in conflict. An example of the latter is the scream of an elderly woman discovering a body and the sound of a train whistle passing through a tunnel in Hitchcock's *The 39 Steps* (1935). In either case the juxtaposition is used to shock the audience. Here intense emotion, rather than key information, is the goal.

The first instance of this strategy is the disappearance of American Flight 11 from the radar screen. Until that point, the scene has been constructed of shots of screens and close-ups of controllers tracking American Flight 11 as well as other aircraft. The shot where American Flight 11 is suddenly off the screen is a shock because we in the audience know before the characters do the meaning of the shot: The first World Trade Center building has been hit by the missing aircraft.

Another example of powerful juxtaposition is the scene where the first, bomb-bearing hijacker is overpowered. The elevation of the trigger device has been used to keep the passengers at bay and in a state of fear. At the end of the attack, one passenger elevates the trigger mechanism, now ripped away from a dying hijacker. Clearly, it is a fake. The close-up of the trigger mechanism provides us with a sense of emotional release. There is no bomb to be detonated!

A third example of juxtaposition is in the last two shots of the film. The hijacker pilot has been wrested from the seat, and the passenger pilot is trying to take over the plane. But the ground is rapidly approaching; clearly the plane is about to crash nose first. The next shot is a cut to black. We know that the juxtaposition means the plane has crashed—United 93 is no more. The emotional implication of this juxtaposition is unmistakable horror.

Pace

The faster a scene is cut, the more important it feels in relation to scenes that have a slower pace. Because United 93 is cut with primarily short takes in order to simulate captured documentary-like footage, it is more difficult to discern how pace is deployed to orchestrate dramatic emphasis. Nevertheless, pace is deployed but in a more subtle fashion. For example, the scenes at Air Traffic Control, Newark and Central, are cut faster than the scenes at the Military Command Center. Not only are the shots shorter, but the handheld camera work also draws more attention to itself in the Air Traffic Control scenes. The consequence is that the Air Traffic Control scenes seem more pivotal, more important than the Military Command Center scenes. The result is also a more energetic, deterministic sense in the Air Traffic Control scenes, whereas the feeling in the Military Command Center scenes implies a conflicted, confused, even impotent sense. Here pace contributes to the sense of importance and effectiveness of these two official organizations.

Pace is also used to build up the tempo and sense of climax in the key takeover and takeback scenes on United 93. As in the classic robbery/last stand in Peckinpah's *The Wild Bunch,* the gradual acceleration of the pace through the key scenes takes us from the introduction of the dramatic purpose to the narrative center of the scene, and on to its resolution via the pace. Both the hijacker takeover and the hostage takeback of the plane operate in this way.

Finally, Greengrass uses a pattern of crosscutting between scenes at Air Traffic Control, the Military Command Center, and on the airplane to increase the tension. Variations in pace between the locations modulate the atmosphere in each location. The contrast between these modulations increases the general sense of tension throughout these interconnected scenes. They provide a larger palette for Greengrass to use pace to highlight details, events, or people that are more important than the other details, events, or people in the sequence.

FROST/NIXON

Ron Howard's *Frost/Nixon* follows a broadcaster and a politician at a point in their respective careers at which they need a catalyst to prevent their careers from continuing in decline. Each looks to the other to provide that catalyst. Each has known power and influence, and fears the personal consequences of their loss. In short, each is a desperate man, and only one of them can emerge into the sun at the expense of the other.

Frost/Nixon begins with the background of each man; in the case of Richard Nixon, this includes the events that led to his likely impeachment and consequent resignation from the presidency. David Frost is the host of a sort-of news show in Australia presented in an entertaining fashion (his caustic style). The nature of the news so far from the center illustrates the dissonance between where Frost is (the periphery) and where he believes he should be (the center). He asks his Australian producer to get him the numbers as to how many people watched the Nixon resignation speech and departure from the office of the presidency. In short order, Frost shares with his favorite British producer his new idea: to interview Richard Nixon.

Leaving office and resettling in his native California does not sit well with Nixon. Not only is he away from the action, but he experiences a medical emergency—phlebitis. Hospitalization only crystallizes for Nixon his fall. His agent, Swifty Lazar, who has negotiated a good book deal for Nixon, mentions the communication from Frost, trying to secure an interview. Lazar mentions the possibility to get a good financial offer from Frost, who needs Nixon to boost his flagging career.

Frost and his producer fly to the United States to meet Nixon. On the flight, Frost meets an attractive young woman, Caroline. He invites her to join him for the Nixon visit. At the meeting, aside from the pleasantries, Nixon receives a check for $200,000. It seals the contract and obliges Frost to give Nixon $400,000 more if the interview takes place. The Nixon camp is dubious whether Frost can deliver the rest of the money necessary. Frost's efforts to secure backers reinforce the Nixon position—the interviews are unlikely to happen. All the networks say no to Frost.

To earn money, Nixon makes a speech to a paying audience. It is clear that he doesn't enjoy this kind of activity. After he complains to his Chief of Staff, the Chief of Staff tells him Frost has raised the necessary money. It's a real opportunity to get back on top. Nixon is appeased.

Frost assembles a writing and producing team. It includes two Americans, Bob Zelnick and James Reston, who have great antipathy for President Nixon. These men represent the liberal American media, intellectual and very angry about Nixon getting off scot-free via Gerald Ford's presidential pardon. For Reston, these interviews represent the trial Nixon never had. The two men, particularly Reston, question Frost's motives and intentions with Nixon. Nevertheless, Frost is willing to work with them, even though they are outside his comfort zone.

While the research proceeds, the two Americans work 150 percent; they notice Frost is attending to other matters. It seems to them that Frost is less committed. Perhaps his party-boy reputation and glib personality allude to lesser motives than their own. Reston particularly is challenging about Frost's sincerity and intentions around the interview. Instead of pushing back, Frost's response seems as glib as the accusation. There is tension inside the group preparing for the interview.

Frost receives a call from Nixon's Chief of Staff. He seeks to limit the conversation about Watergate to a broader-defined 25 percent of the interview. This new limitation is rejected by Frost, who threatens to sue. The Chief of Staff warns Frost that if he feels Frost has pushed to advantage himself over Richard Nixon, he (the Chief of Staff) will devote himself to ruining Frost. Tensions rise as the first interview is imminent.

The first interview day arrives. Richard Nixon seems relaxed and answers questions in as lengthy and anecdotal a manner as possible. Frost doesn't intercede. The stories are soft; Frost is clearly not getting even close to controversy. He is unhappy with the day's work, as is his team. He rationalizes that at least Nixon will feel softened up for the next interview. Between sessions, Frost rushes off to try to sell ads for the program. His team feels the time should be used to prepare better.

The second interview day proceeds no better for the Frost team. The day opens with questions about the bombings on Vietnam and Cambodia. Nixon is aggressive and effective. The Frost team's sense of worry grows. The third interview day, with its focus on foreign affairs (Nixon's forte), goes even worse. The discord among the Frost team grows, although

FIGURE 18.1
Frost/Nixon (2008). Universal Studios/PhotoFest. © Universal Studios.

Frost disagrees. James Reston, in an effort to insult him, calls Frost nothing but a talk show host (as opposed to a journalist).

In the days before the fourth interview, despair sets in. Frost himself shares self-doubts and his sense of professional and financial doom with Caroline. She goes out to buy food and Frost picks up a call, believing it's her. He asks for a cheeseburger, but it's not Caroline—it's Richard Nixon. Drunk, he rages about how he and Frost are outsiders, and no matter what they do, they will never be accepted. Frost is shocked but strangely affected by the call. He receives it as a call to arms; at last he is energized. As Caroline arrives with the food, he tells her he has a lot of work to do. He will be the worthy adversary Nixon has challenged him to be. Frost enlists Reston to look for records in Washington about a particular meeting Nixon held with Charles Colson. As the day arrives, Frost and Reston are ready for battle. It is clear as Nixon arrives with his entourage that he too is ready to do battle. All but ignoring Frost's offer of a handshake, Nixon walks right past him.

The interview today, to be about Watergate, begins aggressively, with Frost suggesting a number of inconsistencies in the public record. Together, they imply a cover-up. In rapid order, Frost makes the case that Nixon participated in the cover-up, that his actions may have been criminal, and that he has betrayed the trust of the American people. The Frost team is elated and Nixon and his team are speechless and disarmed. Just as Nixon is to respond, fearing a confession, his Chief of Staff orders a pause. He speaks to Nixon, warning him of the consequences of a misstep right now.

As the interview resumes, Nixon is contrite and, on camera, confesses inappropriate, disappointing behavior, implying worse. What he had never done all the months before his resignation he does today to Frost.

For Nixon, the interview ends a failure to revive his career; indeed, if there was a hope to be restored, that hope is now ended. For Frost, it is a great success. He has achieved what no other interviewer or journalist has been able to do. His career will now not only recover but go into overdrive. His belief in these interviews has been justified. He's gambled and won. He is not the ideologue that his colleagues are, but his instinct for great television has trumped ideology; in fact, it has surpassed it.

The film ends with Frost and Caroline visiting Nixon to say goodbye. He brings Nixon a pair of Italian shoes as a gift. Touched, Nixon confides that maybe he and Frost should have swapped careers. Frost likes people and Nixon is uncomfortable with them. Nixon thrives in the world of the intellect; Frost, with his common touch, should have been a politician. Frost leaves Nixon to reflect while he goes off to the next phase of his career.

Different Goals, Different Strategies

Frost/Nixon has quite different source material than *United 93*, narratively speaking. *Frost/Nixon* began as a play, essentially as a character study of two titans clashing, whereas *United 93* has a full-fledged plot with minimal characterization of a multiplicity of characters. The consequence is that the focal point for *Frost/Nixon* isn't so much the plot of the debates as it is the inner workings of two famous men, neither of whom we admire or even like at the outset. The usual empathy approach to the characters of the narrative is out. What this means for the editing principle of dramatic emphasis is consequently less clear than in a film such as *United 93*.

Because the emphasis is on character rather than plot, those points of great importance in the story are revelations of character and surprise rather than a plot device. Further behavior is surprising, and not initially expected of the two adversaries. More specifically, those revelations should lead us beyond understanding toward admiration, even caring, for each of these two characters. In the case of Richard Nixon, this means his humor and his self-awareness. In the case of David Frost, the direction is toward his understanding that his callowness is no barrier to his capacity to stretch himself in order to succeed. The nuance in *Frost/Nixon* is to move us toward caring about two characters who make caring about them more than difficult.

The Close-up

As the criteria for dramatic emphasis in *Frost/Nixon* focus on character revelation, they also focus on character movement along an arc of quiet desperation, to ascent for David Frost, and of not so quiet desperation to final resignation to the implication of his political resignation for Richard Nixon. In this sense, the close-up is used to reveal those states and their implications for each character.

When Frost first meets his associates, Ron Howard uses close-ups to capture how Frost responds (or chooses not to respond) to their clear contempt for him. He chooses to work with them to prove he can take opposition and challenge in his ranks. Similarly, Howard uses close-ups when we first see Nixon, consulting with his Chief of Staff. Here too the reaction shots of Nixon reveal his need to be understood. The early scenes are all about his having been misunderstood.

Later in the film, the reaction shots focus on Nixon reacting to Frost's accusations of knowing and participating in the cover-up. In this section of the film, whether it's Frost's intense research in preparation for his attack on Nixon about Watergate or his reveling in skewering his prey during the fourth interview, the close-ups are all about Frost's power. Equivalently, the close-ups of Nixon during the interview are all about his sudden downturn from victor to victim.

At each stage of character surprise—Frost's self-doubt, Nixon's self-reflection and self-revelation in the last scene of the film—Howard uses the close-up to bring us closer to the characters, and in these private moments, to encourage us to care for the characters.

Dynamic Montage

Ron Howard uses dynamic montage more in line with its use in *United 93* to emphasize the importance of a great deal of information, presented in an intense, engaging fashion, to the overall story. The very opening of the film exemplifies Howard's use of dynamic montage. In this case the events that led to President Nixon's resignation, from the Watergate burglary itself to the testimony of his staff, including Chief Counsel John Dean. This montage is specific and visual, and the details and people are presented in adversarial as well as confessional moments. The consequence is to set the context not only for Richard Nixon's political tragedy but also to establish that he was the first president to leave office in disgrace prior to the end of his term. The unprecedented nature of what led to the resignation is consequently given weight by this dynamic montage.

Another example is the sequence that precedes the fourth interview. Frost at a low point has just had a late-night call from Nixon. His refocus on the interview is presented in a montage sequence in which he listens to tapes, watches video footage, and enlists James Reston in the intensified research effort that will arm Frost for his fourth interview that will focus on Watergate. Close-ups of dates and names are part of the montage. The sequence conveys Frost's renewed engagement with the interviews. The montage conveys his energy and commitment to his original goal, to use the interviews to resurrect his flagging career. If he can nail Nixon on the Watergate cover-up issue, Frost will save himself.

Juxtaposition

Because *Frost/Nixon* is essentially a character-driven story, the notion of juxtaposition à la Eisenstein or Peckinpah is simply not appropriate, as juxtaposition in their films—when it works most strongly—is in response to plot turns. The juxtapositions that are most powerful in *Frost/Nixon* are in the reactions of the key people around Frost and Nixon in the interviews. For David Frost, the people who count are Bob Zelnick and James Reston, his American producing team. Although Caroline is present throughout, her reactions don't have the meaning that those of Zelnick and Reston do. In the case of Richard Nixon, the people who count beyond his Chief of Staff are never introduced. They are his two daughters and their husbands, who are present for the interviews.

In the case of Frost, the responses of Zelnick and Reston are registered throughout each interview. In the first three their disappointment isn't so much so as it is anger at Frost. There is little question that they view his performance as an utter failure and a lost opportunity. Their response to the fourth interview is equally passionate, as if the interviews were a sporting event. Finally, in the fourth interview, their side is winning and they are passionate about victory.

For Nixon, the first three interviews are successful and his family responds with pride in their father and father-in-law. On the fourth and final interview, however, the reaction shots of Nixon's family register not so much disappointment as the pain of watching their hero humiliated, defeated. Although the daughters and sons-in-law are not introduced to us, we can feel their pain at those moments. They reflect on a personal level how defeated Nixon is by the effective barrage by Frost. And when he does admit wrongdoing and disappointment, it is the reactions of his family that touch us.

Pace

As with the use of juxtaposition and close-up, the usage of pace in the character-driven story proceeds differently than in a plot-driven story such as *United 93*. Looking at the four interviews as the most obvious area for dramatic emphasis, a pattern emerges, but it's driven by the relative screen time spent on each of the four interviews rather than the rising action demands of a film such as *United 93*. Consequently, the amount of screen time devoted to Interview 4 far exceeds the screen time devoted to each previous interview day. The shortest interview day in terms of screen time is Interview 3, with Interview 2 only slightly longer than Interview 3.

Within the four interview days, although Interview 4 is the longest and therefore the most important, pace does not really come into play in this lengthy sequence. In fact, reaction shots of Nixon to Frost's attack are quite long. Nor are the reaction shots of his family short. Indeed, there is a painfully long sense to these shots as Howard allows the emotion within these reaction shots to register. Rather than use a faster pace to create emotion, Howard relies on performance to register that emotion. In this sense, he seems to sidestep the use of pace in the more traditional sense for reliance on close-ups and reaction shots, and juxtaposition to register dramatic emphasis in these sequences.

Ron Howard, given the nature of his subject matter, opted to use the tools for dramatic emphasis in a different mix than did Paul Greengrass in *United 93*. Both are strong in their choices, but different. The suggestion then is that deploying dramatic emphasis as a tool will be determined very much in service to the narrative, rather than in a more prescriptive fashion.

CHAPTER 19

Editing for Subtext[i]

Editing is all about telling the story with images and sounds, just as screenwriting is telling the story with words and directing is telling the story with performance and camera. Editing can have straightforward goals or less straightforward goals. Editing with a less straightforward goal or secondary goal is editing for subtext. To understand how such a goal is achieved, we need first to understand how more straightforward goals are achieved in editing.

The history of editing is the creation of a series of discoveries that first addressed technical problems—continuity through place and time shifts, how to achieve dramatic emphasis, how to introduce a new idea into a scene, how to create identification with a character, and how to build growing tension through the narrative. Along the way, aesthetic insights were achieved—how random shots could collectively achieve greater power than individual shots, how shock juxtapositions could alter meaning, the range of possible meaning that was possible from discontinuity editing (the jump cut), the power of sound to shape as well as to alter meaning. But throughout that history, two guiding editing principles dominated—narrative clarity and dramatic emphasis.

The apogee of classic film editing is the D-Day sequence in Steven Spielberg's *Saving Private Ryan* (1997). The 24-minute sequence has as its overarching purpose to recreate the brutality and human cost of the first day of the European invasion. The 24-minute sequence breaks down into nine 2- or 3-minute sequences, each with its own narrative purpose. They are as follows:

1. In the Landing Craft: The purpose of the sequence is to convey the intensity and fear among the soldiers who will soon be on the beach.
2. In the Water: The purpose of the sequence is to convey the surprise that death can't be evaded.
3. At the Edge of the Beach: Not only can death not be evaded, but its omnipresence makes of the soldiers on the beach helpless victims.
4. Movement Off the Beach: Chaos, violent death, and growing helplessness imply that so far, the landing is an unmitigated disaster.

---

[i]Originally written as an article for *CINEASTE*, March 2009.

The Technique of Film and Video Editing: History, Theory, and Practice. DOI: 10.1016/B978-0-240-81397-4.00019-4

5. Up to the Perimeter: The transitional sequence where a feeling of power displaces the powerlessness felt up to this point.
6. Gather Weapons: The main character and his men prepare to take the battle to the enemy.
7. Advance on the Pillbox: Professionalism and competence in the platoon create hope for the first time.
8. Take the Pillbox: The violence of the American attack displaces the chaos of the earlier sequences.
9. The Beach Is Taken.

Throughout the overall sequence, close-ups are used to emotionalize each sequence, and increasing pace is used to punctuate the chaos and carnage. Increasing pace is important to build the tension as we move through the different 2- and 3-minute sequences. Only in the last sequence does the pace at last slow. This 24-minute sequence reflects 90 years of editing innovation utilized to the peak of the possibilities of edition conventions.

Terence Malick's *The Thin Red Line* (1998), a war film made in the same year as the Spielberg film, exemplifies a very different set of editing goals. Although the overall shaping device is the battle for Guadalcanal in the Pacific, Malick's narrative goals are totally different from those of Spielberg. Instead of tension about who will win the battle, how it will be won, and a focus on the human cost, Malick instead opts for a meditation on life, death, man's relation to the natural world, the humanity even of the enemy, and how personal ideology struggles often supersede the collective ideology so necessary in the effective functioning of an organization such as the army. To achieve these subtextual ideas Malick moves away from editing goals such as identification with a character and pace to build suspense within a scene or a sequence. Even though the war film as a genre is about the central question of survival of the main character, Malick implies the irrelevance of the question by focusing instead on the character within a natural order of humanity within the natural world rather than humanity transcendent over the natural world. In the latter, the struggle of men for primacy is central. In the former, the struggle of man for primacy seems arrogant and foolish. Here editing for the subtext takes us away from the progress of the battle to the question of the progress of humankind by its sideline journey into warfare as the be all and end all of existence.

Other examples of editing for subtext include Federico Fellini's *8½* (1962), Baz Luhrman's *Moulin Rouge* (2001), and Jonathan Demme's *Rachel Getting Married* (2008).

In Fellini's *8½*, the narrative focuses on the central character, Guido's creative logjam. His life is brimming with pressure, from his producer, his wife, his mistress, and his potential actors. He ruminates through his past in a series of fantasies that focus on his relationships with religion, his parents, and women. In the fantasies, retribution for desire is the primary thread. This description would suggest a film overly weighted in the direction of victimization. But that's not the experience of *8½*. On the contrary, the editing focuses in a playful manner on the richness of Guido's inner life. Fellini juxtaposes an image of himself floating high in the sky, with an image of his producer pulling on the rope. He then cuts to Guido's body plunging to earth. Fellini uses sounds cues ("asa nisi masa") or a visual cue, the raising of eyeglasses higher on the bridge of his nose, to move us from Guido's present reality into his fantasy. The juxtapositions, the playful visual cues, and the mysterious use of a phrase from the past all convey a subtext that differs substantially from Guido's present. His inner life is rich; his outer life seems barren.

In Baz Luhrman's *Moulin Rouge*, a man comes to Paris to become a writer. And, of course, in order to write about love, the writer must suffer and lose his lover. This is the narrative of *Moulin Rouge*. The subtext of *Moulin Rouge* is all about the excitement and energy of the musical theatre. The joy, the energy, and the pleasure of music and dance are conveyed by pace. The camera moves, the actors move, and the pace moves them faster. Far more memorable than the lovers' loss is the writer's gain. The pleasure of *Moulin Rouge* is the legacy of the edit for its subtext.

In Jonathan Demme's *Rachel Getting Married*, the drug-addicted sister gets a pass to attend her sister's weekend wedding. Can past traumas, parents' reconstituted marriages, and liberal Connecticut be outweighed by the joy of the occasion of the wedding? The answer is no, as Rachel returns to rehab at the end of the film. The edit of the film, however, suggests the messy energy of music, feeling, both of love and anger, and what we're left with is the sense of the relentlessness of life in the face of tragedy in life. The editing for subtext emphasizes the vitality of the life force in spite of those tragedies. In fact, in each of these three films, the sad narrative content is subverted by an editing strategy that captures the vitality and creativity that characters need to call upon to deal with the problems of living. In each case, it's the subtext that makes the film a surprising and rewarding experience for its audience.

In order to understand editing for subtext more deeply we need to pose this question: Is the editor his own agent or is he the agent of the director? Although I'd like to say it's the former, I tend to believe the latter to be the case. How else can we understand the ongoing relationships of the great editors with specific directors? Good examples of this relationship are Walter Murch and Francis Coppola, Thelma Schoonmaker and Martin Scorcese, Sam O'Steen and Mike Nichols. The list is far longer, but I hope my point is made.

What also needs to be said is that good directors are all about deepening or transforming meaning in narrative content. Two examples from my book *The Director's Idea* (Focal Press, 2006) make the point. Because a director faces many decisions about where to place the camera, how to modulate performance, and shot selection or organization for the edit, what she needs is a shaping idea or prism through which to filter and make those decisions. I've called this prism "the director's idea." For John Ford, that idea is a poetic view of heroism; for Stanley Kubrick, it's a dark view of modern life; for Catherine Breillat, it's the view that sexuality is a battle for power between the sexes. Good and great directors use a director's idea to achieve a deep subtextual interpretation of their films and to shape and to personalize the narrative content in line with that idea.

Looking at the work of George Stevens and Roman Polanski, we have two directors with very different editing styles and yet clear subtextual interpretations of their work.

In the case of George Stevens, the director's idea is to explore two contradictory aspects of the American character—desire and conscience. Whether he is working in the action-adventure film (*Gunga Din*, 1939) or in the situation comedy (*The More the Merrier*, 1943), Stevens focuses on characters who represent desire—McChesney (Victor McLahglan) and Ballantyne (Douglas Fairbanks Jr.) and Cutter (Cary Grant)—and conscience—Gunga Din (Sam Jaffe) in *Gunga Din*—and the editing choices illustrate the conflict between these two forces. In *The More the Merrier*, desire is represented by the men, Benjamin Dingle (Charles Coburn) and Joe Carter (Joel McCrea), and conscience by Connie Mulligan (Jean Arthur). Here too the editing style pits one force against the other.

In the case of Roman Polanski, the director's idea is to take us to that existential space that is the aloneness of existence. Whether we look at *Tess* (1981) or *The Pianist* (2002), Polanski uses an editing style that juxtaposes the main characters, Tess (Natassia Kinski) and Wladyslaw Szpilman (Adrien Brody) crowded by the camera in the foreground with the vast wide-angle long shots of the characters they long for in the deep background, or alternately, extreme long shots devoid of humans. Although Polanski sidesteps pace to generate emotion in his work, the reliance on powerful juxtaposition together with subjective point of view camera placements creates the overwhelming pain of his director's idea. This deeper interpretation and its consequence, a deeper experience for the audience, is well understood by good and great directors. It is here that the notion of editing for subtext begins.

To get even more specific about the operation of this subtextual interpretation, we look at the work of Elia Kazan as it operates in a deeply conflictual interpretation of life and relationships. In every relationship in *America, America* (1961), a character is either master or servant. This means father and son, man and woman, political master and powerless citizen. Taking this idea to a deeper level, let's look at the collegial relationship between Blackie, the head of a gang seeking information from a gang member, and Poldi in *Panic in the Streets* (1950). Poldi is dying from the bubonic plague. To cull the secret from him, Blackie (Jack Palance) embraces Poldi, whispers to him, in an all-but-sexual embrace. Shortly after, he dumps Poldi on the street, killing him. Sexuality and hate mix and amplify Kazan's director's idea. In *Splendor in the Grass* (1961), two lovers, Deannie (Natalie Wood) and Bud (Warren Beatty), are discouraged by their parents from seeing each other again. Deannie's mother embraces Deannie as she rails against the repulsiveness of the sexual act. Bud's father pounds Bud's shoulders as he encourages him to see a prostitute for his sexual needs while telling him not to throw his life away for Deannie. Sexuality and aggression partner as shot selection focuses on intimacy, while the editing style illustrates the conflictual dimension of the narrative content. In this manner, Kazan sexualizes the relationships to represent their deepest element while positioning relationships in an adversarial frame in the edit. Here, directing as well as editing for these subtextual dimensions makes Kazan and his editors' work richer for that subtext.

To restate the key idea thus far: subtext deepens our narrative experience. For good directors and editors, making the subtext manifest is an important goal. Three contemporary films—Martin Scorsese's *The Departed* (2006), edited by Thelma Schoonmaker; Ang Lee's

FIGURE 21.4
Raiders of the Lost Ark, 1981. Courtesy Lucasfilm Ltd.™ and © Lucasfilm Ltd. (LFL) 1981. All rights reserved.

He positioned the camera in these shots to film both in focus. When he wanted to use a long shot more dynamically, however, he adjusted the depth of field to lose the foreground and the background. An example of such a shot occurs in the opening scene of the chase when Jones is mounted on a horse. The loss of foreground combined with the jump cutting makes his pursuit on horseback seem faster and more dynamic. For the most part, however, individual scenes are constructed from midshots and close-ups, including cutaways that make a point in the narrative—for example, the German commander giving the truck more gas to go faster in the hopes of crushing Jones between the truck and the command car. Close shots are very important in the creation of this sequence. They are used to enhance narrative clarity but also to intensify the narrative.

Besides the close-ups, the camera position often puts us in the position of Indiana Jones. Not only do we see his reactions to events, but we also see the events unfolding as he sees them. This subjectivity of camera placement gives us no choice but to identify with the character.

Another important element in the sequence is the pace. Shots often last no longer than a few seconds. In general, the pace quickens as we move through the sequence. In the first scene, the average shot is just under 4 seconds. In the last scene, the average shot is just under 5 seconds. In between, however, the pace varies between just under 2 seconds to just over 1 second. In the second scene, when Jones has reached the truck and is struggling to capture it, the scene has 31 shots in 45 seconds. In the next scene, his struggle with the half-truck and the motorbike, the pace is maintained with 48 shots in 80 seconds. This pace eases only slightly as the soldiers who have been guarding the Ark try to take the truck from Jones. Here, there are 38 shots in 65 seconds. The greatest personal threat to Jones occurs when he is literally thrown out of the truck by the German commander. This more personal combat takes longer and is more complex. The scene has 57 shots in 2 minutes, and it is the climax of the sequence. Once Jones's personal safety is no longer at risk, the pace shifts into a more relaxed final scene. Pace plays a very critical role in the effectiveness of this action sequence.

In the entire sequence, Spielberg used 210 shots in 7½ minutes. He included all of the elements necessary to get us to identify with Indiana Jones, to understand his conflict, and to struggle with him for the resolution of that conflict. Spielberg succeeded with this sequence in terms of entertainment and identification. It represents the exciting possibilities of the action sequence.

What can be learned from comparing the Keaton sequence and the Spielberg sequence? At every point of both action sequences, the filmmaker's goal is narrative clarity. The audience must know where they are in the story. Confusion does not complement excitement. Good directors know how the action sequence helps the story and positions the audience. Is the sequence intended for entertainment, as both of these sequences are, or is it meant solely for identification, like Frankenheimer's action sequences in *Black Sunday* and the assassination sequence that ends *The Manchurian Candidate* (1962)? The filmmaker's goal is critical.

Another element that seems similar in both sequences is the role of moving vehicles. Both filmmakers were fascinated with these symbols of technology and how they act as both barriers and facilitators for humans. Both filmmakers demonstrated a positive attitude about technology—unlike Stanley Kubrick in *Dr. Strangelove* (1964) and *2001: A Space Odyssey* (1968)—and their approach to the trains and trucks is rather joyful. This attitude infuses both sequences.

Perhaps the greatest differences between the two approaches are in how manipulative the filmmaker wanted to be in making the action sequence more exciting and the identification more important. Spielberg clearly valued pace, the close-up, and the importance of subjective camera placement to a far greater degree than did Keaton. This is the recent pattern for action sequences: to use all of the elements of film to make them as exciting as possible. The interesting question is not so much why Spielberg needed to resort to these manipulative techniques, but rather why Keaton didn't feel the same way.

Both sequences are very exciting despite the 50 or so years between the two productions, but their approaches differ considerably. It is here that the artistic personality of the director comes into play. It also suggests that the modern conventions of the action sequence, albeit strongly skewed in the direction of Spielberg's approach, may be wider than we thought.

The Bourne Ultimatum: The Ultimate Use of Pace in an Action Sequence

The Bourne trilogy (2004–2007) sets a new standard for the realistic treatment of action. Paul Greengrass, the director of the last two films in the series, deploys a docudrama sensibility to the thriller genre, and the results are a mixture of being there together with a veracity that deepens our identification and our concern for the fate of the main character. That means a handheld camera, lots of mobility, close-ups, and jump cuts to create a feeling level that helps us overcome our James Bond conditioning to this kind of central character.

The Bourne Ultimatum (2007) continues a narrative where a CIA-trained assassin, Jason Bourne, is seeking to recover his humanity and yet remain alive to the active threat the CIA poses for him. Certain high-level operatives (men) want Bourne dead, while others (women) want to help him.

The sequence we focus on here is a 20-minute set-piece that occurs in Tangier, Morocco. Bourne and a reluctant CIA accomplice, Nicky Parsons, are in pursuit of one Neal Daniels, a man very familiar with Bourne's past. He in turn is being pursued by Noah Wilson, a high-level New York–based CIA manager. Wilson wants Bourne and Daniels dead. He has commissioned a Casablanca-based asset named Desh to kill Daniels. When Bourne and Parsons intrude, he orders the asset to kill Bourne and Parsons as well.

In the 20-minute sequence there is a narrative progression as follows:

1. Bourne and Parsons arrive in Tangier.
2. Wilson orders asset to kill Daniels.
3. Nicky Parsons hacks into CIA files to find Daniels's location.
4. Bourne suggests Parsons contact Desh to pick up a new phone (so that they will be able to follow Desh to find Daniels).
5. CIA in New York learns of Parsons's computer interdiction.
6. Wilson orders asset to kill Parsons and Bourne.
7. Asset picks up new phone.
8. Bourne follows asset.
9. Asset drops packet (bomb?) to capture Bourne's interest.
10. Bourne tries to stop Daniels.
11. Asset detonates explosives in his motorbike and kills Daniels.
12. Bourne possibly hurt, follows Desh.
13. Police pursue Bourne.
14. Bourne steals motorbike to evade police and pursue Desh.
15. Asset spots Nicky Parsons.
16. She destroys her phone and flees on foot as asset pursues her.
17. Bourne sees Parsons's phone destroyed and pursues her and the asset on foot.
18. Police continue their pursuit of Bourne.
19. Now moving through souk and local Arab neighborhood, the asset spots Parsons and she continues to try to evade him.
20. Police on rooftops pursue Bourne, but he successfully evades them.
21. The pursuit tightens to a single location.
22. Bourne sees where Parsons is and jumps into the building where she and the asset are close.
23. Bourne fights with the asset.

24. Parsons tries to help but fails.
25. Bourne kills Desh.
26. Bourne takes Desh's phone.
27. Bourne sends information to CIA headquarters that Parsons and Bourne are dead.
28. Wilson asks that local CIA operatives get confirmation on the bodies. He wants to make sure Parsons and Bourne are dead.

This is a complex and elaborate sequence. Aside from the veracity issue, Greengrass wants to make sure his audience knows exactly where we are in the narrative, who is following whom, and who has the upper hand at any given point. To do so in a 20-minute sequence that has approximately 650 edits, Greengrass must use differing strategies to hold us within the sequence and to punctuate changes.

To make sure we know what's most important, Greengrass resorts to a close-up. He uses close-ups to show us Daniels's location in Tangier; he uses close-ups to show us Parsons destroying her phone.

Another strategy Greengrass uses to follow action is a slow swish pan with the key action or players in the foreground. When he needs to suggest a change in tempo, he jump cuts on a character or action. A third strategy is to step up the pace. Although the total set-piece is 650 edits, the last 11¾ minutes, the point of greatest danger and threat to Bourne and Parsons proceeds with double the number of edits in the first 8 minutes. The increase in pace is in proportion to the threat to our main character. In both sections of the set-piece there is also movement within the frame as well as movement of the camera. That movement within the frame is also accelerated in the second part of the set piece.

Close-ups, camera movement, movement within the frame, and jump cutting are complemented by a tendency to downplay establishing shots or camera placements distant from the action. In all the choices, Greengrass opts for intensity over context or objectivity. All the while, however, he wants to be sure not to lose the narrative thread. It's a balancing act in which clear goals and edit choices assure audience involvement and excitement. This sequence may very well be the ultimate in action sequences.

CASE STUDY: *A HISTORY OF VIOLENCE*: AN ALTERNATIVE ACTION SEQUENCE

Both the Keaton and Spielberg sequences follow a developmental arc. Each is almost a self-contained dramatic sequence within the larger film. They have build, and use pace to bring the audience along progressively, paying off the core idea of the sequence and then backing out of the sequence. In this sense, each is classic in its approach to the action sequence. Our third example, David Cronenberg's *A History of Violence* (2005), is quite different in shape and presentation. Whether described as postmodern or as an action sequence without prologue or epilogue, Cronenberg's approach is surprising and shocking.

A History of Violence (Figure 21.5) tells the story of a man with a past. Tom Stall runs a diner in Millbrook, Indiana. Although his 10-year-old daughter has violent nightmares and his teenage son is harassed by two school sports stars, the Stall family is the American ideal— peaceful, happy in marriage and in life. When two violent hoodlums come into his diner with malice on their minds, Tom not only stops them but kills them both with their own weapon. Now that he's a town hero, his publicity prompts the arrival of a higher class of criminal. Their leader claims that Tom is not Tom but rather Joey Cusack of Philadelphia,

FIGURE 21.5

A History of Violence, 2005. New Line Cinema/Photofest. © New Line Cinema.

a violent criminal from a criminal clan. The truth about Tom-Joey rocks his family and takes Joey back to Philadelphia for a violent confrontation with his brother, Richie. The story ends with the Stall family reassessing their identities.

The sequence addressed in this chapter is the act of violence that is the first clue to Tom Stall's true identity, his victory over the two hoodlums who try to take over the diner. Because the scene early in the film radically changes the course of the narrative, I consider it the catalytic—even the inciting—incident. I also consider it the beginning of the plot. Up to this point, the characters involved in the scene have been introduced. The two hoodlums kill the staff at the motel they have been staying at. For the most part, the violence is matter of fact. Also introduced are the Stall family. Here the emphasis is on "gentle" Tom Stall and his love for his family and his life.

The scene under consideration shows the two hoodlums arriving in town and their desperation for money. In the diner, Tom is getting ready to close. Young lovers and two staffers are present. The atmosphere is peaceful until the two hoodlums enter. They demand coffee and pie and ignore Tom's insistence on closing. As he give them coffee, the younger hoodlum stops the waitress from going home. He pulls his weapon and begins to manhandle the waitress. His older accomplice also pulls a weapon. The older hoodlum gives his accomplice permission to sexually assault the waitress. At this point, Tom hurls scalding coffee at the older hoodlum, who consequently drops his pistol. Tom grabs the pistol and shoots the young hoodlum. When the older hoodlum plunges a knife into Tom's foot, Tom shoots away the man's face. The violent incident is over. Tom has saved the day.

The scene itself has two phases: the introduction of the hoodlums into the town and Stall's diner, leading up to the intent to do violence in the diner, and Tom's response: to stop their violence by his own violence. Let's call the first phase the lead-up to the violence and the second phase the violence.

In terms of the breakdown of time and shots, the specifics are as follows:

1. The lead-up to violence.	4 minutes	61 shots
2. The violence.	1 minute	27 shots

The first phase is marked by verbal and emotional violence; the second phase is marked by physical violence. In the first phase, the emotional violence is gradual, initially generated by the aggressiveness of the older hoodlum—his insistence on having coffee in spite of the fact that the shop is closing. The younger hoodlum raises the stakes by demanding dessert as well. When he also reveals a weapon and stops the waitress from leaving, the situation is escalating. When he sexually caresses the waitress' body, it worsens. The scene peaks with the older hoodlum drawing his weapon and pointing it at Tom.

Within this scene, the visual focus is on reaction shots—Tom, his cook, the waitress, and the young couple all respond to the increasingly aggressive tone of the hoodlums. Once weapons are drawn, the reaction shots focus on the fear all but Tom exhibit. Tom is pliant and his reaction shots register his efforts to appease the hoodlums. All the shots, of the hoodlums and of the workers and customers in the diner, are presented as medium shots. The characters are presented from Tom's point of view and eye line.

In phase two, the pace accelerates from an average length of shot of 4 seconds to an average length of 2 seconds (approximately). The shots are primarily close-ups rather than medium shots. And the close-ups are specific: the hot coffee carafe Tom uses to stun the older hoodlum, the knife the hoodlum thrusts into Tom's foot, the damage the bullet does to the hoodlum's face. The shots are physical and the outcomes are extremely violent. The point of view remains Tom's, as does the eye line. Reaction shots of the "civilians" in the diner are included, but they are not as important as the acts of violence done to the hoodlums and to Tom. The rapidity of this scene moves us away from the "balletic" approach to violence of *The Wild Bunch*. The focus is on the shock of physical violence.

This action sequence differs from the early action sequences in this chapter in a number of ways. Both the Keaton and Spielberg sequences have a dramatic arc; they also have an exhilaration to them. They are exciting to watch and to experience. That's not the case in the Cronenberg film. Here we are almost sickened by the rapidity of the violence, its shift from an emotional to a physical base. There is no reflective or aesthetic distancing here—only shock.

NOTES/REFERENCES

1. A. Sarris, The American Cinema, University of Chicago Press, Chicago, 1968, p. 137.

2. Conjecture and reputation have credited the success of that film to editor Elmo Williams, although the assassination attempt on Charles De Gaulle in Zinnemann's *The Day of the Jackal* (1973) is as great a sequence.

CHAPTER 22

Dialog

The dialog sequence is one of the least imaginatively treated types of sequences, although this has started to change. The editor must understand what is most important in a dialog sequence. Generally, a director can opt to film a dialog sequence in a two-shot or in a series of midshots from over the shoulder of each of the participants. Most dialogs proceed as two-character dialogs; occasionally, more than two characters interact in a dialog sequence. Margo's party for Biull in *All About Eve* (1950) is a good example of the latter type of dialog sequence.

The choices, then, are not many. The director might include an establishing shot to set up the sequence or might provide close-ups of the key lines of dialog for emphasis. Many directors do not include close-ups because if the script is well written, the lines and performances can carry themselves. It's quite another matter if the dialog is poor. In this case, the sequence will need all the help the director and the editor can provide.

Additional issues for the editor include whether to use more close shots than medium shots and whether to use an objective shot watching a conversation rather than a subjective shot—that is, an over-the-shoulder shot watching the speaker. Should the editor use the reverse shot of the listener? Is variety between listener and speaker possible and advisable? Is a crossover from speaker to listener and then back possible and advisable? These are the types of questions that the editor faces when cutting a dialog sequence. The meaning of the dialog to the story as a whole helps the editor make those decisions. A piece of dialog that is important for advancing the plot requires a close-up or some shift in the pattern of shots to alert us that what we are hearing is more important than what we've heard earlier in the sequence.

A piece of dialog that reveals key information about a character calls for a similar strategy. The editor must decide whether the piece of character information or plot information could be conveyed visually. If the point of the dialog cannot be conveyed visually, editing strategies are critical. If the dialog can be reinforced visually, editing strategies become unnecessary. If the dialog is used to provide comic relief or to mask character intentions, other editing strategies are required. In this case, the reaction of the listener may be more important than watching what is being said.

301

The Technique of Film and Video Editing: History, Theory, and Practice. DOI: 10.1016/B978-0-240-81397-4.00022-4

The editor and the director must always be in accord about the meaning of the sequence, the subtext, or any other interpretation of the dialog, and they must be able to break down the dialog sequence in the filming and reconstitute it in the editing to achieve that meaning. Dialog is not always used in the most obvious manner. The relationship between dialog and the visualization of the dialog has broadened and become more interesting.

DIALOG AND PLOT

The direction of a dialog sequence is influenced by the genre, and certain genres (the melodrama, for example) tend to be more sedentary and dependent on dialog than others. The action-adventure genre, which is less reliant on dialog, offers an example of more fluid editing.

In *The Terminator* (1984), James Cameron used an interesting dialog sequence to advance the plot. Reese and Sara Connor are being chased by the Terminator. Their car weaves and crashes throughout this sequence. They are under constant threat. Cameron intercut between the excitement of the car chase and Reese and Sara talking to one another. This dialog fills in a great deal of the plot. Reese told Sara earlier that he and the Terminator are from the future. During this sequence, he describes John Connor, who is leading the fight against the robots and technocrats who dominate the future. Sara discovers that she will become John Connor's mother and that the Terminator was sent back in time to kill her before she could have the child. If she dies, the future will change, Reese explains. This is why it's critical that he protect her.

The dialog itself is presented as we would expect, with over-the-shoulder shots mostly of Sara as she listens and reacts, but also of Reese, who will be John Connor's father. Because the shots are in the car, they are in the midshot to close-up range. Subjective camera placement is the pattern. The dialog here is important, and there is a lot of it. By intercutting with the chase, Cameron masked the amount of dialog and conformed to the conventions of the genre: Don't slow down the action with conversation.[1] The dialog is presented in a classic manner, but because it's crosscut with its context, the chase helps mask it.

A more direct approach to the dialog sequence is exemplified by Woody Allen in the climactic scene toward the end of *Manhattan* (1979). In this contemporary story of New York relationships, the main character, Ike (Allen), has committed to a relationship with Mary (Diane Keaton), a writer close to his age. He has put behind him relationships with 17-year-old Tracy (Mariel Hemingway) and his two ex-wives. Mary, who was formerly the mistress of Ike's closest friend, Yale (Michael Murphy), has decided at Yale's prompting to take up with him again. His 12-year marriage does not seem to be an impediment. In this dialog sequence, Ike confronts Yale and accuses him of immaturity and self-indulgence: "But you— but you're too easy on yourself, don't you see that? You know ... that's your problem, that's your whole problem. You rationalize everything. You're not honest with yourself. You talk about ... you wanna write a book, but, in the end, you'd rather buy the Porsche, you know, or you cheat a little bit on Emily, and you play around with the truth a little with me, and the next thing you know, you're in front of a Senate committee and you're naming names! You're informing on your friends!"

This dialog sequence is in many ways the climax of the film because the main character has finally come to realize that relationships that proceed without a sense of morality and mutual respect are doomed and transitory and that the maturity that leads to healthy relationships is not related to age.

The dialog sequence begins with three camera setups and a long establishing shot of the location where the conversation takes place. The two characters approach a blackboard, which has two skeletons hanging in front of it. The long establishing shot (after the two enter the classroom) sets up the sequence. After the establishing shot, the film moves into two tight midshots: one of Yale, the other of Ike. The frame with Ike includes the head of one of the skeletons so that the shot presents as a two-shot with Ike and the skeleton. For the balance of the dialog sequence, the two midshots of Yale and Ike are intercut. The sequence ends with Ike leaving the frame so that all we see is the skeleton. Ike's last line refers to the skeleton; he says that when he looks like the skeleton, when he thins out, he wants to be sure "I'm well thought of."

This sequence, like the dialog sequence in *The Terminator*, advances the plot, but its presentation is much more direct. It is not presented in an overly emotional manner. The direction makes it clear that we must listen to the dialog and consider what is being said. The presence of the skeleton adds a visual dimension that adds irony to the dialog. This dialog sequence exemplifies the simplicity that allows the dialog to be heard without distraction.

DIALOG AND CHARACTER

Black Sunday (1977), directed by John Frankenheimer, is the story of a terrorist plot to explode a bomb over the Super Bowl. The plot is uncovered by an Israeli raid in Beirut, and the story that unfolds contrasts the terrorists' attempts to carry out the attack and the FBI's efforts to prevent it. For the authorities, this means finding out how the attack will be conducted and who will carry it out. Dalia (Marthe Keller) and Michael (Bruce Dern) are the primary terrorists. She is a Palestinian, and he is an American, a pilot of the Goodyear blimp used at the Super Bowl. Michael is very unstable, a characteristic illustrated through a dialog sequence.

Dalia has returned to Los Angeles from abroad. She has arranged for the explosives necessary for the attack. Michael is very distressed because she is three days late. He worries that something is wrong. He is very angry and threatens her with a rifle. She tries to pacify him and manages to calm him down. This scene is filmed in midshots to close shots. The shots are primarily handheld, and the camera always has some degree of movement, even in still shots. There are moving shots as well.

Within this highly fragmented sequence, Dalia enters a dark room. When she turns on the light, she is confronted by Michael, who is aiming a rifle at her. The rapid series of handheld shots underscores the nervousness of the scene and principally Michael's instability. She moves, he moves, the camera moves. They do things: Dalia unpacks a small statue that holds explosives, Michael examines the statue, she undresses, he puts down the rifle. Throughout the scene, they are speaking, he belligerently and she in a soothing way to assure him that all is well.

The sequence, which is highly fragmented with lots of movement, seems realistic with its heightened sense of danger. The movement supports the goal of establishing Michael's instability, which is a prime quality in his role as terrorist. The goal of the sequence comes across clearly, as does a sense of urgency and realism.

A very different type of sequence establishes character but does not provide as clear a sense of the dialog's role in its establishment. In Robert Altman's *McCabe and Mrs. Miller* (1971), we are introduced to gambler John McCabe (Warren Beatty) as he enters the small mining town of Presbyterian Church. He takes off his coat and searches for the bar. He is dressed differently than the others in the bar. In the first scene in the bar, there is a dialog exchange.

The dialog is neither textured nor localized; it's about the price of liquor and the price of playing a card game. The goal of the scene is to position McCabe among the town's occupants as a negotiator and as something of an entrepreneur. The scene establishes this.

The scene proceeds in a highly fragmented fashion, with only a short establishing shot. Many close-ups feature McCabe and the miners; McCabe is seen as something of a dandy, and the miners appear dirty, wild-eyed, and something less than civilized. The scene does establish McCabe's importance with a number of close-ups, but the dialog itself is not direct enough to characterize him. The intensity of the scene comes from the visual elaboration of his appearance among the miners of Presbyterian Church.

Another element that pushes us to the visual in this scene is the use of overlapping dialog. Many characters speak simultaneously, and we are aware of the discreteness of their conversations, but as their comments bleed into those of others, the effect is to undermine the dialog. The scene moves dialog from the informational status it usually occupies to the category of noise. Language becomes a sound effect. When we do hear the dialog, it is the speaker who is important rather than what is being said.

Like the dialog sequence in *Black Sunday*, we come away from this sequence with a definite sense of McCabe's character. However, unlike the scene in *Black Sunday*, the meaning of the dialog becomes trivialized and expendable.

MULTIPURPOSE DIALOG

Mike Nichols was very creative about the editing of his dialog sequences in *The Graduate* (1967). In the first dialog sequence, Benjamin (Dustin Hoffman) confesses to his father that he is worried about his future. The entire scene is presented in a single midshot of Benjamin. When the father joins the conversation, he enters the frame and sits out of focus in the foreground.

More typical is the famous seduction scene in which Mrs. Robinson (Anne Bancroft) proposes an affair to Benjamin. This scene fits into the overall story about Benjamin Braddock, a college graduate who is trying to develop a set of values that make sense to him. He rejects the materialistic values of his family and their peers, but he doesn't know what should replace them. In his confusion, he becomes involved in an affair with the wife of his father's partner. He later develops a relationship with her daughter. His behavior suggests his confusion and his groping toward the future. His affair with Mrs. Robinson is the first relationship in the film that suggests his state of confusion.

The seduction scene can be broken down into three parts, all of which depend on dialog. In the first, Mrs. Robinson invites Benjamin, who has driven her home, inside for a drink. She offers him a drink, plays some music, and sits with her legs apart in a provocative position. Benjamin asks if she is trying to seduce him, but she denies it.

In the second part, Mrs. Robinson asks him up to her daughter's bedroom, offering to show him a portrait of her. She begins to undress and throws her watch and earrings on the bed. She asks him to unzip her dress, and her intentions are unmistakable. He unzips her dress but then leaves the room and goes downstairs.

In the third part of the sequence, Mrs. Robinson speaks to him from the bathroom upstairs. She asks that he bring her purse. He does, but he refuses to take it into the bathroom. She asks that he take her purse into Elaine's bedroom, where she joins him, naked. He is shocked and wants to leave. She tells him that she will be available to him whenever he wishes. Only the arrival of her husband ends the sequence with Benjamin's virtue unsullied.

Dialog can be used to advance the plot, to reveal a character's nature, or to provide comic relief. In this sequence, dialog is used for each of these purposes. The advancement of the plot is related to Mrs. Robinson's proposal of an illicit affair, which will take Benjamin further down a particular path. In terms of characterization, the sequence illustrates how manipulative Mrs. Robinson is and how naïve Benjamin can be. His youth and inexperience are such that he can be manipulated by others. As to the humor, the sequence abounds in surprises. When Mrs. Robinson confesses that she is neurotic, Benjamin responds, "Oh, my God!" as though she had confessed to a capital crime. Mrs. Robinson's lying—the dissonance between what she says and does—is also a continuing source of humor.

The sequence, then, has many purposes. How was it edited? Nichols and his editor, Sam O'Steen, cut the film subjectively. The foreground–background relationship was used to highlight power relationships as well as Benjamin's subjective perspective. Benjamin appears in the foreground when Mrs. Robinson speaks from the background, or he is in the background speaking when she is in the foreground. The famous image of Mrs. Robinson's uplifted leg in the foreground with Benjamin in the background provides a good example of how the dialog is presented. This foreground–background relationship is maintained throughout the different phases of this sequence. It is most clearly manifested in the final sequence, in which the naked Mrs. Robinson appears in the foreground and there is an intense close-up of Benjamin in the background. In this scene, the focus is on Benjamin throughout, with quick intercutting of her breasts or belly almost presented as flash frames. This quick cutting, which implies the wish to see and the wish to look away, is only part of the sequence in which pace plays an important role. In the balance of the sequence, the rule is subjectivity and the foreground—background interplay of reverse angle shots to highlight the dialog and the speaker.

The sequence exhibits complex goals for the dialog, yet manages to have sufficient visual variety to be stimulating. Nichols did use distinct close-ups of Mrs. Robinson and Benjamin at one point, but the dialog itself doesn't warrant them. The close-ups seem to be offered as variety in a lengthy sequence that relies on subjective foreground—background shots.

TROUBLE IN PARADISE: AN EARLY DIALOG SEQUENCE

As stated earlier, the very first dialog sequences were visually structured to facilitate the actual recording of the sound. Consequently, the midshot to long shot was used to record entire dialog sequences.

As the technology developed, more options complemented the midshot approach to the dialog sequence. But as important as the technology proved to be, the creative options developed by directors were equally effective in broadening the editing repertoire of the dialog sequence.

By examining the creative style of an early dialog sequence and following it with the examination of a contemporary dialog sequence, the reader gains perspective on the developmental nature of editing styles. The reader can also appreciate how much those changes have contributed to the spectrum of current editing styles.

Trouble in Paradise (1932) was written by Samson Raphaelson and Grover Jones and directed by Ernst Lubitsch. Lubitsch's direction of the dialog sequences in *Trouble in Paradise* represents an economy of shots unprecedented in film with the possible exception of Luis Buñuel's work (Figure 22.1).

When he wished, Lubitsch could be very dynamic in his editing of a dialog scene. For example, toward the end of the film, two of the three main characters are committing themselves to one another. Madame Colette (Kay Francis) speaks. She has been trying to seduce her secretary, Gaston (Herbert Marshall), and this is her moment of triumph. She doesn't realize that he is a thief whose interest, thus far, has been her money. The two embrace, and she says they will have weeks, months, and years to be together. Each word—weeks, months, years—has a different accompanying visual. The first is of the two embracing, as seen in a mirror in the bedroom. The second shows the two of them in midshot embracing. The third shot is of their shadows cast across her bed as they embrace. Not only is the sequence dynamic visually, it is also suggestive of what is to come.

Lubitsch usually did not take quite as dynamic an approach. He tended to be more indirect, always highlighting through the editing the secondary meaning or subtext of the dialog. An excellent example is the second scene in the film, which follows a robbery. It opens on Gaston, posing as a baron, instructing a waiter about the food and the champagne and about how little he wants to see the waiter. The anticipation is crosscut with a scene that reveals that a robbery has taken place. The baron's guest, Lili (Miriam Hopkins), arrives. She seems

FIGURE 22.1

Trouble in Paradise, 1932. Copyright © by Universal Studios, Inc. Courtesy of MCA Publishing Rights, a Division of MCA Inc. Still provided by British Film Institute.

to be a very rich countess who is spending time in Venice, but she is not what she appears to be. We realize this when she receives a call and pretends that it's an invitation to a party, but the cutaway shows that it is her poor roommate.

During this sequence, which appears to be a romantic interlude between the baron and Lili, there is a lengthy cutaway to the victim of the robbery (Edward Everett Horton) as he is being interviewed by the police. He provides some detail about the thief, a charming man who pretended to be a doctor.

When the film cuts back to the baron's suite, the relationship has progressed. The two are eating dinner, and the talk seems to be less about gossip and more reflective of the baron's unfolding romantic agenda for the evening.

The dialog sequence is presented as a mid-two-shot with both parties seated. During the meal, Lili tells the baron that she knows he is not who he appears to be: He is a thief who stole from the guests in suites 203, 205, 207, and 209. The baron is calm and notes that he knows that she knows because she stole the wallet he had stolen from the guest.

A short sequence of shots follows as the baron locks the door, closes the curtains, and approaches Lili in a menacing fashion. He raises her from her seat and shakes her. A close-up of the floor shows the wallet that falls from her dress.

Seated again in midshot, but now in a different tone, they profess their affection for one another and describe other items they have stolen from one another: a brooch, a watch, a garter belt. He introduces himself as Gaston, revealing his true identity, and now they really do seem to be in love. They have shed their facades and discovered two like-minded thieves. A series of silent shots follow that suggests the consummation of the relationship and the consolidation of a partnership.

This sequence used crosscutting to suggest another meaning to what was said through the dialog. Where possible, Lubitsch also used short visual sequences to build up dramatic tension in the scene, but for the most part, he relied on the midshot to cover the sequence. In the entire 15-minute sequence, there are no more than four or five close-ups.

Later in the film, Lubitsch shed his reliance on crosscutting to suggest the subtext of a dialog sequence. It's useful to illustrate how he undermined the dialog in this sequence to get to the subtext.

Gaston and Lili are now a team. They have stolen a diamond-studded handbag from a rich widow, Madame Colette. When they read in the paper that she is offering a reward of 20,000 francs for the bag, Gaston decides to return it. Madame Colette is a young romantic widow who is pursued by older, more serious suitors who are not to her taste. When she meets Gaston as he comes to return the bag, she is clearly charmed by him.

In the scene that follows, Lubitsch allowed the performances and the consistent use of a two-shot of the characters to communicate all of the nuances of meaning. In the scene, Madame Colette is taken with Gaston, but he must convince her that (1) he is a member of her class and (2) his intentions are honorable. The two talk about the contents of her purse; Gaston criticizes one of her suitors as well as her makeup. She seems to appreciate his interest, and when she is embarrassed about giving him the reward, he assures her that she needn't be: as a member of the nouveau poor, he needs the money.

He follows her up the stairs, where she looks for her checkbook. In this scene, she demonstrates her reliance on others. She can't find her checkbook, and she alludes to the ineptitude of the secretary she had to fire. While she looks for the checkbook, Gaston looks for the safe. It is in the secretary desk in the bedroom. Although he speaks of period furniture, he is obviously scouting a new location for robbery.

As she opens the safe, Lubitsch cuts to a close-up of Gaston's fingers as they mimic the turns of the dial on the safe. Once she gets the safe open, he scolds her for keeping only 100,000 francs in the safe. She is indifferent to his criticism, and the following dialog closes the scene. The two characters are seated on a chair. The midshot is tight on the two of them.

```
GASTON (sternly, an uncle): Madame Colette, I think you
deserve a scolding. First you lose your bag——
COLETTE (gaily): Then I mislay my checkbook——
GASTON: Then you use the wrong lipstick——
COLETTE (almost laughing): And how I handle my money!
GASTON: It's disgraceful!
```

```
COLETTE (with a flirtatious look): Tell me, M. Laval,
what else is wrong?
GASTON Everything! Madame Colette, if I were your father——
(with a smile) which, fortunately, I am not——
COLETTE (coquettish): Yes?
GASTON: And you made any attempt to handle your own
business affairs, I would give you a good spanking——in a
good business way, of course.
COLETTE (complete change of expression; businesslike): What
would you do if you were my secretary?
GASTON: The same thing.
COLETTE: You're hired!
FADE OUT
```

This elaborate scene, which reveals the character of Madame Colette and Gaston as well as advances the plot, has a very specific subtext: the verbal seduction of Gaston by Madame Colette and of Madame Colette by Gaston. The dialog contributes to the progress of this new relationship. Consequently, by focusing on a midshot of the two characters together, first standing and then sitting, Lubitsch directed for subtext regardless of the actual lines of dialog. Because of his direction of the actors in this sequence, he relied less on editing than he had to in the Gaston–Lili seduction sequence.

Both approaches are options for the editor. The earlier sequence relied more on editing; the second sequence relied more on performance and direction.

CHINATOWN: A CONTEMPORARY DIALOG SEQUENCE

The dialog sequences in *Chinatown* (1974) differ considerably from those in *Trouble in Paradise*. Although the sequences described here are also about seduction, the approach that director Roman Polanski took in the dialog scenes is more aggressive than that of Ernst Lubitsch. Although the differences are, in part, related to the different genres or to preferences of the directors, contemporary conventions about the dialog sequence also suggest a more assertive, less subtle approach to its editing.

Robert Towne's script for *Chinatown* is film noir, with all of its highly stylized implications, whereas the Raphaelson/Jones script for *Trouble in Paradise* is a romantic comedy closely aligned with a theatrical comedy of manners. Lubitsch's direction was subtle and slightly distant, but Polanski's direction verged on the claustrophobic. To be more specific, Lubitsch set up shots so that the action takes place in front of the camera, an objective position.

He rarely resorted to subjective camera placement. Lubitsch also relied on the midshot to long shot for his sequences. Polanski, on the other hand, favored subjective camera placement. When Gittes (Jack Nicholson) speaks, the camera sees what he sees. Polanski crowded the camera up against Gittes shoulder at his eye level, so that there would be no mistake about the point of view. Polanski used the foreground–background relationship to set the dialog sequence in context. He also favored the close-up over the midshot. The result is a dialog sequence of intense emotion and pointed perspective.

The following sequence occurs about an hour into the film. Evelyn Mullwray (Faye Dunaway) has arrived at the office of private investigator Jake Gittes. She wants to hire him. Earlier in the film, another woman claiming to be Evelyn Mullwray had hired Gittes to watch her husband, whom she suspected of infidelity. The husband was then killed.

The first part of the scene presents Gittes pouring himself a drink with his back to Evelyn or reading his phone messages while speaking to her. She, on the other hand, is presented entirely in close-up. She wants to hire Gittes to find out why her husband was killed. He suggests that it was for money; when he says this, we see him in midshot reading his phone messages.

When she offers him a substantial sum of money, he looks up and begins to talk about her background, about her marriage to Hollis Mullwray, who was considerably older, and about the fact that Mullwray was her father's former partner. When Gittes mentions her father's name, Noah Cross (John Huston), the shot shifts to a close-up of her reaction. The camera holds on her while Gittes mentions her father's name, then the film cuts to a close-up as she fumbles with her handbag to remove a cigarette holder and lighter.

There is a close-up of Gittes as he says, "Then you married your father's business partner." A quick series of close-ups follows. Gittes refers to Evelyn's smoking two cigarettes simultaneously, and this part of the sequence suggests how nervous she is about the topic of her father. The visual holds on a close-up of Evelyn while Gittes asks her about the falling out between her husband and her father. The secretary enters with a service contract for Evelyn to sign. The conversation continues over a midshot of Gittes looking over and signing the contract. When he offers Evelyn the contract, she enters the foreground of the shot while Gittes remains in midshot in the background.

By relying on close-ups of Evelyn as often as he did, Polanski suggests the importance of her truthfulness in the scene. She is closely scrutinized by the camera for clues as to whether she is telling the truth.

Polanski also supported this search for clues by focusing on Evelyn while Gittes speaks. At the end of the scene, the camera is focused on Gittes and the legal dimension of their relationship: the service contract. By editing this sequence as he did, Polanksi gave the meeting a subjective character and intensity that the dialog itself does not have. Like Lubitsch, he has tried to reveal the subtext through the editing of the sequence.

Later in the film, when the relationship between Gittes and Evelyn has taken a more personal turn, Polanski uses a different approach. In one scene, Gittes is under the impression that Evelyn is holding against her will a young woman whom he believes was Hollis Mullwray's mistress. In fact, the young woman is Evelyn's daughter. The scene is one of confrontation between Evelyn and Gittes (Figure 22.2).

Polanski used a moving camera here. The camera follows Gittes as he enters the house. It follows him as he telephones the police about the whereabouts of the girl. The camera

FIGURE 22.2
Chinatown, 1974. Courtesy of Paramount Pictures. Copyright © 1974 by Paramount Pictures. All Rights Reserved.

continues to move until Gittes sits down. In this first phase of the scene, we see Evelyn in tight midshot in the background with Gittes crowded into the foreground. Their relationship is visually reinforced. They speak strictly about the whereabouts of the girl. Once Gittes calls the police and takes a seat, the conversation shifts to the identity of the killer.

This portion of the dialog sequence begins with Gittes seated in the background and Evelyn in the foreground. Once he makes his accusation, he stands, and close-ups of Gittes and Evelyn are intercut. He accuses her of accidentally killing her husband. She denies it. The dramatic intensity is matched by the cutting of close-up to close-up. Gittes shakes her, and she denies the charges.

Gittes now shifts the conversation to the identity of the girl she claimed was her sister. The close-ups continue. Evelyn states that the girl is her daughter. Gittes slaps her. The film cuts to a tight two-shot with Gittes in the foreground and Evelyn in the background. Now, in a single shot within this frame, she claims that the girl is her sister and her daughter. She makes this statement again, and again Gittes slaps her. The camera moves as Gittes pushes her down. The entrance of her servant works as a cutaway to break the tension. She sends him away, and the film cuts to a close-up of Evelyn, who explains that her father was the father of her daughter, Catherine. A reaction close-up of Gittes allows the audience to see his emotional shift from anger to pity for Evelyn. Now, the close-ups are principally of Evelyn while she explains about her marriage and Catherine's birth.

Gittes agrees to let Evelyn go. She will go to her servant's home. As she begins to walk around, she tells Gittes that the glasses he found were not her husband's. She couldn't have been the killer. The sequence shifts to a close-up of Gittes and then of the glasses. She returns with Catherine, introduces her, and gives Gittes her servant's address. She asks if he knows where it is. The camera moves in on Gittes as he says it is located in Chinatown.

The sequence ends with Gittes in the foreground dropping the window blind with Evelyn and Catherine in the background as they prepare to drive off. This sequence is presented in a much more intense manner than the first sequence described. The subjectivity, the moving camera, and the abundance of close-ups and cutting all support the notion of a scene of great dramatic importance. The editing is very dynamic, and yet everything we learn is revealed through the dialog. The scene exemplifies the dynamic possibilities where plot is revealed. It is, however, a scene that has tremendous emotional impact, principally because of the editing of the sequence.

It offers a very different editing model from the seduction scene between Madame Colette and Gaston in *Trouble in Paradise*. The direction is far more aggressive and the editing is less subtle. It also illustrates the more aggressive approach currently being taken to the dialog sequence.

MICHAEL CLAYTON: DIALOG AS TRANSFORMATIVE DEVICE

Generally, dialog can characterize, and it can advance the action, but rarely is it as important as the antagonist, the main character, or the plot. The film *Michael Clayton* is the exception to the previous statement. In Tony Gilroy's *Michael Clayton*, the dialog is the most important narrative tool, as transformational as a love interest, an antagonist, or a plot.

Tony Gilroy's *Michael Clayton* is a contemporary thriller focusing on corporate malfeasance. The main character, Michael Clayton, is a "fixer," or a problem solver, for a large corporate law firm. His firm represents a large agro-business corporation in a six-year lawsuit. The lead lawyer in the suit, Arthur Eden, has a breakdown and turns against his own client. His actions cost him his life, and when Michael Clayton begins to look into Arthur's accusations, he too is in danger.

Michael Clayton is a man who can solve problems but seems beset by personal challenges (his brother's debts, his own gambling habit, a failed marriage). He hovers between pragmatic accommodation and moral responsibility. It is his commitment to Arthur (personal) that pushes him to finish what Arthur began (moral redemption).

The dialog throughout Michael Clayton is energetic. It's used to express a yearning for redemption (in the quasireligious sense). The dialog also reflects the degree of damage living inflicts on the characters. It is the yearning and the damage that gives Gilroy's dialog its power.

To examine the unusual usage of the dialog in *Michael Clayton*, I focus on a single character, Arthur Eden. In the film's opening, Arthur is reading a letter addressed to Michael Clayton. The letter is confessional and may very well have been found by Michael after Arthur's death.

The other scene I use is the first actual conversation between Arthur and Michael; Arthur is in jail for his inappropriate lewd behavior at a deposition in Minneapolis. Michael has arrived to "fix" the situation, to encourage Arthur's team to continue the depositions and to hustle Arthur out of Minneapolis back to New York with as little professional damage as possible. His law firm is in takeover talks—and bad publicity might jeopardize the firm's potential to be bought out. Arthur's behavior represents that threat.

In the letter, Arthur describes rushing out of his office with 38 minutes to make it to the airport. There crossing a busy Manhattan street he has an epiphany: "It's not an episode or a relapse; it's not just madness." He is referring to his ongoing struggle with manic depression. He talks about then and there being reborn. He speaks of being "covered in a coating of amniotic fluid." But "this is not a rebirth; it's the final moment before death." He speaks of it as "a moment of clarity" when he "excretes the poisons that are necessary for other organisms to destroy the miracle of humanity."

Exactly where this epiphany comes from is explained in the first conversation Arthur has with Michael. Now confined probably for psychiatric reasons as much as lewd behavior, Arthur explains that he simply has become fed up with what he was doing and why he was doing it. He found the light when he had been invited to celebrate that he billed for 30,000 hours in the past six years on this case. He speaks of the depth of the pathology. He states, "If I tear off my f***ing skin, I could not get down to where this thing is living. Four hundred depositions, 85,000 documents and 30,000 billable hours ... $50 million ... it's years, it's lives ... I'm trying not to think ... four years ... to protect ... this carcinogenic moment ... I have blood on my hands."

He then becomes specific about the plaintiff, her dead parents, and her dying mother. Regardless of whether he is overwhelmed with guilt, what is clear is that Arthur has crossed over and decided to act for the plaintiff rather than to do what he is hired for, to act for the defense. Although there is much talk about taking or not taking his medication, Arthur Eden has give up his corporate ways and embraced what for him is a path to redemption; he has embraced a new morality and rejected his former values and way of being in the world. Whether it is madness or the ultimate sanity is what the rest of the film is about. For our purposes, Arthur and his words are the transformational devices that pressure Michael Clayton to act as Arthur would have acted. And he does.

NOTE/REFERENCE

1. I am indebted to my colleague, Paul Lucey from the University of Southern California, for drawing this example to my attention. He calls this "torquing the dialog," an apt mechanical image appropriate to the location of the dialog and to what the chase does to it as the intercutting proceeds.

CHAPTER 23

Comedy

When examining the editing of a comedy sequence, it is critical to distinguish the role of the editor from the roles of the writer and the director. The burden of creative responsibility for the success of verbal humor, whether a joke, a punch line, or an extended witty repartee, lies with the writer for the comic inventiveness of the lines and the director and the actor for eliciting the comic potential from those lines. The editor may cut to a close shot for the punch line, but the editor's role in verbal humor is somewhat limited. With regard to visual humor, the editor certainly has more scope.[1] Indeed, together with the writer, director, and actors, the editor plays a critical role.

It is important to understand that *humor* is a broad term. Unless we look at the various types of comedy, we may fall into the trap of overgeneralization.

CHARACTER COMEDY

Character comedy is the type of comedy associated with Chaplin, Keaton, Lloyd, and Langdon in the silent period, and with the Marx Brothers, W. C. Fields, Mae West, Martin and Lewis, Laurel and Hardy, Abbott and Costello, and Woody Allen in the sound period. Abroad, these ranks are joined by the great comedians Jacques Tati, Pierre Etaix, Peter Sellers, and John Cleese.

The roles of these character comics were associated with the particular personae that they cultivated, which often did not change throughout their career. A character role is somewhat different from a great comic performance by a dramatic performer—for example, Michael Caine in *Alfie* (1966)—in the sense that this screen persona provides a different relationship with the audience. It allows Woody Allen to address and to confess to the screen audience in *Annie Hall* (1977); it allows Chaplin's Littlet Tramp to be abused by a lunch machine in *Modern Times* (1936); it allows Groucho Marx to indulge in nonsequiturs and puns that have nothing to do with the screen story in *Duck Soup* (1934). The audience has certain expectations from a comic character, and it is the job of the editor to make sure that the audience isn't disappointed.

315

The Technique of Film and Video Editing: History, Theory, and Practice. DOI: 10.1016/B978-0-240-81397-4.00023-6

SITUATION COMEDY

The most common (on television and in film) is the situation comedy. This type of comedy tends to be realistic and depends on the characters. As a result, it is generally verbal, with a minimum of pratfalls. The editing centers on timing to accentuate performance; the editor's role with situation comedy is more limited than with other types of comedy sequences.

SATIRE

A third category of comedy is satire. Here, because anything goes, the scope of the editor is considerable. Whether we refer to the dynamic opening of Paddy Chayefsky's *The Hospital* (1971) or Terry Southern and Stanley Kubrick's *Dr. Strangelove* (1964), which ranged from absurdist fantasy to cinéma vérité, the range for the editor of satirical sequences is challenging and creative.

FARCE

The editor is also very important in farce, such as Blake Edwards's *The Pink Panther* (1964), and in parody, such as Sergio Leone's *The Good, the Bad, and the Ugly* (1967). In *The Pink Panther*, for example, the quick cut to Robert Wagner sneaking out of Inspector Clouseau's bedroom, having hidden in the shower, is instructive. Earlier, Clouseau had turned on the shower without noticing its occupant. When the wet Wagner sneaks from the room, his ski sweater, which, of course, is now wet, has stretched to his toes. Logically, such an outcome is impossible, but in farce, such absurdity is expected.

EDITING CONCERNS

Beyond understanding the characteristics of the genre he is working with, the editor must focus on the target of the humor. Is it aimed by a character at himself, or does the humor occur at the expense of another? Screen comedy has a long tradition of comic characters who are the target of the humor. Beyond these performers, the target of the humor must be highlighted by the editor.

If the target is the comic performer, what aspect of the character is the source of the comedy? It was the broad issue of the character's sexual identity in Howard Hawks's *Bringing Up Baby* (1938). The scene in which Cary Grant throws a tantrum wearing a woman's housecoat is comic. What the editor had to highlight in the scene was not the character's tantrum, but rather his costume. In Sydney Pollack's *Tootsie* (1982), the source of the humor is the confusion over the sexual identity of Michael (Dustin Hoffman). We know that he is a man pretending to be a woman, but others assume that he is a woman. The issue of mistaken identity blurs for Michael when he begins to act like a woman rather than a man. Here, the editor had to keep the narrative intention in mind and cut to surprise the audience just as Michael surprises himself.

Comedy comes from surprise, but the degree of comedy comes from the depth of the target of the humor. If the target is as shallow as a humorous name—for example, in Richard

Lester's *A Funny Thing Happened on the Way to the Forum* (1966), two characters are named Erronius and Hysterium—the film may elicit a smile of amusement. To develop a more powerful comic response, however, the very nature of the character must be the source of the humor. Jack Benny's vanity in Lubitsch's *To Be or Not to Be* (1942), Nicolas Cage's sibling rivalry and the anger it engenders in Norman Jewison's *Moonstruck* (1987), and Tom Hank's immaturity and anger in David Seltzer's *Punchline* (1989) are all deep and continuous sources of comedy arising from the character.

When comedy occurs at the expense of others, the degree of humor bears a relationship to the degree of cruelty, but only to an extent. If the character dies from slipping on a banana peel, the humor is lost. The degree of humiliation and pain is the variable. Too much or too little will not help the comic situation. This is why so many directors and editors speak about the difficulty of comedy. Many claim that it is the most difficult type of film to direct and to edit.

Examples of this type of humor range from the physical abuse of the Three Stooges by one another to the accidental killing of three little dogs in *A Fish Called Wanda* (1988). This type of humor can be present in a very extreme fashion, such as in the necessity of Giancarlo Giannini's character in *Seven Beauties* (1976) to perform sexually with the German camp commandant. Failure will mean death. This painful moment is excruciatingly funny, and the director and editor have wisely focused on the inequity, physical and political, in the relationship of the momentary lovers. The reversal of the conventions of gender roles is continually reinforced by images of her large form and his miniature one. The editing supports this perception of the power relationship and exploits his victimization.

Equally painful and humorous is the situation of the two principal characters in Ethan Coen and Joel Coen's *Raising Arizona* (1987). The husband and wife are childless, and to solve their dilemma, they become kidnappers and target a millionaire with quintuplets. The abduction of one of the children is a comic scene in which the editor and the director reverse the audience's perception of who the victim is. The kidnapper is presented as the victim, and the child is presented as the aggressor. He moves about freely, eluding the kidnapper, and the implication is that his movement will alert his parents.

Whether the source of the comedy is role reversal, mistaken identity, or the struggle of human and machine, the issue of pace is critical. When Albert Brooks begins to sweat as he reads the news in *Broadcast News* (1987), the only way to communicate the degree of his anxiety is to keep cutting back to how much he is sweating. The logical conclusion is that his clothes will become wringing wet, and of course, this is exactly what happens. Pace alerts us to the build in the comedy sequence. What is interesting about comedy is that the twists and turns require build or else the comedy is lost. Exaggeration plays a role, but it is pace that is critical to the sequence.

Consider the classic scene in *Modern Times* in which Chaplin's character is being driven mad by the pace of the assembly line. His job is to tighten two bolts. Once he has gone over the edge, he begins chasing anything with two buttons, particularly women. The sequence builds to a fever pitch, reflecting the character's frenzied state.

Pace is so important in comedy that the masterful director of comedy, Frank Capra, used a metronome on the set and paced it faster than normal for the comedy sequences so that his actors would read the dialog faster than normal.[2] He believed that this fast tempo was critical to comedy. Attention to pace within shots is as important to the editing of comic sequences as is pace between shots.

If we were to deconstruct what the editor needs to edit a comedy sequence, we would have to begin with the editor's knowledge. The editor must understand the material: its narrative intention, its sources of humor, whether they are character-based or situation-based, whether they are the target of the humor, and whether there is a visual dimension to the humor.

The director should provide the editor with shots that facilitate the character actor's persona coming to the forefront. If the source of the humor is a punch line, has the director provided any shots that punctuate the punch line? If the joke is visual, has the director provided material that sets up the joke and that executes it? Unlike other types of sequences, a key ingredient of humor is surprise. Is there a reaction shot or a cutaway that will help create that surprise? The scene must build to that surprise. Without the build, the comedy might well be lost.

Another detail is important for the editor: Has the director provided for juxtaposition within shots? The juxtaposition of foreground and background can provide the surprise or contradiction that is so critical to comedy. Blake Edwards is particularly adept at using juxtaposition to set up the comic elements in a scene. The availability of two fields of action, the foreground and background, are the ingredients that help the editor coax out the comic elements in a scene. For example, if the waiter pours the wine in the right foreground part of the frame, the character begins to drink from the wine glass in the middle background of the frame. The character drinks and the waiter continues to pour. This logical and yet absurd situation is presented in *Victor Victoria* (1982). Edwards often resorts to this type of visual comedy within a shot. These elements, combined with understanding how to pace the editing for comic effect, are crucial for editing a comedy sequence.

THE COMEDY DIRECTOR

Comedy may be a difficult genre to direct, but there are some directors who have been superlative. Aside from the great character comics who became directors—Chaplin, Keaton, and, in our time, Woody Allen—a relatively small number of directors have been responsible for most of the great screen comedies. Ernst Lubitsch was the best at coaxing more than one meaning from a witty piece of dialog. His films, including Noel Coward's *Design for Living* (1933), Samson Raphaelson's *Trouble in Paradise* (1932), and Ernst Lubitschs's *Ninotchka* (1939), are a tribute to wit and civility. Howard Hawks, particularly in his Ben Hecht films (*His Girl Friday*, 1940; *Twentieth Century*, 1934) and his screwball comedies (*Bringing Up Baby*, 1938; *I Was a Male War Bride*, 1949; *Monkey Business*, 1952), seemed to be able to balance contradictions of character and the visual dimension of his scenes in such a way that there is a comic build in his films that is quite unlike anyone else's. The comedy begins as absurdity and rises to hysteria. He managed to present this comedic build with a

nonchalance that made the overt pacing of the sequences unnecessary. His performers simply accelerated their pace as the action evolved.

In his films (*Mr. Smith Goes to Washington*, 1939; *Mr. Deeds Goes to Town*, 1936), Frank Capra was capable of relying on lively dialog and surprising behavior by his characters to generate the energy in his comedy sequences. Capra, however, was more likely than other directors to use jump cutting within a scene to increase its energy. Preston Sturges was similar to Capra in that he resorted to editing when necessary (*The Great McGinty*, 1940; *Sullivan's Travels*, 1941), but he usually relied on language and performance to develop the comedy. He differed from the aforementioned directors in the satiric energy of his comedy. Whether it was heroism (*Hail the Conquering Hero*, 1944) or rural morality (*The Miracle of Morgan's Creek*, 1944), Sturges was always satirizing societal values, just as Capra was always advocating them. Satire is always a better source of comedy than advocacy, and consequently, Sturges's films have a savage bite rare among comedy directors.

Billy Wilder was perhaps most willing to resort to editing juxtapositions to generate comedy. That is not to say that his films don't have other qualities. Indeed, Wilder's work ranges from the wit of Lubitsch (*The Apartment*, 1960), to the absurdism of Hawks (*Some Like It Hot*, 1959), to the satiric energy of Sturges (*Kiss Me, Stupid*, 1964). Like Hawks, Wilder also made films in other genres. Consequently, the editing of his films is more elaborate than that of the directors mentioned previously.

Contemporary directors who are exceptional at comedy include Blake Edwards (the *Pink Panther* series) and Woody Allen. Edwards is certainly the more visual of the two. We will look at an example from his body of work later in this chapter. Woody Allen, on the other hand, is interested in performance and language in his films. Consequently, the editing supports the story and highlights the performance of his actors. His work is most reminiscent of Ernst Lubitsch in its sense of economy. Although there are marvelous sequences that rely on editing in *The Purple Rose of Cairo* (1985) and *Radio Days* (1987), editing rarely plays a prominent role in the creation of comedy in his films.

Another director who should be mentioned here is Richard Lester (*A Hard Day's Night*, 1964; *Help!*, 1965). Of all of the directors mentioned, Lester most relies on editing to achieve juxtaposition and surprise. It would be an exaggeration to say that this makes him the most filmic of the comic directors, but his use of editing does make him particularly interesting.

The aforementioned are the great American directors of comedy. There are exceptional foreign directors as well, particularly the French actor–director Jacques Tati, whose films (*Mr. Hulot's Holiday*, 1953; *Mon Oncle*, 1958) are classics of screen pantomime. Also important to mention are some individual directors who are not known for comedy but have directed exceptional film comedies. They range from George Stevens (*The More the Merrier*, 1943) to Lewis Gilbert (*A Fish Called Wanda*). Joan Micklin Silver directed the comedy-drama *Crossing Delancey* (1988), and George Roy Hill directed the broad, outrageous *Slap Shot* (1977). The best comedy on screen recently has been directed by comedy performers who became directors: Woody Allen, Steve Martin, Rob Reiner, and Danny De Vito. Although there has been good comic writing by James Brooks, John Hughes, and John Patrick Shanley, comedy in the 1980s and 1990s has not had the resurgence of the action film. Comedies are being produced, but with the exception of Woody Allen and John Cleese, great screen comedy is still elusive. There are new comic characters—Bill Murray, Robin Williams, Jim Carrey, Mike Myers—but their screen personae have not been as powerful as those of their predecessors.

THE PAST: *THE LADY EVE*—THE EARLY COMEDY OF ROLE REVERSAL

The Lady Eve (1941), by writer–director Preston Sturges, tells the story of a smart young woman (Barbara Stanwyck) who is a professional gambler. She meets a rich young man (Henry Fonda) aboard an ocean liner. She determines their fate; they fall in love. When he learns that she is a gambler, he breaks off the relationship. Ashore, filled with the desire for revenge, she dons a British accent and visits his home. She convinces him that, because she looks so much like the first woman, she must be someone else. He falls in love with her again. On their honeymoon, she confesses to a string of lovers, and he leaves her. He sues for divorce, but she refuses his settlement. He goes away. They meet again aboard a ship. Believing that she is his first love, he falls for her again. As they confess to one another that they are married, the door closes and the film ends.

Although the film relies strongly on verbal comedy, Sturges also exploited the dissonance between the verbal and the visual. When Pike (Fonda) takes his first meal on the ocean liner, every woman in the dining room tries to capture his attention. In an elaborate sequence, Eve (Stanwyck) watches in her makeup mirror as Pike avoids the attention of various women. She seems dispassionate until the film cuts to a midshot that reveals her indignation at the situation. This is followed by a close-up of her foot, which she has extended to trip Pike. In the next shot, he is flat on his face, having smashed into a waiter bearing someone's meal (Figure 23.1). The contrast between her dispassionate appearance and her behavior provides the surprise from which comedy springs. The indignation he expresses after his fall turns into an apology as she accuses him of breaking the heel of her shoe. He introduces himself, but she dismisses it, saying that everyone knows who he is.

The verbal twists and turns in this sequence are typical of the surprise that characterizes the film. The wittiness of the dialog, the visual pratfalls, the verbal twists, and the superb performances are the major sources of humor in the film.

Aside from the exceptional quality of the script, Sturges's approach to the editing of the film is not unusual. Later in the film, however, there is a sequence that relies totally on the editing to create comedy. Pike is now married to Eve, who is posing as Lady Sedgewicke. They are on their honeymoon. To avenge herself for the first round of their relationship in which he left her because she was a gambler, Eve has decided to confess to a string of lovers. She begins slowly and tells him about eloping with a stable boy at the age of 16. Instead of cutting directly to a shot that reveals Pike's disappointment, Sturges cut to a shot of the train rushing through the night. This first confession is paced slowly, but as the confessions come faster, Sturges cuts

FIGURE 23.1
The Lady Eve, 1941. Copyright © by Universal City Studios, Inc. Courtesy MCA Publishing Rights, a Division of MCA Inc. Still provided by British Film Institute.

to the train rushing through a tunnel. The pace of editing quickens between her confession, his response, and the train. It leads us to the aching disillusionment of the new husband.

The entire sequence concludes with the train stopping and Pike leaving the train and the marriage. After the first story of the elopement with the stable boy, the cutting takes over, illustrating Pike's rising temper and her candor. The motion of the train underscores the emotion of the situation. It also provides a visual dimension beyond the verbal interchange. The rushing train implies the termination of the relationship rather than the consummation of the marriage. The result is comedy.

The approach that Sturges took, with its reliance on verbal humor and the occasional use of visual humor, is typical of the comedy sequences of his time.

THE PRESENT: *VICTOR VICTORIA*—A CONTEMPORARY COMEDY OF ROLE REVERSAL

In 1982, Blake Edwards wrote and directed *Victor Victoria*. In the 40 years between *The Lady Eve* and *Victor Victoria*, the balance between the verbal and visual elements of comedy shifted. Today's films have a much greater variety of visual humor.

Victor Victoria is the story of a young performer, Victoria (Julie Andrews), who is not very successful in 1930's Paris until she meets a gay performer, Toddy (Robert Preston), who suggests that she would improve her career if she pretended to be a man who pretended to be a female performer.

She follows his advice, pretends to be a Polish count, and under Toddy's tutelage, she is an instant success. An American nightclub entrepreneur, King Marchand (James Garner), sees her perform and is very taken by her performance and by her female stage persona until he discovers that she is "Victor." He doesn't believe that she is a man and tries to prove that she really is a woman.

This story about mistaken identity and sexual attitudes has a happy conclusion. The humor, both verbal and visual, usually generates from the confusion about sexuality. For example, one of the best visual jokes in the film is a close-up of King and "Victor" dancing cheek-to-cheek (Figure 23.2). They are clearly romantically involved with one another. In a preceding scene, she had acknowledged that she is a woman, and they initiated their relationship. The dancing shot begins in a close-up of the two lovers, and when the camera pulls back, we see that they are dancing cheek-to-cheek in a gay bar. All of the other loving couples are male.

A more typical comedy sequence occurs early in the film. Victoria and Toddy are eating a meal that they can't afford in a French café. The sequence illustrates their hunger and the

FIGURE 23.2
Victor Victoria, 1982. © 1982 Turner Entertainment Company. Still provided by British Film Institute.

instrument of their escape: a cockroach that Victoria intends to put onto her salad. She tries to dump the cockroach from her purse onto the salad, but a close-up shows that she has failed. When the suspicious waiter asks her how her salad is, she is jumpy. Toddy asks for another bottle of wine to distract the waiter, who notices they haven't finished the first bottle yet. In a close-up, the cockroach moves from the purse to the salad. Victoria sees the cockroach and screams. The suspicious waiter collides with another waiter, and the cockroach is flung onto another table. Attracted by the commotion, the manager comes to the table. In midshot, he attempts to calm the situation, but he, too, is suspicious. The following shots of Toddy defending Victoria and of the manager handling the accusation create the sense that either Toddy or Victoria will be held responsible for the bill. Just as the situation seems to be lost, the film cuts to a close-up of the cockroach on a patron's leg. The dialog of Toddy and the manager continues on the sound track, but the visuals shift to the cockroach. The film cuts to a close-up of the patron as she screams and then quickly cuts to an exterior shot of the restaurant, where we see the growing pandemonium from afar.

The twists and turns of this sequence provide the context for the humor. The waiter's behavior and the cockroach constitute the surprises that give rise to the comedy. Edwards clearly understood the role of conflict and contrast in the creation of comedy. The editing follows the development of the conflict and at strategic points introduces the necessary elements of surprise. The comedy in this sequence is primarily visual, although there is some verbal humor, particularly from the waiter.

Edwards's use of visual humor to bypass the obligatory but uninteresting parts of the narrative demonstrates how useful the comedy sequence can be. The obligatory part of the narrative is the introduction of "Victor" to a music impresario who can help her career. Toddy takes her to the impresario's office, where the secretary tells them that her boss is unavailable. The scene has been played many times before: The characters lie to or charm the secretary, the would-be performer wows the impresario, and a career is launched. To avoid this trite approach, Edwards introduced a new element. While Toddy and "Victor" wait to see the great man, another would-be star enters: a tuxedo-clad gentleman with a bottle of champagne who claims to be the greatest acrobat in the world. The secretary refuses him entry as well.

The man opens the bottle of champagne, offers the secretary a glass, and proceeds to do a handstand, cane placed in the champagne bottle, his other hand on the secretary's head. This distraction has allowed Toddy and "Victor" to join the impresario in his office. On the sound track we hear Toddy's pitch and the impresario's skepticism. As "Victor" sings, the acrobat is a tremendous success; he has let go of the secretary and is supporting himself with only the cane in the champagne bottle. As Victor hits a high note, a close-up of the champagne bottle shows it shattering, and a long shot shows the acrobat falling. His fall brings everyone out of the inner office, and the scene ends. "Victor" is a success. The humor of this scene masks its obligatory narrative role.

Later, when King Marchand is attempting to prove Victoria's real identity, his ruse to get into her apartment is presented visually. In the hallway, King and his bodyguard attempt to follow a housecleaner into the apartment. Victoria's neighbor, who is interested only in putting his shoes out in the hallway for cleaning, is a reappearing character. Whenever either King or the bodyguard is in the hallway entering or exiting Victoria's apartment, the film cuts to the neighbor and his shoes. Straight cutaways show his evolving fears, which range from concern about his shoes to fear about the type of friends his neighbors have. Inside the apartment, the potential consequences of Victoria and Toddy's discovery of King develop the tension that is the source of the humor.

All of the comedy in this lengthy sequence is visual, and thus the editing is crucial. Cutting away from the action to provide necessary plot information keeps the sequence moving. The twists and turns of the plot are highlighted by ample close shots and visual juxtapositions that give the sequence a visual variety that differentiates it from Chaplin's style of filmed pantomime performance. In this sequence, performance is important, but the staging and editing are the sources of the humor. Repetition of characters and situations—for example, the neighbor and his shoes—helps to flesh out the sequence and add humor. The neighbor is not necessary to the narrative story; his only purpose is comic. Both narrative and comedy fuse in this sequence. We discover that King knows "Victor" is really a woman (the narrative point of the scene), and we've had an amusing sequence that entertains while informing.

FORGETTING SARAH MARSHALL: EMOTIONAL ROLE REVERSAL

If *The Lady Eve* focuses on sexual role reversal and *Victor Victoria* focuses on role reversal as an opportunity to poke fun at gender stereotypes, Nicholas Stoller's *Forgetting Sarah Marshall* (2008) explores emotional role reversal. In this film, it is the women who are stoic, decisive, and manipulative, while the male main character is emotional, indecisive, and a victim.

Peter, a musician has a steady girlfriend, Sarah Marshall. Sarah is the television star of a successful crime series. Peter writes the music for the crime series. As the film opens, Sarah breaks up with Peter. Inconsolable, he seeks consolation from his stepbrother and casual sexual partners. Nothing works. His stepbrother suggests a holiday. He goes on holiday to Sarah's favorite Hawaiian island. There he finds Sarah and her new rock star boyfriend. He stays at the resort for the following four days. There he falls out of love with Sarah and into love with a hotel employee. Getting over Sarah also means getting back to what he really wants to do: write a musical about Dracula.

In *Forgetting Sarah Marshall*, the actor (Jason Segel) is also the writer of the screenplay. What is important to note is that Peter is a physically imposing character, not the type one imagines to be emotionally vulnerable. Consequently, the writing and performance needs to be skewed against type. The result is that when Sarah tells Peter the bad news, he is naked. He offers his postshower body, but it is rejected. Although Sarah insists that he dress so they can talk about this, he retorts that if he dresses, she will break up with him. Consequently, Jason-Peter plays the breakup scene in the nude. His full frontal nudity is intended to make his character appear vulnerable—and it does. The scene also in its surprising attention to his nudity masks the banality of the breakup. Aside from its narrative purpose, it also characterizes him as a victim and Sarah as a callow television personality (why would he be in love with her?). The fact that he is naked and begging Sarah not to leave him generates a sense that Peter is "young," not mature, unable to handle disappointment in life—in short, that he is one of life's victims rather than a master of the universe (the ultimate male fantasy).

Stoller films this painful scene with Peter in tight long shot in midframe. There is no way to avoid his imposing physical presence. Sarah Marshall, on the other hand, is further back in the frame, making her appear smaller. This makes the situation and their behavior even more ironic.

In the scenes that follow, the focus is on Peter in a bar with his stepbrother. Peter is focused on finding a partner with whom he can have sex. He succeeds, but rather than the scene bringing him relief, it serves only to remind him about the life he has lost. A cutaway to a happy Peter with Sarah in the past serves to make the point that he is not getting over Sarah. A montage of other sexual partners does not do the trick either. He states as much to his stepbrother, who recommends a vacation.

At the Hawaiian resort, he almost immediately runs into Sarah and her new boyfriend. The scene deepens Peter's sense of humiliation. Not even a luxury room at a reduced rate helps Peter. In his new room, with Sarah in a room nearby, he cries like a baby. When he gets a call from the hotel employee who facilitated his being in this room, he tells her he also hears someone crying upstairs. She tells him that he is on the top floor. Humiliated, he assures her he will try to keep the noise of crying lower. But he can't.

Peter's emotional pain continues until he begins a relationship with Rachel, a hotel employee. But until then, the narrative focus is on Peter, the emotional basket case, stuck in his pain, loss, and humiliation. Sarah, on the other hand, is feeling no pain—only irritation about Peter's presence.

The presentation of the former lovers, Peter and Sarah, as opposite to our physical and gender expectations about their behavior, is the primary source of humor in *Forgetting Sarah Marshall*.

CONCLUSION

A comparison of *The Lady Eve* and *Victor Victoria* reveals the decline in the importance of the spoken word. Dialog, whether comedic or not, is no longer written as Sturges, Wilder, and Raphaelson wrote dialog. Although also true of television programming, television commercials, and media presentations, films in particular now rely more on the visual for humor than they did in the past. This shift away from the verbal is evident in *Victor Victoria*. Visual comedy implies a greater role for the editor than verbal comedy does.

The pace of the cutting for comic effect in *The Lady Eve* is not very different from the pace in *Victor Victoria*. In addition, both films emphasize cutting that highlights character-related sources of humor. In a sense, both films are about gender politics, and just as Sturges was quick to emphasize the primacy of Eve over Pike, so too was Edwards quick to cut to King Marchand's unease and insecurity when he thinks he is falling in love with a man. In the case of Stoller's *Forgetting Sarah Marshall*, the emphasis on the emotional nature of the two principals, Peter and Sarah, along with the fact that Peter acts in a "feminine" emotional way and Sarah behaves in a "masculine" emotional pattern, pushes the edit to emphasize those reversals.

Editing to highlight the source of the tension and therefore of the comedy was a primary concern for both Sturges and Edwards. Surprise and exaggeration are critical dimensions in the creation of their comedy. The editor does not play as important a role in the comedy sequence as in other types of sequences. However, as the work of both Sturges and Edwards illustrates, the editor can make a creative contribution to the efficacy of comedy.

Other filmmakers continue to use role reversal as the basis for their comedy. Recently, writer–director–producer Judd Apatow has put his own particular stamp on the issue. In a film he produced, *I Love You, Man* (2009), he explores the female dimension in men as his male character who has no male friends seeks a friend to be the best man at his wedding. In the Apatow-written and -directed *Funny People* (2009), his main character is a nurturing male whose nature interferes with his career and his love life.

Another filmmaker who looks at the crossover in men and women's personal and professional lives is Jason Reitman, in his films *Juno* (2007) and *Up in the Air* (2009). Male and female behavior continues to be an important source of comedy for writers and directors.

NOTES/REFERENCES

1. Ralph Rosenblum's discussion of working with directors William Friedkin and Woody Allen in his book *When the Shooting Stops . . .* (New York: Da Capo Press, 1986) illustrates how critical the editor can be in transforming the same material from unfunny to funny.
2. F. Capra, The Name Above the Title, Macmillan, New York, 1971, pp. 35–56, 244–252.

CHAPTER 24

Documentary

The documentary sequence has very different criteria for success than those of the dramatic sequence. Both must follow certain rules of editing to communicate with the audience, but beyond simple continuity, the differences far outweigh the similarities. As Karel Reisz suggested, "A story-film—and this will serve as a working distinction between documentary and story-films—is concerned with the development of a plot; the documentary is concerned with the exposition of a theme. It is out of this fundamental difference of aims that the different production methods arise."[1]

The production of the dramatic film is usually much more controlled than that of the documentary. The story is broken down into deliberate shots that articulate part of the plot. Performance, camera placement, camera movement, light, color, setting, and juxtaposition of people within the shot all help advance the plot. The editor pieces together the shots, orders them, and paces them to tell the story in the most effective way.

The documentary generally proceeds in the opposite manner. There are no performers, just subjects that the filmmaker follows. Camera positioning tends to be a matter of convenience rather than intention, and lighting is designed to be as unobtrusive as possible. Documentary filmmakers tend to adhere to their definition of a documentary: a film of real people in real situations doing what they usually do. Consequently, the role of the director is less that of the orchestra conductor than that of the soloist. He tries to capture the essence of the film by working with others—the cinematographer, the sound recordist, and the editor. The documentary film is found and shaped in the editing.[2]

There are exceptions. Some documentaries are staged—Robert Flaherty's *Man of Aran* (1934), for example—and some dramatic films proceed in an extemporaneous fashion—John Cassavetes's *Faces* (1968), for example. Whether the staging of Flaherty's work made it less reliant on the editor is questionable.[3] These crossovers have become increasingly notable with the docudrama work of Peter Watkins, Ken Loach, and Don Owen. The editors played an important part in those films.

In the documentary sequence, then, the editor has a crucial and creative function. Given the goals of the documentary, that function gives the editor more freedom than the editing of a dramatic film. With freedom comes responsibility, however.

327

The Technique of Film and Video Editing: History, Theory, and Practice. DOI: 10.1016/B978-0-240-81397-4.00024-8

QUESTIONS OF ETHICS, POLITICS, AND AESTHETICS

Documentary filmmakers go out and film events that affect the lives of particular people. They film in the place that the event occurs with the people who are involved. They then edit the film. Questions immediately arise. Would the truest representation of the facts be obtained by simply stringing all of the footage together, or is some shaping necessary?

As soon as the shaping process begins, ethical questions arise. Is the event honestly presented? Does it accurately reflect the perceptions of the participants? How much ordering of the footage is necessary to make the event interesting to an audience? Do the filmmaker and editor betray the event and the participants when they impose dramatic time on the footage?

The editing of documentary footage often leads to a distortion of the event. The filmmaker's editorial purpose often supersedes the raw material. From Leni Riefenstahl in *Triumph of the Will* (1935) to Michael Moore in *Roger and Me* (1989), filmmakers have edited documentaries to present their particular vision. For them, the ethical issue is superseded by the need to present a particular point of view.

The documentary is sometimes referred to as a sponsored film. Whether it is a public affairs documentary or a documentary underwritten by a local church, the sponsor has a particular goal. That goal may be journalistic, humanistic, or mercenary, but it always has on impact on the film that the director and the editor make.

Unlike the dramatic film, the goals of the documentary are not entertainment and (ultimately) economic success. Nevertheless, those goals must be met, or the sponsor may claim the footage from the director, just as Sinclair Lewis took Eisenstein's Mexican footage. This is one of the reasons that some filmmakers finance their own documentaries. Financial independence may mean low-budget filmmaking, but it also gives rise to a personal filmmaking style that only independence can provide. Most documentary films are sponsored, however, and the sponsor usually has an impact on the type of film that is created.

One of the most interesting dimensions of the documentary is the aesthetic freedom that is available even within the ethical and political bounds. Filmmakers are basically free to experiment with any mixture of sound and visuals that captures an insight they find useful. Their choices may be incidental to the overall shape of the film. When Leni Riefenstahl decided that the beauty of the human form was more important than the Olympic competition and its outcome in *Olympia* (1938), she made an aesthetic decision that influenced both the shape of the overall film and the content of the individual sequences.

When Humphrey Jennings decided to use music as the predominant sound in his wartime propaganda film *Listen to Britain* (1942), he opted to omit the interviews and footage of political leaders and instead selected a freer presentation of the images and the message of the film. This aesthetic choice influenced everything else in the film.

The range of aesthetic choices in the documentary is far wider than is available in the dramatic film. Consequently, in the documentary, the editor can stretch her editing experience. It is in this type of film that creative editing is most encouraged and learned.

ANALYSIS OF DOCUMENTARY SEQUENCES—*MEMORANDUM*

This chapter uses a single film, *Memorandum* (1966), to examine the documentary. *Memorandum* was produced at the National Film Board of Canada. Donald Brittain and John Spotton directed it, and Spotton also photographed and edited the film. The documentary examines the Holocaust from a retrospective point of view. The film centers around the visit of a concentration camp survivor, Bernard Lauffer, to Bergen-Belsen, the camp from which he had been liberated 20 years earlier. In April 1965, Lauffer traveled to Germany with his son and other survivors.

The filmmakers built on his visit to present modern Germany at a time when Israel was opening its embassy for the first time and war criminals from Auschwitz were on trial. Interviews with Germans who served in the war intermingle with newsreel footage of Hitler and the concentration camps. Old and new footage are unified by the narrator. Always, the question is asked: How could the Holocaust happen in a land as cultured as Germany? The role of the doctors and the churches is also explored.

In a film of less than an hour, the filmmakers presented an examination of the Holocaust. They used the film to remind the audience that once such an event enters the public consciousness, it becomes part of that consciousness. The film warns that those who were responsible for the Holocaust were ordinary men who loved their wives and children, men who killed by memorandum rather than pull the trigger themselves.

The commemoration of the twentieth anniversary of the liberation of Bergen-Belsen ties the film together. *Memorandum* does not pretend to be a cinéma vérité treatment of the life of a concentration camp survivor. That would be another film.

Simple Continuity and the Influence of the Narrator

In the prologue to *Memorandum*, we watch a waitress washing beer mugs and preparing service for the beer garden. We see close-ups of what she is doing, and then a series of shots follows her as she goes about her duties. This simple continuity presents a young woman performing one aspect of her job. The size of the beer mugs and her uniform tell us that the setting is Germany (Figure 24.1).

On the sound track, the narrator introduces the place and time: Munich, summer of 1965. The young woman is Fräulein Bellich. The narrator says, "She was born in 1941, the year Hitler decided she should never see a Jew. But that's finished now."

Without the narration, the footage of Bellich might have opened a film about Munich, beer gardens, or German youth. However, when the narrator Donald Brittain mentions Hitler, he adds direction to the visuals. When Brittain says of the Holocaust, "But that's finished now," he adds irony to the narration because the film is dedicated to the proposition that it isn't finished. As this sequence shows, even simple visual continuity can be directed and shaped by sound.

A sequence that follows the prologue illustrates how simple continuity can be supported by the narration. The sequence, which features a Jewish funeral in Hanover, begins with a shot

FIGURE 24.1
Memorandum, 1966. Courtesy National Film Board of Canada.

of the Hebrew markings on gravestones in the Jewish cemetery. This provides visual continuity with the prior scene, which ended on the Hebrew lettering of the Israeli embassy sign in Cologne. All of the participants of the funeral seem to be elderly.

The shots detail the funeral procession, which is led by a rabbi. We see the German police on guard, and we see the mourners, primarily the widow. The sequence ends with the widow grieving, dropping a shovelful of dirt on the lowered casket.

The visuals are primarily close-ups except for the long shot of the procession as it nears the grave site. The close-ups give the sequence an intensity that underscores the feelings of the participants of the funeral.

The narrator introduces the funeral and speaks about the right to hold a Jewish funeral in modern Germany, a right that was denied to all who died in the concentration camps. He also talks about the number of people who died. The German Jewish community of 500,000 before the war became a community of 30,000 in 1965, and most of the survivors are elderly. With a tone of irony, the narrator implies that it is a special privilege for a Jew to be buried in Germany.

These two sequences illustrate how the narration can support the visual or direct it to another meaning. They also illustrate the importance of sound in the documentary.

The Transitional Sequence
To move from the present into the past, Spotton and Brittain adopted a gradual approach that embraces new footage and slowly moves into archival footage. The narration plays a key

role in identifying the time period, but in this sequence, the visuals play a stronger role. One sequence begins with close-ups of the telephone operators of a German hotel. The camera passes through the doors of a fancy hotel where elegance and propriety are clearly elements of modern German life. The narrator introduces Lauffer, who is dining with his colleagues in the hotel. The narrator describes how Lauffer was unwelcome in Germany 24 years earlier and how his treatment and the treatment of other Jews "has drained the German landscape of its humanity." This sound cue leads to a German announcement from the war that Communists, partisans, and Jews are to be arrested and confined in concentration camps.

We see a radio, a military cap, and symbols of the authority that the Germans exercised over the Jews. The film then cuts to visuals of artifacts and monuments to the victims of the Holocaust: a towering statue in Austria, a torture instrument in Warsaw. The narrator tells us that torture was too dignified a fate for the Jews and that there were other places than torture chambers for the Jews.

The next scene is of the museum at Dachau, where visitors walk past enlarged pictures of the inmates. Visuals of medical experiments are explained by the narrator. Shots of the museum visitors are interspersed with images of "medical experiments." Images of an experiment in which the human subject dies conclude this scene. The narrator's explanation underscores the inhumanity of the closely shot images (Figure 24.2).

From the still image of death, Brittain and Spotton cut to the moving image of Hitler opening the Dachau camp in 1933. The footage was shot on a large scale and seems rather operatic. The narrator takes us from the opening of the camp to a newsreel celebrating Hitler's accomplishments, particularly the opening of the Autobahn in 1936 (Figure 24.3).

This scene is followed by archival shots of the large-scale destruction of Jewish property in 1938: Krystallnacht. This event is downplayed by Joseph Goebbels in archival footage. The visuals are calm and rather benign, but the narration is ominous. Brittain describes Hitler's comment that war will bring the annihilation of Europe's Jews and discusses how this remark was interpreted as a figure of speech. The final shot is of a crowd cheering Hitler. The next sequence begins with a shot of a modern crowd.

The narrator takes the lead in this sequence to move us between periods: from Lauffer to the artifacts of the camps, from the artifacts to the modern tour of Dachau, from Dachau to the newsreel footage of Germany in the 1930s. Within each scene is a visual variety that punctuates a world of contrasts. The first contrast is of modern, affluent Jews and older, apprehensive concentration camp survivors; the second is of the symbols of torture in the past and of the victims. The third contrast is of the museum, where healthy visitors look at photographs of the most grotesque medical experiments ever undertaken on humans, and the final contrast is the footage of Hitler and Germany in the 1930s and the progress of modern Germany. The narration provides the contrast between what we see and what we know will happen.

Throughout this sequence, the issue of conflict and contrast in each scene carries us toward the fuller introduction of the past. This sequence visually introduces the history of the Holocaust, and it marks the beginning of the shift toward a greater emphasis on the past

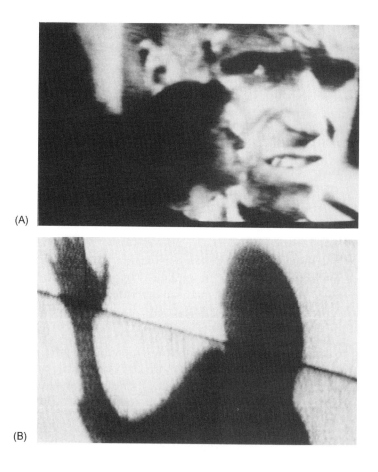

(A)

(B)

FIGURE 24.2
Memorandum, 1966. Courtesy National Film Board of Canada.

than on the present. The narrator is important in this sequence, but not as important as the visuals in preparing the transition to the past.

The Archival Sequence

When archival footage is used, the narrator becomes critical. In the sequence where the narrator begins to tell us Lauffer's story, the film focuses on Lauffer's hands and the documents he holds. The narrator tells about the Germans' offer to sell Lauffer's brother's ashes to the family for 24 marks. The Warsaw ghetto was the first of 11 places where Lauffer was confined during the war. The film cuts to archival footage of a close-up of a Jew holding his documents. The cut from an image of documents in 1965 to a similar image of documents in 1942 provides a visual continuity for the transition into the past.

The narrator and Lauffer both speak of life in the ghetto. We see a Jewish committee meeting with German officials as Lauffer describes that the committee was composed of good people.

FIGURE 24.3

Memorandum, 1966. Courtesy National Film Board of Canada.

The narrator suggests that centuries of oppression have trained the Jews to wait for a bad situation to improve.

The narrator editorializes about the deterioration of life in the ghetto and how it was the children who suffered the most. The images support the narration. When Brittain speaks of dehumanization in the ghetto, the footage illustrates that dehumanization.

Archival footage shows Hitler at Berchtesgaden greeting a young child. Over this footage, the narrator tells us that Hitler decided in 1941 that all of the Jews of Europe were to be systematically exterminated. He details Lauffer's losses: his four brothers, four sisters, and parents were killed. In this sequence, the juxtaposition of the visuals and their tranquility contrast with the narration. The sequence ends with visuals of children playing. The narrator tells us that they were photographed for propaganda purposes and then led into the gas chambers. The narration thus goes beyond the visuals to rectify misinformation that the visuals present (Figure 24.4).

The archival sequence is presented carefully. It begins with a direct correlation between visuals and narration and gradually begins to use the images as a counterpoint to the narration. The film returns to an almost direct correlation between narration and visuals as the sequence ends. The sound track is thus the critical shaping device in this archival sequence.

A SEQUENCE WITH LITTLE NARRATION

One sequence in Memorandum documents a visit to Auschwitz. Lauffer had grown up 9 miles from Auschwitz, he had helped build it, and his parents had died there. This narration

FIGURE 24.4
Memorandum, 1966. Courtesy National Film Board of Canada.

serves as the transition into the visual sequence at Auschwitz. The narrator's few comments primarily prepare the audience for the sequences to come; he mentions two of the featured topics: Papa Kadusz's chapel and Wilhelm Bolge's cruelty to inmates. Both men went on trial in Hamburg. The trial itself is featured in a later sequence. The narrator also explains about the location where Rudolf Hess was hanged by the Poles; he speaks about Hess as a family man. This commentary takes us into the next sequence, which is archival and concentrates on Heinrich Himmler's paternal attitude toward the S.S. men who carried out the killings of Jews. The narration leads to an articulation of the methodology of death. The principal goal of the narration in the Auschwitz sequence is to provide a transition or foreshadowing for later sequences (Figures 24.5 and 24.6).

The visuals in the Auschwitz sequence, which is organized as a tour of the camp, are presented very differently than in every other sequence. The sequence follows visitors and their Polish guides through the different areas of the camp to see the locations where Jews entered the camp and where they were killed. Because they were filmed primarily as long shots, the human images seem distant and dispassionate. There is little camera mobility compared to earlier sections, and as a result, the sequence proceeds visually at an unhurried pace.

When children's artifacts are shown, the shot is a slow, handheld shot that lingers. The camera moves to animate the statue of a child, but for the most part, movement follows action. Natural sound allows us to listen to the guides explain about the concentration camp. It is only when the narrator speaks of the torture that Bolge inflicted on the Jews in the camp that we see the first close-ups of the visitors. Two or three shots of the faces of the visitors are the

FIGURE 24.5
Memorandum, 1966. Courtesy National Film Board of Canada.

FIGURE 24.6
Memorandum, 1966. Courtesy National Film Board of Canada.

closest that Brittain and Spotton come to using any visual intensity in the sequence. These shots stand out in contrast to the predominance of long shots in the sequence.

The Auschwitz sequence was designed to be as similar to cinéma vérité as possible. It is one of the most journalistic-like sequences in the film.

The Reportage Sequence

Toward the end of *Memorandum*, the sequence about Lauffer's visit to Bergen-Belsen is presented as straight reporting (Figures 24.7 to 24.12). The narrator relinquishes his editorial role and simply introduces people and places. Although he fills in the details of Lauffer's survival in Bergen-Belsen before liberation, the narrator's role is principally to support the visuals and synchronous sound of the participants as they speak or are interviewed. The sequence begins with a cocktail party held the night before the visit.

The organizers and participants greet one another, and we are introduced to Brigadier Glynn Hughes, who led the British forces that liberated Bergen-Belsen in April 1945. We are also introduced to two former inmates who survived. The next scene is of the town of Belsen in 1965. The visuals show its citizens pouring out of a church after Sunday Mass. The majority appear to be older people. The narrator talks of their not knowing of the camp during the Holocaust, although there was too much evidence toward the end of the war to deny. Brittain also editorializes about the appeal of Nazism in this rural region.

On the bus ride to Belsen, Lauffer speaks of his views about Germany, how it appears, and how he feels. The rain continues as the group leaves the buses.

FIGURE 24.7
Memorandum, 1966. Courtesy National Film Board of Canada.

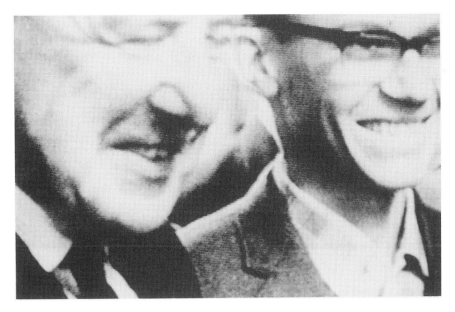

FIGURE 24.8
Memorandum, 1966. Courtesy National Film Board of Canada.

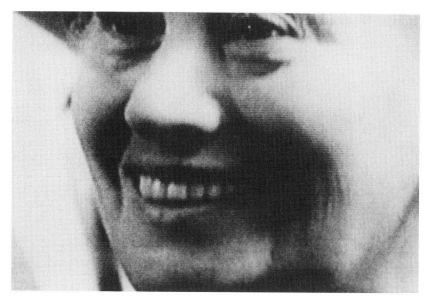

FIGURE 24.9
Memorandum, 1966. Courtesy National Film Board of Canada.

FIGURE 24.10
Memorandum, 1966. Courtesy National Film Board of Canada.

FIGURE 24.11
Memorandum, 1966. Courtesy National Film Board of Canada.

FIGURE 24.12
Memorandum, 1966. Courtesy National Film Board of Canada.

On the site, Brigadier Hughes is interviewed about the day of liberation. He is jovial and jokes about still having Commandant Kramer's desk. The interviewer asks him whether this makes him feel strange. Hughes replies, "Not at all. It's a very good, heavy desk." Lauffer and Silvernick watch with pained expressions.

In the next scene, Lauffer and his son visit the grave of an uncle who died three days after liberation. A young Christian penance group is introduced. The members are helping to build an information center at Belsen. They are disillusioned with the values of their parents. They are young, yet they seem to be tentative about being photographed at the Bergen-Belsen camp.

The site visit officially begins. The survivors walk past mounds of buried dead. In one of these mounds, Anne Frank is buried, the narrator tells us.

Handheld shots follow Lauffer and his son. The survivors take on a somber tone as they approach the monument to the dead. The group approaches the site, lays down a wreath, and says a prayer for the dead. The camera films the scene as a long shot, and a series of close-up shots includes Hughes and Rosenzafft. A moving shot catches the survivors consoling one another.

The synchronized sound scene gives way to another. A frustrated Lauffer speaks of the mounds of buried dead as the group walks back to the bus. He can't find the proper words, but his son helps him. "Here lie five hundred," he says. "Next year, it will be four hundred. They want to minimize what happened here." Lauffer suggests that the Germans should not have beautified the site; they should have left it as they found it in 1945. The film cuts to the hotel in Hanover, and the sequence is over.

Perhaps more than any other part of the film, this sequence featuring the commemorative visit to Bergen-Belsen proceeds as straight reporting of the events. The archival footage of the camp at the time of liberation and the shots of the town in 1965 flesh out the sequence, providing context for the visit. In a sense, the entire film leads up to this sequence. In it, Brittain and Spotton let the footage speak for itself. There is a minimum of editorializing in the narration and minimal use of the kind of juxtaposition of sound and picture used extensively earlier in the film.

This sequence, however, does conform thematically with the other sequences described in this chapter. They all examine the Holocaust from two perspectives—past and present—and they all remind the viewers of the character of the Holocaust as well as of the deep feeling of its survivors, like Bernard Lauffer, and their commitment to not forget.

NOTES/REFERENCES

1. K. Reisz, G. Millar, The Technique of Film Editing, Focal Press, Boston, 1968, p. 124.

2. Reisz's suggestion in *The Technique of Film Editing* has not been challenged by time. The documentary remains an editor's medium.

3. Helen Van Dongen, Flaherty's editor on *Louisiana Story* (1948), is credited with having made key contributions to the effectiveness of that film.

Imaginative Documentary

As discussed in Chapters 7, realism is the basis of the documentary. When a documentary is edited, the footage of an event is made to conform to an interpretation of the event that, within the parameters of sponsorship, is truthful. The greatest expression of this characteristic of the documentary is found in cinéma vérité works.

What if the filmmaker's goal is to reveal an insight or an interpretation that wouldn't be available from a straightforward editing of the footage? What if the filmmaker wishes to deconstruct a wrestling match so it can be viewed as a struggle of good against evil? This isn't quite the interpretation we would derive from straight documentary footage of a wrestling match, but with the addition of a sound track and with a ritualized pattern of editing, this is precisely the interpretation we derive from *Wrestling* (1960).

ALTERING MEANING AWAY FROM THE LITERAL

The imaginative documentary uses the tools of editing to fashion a unique interpretation from documentary footage. That this can be done is a tribute to the power of editing and to the imagination of such filmmakers as Robert Flaherty, Humphrey Jennings, and Lindsay Anderson.

The editor has many options for creating a new interpretation of reality. The editing style of Leni Riefenstahl in *Olympia* (1938) is an excellent example. Sound offers many options, as does the juxtaposition of sequences and the use of different types of shots. Close-up can be used effectively, and pace can be used to create a fresh interpretation.

Sound effects and music play a role in the success of Basil Wright's *Night Mail* (1936). A poem that is written and read to simulate the motion of the wheels of a train creates a mythology in that film about the delivery of mail. The playful sounds of the amusement park are modulated to underscore the fun and to emphasize mystery and danger in Lindsay Anderson's *O'Dreamland* (1953). Narration and sound are used ironically to alter the meaning of Basil Wright's *Song of Ceylon* (1934), and sound is used to undermine what is being shown in *I Was a 90-Pound Weakling* (1964). In all of these examples, sound shifts the images to another level of meaning.

341

The Technique of Film and Video Editing: History, Theory, and Practice. DOI: 10.1016/B978-0-240-81397-4.00025-X

The editor can also choose to crosscut sequences or shots to elicit another meaning from the visuals. In *Diary for Timothy* (1945), Humphrey Jennings crosscut between a theatrical performance of Hamlet and a dispassionate canteen discussion about the mechanics of a V1 rocket as it is launched. On one level, this sequence connects culture and everyday life, but on another level, it allows the content of each sequence to comment on the other. The gravedigger scene in *Hamlet* is black humor about loss; the canteen conversation about the destructive power of an enemy rocket connects to that scene with its anticipation of death. The explosion of the rocket during the sequence accentuates the imminence of death. By crosscutting the two scenes, Jennings linked past and future in a present that, although it might be momentary, embraces both high culture and the everyday pleasure of a canteen conversation.

Robert Flaherty's *Louisiana Story* (1948) is instructive about the power of juxtaposing individual shots. As he did in *Man of Aran* (1934), Flaherty juxtaposed a tranquil image of great beauty with an image of great danger. In *Louisiana Story*'s opening series of shots, an image of a beautiful leaf is followed by an image of an alligator slinking through the dark water. A bright shot is followed by a dark shot, and in this brief juxtaposition, which Flaherty resorted to more than once, he revealed the natural order of the bayou. Wonder and danger coexist, and neither is preeminent over the other. Because Flaherty and editor Helen Van Dongen don't pace the footage to editorialize, there is an egalitarian sense about this natural order. Tension is evident, but it is not an inordinate tension. This sense of the egalitarian is at the heart of Flaherty's work, and in his juxtaposition of shots, we see how it is suggested in microcosm.

The close-up can also help shift the meaning of documentary footage away from the most truthful interpretation. This is accomplished by using the close-up as a cutaway—a new idea—introduced into a sequence of shots with a general continuity. Flaherty's famous opening sequence of *Louisiana Story* proceeds in a gentle but mysterious way to introduce us to the bayou and its natural inhabitants: the flowers, the insects, the alligators, and the snakes. Into this milieu, Flaherty positioned the main character of the film, a Cajun boy named Alexander Napoleon Ulysses Latour. The boy's presence in the scene increases until he is as natural a part of the bayou as are the flora and fauna. Flaherty and Van Dongen then introduced two images of bubbles coming to the surface of the water. The first time, the narrator refers to the bubbles as "mermaid bubbles," but the second time, there is the sense that the bubbles signal a new presence. We don't know yet that the film is about the construction of an oil rig in the bayou and about how the discovery of oil affects Alexander and the creatures and plants of the bayou. Nor do we necessarily know that the film was sponsored by a large oil company involved in oil exploration. At this early stage of the film, the close-ups of the rising bubbles suggest that another, as yet unidentified, element will join the boy and the other inhabitants of the bayou.

Finally, pace can alter the meaning of documentary footage. The director and editor have the option of slowing down or accelerating the pace of the footage. These options will affect meaning in different ways. The slow motion shot is an alternative to slowing down the edited pace of the footage. The impact of picking up the pace is perhaps most readily understood.

Consider, for example, the stop-motion sequence in Godfrey Reggia's *Koyaanisqatsi* (1983), with its accelerated speed of urban traffic, or the quick pace of the cutting in Arthur Lipsett's *Very Nice, Very Nice* (1961). Both film sequences give the impression of an urban metropolis rushing to its demise. Pace of this speed changes a film from a document of life in New York, for example, to a comment on the quality of life in New York. So great is the strength of the pacing in these films that we must draw the conclusion that speed is destructive to humans and to the human spirit.

THE WARTIME DOCUMENTARY: IMAGINATION AND PROPAGANDA

The remainder of this chapter provides a more detailed examination of Humphrey Jennings's *Listen to Britain* (1942). It explores how Jennings edited his film to be more than a record of everyday life in war-torn Britain (Figure 25.1).

Listen to Britain was one of many documentaries made during World War II. The most prominent documentary filmmakers in the United States were Frank Capra, John Huston, and William Wyler. These filmmakers came from Hollywood and used the techniques Hollywood knew so well. They applied what had primarily been narrative or dramatic techniques to the documentary to create propaganda films that supported the Allied cause. The *Why We Fight* series, with its reliance on newsreel footage, best exemplifies that wartime effort. The series borrowed heavily from Nazi propaganda films and consequently relied on an editing style of juxtaposition and pace. Narration for content and style was also very important.

FIGURE 25.1
Listen to Britain, 1942. Courtesy Museum of Modern Art/Film Stills Archive.

The German propaganda film, particularly the work of Leni Riefenstahl, was highly visual and dynamically cut. German films focused on the creation of a cult of leadership around Hitler and on the supernatural power with which he was supposedly endowed. Both the German and the American propaganda films were highly effective and given to metaphor.

THE CASE OF *LISTEN TO BRITAIN*

The British war documentary ranged from direct, narration-driven films such as *Desert Victory* (1943) to the nonnarrative treatment of *Listen to Britain*. Jennings's treatment of a Britain under assault from the air and under threat of invasion was unhurried and indirect. As Alan Lovell and Jim Hillier write,

> It is a most unwarlike film. Its basic motivation is a balance between menace (to a culture rather than to material things) on the one hand and harmony and continuity from the past on the other. Images of menace are constantly juxtaposed with the images of the population's reactions. Almost all images gain complete meaning only when seen in context. Thus the fighter planes fly over harvesters and gunners in the fields, working side by side; the sandbags, empty frames and fire buckets at the National Gallery are intercut both with steady tracking shots of the calm faces of the audience or shots of people eating sandwiches or looking at paintings and accompanied by Mozart.[1]

Jennings was unique in his approach to the documentary. His colleagues at the Crown Film Unit, although they admired him, did not understand how he could achieve so great an impact in his films. As Pat Jackson, a colleague of Jennings, suggests, a good part of his success was achieved in the editing room: "Humphrey would interpret a situation in disconnected visuals, and he wouldn't quite know why he was shooting them, probably until he got them together. Then he created a pattern out of them. It was as though he were going out to collect all sorts of pieces, cut already, for a jigsaw puzzle, and wasn't quite certain about the picture that jigsaw puzzle was going to be until he had it in the cutting room, and here he was enormously helped by [Stewart] McCallister."[2] This view is echoed by the producer of *Listen to Britain*, Ian Dalrimple,[3] and the impact of the film abroad is discussed by filmmaker Edgar Anstey.[4]

The key to the success of *Listen to Britain* is its imaginative use of sound and image. As Paul Swann suggests, "[Jennings's] subtle cross structuring of sound and visual images instilled a uniquely poetic element in his films."[5]

Listen to Britain, a film of 21 minutes in length, does not focus on any particular character or event. It depicts wartime Britain with a focus on London, pastoral farmland, the industrial heartland, and the vulnerable coast. Jennings included shots of civilians at work and soldiers enjoying themselves in individual recreation and marching in organized columns as they pass through a small town. Many of the people included are women, principally because the men were away at war. The film focuses on culture, both popular culture—a dance in

Blackpool, luncheon entertainment by Flanagan and Allen—and high culture—Myra Hess performing Mozart at the National Gallery. Jennings also included sequences of individuals and groups passing the time by singing.

Throughout the film, work and leisure activities are presented in an unhurried fashion. Whether people are working on an assembly line manufacturing Lancasters or sitting in the audience listening to a lunchtime concert, there is no anxiety—only a concentrated involvement in the tasks of war and everyday life. The film gives the impression of a calm, strong, determined population, a population in which the queen can sit at a lunchtime concert as one of her people rather than the cult of leadership central to the German propaganda film or, for that matter, the cult of ideology so central to the dramatic fabric of the American propaganda film. Jennings managed to transcend politics and economics to present a purely aesthetic, cultural response to the problem of war, and it's a very powerful response.

Central to the structure of *Listen to Britain* is a dialectic set of sequences. Each sequence interacts with the next through sound and juxtaposition. Pace is never relied on too heavily.

The film can be broken down into the following sequences:

1. Farming goes on in spite of the war.
2. Soldiers relax at the Blackpool dance hall.
3. The work for war goes on at night.
4. Canadian soldiers wait for an assignment.
5. The manufacture of the Lancaster bomber is ongoing.
6. Ambulance workers wait.
7. The British Broadcasting Corporation (BBC) speaks to and for Britain in the world.
8. The work of war proceeds from dawn forward.
9. Families are left behind while loved ones go to war.
10. War workers are mostly women.
11. Popular performers entertain workers at the lunch halls.
12. Guest artists perform in museums at lunch.
13. War and great culture have intermingled in the past.
14. The British people serve in the factories and in the armed forces.
15. "Rule Britannia": the determination of a nation.

Every sequence reminds us that Britain is at war. In the first sequence, the rustle of the trees and of the wheat fields is complemented by the roar of a Spitfire flying overhead. Toward the end of that sequence, a shot of spotters at their posts on the coast facing the English Channel is a reminder of Britain's vigilance against potential invaders.

Either a sound effect or a visual acts as the reminder of war: soldiers in uniform at Blackpool, the morning march of civilians carrying helmets along with their lunchbags, the sandbags piled high against a tall window in the National Gallery. In one sequence, children play in the schoolyard of a sleepy town as if there were no war, but the shot of a woman looking at a photo of her uniformed husband and the sound of a motorized column moving through the town are reminders about how close the war is.

Between each of the first three sequences, Jennings referred to the spotters and those on guard watching the skies and the sea for the enemy. These shots support the idea that although the sequences may be about recreation or rural beauty, the real theme of the film is war. The waiting and watching and civilian preparation are part of the process of being at war. So is the ambulance service and the war manufacturing.

Gradually, Jennings shifted the focus from waiting for war to preparing for war. Beginning with the sequence that shows the manufacture of the Lancaster bomber, Jennings began to concentrate on the war effort. Sequences 5, 8, 10, and 14 are about the effort at home to prepare for war. Although less obvious, sequences 6, 9, 11, and 12 are also about people involved in the war effort. However, these sequences do not show them at work, but rather at lunch or listening to a noontime concert. Jennings seems to have been saying that the British know how to prepare for war, and they are confident enough to enjoy a respite from the lathe, the iron furnace, and the assembly line. The British value culture and companionship.

Sequences 7 and 13, the sequences about the BBC and about the past—Horatio Nelson and Trafalgar, the architecture of the Empire—all suggest the power and influence that is Britain. These two sequences rely heavily on sound. In sequence 7, a series of sound dissolves suggest not only that the BBC is important within England, but also that it reaches in every direction; the last sound reference, "This is the Pacific Services," represents the BBC's influence on the land, air, and merchant navy forces in that region. In sequence 13, the soaring orchestral treatment of Mozart's Concerto Piano Forte in C Major accompanies images of Trafalgar Square; the monument to Nelson seems almost to come alive as the dynamic cutting suggests a historical continuity that is irresistible in its power. In sequences 7 and 13, the abstract idea of Great Britain is a long-standing, far-reaching, and impregnable nation. Although nothing is said verbally, the juxtaposition of these sequences acts as an apex for the ideas arising out of the film as a whole. There is something emotional about Jennings's reliance on music in sequence 13. This sequence prepares us for the anthem-like quality of the last sequence, in which the manufacturing for war is presented to the sounds of "Rule Britannia."

A notable characteristic of *Listen to Britain* is the level of feeling Jennings achieved without the use of even a single close-up. Much of the film is presented in midshots and slow-moving shots.

Through the juxtaposition of sequences and a gradual build-up caused by the pattern of filming and editing, Jennings created a sense of Britain's invincibility. To appreciate how indirect his editing is, we must look at a single sequence. Many sequences are unified by a single piece of music, for example, the Blackpool sequence, the two lunchtime concerts, the sequence in which the Canadian soldiers are waiting. Other sequences are less obviously unified, such as the sequence featuring the manufacture of the Lancaster bomber.

The transitional image of spotters watching for German planes dissolves to the sight and sound of a train pulling out of a station. The trains move without lights. The film cuts to the manufacture of an airplane and then to a Lancaster taking off. The film pans to an ambulance station, and we are into the next sequence.

This sequence is flanked by images of civilians preparing for war. In between, the images are of the production for war. The sound throughout highlights the natural sounds of the production process and of an airplane in flight. The sounds of the preceding and following sequences are overlapped to create a smooth flow into and out of the sequence. Although the sequence has no visuals in common with the preceding and following sequences, the sound overlaps provide continuity.

As is so often the case in the documentary, the continuity of ideas flows from the sound track. Jennings may juxtapose visual sequences to one another, but the ideas are more directly ordered by sound continuity. His approach is less direct, but nevertheless not confused, because the overall pattern of the juxtapositions has a sound continuity.

CONCLUSION

A direct plea for help for Britain might have seemed logical for a film like *Listen to Britain*, but Jennings succeeded with a different approach. He wanted to communicate the qualities of Britain that made it worth helping: the dignity and culture of the great nation. By using an imaginative approach to this goal, Jennings fashioned a film that even today exemplifies the possibilities for sound and image. Jennings undertook in 1942 with *Listen to Britain* what Francis Ford Coppola would undertake in 1979 with *Apocalypse Now*: the creation of an entire world (or at least the image of that world). In Jennings's case, it was a world worth saving; in Coppola's, it was not.

NOTES/REFERENCES

1. A. Lovell, J. Hillier, Studies in Documentary, Martin Secker and Warburg, London, 1972, p. 86.
2. Quoted in E. Sussex, The Rise and Fall of British Documentary, University of California Press, Los Angeles, 1975, p. 144.
3. Ibid.
4. Anstey felt the film was too oblique, but it was far more successful abroad than Jennings's more direct film *Fires Were Started*; see Sussex, The Rise and Fall of British Documentary, 1943, p. 146.
5. P. Swann, The British Documentary Film Movement, 1926–1946. Cambridge University Press, Cambridge, 1989, pp. 162–163.

CHAPTER 26

Innovations in Documentary I

Too often in the past two decades, the announcement has been made, "The documentary is dead." But stubbornly, it has held on. The reason, principally, is the documentary's flexibility. Associated so long with educational and political goals, the documentary has more recently aggressively embraced the entertainment impulse that has swept through broadcast news and reality programming. Less obvious but no less important is the documentary's hold on past generations. Its affiliation with political, social, and educational goals has given the documentary a gravitas or weight that is deeply meaningful. The form consequently has not lost its audience as so many other story forms have. Whatever the reason, the announcement that the documentary is dead has been an empty one. The documentary is alive and evolving. In this chapter, we will address a number of its innovations: the changes in the personal documentary, the expansion in the use of narration in a fashion differing from earlier uses, and the interface between documentary and drama. First, we turn to the shifts in the personal documentary.

THE PERSONAL DOCUMENTARY

The personal documentary is different from the social/political documentary or the cinéma vérité documentary. The cinéma vérité documentary, which is rooted in the philosophy of filmmaking of Dziga Vertov, suggested that the great strength of the documentary and of film was its capacity to capture real-life events as they happen. For Vertov, this represented the highest aesthetic of the medium. The result is films such as *The Man with a Movie Camera* (1929), which was the inspiration for a school of documentary, principally the cinéma vérité school. The Free Cinema movement in England in the 1950s, the Direct Cinema in France in the late 1950s and early 1960s, and the Candid Eye series in Canada in the 1950s all essentially owed a debt to Vertov. In the United States, the work of Richard Leacock and D. A. Pennebaker in the 1960s gave way to the work of Barbara Kopple in the 1970s and to the self-reflexive filmmaking of Ross McElwee (*Sherman's March*, 1986) in the 1980s and of Rob Moss (*The Tourist*, 1992) in the 1990s. All are fundamentally cinéma vérité filmmakers. Finally, the Dogme films of Lars von Trier, Thomas Vinterberg, and Kristian Levring owe much in terms of their style to the work of Vertov. They are, however, dramatic films rather than documentaries. Cinéma vérité represents one of the three "paths" of the documentary.

349

The Technique of Film and Video Editing: History, Theory, and Practice. DOI: 10.1016/B978-0-240-81397-4.00026-1

The second ideology of the documentary is based on the ideas of John Grierson, the British filmmaker and executive producer who first established government film units in Great Britain and later in Canada. Grierson believed the documentary should have an educational purpose. If we broaden the term *education* to include social and political education, we see how this ideology also embraces the propaganda film (a particular type of education, or one we don't necessarily believe in, we call *propaganda*). Whether one looks at the British-sponsored documentaries of the 1930s, or the work of Leni Riefenstahl, or of Frank Capra, or the later work of Grierson at the National Film Board of Canada, we see a continuation of this philosophy of documentary. Sponsored films, educational films, and corporate films all fall under this category. Perhaps a more precise term for this ideology of documentary would be *purposeful documentary*.

The third ideology or "path" of documentary is that of the personal documentary, which we associate with the work of Robert Flaherty (*Nanook of the North*, 1922). Although he filmed on location in the Arctic, Flaherty shaped *Nanook* to fit his vision of the struggle of man against nature. This noble, romantic, epic struggle is repeated in Flaherty's films about life in the South Sea Islands, the Aran Islands, and the bayous of Louisiana. Flaherty chose real subjects, but cast, filmed, and staged his work to suit his sensibility, as opposed to recording what he found in those far-flung settings. This is the nature of the personal documentary: Its tone is personal, based on the views of the filmmaker rather than on the anthropological actuality in the field. This particular approach is clearly at the heart of Luis Buñuel's *Las Hurdes* (*Land without Bread*, 1933), the work of Humphrey Jennings (*Diary for Timothy*, 1945), and the docudrama work of Peter Watkins (*Culloden*, 1964) in the 1960s. Buñuel and Jennings use their subjects to convey their ideas about society and its obligation to its people, and Watkins uses his subjects to convey his ideas about Scottish nationalism and British imperialism, just as Flaherty used his Louisiana story to convey his own ideas about childhood and its innocence. We now turn to the recent work in the area of the personal documentary.

A good starting point is to define particular characteristics that don't so much delimit personal documentary as together distinguish this particular branch of the documentary. First, is the striking visual character of the personal documentary. Most documentaries are content-driven, although the visual dimension has been critical in the propaganda documentary work of Riefenstahl and Jennings. In the personal documentary, the visual aesthetic of the work is prominent. Flaherty had a poetic style suitable to his approach to his subject matter. Peter Watkins has a pseudorealistic style that supports the seriousness of intention in his work. In the case of Errol Morris, whose work we will turn to shortly, the style is distinctly oblique. In each case, the visual aesthetic is so powerful that it draws great attention to itself beyond the organization of the content.

A second characteristic of the personal documentary is the mixed use of staged or performed footage with actuality footage. This finds its extreme form in Flaherty's work and in the more recent work of Peter Watkins. All of Watkins's *Edvard Munch* (1974) is staged, but it is filmed as if it were captured or cinéma vérité actuality footage. More often the film is a mix, as in

Errol Morris's *The Thin Blue Line* (1988). How the two styles of footage blend is often masked, although Morris's staged material is so stylized (e.g., the murder scene) that it is clearly not documentary footage. The models for other extreme footage that blends easily with documentary footage are John Cassavetes's *Shadows* (1959) and Gillo Pontecorvo's *The Battle of Algiers* (1965), both films that are entirely staged.

A third characteristic of the personal documentary is the use of irony. The source for this impulse is Luis Buñuel's *Land without Bread*. More recent examples include Errol Morris and Werner Herzog, whom we will turn to shortly. Herzog was very influenced by the documentary work of the West Coast filmmaker Les Blank, who documented Herzog's own filmmaking practice in *Werner Herzog Eats His Shoe* (1980).

The most vigorous characteristic of the personal documentary is the issue of voice. Voice can be established directly through the narration, or generated out of a distinctive visual style, or through the deployment of irony generated out of the counterpoint of the narration or music with the visual, or out of a combination of any or all of the above. Clearly the singularity of the personal documentary emanates from its distinctive voice. That voice may be grounded in the political, as in the docudramas of Peter Watkins, or it may allude to the political to highlight the personal, as in the work of Michael Rubbo (*Waiting for Fidel*, 1974), or it may be entirely personal, as in Herzog's *My Best Fiend* (1999). In each case, the voice is so pronounced that it overwhelms the more objective or general intentions of the documentary.

We turn now to the films and their filmmakers, beginning with Herzog's film *My Best Fiend*. Herzog is best known as the dramatic filmmaker of a series of films—*Aguirre: The Wrath of God* (1973), *Nosferatu: The Vampyre* (1979), *Fitzcarraldo* (1982), and *Woyzek* (1979)—all made with the actor Klaus Kinski. Although Herzog made other dramatic films and documentaries, he is best known for these films made with Kinski. *My Best Fiend* is a personal documentary about his relationship with Kinski. As Kinski died in 1991, the film is an amalgam of clips from the films he made with Herzog: broadcast footage of a Kinski performance, amateur footage, and excerpts from *Burden of Dreams* (1983), the documentary by Les Blank about the making of *Fitzcarraldo*. Contemporary footage consists of interviews with two of Kinski's costars, Eva Mattes from *Woyzek* and Claudia Cardinale from *Fitzcarraldo*. Herzog also retraces the places of some of his work with Kinski, including South America for *Aguirre: The Wrath of God* and *Fitzcarraldo*, and Austria for *Woyzek*. He even visits the home where the would-be actor Kinski, as a boy of 13, rented a room.

My Best Fiend is not so much a biography or a vanity portrait of an important actor as it is an examination of a difficult, almost impossible relationship between a director and an actor. Were they friends or enemies? Did they creatively unleash a talent in the other that was more than the sum of their individual abilities? Is the film the portrait of madness as genius, or all of the above?

At no point does Herzog question his own attraction to extreme subject matter—the dictatorial impulse of a Spanish soldier 8000 miles from home in *Aguirre: The Wrath of God*, or the mad act of dragging a boat over a mountain so that a town can have what the main character feels the town needs—opera—in *Fitzcarraldo*. What is clear is that Herzog himself is attracted to the madness in genius and to the genius in madness. Rarely does he approach the madness issue directly, but what lingers about Herzog's work is that there is a magical quality to those who struggle against nature, man, and their own nature to achieve their goals. What better actor could he choose to portray these complex but fascinating characters than the complex, fascinating Klaus Kinski?

This personal examination of the relationship between director and actor leads Herzog to conclude that he and Kinski were alter egos. They needed each other to make the magic they achieved in the five films they made together. As Herzog journeys back geographically to the places he made films with Kinski, we begin to understand that although Herzog is speaking about Kinski, he is in fact revealing himself. *My Best Fiend* begins to look more like a portrait of a director's creative state, one fueled by an emotional war with his primary actor, Klaus Kinski. That state, however achieved, is the basis for one of international cinema's great careers. The play on words in the title, "best" and "fiend," one word implying pleasure and the other torture, begins to take on a layered meaning: Is Herzog invoking contradiction and chaos or constructed creativity? Whichever is his goal, Herzog creates a paradox—the triumph of the personal demons of each man to create together great art.

Whether personal documentary is about self-revelation, self-exploration, or simply self-promotion, voice is central to its articulation. Few documentarians have as singular a voice as does Errol Morris. In many ways he uses his voice to explore eccentricity in the American character. In *Fast, Cheap and Out of Control* (1998), Morris celebrates eccentricity. In *Mr. Death* (2000), the exploration implies the tragic in eccentricity.

Mr. Death has as its subtitle *The Rise and Fall of Fred A. Leuchter, Jr.* In the first half of the narrative, Leuchter, the son of a prison worker, grows up in Massachusetts to become a leading expert in execution equipment. He explains his mission: to make execution humane, whether by electrocution or lethal injection. Leuchter alludes to a creative touch that will bring death quickly and efficiently. As a tour guide of the mishaps and messy nature of execution, Leuchter takes a me-against-them attitude. "They" are the wardens, state officials, and so-called professionals who have been cruel and unusual in their punishment of death-house convicts. His matter-of-fact description of heads blowing off and eyes popping out is intended to support his mission as a humane hero to the soon-to-be-dispatched and their families. As Leuchter describes his growing professional success, his personal success, and a marriage—all of which become the final act of his ascent—Morris intercuts black-and-white with color footage. By doing so, Morris is implying a layer of artifice, mixed in with realism. The irony is unavoidable. The execution room scenes are highly stylized through the use of backlight. Mock heroism is the tone in this section of the film.

The second phase of the narrative takes up the late 1980's request by Ernst Zundel, a Holocaust denier in Canada, for Fred Leuchter to act as his expert witness. The mission is to visit Auschwitz and Birkenau to explore whether gas executions actually took place there. The visit becomes the honeymoon for the newly married Leuchters. The location scene is filmed in handheld cinéma vérité style. TV footage of the infamous Zundel trial, a trial prompted by

Zundel's campaign against Holocaust denial, in Toronto is intercut with a more recent interview with Ernst Zundel.

To substantiate his investigation, Leuchter takes numerous rock samples at locations claimed to be gas chambers or adjacent to gas chambers. Back in Massachusetts, he tests these samples and finds no trace of Cyclon B, the gas used to kill the inmates at Auschwitz. Leuchter writes a report claiming that no gassing of inmates took place at Auschwitz or Birkenau. The Leuchter report is submitted to the trial in defense of Zundel's claim that the Holocaust never took place. Historian and Holocaust denier David Irving is interviewed to illustrate the receptivity for Leuchter's report among a certain constituency, neo-Nazis in Europe and Latin America. The Canadian Court, on the other hand, found Zundel guilty, impugning its own assessment of the Leuchter report. In short order, Leuchter moves from being a useful contributor to society to a pariah. First, his business suffers due to the bad publicity his expert testimony yields, and indeed, he becomes a laughingstock. His business fails, and then his marriage fails. He moves west in an effort to restore himself, but the occasional speaking engagement isn't enough, and by the end Leuchter is destroyed. He remains provocative and unapologetic about his report, and by the end of the film we leave him on a road somewhere in California, a lonely and alone figure of ridicule. Only in this last phase of the narrative does Morris return to stylization.

Morris's voice is focused on two devices—the mix of stylized or dramatized footage with cinéma vérité footage and the use of irony. Irony permeates the structure of the narrative. By elevating the creation of killing machines with a humane goal, Morris undermines the seriousness with which he constructs Leuchter, the hero, in the early half of the film. Morris carries on using irony as Leuchter chips away at the concrete bunkers at Auschwitz, earnest in his pursuit and tickled to be away from the United States for the first time. Although Leuchter is on his honeymoon, we never see him with his wife. He acts like a kid in a playground. But it's not a playground, it's Auschwitz—where 3 million people were killed. The irony is lost on Leuchter, who increasingly appears to be a naïf rather than an expert on anything. Zundel and Irving both appear to be canny, knowing, and unironic. Beside them, Leuchter looks more and more like the rube who's been had.

Death and the Holocaust: weighty matters, yet Morris has chosen Fred Leuchter as his prism. Leuchter is an eccentric, but the subject—death—makes *Mr. Death* no laughing matter. Rather, it's a human tragedy.

Fast, Cheap and Out of Control is Morris's celebration of eccentricity. The film is basically a portrait of four men who are enthusiastic about their work. Each has a rather out-of-the-ordinary vocation, and each is a zealot about his work. Dave Hoover is a wild animal trainer; George Mendanca is a topiary gardener; Ray Mendez is a mole rat expert; and Rodney Brooks is a robot designer. Aside from their enthusiasm for their work, the animal kingdom is the linkage. The robots that Rodney designs look like large insects, and the leafy sculptures that George creates are in the image of animals, such as a dinosaur. Less apparent but no less common among the four men is a sense of play. Ray and Rodney are almost childlike in their enthusiasm. George and Dave are more mature in their approach to their work.

Although the major focus of the film is the interviews with the four men with visual illustration of their work, Morris intertwines two additional thematic threads in the story. First, he cuts away to film serials, such as "King of the Jungleland" and "Zombies of the Stratosphere." "King of the Jungleland" stars Clyde Beatty, best known as a lion trainer prior to and during his Hollywood career. In the serial, Beatty has to fight lions and many human adversaries. Morris's second intervention is circus footage, from clowns to lion acts to trapeze acts. The reaction of the audience is also a visual element. Both visual interventions are entertainments, both attract a young audience, both are about the dangerous interface between the natural or animal world and man, and both are about adults playacting at being adults—they are really all kids at heart.

Fast, Cheap and Out of Control has a very distinctive style. Whereas Morris mixed cinéma vérité and a dramatic style in *Mr. Death*, in *Fast, Cheap and Out of Control* he uses mostly interviews that are presented in traditional documentary style. The balance of the material runs from the dramatic (the serial) to almost hyperstylized footage. The circus material in particular is presented using oblique camera placements and angles. Whether Morris is trying to introduce the notion of instability or danger or both, he moves far from realism in the circus footage. The same can be said for the robot laboratory footage, where Morris tries to impute point-of-view shots that "humanize" the robot. He also uses oblique angles to film the topiary garden. The use of extreme angles and wide-angle lenses "animates" the animal sculptures. It also gives them a looming, menacing presence.

In the case of the actual animals—the mole rats, lions, and tigers—Morris approaches them with a naturalistic visual style that emphasizes their being captive. The consequence is to create empathy for these animal "victims" of man. Camera placements and lens selection are utilized to capture this sense of the animals. The style distinctively sets up a sense of play about representing reality; indeed, the style seems the playful equivalent of the zeal the interviewees feel for their professions. Errol Morris isn't going to be left out. He feels equally zealous about his profession: filmmaking.

The clash of dramatic footage, from the serial, with the documentary or actuality footage is not quite as great as it was in *Mr. Death*. Morris's approach to the actuality footage is so stylized that it seems more in harmony with the artifice of the serial than it does in conflict.

As in *Mr. Death*, irony is plentiful in *Fast, Cheap and Out of Control*. Each of the interviewees is a grown man, but Morris chooses to focus on only one dimension of their adult lives—their profession, and the how and the why of it. As in the case of Fred Leuchter, these men have a vocation where they don't have to interface with others. They are loners working at an unusual profession that is enormously gratifying to them. But as in the case of Leuchter, they are not adding obvious value to mankind. They are marginalized men gaining their status from their work as an act of individuality, of free will. In a sense, the irony is that—regardless of the vocation—Morris is looking at each of these men as a purveyor as well as a victim of his acts of free will. I don't mean to overemphasize Morris as a film moralist, but on one level that's exactly what he's doing, and it's his sense of irony about man and animal that is pointing us in this direction, which brings us finally to the issue of voice in Morris's work.

We can say that Errol Morris wants to explore the American character, that he wants to look at men at the margin of society, that he wants to look at the eccentric in this society. I believe that Morris, as in the case of Werner Herzog, is looking at his own psychology. He sees wonderment, he sees difference, he sees play, and he sees the downside to excess. All these are themes he explores in his characters, and all these characteristics capture his approach to filmmaking. In a sense his films are probes: How excessive can I be, before I too suffer the fate of a Fred Leuchter? This is the creative path Morris walks down. He has chosen the documentary as his medium, but he has modified it to such an extent that it is barely recognizable as a documentary. This is Errol Morris's contribution to the personal documentary.

CHANGES IN THE USE OF NARRATION

Although narration is totally absent (by definition) in cinéma vérité, it is a formative presence in the other genres of documentary. Narration, as one of the three layers of sound (dialog and music are the others), is a very powerful tool. Narration has the capacity to alter the meaning of the visual. The classic role of narration, "the Voice of God," was essentially interpretive. As filmmakers have begun to range in their use of narration, it is useful to look at the possibilities for narration and then to move on to novel examples of these uses.

If we were to summarize the uses of narration we could categorize the narrator as observer, as investigator, as guide, or as provocateur. Within these larger categories the narrator can be objective or subjective, intimate or distant, harsh or ironic, young or old, professional or anecdotal. Every choice will influence our perception and experience of the film. Consequently, the filmmaker must make a decision about how he or she wants us to experience the film narrative.

The Narrator as Observer

Narrators as observers presume that their mission is to allow us to accompany them on a tour of a place, a person, or an idea. The position of the narrator can be as an expert, a companion, or an innocent in the process of discovery. This latter notion was made famous by Michael Rubbo, the Australian documentarian who made films for the National Film Board of Canada for two decades. Rubbo himself becomes a character in his work; he is a participant—observer. This is his approach in Vietnam with *Sad Song of Yellow Skin* (1970), in Cuba with *Waiting for Fidel* (1974), and in Paris with *Solzhenitsyn's Children ... Are Making a Lot of Noise in Paris* (1979).

Thematically, each film has rich subject matter: the effect of the war or the quality of life issues for expatriates trying to live in Vietnam; the potential meeting of a capitalist and politician from Canada with Premier Fidel Castro; the intellectual currents of a city where ideas mean everything in *Solzhenitsyn's Children ... Are Making a Lot of Noise in Paris*.

Rubbo is an ingenuous observer. In order to personalize complex material, but also to explore that material, Rubbo sets himself up as a curious observer who hasn't quite made up his mind. We know that his experiences will shape his views, and by acting as a guide who is processing the material as he discovers it, Rubbo, at times naïve, at other times skeptical, provides us with an avenue into material that otherwise would be heavy slogging for the audience. His role as observer also makes his documentaries lighter and more entertaining.

Amir Bar-Lev's *Fighter* (2000) is no less ambitious than Rubbo's work, but his approach is to use a constant on-camera observer. *Fighter* is the story of two Czech Holocaust survivors, Jan Weiner and Arnost Lustig. Bar-Lev films their contemporary return to Czechoslovakia in order to trace Weiner's escape during World War II. They travel from Czechoslovakia to Croatia and then to Italy, where Weiner was imprisoned as an undesirable alien, and finally from Italy, his escape to join the British Air Force, where he participated in the Allied bombing of Germany. Bar-Lev intercuts archival historical footage as well as family photographs of Weiner. Arnost Lustig, now a friend of Weiner's as well as a fellow Holocaust survivor, is the observer for the film.

Because Lustig is a writer, he tries to interpret Weiner's actions throughout the journey. Weiner, the fighter of the title, is a man of action rather than words. The journey stirs up deep feeling and multiple wounds—the tragic loss of his mother in a concentration camp in Czechoslovakia; the awful fact of the suicide of his father in Croatia in 1942 while Weiner is staying with him. His father commits suicide to allow the young Weiner to travel west, unburdened by an elderly, less able, parent. Lustig attempts to give words to the feelings of Weiner, but Weiner turns against his friend. Words detract and undermine Weiner's capacity to cope, to hold on, to go forward. He breaks with Lustig and, in effect, walks out on the film.

What is important about the use of Lustig as a character and observer is that the contrast between the two men allows the audience to feel the pain of a man who refuses to see himself as a victim. Jan Weiner sees himself as a fighter. We see this side of him, but thanks to the presence of Arnost Lustig as an observer, we also feel the depth of the tragedies in his life, and he becomes all the more admirable a character for that contrast.

The Narrator as Investigator

Investigations imply a goal: to come to an understanding of an issue or person by means of the investigation. The consequence is a more purposeful documentary. Unlike the political or social issue documentary, the investigative documentary does not endeavor to make a case. Consequently, the investigative documentary is not at all a polemic.

In *The Ballad of Ramblin' Jack* (2000), Aiyana Elliott is trying to understand her father, the singer Jack Elliott. Mixing home movies, archival footage, contemporary interviews, and the equivalent of a current concert tour, Aiyana Elliott seeks to know a man she barely knows, her father.

By looking at his professional and personal life, she may find the key to connecting with the most elusive significant person in her own life. Her father divorced her mother when Aiyana was a small child. Today, as a filmmaker, five years out of film school, Aiyana wants to reconnect with her father, and making a film about him is the logical vehicle for that attempt. Jack Elliott, the son of a Jewish doctor in Brooklyn, decided he wanted to be a cowboy and eventually a cowboy balladeer. Elliott lived and performed with Woody Guthrie in the 1950s, and as his fame grew he became a powerful influence on Bob Dylan in the 1960s. But by the 1970s Elliott is a forgotten man, only to be rediscovered 20 years later by no less a fan than President Bill Clinton. Aiyana Elliott tries to understand the why of her father's career: his lack of ambition; his disorganized approach to his career; his chaotic personal life, including four wives. But in the end she sees that Jack Elliott is a man who is most comfortable on stage making up the set as he goes along; he is a great performer and a poor father. Although she doesn't seem to come to a deeper understanding of their relationship, she has made a film that is a tribute to an artist who was a transitional figure in folk music: the man between Woody Guthrie and Bob Dylan.

Ray Muller also strives for understanding in his film *The Wonderful, Horrible Life of Leni Riefenstahl* (1995). Leni Riefenstahl, one of the towering figures in film history, is the subject. Muller interviews Riefenstahl, aged 90, at many of the locations of her films, and of course at an editing bench. He also interviews her at various Berlin locations. Interspersed with the interviews are clips from her films, the two most important being *Triumph of the Will* (1935) and *Olympia, Parts I and II* (1938).

The goal of Muller's investigation goes beyond a portrait of the filmmaker. Muller wants to know how involved she was with the Nazi party, with Hitler, and his goals. He wants to test the idea, how much did you know, and how much responsibility should you bear for making films for the Nazis? These are issues Muller goes back to around the two key films but also around a supportive letter Riefenstahl wrote to Hitler in the early 1940s. He also returns to these questions when dealing with Riefenstahl's postwar hearing at the hands of the Allies (she was cleared), which resulted in the end of her filmmaking career, and her consequent efforts to restore her reputation right up until this film is made. To the end, Riefenstahl claims her goals were artistic not political, that had she known about the fate of the Jews and other persecuted minorities, she would have felt differently. She never recants, but does lament the suffering she has experienced for the past 50 years.

Muller draws no conclusion, but his continual probing poses the key questions about art and morality. He leaves us, his audience, with the conclusion we ourselves wish to come to.

Michael Moore in his films *Sicko* (2007) and *Capitalism: A Love Story* (2009) represents the most interventionist representation of the narrator as investigator. Moore has a very definite point of view and makes his case pointedly in these films.

The Narrator as Guide

If the investigator is looking for understanding, the guide already has it. Through the narration the guide helps us understand. Multiple guides are used to layer that understanding, usually first on an intellectual level, then on an emotional level. Mark Jonathan Harris uses multiple guides to engage us with his films in both of his Oscar-winning documentaries, *The Long Way Home* (1997) and *Into the Arms of Strangers* (2000).

The Long Way Home is the story of the survivors of the Holocaust from the end of the war in 1945 to the birth of the State of Israel in 1948. It is the story about people who survived Hitler's death camps only to discover they could not return to their former homes. Many who did not return were killed. And so their hopes turned principally to the West and to Palestine.

The British Mandate resisted Jewish immigration into Palestine, and the consequent civil disturbance eventually caused Britain to end the mandate, the precursor to a UN-supported partition of Palestine with a homeland for the Jews and a homeland for the Arabs. The film ends with the birth of the state of Israel, implying that at last the survivors of the Holocaust have a home in Israel.

This brief précis of the narrative provides the skeleton. How does the filmmaker use narration to shape and to layer the narrative? First, to provide unity and transition for the entire narrative, Harris uses the classical, informative guide who can explain the politics of President Truman's choice to support first Jewish immigration and then the State of Israel against the advice of his Departments of State and Defense. The narrator can also detail the story of the 1946 Kelce massacre of 41 Jews who had returned to their homeland in Poland after the war. These narrative knots, where considerable visual material would be needed to capture the issue, are explained by the principal narrator. The history, if you will, is the principle responsibility of the narrator. The actor Morgan Freeman reads the narration.

The other narrators are more personal. Here memoirs, letters, diaries, and oral histories of the 1945–1948 period provide the emotional texture of the narrative. These guides—survivors of the Holocaust, and American soldiers who liberated the camps, who guarded and supervised the camps, including the initial commander, General George Patton—offer deep insights into the emotional states of survivors and liberators. Despair, loss, hope, a future, all the planes of human feeling and existence are explored by these guides. Often actors are used to render these confessional pieces of narration. These "sound close-ups" emotionalize the archival footage. There are also interviewees: survivors, including the chief rabbi of Israel; two American rabbis who were instrumental in helping the survivors; an American volunteer who helped Jews escape illegally from Europe to Palestine; and Clark Clifford, who worked diplomatically for President Truman.

In *The Long Way Home*, it is the multiple or layered use of narrators that guides us through the complex history of the period as well as its equally complex emotional turbulence. Harris uses the same layered strategy for his narration in *Into the Arms of Strangers*. But in this film, the more personal guides also appear on camera. They are the children of the Kindertransport, now adults, 50 years after the traumatic war years. The story begins in 1933 with the ascent of Hitler to power in Germany. For children, the changes under the Nazis were subtle and not always apparent. But all that changed with the pogrom in November 1938, the night of shattered glass known as Kristallnacht. Throughout Germany and Austria and the Sudentenland, the annexed portion of Czechoslovakia, Jewish businesses were looted, Jewish synagogues were burned, and Jews were harassed, beaten, and killed. Many died. It proved to be a turning point for the Jews in Germany.

Consequent to Kristallnacht, Jews tried to leave Germany, but exit visas were hard to come by and entry visas to other countries even harder. Great Britain decided that it would accept as many children from Germany as possible. The conditions were that the children had to be under 17, that £50 had to be paid for their support, and that a British home must be willing to take them in. The program, which began in December 1938 and continued until the beginning of World War II in 1939, was known as the Kindertransport. Children from Germany, Austria, and Czechoslovakia participated in the transport.

Into the Arms of Strangers tells the story of the Kindertransport and follows 10 children who participated. Their interviews as well as archival footage, home movies, and photographs provide the visuals for the film.

As in *The Long Way Home*, there is a primary narrator who explains the historical progression. The narration, read by Judi Dench, provides the general informational shape for *Into the Arms of Strangers*. With the overarching narrative as the guide track for the film, Harris proceeds to use the 10 participants as the personal guides to the story of the Kindertransport.

They include six women and four men: five are from Germany, three from Austria, one from Czechoslovakia, and one from Poland, who had made his way to Germany by 1939. Their stories focus on life prior to 1938, Kristallnacht; their leave-taking from their parents; the transport itself; life in England; in the case of the young man from Poland, his transport to Australia on the *HMS Deruna*, and his return to join the army; the reunion with parents where the parents survived, or the experience of learning of the death of the parents; and the aftermath of the Kindertransport experience. What is clear from the stories is that the Kindertransport saved thousands of children's lives, but that it was a scarring event for the children; in a sense, it was the seminal event in the lives of these 10 people.

In *Into the Arms of Strangers*, the narration provides multiple points of entry into a complex historical event. By using a general narration for historical information and participants for personal information, Harris has created a tiered entry into the narrative—informational and emotional lines emanate out of the two layers of narration. Although the narrators are on camera in *Into the Arms of Strangers*, they serve the same purpose as the off-camera readings of letters, diaries, and memoirs in *The Long Way Home*—to personalize a complex historical event and to give emotional resonance to a Holocaust event too easily overwhelmed by statistics and scale. By using multiple narrators as guides, Harris brings us to the emotional core of the issue and we begin to understand.

The Narrator as Provocateur

The provocateur has a specific goal in his documentary: to promote change. The nature of the narration may be direct or ironic, but in both cases the goal remains the same. Justine Shapiro and B. Z. Goldberg, in their film *Promises* (2001), are very direct. They want their film to contribute to the possibility of peace in the Middle East. Goldberg is the narrator, both on and off camera.

Promises was filmed in Israel and in the West Bank from 1997 to 1999. The film follows eight children: four are Israeli and four are Palestinian. In Israel, the children include an ultra-orthodox child, the son of a West Bank settler, and a set of twins who are grandchildren of Holocaust survivors. In this sense, the full political spectrum, from liberal to conservative, is represented. Among the Palestinian children, the spectrum is from urban (settled) to refugee (unsettled) and includes a young girl. All other participants on both sides are male. Shapiro and Goldberg are interested in the attitudes of the children toward one another. The film includes their families but only in a limited sense. The major part of the film focuses solely on the children. The film's last section brings together the Israeli twins with the two children (male and female) from the West Bank refugee camp. The implicit question is whether the children can get along for an afternoon. They do, but when the filmmakers return to interview them two years later, they have not maintained contact and their attitudes have hardened.

Shapiro and Goldberg have tried with *Promises* to illustrate the complexity and depth of opposing attitudes in the Middle East between Israelis and Palestinians. They are also attempting to say, by the nature of the film's structure, that it begins with the next generation. We have to get them together if there is to be hope for peace in that region. Their direct approach is an emotional provocation to try.

Ron Mann's *Grass* (2000) takes a very different approach. *Grass* is an exploration of American attitudes toward marijuana from the 1930s through the 1990s. Both the government's and the public's attitudes are examined. The information line is essentially to trace the history of marijuana in the United States, from its entry via Mexican migrant workers at the turn of the century to its status today—as a criminalized drug that the government spends billions of dollars to eradicate. The dramatic line of the narrative is how marijuana has been affiliated with dangers to society. Over time it has been affiliated first with the outsider (Mexicans); then with a scapegoated minority (the black community); then with murder; then with mental illness and its consequences; then with heroin use; and finally, with "never fulfilling your potential" or, to put it another way, "to be a loss to society." The government, primarily through the Commissioner of the Federal Bureau of Narcotics from 1930 onward, mounted a vigorous attack to criminalize the drug. The head of that department, Commissioner Harry J. Anslinger, made it his personal mission to eradicate marijuana from the American landscape. Although there are powerful figures, such as Mayor Fiorella LaGuardia of New York, who question and commission scientific studies to evaluate the drug, the government continues a 45-year assault on the drug and its users. The expense of this war and the number of users grow anyway. In 1977, President Jimmy Carter attempted to decriminalize the drug, but his effort failed. Nevertheless, a number of states have since decriminalized marijuana usage. But until the end of the century, marijuana use remained a criminal activity from the point of view of the federal government.

Grass is a provocation to change the law and align it with scientific knowledge about the drug. The film takes an adversarial position to the law. To flesh out this position, filmmaker

Ron Mann uses as his narrator Woody Harrelson, an actor with a liberal reputation and a knack for portraying antiestablishment characters. The more extreme layer of provocation, however, comes from the visuals. Mann uses film clips from archival antimarijuana films as well as graphics to make his case. The film opens with a clip about marijuana that poses the question "Marijuana, Threat or Menace?" The clips increasingly become extreme, melodramatic illustrations of the madness, rapacity, and murder that follow from marijuana usage. The irony and provocation then arises principally from the visuals. But the narration also is provocative in its use of language. Mexicans are characterized as blood-curdling murderers. Commissioner Anslinger is called a "prohibitionist" and a "law-and-order evangelist." Mayor LaGuardia, on the other hand, is "skeptical about government claims" about marijuana.

Commissioner Anslinger is portrayed as a villain; Mayor LaGuardia is a fair-minded hero. This kind of characterization also presents the opposition of Presidents Nixon, Ford, and Reagan to marijuana and the youth movement and the movement for decriminalization as heroic. The narration, although more tempered than the visuals, advocates changing the marijuana laws in the United States. This is the provocation of the narration in *Grass*.

CONCLUSION

The changes in the narration imply the richness that has kept the documentary lively and alive as a genre. It is important, however, to understand that just as there are subgenres within the documentary, innovation in techniques such as narration, as much as the movement to explore voice in the documentary, are responsible for keeping the genre alive and as critical a center for innovation as it was in the 1920s, 1930s, and 1950s.

CHAPTER 27

Innovations in Documentary II

Fahrenheit 9/11 (2004), by Michael Moore, represents a watershed in documentary film history. On one level, having earned almost $200 million, including ancillary revenue, it is the most commercially successful documentary of all time. Earnings rivaled the vast majority of dramatic films made in 2003. On another level, however, the film demarks the adoption of dramatic-entertainment values as opposed to the educational-informational values more often associated with the documentary. *Fahrenheit 9/11* was certainly not the first documentary to do so; Moore's film was simply the documentary that garnered the most attention for doing so.

Other areas of the media, particularly news broadcasts on television, have softened their approach to the news. They, too, have adopted "entertainment" values. Simultaneously, TV drama and a segment of the feature film industry have adopted "information-documentary" values: witness reality TV and the rise of a documentary approach on shows such as *Law and Order* and the CSI series.

In this chapter, our interest is this trend toward entertainment values in the documentary. Is it a new trend? Is it a progression or a regression? To contextualize these questions, it's important to acknowledge that the documentary has flirted with entertainment and dramatic values from the outset. If we use Dziga Vertov's *Chelovek s kino-apparatom* (*Man with a Movie Camera*) (1929) as the antithesis of dramatic values in the documentary, we note that Vertov's film has no main character in the traditional sense, that there are no antagonists, and that there doesn't seem to be a plot—only a slice-of-life approach to a day in the life of a cameraman and a day in the life of a city.

Vertov represents the classic cinéma vérité sensibility that reemerges in direct cinema in England, in the candid eye series in Canada, and in the American work of Fred Wiseman and the Maysles brothers. But other visions of documentary emanated from the work of Robert Flaherty and John Grierson, working in the same era as Vertov. In the case of Robert Flaherty, a romantic vision was applied to Eskimo life in the Arctic. In *Nanook of the North* (1922), Nanook heroically makes his way in spite of the hardships of securing food and shelter in the world's harshest environment. Grierson, too, plied his heroic humanist agenda to labor relations and to the delivery of the mail, in *Night Mail* (1936). In each of these films, dramatic ideas are used to enoble the documentary subject.

The Technique of Film and Video Editing: History, Theory, and Practice. DOI: 10.1016/B978-0-240-81397-4.00027-3

The stakes as well as the dramatic techniques employed become more evident in Leni Riefenstahl's *Triumph des Willens* (*Triumph of the Will*, 1934) and Frank Capra's *Why We Fight* series (1942–1944). In Riefenstahl's film, Adolph Hitler is the heroic main character who arrives from somewhere above the clouds to save his nation. The same Adolph Hitler is the principal antagonist in Capra's *Divide and Conquer* (1943). Capra uses Riefenstahl's own footage as well as newsreel, even Hollywood, film footage to illustrate what a duplicitous bad guy Hitler really is.

Alain Resnais used a dramatic strategy to juxtapose 1954 Auschwitz (color) with 1944 Auschwitz (black and white) in his *Nuit et brouillard* (*Night and Fog*, 1955). The raw footage itself was sufficiently shocking—the conflictual strategies hardly seemed necessary. The same can be said for Marcel Ophül's *Chagrin et la pitié* (*The Sorrow and the Pity*, 1969), in which the juxtaposition of the Vichy government's behavior toward its Jews was in stark contrast to the nationalistic resistance claims made by French politicians after World War II.

By the late 1980s, however, particularly with the work of Errol Morris (*The Thin Blue Line*, 1988; *Mr. Death: The Rise and Fall of Fred A. Leuchter, Jr.*, 1999), the use of dramatic strategies in the documentary became more novel and appealing to documentary makers. Morris principally used a protagonist or antagonist model in his films. In *Mr. Death*, holocaust deniers, including Mr. Death, are the antagonists. In *Fast, Cheap & Out of Control* (2001), the four main characters are nonconformists in an increasingly conformist world. In Morris's *The Fog of War: Eleven Lessons from the Life of Robert McNamara* (2004), McNamara is a protagonist who is his own antagonist.

Similarly, in *Grizzly Man* (2005), Werner Herzog investigates the death of Timothy Treadwell, a wildlife preservationist killed by a grizzly after spending 13 summers among the bear population in Alaska. Here the conflict is man versus animal; man, advocate of animal life; or, to put it another way, friend or food—what is the nature of man in nature? Herzog structures the film as an investigation into this relationship, and what he concludes is that Treadwell and the grizzly saw the relationship differently and therein lays the tragedy of Treadwell. And by using the chronology of the relationship as the plot, Herzog is able to create the conflictual tension that plot always brings to the goal of the main character.

This use of plot as a shaping device is rarely as powerfully used as it is in Andrew Jarecki's *Capturing the Friedmans* (2003). The film relies on the protagonist–antagonist relationship as well as on a plot. The main character is definitely Jesse Friedman, a teenager when he is sentenced to go to jail as a pedophile, having been found guilty of abusing children in the basement of his home together with his father, Arnold Friedman. Ostensibly, the children (boys) were there to be tutored in computer and math skills by their teacher, Arnold Friedman. The antagonist is Arnold Friedman, the main character's father. The plot is the accusation of child molestation, the investigation, the trial, and the impact of these events on the Friedman family.

Director Jarecki clearly sympathizes with Jesse and believes he is innocent, even though Jesse, along with his father, is sentenced to significant jail time. Jarecki is also interested in the impact of the events upon the Great Neck, New York, community in which they took place.

From the point of view of the narrative choices and editing style, Jarecki has treated *Capturing the Friedmans* as a thriller.

Another example of a documentary film structured as a thriller is Nathaniel Kahn's *My Architect*. The film begins with the director discovering, at the death of his father, the architect, Louis Kahn, that the father had two other families (two other wives and two other children). As the youngest of all of Kahn's children, Nathaniel sets out to find out who his father was, personally and professionally. In the course of his investigation, he and his audience learn a great deal about Louis Kahn. We learn he was one of the great American architects of the twentieth century. We also learn that he was utterly unorthodox in how he conducted his personal life. Aside from structuring the film as an investigation into a mystery, Nathaniel poses as the naïve narrator of the investigation. By doing so, he is attempting to dramatize the sense of surprise and wonder at each revelation. By assuming this pose, Kahn lightens what might have become heavy, even tragic, in the unfolding. The pose lightens the tone of this documentary, and by doing so, Kahn moves us away from realist interpretation and judgment of his father. The alternative, creative tolerance, is the upshot of Kahn's narrative choices.

Jeffrey Blitz's documentary *Spellbound* (2002) has launched two dramatic films and a Broadway musical. Rarely has a documentary spawned as much emulation. *Spellbound* follows the lives of eight diverse American teenagers as they move from the regional to the national spelling bee competition. And so, there are eight main characters, each humanized and individualized.

And there is a plot—the regional competitions and the national competition. Clearly, there can be only one winner, but the pride of each of the families in their children is so strong that it outweighs the disappointment of the seven who have lost the competition. Blitz has managed to make each of these main characters a winner in their own right. *Spellbound* abounds in dramatic values. One of the students is the local genius in his small rural school. Only his size protects him from the taunts of his classmates. A Hispanic girl, the child of Spanish-speaking illegal immigrants, is proud to be the "educated" child in her family. Each of these children faces challenges in their own environment. Again, the drama doesn't emanate from the competition alone.

Each of the films discussed so far has dramatic and entertainment values unusual in a documentary film. But to capture the sense of crossover between the documentary and the drama, the rest of this chapter focuses on two films about the same subject—the Munich massacre of Israeli athletes at the 1972 Olympic Games. This tragedy is the subject of Kevin Macdonald's 1999 documentary, *One Day in September*. It is also the subject of Steven Spielberg's 2005 drama *Munich*.

Let's look at the dramatic film first. Although *Munich* focuses on the aftermath of the massacre, the presentation of the massacre itself is the baseline for all that follows. An Israeli assassination team is organized with its goal to kill not only the assassins (three survived the day of the massacre), but also the Palestinian planners of the massacre. The revenge killings take place principally in Europe, but there is at least one attack in the Middle East. In the course of those assassinations, half of the Israeli team is killed, and, in the end, the leader of the team refuses to carry on. He joins his wife and child in Brooklyn, where the film ends inconclusively.

From the point of view of the narrative choices Spielberg makes, he is clearly opting for documentary-informational choices as opposed to dramatic-emotional choices when it comes to the main character, the antagonist, the use of plot, and the story form or genre he uses to frame the narrative. Let's begin with the main character, Avner (Eric Bana).

If we contextualize the Spielberg approach to the main character, we note the heroic nature of an ordinary main character in Sheriff Brody (Roy Scheider) in *Jaws* and in John Miller in *Saving Private Ryan*, or the heroic nature of an outsider in the young boy (Henry Thomas) in *E.T. the Extra-Terrestrial* (1982) or in Oscar Schindler (Liam Neeson) in *Schindler's List*. In every case, the main character becomes a reluctant hero. That is not the case of the Avner character in *Munich*. If anything, Avner's commitment at the outset not only softens but, over time, he also questions the mission to which he has been assigned. He is reluctant, but he is certainly not heroic by the end of this narrative.

Turning to the issue of an antagonist, we find a similar outcome. In *Saving Private Ryan*, the German spared by Miller's patrol ends up cruelly killing the Jewish member of the American company. He is the vicious face of Nazism, just as Amon Goeth is its face in *Schindler's List*. Each of Spielberg's films has a definite antagonist, human or otherwise, with the exception of *Munich*. In a situation where we would expect a Palestinian antagonist, there is no such character. In fact, Spielberg humanizes two of the Palestinians to be killed, one with a daughter and the other with his impassioned speech about the Palestinian cause. There is tragedy in *Munich*, but no clear antagonist.

Turning to the plot, the assassination of the assassins and their planners, there is no rising arc here. Although the early assassinations have a powerful sense of revenge, this softens over time. The last visualized attempt at assassination actually fails and it is clear by the end that the mission is incomplete. There is no climactic battle (*Saving Private Ryan*) or clear resolution (*Jaws*) to the plot. Consequently, as in the case of the main character and the use of an antagonist, the use of plot in Munich has been intentionally muted.

The reason is not unclear—Spielberg intends *Munich* to be a meditation on vengeance. Does an eye for an eye work for political goals? Spielberg's answer is clearly "no." Consequently, Spielberg uses the docudrama as the story form of choice in *Munich*. Rather than telling a story of vengeance and power, Spielberg seems more interested in examining that pattern of political behavior in the Middle East and in challenging its purposefulness. Using the docudrama allows Spielberg to embrace realism without relying on pulp or pop dramatic effects to make his point. Although the result may disappoint fans of earlier Spielberg films, it is clear that by embracing documentary-educational goals, Spielberg is trying to wean his audience from the facile answers that so often emanate from the simplification of political issues when they are framed by dramatic considerations. Clearly, Spielberg is looking to change the paradigm and to present a serious, thoughtful meditation on the intractable history of the Middle East in the twentieth century.

One Day in September is Kevin Macdonald's documentary treatment of the single day at the Olympics in Munich when the kidnapping and killing of the Israeli athletes occurred. Aside from the detailed treatment of the events of that day, Macdonald includes contemporary interview material with the Dutch wife of one of the victims and the Israeli daughter of another victim, plus interview material with the sole surviving Palestinian who participated in the massacre, as well as a number of the Germans who participated either as police or government officials that day in September. And also interviewed is the Israeli sent by Mossad to represent Mossad's interests at the site of the kidnapping and, later, at the airport where the Germans attempted to rescue the hostages.

Macdonald begins his documentary by introducing the site, Munich, of the 1972 Olympics. Thirty-six years after the 1936 Olympics that Hitler used to glorify the new Nazi Germany, Germany would now use the 1972 Olympics to show how the country had changed consequent to the end of World War II. Problematic was the decision to have unarmed security people at the Olympic village, rather than a trained security force. After giving the background of the fencing coach and the wrestling coach, both having been child Holocaust survivors who emigrated to Israel after the war, Macdonald contextualizes the significance for these men to return to Germany as free men, as equals to their German hosts.

Having given the victims a human face, Macdonald proceeds with the events of that fateful day. He begins by describing the Olympic village and how the Palestinian team gained access to the village (a subterfuge orchestrated by the Eastern German authorities). The narrative then proceeds with entry into the first Israeli apartment. There the injured wrestling coach is forced to take the Palestinians to another apartment, that of the wrestlers, who he feels might be able to overwhelm the Palestinians. And so, the Palestinians gain entry to two apartments, those of the coaches and of the wrestling team. In the ensuing struggle, two of the eleven Israelis are killed (not at the same time). The body of the wrestling coach is dumped off of the apartment balcony and in this way the world is informed that the kidnapping has taken place. A ransom demand (the freedom of 200 Palestinians from Israeli jails) is made.

What follow is Israel's refusal to negotiate and the efforts of the Germans to negotiate with the terrorists. Israel offers to dispatch a team to rescue the hostages, but Germany refuses. There are no trained German military personnel to deal with the circumstance that has arisen. Naïvety and surprise characterize the German response throughout the day. Olympic officials decide in spite of events that the Games should continue. The hostage-taking has nothing to do with the events. Media reportage of the events of the day falls to Jim McKay, a network sports commentator. Occasional audio of Peter Jennings, reporting for ABC News, is also included.

The deadline passes three times as negotiators secure an extension. By the third time, Olympic officials, under pressure, decide to suspend the Games in the face of the crisis. A deal is struck to transport the Palestinians and their prisoners out of Germany to an Arab country. The deal is a ruse to get the terrorists and prisoners out of the Olympic village and to relocate them to a place where a rescue will be attempted. The ambush site, however, is staffed by too few snipers, and the German volunteer force aboard the plane intended to overcome the terrorists' votes to abandon the plane minutes before the terrorists arrive by helicopter at the airport and awaiting aircraft. Without communications equipment, without experience and knowledge of the terrorist numbers, the Germans do not effect a rescue, and although five of the terrorists are killed, all nine Israeli hostages are murdered. The rescue attempt has failed. Within three weeks, the German authorities make a deal to get the three surviving terrorists out of Germany.

They are never put on trial. Two are consequently killed by an Israeli assassination squad. Although it's unstated, the age of global terrorism began in September 1972 in Munich. Now, more than 30 years later, it's more global than ever, and far more lethal.

How does Kevin Macdonald rely on dramatic strategies in his editing choices of *One Day in September*? How does he deal with his main character? Macdonald chooses the two coaches, the fencing coach and the wrestling coach. Both men will die in the attack, but although each is a victim, it is their love of life that Macdonald embraces. Each of these men was a very positive person who changed lives, especially the lives of their families. And it is the families of each man, the wives and the children, who represent the men in the film. By approaching the main characters in so personal a way, Macdonald deepens our emotional connection with the victims. It takes their deaths out of the political realm and very much makes *One Day in September* a personal story.

Turning to the antagonists of *One Day in September*, one would expect that the antagonists would be the terrorists who killed the eleven athletes. I didn't find this to be the case. Instead, Macdonald surprises us. It is the German authorities responsible for the conduct of the Games and for the safety of the athletes who are the antagonists. Not far behind are the Olympic Committee members, who continually try to wash their hands of the event of the kidnapping and massacre. By doing as he does, Macdonald points out that nations have political responsibilities for the safety of guests and of their own citizens. When the three surviving terrorists are flown out of Germany, even the Germans interviewed are embarrassed by the moral implications of their government's actions. And so Macdonald has framed events in a very personal way. The hosts have let down their guests and that has led to a tragedy that continues to resonate throughout the world. East/West, Arab/Israeli, new Germany/old Germany—each is sidestepped to tell this story in the most personal, emotional manner possible.

Turning to how Macdonald has used the plot, the events of that tragic day: He treats the events as a thriller. Although we who are watching know the outcome, Macdonald's introjections of options and opportunities suggest that events did not have to turn out the way they did. And by using the overlay of indifference from athletes and Olympic officials to those events, Macdonald implies the age-old maxim of anti-Semitism. Would these events have occurred if the athletes had been another nationality rather than Israeli? His implication is unmistakable: In Munich, there is the wish that Israelis and Arabs handle their own problems—anywhere but here. And that, too, becomes part of the tragedy of the events of that day.

Macdonald uses plot as dramatically as Costa-Gavras does in *Z* (1969) and as Alan Pakula does in *All the President's Men* (1976). The result is that Macdonald's use of dramatic strategies makes his film entertaining, in spite of its horrific events, whereas the documentary strategies Steven Spielberg adopts in *Munich* make his dramatic film less entertaining and more documentary-educational.

These two films capture an important trend—the movement of the documentary toward the dramatic film, and, conversely, the movement of a segment of the dramatic film industry toward the documentary.

4

Principles of Editing

28. The Picture Edit and Continuity 371
29. The Picture Edit and Pace 381
30. Nonlinear Editing and Digital Technology I 391
31. Nonlinear Editing and Digital Technology II 399
32. Conclusion 413

CHAPTER 28

The Picture Edit and Continuity

Much has been written suggesting that the art of film is editing,[1] and numerous filmmakers from Eisenstein to Welles to Peckinpah have tried to prove this point. However, just as much has been written suggesting that the art of film is avoidance of editing,[2] and filmmakers from Renoir to Ophuls to Kubrick have tried to prove that point. No one has managed to reconcile these theoretical opposites; this fascinating, continuing debate has led to excellent scholarship,[3] but not to a definitive resolution. Both factions, however, work with the same fundamental unit: the shot. No matter how useful a theoretical position may be, it is the practical challenge of the director and the editor to work with some number of shots to create a continuity that does not draw unnecessary attention to itself. If it does, the filmmaker and the editor have failed to present the narrative in the most effective possible manner.

The editing process can be broken down into two stages: (1) the stage of assembling the shots into a rough cut and (2) the stage in which the editor and director fine-tune or pace the rough cut, transforming it into a fine cut. In the latter stage, rhythm and accentuation are given great emphasis. The goal is an edited film that is not only continuous, but also dramatically effective. The goal of the rough cut—the development of visual and sound continuity— is the subject of this chapter; the issue of pace is the subject of Chapter 29. Both chapters attempt to present pragmatic, rather than theoretical, solutions to the editing problem, because, in the end, the creativity of editing is based on pragmatic solutions.

The editing problem begins with the individual shot. Is it a still image or a moving image? Is the foreground or the background in focus? How close is the character to the frame? Is the character positioned in the center or off to one side? What about the light and color of the image and the organization of objects or people relative to the main character? A great variety of factors affect the continuity that results when two shots are juxtaposed. The second shot must have some relationship to the first shot to support the illusion of continuity.

The simplest film, the one that respects continuity and real time, is the film that is composed of a single, continuous shot. The film would be honest in its representation of time and in its rendering of the subject, but it probably wouldn't be very interesting. Griffith and those who followed were motivated by the desire to keep audiences involved in the story. Their explorations focused on how little, rather than how much, needs to be shown. They

The Technique of Film and Video Editing: History, Theory, and Practice. DOI: 10.1016/B978-0-240-81397-4.00028-5

discovered that it isn't necessary to show everything. Real time can be violated and replaced with dramatic time.

The premise of not needing to show everything leads quite logically to the question of what it is necessary to show. What elements of a scene will, in a series of shots, provide the details needed to direct the audience toward what is more important as opposed to less important? This is where the choice of the type of shot—the long shot versus the midshot, the midshot versus close-up—comes into play. This is also where decisions about camera placement—objective or subjective—come into play. The problem for the editor is to choose the shot that best serves the film's dramatic purpose. Another problem follows: Having chosen the shot, how does the editor cut the shot together with the next one so that together they provide continuity? Without continuity (for example, if the editor cuts from one close-up to another that is unrelated), viewers become confused. Editing should never confuse viewers; it should always keep them informed and involved in the story.

Narrative clarity is achieved when a film does not confuse viewers. It requires matching action from shot to shot and maintaining a clear sense of direction between shots. It means providing a visual explanation if a new idea or a cutaway is introduced. To provide narrative clarity, visual cues are necessary, and here, the editor's skill is the critical factor.

CONSTRUCTING A LUCID CONTINUITY

Seamlessness has become a popular term to describe effective editing. A seamless, or smooth, cut is the editor's first goal. A seamless cut doesn't draw attention to itself and comes at a logical point within the shot. What is that logical point? It is not always obvious, but viewers always notice when an inappropriate edit point has been selected. For example, suppose that a character is crossing the room in one shot and is seated in the next. These two shots do not match because we haven't seen the character sit down. If we saw her sit down in the first shot and then saw her seated in the second, the two shots would be continuous. The critical factor here is using shots that match the action from one shot to the next.

PROVIDING ADEQUATE COVERAGE

Directors who do their work properly provide their editors with a variety of shots from which to choose. For example, if one shot features a character in repose, a close shot of the character as well as a long shot will be filmed. If need be, the props in the shot will be moved to ensure that the close shot looks like the long one. The background and the lighting must support the continuity.

Similarly, if an action occurs in a shot, a long shot will be taken of the entire action, and later a close shot will be taken of an important aspect of the action. Some directors film the entire action in long shot, midshot, and close-up so that the editor has maximum flexibility in putting the scene together. Close-ups and cutaways complete the widest possible coverage of the scene.

If the scene includes dialog between two people, the scene will be shot entirely from one character's point of view and then repeated from the other's point of view. Close-ups of important pieces of dialog and close-up reaction shots will also be filmed. This is the standard procedure for all but the most courageous or foolhardy directors. This approach provides the editor with all of the footage needed to create continuity.

Finally, considerations of camera angles and camera movement dictate a different series of shots to provide continuity. With camera angles, the critical issue is the placement of the camera in relation to the character's eye level. If two characters are photographed in conversation using a very high angle, as if one character is looking down on the other, the reverse-angle shot—the shot from the other character's point of view—must be taken from a low angle. Without this attention to the camera angle, the sequence of shots will not appear continuous. When a film cuts from a high-angle shot to an eye-level reaction shot, viewers get the idea that there is a third person lurking somewhere, as represented by the eye-level shot. When that third person does not appear, the film is in trouble.

MATCHING ACTION

To provide cut points within shots, directors often ask performers to introduce body language or vocalization within shots. The straightening of a tie and the clearing of a throat are natural points to cut from long shot to close-up when there is no physical movement within the frame to provide the cut point. Where movement is involved, "here-to-there" is a trick directors use to avoid filming an entire action. When an actor approaches a door, he puts his hand on the doorknob; when he greets someone, he offers his hand. These actions provide natural cut points to move from long shot to close-up. A favorite here-to-there trick is raising a glass to propose a toast. Any action that offers a distinct movement or gesture provides an opportunity within a shot for a cut. The more motion that occurs within the frame, the greater the opportunity for cutting to the next shot.

It is critical that the movement in a shot be distinct enough or important enough so that the cut can be unobtrusive. If the move is too subtle or faint, the cut can backfire. A cut is a promise of more information or more dramatic insight to come. If the second shot is not important, viewers realize that the editor and director have misled them.

Match cuts, then, are based on (1) visual continuity, (2) significance, and (3) similarity in angle or direction. A sample pattern for a match cut is shown in Figure 28.1. The first cut, from the long shot to the close-up, would be continuous because character 1 continues speaking in the close-up. The next shot is a reverse-angle reaction shot of character 2 from her point of view. After the reverse-angle shot of character 2, we return to a midshot of character 1, and, in the final shot, we have a midshot of character 2 speaking. The cuts in this sequence come at points when conversation begins, and the cutting then follows the conversation to show the speaker.

The camera position used to film this sequence must not cause confusion. The straightforward approach, in which character 1 is photographed at a 90-degree angle, is easiest. The reverse-angle shot of character 2 would also be a 90-degree angle (Figure 28.2). If the angle for the reverse shot is not 90 degrees (head on), but rather is slightly angled, it will not appear continuous with

FIGURE 28.1 Sample pattern for a match cut.

(A) Long shot of character 1. (B) Close-up of character 1. (C) Reaction shot of character 2; includes character 1 in profile.
(D) Midshot of character 1. (E) Midshot of character 2.

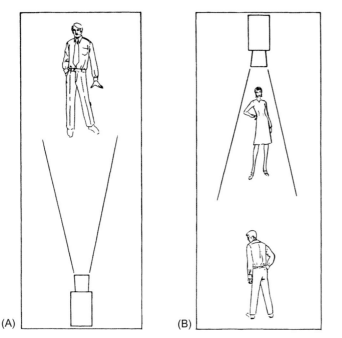

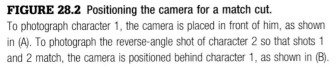

(A) (B)

FIGURE 28.2 Positioning the camera for a match cut.
To photograph character 1, the camera is placed in front of him, as shown in (A). To photograph the reverse-angle shot of character 2 so that shots 1 and 2 match, the camera is positioned behind character 1, as shown in (B).

the 90-degree shot of character 1. Strict continuity is possible only when the angle of the first shot is directly related to the angle of the next shot. Without this kind of correlation, continuity is broken.

PRESERVING SCREEN DIRECTION

Narrative continuity requires that the sense of direction be maintained. In most chase sequences, the heroes seem to occupy one side of the screen, and the villains occupy the other. They approach one another from opposite directions. Only when they come together in battle do they appear in the same frame.

Maintaining screen direction is critical if the film is to avoid confusion and keep the characters distinct. A strict left-to-right or right-to-left pattern must be maintained. When a character goes out to buy groceries, he may leave his house heading toward the right side of the frame. He gets into his car and begins the journey. If he exited to the right, he must travel left to right until he gets to the store. Reversing the direction will confuse viewers and suggest that the character is lost. Preserving this sense of direction is particularly important when a scene has more than one character. If one character is following another, the same directional pattern will work fine, but if they are coming from two different directions and will meet at a central location, a separate direction must be maintained for each character.

If a character is moving right to left, he exits shot 1 frame right and enters shot 2 frame left (Figure 28.3). The cut point occurs at the instant when the character exits shot 1 and enters shot 2. The match cut preserves continuity and appears to be a single, continuous shot. If there is a delay in the cut between when the character exits shot 1 and when he reappears in shot 2, discontinuity results, or the cut suggests that something has happened to the character. A sound effect or a piece of dialog would be necessary to explain the delay.

Equally as interesting an issue for the editor is whether to show every shot in the sequence with the character moving across the frame in each shot. Editors often dissolve one shot into another to suggest that the character has covered some distance. Dissolves suggest the passage of time. Another approach, which was used by Akira Kurosawa in *The Seven Samurai* (1954)

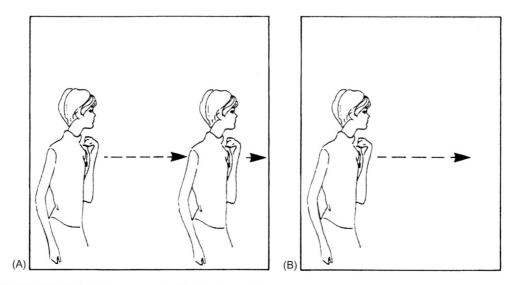

FIGURE 28.3 Maintaining screen direction for the match cut.
If a character exits frame right (A), she must enter the next shot frame left (B).

and Stanley Kubrick in *Paths of Glory* (1957), is to show the character in tight close-up with a panning, trucking, or zoom shot that follows the character. As long as the direction in this shot matches that of the full shot of the character, this approach can obviate the need to follow a character completely across the frame. Cutaways and the crosscutting of a parallel action can also be used to avoid continuous movement shots. If a character changes direction, that change must appear in the shot. Once the change is shown, the character can move in the opposite direction. The proper technique is illustrated in Figure 28.4.

These general rules are applicable whether the shots are filmed with the camera placed objectively or with it angled. Movement need not occur only from left to right or right to left. Diagonal movement is also possible. The character might enter at the bottom-left corner of the frame and exit at the upper-right corner. Here, the left-to-right motion is preserved. Filmmakers often use this camera position because it provides a variety of options. There is a natural cut point as the character begins to move away from a point very close to the camera. In this classic shot, we see the character's back full frame, and as she walks away from the camera, she comes fully into view. The shot starts as a close-up and ends as a long shot. The director can also choose to follow the character with a subjective camera, or the director can use a zoom to stay with the close-up as the character moves through the frame. In all of these cases, diagonal movement across the frame provides more screen time than left-to-right or right-to-left movement. This makes the shot economically more viable, more interesting, and, because it's subjective, more involving. The shot lasts longer on screen, thereby implying more time has passed. Also the costs of production are so great that a shot that is held on screen longer is better from a production cost point of view.

A shot with diagonal movement that starts as a long shot and ends as a close-up is also involving, and it allows the most literal rendering of the movement (Figure 28.5). An alternative would be to follow the actor's movement with the camera or zoom, maintaining a

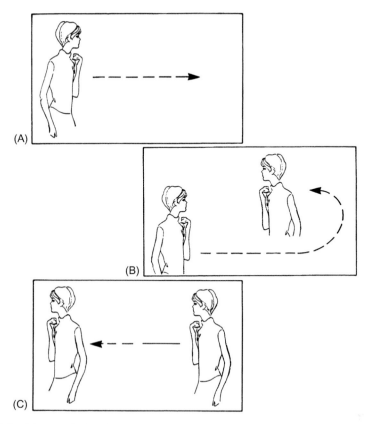

FIGURE 28.4 Maintaining continuity with a change in direction.
(A) Character moves left to right. (B) Character is shown changing direction. (C) Character moves right to left.

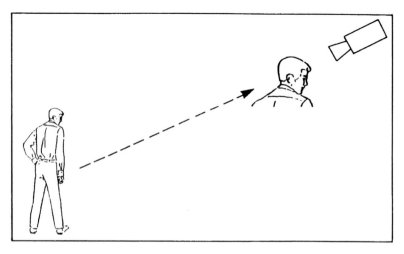

FIGURE 28.5 Following diagonal movement.
The shot shown begins as a long shot and ends as a close shot.

midshot or close-up throughout the shot. Any of these options will work as long as screen direction is preserved from shot to shot and continuity is maintained.

SETTING THE SCENE

Match cutting and directional cutting help the editor preserve continuity. The establishing shot, whether it is an extreme long shot or long shot that sets the scene in context, is another important tool. Karel Reisz refers to the scene in *Louisiana Story* (1948) that begins in a close-up. The setting for the sequence is not established until later.[4] What about stories that take place in New York or on Alcatraz or in a shopping mall? In each case, an establishing shot of the location sets the context for the scene and provides a point of reference for the close-ups, the follow action shots, and the visual details of the location.

Most filmmakers use an extreme long shot or a long shot to open the scene. It provides a context for the scene and allows the filmmaker to explore the details of the shot. The classic progression into and out of a scene (long shot/midshot/close-up/midshot/long shot) relies on the establishing shot. The other shots flow out of the establishing shot, and thus a clear continuity is provided. Classically, the establishing shot is the last shot in the scene as well as the first. Many filmmakers and editors have found ways to shorten the regimentation of this approach. Mike Nichols, for example, presented an entire dialog scene in one shot. By using the zoom lens, he avoided editing. Notwithstanding novel approaches of this type, it is important that editors know how to use the establishing shot to provide continuity for the scene.

MATCHING TONE

Variations in light and color from shot to shot can break continuity. These elements are under the cameraperson's control, but when variations do exist between shots, they can be particularly problematic for the editor. Laboratory techniques can solve some minor problems, but there are limits to what is possible. Newer, more forgiving film stocks have improved the latitude by overcoming poor lighting conditions and lessened the severity of the problem. The best solution, however, is consistency of lighting, cameraperson, and the sensitivity of the director to that working relationship. If all else fails, it may be necessary to reshoot the affected scenes. This requires the flexibility and understanding of the film's producers.

The editor's goal is always to match the tone between shots, but the editor's ability to find solutions to variations caused by poor lighting control is limited.

MATCHING FLOW OVER A CUT

What is the best way to show action without making the continuity appear to be mechanical? Every action has a visual component that can be disassembled into its various parts. Having breakfast may mean removing the food from the refrigerator, preparing the meal, laying out the dishes, eating, and cleaning up. If a scene calls for a character to eat breakfast, all of these sundry elements would add up to some rather elaborate action that is probably irrelevant to the scene's dramatic intention.

To edit the sequence, the editor will have to decide two things: (1) which visual information is dramatically interesting, and (2) which visual information is dramatically necessary. The length of the scene will be determined by the answer to these two questions, particularly the latter. Dramatic criteria must be applied to the selection of shots. If a shot does not help to tell the story, why has it been included in the film?

For example, if it is important to illustrate the fastidious nature of the character, how that character goes about preparing breakfast, eating, and cleaning up might be important. If the character is a slob and that is the important point to be made, then here too the various elements of the breakfast might be shown. However, if it is only important to show how quickly the character must leave home in the morning, the breakfast shots will get short shrift. The dramatic goals, first and foremost, dictate the selection of shots.

Once shots are selected, the mechanical problem for the editor is to make the cuts in such a way that undue time is not spent on shots that provide little information. Is there a way to show the character eating breakfast quickly? The answer, of course, is yes, but the editor does not accomplish this goal by stringing together shots of the character involved in each element of the activity. The screen time required for all of these shots would give the impression of the slowest breakfast ever eaten.

The editor has to find elegant ways to collapse the footage so that the scene requires a minimum of screen time. The shots of the breakfast, for example, can be cut down to a fraction of their previous length, and the scene can be made to flow smoothly and quickly. Consider a shot in which the character enters the kitchen, approaches the refrigerator, removes the milk and juice, and places them on the counter. It is not necessary to watch him traverse the kitchen. By cutting the long shot when he still has some distance to go, moving to a close shot of the refrigerator, holding for a second, and then showing his hand enter the frame to open the refrigerator door, we have collapsed the shot into a fragment of its original length. If the shot that follows this shows the character placing the milk and juice on the counter, we can drop the part of the previous shot where he removes the milk and juice from the refrigerator and carries them to the counter.

In this hypothetical example, we used a fragment of a shot to make the same point as the entire shot, using considerably less screen time as a result. By applying this approach to all of the shots in the breakfast scene, the vital information will be shown, and the screen time will suggest that the character is having a very quick breakfast. Continuity and dramatic goals are respected when the editor cuts each shot down to its essence. The flow from shot to shot is maintained without mechanically constructing the scene in the most literal sense of the shots. Literal shots do not necessarily provide dramatic solutions.

CHANGE IN LOCATION

This principle of cutting down each shot to its essence can be applied to show a character changing location. Rather than show the character move from point A to point B, the editor often shows her departing. If she is traveling by car, some detail about the geography of the area is appropriate. Unless there is a dramatic point to the scene other than getting the character from point A to point B, the editor then cuts to a street sign or some other indication of the new location. If the character traveled from left to right, the street sign will be positioned toward the right of the frame. Directors often use a tight close-up here. After holding a few seconds on the close-up, the character enters from frame left, and the zoom back picks up her arrival. If the shot is not a zoom, the character crosses the frame until she stops at the destination within the frame. With these few shots, the audience accepts that the character has traveled from one location to another, and little screen time was required to show that change in location.

CHANGE IN SCENE

To alert the audience to a change in scene, it is important to provide some visual link between the last shot of one scene and the first shot of the next. Many directors and editors now cover this transition with a shift in sound or by running the same sound over both shots. However, this inexpensive method shouldn't dissuade you from trying to find a visual solution.

If there is a similarity in movement from one shot to another, visual continuity can be achieved. This works by tracking slowly in the last shot of the first scene from left to right or from right to left. Because the movement is slow, the details are visible. The cut usually occurs when the tracking shot reaches the middle of the frame. In the next scene, the movement is picked up at about the same point in midframe, but as the motion is completed, it becomes clear that a new scene is beginning.

A change in scene can also be effected by following a particular character. If he appears in a suit in the last shot of one scene and in shorts in the first shot of the next scene, the shift occurs smoothly. Other elements help ease the transition; for example, the character might be speaking at the end of the first scene and at the beginning of the next.

Finally, a straightforward visual cue, such as a prop, can be used to make the transition. Suppose, for instance, that one scene ends with a close-up of a marvelous antique lamp. If the next scene begins with a close-up of another antique lamp and pulls back to reveal an antique store, the shift will be effective. The visual link between scenes allows a smooth transition to take place. The scenes may have very little to do with one another, but they will appear to be continuous.

NOTES/REFERENCES

1. Eisenstein and Pudovkin have written extensively on this point.
2. A. Bazin, What Is Cinema, vols. I, II, University of California Press, Berkeley, 1971.
3. B. Henderson's, The long take, in: E. P. Dutton (Ed.), A Critique of Film Theory, E. P. Dutton, New York, 1980.
4. K. Reisz, G. Millar, The Technique of Film Editing, Focal Press, Boston, 1968, p. 225.

CHAPTER 29

The Picture Edit and Pace

Pace is most obvious in action sequences, but all sequences are shaped for dramatic effect. Variation in pace guides viewers in their emotional response to the film. More rapid pacing suggests intensity; slower pacing, the reverse. Karel Reisz explores the opposite of editing for pace in his discussion of Hitchcock's *Rope* (1948), a film that was directed to avoid editing.[1] The entire film looks like a single long take. Reisz argues that too much screen time, which could have been used more productively, is wasted moving the camera from one spot to another.

Once the rough assembly is satisfactory, the question of narrative clarity has, to a certain extent, been satisfied. Shots flow from one to another and suggest continuity. What is still lacking is the dramatic emphasis of one shot relative to another. This is the role of pace, which is fine-tuned in the second editing stage. The product of this stage, the fine cut, is the culmination of all of the editor's decisions. At the end of the fine cut, the choices have all been made, and the sound tracks have been aligned and prepared for the mix. The stage between rough cut and final sound mix is the subject of this chapter. The goal of this stage is to introduce dramatic impact through the editing decisions.

This notion may seem obvious, but when we look at the opening of Welles's *Touch of Evil* (1958), we may back away from too general a statement about using camera movement to avoid editing. This three-minute sequence follows a car from a scene in which a bomb is planted in its trunk, to a scene showing the owner returning with a guest, to a scene in which they drive from Tijuana across the border into California. During the drive, we see Varguez (Charlton Heston), a Mexican policeman, cross the border with his new wife (Janet Leigh). They occupy the foreground while the doomed car moves across the border in the background. Soon after, the car passes them and explodes. The explosion leads to the first cut in the film.

Welles chose to begin his film with an elegant tracking shot through town and across the border. He could have fragmented the scene into shots that showed the bomb being planted and the owner returning and intercut the car with Varguez as each progressed across the border. If he had taken this approach, the pacing would have progressively quickened as we moved toward the explosion. The pace, rather than the contradiction between foreground and background, would have heightened the tension of the film.

381

The Technique of Film and Video Editing: History, Theory, and Practice. DOI: 10.1016/B978-0-240-81397-4.00029-7

In *Touch of Evil*, Welles avoided editing, and avoided the pacing, yet opened the film with a mesmerizing and powerful sequence. This example suggests that pace isn't everything. It reminds us that composition, lighting, and performance also count.

Having suggested the limits of pace, let's turn now to the possibilities of pace. Many directors specializing in political thrillers have used pace to empower their message. Costa-Gavras's exposé of Greek injustice in *Z* (1969) and Oliver Stone's exploration of political assassination in *JFK* (1991) both rely on juxtaposition and pace to drive home a particular point of view.

Another genre in which pace plays a central role is the adventure film. In both, the mixed genre adventure film, such as Joel Coen and Ethan Coen's *Raising Arizona* (1987), and the straightforward adventure film, such as Steven Spielberg's *Raiders of the Lost Ark* (1981), pace helps provide the sense of energy and excitement that is at the heart of the genre's success.

Whether it is the excitement of an adventure film or the indignation of a political thriller, pace is the key. The role of pace varies in different genres, but it always comes into play to some degree.

TIMING

One element of pace is the timing of particular shots. Where in a sequence should a particular close-up or cutaway be positioned for maximum impact? When is a subjective shot more powerful than an objective one? What is the most effective pattern of crosscutting between shots or juxtapositions within shots? These are editing decisions that directly affect the issue of dramatic effectiveness.

The editor's understanding of the purpose of the sequence as a whole helps her make these decisions. The purpose of the sequence might be exposition or characterization. Within these broad categories, the editor must decide how much visual and aural explanation and how much punctuation are needed to make the point. Finally, she must decide whether to take a straightforward editing strategy or use its alternative: a more indirect, layered strategy. For example, in a comedy film, the strategy of editing for surprise might be most appropriate. In comedy, surprise is critical. If the edit is not properly timed, the comedy is lost. Surprise is also useful in the thriller. In most other genres, though, a more straightforward approach is generally taken.

An example of surprise used for comic purposes can be found in the Coen brothers' *Raising Arizona*. A six-minute comedy sequence is difficult to sustain, particularly if it is an action sequence, but it succeeds in *Raising Arizona*. In the film, Hi (Nicholas Cage) and Ed (Holly Hunter), a childless couple, have stolen a baby from a rich businessman whose wife has had quintuplets. Hi is a former criminal, and Ed is a law-enforcement officer.

In this sequence, Hi decides to revert to crime in his old milieu, the local convenience store. Ed is not happy about this decision. Not only would Hi be breaking the law, but if caught, his actions would deprive their new child of its "father."

The sequence begins with Hi and Ed expressing concern about the future. They stop at a convenience store to buy disposable diapers for the baby. Ed plays with the baby while Hi enters the store. The first surprise comes when Hi decides to rob the store of a box of diapers and as much cash as he can get. The clerk pushes a silent alarm.

The next surprise is Ed's response once she sees Hi robbing the store. She becomes angry and leaves, deserting him. Hi is surprised by Ed's action, but not as surprised as he is by the store clerk, who has now a Magnum .357 in his hand and is trying to kill him. Hi flees on foot, but the police sirens suggest he is in trouble. He runs after Ed, with the police cars in pursuit.

Hi escapes into a backyard, only to be accosted by a watchdog. The dog lunges, but it is chained to an anchor, which saves Hi's life. Hi continues to run, but the dog is persistent and pulls the chain's anchor from the ground. The dog joins the police and the clerk in their pursuit of Hi. At this point, Ed, who has gotten over her anger, returns to pick up Hi, but she can't find him. Hi, now desperate, stops a truck on the road. He threatens the driver, who takes him into the truck.

Other neighborhood dogs take off after Hi, who is now being chased by dogs, the police, a store clerk, and his wife. The clerk fires his gun and shatters the truck's windshield. As the driver turns to avoid the onslaught, the first dog jumps the armed clerk by mistake. To avoid the police, the truck driver changes direction, putting the truck on a collision course with a house.

The truck driver, terrified by threats approaching from all sides, puts on the brakes. The sudden stop sends Hi flying through the front of the truck. The truck driver backs up and escapes. Meanwhile, Hi has been deposited on the front steps of a house. He runs through the house, closely pursued by the police and the dogs.

He escapes into a supermarket, where he picks up another box of diapers (he lost the other package). The police and the dogs are still in pursuit, and now the supermarket manager begins firing at Hi with a shotgun. The panicking customers add to the chaos, and Hi escapes. He loses the second box of diapers, but he is picked up by Ed outside the supermarket. They escape.

In this sequence, the timing of the surprises—the clerk's gun, the dog's tenacity, the truck driver's panic—all depend on the editing of the scene. In each case, a quick cut introduces the surprise, often in an exaggerated visual. The clerk's Magnum, for example, seems like a cannon due to its proximity to the camera and the use of a wide-angle lens. The quick cut and the visual exaggeration yield the desired comic effect.

RHYTHM

In general, the rhythm of a film seems to be an individual and intuitive matter. We know when a film does not have a rhythm. The jerkiness of the editing draws attention to itself. When the film has an appropriate rhythm, the editing appears to be seamless, and we become totally involved with the characters and the story. Of course, intuition alone is not enough. Some practical considerations help determine an appropriate length for particular shots within a sequence.

The amount of visual information within the shot often determines the length of the shot. A long shot, which has more visual information than a close-up, will be held for a longer time to allow the audience to absorb the information. If the information is new, it is appropriate to allow the shot to run longer so that the audience can become familiar with the new milieu. Moving shots are often held on screen longer than static images to allow the audience to absorb the shifting visual information. A cutaway that is important to the plot is generally extended to establish its importance.

Conversely, a close-up with relatively little information will be held on screen for only a short time. The same is true for static shots and repeated shots. Once the shot's visual information has been viewed, it's not necessary to give equal time to a second or third viewing.

It's not possible to provide absolute guidelines about the length of shots. However, it is important that the editor develop a sense of the relative lengths of shots within a sequence. Shots should never be all the same length. If they are all long or all short, the lack of variety deadens the impact of the sequence. It will have no rhythm. In the pacing of shots, rhythm requires the variation of the length of the shots.

Rhythm is also affected by the type of transition used between sequences. A straight cut can be jarring; it leaves us confused until a sound or visual cue suggests that a change has taken place. A dissolve at the end of one sequence into the beginning of the next makes a smooth transition and provides a visual cue. The dissolve, which is often associated with the passing of time, can also imply a change of location. The rhythm between sequences is smoother when dissolves are used.

A fade-out is occasionally used at the end of a sequence. Although it is clearly indicative of the closure of one sequence and the beginning of the next, the fade is currently not as widely used as it once was. It is still more popular than the wipe or iris shot, but it is certainly less popular than the dissolve.

If the editor's goal is to make a sequence seamless, his first criterion is to understand and work to clarify the emotional character of the scene. To do so most effectively, the editor must respect the emotional structure of the performances. This means trusting that a pause between two lines of dialog is not necessarily a lapse, but rather part of the construct of the performance. To edit out the pause may make superficial sense, but makes no sense whatsoever in terms of the performance. The editor must learn to distinguish performance from error, or dead space. It may be as simple as following action to its conclusion, or it may be more complex, involving the subtle nuances of the delivery of dialog or nonverbal mannerisms. Cutting into the performance may break the rhythm established by the performer in the scene or sequence.

Understanding both the narrative and the subtextual goals of a scene will also allow the editor to follow and modulate the editing so that it clarifies and emphasizes rather than confuses. The editor will be able to determine how long the shots need to be held on screen and how much modulation is necessary to make the point of the scene clear. The editor will then be able to use the most dynamic tools, like crosscutting, and the most minimal, the long shot, for maximum effect.

A simplified example of rhythmic pacing can be found in the "Tomorrow Belongs to Me" sequence in Bob Fosse's *Cabaret* (1972). A young boy stands up in a rural beer garden in 1932 Germany. He is dressed in a Hitler Youth uniform, but he is young enough to have an innocent, prepubescent voice. The impression he gives is of youthful beauty and optimism. As the song progresses, the orchestration becomes more elaborate, and the young man is joined by others. By the end of the song, Germans of all ages have joined in a defiant interpretation of the lyrics. By editing rapidly, using many close-ups, and cutting to Germans of all ages, Fosse produced a powerful sequence foreshadowing Nazism. The editing helps create the feelings of both innocence and aggression as the singers shift from a simple, innocent interpretation of the song to an aggressive one. The shifting emotional tone of the scene is modulated, and the result illustrates not only the power of pacing, but also how the modulation of pace enhances the power of a scene.

A more subtle and complex example is the nine-minute sequence that serves as the dramatic climax of Bernardo Bertolucci's *The Conformist* (1971). Marcello (Jean-Louis Trintignant) is an upper-middle-class follower of Mussolini in pre—World War II Italy. He wants to be accepted by the Fascists, but at his initiation, they ask him to help in assassinating an exiled dissident in Paris. The man is Marcello's former professor. On his honeymoon in Paris, Marcello reestablishes contact with Professor Quadriand and gains his trust. He also falls in love with the professor's young wife, Anna (Dominique Sanda). He warns her not to accompany her husband on his trip, but at the last minute, she chooses to travel with him.

The assassination sequence that follows reveals Marcello's true nature as a coward and Facism's true nature as a brutal ideology that does not tolerate dissidence. The sequence can be broken down into five sections plus a prologue: prologue (2 minutes, 45 seconds), (1) the trap (2 minutes), (2) the murder of the professor (1 minute, 25 seconds), (3) Anna's attempt to be saved (1 minute), (4) Bangangan's response (40 seconds), and (5) the murder of Anna (1 minute, 30 seconds).

Given the extreme dramatic nature of the events, Bertolucci did not rely on rapid pace. Instead, he varied the shots between subjective close-ups and objective traveling shots. Only in the last sequence, the murder of Anna, did he use subjective camera movement. Bertolucci also varied foreground and background. The long shots are wide-angle shots of the fog- and snow-shrouded road through the forest. The early morning light throws shadows that are as stately as the trees of the forest. In the close-ups, Bertolucci used a telephoto lens that collapsed and blurred the context. The close-ups are interior shots in Marcello's car or in Professor Quadri and Anna's car. By varying close-ups, long shots, and point-of-view shots, Bertolucci set up a visual tension that is every bit as powerful as if he had relied on pace alone.

In the first scene in the sequence, Marcello muses about Quadri and Anna. He wishes he were not there. His driver, Bangangan, is a Fascist to the core. He has no dreams, only memories of his induction into the ideology that organizes his interior and exterior lives. The reverie of this scene was created with very lengthy takes, including a 50-second close-up of Marcello. In this shot, Bertolucci dropped the focus and slowly panned to Bangangan, also in close-up. Bertolucci avoided editing the interior car shots to create a greater sense of unity inside the car. He alternated the interiors with wide-angle objective tracking shots of the car moving through the forest. The result is a highly emotional stylization. The scene has an emotional reality but seems almost too beautiful to be real.

The next shot shifts to the interior of Quadri's car. Anna and Quadri appear in a crowded close-up. The subjective point of view shows the road ahead as Anna looks back and tells Quadri that she thinks they are being followed. He dismisses the idea. Anna's sense of the danger ahead is offset by his assurance that he sees nothing.

The scene proceeds in a very stylized manner to show their car cut off by a feigned accident in front of them and Marcello's car stopped behind them. Close-ups of each statically present the stand-off that precedes the murder. Only Quadri's insistence on seeing to the well-being of the other driver breaks the stillness. Anna asks him not to go. He finds the driver unconscious and the car locked. Anna locks her car. The static shots stretch out the sequence, which is long, at 2 minutes. This pause is emotionally tense because we see the scene through Marcello's eyes. He knows what is coming. Although the scene is more rapidly cut than the prologue, it is nevertheless slowly paced.

The murder of Quadri is cut much faster. The killers come from the woods. They are joined by the driver of the front car. The killing itself is presented as a version of the killing of Shakespeare's *Julius Caesar*. All of the killers participate. They use knives, and the death is drawn out. Because of the nature of the content, this scene is more rapidly paced than the previous scenes in this sequence.

The next scene, Anna's attempt to save herself, relies less on pace than on performance and close-ups. The pain and poignancy of Anna screaming for Marcello to save her is accentuated by their relationship and by the situation. She pulls on the door of his car, facing him, screaming for her life. His inability or unwillingness to help her represents the emotional high point of the sequence. This is Marcello's moment of truth, his opportunity for salvation, but it is not to be. Love is not great enough to overcome politics. He does not rescue her, and she runs off to her fate. The shots in this scene are held much longer than the shots of the preceding murder scene.

The next scene is short. Bangangan editorializes on his disdain for Marcello and categorizes him with every other group that the Fascists hate. This scene is not very long, but it provides an opportunity to pause between the two most powerful scenes in the sequence. It allows the audience to recover somewhat from the shock of Marcello's failure to save Anna.

The final sequence, the murder of Anna, does not rely on pace, although it is one of the most powerful scenes in the film. Instead, Bertolucci used subjective camera footage of the murderers as they chase Anna through the woods. The camera is handheld, and consequently, the action seems all the more real. The Fascists fire at her, passing the automatic pistol to one another. She is shot, falters, and then falls. The camera moves unsteadily around her bloodied body, and even after her death, it continues to circle before finally retreating from the woods with the killers. The shifts in pace in this scene have more to do with the pace of the movement itself than with the editing. That movement slows once Anna has been shot and continues at a slower pace until the end of the sequence.

This sequence uses a varied pace to carry us through a wide range of emotions. It also identifies a clear emotional role for each of the characters. In fact, Bertolucci remained very close to those roles through his use of close-ups. By varying the close-ups with objective long shots of the forest, Bertolucci added a layer of tension that supported the pace when he chose to rely on it.

This entire sequence is nine minutes long on the screen. To the extent that we are involved in the sequence, we suspend our sense of real time. In real time, the sequence might have taken five minutes or five hours. Certain parts of the sequence are given more time than might have been expected. Anna's plea for help, for example, is as long as each murder. Realistically, it would not have taken so long given the proximity of the murderers. However, Bertolucci felt that it was important to give Marcello a chance for redemption and a chance to be incapable of it. This, as much as the loss of a woman he loves, is Marcello's tragedy. The length of Anna's plea for help is thus dramatically important. Pace is affected by the importance of the scene to the film. If the scene is sufficiently important, it may be extended to suit its dramatic importance to the story.

TIME AND PLACE

Pace can help establish a sense of time and place. Examples from Stanley Kubrick's *2001: A Space Odyssey* (1968) and *Barry Lyndon* (1975) were discussed in Chapter 10. Kubrick exploited pace to the same extent in the battle for Hue in *Full Metal Jacket* (1987) (Figure 29.1) as he did in his earlier works. The pace of the sequences, the cinéma vérité camera style, the set design, and the sound create the setting of Hue, Vietnam, in 1968. The actual city was recreated on a set in England for the film. Martin Scorsese relied heavily on pace to help him create his version of New York in *Mean Streets* (1973), and George Lucas relied on music and pace to create his view of Northern California in the early 1960s in *American Graffiti* (1973).

Few filmmakers have been more effective at using pace to create a sense of time and place than Carroll Ballard was in *The Black Stallion* (1979). The first 45 minutes of the film are largely silent. The first third of the film tells the story of young Alec, who is on a ship near the coast of North Africa. The year is 1946. Alec becomes fond of a black horse on board the ship. It is an Arabian, untamed and seemingly untamable. The ship encounters bad weather, and a fire on board threatens the passengers' lives. Alec's father saves his life, and the boy saves the horse's life.

For the next 30 minutes, the scene shifts to a deserted island where the boy and the horse, seemingly the only survivors of a shipwreck, become friends, and in so doing save each other. Two primary locations are featured in this section of the film: the ship and the island. Ballard realized that he had to create both from the perspective of an inquisitive 11-year-old child. He did this with a magical realism. The images are almost otherworldly, and the editing recognizes Alec's sense of the importance of particular details about the horse, his father, and the world. He is not afraid of the world; rather, he is part of it.

Time is collapsed for all but the important events. We know that much real time has passed, and we accept the mundane details of life on the island: food, shelter, and warmth. Alec's relationship with the horse, which is carefully developed in the sequence, is detailed in an almost magical progression. The boy gains the horse's trust by offering him food and later takes him

FIGURE 29.1
Full Metal Jacket, 1987. Courtesy British Film Institute.

into the water where he gradually mounts the horse. The magical character of this part of the film is enhanced by shots of the boy and the horse from the perspective of the sandy ocean bottom. They appear as intruders, and somehow it unifies them in the context of the mysterious sea. Ballard alternated this sequence with traveling shots of the boy and the horse filmed from high above the water. The effect is to reinforce the specificity of the time and place.

THE POSSIBILITIES OF RANDOMNESS UPON PACE

One of the remarkable elements of editing is that the juxtaposition of any grouping of shots implies meaning. The pacing of those shots suggests the interpretation of that meaning. The consequence of this is seen in microcosm when a random shot or cutaway is edited into a scene: it introduces a new idea. This principle is elaborated where there are a number of random shots in a scene. If edited for effect, the combination of shots creates a meaning quite distinct from the sum of the individual parts. This shaping is, in effect, pure editing.

A specific example suggests the possibilities. Francesco Rosi's *Three Brothers* (1980) opens with an image of an artificial building—a parody of a building suitable to a dream—in the background and a group of large rats in the foreground. The rats approach the camera. The cut to the next shot, a close-up of a young man asleep, suggests that he is dreaming of the rats. The scene that follows shows that he lives and works in an institution for juveniles. Was he dreaming that his wards are rats or that the other members of society are?

The two opening shots are set into context by the scene that follows, but the juxtaposition implies potential meanings beyond the content of either shot.

In Ingmar Bergman's *Winter Light* (1962), a disillusioned minister serves a small parish. One man has lost his faith and contemplates suicide. Others want to relate to the minister, but he is unable to relate to them. Bergman used juxtapositions to detail the minister's disillusionment. A series of exterior dissolves at the end of the sermon imply his distance from the parishioners. Later, a parishioner who wants to take care of him (the minister's wife has died) has left him a letter. He reads the letter, which explains how she feels about him. Bergman cut from his reading the letter to the woman in midshot confessing her feelings. By cutting in that second shot, Bergman moved us from the minister's dispassion and indifference to the parishioner's passion. He altered the meaning of one shot by shifting to another. The shots don't necessarily provide continuity; the contradiction between the shots alters the meaning of the scene.

The films of Rosi and Bergman suggest how the juxtaposition and organization of shots can layer meaning. The pacing of the shots themselves deepens the effect of juxtaposing random shots.

NOTE/REFERENCE

1. K. Reisz, G. Millar, The Technique of Film Editing, Focal Press, Boston, 1968, pp. 233–236.

CHAPTER 30

Nonlinear Editing and Digital Technology I

Today we no longer speak of the coming technological revolution or how digital technology will transform sound, special effects, film, and video editing. The revolution is here. Our concerns in this chapter are the issues of technological revolution in film and video and its potential for aesthetic evolution.

THE TECHNOLOGICAL REVOLUTION

Film and video, the two most technology-dependent art forms of the twentieth century, have witnessed a profound acceleration in change, the shift from analog- to digital-driven technology. The implications are enormous. In preproduction, computer software is available for previsualization of scenes. Color and design opportunities—in essence, computer animation—deepen the predictability of the potential elements of an image. During production, nonlinear editing allows for rapid assemblies that provide feedback on the question: Am I making the intended dramatic point in the scene? Digital cameras will replace film- and electronic-based videotape as the originating source of the image. The digitization process allows any part of the image to be withdrawn, an additional element to be added if necessary. In postproduction, it is possible for the editor to consolidate in his role, sound editing, picture editing, sound mixing, special effects, and printing, at least if the release form is videotape. The editor could also write and input the music track using her nonlinear editing system! The degree of consolidation that is possible is probably not wise for one person to undertake, but the critical point is that the digital revolution makes it possible.

Digital opportunities include delivery systems (films will be beamed digitally over fiber optic lines to theatres, thus bypassing standard projection systems) and the interface between entertainment, education, and economics (they can meet on the Internet). Movies will be available on demand (satellite or phone line) and editing will occur between client and producer on the Internet rather than in an office in Los Angeles or New York. The means to produce quality visual stories will drop, democratizing the cost of production. Who will dominate this system, if anyone, remains to be seen. Web sites may become the Cannes Film Festival marketplaces of tomorrow. All this is possible because of the digital revolution.

391

The Technique of Film and Video Editing: History, Theory, and Practice. DOI: 10.1016/B978-0-240-81397-4.00030-3

The Limits of Technology

The best place to begin is to state the obvious—that a computer-driven editing machine such as an Avid or Lightworks station, no matter how sophisticated, cannot make the creative decision of where to cut and why. The decisions for continuity or dramatic emphasis are creative—aesthetic, if you wish—choices. They are made by the editor or by the editor with the director or producer. The speed of computer-assisted editing will enable creative decisions to be arrived at more quickly than earlier editing technology, but it will not make the creative decisions. Here then lie a number of fallacies about nonlinear editing.

A second issue that devolves from the new technology is that it will yield new forms of storytelling, new levels of interactivity, and a more democratic relationship between storyteller (film- or videomaker) and audience. Although much progress has been made in video games, and on the CD entertainment and education fronts, for the most part that work to date has not been particularly interesting nor creative. It has been game-oriented and youth-oriented. This may change, but the promise of interactivity has yet to be fulfilled.

On the other hand, just as the invention of the printing press did not necessarily lead to a proportional increase in writers, but rather to a spread in ancillary effects—secularization, rationality, and democratization via communication—so the result of the digital revolution is the growth of the Internet and its impact on communication, democratization, and, hopefully, rationality. These changes may or may not have an impact on storytelling.

On a more positive note, there is no question that nonlinear editing and digital technology will have positive effects on the editing process and on the outcome of that process, the screen story. In technical terms, time is money, and the speed of nonlinear systems should have a positive impact on postproduction budgets. So too will the capacity for the editor to build up his own tracks and mix them down on his nonlinear systems. The capacity to work in a more complex way with sound and picture can only help the postproduction process and budget. Digital technology also helps in the creation of special effects. The famous shots of Gary Sinise legless in the second half of *Forrest Gump* (1994) were produced in a digitized set of images reconstituted frame by frame to eliminate his legs from each frame. Equally possible today is the removal of any portion, small or large, of the image. This same technology can be used in film or sound restoration as well.

The Aesthetic Opportunities

To begin to understand the aesthetic opportunities of the nonlinear digital age, we should begin by stating that, to date, interactive technology has had a more profound impact on video games and on making available art and photographs for specific educational goals than upon mainstream film and video. Consequently, its impact has been relegated to special effects and animation. That is not to say that these special effects in *Terminator 2: Judgment Day* (1991) or in *Jurassic Park* (1993) were not spectacular in aiding the dynamism and credibility of the story. What it does mean, however, is that those stories, *Terminator 2* and *Jurassic Park*, remained conventional screen stories, neither challenging old forms nor old ideas. The special effects simply made the films more sensational for their audiences.

Are there aesthetic opportunities in the digital technologies? Yes and no. Certainly the capacity to tell stories of which the scale or expanse was not previously possible could add to the range of filmic experience. Stories such as Dostoyevsky's *Crime and Punishment* and Coetzee's *Foe* might focus on the interior life of the characters, thereby bringing two wonderful psychological novels to film in the richest manner rather than as plotted narratives flattened by the current conventions of filmic narrative. There are far less aesthetic opportunities where linearity as a dramatic shaping device dominates. And because the linear story, the plot-driven story, today reigns supreme, the likelihood is that digital technology will be used in support of linear tales rather than to subvert or emend the narrative conventions of today.

THE NONLINEAR NARRATIVE

Nonlinear storytelling has been a factor at least since Luis Buñuel's *Un Chien d'Andalou* (1929). Although unusual and the exception to the rule, it is by no means unimportant, as a film such as Orson Welles's *Citizen Kane* (1941) attests. However, to understand the notion of nonlinearity, it is important to first define the linear narrative.

One feature of the linear narrative is its reliance on plot and upon our involvement with the main character. A second, equally important feature of the linear narrative is its dramatic shape. Whether one describes that shape as restorative three-act structure[1] or as the marriage of goal-directed characters and resolution-oriented plotting, the outcome is the same, a linear narrative arc. This linearity transcends story form and links film and video narratives to the Aristotelian equivalents in theatre and in the novel.

The consequence of the linear narrative is the fulfillment of a particular style of experience for an audience. In spite of surprising twists and turns in the plot, the audience knows at the outset the kind of resolution to anticipate. It in essence expects and experiences a predetermined outcome that we associate with linear narrative. That is not to say that linear narrative is boring or blasé; often it is exciting and satisfying. But it is always satisfying within predictable parameters.

The nonlinear narrative may not have a resolution; it may not have a single character with whom to empathize and identify; it may not have characters who are goal-directed; and it may not have a dramatic shape driving toward resolution. Consequently, the nonlinear narrative is not predictable. And here lies its great aesthetic potential: Because of that unpredictability, it may provide an audience with a new, unexpected experience. This is the potential aesthetic upshot of nonlinearity—new, unpredictable experiences. This will never happen, however, if nonlinearity remains a technological fact rather than a philosophical and aesthetic attitude.

Past Reliance on Linearity

In the period in which film and video narratives were popular cultural forms intended for the largest mass audiences on an international as well as national level, linearity as a narrative principle was critical. The codes of linear narrative—the goal-directed main character, the antagonist so superior in his countergoal as to make a hero of the main character, the linear plot veering from point to counterpoint with an accelerating speed, and, of course, the inevitable resolution that justified all that had proceeded it—are portable, moving from one story to another, transported form one country to another, and from one medium to another. This is the system of storytelling that is necessary in a period of mass audiences.

But what happens when the audience fractures? What happens when there are films and videos produced for particular age groups, interest groups, gender groups, educationally leveled groups, corporate culture groups, media-suspicious groups? In the digital age, with many channels (more than 500), the audience will fragment into a large number of specialty audiences. Under these circumstances, modes of storytelling also can be modified to take into account the patterns of desire, thought, and belief of these subgroups. In this new environment, the opportunity to move away form linear narrative and to experiment with narrative styles is simply a fact of the digital age. If the makers don't experiment with new styles, they may find the audiences taking the means of production into their own hands. The accessibility of the means of production in the digital age will force filmmakers to reach out and to define those means with their audience. This very impulse lies at the heart of the success of Quentin Tarantino, Mary Harron, and Spike Lee. They have fashioned a style that helps them define and communicate with their audience.

Linearity served its purpose. It will not disappear, but nonlinearity will now assert itself more aggressively. The digital age demands new narrative styles for the new but fragmented audience of the age.

A Philosophy of Nonlinearity

Perhaps the most useful way to suggest a philosophy on nonlinearity is to begin with an operating principle related to expectations. Just as nonlinear editing has been called random-access editing, sourcing shots, scenes, and sounds on an as-needed basis, we can view the narrative style of the nonlinear narrative as having an equally random quality. A does not follow B; cause is not followed by effect. The result is an altered narrative shape sufficiently unpredictable as to create a spontaneity or artifice that alters meaning.

A second characteristic of nonlinearity is the use of opposites to propose the different narrative shape. Opposites, because of their nonfluid relationship to what had proceeded them, undermine expectations. The opposite may be used as a counterpoint, clearly related to its predecessor, or may in fact be more random.

A third characteristic of nonlinearity is the break from character identification. This may be achieved through the use of an ironic character. It may be achieved through the focus on a place or event rather than the experience of the character. It may be achieved by overbuilding the secondary characters at the price of the main character.

A final characteristic is the replacement of linear plot by elevated incident, set-pieces over developmental narrative, feeling-state scenes over expository scenes. This approach undermines the notion of plot and of main character-driven narrative.

The nonlinear narrative is intuitive rather than purposeful, random rather than developmental, and emphasizes feeling over action. When added to a group of characters, the nonlinear narrative embraces politics over psychology and aesthetics over ethics. The experience of the nonlinear narrative is also less susceptible to the gestalt of Aristotelian dramatic principles.

The Artists of Nonlinear Narrative

The contributions of Porter, Griffith, and Vidor to the history and practice of film editing are a series of editing choices that underpinned linear narratives—the close-up to articulate clearly the goal of the main character, a cutaway to provide an analogy for what the character was thinking about, and pace to provide an emotional rhythm for the clash of the main character's goal with the barriers to that goal. All these choices, including extreme long shots, camera placement, and camera movement, provided the code for the linear narrative.

It was the work of the Russian Revolutionary filmmakers, particularly Eisenstein, Pudovkin, and Dovshenko, that clarified the nonlinear possibilities. Images could be juxtaposed and, although random, the juxtaposition and sometimes the clash of images created new ideas and perceptions of narrative. The presence of nature—flowers, apples, cows—acts as a counterweight to the death of a patriarch in Dovshenko's *Earth* (1930); the playful camera/eye of the cinematographer as a character in Vertov's *The Man with a Movie Camera* (1929); and Eisenstein's stylized executions near the beginning of *Alexander Nevsky* (1938)—the casual introduction of the character Nevsky acts as a visual counterpoint to those executions. Each example illustrates how thinking in terms of juxtaposition opens up the story to new interpretations. The result is greater than the parts (shots) in each case.

Perhaps no filmmaker took this principle of nonlinearity as far as Luis Buñuel, who in his work with Salvador Dali set as his primary goal to destroy linear narrative and the restorative resolution it implies. There is no peace of mind for the audience when they view *Un Chien d'Andalou*. There is only the unpredictable sense while watching the film that anything can happen next. Whether Buñuel wishes to launch an attack on the Parisian bourgeoisie or to create an anarchy of experience, his images of sexuality, death, and horror are provocative and unforgettable. The totality of the experience of *Un Chien d'Andalou* is a true nonlinear experience. There had been vestiges of such an experience in Eisenstein's *Strike* (1924) and in Dovshenko's *Earth*, but no film experience was as devoted to a nonlinear experience as Buñuel's film. He was to continue this pattern of narrative experience through *Belle de Jour* (1967) and *The Discreet Charm of the Bourgeoisie* (1972).

Other filmmakers have digressed from linear narrative: the Shakespeare performance sequence in Ford's *My Darling Clementine* (1946), the closing sequence in Antonioni's *L'Eclisse* (*The Eclipse*) (1962), the introduction of a second but different story and genre in Woody Allen's *Crimes and Misdemeanors* (1989). More often when the intention was a nonlinear narrative, filmmakers have found an orderly approach to the issue—the multiple narrators in Welles's *Citizen Kane* and Kurosawa's *Rashomon* (1951), or the overreliance on rituals and time in Davies's *Distant Voices, Still Lives* (1988). In the evolution of nonlinear narrative, however, few filmmakers have been as bold as Humphrey Jennings.

In his documentary *Listen to Britain* (1942) (see Chapter 25), Jennings achieves a remarkable film that is notably nonlinear. A war documentary that emphasizes the survival capacity of the British Isles against the Axis threat, would, in a linear narrative, highlight the Battle of Britain, focus on a single character or place at a particular time, or use a political figure such as Winston Churchill as the unifying voice. Jennings does none of these. Instead, he uses music—orchestral, dance hall, pianists, guitar-strumming soldiers—to unify the film. Music is not warlike, but it does create a counterpoint sound and idea in the light of the sights and sounds of war.

Jennings sidesteps the single character, but shows many characters at work and at leisure. Again, the counterpoint is to people at work for war and people at leisure from war. Jennings creates an attitude rather than an act, and the consequences are powerful and moving.

Another dimension of his nonlinear approach is that he moves geographically from place to place, from time to time, in a random fashion. There is no obvious cause and effect here. Instead, the geography, whether urban or rural, is a unity rather than a specific place. Trafalgar Square is as important as a beach looking out to the English Channel and the North Sea. Time is managed rather than being viewed as a dramatic end game of fighting the war. The cause-and-effect relationship between time, place, and history is sidestepped, undermined, and thus Jennings can step away from the actual event and present an attitude that, in the end, will persevere and assure Great Britain's allies that she will triumph. The result of Jennings nonlinear approach to the subject is a film as fresh and innovative today as it was in 1942.

The next figure that is critical in nonlinear narrative is Jean-Luc Godard. Although others in the New Wave were interested in genre subversion (François Truffaut in *Shoot the Piano Player*, 1962) and expansion of the interplay between the past and the present and how memory defines one and redefines the other (Alain Resnais in *Last Year at Marienbad*, 1961), no one was as radical about narrative as Jean-Luc Godard.

Whether using essay as a formal structure (*Two or Three Things I Know About Her*, 1966), or a polemic (*La Chinoise*, 1967), or a musical (*Tout Va Bien*, 1970), Godard would always subvert that narrative invention with another. The result was to move us away from character toward ideas. His overriding concern with the journey in *Weekend* (1967) is subverted by his shifts in time from one place to another, leading us to question meaning in the film. An early scene, the leave-taking on the journey, is a farce; a middle scene, the Leonard character, meditates on history, academia, and the future; in a late scene, a husband in the traditional family considered the breadwinner is actually consumed by his wife—he is "bread" rather than the breadwinner. These radical shifts take us away from the literal meaning of content (so often the core of the linear narrative) toward a experimental, almost explosive, set of new narrative ideas. As with nonlinear narratives already highlighted, the key to this new perception is to undermine the relationship between the audience and the main character. The jump cut, the overuse of the long shot, and the long take underscore our distance from the character.

In Great Britain, Lindsay Anderson (*O Lucky Man!*, 1973) was the greatest proponent of a nonlinear style. His use of music interludes as well as outrageous set-pieces moving away from the narrative action line highlighted an anarchistic style that was in part nonlinear. In Germany, Wim Wenders (*The Goalie's Anxiety at the Penalty Kick*, 1971; *Alice in the Cities*, 1974) best exemplify the nonlinear impulse. In the former Yugoslavia, Dusan Makavejev fuses documentary and drama, psychology and politics in *WR: Mysteries of the Organism* (1971), creating a disorderly portrayal of the life and ideas of Wilhelm Reich. Here too the nonlinear overwhelms the linear.

But in order to see the nonlinear aesthetic fully flower, we have to move beyond the experiments and flirtations of Arthur Penn (*Little Big Man*, 1970), Peter Brook (*Marat/Sade*, 1966), and Nicholas Roeg (*Don't Look Now*, 1973). When we approach the recent work of Quentin Tarantino (*Pulp Fiction*, 1994), Milcho Manchevski (*Before the Rain*, 1994), and François Girard (*Thirty-two Short Films about Glen Gould*, 1993), we see the nonlinear aesthetic in full bloom. Single character–driven stories are abandoned in both *Pulp Fiction* and *Before the Rain*. Although *Pulp Fiction* has a series of main characters who are criminals wrestling with an ethical question or problem, the affiliation of main characters in Manchevski's film are much looser. All are Macedonian and all are in love, but there the similarity ends. Age, education, geography all differentiate the characters from one another. In both cases, the multiple characters undermine the opportunity for identification. Although *Thirty-two Short Films about Glen Gould* clearly has a single main character, that character is posing in each film in such a way as to preclude identification. He distances himself from us and so no ongoing identification is possible.

A second dimension of these films is that the dramatic shape is subverted. In *Pulp Fiction*, we expect the gangster story to proceed according to tradition—crime, rise, fall—but this doesn't happen. The crime section is undermined by a debate between the two main characters—Travolta and Jackson. The extent of the discussion/debate, its philosophical nature, undermines any developing sense of anxiety related to what these men are going to do—kill people. Similarly, the dramatic arc of each story in *Before the Rain*—tales of intrareligious conflict—is undermined by a love story or the aftermath of a love relationship. This introjection of a relationship into a tense and probably violent conflict between Muslims and Christians is a counterpoint that actually makes more powerful the final outcome of each of the stories.

A third dimension of these films is that each scrupulously avoids a cause-and-effect relationship in their stories. In both *Pulp Fiction* and *Before the Rain*, the time line is violated. In *Pulp Fiction*, we join the story in midstream and return to the same point later in the narrative. In *Before the Rain*, we begin in one story only to rejoin the late phase of that story at the end of the third narrative. In both cases, we did not know this until a visual cue, or repetition, presents the return to the earlier time to us.

In *Thirty-two Short Films about Glen Gould*, we loosely follow a standard linear chronology of Gould's life, but the prologue and the epilogue may be a vision of Gould in a kind of Arctic heaven, speaking to himself and, in his fashion, to us, or it may be a metaphor for his status as visionary vis-à-vis the rest of us. In either case, these scenes frame the film in a way that subverts the chronological line of his life and of the organization of the films about his life. This nonlinear approach is deepened by using documentary films, abstract films, and dramatized narratives. The mix of styles further subverts the time line and any remaining linearity. Radical shifts in tone between the absurd and the studied or formal also act as a counterpoint to our impulse to organize the material so we can understand it in a linear fashion.

This latter brings us to the final dimension of nonlinearity—feeling overexposition. In these very abbreviated insights into Glen Gould, the filmmaker goes with a feeling—his perfectionism in the playing of a record in his hotel room in Germany, his eccentricity in the film about the truck stop. What Gould hears illustrates the extent that he tuned out of the kind of observation we associate with such a casual experience (eating breakfast at a diner). When the most obvious becomes surprising, when a recording session isn't about the recording but rather the sense of ecstasy of the artist, we, the viewers, face a different kind of experience. This is the true possibility of the nonlinear revolution, the opportunity to give us a new, surprising experience.

Godard, Tarantino, and Manchevski understand that to do so means not only creative risk, but the subversion of the linear expectation of the audience. But just as the more media-experienced audiences grow, the opportunity of accessing specialty audiences via satellite and multichannel television will encourage filmmakers to continue to experiment with new narrative styles to reach them. Here lies the true potential for a nonlinear aesthetic. The future is here. The technology is available. Filmmakers need only take the risk.

NOTE/REFERENCE

1. K. Dancyger, J. Rush, Alternative Scriptwriting, second ed., Focal Press, Boston, 1995 (Chapters 2, 3, and 4).

CHAPTER 31

Nonlinear Editing and Digital Technology II

In the last chapter, I introduced the notion that there is a tradition of nonlinear storytelling and that the technological shift to nonlinear editing has accelerated the consideration that this alternative approach to story is a viable option. As an option, however, it proceeds differently regarding shot selection and pace principally because the audience no longer experiences the narrative through a single main character; nor is the audience following the experience of that character from crisis to resolution.[1] Indeed, we may be following multiple main characters, and there may or may not be a resolution. The conventional story arc, with its implications for editing, may simply not be relevant in the nonlinear narrative.

In order to understand the different editing choices made in nonlinear narratives, we will look at four nonlinear films. To explore those choices in detail and to highlight their differences from the classic narrative, we will use the following framework.

THE FRAMEWORK

If there is no main character, no resolution, what are the goals of the editing of the nonlinear film? The first goal must be to assure that the narrative coheres, that it holds together. Each of the narrative tools of character, structure, genre, and tone may be used, but it is structure that is most critical in a macro sense.[2] The structural option most directly applicable to the nonlinear film is a shaping device. The murderous career of Mickey and Mallory is the shaping device in *Natural Born Killers* (1994); the battle for Guadalcanal is the shaping device of *The Thin Red Line* (1998); identity crises are the shaping device in *Pulp Fiction* (1994); an Atlantic island off of Georgia is the geographical shaping device and the day of migration is the temporal shaping device in *Daughters of the Dust* (1991). Whether the shaping device is an event, a place, a time, that device is the most general structural tool that helps the narrative cohere.

The second macro device is the voice of the filmmaker. As we saw in Chapter 1, Buñuel's narrative goal was to subvert narrative, and this dialectic highlighted his voice. Godard undermined the narrative to interject his political views through the narrative. The Coen brothers use irony to loosen us from our genre expectations in their work. Voice is the second important device that makes clear how we should experience the nonlinear narrative.

The Technique of Film and Video Editing: History, Theory, and Practice. DOI: 10.1016/B978-0-240-81397-4.00031-5

On a more detailed or micro level, the nonlinear filmmaker has to concern himself with the issue of energy. Every narrative, linear or nonlinear, must engage the audience in an energetic experience. In the linear narrative, this is far easier. The goal-directedness of the main character, the barrier of the antagonist, and the barrier of plot provides a structure that keeps the dramatic arc moving from the critical moment of entry into the narrative and on to the culmination and resolution of the narrative. Each device implies the critical role that pace and camera movement and placement will play in energizing the narrative. The filmmaker and editor know that the close-up punctuates the most important events of the narrative.

Because the filmmaker has opted for a nonlinear narrative does not mean she can sidestep the energy issue. What is removed from the narrative approach must be compensated for elsewhere, as an example will illustrate. The gangster film gains enormous energy from its plot: the rise and fall of the main character, the gangster. The gangster's career is in essence the plot of the film. In *Pulp Fiction*, however, which is a nonlinear narrative, the first thing we notice is that it has very little plot. In fact, the major plot is concentrated in the second of three stories that make up the narrative. Those stories occur out of chronological order, thereby taking temporal momentum out of the structural mix as a potential source of energy. Instead, the energy in *Pulp Fiction* comes from its dialog, from the conflictual and conflicted nature of the characters. It also comes from considerable camera movement. It does not come from the traditional narrative source, the plot.

Filmmakers must replace the energy that would be more easily generated in the linear narrative. Here is an important role for the filmmaker and editor in the nonlinear edit—to find new sources to energize the narrative. The issue for us then is to look for and to highlight those macro and micro editing strategies that make the nonlinear film connect with its audience. We turn now to our case studies.

THE CASE OF *THE ICE STORM*

Ang Lee's *The Ice Storm* (1997) takes place in upper-middle-class suburban Connecticut. The time is 1974, just prior to Nixon's resignation. The narrative focuses on two families, the Hoods and the Carvers. Both have two teenaged children. The families are dysfunctional, in the sense that no one seems to be able to help one another. Consequently, Ben Hood and Janie Carver are having an affair; their children Wendy Hood and Mikey Carver are trying to echo their "parental units." The others in the couples, Helena Hood and Jim Carver, fluctuate between depression and a search for escape—into spirituality, into work, anywhere except the battleground of family life.

The other children, Paul Hood and Sandy Carver, also look for escape—into violent fantasies, in the case of Sandy. Paul Hood makes do with sexual fantasies. Sexuality as currency ties all these characters to one another: sexuality as power, as a weapon, as compensation for the sense of loss or failure, is felt by each of these characters.

The ice storm of the title refers to the storm that takes place in the last third of the narrative. The event is a natural expression of the despair of these characters. Because of the storm, an electrical wire fractures and kills Mikey Carver. But his death is as much a result of emotional neglect. He is out of it and does seem drugged out, but Mikey suffers from parents who can't help him or satisfy themselves and consequently they are disconnected from the lives of their children. Mikey is a casualty of materially rich, spiritually despairing America. His death punctuates a narrative filled with desperation and unhappiness. In this sense, the sexual arc that runs through the narrative is compensatory rather than empowering its characters. In terms of shaping devices, Ang Lee relies on one critical week in the life of the characters. It is significant that the week includes Thanksgiving, the most meaningful secular family holiday. The narrative focuses on how separate the members of two families can be, and the shaping event implies the opposite—togetherness. The dramatic conflict that runs through the narrative is generated out of this ironic paradox.

The second shaping device is to focus on two families, both with socioeconomic goals and status in common. They both have two teenagers, and they both are tied to each other by adultery and desire. Both families also have one parent who is aggressive and the other who is intelligent and marginalized within the family.

The third shaping device is behavioral. The characters all are upstanding members of the community, but all become transgressive in their behavior. The most obvious transgressors are Ben Hood and Janie Carver. Both are involved in adultery. They are not alone—the concluding social event in the film is a neighborhood post-Thanksgiving party. The focus of the party is organized adultery: a key-swapping lottery for a new partner for the night. But adultery isn't the only transgression. Early in the narrative Wendy Hood steals cosmetics from the local pharmacy. Later her mother, Helena, does the same and is caught. Sandy Carver indulges in violence, blowing up his toys and fantasizing about blowing up his teacher and classmates. Even the innocent Paul Hood drugs a friend to eliminate a sexual rival. Transgression unites these characters as much as their unhappiness and socioeconomic status.

In terms of voice, Ang Lee is both genre specific and distinctly authorial in *The Ice Storm*. The dysfunctional American family was the subject of two satires that followed Lee's film, *Happiness* (1998) and *American Beauty* (1999). Lee, on the other hand, opted to treat *The Ice Storm* as melodrama.

All eight characters in *The Ice Storm* are treated as the main character in a melodrama would be treated: as a powerless person attempting to secure power from an intractable power structure. As a result, Lee invites us to empathize at one point or another with each of these characters. Even in the most extreme cases, Janie and Sandy Carver, Lee gently pokes fun at them, but not so much that we can't see their pain. To feel their pain is to be with them. The other characters are easier to relate to, and they too display their vulnerability to us. Consequently, the dominant tone of *The Ice Storm* is realistic, and we are invited to care about each of these characters. I have written elsewhere about Ang Lee's capacity to be inclusive of characters who too often occupy the margins of society or whose actions justify our contempt.[3] This sense of inclusiveness is the voice of Ang Lee.

The issue from an editing point of view is how that voice is established. The most direct path to inclusiveness is to care about the characters. Aside from the content of the shot—we do see Ben Hood totally break down in tears near the end of the film—the issue is the use of close-ups. Lee does not go overboard in his use of close-ups, but he does use them strategically. When he wants to tell us that Sandy is sexually aroused by Wendy he uses a close-up and a point-of-view shot. The two are performing in the high school band, but the shot is of Sandy looking not at the conductor but rather at Wendy's exposed underwear, which is visible as he looks down at her (she is seated to play her instrument while he stands to play his). When Lee wants us to feel for the characters, he resorts to a close-up. When the agitated Sandy is confused and overwhelmed by the straightforward Wendy's exhibitionist sexual proposal, Lee simply holds on Sandy's face as desire turns to terror and confusion and anger. We understand Sandy and feel his emotional confusion. It would have been far easier to treat Sandy broadly and stereotypically as an unprepared teenager. Lee instead opts to stand with Sandy rather than against him. Consequently, we stand with him as well. This is a pattern Ang Lee follows with all the characters.

Lee also uses context to tell us more about the characters and their feeling states. When Helena Hood is stealing from the pharmacy, we see in the security mirror above her the reflection of the pharmacist observing her while she perpetrates the theft. When Wendy Hood steals, an older woman glares at her implying that she will be caught, but Wendy glares right back, ignoring the guilt implicit in her earlier actions. By providing a social context, Lee suggests that these characters are not isolated from their society. They are simply transgressive, regardless of the views of society. Context also provides clues to the aspirations of the characters. When Helena bumps into Reverend Phillip Edwards, a man clearly interested in her as a woman, they chat over books that are being sold in the foreground, but in the background the community church looms. Helena's search for spiritual values is highlighted, as much as her quest for freedom is highlighted by the open road before her and behind her as she rides her bike in search of the feeling of freedom she associates with her daughter more than with her own desires.

Ang Lee also uses deep focus or contextual shots to suggest power. The closer he places the camera to a character, the more powerful they are. The image of Janie Carver, foregrounded in bed with Ben Hood in the background, implies who has the power in this relationship. So too in the case of the relationship of children to adults. Very often the adults are foregrounded with the children in the background. When Lee wants to render a character even more powerless, the camera is placed farther from the character. In the last shot, the Hood family is waiting for Paul Hood to get off the train. They, the adults and Wendy, are on the same plane, and the camera is far from them. The parents here are virtually equivalent to the children in their powerlessness, in their inability to help one another. The voice of Ang Lee is clear and powerful in the choice of these visuals.

As to the issue of energy, Lee uses a dual strategy to create energy in *The Ice Storm*. As mentioned earlier, he has adopted as one strategy the genre of melodrama. This realist approach, however, is broken intermittently by irony—an exaggeration strategy that breaks away from a connection with the characters. A scene between Ben Hood and Janie Carver makes the point. The couple has made love and Ben speaks obsessively about his antagonism toward a colleague at work, a colleague who is besting him on the golf course. Whether this is an expression of Ben's more general aggressiveness or insecurity about the implications of a rival in the workplace, Janie's response is boredom. She tells him she already has a husband, implying the boredom of the state of marriage. The aggressive humor puts Ben in his place, and for that instant the two characters are joyless adulterers. Although we quickly move back into realist mode, and consequently an engagement with the characters, this tonal shift unsettles as well as energizes our experience of the narrative. Similar scenes are initiated with Paul Hood, Sandy Carver, and the friends and colleagues of the Hoods and the Carvers.

A second strategy Lee uses to generate energy in the narrative is more expected. He places the camera close to the characters. His use of deep focus assures a context for the actions of these characters, and he uses point of view to create energy, as well as cutaways and strategic close-ups. A good example is the scene where Paul drugs his sexual rival for Libitz, the girl of his dreams. There they are in her empty apartment, but the plan goes awry when Libitz also drinks a drugged drink. Rather than the night on the town that Paul expected, he ends up with Libitz asleep in his lap. The desirable goal looks promising, even visually; the only problem is that she is asleep. Thwarted by his own clever plan, Paul ends up as he began, alone.

THE CASE OF *HAPPINESS*

Todd Solondz's *Happiness* (1998) is a portrait of a suburban family, the Jordans. The story focuses on the parents, Mona and Lenny Jordan; their adult daughters, Joy, Helen, and Trish; Bill Maplewood, a psychiatrist and the husband of Trish Jordan; Billy, the son of Bill and Trish Maplewood; Andy, Joy's boyfriend; and Allen, a patient of Bill Maplewood. The prism for the narratives is relationships—love relationships, relationships of desire, parent–child relationships, and sibling relationships. The experience of the film suggests the irony of the title: The relationships are doomed by the self-absorption of the participants and by the imbalance between the pleasure and pain principles as they operate in the lives of these characters. In other words, this is a deeply neurotic set of characters.

The film is structured initially as a number of set-pieces fluctuating between the obsessive goal of one of the characters and the indifference of the character to whom they look for help. In the second half of the film, the momentum of three sexual obsessions is the focus: the lust of Joy, Bill, and Allen. In each case the relationship is transgressive. Joy has an affair with a married Russian cabbie, a student in the English-as-a-second-language class she teaches. Bill pines for Johnny, his 11-year-old son Billy's friend. In fact, Bill drugs and rapes the boy. And Allen is obsessed with Helen. When she responds positively to his obscene phone call, he is frightened into the arms of an obese neighbor, Kristina, who has in turn murdered and mutilated the building's doorman for attempting to rape her. At best the relationships are exploitative, and in the case of the child rape at the hands of a pedophile psychiatrist, the result is obscene and abusive. Ironically, this is the relationship that Solondz treats with the greatest empathy.

The narrative as I've described it doesn't fully capture the shaping devices Solondz relies upon to pull this nonlinear story together. The primary shaping device is to follow the course of a number of sexual relationships. We don't enter those relationships at the same point. Where they are more conventional relationships, a marriage or a male–female relationship of equals, we see only a fragment of the relationship and the emphasis is on its failure.

A second shaping device is to look at power relationships: a parent–child relationship, a therapist–patient relationship, and a teacher–student relationship. In each case, the more powerful character crosses the line, thereby exploiting the relationship.

A third shaping device is the tone that assumes the ironic position so often associated with satire. This tone permeates character, dialog, and narrative structure.

Although I have addressed the issue of voice elsewhere in my work, it requires elucidation in this chapter as well. Todd Solondz exhibits a very distinctive voice in *Happiness*.[4] He is ironic and humorous about the Jordan sisters. The sister most likely to fail, Joy, is the character who dominates screen time. The other sisters, Trish and Helen, have what might appear to be privileged lives. Trish has a husband and a family, and Helen has beauty and job success. But their surface successes belie a husband who is a pedophile and, in Helen's case, a dangerous promiscuity that implies failure rather than success. Both Trish and Helen are treated ironically; only Joy is allowed to become real for the audience. She has ironic moments—the relationship breakup with Andy, for example, or the kitchen conversation with Trish about happiness—but eventually Solondz relents and allows Joy moments of deep feeling—her created song, "Happiness," and her sexual relationship with the cabbie are both treated with real feeling.

The same can be said for the male characters. Allen, the patient, is excessive and ironic, and although the treatment of Bill the psychiatrist may be ironic, the treatment of Bill as father and as sexual predator is treated more realistically. These shifts in tonal expectations imply that irony and empathy can coexist in the same narrative. Surprise and satire are both narrative goals for Solondz, and both go to the heart of his voice in the narrative. He heaps scorn on conventional people and on conventional behavior, but his empathy for the outsider is constant, and that empathy can be generated from the behavior of a character or from a group reaction to the behavior of a character.

The fact that Solondz uses sexuality as the currency for relationships as well as an expression of power that allows us to assess the behavior of a character only intensifies our response. By viewing Bill and Andy as sexual predators, and by viewing Kristina and Helen as castrating females, Solondz is demythologizing the notion of romantic love and bringing relationships down to the level of rough sex and abusive exploitation. But this does not dim the desire of any of these characters; rather it creates a self-absorbed context that sets up a new paradigm— sex without love, love of self over love between two individuals, and finally instant gratification over a lasting commitment to a relationship. This is the destination to which Solondz's narrative and voice take us.

A great deal of energy is generated in the narrative in the conflictual shifts in tone from irony to empathy. Although Solondz sidesteps pace, using classic editing strategies such as faster pace to generate energy, he does shift from one character to another. As an episode ends with Joy and Trish, for example, another begins with Bill and his son Billy. The dissonance between scenes generates a sense of narrative conflict. Within each scene, another level of conflict is generated. In the scene between Trish and Joy, the conflict is sibling rivalry focused on Joy's unhappy state. In the next scene, the conflict emanates from Billy's state of sexual ignorance. As he punishes himself for that ignorance, his father, Bill, tries to assure him that all will be well. Bill, a psychiatrist, plays sexual scientist and plies his son with information. All the while we know Bill to be a sexual predator, and his questions to his son take on a distinct ironic edge. Although the focal point of the energy in these scenes is the dialog, the complication of the subtext for one character in each scene raises the meaning of the dialog and the conflict level. The energy that is usually generated from pace is nevertheless a powerful dimension of these scenes; only the source of that energy differs.

Solondz also uses the contrast of fantasy and reality to energize *Happiness*. Allen's verbal sexual fantasies, which are aggressive and abusive, give way to his telephone search for Helen. When he eventually finds she is his neighbor, he is petrified by her positive response to his abuse. Her sadomasochistic disposition, in fact, meshes well with his sadomasochistic fantasies. But the reality is too much for him. He cannot succeed with the reality of Helen and he retreats to the less threatening Kristina.

Allen's psychiatrist, Bill, also has destructive fantasies, such as a walk through Central Park with an M16. His violent fantasies have many victims but a positive dimension—at least he doesn't kill himself. Here too, the mix of fantasy and reality generates energy in the narrative.

Finally, the inclusion of the MTV style yields considerable energy. In the opening scene of Joy and Andy in a restaurant, for example, he proposes marriage, but she then rejects his proposal, which in turn leads him not to offer her the friendship gift he would have given to the woman who loves him—all of which is presented with the quality of a TV sitcom being filmed before a live audience. There are few shots, but the lengthy sequence is the story of an entire relationship. In intention, the scene is reminiscent of the breakfast scene in *Citizen Kane*: an entire relationship of five years is spun out in five minutes. And in its flat TV style, filmed as if the viewer sat in a live audience in front of the two characters, the scene has an intensity and a feeling level that isn't shared by what follows. It is in effect an MTV movie unto itself.

This MTV pattern, which Solondz follows in the first half of the film, gives each scene a powerful intensity. The MTV style generates the energy that ordinarily proceeds via identification with the main character in a linear story.

THE CASE OF *THE THIN RED LINE*

Terry Malick's *The Thin Red Line* (1998) is a war film about the battle for Guadalcanal. War films, whether they focus on a battle, a war, or a patrol that is a minor piece of a war, have a beginning, middle, and end. The end or resolution addresses whether the main character survived or did not. The tone of such films usually varies, ranging from patriotic films such as

Guadalcanal Diary (1942) to the antiwar polemic of films such as *Too Late the Hero* (1970), a Pacific war film made while the United States was fighting the war in Vietnam. Forty-five years after the event, Malick's film is quite different from either of these extremes. In addition, rather than having a beginning, middle, and end, it is nonlinear in its presentation.

The film's nonlinearity is defined by its conscious attempt to sidestep linear structure. If the film were linear it would follow a land-on-the-island, battle-for-the-island, and win-the-island structure. Instead, Malick opens the film on a soldier, Private Witt, who has gone AWOL to another Pacific island. There he and a few army friends collude with the natives. They try to be part of the native community as opposed to that of the U.S. soldiers. When they are taken by U.S. forces, we have no idea how much time passes before they are shipped to Guadalcanal. Certainly this soldier's outfit is shipped to Guadalcanal for the upcoming conflict. His sergeant, Ed Welsh, reluctantly takes him back into the company. From here the narrative progresses not on a time line but rather through a series of incidents: the landing; the first encounter with the enemy; the struggle to take an enemy bunker high atop the American position; the departure from the battlefield; the capture of a native village occupied by the Japanese; a patrol on which Private Witt sacrifices his life to save his patrol. But these incidents focus on the inner thoughts of a variety of soldiers in the company as well as their behavior. It's as if these inner thoughts create the private world of these characters. Rather than deal with the battle and the camaraderie that battle forges, their inner thoughts fragment the sense that the company is a unit. Instead, it becomes a collection of individuals with distinct and differing goals.

Colonel Gordon Tall, who commands the company, is concerned only with the injustice of having commanding officers who are younger than he. For him the battle is an opportunity to secure the promotion that for too long has eluded him. Captain Staros, who answers to the colonel, is totally different. He is consumed by guilt and responsibility toward his men and their well-being. Captain Gaff, who is also responsible to the colonel, is not racked by anything but doing the job that needs to be done. He is brave to the point of foolhardiness. Moving down the chain of command, Sergeant Welsh, who works most directly with the soldiers of the company, is survivalist and cynical. He has been disappointed in his superiors and consequently works to help his men deal with the threat of the enemy as well as the threat of the chain of command. Above all, he wants to live, and he wants to help his men live.

The film focuses on three privates in the company. One is Private Witt, whom we meet at the opening of the narrative and who dies at its close. Witt is concerned about his place in the world. He feels he belongs in the outfit and has a responsibility to his fellow soldiers, as well as to his family at home and to the natives he meets on the Pacific islands. This is a man looking to define his place in the universe. Another soldier, Corporal Fife, has a narrower field of focus: he looks beyond himself only to look at death in the universe. He is fearful and obsessed by the meaning of death. Yet another, Private Jack Bell, thinks only about home, specifically about his wife. He yearns for her, reveling in memories of his recent marriage, bathed in the recollection of the aliveness of her sexuality. Unfortunately, his feelings are not shared by his wife. Late in the narrative he receives a letter from her; she writes that she is leaving him for another man, an available stateside man.

Each man acts as a narrator, giving voice to his inner thoughts. The multiple points of view push the experience of the film as a nonlinear, discontinuous experience. Together with an episodic structure, *The Thin Red Line* in fact becomes an impressionistic tone poem rather than a polemic putting forward a particular position on a particular battle in a particular war.

In order to give the film shape, Malick poses a series of relationships, keying in on those relationships to break down the geography and the chronological progress of a significant World War II battle. Private Witt in the company relates to humanity in general, as we have seen. He relates to the native islanders as he does to his own comrades; he relates to them as people, as a part of humanity rather than as the enemy separated out of humanity. He even relates to the enemy, who in the end will kill him. Private Bell, on the other hand, relates more to the home front than he does to his comrades or to his presence on the islands. American soldiers are not the only relationships Malick explores. Enemy soldiers when captured express the pain, the unbearable pain of losing their comrades. This particular scene humanizes the enemy, just as the later death scene of Private Witt humanizes Witt as well as the enemy. Throughout the narrative Malick humanizes and individualizes so that the soldiers become individuals and people rather than soldiers. Each of the relationships portrayed mitigates against the solidarity of viewing the company of man as a war machine. Malick views the enemy, the U.S. soldiers, and the natives as individuals, as human beings.

But humans are nothing more than part of the natural order, a part of the natural world. Consequently, his film nature, whether it be birds or bats or overgrown fields and outsized trees, plays an omnipresent role, as if to say that nature will endure, whatever man does to his fellow man. This is the voice of Terrence Malick. Relationships are the vehicle for this meditation. The war story is the genre he has used to explore these ideas about man and nature.

Voice can be genre-specific, but many filmmakers challenge genre expectations in order to strengthen their voices. The Coen brothers, for instance, use satire to undermine the expected realism of the police story in *Fargo* (1996). Martin Scorsese uses a dark hyper-realism to undermine the heroism of the sports film in *Raging Bull* (1980). War films tend to realism, although Agnieszka Holland has used satire to make *Europa Europa* (1990) a child's nightmare come true. In *Come and See* (1985), Elem Klimov also takes the point of view of an adolescent's experience of war, but he creates a more intense nightmare. Terry Malick sees war differently, more philosophically. The tone he chooses for *The Thin Red Line* is poetic, stirring, and yet never nationalistic or patriotic. Malick is interested in questions of life and death, questions of friendship and of love. He is also concerned with man's place in the natural world. Consequently, he doesn't see the battle for Guadalcanal in political, military, or economic terms. The result is an unhurried meditation on human behavior as well as of human behavior during unnatural events such as war. If there is antagonism here, it is also philosophical: What is death? What is life? What does it mean to help another or to empathize with another? These questions consume the narrative, influence behavior, and generally drive the shape of the narrative. This is a war film, but Malick had made it the most unusual of war films—a meditation rather than a melodrama. This is Malick's unique voice in *The Thin Red Line*.

Malick has supported that voice by changing the balance between plot and character layers in *The Thin Red Line*. For the most part, the war film is a genre dominated by plot. The patrol to find Private Ryan in *Saving Private Ryan* (1997), the attack on the Ant Hill and its aftermath in *Paths of Glory* (1957), the attempted escape through the sewers of Warsaw in *Kanal* (1957), are all plot-driven narratives. That is not to say that the character layer isn't important in the war film, as it is in all the abovementioned films. But plot dominates the war film. *The Thin Red Line* is an exception. Malick raises the character layer of all characters, thereby downgrading the importance of plot. How this works is that the plot of the attack on the bunker, for example, is undermined by the elevation of the relationship stories of Captain Staros and Colonel Tall. The colonel will sacrifice any relationship to advance his ambition. His unwillingness to provide water for the company attacking the bunker supports his lack of care for others. The captain, on the other hand, refuses to send his men into battle. He cares too much. In both of these cases, the scenes highlight the nature of each character, as opposed to the progress of the battle.

A similar result is created in the attack on the village on Guadalcanal. Rather than detailing the progress of the attack, Malick focuses on the feelings of the captives, the Japanese, their pain, their sense of loss with regard to dead comrades, their fear about their own fates. Instead of demonizing the enemy, Malick humanizes the enemy, thereby undermining the sense of victory for the main characters. This upgrade of character layer and downgrade of plot undermines genre expectations and accentuates Malick's voice.

Besides changing the balance between the plot and character layers, Malick uses narrative detail that pushes voice forward is his emphasis on two extreme states: living and dying. Particular sequences engender both phenomena. Movement through the tall grass conveys the awareness that in one instant you are totally alive, but in the next instant you could be dead. Living soldiers came upon the dead, or at least parts of the dead. The sequence of moving through the fog has a similar feeling—a heightened sense of the danger that brings death. During the battle for the bunker, Sergeant Keck falls on a grenade that accidentally explodes. Malick lingers over his dying. So too the death of Private Witt, who dies to save his patrol. But here Malick moves away from the moment of death to the elements of life dear to him: nature, the island natives, and animal life. These elements live on while he dies.

In this latter scene, we see a recurring theme for Malick—the natural order. Although there are war films that embrace technology, such as *Full Metal Jacket* (1987) and *Apocalypse Now* (1979), Malick's narrative seems the opposite. It is environmental in its concerns rather than nationalistic or technological. It should come as no surprise that he ends the film with three shots of nature rather than of characters or machines.

Malick also uses narration to give voice to his philosophical concerns. "Who's killing us, robbing us of life and light?" "Is this darkness in you too?" "You are like my sons. My dear sons.

I'll carry you around wherever I go." "War turns men into dogs. It poisons the soul." These words are spoken by a variety of characters who probe for meaning. They are both personal and poetic. These are the deep issues that Malick associates with war.

Malick's nonlinear approach to the narrative means giving up the natural strengths that plot and a main character yield: involvement. To do so means finding other means to energize the experience of the narrative. What alternative technologies does Malick use to energize the narrative? The first strategy Malick uses is to provide contrast between sequences. As mentioned earlier, the sequences are not organized in a progressive or linear fashion. Although they generally follow the time line of an invasion, neither the proportion of film time spent on each sequence nor the narrative approach to those sequences builds progressively to a climax. Indeed, the focus in the scenes will vary from pain and loss among the enemy in the taking of the village to the opposite goals of a captain and a colonel as they face the challenge of capturing a hill dominated by an enemy bunker. The contrast at times is so great that the viewer is faced always with the unexpected. More conventionally but no less effectively, Malick relies on the moving camera, particularly in the military movement through the fog, the advance through the overgrown fields, and the attack on the bunker as well as the village. Subjective movement places us with the soldier Corporal Fife as he advances. The anticipation and the anxiety are captured by the moving camera. As much as possible, the pace of the movement simulates human movement, resulting in an identification with the feeling level of the soldier in each case.

Malick also relies on close-ups to intensify the emotion and the energy in particular scenes. Sergeant Welsh talking to his men, whether it is about belonging to the company or carrying morphine to a dying man on the battlefield, is presented in close-up. So too is Private Bell, who is obsessed with his wife at home. When the flashbacks occur they contain movement as well as off-center framing, as if the soldier struggles to contain the memory and also to possess the sexuality, the life force, he associates with his wife. Close-ups intensify his desire to hold on to those memories and to that desire. Finally, Malick uses cutaways to remind us that there is a world beyond the battlefield—a world with families and with children, and a world where nature not only exists but prevails. Again and again, Malick cuts away to images of that natural world, the context for his soldiers' story.

THE CASE OF *MAGNOLIA*

Paul Thomas Anderson's *Magnolia* (1999) functions as a nonlinear drama but, as in the case of Anderson's other films, it also functions as a movie about moviemaking (a constructed reality), or more broadly the media. In the case of *Magnolia*, the prologue consists of narration. A skeptical narrator describes in detail three remarkable coincidences from the past. Each is framed as a past "how-done-it" as opposed to a who-done-it. Each incident ends in a death: the first a murder, the second an accident, and the third a suicide. Then Anderson proceeds to question, and in the case of the last incident prove, that it was something else: a murder rather than a suicide.

Each case is a puzzle that is deconstructed to challenge or alter the first impression. The prologue also implies that the media creates illusions and that we, the viewers, should be skeptical about such constructed realities. Stories are told in the media but can be reconfigured to alter their impact and meaning. Anderson uses pace and detailed close-ups to make the experience of the three stories of the prologue exciting. They leave us winded, not having had enough time to digest and process the visual and aural information.

Using the same sense of dynamic pace, he launches us into the multiple stories of the main body of the narrative. What proceeds are the stories of eight characters who will participate in essentially three story lines. By coincidence each story will link to the others. The first story is the story of the Partridge family. The son, Jack, is now known as Frank Mackie, a media phenomenon. Frank is the voice for men being aggressive toward women, but his version of aggressiveness is as close as possible to rape yet just shy of being charged with a crime. His program is, needless to say, called "Seduce and Destroy." Frank (Jack) is alienated from his father Earl, who is dying. Before he dies, Earl would like to reconcile with his son, whom he deserted when he discovered that his wife, Jack's mother, was dying of cancer. Earl's new wife, Linda, who married him for his money, is now disintegrating because the man she's come to love is dying, and she is overwhelmed by the knowledge that she will lose him.

The second story is the story of Jimmy Gator, a famous TV game show host. Professionally, he is immensely popular; personally, he is dying of cancer and wants to reconcile with his daughter, Claudia. Claudia is a promiscuous coke addict who hates her father for sexually abusing her when he was drunk. Jim is a police officer who is earnest about his work. He is called to Claudia's apartment because of a complaint about noise from the stereo. Jim, rather than charging Claudia, falls in love with her. Their relationship rescues her from the self-destructive arc of her life.

The third story is that of Donnie, an adult former child star made famous on an earlier TV game show. Today he has ruined his work life and his love life is even less successful. Stealing money from his current employer seems to be the solution to all his problems. It's not. Parallel to this story is the story of Stanley, a contemporary child star on Jimmy Gator's TV show. He is so knowledgeable that his two child teammates depend on him to win. But Stanley is driven to win by a relentless, cruel father. When Stanley has to go to the bathroom, no one on the show is empathetic, and when he finally urinates in his pants, his father goes ballistic. Stanley refuses to "play" genius for television or for his father. He just wants to be treated like the child he is.

All these stories are linked because Earl Partridge owns the TV game show, the setting for parts of two of the stories. In addition, Jim from the second story rescues Donnie from becoming a thief in the third story.

The best way to frame the stories is to consider each of the eight characters as a character in crisis. Anderson for the most part treats the stories realistically. The dramatic arc of the stories leads the characters to help each other. Jim and Claudia help each other, and Jim helps Donnie return the stolen funds. One event or coincidence that is notable is that the narrative occurs in the late stages of each story. We can correlate the moment at which Anderson enters the narrative to the point of deepest despair for Jack, for Claudia, for Jimmy, and for Donnie. At this moment, during an intense storm, the rain is replaced by frogs falling from the sky. This event, analogous in tone to the plagues Moses called forward to punish Egypt for retaining the Jews as slaves, has a shocking, surreal quality, although Anderson treats the storm of pests realistically. After this event, reconciliation and recovery begin.

Stanley tells his father that he wants to be considered as a child. Jack (Frank) cries for his father. And Jim helps Donnie return the stolen money. The film closes with Claudia breaking out in a smile. All of these signals of hope for the despairing characters seem to pivot on this act of God, the storm of pestilence. The storm and its character, together with the prologue, shifts *Magnolia* from the melodrama that it appears to be to a moral fable, a hyperdrama.[5]

The principal shaping device Anderson uses is the notion of three interconnected narratives. As in stories told in the prologue, each can lead to death. In the first story, Earl Partridge will die, probably never forgiven by the son he deserted. In the second story, Jimmy will certainly die of cancer, but his daughter Claudia may also die, given the level of her self-destruction. In the third story, it is the dignity of the character that is being destroyed: both Donnie and Stanley are being destroyed by their dependency upon the fame television has brought them. And in each case, divine intervention or its equivalent—profound empathy for the other—saves the character from what appears to be their inevitable fate.

A second shaping device is the state of despair shared by so many of these characters. Even Frank Mackie, who was Jack Partridge in a former life, seems to be overwhelmingly defensive in his aggressive "Seduce and Destroy" posturing. We discover that he has never gotten over the wound of being abandoned by his father. He speaks of caring for his sick mother, but he has been abused by his father no less than Claudia has been by hers. Donnie longs for a lost past as much as he longs for the local muscular bartender. Stanley despairs for a lost childhood, and Earl despairs for his past sins, principally abandoning the wife, who died of cancer, a woman he loved deeply.

A third shaping device is the presence of the media in all these stories. Its presence provides a public–private forum to consider each of the characters. In the first story, Earl is a public success, for he owns successful television shows; but privately, as a husband and father, he is a failure. His son Jack (Frank) is a media star, a man's man, but privately he is a posturing, defensive boy, fearful of his deepest feelings. In the second story, Jimmy is the most long-lasting TV game show host. Publicly, he is a star; privately, he is a failed father and a failing husband. In the third story, Stanley is the most brilliant child contestant on the Jimmy Gator show, but privately he is a young boy who wants to go out and play—to be a boy, rather than to be a "star," the role his father clearly needs him to be.

Anderson for the most part treats these stories realistically, as we would expect in a melodrama. The result is that we become emotionally engaged with the characters, thereby masking voice as a key shaping device.[6] On the other hand, Anderson's use of the prologue together with the narrative intervention of the pestilence late in the narrative provides a constructed overlay to the realism of the narrative. It is here in the narration, in the skepticism about coincidence and the implicit skepticism about the manipulative capabilities of what we think we see (i.e., a construction, an anecdote, or a movie), that Anderson's voice is given its freest rein. By implying that a filmmaker can construct and alter perception, Anderson is alerting us to the power he yields in the film. Consequently, what we will watch is also a construction, albeit a powerful one. The dissonance between the prologue, the pestilence intervention, and the stories of these eight desperate characters allows us to be involved with their stories but also to remember that we are watching a film, a construction, an intentional coincidence. In this way, Anderson allows us to have a powerful film narrative experience as well as his voice—which cautions that what we are watching is a construction, as all films are.

The energy in *Magnolia* comes from rather classic sources. The most important is pace. Anderson uses, and even overuses, pace, as early as the prologue. The cutting is so rapid that we can barely keep up with the three stories of coincidence. That breathless sense of pace carries on as he introduces all of the characters. Not only does Anderson introduce them quickly via rapid crosscutting, but within each of the individual stories he also uses rapid camera motion and intense close-ups. This is a pattern he will use throughout the narrative: motion, close-up motion, and cutting on movement. Whatever the mood, the pace raises the energy level in the presentation of each of the stories.

Whenever Anderson wants to make an important point, however, he holds on a shot to register that point. When Donnie realizes that he is trapped, he says: "The past is not through with us." When Frank is caught up in a lie about his past (about caring for a dying mother, or about growing up locally), he glares at the documentary reporter who has thrown his past back at him. Each of these scenes works with the notion of reversing the pace that has prevailed in the narrative, and Anderson's point is made.

Anderson also generates energy from the proximity of the camera to the characters in the different stories. A created song for the film, "It's Not Going to Stop Until You Rise Up," is sung by all of the characters. Anderson cuts from character to character as the song proceeds, each taking his or her turn singing the words. This artifice links each to the other and to the notion that they are each characters in a film as well as performers for a film. Just as the film begins with a prologue, it ends with an epilogue. The epilogue is about confession, about characters revealing themselves; it states, "Sometimes people need to be forgiven."

NOTES/REFERENCES

1. Identification and the goal-directedness of a main character have particular editing implications, with respect to the use of the close-up, subjective camera placement, and movement and pace. Each of these editing choices creates a more emotional or dramatically meaningful experience. This classic approach to editing has less relevance in the nonlinear narrative.

2. K. Dancyger, *Global Scriptwriting*, Focal Press, Boston, 2001 (chapter 1).

3. Ibid., p. 77.

4. Ibid., pp. 161–163.

5. P. Cooper, K. Dancyger, *Writing the Short Film*, Focal Press, Boston, 1999 (chapter 14).

6. As a relationship between the character and the audience takes hold, that identification masks voice. The opposite is the basis for the clarity of the voice of the filmmaker: distance from character and structure reveals voice.

CHAPTER 32

Conclusion

This book covers the theory and practice of editing from the beginning to 2010. We have far surpassed the skepticism that Rudolph Arnheim expressed when he said that technological changes such as sound could add nothing to the advancement of the silent film. Sound is now an artful addition to the repertoire of the film experience. This is also true of video.

Although they are different technologies, film and video have begun to merge. Movie screens are now smaller and television screens are larger than they once were, and the film audience is increasingly viewing films on a video format. Movies that were once shot and edited on film are now shot on film and edited on video. Television shows that were once shot on video using three-camera studio techniques are now shot on video using single-camera filmic techniques. They are edited on tape, but have the look of a filmed show. The editing styles of films and taped television shows are becoming indistinguishable.

Much is different today from Alfred Hitchcock's time. Today's emphasis on technology—whether sound, image, or special effects—has placed a premium on sensation. On one level, the sensation of sound and image is what editing is about.

Because of its power, editing without an ethical dimension can only further the trend to use it to further sensation over more complex responses to film. This is the dangerous point at which we find ourselves today. In a sense, it places the artfulness of all that we have discovered—the power of film and television—in a spiritual vacuum.

When Eisenstein, Welles, and Buñuel created their works, they aimed to move the minds and emotions of their audiences. They used editing in a manipulative way, yet their works had an ethical foundation. They deployed their creativity in a world of ethical choices. The music video—the apogee of sensation—encourages sensation with contextual reference but seems to have no ethical goals beyond the stimulus of the sound and image. Eisenstein, Welles, and Buñuel did not live in a less difficult time than we do today. They managed to create works that speak to us vividly about ethics as well as aesthetics. The same is true for Truffaut and Antonioni and Kurosawa.

When I look at today's work, I see the height of technological achievement in such films as *Terminator 2* (1991), *Titanic* (1997), and *Avatar* (2009). I am entertained, but I am not

413

The Technique of Film and Video Editing: History, Theory, and Practice. DOI: 10.1016/B978-0-240-81397-4.00032-7

moved to consider the ethics of violence or technology or relationships. The sensations of ear and eye are everything. Is that all there is? It seems to be. The postmodern world has arrived.

Here is the challenge. We have learned a great deal *from* and a great deal *about* the greatest art of this century. How do we want to use our knowledge?

Filmography

Addams Family, The (1991), Barry Sonnenfeld, United States

Adventures of Dolly, The (1908), D. W. Griffith, United States

Age d'Or, L' (1930), Luis Buñuel, France

Aguirre: The Wrath of God (1972), Werner Herzog, West Germany

Alexander Nevsky (1938), Sergei Eisenstein, Russia

Alfie (1966), Lewis Gilbert, Great Britain

Alice in the Cities (1974), Wim Wenders, Germany

Aliens (1986), James Cameron, United States

All About Eve (1950), Joseph Mankiewicz, United States

All That Jazz (1979), Bob Fosse, United States

All the President's Men (1976), Alan Pakula, United States

America, America (1963), Elia Kazan, United States

American Beauty (1999), Sam Mendes, United States

American Graffiti (1973), George Lucas, United States

American in Paris, An (1951), Vincente Minnelli, United States

An Affair of Love (2000), Frederick Fonteyne, Belgium

And Now for Something Completely Different (1972), Ian McNaughton, Great Britain

Andrei Rublev (1969), Andrei Tarkovsky, Russia

Apartment, The (1960), Billy Wilder, United States

Apocalypse Now (1979), Francis Ford Coppola, United States

Applause (1929), Rouben Mamoulian, United States

Armageddon (1997), Michael Bay, United States

Arrivée d'un Train en Gare, L' (Arrival of a Train at the Station) (1895), Louis Lumière and Auguste Lumière, France

Atonement (2007), Joe Wright, United States

Aviator, The (2004), Martin Scorsese

Avventura, L' (1960), Michelangelo Antonioni, Italy

Back-Breaking Leaf (1959), Terence McCartney-Filgate, Canada

Bad Day at Black Rock (1955), John Sturges, United States

Ballad of Cable Hogue, The (1970), Sam Peckinpah, United States

Ballad of Ramblin' Jack, The (2000), Aiyana Elliott, United States

Bandit Queen, The (1994), Shekhar Kapur, India

Barry Lyndon (1975), Stanley Kubrick, United States

Battle of Algiers, The (1965), Gillo Pontecorvo, Italy

Battle of Culloden, The (1965), Peter Watkins, Great Britain

Beach Red (1967), Cornel Wilde, United States

Bear, The (1989), Jean-Jacques Annaud, France

Before the Rain (1994), Milcho Manchevski, Macedonia/United Kingdom

Belle de Jour (1967), Luis Buñuel, France/Italy

Ben Hur (1959), William Wyler, United States

Berlin: Symphony of a Great City (1927), Walter Ruttmann

Best Years of Our Lives, The (1946), William Wyler, United States

Bicycle Thief, The (1948), Vittorio de Sica, Italy

Big Chill, The (1983), Lawrence Kasdan, United States

Big Parade, The (1925), King Vidor, United States

Billy Liar (1963), John Schlesinger, Great Britain

Billy the Kid (1930), King Vidor, United States

Bird (1988), Clint Eastwood, United States

Birds, The (1963), Alfred Hitchcock, United States

Birth of a Nation, The (1915), D. W. Griffith, United States

Black Robe (1991), Bruce Beresford, Canada/Australia

Black Stallion, The (1979), Carol Ballard, United States

Black Sunday (1977), John Frankenheimer, United States

Blackmail (1929), Alfred Hitchcock, Great Britain

Blood and Fire (1958), Terence McCartney-Filgate, Canada

Blood on the Moon (1948), Robert Wise, United States

Bloody Sunday (2002), Paul Greengrass

Blue Steel (1989), Kathryn Bigelow, United States

Blue Velvet (1986), David Lynch, United States

Body and Soul (1947), Robert Rossen, United States

Body Snatcher, The (1945), Robert Wise, United States

Bonnie and Clyde (1967), Arthur Penn, United States

Boomerang! (1947), Elia Kazan, United States

Born on the Fourth of July (1989), Oliver Stone, United States

Bourne Identity (2002), Doug Liman

Bourne Supremacy (2004), Paul Greengrass, United States

Bourne Ultimatum (2007), Paul Greengrass, United States

Boxing Bout, A (1896), unknown, United States

Braveheart (1995), Mel Gibson, United States

Brazil (1985), Terry Gilliam, Great Britain

Breathless (1959), Jean Luc Godard, France

Bridge on the River Kwai, The (1957), David Lean, Great Britain

Bridges of Madison County, The (1995), Clint Eastwood, United States

Brief Encounter (1945), David Lean, Great Britain

Brighton Rock (also called *Young Scarface*) (1947), John Boulting, Great Britain

Bring Me the Head of Alfredo Garcia (1974), Sam Peckinpah, United States

Bringing Up Baby (1938), Howard Hawks, United States

Broadcast News (1987), James Brooks, United States

Broken Blossoms (1919), D. W. Griffith, United States

Bullitt (1968), Peter Yates, United States

Burden of Dreams (1983), Les Blank, United States

Cabaret (1972), Bob Fosse, United States

Cabinet of Dr. Caligari, The (1919), Robert Wiene, Germany

Candidate, The (1972), Michael Ritchie, United States

Capitalism: A Love Story (2009), Michael Moore, United States

Capote (2005), Bennett Miller

Capturing the Friedmans (2003), Andrew Jarecki

Carnal Knowledge (1971), Mike Nichols, United States

Catch 22 (1970), Mike Nichols, United States

Caught (1949), Max Ophuls, United States

Celebration, The (*Festen*) (1998), Thomas Vinterberg, Denmark

Champion (1949), Mark Robson, United States

Chant of Jimmy Blacksmith, The (1978), Fred Schepsi, Australia

Chaos (2001), Coline Serreau

Charlie's Angels (2000), McG

Chelovek s kino-apparatom (Man with a Movie Camera) (1929), Dziga Vertov, Russia

Chien d'Andalou, Un (An Andalusian Dog) (1929), Luis Buñuel, France

Chinatown (1974), Roman Polanski, United States

Cinderella (1899), unknown, France

Citizen Kane (1941), Orson Welles, United States

City Lights (1931), Charlie Chaplin, United States

City, The (1939), Willard Van Dyke, United States

Clerks (1994), Kevin Smith, United States

Clockwork Orange, A (1971), Stanley Kubrick, Great Britain

Clueless (1995), Amy Hockerling, United States

Cobweb, The (1955), Vincente Minnelli, United States

Collateral (2004), Michael Mann, United States

Come and See (1985), Elem Klimov, Russia

Conformist, The (1971), Bernardo Bertolucci, Italy

Conversation, The (1974), Francis Ford Coppola, United States

Cows (1991), Julio Medem, Spain

Cries and Whispers (1972), Ingmar Bergman, Sweden

Crimes and Misdemeanors (1989), Woody Allen, United States

Crimson Tide (1995), Tony Scott, United States

Crooklyn (1994), Spike Lee, United States

Cross of Iron (1977), Sam Peckinpah, United States

Crossing Delancey (1988), Joan Micklin Silver, United States

Crouching Tiger, Hidden Dragon (2000), Ang Lee, United States/Taiwan

Crowd, The (1928), King Vidor, United States

Culloden (1964), Peter Watkins, Great Britain

Dances with Wolves (1990), Kevin Costner, United States

Daughters of the Dust (1991), Julie Dash, United States

Day after Day (1965), Clement Perron, Canada

Day of the Jackal, The (1973), Fred Zinnemann, United States

Day the Earth Stood Still, The (1951), Robert Wise, United States

Days of Heaven (1978), Terence Malick, United States

Dazed and Confused (1993), Richard Linklater, United States

Dead Calm (1988), Phillip Noyce, United States/Australia

Dead End (1937), William Wyler, United States

Dead Ringers (1988), David Cronenberg, Canada

Deer Hunter, The (1978), Michael Cimino, United States

Departed, The (2006), Martin Scorcese, United States

Desert Fox, The (1951), Henry Hathaway, United States

Desert Victory (1943), Roy Boulting, Great Britain

Design for Living (1933), Ernst Lubitsch, United States

Desperately Seeking Susan (1985), Susan Seidelman, United States

Diary of a Country Priest (1945), Robert Bresson

Diary of a Lost Girl (1929), G. W. Pabst, United States

Diary for Timothy (1945), Humphrey Jennings, Great Britain

Die Hard (1988), John McTiernan, United States

Dirty Harry (1971), Don Siegel, United States

Discreet Charm of the Bourgeoisie, The (1972), Luis Buñuel, France

Distant Voices, Still Lives (1988), Terence Davies, Great Britain

Diva (1982), Jean-Jacques Beineix, France

Divide and Conquer (1943), Frank Capra and Anatole Litvak, United States

Divorce—Italian Style (1962), Pietro Germi, Italy

Do the Right Thing (1989), Spike Lee, United States

Doctor Zhivago (1965), David Lean, United States

Dodes' Ka-Den (1970), Akira Kurosawa, Japan

Dogs of War, The (1980), John Irvin, United States

Dogville (2003), Lars von Trier

Don't Look Now (1973), Nicholas Roeg, United States

Double Indemnity (1944), Billy Wilder, United States

Downhill Racer (1969), Michael Ritchie

Dr. Jekyll and Mr. Hyde (1932), Rouben Mamoulian, United States

Dr. Strangelove (1964), Stanley Kubrick, Great Britain

Draughtsman's Contract, The (1982), Peter Greenaway, Great Britain

Dreamlife of Angels, The (1998), Erick Zonca, France

Drifters, The (1929), John Grierson, Great Britain

Duel in the Sun (1946), King Vidor, United States

Earth (1930), Alexander Dovshenko, Russia

East of Eden (1955), Elia Kazan, United States

Eclisse, L' (1962), Michelangelo Antonioni, Italy

Edvard Munch (1974), Peter Watkins, Norway

8½ (1963), Federico Fellini, Italy

El Cid (1961), Anthony Mann, United States

Elizabeth (1998), Shekhar Kapur, Great Britain

Empire of the Sun (1987), Steven Spielberg, United States

Enfant Sauvage, L' (The Wild Child) (1970), François Truffaut, France

Enigma of Kaspar Hauser, The (1974), Werner Herzog, West Germany

Enoch Arden (1908, 1911), D. W. Griffith, United States

E.T. the Extra-Terrestrial (1982), Steven Spielberg, United States

Europa, Europa (1991), Agnieszka Holland, France/Germany

Every Day Except Christmas (1957), Lindsay Anderson, Great Britain

Excalibur (1981), John Boorman, Great Britain

Exodus (1960), Otto Preminger, United States

Exorcist, The (1973), William Friedkin, United States

Exotica (1994), Atom Egoyan, Canada

Eyes Wide Shut (1999), Stanley Kubrick, United States

Faces (1968), John Cassavetes, United States

Fahrenheit 9/11 (2004), Michael Moore, United States

Fall of the Roman Empire, The (1964), Anthony Mann, United States

Fame (1980), Alan Parker, United States

Family Life (*Wednesday's Child*) (1972), Ken Loach, Great Britain

Farewell to Arms, A (1957), Charles Vidor, United States

Fast, Cheap and Out of Control (1998), Errol Morris, United States

Fast Times at Ridgemont High (1982), Amy Heckerling, United States

Father (1966), Istvan Szabo, Hungary

Fellini Satyricon (1970), Federico Fellini, Italy

Fighter (2000), Amir Bar-Lev, United States

Fireman's Ball (1968), Milos Forman, Czechoslovakia

Fires Were Started (1943), Humphrey Jennings, Great Britain

Fish Called Wanda, A (1988), Lewis Gilbert, Great Britain

Fitzcarraldo (1982), Werner Herzog, Germany

Five Fingers (1952), Joseph Mankiewicz, United States

Flashdance (1983), Adrian Lyne, United States

Fly, The (1986), David Cronenberg, Canada

Fog of War, The: Elevens Lessons from the Life of Robert McNamara (2004), Errol Morris, United States

For the Boys (1991), Mark Rydell, United States

Foreign Correspondent (1940), Alfred Hitchcock, Great Britain

Forgetting Sarah Marshall (2008), Nicholas Stoller, United States

Forrest Gump (1994), Robert Zemeckis, United States

400 Blows, The (1959), François Truffaut, France

French Connection, The (1971), William Friedkin, United States

Frenzy (1972), Alfred Hitchcock, United States

From the Life of the Marionettes (1980), Ingmar Bergman, Sweden

Front Page, The (1931), Howard Hawks, United States

Frost/Nixon (2008), Ron Howard, United States

Full Metal Jacket (1987), Stanley Kubrick, Great Britain

Funny Face (1957), Stanley Donen, United States

Funny People (2009), Judd Apatow

Funny Thing Happened on the Way to the Forum, A (1966), Richard Lester, Great Britain

Gattopardo, Il (*The Leopard*) (1963), Luchino Visconti, Italy

General, The (1927), Buster Keaton, United States

Get Shorty (1995), Barry Sonnenfeld, United States

Getaway, The (1972), Sam Peckinpah, United States

Gimme Shelter (1970), The Maysles Brothers, United States

Gladiator (2000), Ridley Scott, United States

Gloria (1980), John Cassavetes, United States

Glory (1989), Ed Zwick, United States

Goalie's Anxiety at the Penalty Kick, The (1971), Wim Wenders, Germany

Gold Diggers of 1933 (1933), Mervyn LeRoy, United States

Gold Rush, The (1925), Charlie Chaplin, United States

Golden Boy (1939), Rouben Mamoulian, United States

Goodfellas (1990), Martin Scorcese, United States

Good, the Bad, and the Ugly, The (1967), Sergio Leone, Italy

Graduate, The (1967), Mike Nichols, United States

Grass (2000), Ron Mann, Canada

Greaser's Gauntlet, The (1908), D. W. Griffith, United States

Great Dictator, The (1940), Charlie Chaplin, United States

Great Expectations (1946), David Lean, Great Britain

Great McGinty, The (1940), Preston Sturges, United States

Great Race, The (1965), Blake Edwards, United States

Great Train Robbery, The (1903), Edwin Porter, United States

Greatest Story Ever Told (1965), George Stevens, United States

Grizzly Man (2005), Werner Herzog, Germany

Guerre Est Finie, La (1966), Alain Resnais, France

Guilty by Suspicion (1991), Irwin Winkler, United States

Gunga Din (1939), George Stevens, United States

Hail the Conquering Hero (1944), Preston Sturges, United States

Hallelulah (1929), King Vidor, United States

Hands Up (1965), Jerzi Skolimowski, Poland

Hannah and Her Sisters (1986), Woody Allen, United States

Happiness (1998), Todd Solondz, United States

Hard Day's Night, A (1964), Richard Lester, Great Britain

Having a Wild Weekend (1965), John Boorman, Great Britain

Heaven and Earth (1993), Oliver Stone, United States

Heaven Can Wait (1977), Warren Beatty, United States

Hell in the Pacific (1968), John Boorman, United States

Help! (1965), Richard Lester, Great Britain

Hero (1992), Stephen Frears, United States

High Noon (1952), Fred Zinnemann, United States

High School (1968), Fred Wiseman, United States

Hiroshima, Mon Amour (1960), Alan Resnais, France

His Girl Friday (1940), Howard Hawks, United States

History of Violence, A (2005), David Cronenberg, United States

Hobson's Choice (1954), David Lean, Great Britain

Home of the Brave (1949), Mark Robson, United States

Hook (1991), Steven Spielberg, United States

Hospital (1969), Fred Wiseman, United States

Hospital, The (1971), Arthur Hiller, United States

Hours, The (2002), Stephen Daldry, United States

How the West Was Won (1962), Henry Hathaway, John Ford, and George Marshall, United States

Husbands (1970), John Cassavetes, United States

Husbands and Wives (1992), Woody Allen, United States

Hustler, The (1961), Robert Rossen, United States

I Love You, Man (2009), Judd Apatow

I Want to Live! (1958), Robert Wise, United States

I Was a 90-Pound Weakling (1964), Wolf Koenig and George Dufaux, Canada

I Was a Male War Bride (1949), Howard Hawks, United States

Ice Storm, The (1997), Ang Lee, United States

If . . . . (1969), Lindsay Anderson, Great Britain

In the Mood for Love (2000), Wong-Kar Wai, Hong Kong

In Which We Serve (1942), David Lean, Great Britain

Independence Day (1996), Roland Emmerich, United States

Indiana Jones and the Last Crusade (1989), Steven Spielberg, United States

Inglourious Basterds (2009), Quentin Tarantino, United States

Into the Arms of Strangers (2000), Mark Jonathan Harris, United States

Intolerance (1916), D. W. Griffith, United States

Invictus (2009), Clint Eastwood, United States

Invitation to the Dance (1957), Gene Kelly, United States

Isadora (1969), Karel Reisz, Great Britain

Italiensk for begyndere (Italian for Beginners) (2000), Lone Scherfig

Jaws (1975), Steven Spielberg, United States

Jazz Singer, The (1927), Alan Crosland, United States

Jesus of Montreal (1990), Denys Arcand, Canada

JFK (1991), Oliver Stone, United States

Judith of Bethulia (1913), D. W. Griffith, United States

Jules et Jim (1961), François Truffaut, France

Jungle Fever (1991), Spike Lee, United States

Junior Bonner (1972), Sam Peckinpah, United States

Juno (2007), Jason Reitman

Jurassic Park (1993), Steven Spielberg, United States

Kanal (1957), Andrzej Wajda

Killing of a Chinese Bookie, The (1976), John Cassavetes, United States

Kind of Loving, A (1962), John Schlesinger, Great Britain

King Arthur (2004), Antoine Fuqua

King Is Alive, The (2000), Kristian Levring

King of Kings (1961), Nicholas Ray

King Kong (2005), Peter Jackson

Kiss Me, Stupid (1964), Billy Wilder, United States

Kiss of Death (1947), Henry Hathaway, United States

Kiss, The (1896), Thomas A. Edison, United States

Koyaanisqatsi (1983), Godfrey Reggio, United States

Kundun (1997), Martin Scorcese, United States

La Chinoise (1967), Jean-Luc Godard, France

La Femme Nikita (1990), Luc Besson, France/Italy

La Jetee (1962), Chris Marker, France

La Promesse (1996), Jean-Pierre Dardenne and Luc Dardenne, Belgium

Lady Eve, The (1941), Preston Sturges, United States

Lady from Shanghai, The (1948), Orson Welles, United States

Lady in the Lake (1946), Robert Montgomery, United States

Land and Freedom (1995), Ken Loach, Great Britain

Land without Bread (1933), Luis Buñuel, France

Last Laugh, The (1924), F. W. Murnau, Germany

Last Tango in Paris (1973), Bernardo Bertolucci, France/Italy

Last Year at Marienbad (1961), Alain Resnais, France

Laughter in the Dark (1969), Tony Richardson, Great Britain

Lawrence of Arabia (1962), David Lean, Great Britain

L'Enfant (*The Child*) (2005), Jean-Pierre Dardenne and Luc Dardenne, Belgium

Le Fils (*The Son*) (2002), Jean-Pierre Dardenne and Luc Dardenne, Belgium

Les Liaisons Dangereuses (1988), Stephen Frears, United States

Lesson in Love (1954), Ingmar Bergman, Sweden

Letter from an Unknown Woman (1948)

Letter to Three Wives, A (1949), Joseph Mankiewicz, United States

Life Is Beautiful (1998), Roberto Benigni, Italy

Life of an American Fireman, The (1903), Edwin Porter, United States

Life of Brian (1979), Terry Jones, Great Britain

Lineup, The (1958), Don Siegel, United States

Listen to Britain (1942), Humphrey Jennings, Great Britain

Little Big Man (1970), Arthur Penn, United States

Little Foxes, The (1941), William Wyler, United States

Lives of a Bengal Lancer, The (1935), Henry Hathaway, United States

Lola Montès (1955), Max Ophuls, France

Lonedale Operator, The (1911), D. W. Griffith, United States

Loneliness of the Long Distance Runner, The (1962), Tony Richardson, Great Britain

Lonely Boy (1962), Wolf Koenig and Roman Kroiter, Canada

Lonely Villa, The (1909), D. W. Griffith, United States

Long Good Friday, The (1980), John MacKenzie, Great Britain

Long Goodbye, The (1973), Robert Altman, United States

Long Way Home, The (1997), Mark Jonathan Harris, United States

Look Back in Anger (1958), Tony Richardson, Great Britain

Lord of the Rings trilogy (2001, 2002, 2003), Peter Jackson

Lost Honor of Katharina Blum, The (1975), Volker Schlondorff and Margarethe von Trotta, West Germany

Lost Horizons (1937), Frank Capra, United States

Louisiana Story (1948), Robert Flaherty, United States

Loved One, The (1965), Tony Richardson, United States

Lust, Caution (2006), Ang Lee, Taiwan

Lust for Life (1956), Vincente Minnelli, United States

M (1931), Fritz Lang, Germany

Mad Max 2 (The Road Warrior) (1981), George Miller, Australia

Madigan (1968), Don Siegel, United States

Magician, The (1959), Ingmar Bergman, Sweden

Magnifi cent Ambersons, The (1942), Orson Welles, United States

Magnolia (1998), Paul Thomas Anderson, United States

Mahabharata, The (1989), Peter Brook, France

Major Dundee (1965), Sam Peckinpah, United States

Malcolm X (1992), Spike Lee, United States

Man Bites Dog (1992), Remy Belvaux, Belgium

Manderlay (2005), Lars von Trier

Man on Fire (2004), Tony Scott, United States

Man in the Gray Flannel Suit, The (1946), Nunnally Johnson, United States

Man of Aran (1934), Robert Flaherty, Great Britain

Man Who Knew Too Much, The (1956), Alfred Hitchcock, United States

Man with a Movie Camera, The (1929), Dziga Vertov, Russia

Manchurian Candidate, The (1962), John Frankenheimer, United States

Manhattan (1979), Woody Allen, United States

Marat/Sade (1966), Peter Brook, Great Britain

Marianne and Julianne (1982), Margarethe von Trotta, West Germany

Marnie (1964), Alfred Hitchcock, United States

Marriage Circle, The (1924), Ernst Lubitsch, United States

McCabe and Mrs. Miller (1971), Robert Altman, United States

Mean Streets (1973), Martin Scorsese, United States

Medium Cool (1969), Haskell Wexler, United States

Memorandum (1966), Donald Brittain, Canada

Mephisto (1981), Istvan Szabo, Hungary

Meshes in the Afternoon (1943, 1959), Maya Daren, United States

Michael Clayton (2007), Tony Gilroy, United States

Mickey One (1965), Arthur Penn, United States

Midnight Cowboy (1969), John Schlesinger, United States

Midnight Express (1978), Alan Parker, United States

Minnie and Moskowitz (1971), John Cassavetes, United States

Miracle of Morgan's Creek, The (1944), Preston Sturges, United States

Mo' Better Blues (1990), Spike Lee, United States

Modern Times (1936), Charlie Chaplin, United States

Momma Don't Allow (1955), Karel Reisz and Tony Richardson, Great Britain

Mon Oncle (1958), Jacques Tati, France

Mon Oncle d'Amerique (1980), Alain Resnais, France

Monkey Business (1952), Howard Hawks, United States

Monte Walsh (1970), William A. Fraker, United States

Monty Python and the Holy Grail (1975), Terry Gilliam and Terry Jones, Great Britain

Moonstruck (1987), Norman Jewison, United States

Mountains of the Moon (1990), Bob Rafelson, United States

More the Merrier, The (1943), George Stevens, United States

Morgan: A Suitable Case for Treatment (1966), Karel Reisz, Great Britain

Mother (1926), Vsevolod Pudovkin, Russia

Moulin Rouge! (2001), Baz Luhrman, United States

Mr. Death (2000), Errol Morris, United States

Mr. Deeds Goes to Town (1936), Frank Capra, United States

Mr. Hulot's Holiday (1953), Jacques Tati, France

Mr. Smith Goes to Washington (1939), Frank Capra, United States

Munich (2005), Steven Spielberg, United States

Muriel (1963), Alain Resnais, France

My Best Fiend (1999), Werner Herzog, Germany

My Darling Clementine (1946), John Ford, United States

Nanook of the North (1922), Robert Flaherty, United States

Napoleon (1927), Abel Gance, France

Nashville (1975), Robert Altman, United States

Natural Born Killers (1994), Oliver Stone, United States

Navigator, The (1988), Vincent Ward, Australia

Nevada Smith (1966), Henry Hathaway, United States

Night and Fog (1955), Alain Resnais, France

Night Mail (1936), Basil Wright, Great Britain

Night of the Hunter, The (1955), Charles Laughton, United States

Night Porter, The (1974), Liliana Cavani, Italy

Ninotchka (1939), Ernst Lubitsch, United States

Nixon (1995), Oliver Stone, United States

No Way Out (1987), Roger Donaldson, United States

North by Northwest (1959), Alfred Hitchcock, United States

Northwest Mounted Police (1940), Cecil B. DeMille, United States

Nosferatu: The Vampyre (1979), Werner Herzog, Germany

Notorious (1946), Alfred Hitchcock, United States

O Lucky Man! (1973), Lindsay Anderson, Great Britain

Occurrence at Owl Creek, An (1962), Robert Enrico, France

October (1928), Sergei Eisenstein, Russia

Odds Against Tomorrow (1959), Robert Wise, United States

O'Dreamland (1953), Lindsay Anderson, Great Britain

Oliver Twist (1948), David Lean, Great Britain

Olivier, Olivier (1992), Agnieszka Holland

Olympia (1938), Leni Riefenstahl, Germany

Once Upon a Time in America (1984), Sergio Leone, United States

One Day in September (1999), Kevin Macdonald

One Flew Over the Cuckoo's Nest (1975), Milos Forman, United States

Open City (1946), Roberto Rossellini, Italy

Opening Night (1977), John Cassavetes, United States

Ordinary People (1980), Robert Redford, United States

Our Daily Bread (1934), King Vidor, United States

Pale Rider (1985), Clint Eastwood, United States

Panic in the Streets (1950), Elia Kazan, United States

Parallax View, The (1974), Alan J. Pakula, United States

Paris, Texas (1984), Wim Wenders, West Germany/France

Passage to India (1984), David Lean, Great Britain

Passion of Joan of Arc, The (1928), Carl Dryer, France

Passion of the Christ, The (2004), Mel Gibson, United States

Paths of Glory (1957), Stanley Kubrick, United States

Pawnbroker, The (1965), Sidney Lumet, United States

Performance (1970), Nicolas Roeg, Great Britain

Personal Best (1982), Robert Towne, United States

Petulia (1968), Richard Lester, United States

Pianist, The (2002), Roman Polanksi, United States

Pink Panther, The (1964), Blake Edwards, United States

Pirate, The (1948), Vincente Minnelli, United States

Place in the Sun, A (1951), George Stevens, United States

Plainsman, The (1936), Cecil B. DeMille, United States

Platoon (1986), Oliver Stone, United States

Plow that Broke the Plains, The (1936), Pare Lorentz, United States

Point Blank (1967), John Boorman, United States

Point Break (1991), Kathryn Bigelow, United States

Potemkin (1925), Sergei Eisenstein, Russia

Pour Construire un Feu (1928), Claude Autant-Lara, France

Prelude to War (1942), Frank Capra, United States

Prince of the City (1981), Sidney Lumet, United States

Privilege (1967), Peter Watkins, Great Britain

Promises (2001), Justine Shapiro and B. Z. Goldberg, United States

Proposition, The (2006), John Hillcoat, Australia

Proof (1991), Jocelyn Moorhouse, Australia

Providence (1977), Alain Resnais, France/Switzerland

Psycho (1960), Alfred Hitchcock, United States

Pulp Fiction (1994), Quentin Tarantino, United States

Punchline (1989), David Seltzer, United States

Purple Rose of Cairo, The (1985), Woody Allen, United States

Quo Vadis (1912), Enrico Guazzoni, Italy

Rachel Getting Married (2008), Jonathan Demme, United States

Radio Days (1987), Woody Allen, United States

Raging Bull (1980), Martin Scorsese, United States

Raiders of the Lost Ark (1981), Steven Spielberg, United States

Raising Arizona (1987), Joel Coen and Ethan Coen, United States

Ramona (1911), D. W. Griffith, United States

Ran (1985), Akira Kurosawa, Japan

Rashomon (1951), Akira Kurosawa, Japan

Ray (2004), Taylor Hackford

Reality Bites (1994), Ben Stiller, United States

Rear Window (1954), Alfred Hitchcock, United States

Red and the White, The (1967), Miklós Jancsó, Hungary

Reine Elizabeth, La (Queen Elizabeth) (1912), Louis Mercanton, France

Replacement Killers, The (1998),

Reprise (2006), Joachim Trier

Requiem for a Dream (2000), Darren Aranofsky, United States

Reservoir Dogs (1992), Quentin Tarantino, United States

Ride the High Country (1962), Sam Peckinpah, United States

Rififi (1954), Jules Dassin, France

Rio Bravo (1959), Howard Hawks, United States

River of No Return (1954), Otto Preminger, United States

River, The (1937), Pare Lorentz, United States

Robe, The (1953), Henry Koster, United States

Robo Cop (1987), Paul Verhoeven, United States

Roger and Me (1989), Michael Moore, United States

Romeo Is Bleeding (1993), Peter Medak, United States

Rope (1948), Alfred Hitchcock, United States

Rosemary's Baby (1968), Roman Polanski, United States

Rosetta (1999), Luc Dardenne and Jean-Pierre Dardenne, Belgium

Round-up, The (1965), Miklós Janscó, Hungary

Run Lola Run (1999), Tom Tykwer, Germany

Runaway Train (1985), Andrei Konchalovsky, United States

Running, Jumping and Standing Still (1961), Richard Lester, Great Britain

Ryan's Daughter (1970), David Lean, Great Britain

Sacrifice, The (1986), Andrei Tarkovsky, Russia

Sad Song of Yellow Skin (1970), Michael Rubbo, Canada

Salesman (1969), The Maysles Brothers, United States

Salvador (1986), Oliver Stone, United States

Sand Pebbles, The (1966), Robert Wise, United States

Saturday Night and Sunday Morning (1960), Karel Reisz, Great Britain

Saving Private Ryan (1997), Steven Spielberg, United States

Scarface (1983), Brian De Palma, United States

Schindler's List (1993), Steven Spielberg, United States

School Daze (1988), Spike Lee, United States

Searchers, The (1956), John Ford, United States

Second Awakening of Christa Klages, The (1977), Margarethe von Trotta, West Germany

Seconds (1966), John Frankenheimer, United States

Secrets of a Lost Soul (1926), G. W. Pabst, United States

Sense and Sensibility (1995), Ang Lee, Great Britain

Serpent's Egg, The (1978), Ingmar Bergman, United States/West Germany

Serpico (1973), Sidney Lumet, United States

Set-Up, The (1949), Robert Wise, United States

Seven Beauties (1976), Lina Westmüller, Italy

Seven Days in May (1964), John Frankenheimer, United States

Seven Samurai, The (1954), Akira Kurosawa, Japan

Seventh Seal, The (1956), Ingmar Bergman, Sweden

Seventh Sign, The (1988), Carl Schultz, United States

Shadows (1959), John Cassavetes, United States

Shane (1953), George Stevens, United States

Sherman's March (1986), Ross McElwee, United States

She's Gotta Have It (1986), Spike Lee, United States

Shoot the Piano Player (1962), François Truffaut, France

Sicko (2007), Michael Moore, United States

Singin' in the Rain (1952), Gene Kelly, United States

Sink or Swim (1990), Su Friedrich, United States

Skirt Dance (1898), Cinematograph, Great Britain

Slacker (1991), Richard Linklater, United States

Slap Shot (1977), George Roy Hill, United States

Solzhenitsyn's Children Are Making a Lot of Noise in Paris (1979), Michael Rubbo, Canada

Sombre (1998), Philippe Grandrieux

Some Like It Hot (1959), Billy Wilder, United States

Somebody Up There Likes Me (1956), Robert Wise, United States

Something Wild (1986), Jonathan Demme, United States

Song of Ceylon (1934), Basil Wright, Great Britain

Sons and Lovers (1958), Jack Cardiff, Great Britain

Sorcerer (1977), William Friedkin, United States

Sortie de l'Usine Lumière, La (Workers Leaving the Lumière Factory) (1895), Auguste Lumière and Louis Lumière, France

Specter of the Rose (1946), Ben Hecht, United States

Speed (1994), Jan de Bout, United States

Spellbound (1945), Alfred Hitchcock, United States

Spellbound (2002), Jeffrey Blitz

Splendor in the Grass (1961), Elia Kazan, United States

Stand By Me (1986), Rob Reiner, United States

Stop Making Sense (1984), Jonathan Demme, United States

Strangers on a Train (1951), Alfred Hitchcock, United States

Straw Dogs (1971), Sam Peckinpah, United States

Streetcar Named Desire, A (1951), Elia Kazan, United States

Strike (1924), Sergei Eisenstein, Russia

Sullivan's Travels (1941), Preston Sturges, United States

Summertime (1955), David Lean, Great Britain

Sunday in the Country, A (1984), Bernard Tavernier, France

Sunrise (1927), F. W. Murnau, Germany

Sunset Boulevard (1950), Billy Wilder, United States

Swept Away . . . (1975), Lina Wertmüller, Italy

Swing Time (1936), George Stevens, United States

Tampopo (1987), Juzo Itami, Japan

Ten Commandments, The (1923, 1956), Cecil B. DeMille, United States

Tequila Sunrise (1988), Robert Towne, United States

Terminator, The (1984), James Cameron, United States

Terminator 2: Judgment Day (1991), James Cameron, United States

Terminus (1960), John Schlesinger, Great Britain

Terra Trema, La (1947), Luchino Visconti, Italy

Tess (1981), Roman Polanski, United States

Thelma & Louise (1991), Ridley Scott, United States

There Will Be Blood (2007), Paul Thomas Anderson, United States

Thin Blue Line, The (1988), Errol Morris, United States

Thin Red Line, The (1998), Terence Malick, United States

39 Steps, The (1935), Alfred Hitchcock, Great Britain

Third Man, The (1949), Carol Reed, Great Britain

Thirty-Two Short Films about Glen Gould (1993), François Girard, Canada

This Sporting Life (1963), Lindsay Anderson, Great Britain

Three Brothers (1980), Francesco Rosi, Italy

Three Faces of Eve (1957), Nunnally Johnson, United States

Three Musketeers, The (1973), Richard Lester, Panama

Time Code (2000), Mike Figgis, United States

To Be or Not to Be (1942), Ernst Lubitsch, United States

Tom Jones (1963), Tony Richardson, Great Britain

Too Late the Hero (1970), Robert Aldrich, United States

Tootsie (1982), Sydney Pollack, United States

Top Gun (1986), Tony Scott, United States

Touch of Evil (1958), Orson Welles, United States

Tourist, The (1992), Rob Moss, United States

Tout Va Bien (1970), Jean-Luc Godard, France

Track 29 (1989), Nicolas Roeg, Great Britain

Train, The (1965), John Frankenheimer, United States/France/Italy

Trip to the Moon, A (1902), Georges Méliès, France

Triumph of the Will (1935), Leni Riefenstahl, Germany

Trouble in Paradise (1932), Ernst Lubitsch, United States

Twelve Monkeys (1995), Terry Gilliam, United States

Twentieth Century (1934), Howard Hawks, United States

Two or Three Things I Know about Her (1966), Jean-Luc Godard, France

2001: A Space Odyssey (1968), Stanley Kubrick, Great Britain

Unconquered (1947), Cecil B. DeMille, United States

Under Capricorn (1949), Alfred Hitchcock, Great Britain

Unforgiven (1992), Clint Eastwood, United States

United 93 (2006), Paul Greengrass, United States

Unstrung Heroes (1995), Diane Keaton, United States

Up in the Air (2009), Jason Reitman

Valmont (1989), Milos Forman, United States

Variety (1925), E. A. Dupont, Germany

Vertigo (1958), Alfred Hitchcock, United States

Very Nice, Very Nice (1961), Arthur Lipsett, Canada

Victor Victoria (1982), Blake Edwards, United States

Wages of Fear, The (1952), Henri-Georges Clouzot, France/Italy

Waiting for Fidel (1974), Michael Rubbo, Canada

Walkabout (1971), Nicolas Roeg, Great Britain

Walk the Line (2005), James Mangold

Wall Street (1987), Oliver Stone, United States

War of the Worlds (2005), Steven Spielberg, United States

War Game, The (1967), Peter Watkins, Great Britain

Warrendale (1966), Alan King, Canada

Week End (1967), Jean-Luc Godard, France/Italy

Werner Herzog Eats His Shoe (1980), Les Blank, United States

West Side Story (1961), Robert Wise, United States

What's Up, Doc? (1972), Peter Bogdanovich, United States

White Dawn, The (1974), Phillip Kauffman, United States

White Heat (1949), Raoul Walsh, United States

Whore (1991), Ken Russell, Great Britain

Why We Fight (series) (1943–1945), Frank Capra, United States

Wild Bunch, The (1969), Sam Peckinpah, United States

Wild One, The (1954), Laslo Benedek, United States

Wild Strawberries (1957), Ingmar Bergman, Sweden

Winter Light (1962), Ingmar Bergman, Sweden

Wiz, The (1978), Sidney Lumet, United States

Wizard of Oz, The (1939), Victor Fleming, United States

Woman Under the Influence, A (1974), John Cassavetes, United States

Woodstock (1970), Michael Wadleigh, United States

Working Girls, The (1986), Lizzie Borden, United States

Wonderful, Horrible Life of Leni Riefenstahl, The (1995), Ray Muller, Germany

Woyzek (1979), Werner Herzog, Germany

WR: Mysteries of the Organism (1971), Dusan Makavejev, former Yugoslavia

Wrestling (1960), Michelle Brault, Marcel Carrier, Claude Fournier, and Claude Jutra, Canada

Year of the Dragon (1985), Michael Cimino, United States

Ying xiong (*Hero*) (2002), Zhang Yimou

You Can't Take It With You (1938), Frank Capra, United States

You're a Big Boy Now (1966), Francis Ford Coppola, United States

Z (1969), Constatin Costa-Gavras, France

Glossary

A-B rolls The process used to create optical effects such as dissolves in film and videotape. Two rolls are used alternately. The A roll contains the first shot, and the B roll contains the second. The two rolls overlap for the length of the dissolve.

academy leader Film that precedes the first picture or sound. It contains synchronizing marks and countdown information used by the film lab for processing the composite print.

analog A form of electronic signal composed of varying voltage levels. Analog signals are of lower quality than digital signals.

anamorphic An image that is squeezed laterally so that the width-to-height ratio drops.

answer print The first lab print of a completed motion picture.

aspect ratio The proportion of picture width to height. For television and 16 mm film, the aspect ratio is 1.33:1; widescreen 35 mm, 1.85:1; widescreen 70 mm, 2.2:1; 35 mm anamorphic, 2.35:1.

assembly A rough cut; the organization of shots in rough order according to the script.

asynchronous Sound that is not synchronized to the picture being presented.

automatic dialog replacement (ADR) The process of recording new dialogs. If the original dialog recording has picked up too much ambient noise (such as an airplane), the dialog is rerecorded in a studio under controlled conditions.

back lighting Light directed from behind the subject toward the camera. The effect is to soften the impression of the subject.

back projection The projection of an image, film, or television show on the rear of a translucent screen to be viewed from its front surface.

base For film or videotape, the flexible support on which a photographic emulsion or magnetic coating is carried.

batch number Identification number of a quantity of product that has been manufactured at one time and has uniform characteristics, particularly raw stock.

Betacam Sony's trade name for a broadcast-quality videotape recorder (VTR) system that uses half-inch tape with component recording of luminance and chrominance on separate tracks. The high-speed recording results in a higher-quality image on the videotape.

Beta format The tape used in the Betamax system.

bias In audiotape recording, an ultrasonic signal applied to the record head to reduce distortion.

bidirectional microphone A microphone with equal sensitivity to sound arriving from the front or the rear.

bridging shot A shot used to cover a jump in time or another break in continuity.

broadcast standard In video practice, the highest quality of recording and reproduction; video capable of meeting the stringent requirements of broadcasting organizations.

burn-in The addition of visible time code numerals to a videotape recording.

butt splice A splice in a film or tape in which the two ends are not overlapped.

camera angle The angle of view created by the position of the camera vis-à-vis the subject. The positioning results in a composition that has particular characteristics as a result of the angle.

cement Cellulose solvent used for joining pieces of film.

character generator A device used to issue the signals needed to form alphanumeric characters on a cathode-ray tube. Such characters are used to create time code numbers for establishing edit points and to display letters or graphics used in titles.

cheat shot A shot in which part of the subject or action is excluded from view to make the part that is recorded appear different from what it actually is. Cheat shots are often used in action sequences to create the illusion of danger or disaster.

chroma key An electronic matting process for combining two or more video images into a credible composite form.

CinemaScope A system of anamorphic widescreen motion pictures that makes use of a horizontal compression-expression factor of between 2:1 and 2.5:1.

cinéma vérité See **direct camera**.

clapboard Sometimes referred to as *clapper board*, *clapper*, or *slate*. In motion picture photography, a board with a hinged arm used to identify the correct synchronization of picture and sound at the beginning or end of a scene. The clapboard yields a sharp sound that can be matched to the visual action of the clap.

clean edit list An offline edit list that has had discrepancies, overrecordings, or redundancies resolved, preparing it for efficient online editing.

click track A prerecorded timing track that consists of recorded clicks and is used for dubbing music with precise timing. The click track is generally produced after all of the visual editing decisions have been made.

close-up A tight shot of a person's head and shoulders. An extreme close-up might include a part of the face or a hand, for example.

commentary See **narration**.

control track In videotape, a track used for servo information, synchronization, and scanning rate.

credits Acknowledgments given in titles at the beginning or end of a film or television production, that list the cast, technicians, and organizations involved.

creeping sync In film recording, a progressive error of synchronization between picture and sound track; the steps taken to correct this error.

crosscut Sometimes referred to as intercutting or *parallel editing*. The intermingling of shots from two or more scenes. An alternating of scenes sometimes implies an eventual relationship between them.

crystal sync A method of synchronizing an audio magnetic tape recorder to a motion picture camera.

cut An instantaneous change from one scene to another.

cutaway Also known as an insert shot. A noncritical shot used to break or link principal action in scenes.

cutter An editor.

cutting print Sometimes called the *work print*. The positive print that the editor works within the editing process. Once complete, the print is used to edit the negative for the printing of the film.

dailies Also referred to as *rushes*. The first prints made from the newly processed picture or sound negative, which are used to check content and quality.

depth of field Distance between the nearest and farthest points from the camera at which the subject is acceptably sharp.

digital An electronic signal system composed of voltages that are turned on or off. Data in digital form may be copied many times with virtually no loss of quality (degradation) because the data are not altered or distorted as they go through the electronic system.

direct camera Also referred to as *cinéma vérité*. A style of filming real-life scenes without elaborate equipment. The result is less intrusion into the activities of the subject being filmed than with standard techniques.

dissolve A gradual merging of the end of one shot into the beginning of the next, produced by the superimposition of a fade-out onto a fade-in of equal length.

Dolby A noise reduction system for magnetic and photographic sound recordings.

dolly A movable platform on which a camera may be mounted so that action in front of the camera may be followed. See also **tracking shot**.

double system In cinematography, the system in which picture and sound are recorded on separate films or on film and tape. This system allows greater flexibility in working with sound than a single system in which original sound and picture are recorded simultaneously on the same piece of film.

dub Also referred to as *dupe*. In television, to copy a videotape. In film, to mix and compose audio sound tracks from several elements by balancing them for level, proportion, and equalization.

edge coding Sometimes called *edge numbering* or *footage numbers*. A coding system for numbers printed on motion picture film raw stock by the manufacturer. They are included once every foot on 35 mm film and once every 20 frames, or every 6 inches, on 16 mm film. These letters and numbers are used by the film negative cutter to match a work print film frame to its corresponding negative original. Time code, an electronic form of edge numbers, serves a similar purpose on videotape.

edit controller A keyboard or mouse used to communicate edit commands to the computer and the electronic editing system, including VCRs, VTRs, video switchers, and audio switchers.

edit decision list (EDL) The time code information defining each edit in a sequence. The list may be constructed for use on a computerized editing system.

edit point The position on the tape where two scenes are joined to create an edit. The end of one scene is joined by means of a splice to the beginning of the second scene.

effects track The composite or single track that is reserved for the sound effects to be used with the pictures.

electronic editing A method of electronically transferring pictures and sound from one videotape to another. This new, or edited, copy is regarded as a second-generation copy.

electronic field production (EFP) Remote, as opposed to studio production, techniques that use television cameras and portable video recorders.

electronic news gathering (ENG) The fast and portable electronic photography used in news reporting or in educational or industrial applications.

establishing shot Usually a long shot used near the beginning of a scene to establish the interrelationship of details to be shown subsequently in nearer shots.

fade-in The beginning of a shot that starts in darkness and gradually lightens to full brightness.

fade-out The beginning of a shot that starts in full brightness and gradually darkens to black.

fine cut Also called *final cut*. An editor's last cut of the edited work print after all of the changes have been made and the program is ready for the conforming process.

first generation The original videotape used to record the production. Each subsequent copy loses one generation.

flashback A scene that takes place at an earlier time than the scene it follows.

flash frame An extra frame of film, usually seen at an edit point. It appears as a momentary flash.

focus pull The shift of the subject in focus from the foreground to the background or vice versa.

footage The length of film measured in feet.

format In videotape, there are various systems: half inch, three-quarter inch, one inch. Tape can be Beta, VHS, super VHS, 8 mm, etc. Each has different characteristics and is used in different geographical regions. Various formats also reflect amateur or consumer purposes as well as professional broadcast uses.

frame A single image of film is the still visual composition.

frame rate The rate at which film or video proceeds through a camera or projector. The American standard is 24 frames per second; the European standard is 25 frames per second. For television, the NTSC standard is 30 frames per second; the PAL and SECAM standard is 25 frames per second.

freeze frame At a chosen point in a scene, the effect of freezing the action. It is accomplished by repeatedly printing a particular frame.

full shot A shot in which an entire person or object is visible within the frame.

generation Each copy of the original videotape. A deterioration of quality results from the process of copying.

genlock Short for *generator lock*. A method of synchronizing or electronically locking several video sources together so that they are in electronic time.

guide track A speech track recorded with too much background noise that serves as a guide for the actor to repeat the speech in a studio.

high-definition television (HDTV) A television system that contains 1125 horizontal scan lines per frame. Conventional television displays 525 lines per frame. The screen aspect ratio of HDTV is 1.78:1, as opposed to 1.33:1 for standard television.

insert shot See **cutaway**.

intercut See **crosscut** and **parallel cut**.

interlock A method of connecting a separate sound track and picture by means of electronic or mechanical links between devices such as ATRs, VCRs, and film projectors. Interlock is used in the transfer of film to videotape.

iris An adjustable diaphragm of metal leaves over the lens aperture that controls the amount of light passing through the lens. In the early days of film, the stopping down of the iris was used to fade out on the subject in the center of the frame. The effect was cruder than today's light-to-dark fade-out, which affects the entire frame.

iris-in, iris-out A decorative fade-in or fade-out in which the image appears or disappears as a growing or diminishing oval. This effect was used often in the silent cinema era.

jump cut A cut that breaks the continuity of time by jumping forward from one part of an action to another that is obviously separated from the first by an interval of time.

key lighting (high or low) A high-key image has a characteristic all-over lightness achieved by soft, full illumination on a light-toned subject with light shadows and background.

lap dissolve See **dissolve**.

leader A length of film joined to the beginning of a reel that is used for threading the film through the camera or projector.

library shot A shot used in a film but not recorded specifically for it. Often, newsreel footage is stock, or library, footage filmed previously but copied and used for another film or television show. Journalistic films often rely extensively on library shots.

lip synch The accurate synchronization of a sound track with its corresponding picture. The phrase in *lip synch* means that the sound matches the picture.

long shot A wide, long-distance shot generally used to establish the scene and give the audience a reference point for subsequent shots.

loop A short length of film joined together at its ends to form an endless band. It can be passed through a projector to give a continuous repetition of the subject. Loops are used to rerecord dialog and particular sound effects.

magnetic film A strip of magnetically coated or striped material that has perforation similar to that of photographic film for transport and synchronization. Original audiotape sound is transferred to magnetic film for editing.

magnetic tape A thin plastic or Mylar material coated with a formula of magnetically responsive ferrous oxide that records and preserves electronic signals.

M and E tracks Separate music and sound effects tracks.

married print The composite of optical sound track and a positive print of the complete film. The final laboratory step of printing the film includes the sound track. The synchronization is correct for projection.

mask A shield placed before the camera to cut off some portion of the camera's field of view.

master shot A single shot of an entire piece of dramatic action designed to facilitate the assembly of the closer, detailed shots from which the final sequence will be created.

match cut A cut in which the end of one shot leads logically and visually to the beginning of the second shot. An example is the cut from a character exiting frame right to the character entering frame left.

match dissolve A dissolve in which one object is seen in different settings but occupies the same position on screen throughout the dissolve.

medium close shot A shot with a looser frame than a close shot. A medium close shot of an actor, for example, includes everything from the waist up. A close shot includes only the actor's face.

medium shot For the human figure, a shot from the waist up.

mix To combine the various separate sounds on location or to combine various sound tracks to make a smooth composite.

monitor A video display screen. A monitor usually does not include a tuner.

montage A compilation of images.

MOS Silent shooting (no sound recorded at the time).

Moviola The trade name for a portable editing machine. It is based on the same technical concept as a motion picture projector. Sound is run separately from picture, to allow for editing of each sound or picture individually or of both together.

multiple exposure Repeated exposures made on a single series of film frames.

multitrack A technique of sound recording that uses a separate track for each source to permit subsequent mixing and blending.

narration Also called *commentary*. Descriptive dialog accompanying a film. Voice over serves as a bridging device between sequences. Voice over can also be used to clarify the narrative intentions of the visuals.

negative Refers to the originating material, film and videotape, used to record images. Tone and color values are the reverse of the original.

negative cutting Editing the original negative film from the positive working copy used during the editing. Once the negative cutting is complete, the film is printed from the negative, or an interpositive is printed from the negative.

nonlinear editing Editing videotape out of sequence. It allows the editor to build or switch segments in any manner.

NTSC The North American television standard: a 525-line system that scans 30 interlaced television frames per second.

offline edit Editing video material using low-cost equipment to produce rough cut before using expensive broadcast-standard equipment for the final work.

one light A film print made using the same exposure for every scene and take on a roll without any color correction.

online edit The last stage of videotape editing, which results in a final master tape. Time-coded offline edit decisions are used to create the master tape.

optical Any effect carried out using an optical printer. Opticals are usually performed in a laboratory. Dissolves, fades, and wipes are examples of opticals.

optical printer A high-quality film projector and motion picture camera that are mechanically interlocked so that both synchronously advance the film one frame at a time. Fades, dissolves, and other special effects are recorded on an optical printer.

optical track The sound track mixed from magnetic track onto a magnetic master mix, then transferred to an optical track so that it can be combined with the visuals on a composite print.

original The film exposed in the camera after processing; the first video recording prior to copying or editing.

outtake A shot or scene discarded in the process of editing.

PAL The European color television coding standard: a 625-line, 50-Hz television transmission system.

panning shot A shot in which the camera moves along a horizontal axis. A panning shot is often used to establish location or to follow action.

parallel action A device of narrative construction in which the development of two pieces of action is represented by alternately showing a fragment of one and then a fragment of another. See also **crosscut**.

parallel cut See **crosscut**.

perforation Holes along the edge of a strip of film used for its transport and registration.

postproduction The editing of prerecorded material, including the use of special effects and audio dubbing.

print A photographic copy of a film, usually with a positive image.

random-access editing systems Nonlinear electronic video editing equipment allows the editor to build a segment out of sequence without having to modify material on either side of a shot or sequence. The shot and sound information are stored in computer memory, and when needed, picture and sound are switched from one camera to another.

reaction shot A cut to a performer's face to capture an emotional response.

release print A motion picture positive print that includes picture and sound and is made for general distribution and exhibition.

retake The repetition of a take.

reversal film A special type of direct positive film.

rewind An apparatus for rewinding film.

rushes See **dailies**.

shooting ratio The amount of film or tape exposed or recorded in production compared to the amount actually used in the final edited program.

single system A method of film or videotape recording or editing in which the picture and sound are located on the same piece of film or videotape.

slate A device used in front of the film or television camera to display production information such as scene number, take number, date, and other pertinent information. The clapboard, which also provides a simultaneous sound cue for editing, is one type of slate.

slave A unit designed to function only as ordered by a master unit, for example, a videotape recorder that is controlled by another VTR.

slow motion A movement or shot that takes place more slowly than it did in reality.

sound track A narrow path that normally runs along one side of cinematographic sound film in which sound is recorded in the form of a light trace varying in its light transmission.

special effect A general term for scenes in which an illusion of the action required is created by the use of special equipment and processes.

splice A physical joining in film or tape.

stock shot See **library shot**.

superimpose To add one picture on top of another. Usually, both continue to be visible. To add a caption or graphic over a picture.

sync To match sound and picture.

synchronizer An apparatus that facilitates the mechanical operation of synchronizing two tracks.

synchronous sound Sound that has been synchronized with the picture.

take A single recording or a shot.

tilt To move the camera on a vertical axis: from up to down or from down to up.

time code A coding system, usually binary, recorded on audiotape, videotape, and sometimes on film for subsequent synchronization and editing. It denotes hours, minutes, and seconds and allows frames to be identified.

time code generator An electronic clock that generates and assigns to each video or audio frame a unique identification number of eight digits.

time code reader A device that reads and visually displays the eight-digit SMPTE time code.

track A defined part of the recording medium, photographic or magnetic, that carries discrete information.

tracking shot Also known as a *trucking shot*. A shot taken when the camera is in motion on a truck, dolly, or trolley.

trim The portion of a shot remaining after the selected material has been used in an edit.

trolley A wheeled device on which the camera can be moved while taking a shot.

two-shot A shot framing two people, usually from the waist up.

U-matic The trade name for a videocassette system that uses three-quarter-inch tape.

videocassette A cassette containing video recording tape with separate supply and take-up spools.

videotape Magnetic tape specifically designed for use as a video recording medium.

videotape recorder (VTR) A device used to record and replay television pictures and sound on magnetic tape.

wide-angle lens A lens of short focal length that has a wide angle of view and great depth of field.

wide screen A screen with a ratio greater than 1.33:1.

wild shooting Shooting the picture of a sound film without simultaneously recording the sound of the action.

wild track A sound track recorded independently of the picture with which it will subsequently be combined.

wipe A transition from one shot to another in which a line appears to travel across the screen, removing one shot and revealing another.

work print See **cutting print**.

zoom To magnify a chosen area of the image by means of a zoom lens (a lens with a variable focal length). The camera appears to move closer to the subject.

Selected Bibliography

G. Anderson, Video Editing and Post-Production: A Professional Guide, Knowledge Industries, New York, 1984.

D. Andrew, Concepts in Film Theory, Oxford University Press, New York, 1984.

———, The Major Film Theories, Oxford University, New York Press, 1976.

D. Arijon, Grammar of the Film Language, second ed., Silman-James Press, Los Angeles, 1991.

R. Aruheim, Film, Faber and Faber, London, 1933.

H. Baddley, The Technique of Documentary Film Production, Focal Press, Boston, 1963.

T. Balio (Ed.), The American Film Industry, University of Wisconsin Press, Madison, 1976.

R. M. Barsam (Ed.), Nonfiction Film: A Critical History, E. P. Dutton, New York, 1973.

———, Nonfiction Film: Theory and Criticism, E. P. Dutton, New York, 1976.

A. Bazin, What Is Cinema? vols. I, II, University of California Press, Berkeley, 1971.

M. F. Belenky, B. M. Cliachy, N. R. Goldberger, J. M. Torule, Women's Way of Knowing. The Development of Self, Voice and Mind, Basic Books, New York, 1986.

D. Bordwell, J. Staiger, K. Thompson, The Classical Hollywood Cinema, Columbia University Press, New York, 1985.

D. Bordwell, K. Thompson, Film Art: An Introduction, third ed., McGraw-Hill, New York, 1990.

J. Burder, The Technique of Editing 16-mm Films, Focal Press, London, 1975.

W. E. Cameron, An Analysis of 'A Diary for Timothy', Cinema Studies 1 (Spring 1967) 68.

R. L. Carringer, The Making of Citizen Kane, University of California Press, Berkeley, 1985.

S. Chatman, Antonioni, or the Surface of the World, University of California Press, Berkeley, 1985.

D. A. Cook, A History of Narrative Film, W. W. Norton, New York, 1990.

R. Crittenden, The Thames & Hudson Manual of Film Editing, Thames and Hudson, London, 1981.

K. Dancyger, J. Rush, Alternative Scriptwriting, second ed., Focal Press, Boston, 1995.

K. Dancyger, The Director's Idea, Focal Press, 2006.

E. Dmytryk, On Film Editing, Focal Press, Boston, 1985.

A. Dovzhenko, The Poet as Filmmaker, MIT Press, Cambridge, 1973.

S. Eisenstein, Film Form, Harcourt Brace Jovanovich, New York, 1977.

———, The Film Sense, Harcourt Brace Jovanovich, New York, 1975.

———, Notes of a Film Director, Dover Publications, New York, 1970.

T. Elsaesser, Early Cinema, British Film Institute, London, 1950.

E. Erikson, Identity: Youth and Crisis, Dutton, New York, 1968.

S. Freud, Beyond the Pleasure Principle, Martino Fine Books, 2010.

R. Gottesman (Ed.), Focus on Citizen Kane, Prentice-Hall, Englewood Cliffs, NJ, 1971.

B. Happé (Ed.), Dictionary of Image Technology, Focal Press, London, 1988.

B. Henderson, A Critique of Film Theory, E. P. Dutton, New York, 1980.

A. Innsdorff, François Truffaut, Twayne Publishers, Boston, 1978.

L. Jacobs, The Movies as Medium, Farrar, Strauss and Giroux, New York, 1970.

———, The Rise of the American Film, Harcourt, Brace and Company, New York, 1947.

C. G. Jung, Memories, Dreams, Reflections, Pantheon, New York, 1963.

S. Katz, Film Directors Shot by Shot, Focal Press, Boston, 1991.

O. Kernberg, Severe Personality Disorders: Psychotherapeutic Strategies, Yale University Press, New Haven, CT, 1984.

I. Konigsbertg, The Complete Film Dictionary, New American Dictionary, New York, 1987.

S. Kracauer, Theory of Film, Oxford University Press, New York, 1965.

J. Leyda, Kino, George Allen and Unwin, London, 1960.

A. Lovell, J. Hillier, Studies in Documentary, Martin Secker and Warburg, London, 1972.

E. Lundgren, The Art of the Film, George Allen and Unwin, London, 1948.

R. D. MacCann, Film: A Montage of Theories, E. P. Dutton, New York, 1966.

G. Mast, M. Cohen, Film Theory and Criticism, third ed., Oxford University Press, New York, 1985.

D. Mayer, Eisenstein's *Potemkin*, Da Capo Press, New York, 1972.

J. McBride, Orson Welles, Martin Secker and Warburg, London, 1972.

J. Mellen, The World of Luis Buñuel: Essays in Criticism, Oxford University Press, New York, 1978.

A. Michaelson (Ed.), Kino-Eye: The Writings of Dziga Vertov, University of California Press, Berkeley, 1984.

J. Monaco, Alain Renais, Oxford University Press, New York, 1975.

———, How to Read a Movie, Oxford University Press, New York, 1977.

———, The New Wave, Oxford University Press, New York, 1976.

T. A. Nelson, Kubrick: Inside a Film Artist's Maze, Indiana University Press, Bloomington, 1982.

B. Nichols (Ed.), Movies and Methods: An Anthology, University of California Press, Berkeley, 1976.

V. Nilsen, The Cinema as Graphic Art, Hill and Wang, New York, 1936.

V. I. Pudovkin, Film Technique and Film Acting, Vision Press, London, 1968.

M. Rabiger, Directing the Documentary, second ed., Focal Press, Boston, 1992.

K. Reisz, G. Millar, The Technique of Film Editing, second ed., Focal Press, Boston, 1968.

R. Rosenblum, R. Karen, When the Shooting Stops . . . , DaCapo Press, New York, 1986.

A. Sarris, The American Cinema, University of Chicago Press, Chicago, 1968.

A. Schneider, Electronic Post-Production Terms and Concepts, Focal Press, Boston, 1990.

E. Sussex, The Rise and Fall of British Documentary, University of California Press, Los Angeles, 1975.

P. Swann, The British Documentary Film Movement, 1926–1946, Cambridge University Press, Cambridge, 1989.

A. Tudor, Theories of Film, Martin Secker and Warburg, London, 1974.

N. A. Vardac, Stage to Screen, Harvard University Press, Cambridge, MA, 1949.

E. Weis, J. Belton (Eds.), Film Sound: Theory and Practice, Columbia University Press, New York, 1985.

P. Wollen, Readings and Writings, Versa, London, 1982.

———, Signs and Meaning in the Cinema, Martin Secker and Warburg, London, 1969.

R. Wood, Hitchcock's Films Revisited, Columbia University Press, New York, 1989.

Index

A

Academy aspect ratio, 99, 100f
 foreground-background
   relationship, 102f
acceleration of narrative stories,
   135–136
action genre, 287–300
 The Bourne Ultimatum (2007),
   296–298
 contemporary context for,
   289–298
 The General (1927), 292–294,
   292f, 293f
 A History of Violence (2005),
   298–300, 299f
 pace in, 198–199
actors becoming directors, 72
adventure film, pace in,
   198–199, 382
aesthetics
 in digital technologies,
   392–393
 in documentary filmmaking,
   328
 editing for, 277–284
 Brighton Rock (1947),
   278–279
 The Passion (2004), 282–284
 in personal documentary,
   350
 The Third Man (1949),
   279–282
 in personal documentary, 350
African-American community *See*
   Lee, Spike
L'Age d'Or (1930), 29
Aguirre: The Wrath of God (1972),
   150

Alexander Nevsky (1938), 395
Alexandrov, Grigori, on sound in
   film, 35
Alfie (1966), 315
alienation (character), 143–146
All About Eve (1950), 301
All that Jazz (1979), 199
Allan, Anthony Havelock, 80
Allen, Woody, 238, 319–320
 Annie Hall (1977), 315
 Hannah and Her Sisters (1986),
   248–249
 Manhattan (1979), 302
Altman, Robert, 146–148
 McCabe and Mrs. Miller
   (1971), 304
America, America (1961), 270
American Beauty (1999), 401
American Graffiti (1973), 387
anarchy, portraying in editing,
   143–146
An Andalusian Dog *See* Un Chien
   d'Andalou (1929)
Anderson, Lindsay, 138–140,
   341, 397
Anderson, Paul Thomas
 Magnolia (1999), 409–412
 There Will Be Blood (2007),
   273–275
Anka, Paul *See* Lonely Boy (1962)
Annie Hall (1977), 315
antinarrative editing, feminism
   and, 160–162
Antonioni, Michelangelo,
   108–109, 128–129, 169
Apatow, Judd, 326
Apocalypse Now (1979), 408
Applause (1929), 42–44, 43f

archival sequence in
   documentary, 332–334
Aronofsky, Darren, 230
 Requiem for a Dream (2000),
   230–232
art, ideas about, 51–56
articulation of premise, 243
artificial reality, 233–237. *See also*
   digital reality
 constructed artifice, 235
 imagined as observational,
   235–236
 special effects, use of, 237
 spectacle, use of, 236–237
 video over film, 234–235
aspect ratio, screen *See* wide
   screen format
asynchronism *See* visual
   discontinuity
Atonement (2007), 252–254
Autant-Lara, Claude, 100
The Aviator (2004), 239

B

background-foreground
   relationship, wide screen
   and, 101, 102f
Bad Day at Black Rock (1955),
   105–106
The Ballad of Ramblin' Jack (2000),
   356–357
Ballard, Carroll *See* The Black
   Stallion (1979)
Bandit Queen (1994), 223–225
Bar-Lev, Amir, 356
Barry Lyndon (1975), 149, 149f,
   150, 217, 387

445

The Battle of Algiers (1965), 350–351
The Battle of Culloden (1965), 110
Bay, Michael, 222
Beach Red (1967), 205
the Beatles *See* Help! (1965); A Hard Day's Night (1964)
Beatty, Warren, 72
Before the Rain (1994), 210–211, 397
Belenky, Mary Field, 159
Belle de Jour (1967), 395
Belvaux, Remy, 213
Ben Hur (1959), 289
Benigni, Roberto, 177–178
   Life Is Beautiful (1998), 177–178, 188–190
Beresford, Bruce, 290
Bergman, Ingmar, 137, 138
   Winter Light (1962), 389
Berkeley, Busby, 64
Bertolucci, Bernardo *See* The Conformist (1971)
Besson, Luc, 217
The Best Years of Our Lives (1946), 115
Billy Liar (1963), 141
The Birds (1963), 87
The Birth of a Nation (1915), 6–7, 289
The Black Stallion (1979), 387–388
Black Sunday (1977), 290, 303–304
Blackmail (1929), 36–38, 37f, 38f, 227
The Blair Witch Project (1999), 213
Blank, Les, 351
Blitz, Jeffrey, 365
   One Day in September (1999), 365–368
Blue Velvet (1986), 163
The Body Snatcher (1945), 73
Bogdanovich, Peter *See* What's Up, Doc? (1972)
Bonnie and Clyde (1967), 144
Boorman, John, 108, 166, 290
   Point Blank (1967), 277
Borden, Lizzie, 160
Boulting, John *See* Brighton Rock (1947)

Bourne trilogy (2004–2007), 296–297
   The Bourne Supremacy (2004), 195–197
   The Bourne Ultimatum (2007), 296–298
The Bridge on the River Kwai (1957), 80–83, 222, 223
Brief Encounter (1945), 80, 81
Brighton Rock (1947), 278–279
Bringing Up Baby (1938), 316
Brittain, Donald *See* Memorandum (1966)
Broadcast News (1987), 317
Broken Blossoms (1919), 7–11, 8f, 9f, 10f, 11f, 12f, 255
Brook, Peter, 141, 142, 169–170
Brooks, James, 319–320
Bullitt (1968), 197, 277, 290
Buñuel, Luis, 24–25, 27–31, 227, 350, 351, 395
Burden of Dreams (1983), 351

C

Cabaret (1972), 199, 384–385
The Cabinet of Dr. Caligari (1919), 13
camera blimps, 35
camera placement *See* subjective camera placement
Cameron, James, 290
   The Terminator (1984), 290, 302
Capitalism: A Love Story (2009), 357
Capote (2005), 239–240
Capra, Frank, 56–57, 318, 319, 343, 350
   Lost Horizons (1937), 255
   Why We Fight series (1943–1945), 56–57, 343, 364
Capturing the Friedmans (2003), 364–365
Cardiff, Jack, 71
Carnal Knowledge (1971), 221
Cassavetes, John, 72
   Faces (1968), 327
   Shadows (1959), 350–351
Catch 22 (1970), 221
Caught (1949), 203–204
Cavalcanti, Alberto, 36
Cavani, Liliana, 158

The Celebration (1998), 214–216, 238
Chagrin et la pitié (1969), 364
change in location, continuity on, 379–380
change in scene, continuity on, 379–380
Chaos (2001), 234
chaos, freedom of, 143–146
Chaplin, Charlie, 61–64, 72
   Modern Times (1936), 62, 315, 317
character *See also* relationships (between characters)
   action and, 287–288
   character comedy, 315
   character-driven films, 248–254
     Atonement (2007), 252–254
     Hannah and Her Sisters (1986), 248–249
     Hero (1992), 249–250
     The Hours (2002), 250–252, 252f
     Valmont (1989), 249
   dialog and, 303–305. See also dialog
   environment and
     alienation from context, 143–146
     gaining understanding from environment, 152–153
     interior life as landscape, 125–132
   feeling states vs., 168
   feminism and politics, 158–160
   large number of, continuity and *See* Nashville (1975)
   musicals and, 64
   pace in thriller genre, 197
   preserving screen direction, 375–378, 376f, 377f
   role reversal comedy
     Forgetting Sarah Marshall (2008), 324–325
     The Lady Eve (1941), 320–321, 321f, 325–326
     Victor/Victoria (1982), 321–326, 322f
   romantic relationship stories, 186
   vaudeville and, 63–64

voice, in personal documentary, 351
wide screen format and, 102–104
Chayefsky, Paddy, 316
Chelovek s kino-apparatom See The Man with a Movie Camera (1929)
Un Chien d'Andalou (1929), 27, 27f, 28f, 29f, 227, 393, 395
Chinatown (1974), 309–312, 311f
Chretien, Henri, 100
Chricton, Charles, 287
El Cid (1961), 107, 222
cinéma vérité, 109–114, 137–138, 237–238
  elevating, 213–217
  personal documentary vs., 349
CinemaScope, 100, 100f, 101.
  See also wide screen format
  background-foreground relationship, 101, 102f
cinematographers becoming directors, 71
Cinerama, 100
Citizen Kane (1941), 66–69, 68f, 72–73, 217, 277, 393, 395
The City (1939), 54–56, 54f, 55f
City Lights (1931), 62
clarity of narrative, 72, 372.
  See also editing for narrative clarity; narrative
  in action sequences, 296
  David Lean's use of, 81
  dynamic of relativity, 116–118
Clockers (1995), 156, 157, 157f
A Clockwork Orange (1971), 205
close-up *See also* extreme close-up
  action and, 288
  in Alfred Hitchcock's work, 90–91
  birth of, 5–6
  cinéma vérité and, 109–110
  in dialog *See* dialog
  editing for dramatic emphasis, 258–259, 264–265
  in imaginative documentary, 342
  juxtaposed with long shots, 222–227
  rhythm and, 384

in Sam Peckinpah's work, 144, 145
Clueless (1995), 168
Coen, Ethan and Joel, 399, 407–408
  Raising Arizona (1987), 317, 382–383
Collateral (2004), 234–235
color, matching tone and, 378
Come and See (1985), 227–230, 407–408
comedy genre, 315–326
  directors, about, 318–320
  editing concerns, 316–318
  pace in, 318, 325–326
  role reversal
    Forgetting Sarah Marshall (2008), 324–325
    The Lady Eve (1941), 320–321, 321f, 325–326
    Victor/Victoria (1982), 321–326, 322f
  types of comedy, 315–318
communicating ideas *See* documentary
conflict, in action sequences, 288
The Conformist (1971), 289, 385–387
constructed artifice, 235
constructive editing, birth of, 13–16
context, 402
continuity *See* film continuity
conversation *See* dialog
cornfield sequence *See* North by Northwest (1959)
Costner, Kevin, 72
coverage, adequacy of, 372–373
Coward, Noel, 80
Crimes and Misdmeanors (1989), 395
Cronenberg, David, 290
  A History of Violence (2005), 298–300, 299f
Crooklyn (1994), 154f, 156
crosscutting, in imaginative documentary, 342
Crouching Tiger, Hidden Dragon (2000), 177, 182–186
culture, ideas about, 51–56
cutaway
  in Alfred Hitchcock's work, 92–94

birth of, 5
  rhythm and, 383–384
cutting on motion, 89
cutting pace *See* pace

D

Daldry, Stephen *See* The Hours (2002)
Dali, Salvador, 395
Dalrimple, Ian, 344
Dardenne, Jean-Pierre and Luc, 213, 238. *See also* Rosetta (1999)
Dash, Julie, 161, 162
Dassin, Jules, 289
Daughters of the Dust (1991), 161, 162, 399
Davies, Terence, 395
The Day the Earth Stood Still (1951), 73
D-Day landing sequence *See* Saving Private Ryan (1997)
de Bout, Jan, 71
De Vito, Danny, 319–320
Dead End (1937), 65–66
degraded plot, in MTV style, 168–169
DeMille, Cecil B., 289
Demme, Jonathan, 163
  Rachel Getting Married (2008), 269
The Departed (2006), 271–272, 271f
Desperately Seeking Susan (1985), 160
diagonal movement, following, 377f
dialog, 301–314
  and character, 303–305
  contemporary (*Chinatown*, 1974), 309–312, 311f
  early (*Trouble in Paradise*, 1932), 307f
  multipurpose, 304–306
  and plot, 302–303, 305
  as transformative (*Michael Clayton*, 2007), 312–313
  Trouble in Paradise (1932), 306–309
Diary for Timothy (1945), 55f, 57–60, 342
Dickson, William, 3
digital reality, 233–240

digital reality (*Continued*)
 pushing realism, 237–240
 understanding artificial reality,
  233–237
digital technology, nonlinear
  editing and *See* nonlinear
  editing
diminished plot, in MTV style,
  168–169
direction of screen, preserving,
  375–378, 376f, 377f
directors
 becoming editors, 71–86
  David Lean, 79–85,
   108–109, 222. *See also*
   Lawrence of Arabia (1962)
  Robert Wise *See* Wise, Robert
 of comedy, 318–320
 editor as agent of, 269
 female, 158, 160–162
Dirty Harry (1971), 289
*The Discreet Charm of the
  Bourgeoisie* (1972), 395
disjunctive editing, 169–170
dissolves, 375–376, 384
Distant Voices, Still Lives (1988), 395
distorting lens, reliance on,
  205–206
Divide and Conquer (1943), 57f,
  58f, 364
Do the Right Thing (1989), 153, 154
Doctor Zhivago (1965), 81–82,
  222, 223
docudrama approach, 133–134,
  239
 pace in, 194–195
 in *United 93* (2006), 258
documentary, 45–60, 327–340
 cinéma vérité *See* cinéma
  vérité
 ethics, politics, and aesthetics,
  328
 ideas about art and culture,
  51–56
 ideas about war and society,
  46–51, 56–60
 imaginative documentary,
  341–348
  altering meaning away from
   literal, 341–343
  wartime propaganda, 328,
   343–347, 343f, 350
 innovations in, 349–362

dramatic-entertainment
  values, 363–368
 personal documentary,
  349–355
 use of narration, 355–361
Memorandum (1966),
  329–334
 archival sequence, 332–334
 continuity and narrator
  influence, 329–330
 images, 330f, 332f, 333f,
  334f, 335f, 336f, 337f,
  338f, 339f
 reportage sequence,
  334–340
 transitional sequence,
  330–332
 mixed with policy story *See*
  The Thin Blue Line (1988)
 staged, 327
Dogme, 95, 213, 214, 237–238,
  349
Dogville (2003), 235
Donaldson, Roger, 290
Dovzhenko, Alexander, 24–27,
  107–108, 395
Dr. Jekyll and Mr. Hyde (1932),
  43, 44, 227
Dr. Strangelove (1964), 316
dramatic construction, birth of,
  5–13
dramatic emphasis, editing for,
  255–266
 Frost/Nixon (2008), 261–266
  close-up, 264–265
  dynamic montage, 265
  juxtaposition, 265–266
  pace, 266
 United 93 (2006), 255–261
  close-up in, 258–259
  docudrama event, 258
  dynamic montage, 259–260
  pace, 260–261
dramatic strategies in
  documentary, 363–368
 Munich (2005), 365, 366
 One Day in September (1999),
  365–368
dream states *See* subjective states
The Dreamlife of Angels (1998),
  216–217
dreamstates, in Alfred Hitchcock's
  work, 95–97

Dreyer, Carl, 13, 223
 The Passion of Joan of Arc
  (1928), 13, 223, 255
Duck Soup (1934), 315
Duel in the Sun (1946), 289
Dupont, E. A., 13
dynamic montage, 259–260, 265

E
early sound films, 33–44
 Applause (1929), 42–44, 43f
 Blackmail (1929), 36–38, 37f,
  38f, 227
 Dr. Jekyll and Mr. Hyde (1932),
  43, 44, 227
 technological improvements,
  35
 technological limitations,
  33–34
 theoretical issues, 35–36
Earth (1930), 25–26, 26f, 27f,
  107–108, 395
East of Eden (1955), 104–105
Eastwood, Clint, 72, 207
 Invictus (2009), 246–248
L'Eclisse (The Eclipse) (1962),
  129–132, 130f, 131f, 169,
  395
Edison, Thomas, 3
editing, stages of, 371
editing comedy *See* comedy genre
editing dialog *See* dialog
editing documentaries *See*
  documentary
editing for aesthetics, 277–284
 Brighton Rock (1947),
  278–279
 The Passion (2004), 282–284
 in personal documentary, 350
 The Third Man (1949),
  279–282
editing for continuity, 371–380.
  See also film continuity
 adequacy of coverage,
  372–373
 location change, 379–380
 matching action, 373–375
 matching flow over cuts,
  378–379
 matching tone, 378
 preserving screen direction,
  375–378, 376f, 377f
 scene change, 379–380

seamlessness, 372, 384
setting the scene, 378
time and place, 387–388
editing for dramatic emphasis,
    255–266
    Frost/Nixon (2008), 261–266
        close-up, 264–265
        dynamic montage, 265
        juxtaposition, 265–266
        pace, 266
    United 93 (2006), 255–261
        close-up in, 258–259
        docudrama event, 258
        dynamic montage, 259–260
        pace, 260–261
editing for narrative clarity,
    243–254
    character-driven films,
        248–254
        Atonement (2007), 252–254
        Hannah and Her Sisters
            (1986), 248–249
        Hero (1992), 249–250
        The Hours (2002), 250–252,
            252f
        Valmont (1989), 249
    plot-driven films, 244–248
        Five Fingers (1952),
            244–245
        Invictus (2009), 246–248
        Mountains of the Moon
            (1990), 245–246
editing for pace, 381–390.
    See also pace
    randomness of pace, 388–389
    rhythm, 383–387
    timing, 382–383
editing for subtext, 264, 267–276
    The Departed (2006), 271–272
    Lust, Caution (2006), 272–273
    rhythm and, 384
    Saving Private Ryan (1997),
        267–268
    There Will Be Blood (2007),
        273–275
editors
    as agents of directors, 269
    becoming directors, 71–86
        David Lean, 79–85,
            108–109, 222. *See also*
            Lawrence of Arabia (1962)
        Robert Wise *See* Wise, Robert
    knowledge, in comedy, 318

styles of *See* style
editor's voice *See* voice
Edvard Munch (1974), 350–351
Edwards, Blake, 287, 319
    Pink Panther series
        (1964–1978), 287, 316
    Victor/Victoria (1982),
        321–326, 322f
8½ (1963), 125–128, 126f, 127f,
    128f, 129f, 169, 268–269
Eisenstein, Sergei, 16–23, 222,
    395
    exploring moment of death,
        143–144
    pace, 193
    Potemkin (1925), 8f, 17f, 18, 18f,
        19f, 20f, 21f, 22f, 23f, 289
    screen shape experimentation,
        100
    on sound in film, 35
El Cid (1961), 107, 222
Elizabeth (1998), 223, 225–227
Elliott, Aiyana, 356
emotional states, in MTV style,
    168
energy, in nonlinear narrative,
    400, 402–405, 409, 412
The Enigma of Kaspar Hauser
    (1974), 150, 169–170
Enoch Arden (1908), 5–6
Enoch Arden (1911), 6
entertainment values in
    documentary, 363–368
environment (place) *See also*
    digital reality; time
    character and
        alienation from context,
            143–146
        gaining understanding from
            environment, 152–153
        interior life as landscape,
            125–132
    location change, continuity in,
        379–380
    obliterated, in MTV style,
        169–170
    scene change, continuity in,
        379–380
    sense of, pace and, 387–388
    societal *See* society
    sound editing and, 38–41
    wide screen format and,
        102–106

world building
    of Stanley Kubrick, 148–150
    of Werner Herzog, 150
establishing shots, 378
ethics in documentary
    filmmaking, 328
Europa Europa (1990), 407–408
excitation, in action sequences, 288
Exodus (1960), 103, 103f, 222
extreme close-up, 222. *See also*
    close-up
    in Alfred Hitchcock's work,
        91–92, 96
extreme long shot
    in Alfred Hitchcock's work,
        89–90
    birth of, 5
    establishing shots, 378
Eyes Wide Shut (1999), 217–219

F

Faces (1968), 327
fade-outs, 384
Fahrenheit 9/11 (2004), 363
farce, 316–318
Fargo (1996), 407–408
Fast, Cheap and Out of Control
    (1998), 352–355, 364
Fellini, Federico, 108–109,
    125–132, 169
    8½ (1963), 125–128, 126f,
        127f, 128f, 129f, 169,
        268–269
Fellini Satyricon (1970), 108–109,
    205
female directors, 158, 160–162
female-male reversals *See* role
    reversal comedy
feminism
    antinarrative editing, 160–162
    politics and, 158–160
La Femme Nikita (1990), 169
Festen (1998) *See* The Celebration
    (1998)
Figgis, Mike, 214
Fighter (2000), 356
film, using video instead of,
    234–235
film continuity, 371–380. *See also*
    film continuity; narrative;
    visual discontinuity
    adequacy of coverage,
        372–373

film continuity (*Continued*)
  birth of, 4−5
  cinéma vérité and, 109−110
  collapsing time, 67
  documentary (*Memorandum*, 1966), 329−330
  with large number of characters *See* Nashville (1975)
  location change, 379−380
  matching action, 373−375
  matching flow over cuts, 378−379
  matching tone, 378
  preserving screen direction, 375−378, 376f, 377f
  scene change, 379−380
  seamlessness, 372, 384
  setting the scene, 378
  time and place, 387−388
  wide screen format and, 101
film coverage, adequacy of, 372−373
film noir
  mixed with horror story *See* Blue Velvet (1986)
  mixed with screwball comedy *See* Something Wild (1986)
Film Technique and Film Acting, 36
Le Fils (*The Son*) (2002), 238−239
A Fish Called Wanda (1988), 287
Fitzcarraldo (1982), 351
Five Fingers (1952), 244−245, 289
Flaherty, Robert, 46−48, 350, 363
  Louisiana Story (1948), 342
  Man of Aran (1934), 46−48, 47f, 48f, 49f
Flashdance (1983), 168, 170, 171, 199. *See also* MTV style
flow, matching over cuts, 378−379
The Fog of War: Eleven lEssons from the Life of Robert McNamara (2004), 364
Fonteyne, Frederick, 213
footage, sufficiency of, 372−373
Ford, John, 207, 223
foreground-background relationship, wide screen and, 101, 102f

Foreign Correspondent (1940), 89−90
Forgetting Sarah Marshall (2008), 324−326
Forman, Milos *See* Valmont (1989)
Fosse, Bob, 199
  Cabaret (1972), 199, 384−385
The 400 Blows (1959), 118−119
fragmentation of scenes, birth of, 5−13
Fraker, William, 71
Frankenheimer, John, 217
  Black Sunday (1977), 290, 303−304
Frears, Stephen, 249
  Hero (1992), 198−199
  Les Liaisons Dangereuses (1988), 249
freedom of chaos, 143−146
The French Connection (1971), 197, 290−291
Friedkin, William *See* The French Connection (1971)
From the Life of the Marionettes (1980), 138
Frost/Nixon (2008), 261−266
  close-up, 264−265
  compared to *United 93* (2006), 264, 266
  dynamic montage, 265
  juxtaposition, 265−266
  pace, 266
Full Metal Jacket (1987), 217−218, 277, 387, 388f, 408
Funny People (2009), 326
A Funny Thing Happened on the Way to the Forum (1966), 166, 316−317

G

Gance, Abel, 99
Gavras-Costa, 382
The General (1927), 292−294, 292f, 293f
genres
  adventure film, 382
  comedy *See* comedy genre
  docudrama, 133−134, 239
    pace in, 194−195
    in *United 93* (2006), 258
  documentary *See* cinéma vérité; documentary

imitating, 207−208
mixing, 162−163
Gibson, Mel, 72
  The Passion (2004), 282−284
Gilbert, Lewis, 319−320
Gilliam, Terry, 205−206
Gilroy, Tony *See* Michael Clayton (2007)
Girard, François, 397
Gladiator (2000), 223, 236−237
Godard, Jean-Luc, 121−123, 396, 398
Gold Diggers of 1933 (1933), 64
The Gold Rush (1925), 62
Goldberg, B. Z., 359−360
The Golden Age (1930), 29
The Good, the Bad, and the Ugly (1967), 108, 316
The Graduate (1967), 304−306
Grandrieux, Philippe, 238−239
Grass (2000), 360−361
The Greaser's Gauntlet (1908), 5
The Great Dictator (1940), 62
Great Expectations (1946), 80−82, 84
The Great Race (1965), 287
The Great Train Robbery (1903), 4
Greengrass, Paul, 196
  The Bourne Supremacy (2004), 195−197
  The Bourne Ultimatum (2007), 296−298
  United 93 (2006), 255−261
    close-up in, 258−259
    compared to *Frost/Nixon* (2008), 264, 266
    docudrama event, 258
    dynamic montage, 259−260
    pace, 260−261
Grierson, John, 45−46, 56, 350
  Night Mail (1936), 49−51, 50f, 341, 363
Griffith, D. W., 5−13, 222, 255, 395
  The Birth of a Nation (1915), 6−7, 289
  pace, 193
Griffith, Lawrence, 32. *See also* Griffith, D. W.
Grizzly Man (2005), 364
guide, documentary narrator as, 357−359
Gunga Din (1939), 289

H

handheld style of cinéma vérité, 110. *See also* cinéma vérité
Hannah and Her Sisters (1986), 248–249
Happiness (1998), 401, 403–405
A Hard Day's Night (1964), 134–136, 136f, 166, 170
    pace, 194
Harris, Mark Jonathan, 357–358
    Into the Arms of Strangers (2000), 358–359
    The Long Way Home (1997), 358–359
Hathaway, Henry, 289
Having a Wild Weekend (1965), 166
Hawks, Howard, 207, 318–319
    Bringing Up Baby (1938), 316
Hecht, Ben, 71
Heckerling, Amy, 160, 168
heightened realism, 239
heightened realism, birth of, 13–16
Hell in the Pacific (1968), 108
Help! (1965), 134, 166, 170
    pace, 194
Hero (1992), 249–250
Hero (Ying xiong) (2002), 198–199
The Heroes of Telmark (1965), 222
Herzog, Werner, 148–150, 169–170, 351
    Grizzly Man (2005), 364
    My Best Friend (1999), 351–352
High Noon (1952), 144, 207, 289
Hill, George Roy, 319–320
Hillcoat, John *See* The Proposition (2006)
Hiroshima, Mon Amour (1960), 123–125, 124f, 169
A History of Violence (2005), 298–300, 299f
Hitchcock, Alfred, 36, 87–98, 227
    the chase, 94–95
    cutting on motion, 89
    dreamstates, 95–97
    sound cut, 88–89
    unity of sound, 92–94
Hitchcock, Alfred, films of
    The Birds (1963), 87

Blackmail (1929), 36–38, 37f, 38f, 227
Foreign Correspondent (1940), 89–90
The Man Who Knew Too Much (1956), 92–94
North by Northwest (1959), 94–95, 94f
Notorious (1946), 90–91
Psycho (1960), 91–92, 255
Rear Window (1954), 87–88
Rope (1948), 87–88, 381
Spellbound (1945), 87, 89
Strangers on a Train (1951), 88
The 39 Steps (1935), 88–89, 92–94
Vertigo (1958), 95–97, 96f
Holland, Agnieszka, 161
    Europa Europa (1990), 407–408
Holocaust
    The Long Way Home (1997), 358–359
    Memorandum (1966), 330f, 332f, 333f, 334f, 335f, 336f, 337f, 338f, 329–334, 339f
    archival sequence, 332–334
    continuity and narrator influence, 329–330
    reportage sequence, 334–340
    transition sequence, 330–332
horror mixed with film noir *See* Blue Velvet (1986)
The Hospital (1971), 316
The Hours (2002), 250–252, 252f
How the West Was Won (1962), 100
Howard, Ron *See* Frost/Nixon (2008)
Hughes, John, 319–320
Hurt Locker (2008), 143–144
Husbands and Wives (1992), 238
Huston, John, 343

I

I Love You, Man (2009), 326
I Want to Live! (1958), 75–77, 76f
I Was a 90-Pound Weakling (1964), 341

The Ice Storm (1997), 400–403
ideas, communicating *See* documentary
identification, 288. *See also* character
If . . . (1969), 140
Il Ovotteporno (1962), 108–109
image-sound synchronization, 33–34
imaginative documentary, 341–348
    altering meaning away from literal, 341–343
    wartime propaganda, 328, 343–347, 343f, 350
imagined reality, 233–237.
    See also digital reality
    constructed artifice, 235
    imagined as observational, 235–236
    special effects, use of, 237
    spectacle, use of, 236–237
    video over film, 234–235
IMAX format, 101
imediacy of television, 133
imitating styles *See also* style
    innovation from, 208–211
    innovation vs. imitation, 207–208
In the Mood for Love (2000), 177, 183–186
Indiana Jones and the Last Crusade (1989), 291–292
individual shot, contemplating, 371
influences on editing, 61–64, 66–69
    musicals, 64–65
    popular arts, 61–70
    radio, 66–69
    television, 133–136. *See also* MTV style
    theatre, 65–66, 137–142
Inglourious Basterds (2009), anti-pace of, 201–202
intellectual montage, 20–21
intensification, in action sequences, 288
intercutting, birth of, 4
Into the Arms of Strangers (2000), 358–359
Intolerance (1916), 6, 7, 12
investigator, documentary narrator as, 356–357

Invictus (2009), 246–248
irony, in personal documentary, 351, 353–355
Irvin, John, 290
Isadora (1969), 140
Italiensk for begyndere (*Italian for Beginners*) (2000), 238
Itami, Juzo, 177–178
    Tampopo (1987), 177–178, 190–192

J

Jackson, Michael, 171
Jackson, Pat, 344
Jackson, Peter, 237
Jancsó, Miklós, 221
Jarecki, Andrew, 364–365
Jaws (1975), 108–109, 292
Jennings, Humphrey, 57–60, 328, 343, 350
    Diary for Timothy (1945), 55f, 57–60, 342
    Listen to Britain (1942), 328, 343–347, 343f, 396
JFK (1991), 382
Johnson, Nunnally, 71
Judith of Bethulia (1913), 6
Jules et Jim (1961), 119–120, 120f
jump cuts, 118–121, 277
Jungle Fever (1991), 155, 155f, 156, 206
Juno (2007), 326
juxtaposition
    in comedy, 318
    editing for dramatic emphasis, 260, 265–266
    in imaginative documentary, 342, 346
    long shots with close-ups, 222–227
    randomness of pace, 388–389

K

Kahn, Nathaniel, 365
Kanal (1957), 408
Kapur, Shekhar, 223
    Bandit Queen (1994), 223–225
    Elizabeth (1998), 223, 225–227

Kar-wai, Wong, 177
    In the Mood for Love (2000), 177, 183–186
Kazan, Elia, 72, 104–105, 270
Keaton, Buster, 62, 72
    The General (1927), 292–294, 292f, 293f
Keaton, Diane, 72
Kingdom of Heaven (2005), 236
Kinski, Klaus, 351
Klimov, Elem, 227–228
    Come and See (1985), 227–230, 407–408
Koyaanisqatsi (1983), 343
Kragh-Jacobsen, Søren, 214
Kubrick, Stanley, 107–108, 148–150, 217
    Barry Lyndon (1975), 149, 149f, 150, 217, 387
    A Clockwork Orange (1971), 205
    Dr. Strangelove (1964), 316
    Eyes Wide Shut (1999), 217–219
    Full Metal Jacket (1987), 217–218, 277, 387, 388f, 408
    Paths of Glory (1957), 217–218, 375–376, 408
    The Shining (1979), 217–218
    2001: A Space Odyssey (1968), 107–108, 148, 149, 217, 277, 387
Kuleshov, Lev, 14
Kundun (1997), 219–221
Kurosawa, Akira, 108–109, 116–118, 169
    Rashomon (1951), 116–118, 169, 395
    pace, 193–194
    The Seven Samurai (1954), 277, 289, 375–376

L

La Femme Nikita (1990), 169
The Lady Eve (1941), 320–321, 321f, 325–326
L'Age d'Or (1930), 29f, 30f, 31f
Land without Bread (1933), 351
Lang, Fritz, 38–41
The Last Laugh (1924), 13
Laughton, Charles, 72

L'Avventura (1960), 108–109
Lawrence of Arabia (1962), 79–81, 84–85, 85f, 222, 223, 277
Le Fils (*The Son*) (2002), 238–239
Leacock, Richard, 349
Lean, David, 79–85, 108–109, 222
    Lawrence of Arabia (1962), 79–81, 84–85, 85f, 222, 223, 277
L'Eclisse (*The Eclipse*) (1962), 129–132, 130f, 131f, 169, 395
Lee, Ang, 168, 177
    Crouching Tiger, Hidden Dragon (2000), 177, 182–186
    The Ice Storm (1997), 400–403
    Lust, Caution (2006), 272–273
Lee, Spike, 153–157, 206
    Jungle Fever (1991), 155, 155f, 156, 206
Leone, Sergio, 108, 207
    The Good, the Bad, and the Ugly (1967), 108, 316
Les Liaisons Dangereuses (1988), 249
Lester, Richard, 134, 135, 166, 205, 319. *See also* Help! (1965); A Hard Day's Night (1964)
    A Funny Thing Happened on the Way to the Forum (1966), 166, 316–317
    pace, 194
    Petulia (1968), 135–136, 205
Letter from an Unknown Woman (1948), 217
Levring, Kristian, 214, 349
Les Liaisons Dangereuses (1988), 249
Life Is Beauiful (1998), 177–178, 188–190
The Life of an American Fireman (1903), 4
Life of Brian (1979), 166. *See also* Monty Python
light, matching tone and, 378
linear narrative, about, 393–394
Lipsett, Arthur, 343

Listen to Britain (1942), 328, 343−347, 343f, 396
literal meaning, moving away from, 341−343
The Little Foxes (1941), 65−66
Loach, Ken, 138−139
location change, continuity on, 379−380
Lola Montés (1955), 106−107, 217
The Lonedale Operator (1911), 6
Lonely Boy (1962), 111, 111f, 112f, 113
The Lonely Villa (1909), 6
long shots
 establishing shots, 378
 juxtaposed with close-ups, 222−227
 rhythm and, 383−384
The Long Way Home (1997), 358−359
The Lord of the Rings trilogy (2001−2003), 237
Lorentz, Pare, 51
Lost Horizons (1937), 255
Louisiana Story (1948), 342
Lubitsch, Ernst, 306, 318−319
 Trouble in Paradise (1932), 306−309, 307f
Lucas, George
 American Graffiti (1973), 387
 Raiders of the Lost Ark (1981), 198−199, 294−296, 295f, 382
Luhrmann, Baz *See* Moulin Rouge! (2010)
Lumière, Louis, 3
Lust, Caution (2006), 272−273
Lynch, David, 163
Lyne, Adrian *See* Flashdance (1983)

M

M (1931), 38−41, 39f, 40f, 41f
Macdonald, Kevin, 365
Mackenzie, John, 290
Mad Max 2 (1981), 291
magnetic recording, 35
Magnolia (1999), 409−412
maintaining screen direction, 375−378, 376f, 377f
Makavejev, Dusan, 397

male-female reversals *See* role reversal comedy
Malick, Terence *See* The Thin Red Line (1998)
Mamoulian, Rouben, 42−44, 227
Man of Aran (1934), 46−48, 47f, 48f, 49f
The Man Who Knew Too Much (1956), 92−94
The Man with a Movie Camera (1929), 23, 24f, 25f, 349, 363, 395
Manchevski, Milcho, 210, 397, 398
Manderlay (2005), 235
Manhattan (1979), 302
Mankiewicz, Joseph L., 289
 Five Fingers (1952), 244−245, 289
Mann, Anthony, 102, 107, 222
Mann, Michael, 234
Mann, Ron, 360
man-woman reversals *See* role reversal comedy
Marat/Sade (1966), 141, 142, 169−170
Marianne and Julianne (1982), 159−160
Martin, Steve, 319−320
Marx, Groucho *See* Duck Soup (1934)
match cuts, 277, 373, 374f, 375f
 preserving screen direction, 375−378, 376f, 377f
matching action, 373−375, 374f, 375f
matching flow over cuts, 378−379
matching tone, 378
McCabe and Mrs. Miller (1971), 304
McCallister, Stewart, 344
McElwee, Ross, 349
McTiernan, John, 290
Mean Streets (1973), 387
media, role of, 77
media looking at itself, 171
Méliès, George, 3, 227
Memorandum (1966), 329−334, 330f, 332f, 333f, 334f, 335f, 336f, 337f, 338f, 339f

archival sequence, 332−334
continuity and narrator influence, 329−330
reportage sequence, 334−340
transition sequence, 330−332
metric montage, 17
Michael Clayton (2007), 312−313
middle ground, wide screen and, 101
Miller, George, 290
 Mad Max 2 (1981), 291
mise-en-scéne, 217−222
mixing genres, 162−163
Mo' Better Blues (1990), 153
Modern Times (1936), 62, 315, 317
montage
 birth of theory of, 16−23
 metric montage, 17f
montage for dramatic emphasis, 259−260, 265
Monty Python, 166−167, 170
Monty Python and the Holy Grail (1975), 166
Moonstruck (1987), 316−317
Moore, Michael, 328, 357
 Fahrenheit 9/11 (2004), 363
Morgan: A Suitable Case for Treatment (1966), 139
Morris, Errol, 163, 350−352, 355, 364
 Fast, Cheap and Out of Control (1998), 352−355, 364
 Mr. Death (2000), 352−364
Mosjukhin, Ivan, 14
Moss, Rob, 349
Mother (1926), 14, 15f, 16f
Moulin Rouge! (2010), 165, 269
 pace of, 199−201
Mountains of the Moon (1990), 245−246
Movietone, 33
moving vehicles, 296
Moviola, 35
Mr. Death (2000), 352−353, 364
MTV style, 165−192
 Crouching Tiger, Hidden Dragon (2000), 182−186
 D-Day landing sequence, *Saving Private Ryan* (1997), 178−182

MTV style (*Continued*)
downgrading of plot,
168–169
in *Happiness* (1998), 405
importance of feeling states, 168
Life Is Beauiful (1998),
188–190
In the Mood for Love (2000),
183–186
obliterated time and space,
169–170
Oliver Stone and *Natural Born
Killers* (1994), 171–175
origins of, 166–167
self-reflexivity, 166–167,
170–171
media looking at itself, 171
Tampopo (1987), 190–192
Muller, Ray, 357
multipurpose dialog, 304–306.
See also dialog
Munich (2005), 240, 365, 366
Murnau, F. W., 13
music *See* sound
music videos, 134. *See also* MTV
style
time in, 165
musicals (film genre), 199–201
A Hard Day's Night (1964),
134–136, 136f, 166, 170
pace, 194
Help! (1965), 134, 166, 170
pace, 194
pace in, 199–201
musicals (stage), influence of,
64–65
My Architect (2003), 365
My Best Friend (1999), 351–352
My Darling Clementine (1946),
207, 395

N

Nanook of the North (1922), 350,
363
narration in documentary,
355–361
influence of narrator, 331
in archival sequences,
332–334
narrator as guide, 357–359
narrator as investigator,
356–357
narrator as observer, 355–356

narrator as provocateur,
359–361
narrative *See also* film continuity
acceleration of, 135–136
articulation of premise, 243
challenges to (innovation in),
143–164
alienation and anarchy
(Peckinpah), 143–146
dramatic moment (Martin
Scorsese), 150–152
feminism and antinarrative,
160–162
feminism and politics,
158–160
freedom of chaos (Altman),
143–146
mixing genres, 162–163
pace and social action (Spike
Lee), 153–157
popular and fine art (Wim
Wenders), 152–153
world building (Stanley
Kubrick), 148–150
world building (Werner
Herzog), 150
clarity of, 72, 372. *See also*
editing for narrative clarity
in action sequences, 296
David Lean's use of, 81
dynamic of relativity, 116–118
complexity, in David Lean's
work, 82
MTV style and, 168–169
nonlinear, 393–398. *See also*
nonlinear editing
framework for, 399–400
pace in thriller genre, 197
plot *See* plot
rhythm and, 384
romantic relationship stories,
186
sidestepped in music videos,
165
subtext and, 269–271. *See also*
editing for subtext
supported by style, 203–204
narrator influence in
documentary, 329–330
Nashville (1975), 143–146
Natural Born Killers (1994),
167–169, 172–175, 207,
399

Neame, Ronald, 80
New Wave filmmaking
jump cut and discontinuity,
118–121
objective anarchy, 121–123
Nichols, Mike, 221
The Graduate (1967),
304–306
Night and Fog (1955), 364
Night Mail (1936), 49–51, 50f,
341, 363
nonlinear editing, 391–412
aesthetic opportunities,
392–393
artists of nonlinear narrative,
395–398
framework for nonlinear
narratives, 399–400
Happiness (1998), 403–405
The Ice Storm (1997),
400–403
limits of technology, 392
Magnolia (1999), 409–412
nonlinear narrative, 393–398
philosophy of nonlinearity,
393–394
reliance on linearity, 393–398
The Thin Red Line (1998),
405–409
nonlinear plot *See* visual
discontinuity
North by Northwest (1959),
94–95, 94f
Notorious (1946), 90–91
Noyce, Phillip, 290
Nuit et brouillard (*Night and Fog*)
(1955), 364

O

O Lucky Man! (1973), 140, 141
objective anarchy, 121–123
observational principle,
238–239
observer, documentary narrator
as, 355–356
An Occurrence at Owl Creek
(1962), 144
Odessa Steps sequence
(*Potemkin*), 8f, 18–20, 21f,
22f, 23f, 289
O'Dreamland (1953), 140
O'Dreamland (1953), 341
Oliver Twist (1948), 84

Olivier, Olivier (1992), 161
Olympia Parts I and II (1938), 53–54, 53f, 328, 341
Once Upon a Time in America (1984), 207
One Day in September (1999), 365–368
Ophuls, Max, 106–107, 203–204, 217
optical sonud tracks, 35
Osborne, John, 138–139
O'Steen, Sam *See* The Graduate (1967)
overtonal montage, 20

P

pace, 72, 193–202, 381–390. *See also* pace; style
acceleration of narrative stories, 135–136
in action genre, 198–199, 293, 295–296, 298
in Alfred Hitchcock's work, 92, 95
anti-pace of *Inglourious Basterds* (2009), 201–202
camera placement and subjective states, 227–232
in comedy, 318, 325–326
in David Lean's work, 82–83
in docudrama genre, 194–195
editing for dramatic emphasis, 260–261, 266
evolution of, in filmmaking, 193–201
in imaginative documentary, 342, 343
randomness of pace, 388–389
randomness upon, 388–389
randomness vs., 147
rhythm, 383–387
in Sam Peckinpah's work, 144–145
social action and, 153–157
in thriller genre, 195–197
timing, 382–383
Pale Rider (1985), 207
Panavision format, 101, 107–109
Panavision 70 format, 101
Panic in the Streets (1950), 270
parallel editing
birth of, 5

Strangers on a Train (1951), 88
Paris, Texas (1984), 152–153, 169–170
parody, 316
The Passion (2004), 282–284
The Passion of Joan of Arc (1928), 13, 223, 255
Paths of Glory (1957), 217–218, 375–376, 408
Peckinpah, Sam, 108, 143–146, 222
pace, 194
The Wild Bunch (1969), 143–146, 146f, 277
pace, 194
Pennebaker, D. A., 349
personal documentary, 349–355
Fast, Cheap and Out of Control (1998), 352–355, 364
Mr. Death (2000), 352–353, 364
Petulia (1968), 135–136, 205
Photophone, 33
physical environment *See* environment (place)
picture edit and continuity, 371–380. *See also* film continuity
adequacy of coverage, 372–373
location change, 379–380
matching action, 373–375
matching flow over cuts, 378–379
matching tone, 378
preserving screen direction, 375–378, 376f, 377f
scene change, 379–380
seamlessness, 372, 384
setting the scene, 378
time and place, 387–388
picture edit and pace, 381–390. *See also* pace
randomness of pace, 388–389
rhythm, 383–387
timing, 382–383
Pink Panther series (1964–1978), 287
The Pink Panther (1964), 316
place *See* environment (place)
A Place in the Sun (1951), 204, 223
pleasure, editing for *See* editing for aesthetics

plot
and dialog, 302–303, 305
MTV style and, 168–169
nonlinear narrative, 393–398. *See also* nonlinear editing
framework for, 399–400
plot-driven films, 244–248
Five Fingers (1952), 244–245
Invictus (2009), 246–248
Mountains of the Moon (1990), 245–246
The Plow That Broke the Plains (1936), 51, 52f
Point Blank (1967), 277
Polanski, Roman, 270, 288
Chinatown (1974), 309–312, 311f
political thrillers, pace of, 382
politics, in general *See* society
politics in documentary filmmaking, 328
personal documentary vs., 349
Pollack, Sydney *See* Tootsie (1982)
Pontecorvo, Gillo, 350–351
popular arts, influence of, 61–70
musicals, 64–65
radio, 66–69
theatre, 65–66
vaudeville, 61–64
Porter, Edwin S., 3–5, 395
Potemkin (1925), 8f, 17f, 18, 18f, 19f, 20f, 21f, 22f, 23f, 289
Prelude to War (1942), 56–57
Preminger, Otto, 102, 103, 222, 288
premise, articulation of, 243
preserving screen direction, 375–378, 376f, 377f
Privilege (1967), 110
Promises (2001), 359–360
propaganda, documentary as, 328, 343–347, 350
The Proposition (2006), 243–244
provocateur, documentary narrator as, 359–361
Psycho (1960), 91–92, 255
Pudovkin, Vsevolod I., 12–16
Pudovkin, Vsevolod. I., 395
Pudovkin, Vsevolod I.
Film Technique and Film Acting, 36
on sound in film, 35

Pulp Fiction (1994), 208–211, 222, 397, 399, 400
Punchline (1989), 316–317
purposeful documentary, 350. *See also* propaganda, documentary as

Q

quick cutting *See* pace

R

Rachel Getting Married (2008), 269
radio, influence of, 66–69
Rafelson, Bob *See* Mountains of the Moon (1990)
Raging Bull (1980), 150–152, 151f, 206, 407–408
Raiders of the Lost Ark (1981), 198–199, 294–296, 295f, 382
Raising Arizona (1987), 317, 382–383
Ramona (1911), 6
Ran (1985), 108–109
randomness, 147
randomness of pace, 388–389
Rashomon (1951), 116–118, 169, 395
pace, 193–194
Ray (2004), 239
realism, 237–240
birth of, 13–16, 23–25
Dogme, 95, 213, 214, 237–238, 349
Reality Bites (1994), 168, 169
Rear Window (1954), 87–88
The Red and the White (1967), 221
Redford, Robert, 72
Reed, Carol *See* The Third Man (1949)
Reggia, Godfrey, 343
Reiner, Rob, 319–320
Reisz, Karel, 138–140, 381
Reitmann, Jason, 326
relationships (between characters)
character-driven films, 248–254
Atonement (2007), 252–254
Hannah and Her Sisters (1986), 248–249

Hero (1992), 249–250
The Hours (2002), 250–252, 252f
Valmont (1989), 249
role reversal comedy
Forgetting Sarah Marshall (2008), 324–325
The Lady Eve (1941), 320–321, 321f, 325–326
Victor/Victoria (1982), 321–326, 322f
wide screen format and, 104–106
relativity, 116–118
reportage rearchival sequence in documentary, 334–340
Requiem for a Dream (2000), 230–232
Resnais, Alain, 123–125, 169, 227, 364
rhythm, 383–387
rhythmic montage, 18
Richardson, Tony, 138–139
Riefenstahl, Leni, 53–54, 328, 341, 350, 357
Triumph of the Will (1935), 56, 328, 364
Rififi (1954), 289
Rio Bravo (1959), 207
River of No Return (1954), 102–103
Robbins, Jerome, 77
The Robe (1953), 100, 101
Robocop (1987), 291
Roeg, Nicolas, 71
Roger and Me (1989), 328
role reversal comedy
Forgetting Sarah Marshall (2008), 324–325
The Lady Eve (1941), 320–321, 321f, 325–326
Victor/Victoria (1982), 321–326, 322f
romantic relationship stories, 186
Rope (1948), 87–88, 381
Rosetta (1999), 194–195, 238
Rosi, Francesco *See* Three Brothers (1980)
Rossellini, Roberto, 217
rough cut, 371
Rubbo, Michael, 351, 355, 356
Ryan's Daughter (1970), 108–109

S

The Sacrifice (1986), 221
satire, 316. *See also* Coen, Ethan and Joel
Saving Private Ryan (1997), 178–182, 223, 267–268, 366, 408
scene, setting, 378
scene change, continuity on, 379–380
scene fragmentation, birth of, 5–13
Schepsi, Fred, 290
Schindler's List (1993), 238
Schlesinger, John, 141
Schoonmaker, Thelma *See* The Departed (2006)
Schultz, Carl, 290
Scorsese, Martin, 150–152, 206, 219
The Departed (2006), 271–272, 271f
Kundun (1997), 219–221
Mean Streets (1973), 387
Raging Bull (1980), 150–152, 151f, 206, 407–408
Scott, Ridley, 223, 236
Scott, Tony, 169–170
screen direction, preserving, 375–378, 376f, 377f
screen shape *See* wide screen format
seamlessness (seamless cuts), 372, 384
The Searchers (1956), 223
Seidelman, Susan, 160
Seigel, Don, 289
self-reflexivity, 166–167, 170–171
media looking at itself, 171
Seltzer, David *See* Punchline (1989)
Selznick, David, 71
Sense and Sensibility (1995), 168
The Serpent's Egg (1978), 138
Serreau, Coline, 234
Collateral (2004), 234–235
set-pieces, 178
Crouching Tiger, Hidden Dragon (2000), 182–186
Life Is Beautiful (1998), 188–190

In the Mood for Love (2000), 183–186
Saving Private Ryan (1997), 178–182
Tampopo (1987), 190–192
setting the scene, 378
The Set-Up (1949), 74–75
Seven Beauties (1976), 317
The Seven Samurai (1954), 277, 289, 375–376
The Seventh Seal (1956), 138
70 mm format, 101
Shadows (1959), 350–351
Shane (1953), 207
Shanley, John Patrick, 319–320
shape, screen *See* wide screen format
shaping devices of nonlinear narrative, 399
Happiness (1998), 404
The Ice Storm (1997), 400–401
Magnolia (1999), 411
The Thin Red Line (1998), 407
Shapiro, Justine, 359–360
She's Gotta Have It (1986), 153
The Shining (1979), 217–218
short films, 167
shot coverage, adequacy of, 372–373
shower scene in *Psycho*, 91–92
Sicko (2007), 357
silent period (1885–1930), 3–32
Silver, Joan Micklin, 319–320
situation comedy, 316
65 mm format, 101
Slacker (1991), 168
Smith, Kevin, 214
smooth cut (seamlessness), 372, 384
society *See also* environment (place)
in documentary filmmaking, 328
personal documentary vs., 349
feminism and politics, 158–160
ideas about, 46–51, 56–60
pace and social action, 153–157
Solondz, Todd *See* Happiness (1998)
Sombre (1998), 238–239

Somebody Up There Likes Me (1956), 73
Something Wild (1986), 163
Song of Ceylon (1934), 341
Sonnenfeld, Barry, 71
The Sorrow and the Pity (1969), 364
sound, 152 *See also* entries at music
cinéma vérité and, 109–110
David Lean's use of, 80–81
early sound films, 33–44
Applause (1929), 42–44, 43f
Blackmail (1929), 36–38, 37f, 38f, 227
Dr. Jekyll and Mr. Hyde (1932), 43, 44, 227
M (1931), 38–41, 39f, 40f, 41f
technological improvements, 35
technological limitations, 33–34
Raging Bull (1980), 151
theoretical issues, 35–36
unity of, in Alfred Hitchcock's work, 92–94
sound cut, 380
sound cuts, 88–89, 277
Southern, Terry *See* Dr. Strangelove (1964)
space (physical) *See* environment (place)
special effects, 237
spectacle, use of, 236–237
Spellbound (1945), 87, 89
Spellbound (2002), 365
Spielberg, Steven, 108–109, 223, 235–236, 290
Indiana Jones and the Last Crusade (1989), 291–292
Jaws (1975), 108–109, 292
Munich (2005), 240, 365, 366
pace, 194
Raiders of the Lost Ark (1981), 198–199, 294–296, 295f, 382
Saving Private Ryan (1997), 178–182, 223, 267–268, 366, 408
Schindler's List (1993), 238
War of the Worlds (2005), 235–236, 240
Splendor in the Grass (1961), 270

sponsored films, documentaries as, 328
Spotton, John *See* Memorandum (1966)
Squyres, Tim *See* Lust, Caution (2006)
staged documentaries, 327
personal documentary style, 350–351
staging, importance of, 65–66
Stevens, George, 64, 204, 207, 223, 270, 289, 319–320
Stoller, Nicholas *See* Forgetting Sarah Marshall (2008)
Stone, Oliver, 167, 171–175, 206, 217, 222
JFK (1991), 382
Natural Born Killers (1994), 167–169, 172–175, 207, 399
pace, 194
storytelling *See* narrative; plot
Strangers on a Train (1951), 88
Strike (1924), 16
Sturges, John, 105–106
Sturges, Preston, 319
The Lady Eve (1941), 320–321, 321f, 325–326
style
breaking expectations, 206–207
cinéma vérité, elevating, 213–217
close-ups and long shots, 222–227
digital reality, 233–240
pushing realism, 237–240
understanding artificial reality, 233–237
innovation from imitation, 208–211
innovation vs. imitation, 207–208
for its own sake, 205–206
mise-en-scéne, 217–222
personal documentary, 350–351
realism *See* realism
subjective states, 227–232
supporting the narrative, 203–204
subjective camera placement, 80

subjective camera placement
(*Continued*)
in Alfred Hitchcock's work,
87, 91
for match cuts, 373–375, 375f
pace and subjective states,
227–232
preserving screen direction, 376
subjective states, 227–232
subtext, editing for, 264,
267–276
The Departed (2006), 271–272
Lust, Caution (2006), 272–273
rhythm and, 384
Saving Private Ryan (1997),
267–268
There Will Be Blood (2007),
273–275
survival, moment of, 287–288
Swing Time (1936), 64
synchronization of sound, 33–34

T

Tampopo (1987), 177–178,
190–192
Tarantino, Quentin, 208, 222,
397, 398
Inglourious Basterds (2009),
201–202
Pulp Fiction (1994), 208–211,
222, 397, 399, 400
Tarkovsky, Andrei, 221
Tati, Jacques, 319–320
television, influence of, 133–136.
See also MTV style
The Terminator (1984), 290
dialog in, 302
theatre, influence of, 65–66,
137–142
There Will Be Blood (2007),
273–275
The Thin Blue Line (1988), 163,
350–351
The Thin Red Line (1998), 268,
399, 405–409
The Third Man (1949), 279–282
The 39 Steps (1935), 88–89,
92–94
*Thirty-two Short Films About Glen
Gould* (1993), 397–398
Three Brothers (1980), 388–389
thriller genre, pace in, 195–197
Thriller music video, 171

Tichenor, Dylan *See* There Will Be
Blood (2007)
time *See also* film continuity;
narrative; pace
collapsing, 67
in David Lean's work, 84
dissolves, 375–376
matching real time and screen
time, 74–75
melding past and present,
123–125
obliterated, in MTV style, 165,
169–170
sense of, pace and, 387–388
shower scene in *Psycho*, 92
sound editing and, 38–41
transitional sequence in
documentary, 330–332
timing, 382–383. *See also* pace
To Be or Not to Be (1942),
316–317
TODD-AO format, 101
Tom Jones (1963), 139
tonal montage, 18–20
tone, matching, 378
Tootsie (1982), 316
Top Gun (1986), 169–170, 171
Touch of Evil (1958), 205, 217,
289, 381, 382
tracking shot, birth of, 5
transformative dialog, 312–313
transitional sequence in
documentary, 330–332
A Trip to the Moon (1902), 227
triptych format, 99, 100f
Triumph of the Will (1935), 56,
328, 364
Trouble in Paradise (1932),
306–309, 307f
Truffaut, François, 118–121
Twelve Monkeys (1995), 205–206
2001: A Space Odyssey (1968),
107–108, 148, 149, 217,
277, 387

U

Un Chien Andalou (1929), 27,
27f, 28f, 29f, 227
United 93 (2006), 255–261
close-up in, 258–259
compared to *Frost/Nixon*
(2008), 264, 266
docudrama event, 258

dynamic montage, 259–260
pace, 260–261
Up in the Air (2009), 326

V

Valmont (1989), 249
Van Dyke, W. S., 54–56
Variety (1925), 13
vaudeville, influence of, 61–64
Verhoeven, Paul, 290, 291
Robocop (1987), 291
Vertigo (1958), 95–97, 96f
Vertov, Dziga, 12, 23–25, 349,
363
The Man with a Movie Camera
(1929), 23, 24f, 25f, 349,
363, 395
Very Nice, Very Nice (1961), 343
Victor/Victoria (1982), 321–326,
322f
video, using instead of film,
234–235
Vidor, King, 32, 395
Duel in the Sun (1946), 289
Vinterberg, Thomas, 214, 349
The Celebration (1998),
214–216, 238
violence, 143–146. *See also* war
Visconti, Luchino, 108–109, 217
VistaVision, 100
visual association, editing by,
25–27
visual continuity *See* film
continuity
visual dimension of personal
documentary, 350
visual discontinuity, 118–121.
See also film continuity
birth of, 27–31
visual storytelling *See* narrative
voice
in nonlinear editing, 399, 402,
404, 407–409, 411–412
in personal documentary, 351,
353
von Trier, Lars, 214, 235, 349
von Trotta, Margarethe, 158–160

W

Walk the Line (2005), 239
war *See also* Holocaust
documentary as propaganda,
328, 343–347, 343f, 350

Full Metal Jacket (1987), 217–218, 277, 387, 388f, 408
Holocaust documentary *See* Memorandum (1966)
ideas about, 56–60
Inglourious Basterds (2009), 201–202
Saving Private Ryan (1997), 178–182, 223, 267–268, 366, 408
The Thin Red Line (1998), 268, 399, 405–409
The War Game (1967), 110
War of the Worlds (2005), 235–236, 240
Watkins, Peter, 110, 133–134, 350–351
Week End (1967), 396
Weekend (1967), 121, 122f
Welles, Orson, 66, 217
Citizen Kane (1941), 66–69, 68f, 72–73, 217, 393, 395
Touch of Evil (1958), 205, 217, 289, 381, 382
Wenders, Wim, 152–153, 169–170, 397
Werner Herzog Eats His Shoe (1980), 351
Wertmüller, Lina, 158
West Side Story (1961), 77–79, 78f
Westerns, using CinemaScope format, 102–103

Wexler, Haskell, 71
What's Up, Doc? (1972), 287
Whore (1991), 160
Why We Fight series (1943–1945), 56–57, 343, 364
wide screen format, 99–109
background, 106–107
foreground-background relationship, 101, 102f
character and, 102–104
Cinerama, 100
environment and, 102–106
relationships and, 104–106
Wiene, Robert, 13
The Wild Bunch (1969), 143–146, 146f, 277
pace, 194
Wilde, Cornel, 205
Wilder, Billy, 319
Winkler, Irwin, 71
Winter Light (1962), 389
Wise, Robert, 72–79
I Want to Live! (1958), 75–77, 76f
The Set-Up (1949), 74–75
West Side Story (1961), 77–79, 78f
woman-men reversals *See* role reversal comedy
women as directors, 158, 160–162
The Wonderful, Horrible Life of Leni Riefenstahl (1995), 357

Woo, John, pace of, 194
Working Girls (1973), 160
world building
of Stanley Kubrick, 148–150
of Werner Herzog, 150
Woyzek (1979), 351
Wrestling (1960), 341
Wright, Basil, 36, 49–51
Night Mail (1936), 49–51, 50f, 341, 363
Song of Ceylon (1934), 341
Wright, Joe *See* Atonement (2007)
writers becoming directors, 71
Wyler, William, 65–66, 115, 343
Ben Hur (1959), 289

Y

Yates, Peter, 290
Bullitt (1968), 197, 277, 290
Yimou, Zhang, 198–199
Ying xiong (*Hero*) (2002), 198–199

Z

Z (1969), 382
Zinnemann, Fred, 207
High Noon (1952), 144, 207, 289
Zonca, Erick, 213, 216